SURVEY
OF
SOCIAL
SCIENCE

SURVEY
OF
SOCIAL
SCIENCE

PSYCHOLOGY SERIES

Volume 3
947-1430

Emotion in Primates—Learned Helplessness

Edited by
FRANK N. MAGILL

Consulting Editor
JACLYN RODRIGUEZ
OCCIDENTAL COLLEGE

SALEM PRESS
Pasadena, California   Englewood Cliffs, New Jersey

Library of Congress Cataloging-in-Publication Data
Survey of social science. Psychology series/edited by
Frank N. Magill; consulting editor, Jaclyn Rodriguez.
    p. cm.
    Includes bibliographical references and index.
    1. Psychology—Encyclopedias. I. Magill, Frank Nor-
then, 1907-   . II. Rodriguez, Jaclyn.
BF31.S79   1993   93-34708
150'.3—dc20   CIP
ISBN 0-89356-732-9 (set)
ISBN 0-89356-735-3 (volume 3)

Second Printing

PRINTED IN THE UNITED STATES OF AMERICA

CONTENTS

PSYCHOLOGY

SURVEY
OF
SOCIAL
SCIENCE

EMOTION IN PRIMATES

Type of psychology: Emotion
Fields of study: Cognitive processes; motivation theory

Scientific studies of emotion in nonhuman primates focus on its expression through vocalizations and visual signals, especially facial displays, plus the nervous system control of emotional expression. These studies provide an evolutionary context for the understanding of human nonverbal communication of affect.

Principal terms
AFFECT: the experience of emotion
DISPLAY: a behavior pattern that has been shaped over the course of evolution to communicate or convey information
GRADED SIGNAL: any signal that varies continuously along a quantitative dimension such as pitch, thereby communicating continuously variable information about affective state
HOMOLOGY: any similarity in structure or behavior among species resulting from inheritance from a common ancestor
LIMBIC SYSTEM: an integrated set of forebrain structures (including the amygdala, hypothalamus, hippocampus, and septal area) that plays a vital role in the regulation of emotion and motivation
NONVERBAL COMMUNICATION: communication through any means other than words, including facial expression, tone of voice, posture, and so on

Overview

Contemporary psychologists study patterns of primate emotional expression because they are reliable, conservative characteristics that clarify evolutionary relationships and identify the biological bases of human emotion and its nonverbal communication. Animals communicate how they feel through what are called "emotional displays," which are essential to the coordination of group life. Consequently, expressive repertoires are most diverse in the more socially advanced primates: monkeys, apes, and humans.

Chimpanzees clearly illustrate this. Jane Goodall's decades of study of these apes revealed a rich emotional life encompassing feelings such as contentment, pleasure, joy, sorrow, boredom, apprehension, fear, distress, annoyance, anger, and rage, as well as sexual and social excitement. To express affect (emotion or mood), they draw upon a rich expressive repertoire including at least eleven major facial expressions, thirty-four calls, plus many other signals. Since chimpanzees act on their feelings, an understanding of emotion is vital to understanding their behavior.

Since facial expressions play a key role in close-up interactions in humans and other primates, their study has engrossed behavioral scientists ever since Charles

Darwin's publication of *The Expression of the Emotions in Man and Animals* (1872). The richness and diversity of facial expression evolved in conjunction with the elaboration of the facial musculature. Over the course of primate evolution, facial expressions became ever more important as primates adapted to reliance on vision and group life.

William Redican, in a comprehensive review of Old World monkeys and apes, described eight major facial expressions: the threat display, tense-mouth display, grimace, open-mouth grimace, lipsmack display, grin-lipsmack display, play face, and yawn. Three of these—the grimace, play face, and threat display—illustrate how facial expressions subtly communicate affect. In the grimace, retraction of the lips and mouth corners prominently expose the teeth; the gaze typically alternates between looking at and away from the social partner. Subordinate animals often display a grimace when faced with an attack or the possibility of an attack by a social superior.

Since fear is the chief emotion associated with the grimace, appeasement appears to be its most important function. The play face features a widely open mouth, its corners only slightly retracted, and the avoidance of a fixed gaze. In some cases, the upper lip may curl and tense over the teeth, while the eyelids are lowered, the brow raised, and the forehead retracted. This display, which accompanies vigorous play, signals positive affect. In the threat display, the gaze is fixed and staring, while the mouth is held open. The lips contract to form an "O," while the brow is raised and the ears are flattened against the head. Most observers believe that the threat display indicates a mixture of aggression and fear.

When using facial displays to express affect, primates often combine them with vocalizations and additional visual signals. In many Old World monkeys, the facial threat is accompanied by slapping, lunging, or jerking, as well as particular vocalizations. The body hair of highly aroused, aggressive, or frightened chimpanzees and many other primates becomes erect, a reaction controlled by the autonomic nervous system.

Vocalizations provide an effective way for primates to communicate emotion over long distances and when hidden by foliage. Like facial expressions, calls are closely tied to internal, emotional states. Indeed, Goodall maintains that it is almost impossible to induce sound production in chimpanzees in the absence of appropriate emotions. Primate calls, however, to a greater degree than facial expressions, may be used to designate objects and events external to the signaler. Robert Seyfarth demonstrated that vervet monkeys give acoustically different alarm calls to identify eagles, leopards, and snakes. Also, to a greater degree than facial expressions, primate calls are graded. That is, while calls maintain the same general form among the individuals of a given species, they vary considerably in physical properties such as frequency, amplitude, and duration. The result is that calls intergrade with one another. Boundaries between calls are not always identifiable. Many investigators believe that variation in the acoustic properties of calls correlates with continuous variation in emotional states.

The work of Uwe Jürgens, Detlev Ploog, and their colleagues at Germany's Max Planck Institute for Psychiatry has made the squirrel monkey's vocal repertoire the most thoroughly studied of all. Jürgens classified squirrel monkey calls according to three criteria: similarity of physical structure; probability of one call type following another; and the aversive or pleasurable quality of the underlying emotional state, which was determined by the animal's active preference for inducing or terminating electrical brain stimulation evoking each specific call. The result of this analysis was the identification of five classes of continuously variable, graded vocalizations. Well-defined acoustic and functional features characterized each class, while a continuum of affect from aversiveness to pleasure provided a secondary ordering of call types within the broader classes. According to Jürgens, the five functional classes, each characterized by specific acoustic properties, expressed self-assertiveness, protest, warning/disagreement, desire for social contact, and feelings of companionship. At the same time, aversiveness correlated positively with total frequency range. The experimental work of Jürgens and his colleagues squares with the general trend in mammals and birds (formulated by ornithologist Eugene Morton in 1977): Low-frequency, harsh sounds signify aggression, and pure tones of higher frequency signify fright, appeasement, or friendly approach.

Investigations of the neural control of emotional display in monkeys (mostly rhesus and squirrel monkeys) characterize their facial and vocal expressions as genetically predetermined instincts. Although broad nervous-system involvement characterizes emotional behavior, the central role in the mediation of emotion is played by an inner lobe of the brain, the limbic system. This system includes the hypothalamus, the amygdala, the septal area, and the hippocampus. Numerous studies have linked these brain structures to emotional expression. Hypothalamic mediation of facial expressions prevails among primates, accounting for their rather stereotyped form. Other limbic structures are important, too. For example, Edmund Rolls identified cells in the amygdala that respond to faces. Brain-stimulation studies of squirrel monkeys by Jürgens and Ploog not only demonstrated limbic control of vocalization but also showed that electrical stimulation of specific limbic sites induced emotional changes that were then expressed as distinct vocal expressions.

Applications

The study of emotion in primates promotes understanding of human emotions and their nonverbal communication. Redican notes that Old World monkeys, apes, and humans use remarkably similar facial expressions to express similar emotions in similar contexts. This suggests homology—similarity in structure or behavior caused by inheritance from a common ancestor. Redican's identification of homologies between human smiling and monkey and ape facial displays illustrates how nonhuman primate facial displays can clarify understanding of human facial expression. Human smiles vary with context and underlying affect, and this variance reflects different evolutionary origins. Noting the particular facial muscles involved (the risorius and platysma), Redican argues that the nonhuman primate's grimace is homologous with the human's weak smile or grin of submission, appeasement, and embarrassment. The pleasurable human smile, by contrast, involves contrasting muscular action (zygomaticus contraction) and is deemed homologous with the nonhuman primate's play face. Clearly, the English word "smile" can refer to a variety of anatomically distinct displays communicating different underlying emotional states. The sensitive observer must carefully note facial subtleties; they communicate frequently overlooked dimensions of affect.

The existence of homologous facial displays (which points to their evolutionary antiquity), their relatively stereotyped form and limbic mediation, and, finally, their universality as affirmed in cross-cultural studies by Paul Ekman, combine to suggest that human facial expressions have deeply rooted capacities to communicate affect. Many clinicians and other professional observers who must assess human emotional states are trained to attend carefully to facial expressions. They know that facial expressions, as biologically conservative characteristics, resist dissimulation and have disclosure capacities beyond words.

Demonstrations of parallel vocal correlates for emotional states in both humans and nonhuman primates similarly affirm the evolutionary antiquity of human emotional expression.

The general rule that many birds and mammals, including primates, use higher-pitched sounds when frightened or appeasing, and lower-pitched sounds when hostile or asserting dominance, may apply to humans too. That this relationship is widely held to be true for humans is exemplified by the common advice given in leadership training to lower the pitch of one's speaking voice by at least half an octave when asserting authority. Similarly, Paul Ekman, in his book *Telling Lies: Clues to Deceit in the Marketplace, Politics, and Marriage* (1985), notes that raised voice pitch accompanies fear, anger, and excitement, while voice changes in the opposite direction occur with sadness and perhaps with guilt. Ekman notes that people do exercise considerable voluntary control over nonverbal expressive signs; however, since the neurological tie between voice quality and emotional state is not under the direct control of the higher brain centers that mediate voluntary behavior, control is problematic. A person's true affective state may "leak" out despite great efforts to the contrary. Ekman argues that "leaks" provide vital clues to detecting deceit.

The demonstration of parallels in emotion and its expression between human and nonhuman primates on the basis of single, observable, and measurable dimensions of display provides exact but abstract information. Although less precise, field accounts of complex emotional episodes also point to the evolutionary antiquity, biologically predetermined character, and homology of these emotional expressions. Thus, Goodall observed that some emotional states of chimpanzees are so like humans' that even inexperienced observers can reliably identify them. A young chimpanzee's temper tantrum strongly resembles that of a human toddler. Both species throw themselves to the ground, scream, contort their faces, bang their heads, roll about, and hit out with their arms. Similarly, young chimpanzees and humans express *joie de vivre* in parallel ways. They gambol about their mothers, turn somersaults, pirouette, periodically rush up to their mothers and tumble into their laps, pat them, and pull their mothers' hands to invite tickling. Although the parallel form of such displays and their ready, empathetic recognition by untrained observers may be coincidental, these parallels probably indicate homology.

These observations are reminders that emotion and much of its nonverbal communication are deeply rooted in the biological organization of behavior. This helps explain why nonverbal communication is more difficult to control at will than verbal utterances, and more likely to be evaluated intuitively.

Context

Charles Darwin's classic *The Expression of the Emotions in Man and Animals*, which argued for mental and emotional continuity (homology) between human and subhuman forms, proposed that emotional expressions evolved from movements that at one time served practical ends. Darwin's ideas continue to influence comparative psychology.

Despite the impetus supplied by Darwin, observational studies of emotion in primates did not begin in earnest until the 1930's. In 1931, Ernst Huber's extensive survey of the functional anatomy of primate facial musculature laid the foundation for the study of the evolution of facial expression in primates. In the same year, psychologist C. R. Carpenter began the first modern, observational study of a nonhuman primate, the howler monkey. Many others followed in Carpenter's footsteps, particularly after 1960. Improved methods for recording and analyzing data increased both the quality and the quantity of information. One important advance was the development of the sonogram, or sound spectrogram, which displays the physical properties of sound visually.

Scientific knowledge of primate emotion and its expression developed slowly. After Darwin, the first systematic study of primate calls and facial expressions was Richard J. Andrew's survey of the primates in 1963. Such neglect derived, at least in part, from the reluctance of psychologists to use the term "emotion" in connection with animal expression, particularly for complex emotions. Further, for most primates, naturalistic field descriptions of emotional expression remained embedded as secondary concerns within comprehensive accounts of behavior. Finally, psychological approaches to human emotion have assigned a central role to verbally mediated cognitive appraisal. This potentially devalues the comparison of nonhuman and human emotion by asserting uniqueness to the latter. According to Klaus Scherer and Paul Ekman, however, the tendency of social and behaviorial scientists to shy away from emotion is beginning to dissolve.

Although Darwin and Andrew offered comprehensive accounts of vocal and facial expression of emotion, since the 1970's, specialization has occurred. In general, understanding the evolution of nonverbal communication through facial display has made greater progress, while similar understanding of vocalization has lagged. This probably reflects the simultaneity of affective and cognitive information in vocal expression. That nonhuman primate calls can refer to information in the external

world was convincingly demonstrated in Steven Green's 1975 field study of the vocalizations of Japanese monkeys. Although the blending of affective and cognitive
content in nonhuman primate calls complicates analysis, it also increases their value
in understanding the evolution of human vocal communication.

The component patterning theory of vocal affect expression formulated by Scherer in the 1980's extends the relevance of primate studies by integrating cognitive and
physiological aspects of vocal affect signaling. Scherer argues that animal calls and
human nonverbal vocal behavior are concurrently symptoms of internal states of
physiological arousal, and symbols and appeals based on the nature of a conventional code and the specific context of a particular communication setting.

Exploring integrative links between physiological arousal and symbolic, cognitive
processes in the order Primates promises to advance understanding of human emotional life. First steps have already been taken. For example, Edmund Rolls presents
evidence that limbic system structures are involved in the formation of stimulus-
reinforcement associations. Similarly, Paul MacLean, in concluding a 1986 clinical
study of the limbic system's role in epilepsy, indicated the enduring significance of
explorations of primate emotion with the speculation that the limbic system, a primitive brain region devoid of verbal capacities, may in fact be the source of the feelings
of conviction people attach to their ideas, concepts, and theories.

Bibliography

Andrew, Richard John, and Ernst Huber. *Evolution of Facial Expression.* New York:
Arno Press, 1972. A re-publication of Andrew's study of primate calls and facial
expressions, and Huber's well-illustrated anatomical study of the primate facial
musculature.

Darwin, Charles. *The Expression of the Emotions in Man and Animals.* London:
J. Murray, 1872. Reprint. Chicago: University of Chicago Press, 1965. A true classic; the departure point for any serious exploration of the evolution of emotion.
Vocalization, facial expression, complex emotions, and the general principles governing the evolution of expression are all lucidly treated.

Ekman, Paul, ed. *Darwin and Facial Expression: A Century of Research in Review.*
New York: Academic Press, 1973. This book was published to commemorate the
centennial of Darwin's classic book on emotional expression. Comprehensive, detailed chapters by Suzanne Chevalier-Skolnikoff on facial expression in nonhuman primates, and by Paul Ekman on the cross-cultural universality of facial expressions, demonstrate the continuing relevance of Darwin's ideas.

Goodall, Jane. *The Chimpanzees of Gombe/Patterns of Behavior.* Cambridge, Mass.:
The Belknap Press of the Harvard University Press, 1986. Summarizes findings of
the first quarter-century of Goodall's study of humankind's closest relative. A
comprehensive account of chimpanzee ecology, social behavior, and communication; illustrates primate field studies at their best.

Plutchik, Robert, and Henry Kellerman, eds. *Emotion: Theory, Research, and Experience.* Vol. 3 in *Biological Foundations of Emotion.* New York: Academic Press,

1986. The third volume of a five-volume set by these editors, published between 1980 and 1990. Offers detailed information on the role of the nervous system in emotional expression. Important chapters include Detlev Ploog on the neurobiology of vocal expression, Paul MacLean on affect and its cerebral substrate, Edmund Rolls on the neural systems involved in primate emotion, and two chapters on the amygdala.

Redican, William. "An Evolutionary Perspective on Human Facial Displays." In *Emotions in the Human Face*, edited by Paul Ekman. 2d ed. New York: Cambridge University Press, 1982. An engaging scientific account of the facial expression of emotion by nonhuman primates that discusses homologies with human facial expression.

Rosenblum, Leonard A., ed. *Primate Behavior: Developments in Field and Laboratory Research*. Vol. 4. New York: Academic Press, 1975. A collection of monographs that includes an extensive descriptive account of the facial expressions of nonhuman primates by William Redican, and one hundred pages devoted to the analysis of Japanese monkey vocalizations by Steven Green.

Snowdon, Charles T., Charles H. Brown, and Michael R. Petersen, eds. *Primate Communication*. New York: Cambridge University Press, 1982. Sixteen chapters on nonhuman primate communication summarize the field up to about 1980. Readable throughout. Chapters by Robert Seyfarth and Suzanne Chevalier-Skolnikoff provide excellent summaries of their research. Especially valuable is Uwe Jürgens' contribution on the vocal repertoire of the squirrel monkey, which offers a concise, readable introduction to his extensive research with this species.

Todt, Dietmar, Philipp Goedeking, and David Symmes, eds. *Primate Vocal Communication*. New York: Springer-Verlag, 1988. A good sampling of approaches to the study of vocalization. Includes articles by Detlev Ploog and an accessible summary of Klaus Scherer's component patterning theory of vocal affect expression.

Roy Fontaine

Cross-References

Functions of Emotion, 900; Emotion: Mind-Body Processes, 907; Emotion: Neurophysiology and Neuroanatomy, 914; Emotional Expression, 954; Ethology, 992; Language in Primates, 1407; Nonverbal Communication, 1681.

EMOTIONAL EXPRESSION

Type of psychology: Emotion
Field of study: Interpersonal relations

Emotional expression includes both facial expressions and body movements that accompany the internal experience of emotion and that clearly serve to communicate that emotion to others. Influenced by the work of Charles Darwin, psychologists have long regarded the communication of emotion as an important function with survival value for the species.

Principal terms
DECODING: the perception of cues that signify an emotion in others
EMOTION: a psychological response that includes a set of physiological changes, expressive behaviors, and a subjective experience
ENCODING: the expression of emotion
NONVERBAL COMMUNICATION: silent communication of internal states; accomplished through facial expressions, body posture, and movements

Overview

The study of human emotion is a complex endeavor. It is complex in part because emotion is not a single event or process but is, instead, a collection of discrete events and processes. Humans experience a vast array of emotions, and each of those emotions actually consists of several components—the physiological changes that occur, the nonverbal communication of the emotion, and the subjective or felt experience. The topic of emotional communication or expression includes two related aspects: encoding (the expression of emotion) and decoding (the perception of cues that signify an emotion).

Nonverbal forms of expression play an integral role in the complex human communication system. Examples of emotional expression by nonverbal means are easy to come by. For example, if irritated, people may tense their bodies, press their lips together, and gesture with their eyebrows. With an averted glance or a prolonged stare, a person can communicate intimacy, anger, submission, or dominance.

In his now-classic 1872 book *The Expression of the Emotions in Man and Animals*, Charles Darwin argued that many nonverbal communication patterns, specifically emotional expressions, are inherited and that they evolved because they had survival value. He focused primarily on the expression of emotion through specific changes in the appearance of the face and argued that the primary function of emotional expression is to inform others about one's internal state and, therefore, to inform them of how one is likely to behave. For example, when enraged, individuals commonly grimace and bare their teeth; one's perception of that anger suggests that the individual may behave aggressively. Frequently, such an expression (and the appropriate perception on the part of the target) results in the retreat of the target, thus avoiding an actual fight. For social animals who live in groups, such as humans, this rapid communication of internal states is highly adaptive.

If emotional expressions are a product of evolution and are, therefore, shared by all members of the species, their production and their interpretation should be universal. Cross-cultural research supports the universality of certain facial expressions. People in various cultures agree on how to convey a given emotion and how to convey it most intensely. The universal expression of anger, for example, involves a flushed face, brows lowered and drawn together, flared nostrils, a clenched jaw, and bared teeth. Several researchers have also shown that people from a variety of countries, including the United States, Japan, Brazil, and others, as well as people from several preliterate tribal groups who have had no previous contact with the Western world, have little difficulty identifying the emotions of happiness, anger, sadness, disgust, fear, and surprise, as exhibited in photographs and/or videotapes of members of their own cultures and other cultures. Thus, both the encoding and decoding of certain emotional expressions are the same for people all over the world regardless of culture, language, or educational background.

This universality, however, does not preclude the possibility that certain aspects of emotional expression may be learned. In fact, strong cultural (learned) differences can be found in the intensity and frequency with which certain emotions are expressed and in the situations that elicit certain emotions. For example, in cultures that encourage individuality, as in Western Europe and North America, emotional displays are often intense and prolonged. People express their emotions openly. In Asian and Third-World cultures that emphasize social connections and interdependence, emotions such as sympathy, respect, and shame are more common than in the West, and people in such cultures rarely, and then only briefly, display negative emotions that might disrupt a peaceful group environment. Additional evidence for the role of learning in emotional expression is provided by research suggesting that women express emotions more intensely than men, who tend to hide their expressions to some degree.

People of different cultures also vary in their use of certain other forms of nonverbal cues to express emotion. That is, individual cultures have developed additional signals of emotion that are shared only within those cultures. For example, the psychologist Otto Klineberg reported in 1938 that Chinese literature was filled with examples of emotional expression that would easily be misunderstood by members of the Western world. Such examples include clapping the hands when worried or disappointed, sticking out one's tongue to express surprise, and scratching one's ears and cheeks to express happiness.

The human ability to decode or interpret emotional expressions is, like the expression itself, also partly learned. Evidence for this can be found in the reactions of infants to novel situations and novel toys. Under such circumstances, infants frequently check their mother's facial expressions before approaching or avoiding the novel toy. If she looks happy or relaxed, the infant generally will approach; if she looks frightened, the infant will try to avoid the new situation or will approach the mother. Additional support is found in the research that suggests that women are generally better at detecting emotional undercurrents and at detecting emotion from visual information only (such as facial expressions presented in pictures or in films with no voices) than men are. Such individual differences are probably the result of socialization, with girls socialized to be more sensitive to the feelings of others.

The term "facial expression" is commonly defined as a motor response resulting from an emotional state. That is, the facial expression is believed to be a consequence of the emotion. This is the position implied by most of the theory and research in the area. Yet with regard to the role of the expressive component in the experience of emotion, there is another possibility. Some researchers have suggested that facial expressions not only communicate but also regulate emotion. For example, Darwin, in 1872, wrote that "the free expression by outward signs of an emotion intensifies it. . . . On the other hand, the repression, as far as possible, of all outward signs, softens our emotions." This statement clearly suggests that the outward expression of emotion can either amplify or attenuate the intensity of the emotional experience. Support for this hypothesis is now readily available.

Applications

As more is learned about the subtle changes in facial expression and body movements that are associated with specific emotions, the behavior of individuals in specific situations may be interpreted more accurately. For example, therapists can observe more closely the facial expression changes in their patients, thereby gaining access to emotional reactions that their patients may not discuss openly.

Several researchers have already reported that close scrutiny of changes in facial expression among patients during interviews supports the notion that many expression changes occur too quickly for easy detection. E. A. Haggard and F. S. Isaacs, for example, while searching for indications of nonverbal communication between therapist and patient, ran some film at slow motion and noticed that the expression of the patient's face sometimes changed dramatically within a few frames of the film. These changes were not observable when the film was run at regular speed. Furthermore, these subtle changes appeared to take place at key points during the interview. For example, although the patient's detectable expression included a smile when discussing a "friend," closer inspection of the film suggested that the patient actually exhibited the subtle facial changes associated with the expression of anger during the conversation. These "micromomentary" expressions are believed to reveal actual emotional states that are condensed in time because of repression.

Advanced technology allows researchers to measure the subtle facial changes in other ways as well. For example, when a person is given mild emotional stimuli, electrodes attached to facial muscles can detect the hidden reactions. Thus, although a person's face might not look any different, voltage changes on the skin may reveal micromuscular smiles or frowns underneath; perhaps this procedure will even result in a new approach to lie detection.

In addition to the work being done to develop an understanding of the normal but subtle changes associated with various emotions under normal circumstances, several researchers have looked at how emotional expressions change under abnormal circumstances. For example, the weightlessness experienced by astronauts results in the movement of body fluids toward the upper body, causing their faces to become puffy. Under these circumstances, a reliance on facial expressions for emotional information might increase the risk of misunderstanding. Thus, a full understanding of such changes is necessary for individuals likely to find themselves in such situations.

Nonverbal forms of emotional communication also play an important role in the normal development of the human infant. For example, the facial expressions of both infants and care givers are important in the development of the attachment relationship. That is, the facial expressions of an infant indicate to the care giver the infant's emotional states. Their expressions tell much about how they are "feeling" and thus allow adults to respond appropriately. Furthermore, the early signs of emotional expression in infants are events that clearly contribute to the development of the relationship between infant and care giver. For example, the infant's first smile is typically interpreted in a personal way by the care giver and is responded to with a returned smile and increased interaction on the part of the care giver, thus resulting in a positive interaction sequence. Evidence of the first smile also leads to increased attempts by the care giver to elicit smiling at other times, thus giving the care giver a new topic with which to engage the infant in social interaction.

Context

Throughout history, humankind has acknowledged the existence of discrete emotions and has exhibited acceptance and understanding of the public aspect of emotions—the expressive movements that characterize each individual emotion. For example, sad (tragic) and happy (comic) facial masks were worn by theater players during ancient times to portray the emotional tone of their characters and were correctly perceived by audiences. Similarly, today, in the theater and in everyday life, people accept the notion that the face has a real and definite function in communicating feelings or emotions; people automatically search the face of the speaker, studying facial expressions, to understand more fully what is being communicated in any interpersonal interaction.

Several well-known scientists of the nineteenth century and early scientific psychologists of the twentieth century acknowledged the importance of emotion and emotional expression. It was during the late nineteenth century that Darwin paved the way for theory and research on the facial patterns in emotion. In the early twentieth century, Wilhelm Wundt, the father of psychology, assumed that the face was the chief means of emotional expression. Thus the topic of emotion was considered a topic worthy of scientific investigation during the early years of psychology.

When behaviorism took over as the dominant psychological theory of the twentieth century, however, emotion, as well as all other topics that included "subjective" components, was forced out of the laboratory and out of the range of scientific study. During psychology's period of strong behavioristic orientation (the 1930's through the 1950's), most general theories of behavior and most major personality theories ignored emotion altogether or dealt with it only as a vague, global entity or process of little importance. There was very little scientific investigation into the existence of separate emotions, and therefore there was very little attention paid to the existence of discrete facial patterns for the communication of emotion. This overall lack of interest in facial patterns by behavioral scientists had little influence on common wisdom; people in general have maintained the age-old position that the patterns exist and that they have specific emotional significance.

As theories of emotion began to appear in the scientific literature, and as the potential importance of emotional expressions was considered, the question of innate versus learned facial patterns of emotional expression was addressed. For a substantial period of time, the dominant view was that there were no invariable patterns of expression. It was not until publication of the work of Silvan Tomkins, Carroll Izard, Paul Ekman, and other investigators during the 1960's that conclusive evidence for the existence of universal facial patterns in emotional expression was provided, confirming for science what people have always known. Since then, significant advances have been made in understanding the facial musculature changes associated with the expression of individual emotions and in understanding the development of the ability to interpret those facial musculature changes. It is, moreover, likely that significant advances will continue to be made in the identification of subtle changes in emotional expression and in understanding the important role of such facial patterns in interpersonal communication.

Bibliography

Atkinson, R. L., R. C. Atkinson, E. E. Smith, and D. J. Bem. *Introduction to Psychology.* 10th ed. New York: Harcourt Brace Jovanovich, 1990. An introductory psychology text, aimed at the college-level student; includes a very good discussion of the field of emotion, clear examples of critical issues, and interesting and stimulating discussions of some controversial areas.

Darwin, Charles. *The Expression of the Emotions in Man and Animals.* London: John Murray, 1872. The original theory and scientific evidence of Charles Darwin; includes a discussion of the adaptive value of emotions and emotional expression as well as evidence for the evolution of specific emotional signals. More recent editions of the book are available.

Ekman, Paul. *Darwin and Facial Expression.* New York: Academic Press, 1973. Includes an in-depth discussion of Darwin's theory of emotional expression and presents evidence to support his theory.

Izard, Carroll E. *The Face of Emotion.* New York: Appleton-Century-Crofts, 1971. An excellent presentation of the history of the field of emotion in psychology. Includes a detailed discussion of the evidence regarding the heritability and universality of emotional expression. Presents a general theoretical framework relating neural activity, facial patterning, and subjective experience as the principal components of emotion.

_____. *Human Emotions.* New York: Plenum Press, 1977. A full presentation of Izard's differential emotions theory as well as a detailed discussion of the discrete emotions and their accompanying facial expression.

_____. *Measuring Emotions in Infants and Children.* New York: Cambridge University Press, 1982. A presentation of the measurement procedures commonly used to assess emotional experiences in infants and children. Discusses several important topics regarding the development of emotions and the study of emotions in a developmental context.

Myers, D. G. *Psychology.* 3d ed. New York: Worth, 1992. A general introductory psychology textbook. Contains a good discussion of many aspects of emotion; provides many examples and discusses important issues.

Wortman, Camille B., and Elizabeth F. Loftus. *Psychology.* 4th ed. New York: McGraw-Hill, 1992. A college-level introductory text with a clear presentation of the field of emotion; makes effective use of examples.

Loretta A. Rieser-Danner

Cross-References

Development of Emotion, 810; Emotion: Cultural Variations, 887; Emotion: Definition and Assessment, 893; Functions of Emotion, 900; Emotion in Primates, 947; The Facial Feedback Theory of Emotion, 1019; Nonverbal Communication, 1681.

ENCODING STRATEGIES AND ENCODING SPECIFICITY

Type of psychology: Memory
Field of study: Cognitive processes

Encoding strategies include both intentional and unintentional processes that are used to improve memory performance. Encoding refers to the ways information gets put into memory. Encoding specificity is a theory of memory encoding that predicts that any cue that is present at the time of encoding will serve as an effective cue for retrieval of that memory event.

Principal terms
ASSOCIATION: a combining of two or more items that automatically occur together
CONTEXT: the surroundings or events that are occurring at a particular time
CUE: a specific clue that triggers a memory
ENCODING: the process of transforming sensory information into a code that can be remembered by the memory system
RETRIEVAL: the process of getting information from the memory system
STORAGE: the process of putting events into the memory system to remain until the information is needed
TARGET: in a memory test, a target is the correct word that is being prompted for recall

Overview

Most people find it easy to remember certain events from their past, such as the best vacation they ever had. They would remember their age and the most interesting things they saw or did at that time, even if the events occurred years before. If people could not remember events in their lives, they would have no personal history, skills, or talents. Fortunately, humans are able to take information from the world and store it in a mental representation that allows them to use that past information in a current situation. This ability is a function of the way the human memory system works.

The memory system records events as they occur; this process is called encoding. The information is stored in a memory trace until it is needed. A memory trace remains in storage until a cue for that memory occurs, at which time the memory will be retrieved from long-term storage and outputted for use.

In the model that is often used to illustrate memory systems, information comes into the memory system and is then transported to short-term memory (STM), where it is held for both further encoding into, and interaction with, long-term memory (LTM). There are different encoding strategies for information, depending on whether it is to be used by STM or LTM. Some encoding strategies are unintentional, but others can be used purposefully to increase memory abilities.

One of the characteristics of short-term memory is that it can only store five to nine items and for only about eighteen seconds. Thus, information processed in STM must either be encoded into LTM or be lost from the system. If, for example, one needs the information of a telephone number, one probably will repeat the number until one can dial. This is known as a rehearsal strategy, and it serves to make the information available until one uses it.

One way of overcoming the capacity limitations of STM is by an encoding strategy called chunking: A group of items are chunked into meaningful units, which allows STM to hold more information and to be aided by LTM. For example, if one were asked to remember the letters FCTIIIBWAABM by rehearsing the letters, one would not easily remember the sequence. If, however, one were asked to remember the same letters but arranged as FBI CIA TWA IBM, one would have no trouble recalling the sequence. The letters became chunked into four meaningful units which were small enough for STM and were encoded into LTM because of their meaningfulness.

Another encoding strategy is the use of imagery. In order to remember a list of items, make a visual image of the items. For example, if one is to remember the pair of words "dog" and "ribbon," one might make an image of the dog with a big red ribbon on its neck and tail. Imagery is similar to another encoding strategy called elaboration. This, like imagery, adds details to an event and gives it more meaning so that it is more easily remembered. For example, given directions to a concert, one might start thinking about the time one walked down Main Street and was going to the ice-cream parlor, and so on. By adding these details, one elaborates on the event and increases one's memory. Elaboration is something that people do automatically, because memory is organized so that one event triggers memories of other events. If one hears the word "dog," one automatically begins to retrieve things that one knows about dogs.

Another encoding strategy is called organization. This process groups items into larger categories of relatedness. For example, given a list of words to remember, such as "dog," "knife," "rose," "cat," "horse," "fork," "daisy," "spoon," "pansy," one would likely remember the words in three categories: flowers, utensils, and animals. This could be an intentional encoding strategy, and it aids memory because the retrieval of the larger category also activates all the members of that category that are associated with it.

Yet this is contrary to a theory proposed by Endel Tulving called encoding specificity. He proposes that any cue present and specifically encoded at the time of study will serve as an effective cue for retrieval, even over cues that would seem to be more likely to trigger the memory. For example, Tulving and Thompson in 1971 gave subjects a list of word pairs to remember. One group was given a list of word pairs that were strong associates of each other, such as "hot-cold." The other list had words that were weakly associated with each other, such as "blow-cold." Later, at a test session, the first word was given as a cue, and subjects were asked to fill in the second target word. Each group was given both strong and weak associated cues. It might seem likely that given the cue "hot-_____ ," one would think of the target word "cold" even if one had been given the weakly associated pair of "blow-cold" at the time of study; however, this was not what happened. Subjects given the cue word "blow" at study could not recall "cold" when given "hot" as a cue, but did very well when given their original cue word, "blow." In other words, whatever cue word was encoded at the time of study was the best cue for retrieval of the target word at test regardless of how weakly or strongly associated the cue and target words were. Therefore, Tulving predicted that whatever cues are specifically encoded at the time of the event are the best cues for memory at the time of testing. Thus, encoding specificity can be extended to any context cues specific to the memory event. This includes the subject's mood, surroundings, or cues.

Applications

Encoding strategies aid memory in ways that enable a person either to remember more information or to remember it longer. These strategies are necessary because the human memory system is limited in its abilities. Short-term memory can only handle a limited number of items at a time. If a person is tested by being asked to write down a series of numbers immediately after seeing them, for example, most people can remember somewhere between five and nine numbers without too much trouble. The task becomes far more difficult as soon as encoding strategies (such as rehearsal) are blocked. For example, if people are given a string of numbers (say, "6492035") but must immediately recite the first half of the alphabet before writing the numbers down, most people cannot do this easily. Strategies such as rehearsal are crucial to the effective functioning of short-term memory.

Other intentional encoding strategies that increase the ability to remember include chunking and imagery. Chunking increases the number of items that one can hold in STM. Instead of twelve individual letters, if one can group them into smaller units, then one can be within the five-to-nine-item limit and will have no trouble remembering them. Imagery aids memory because an image has many more details than a word and thus provides more cues for retrieving it. If one is given any of the cues in the image, one will recall the whole image. For example, one could form images of the following two-word groupings by imagining the two things doing something together: "train-seashell," "asparagus-cowboy," "shoe-telephone," "bottle-fish," "tomato-boat." One would then be able to remember the second word if given the first word of the pair ("asparagus-_____ "), because the two words were encoded together. The first word provides a specific cue for the memory event.

Sometimes the information that is encoded into the memory event is related to the context or surroundings of that event; instead of a word cue, the environment at the time of encoding can be a cue for retrieval. For example, in 1975, Duncan Godden and Alan Baddeley found that memory was better if subjects were asked to remember something in the same environment in which they previously had learned the material. They had subjects study a list of words on shore and a list of words underwater. If the list was learned underwater, memory was better if the recall test was also underwater than on shore, and vice versa. They concluded that the context provided additional cues for memory.

These context effects have also been demonstrated to include a person's mood at the time of encoding, known as state-dependent effects. For example, Gordon Bower (1978) hypnotized subjects into either a positive or negative emotional state and tested their memory for material when they were in the same and different emotional states. Students who were in congruent states of mind at study and test sessions had greater memory than students at different states of mind at study and test. Again the contextual cues that were associated with a particular state of mind were present at both encoding and retrieval and served to aid recall by being specifically encoded with the event.

Thus, if one wants to increase one's memory skills, the more types of encoding strategies one uses, the better one will be able to remember. In addition, it is important to remember that using the same cues for both study and test sessions will also result in better performance. Therefore, one might try to do some studying in the same room where one will be taking a test.

Context

Cognitive psychology encompasses the study of all the functions of the human mind, including thinking, problem solving, reasoning, attention, consciousness, and processing information. It is considered a relatively new field of psychology, although its roots go back to the work of early psychologists in the late nineteenth and early twentieth centuries; in a sense they go back even further, to the philosophers of centuries past. In the late 1800's, both the renowned psychologist William James and Sigmund Freud, the founder of psychoanalysis, wrote about aspects of consciousness and attention. In the same time period, Hermann Ebbinghaus began studying verbal learning and memory, while Wilhelm Wundt attempted to research the structure of the mind with his method of introspection.

Another significant contribution to cognitive psychology began in 1904, when Ivan Pavlov proposed his principles of conditioned learning. This led the way for further study into the learning processes of humans and animals; learning became considered to be an overt action, not a process of the mind. Thus, John B. Watson (1913) proposed that behavior was the only suitable topic for psychology to study, and the processes of the mind became a taboo subject for many years.

It was not until World War II that cognitive psychology became a legitimate topic for research again. This occurred because the topic of human error became an important question for the military: Pilots' lives could be saved if more could be known about perception and actions. Researchers were employed to determine how decisions were made and to study the importance of attentional processes on performance. From this an entire field of study emerged, and the study of encoding strategies developed as a by-product of studying other processes of the memory system, such as attention, forgetting, and effective retrieval cues.

In the same time frame, the computer emerged; these areas of psychology were formulated in terms of an information-processing model of human memory. In other words, in order to understand the way memory systems work, a theoretical model of the brain was based on the computer. In 1968, Richard Atkinson and Richard Shiffrin suggested a model of memory which consisted of three memory stores, each with its own characteristics and functions. This consisted of the sensory register, the short-term memory, and the long-term memory. This information-processing model made the concepts of codes, storage capacity, trace duration, and retrieval failures an area of research. In studying these concepts, other areas became new topics of interest.

Research into encoding strategies is concerned with which elements of the environment are selected for encoding and how people can use this information to improve memory performance. The cue environment that is encoded is a topic of great interest, as it can aid performance if it can be predicted. Such components of the cue environment as gestures and emotions that are all encoded below the level of awareness are only beginning to be studied, and they should lead to a much better understanding of how to improve memory.

Bibliography

Anderson, J. R. *Cognitive Psychology and Its Implications.* New York: W. H. Freeman, 1990. Although this book generally has an information-processing framework, it is still a thorough reference book on any area concerned with cognitive psychology. It is written in simple enough terms that a beginning psychology student can easily follow the line of thought.

Ellis, H. C., and R. R. Hunt. *Fundamentals of Human Memory and Cognition.* Dubuque, Iowa: Wm. C. Brown, 1989. This excellent book explains every aspect of cognitive functioning in a clear and precise way. It includes all topics necessary to understand the workings of human processing and illustrates these issues with research findings. It can be easily read and understood by the layperson.

Schwartz, Barry, and Dan Reisberg. *Learning and Memory.* New York: W. W. Norton, 1991. This book is a comprehensive outline of all aspects of psychology that pertain to learning and memory. Includes research and historical review. An excellent reference book.

Smith, Frank. *Comprehension and Learning: A Conceptual Framework for Teachers.* New York: Holt, Rinehart and Winston, 1975. This book is a cognitive textbook on the principles of learning in children. It has both an information-processing format and a psycholinguistic perspective, for a comprehensive presentation of research. It is easily read by student and teacher, and it includes comprehension, language, and concept development.

Tulving, Endel. *Elements of Episodic Memory.* London: Oxford University Press, 1983. A comprehensive overview of the complete theories of Tulving. Contains explanations of both the episodic memory system (which is related to encoding specificity) and the semantic memory system (which is more knowledge-based).

The book is not too technical to be read by the novice, but it serves better as a resource than a book to be read in its entirety.

Donna J. Frick

Cross-References

Forgetting and Forgetfulness, 1049; Long-Term Memory, 1479; Memory: Empirical Studies, 1511; Memory: Long-Term versus Short-Term, 1517; Memory Enhancement, 1556; Memory Storage: Episodic versus Semantic, 1562; Short-Term Memory, 2265.

THE ENDOCRINE SYSTEM

Type of psychology: Biological bases of behavior
Field of study: Endocrine system

Behavior, by definition, includes physiological events which are responses to internal and external stimuli; the endocrine system, through the action of hormones and in cooperation with the nervous system, plays a necessary role in bringing about these reactions in animals and humans.

Principal terms

ADRENAL GLANDS: endocrine glands located above the kidney consisting of a medulla and cortex area, each of which is under pituitary control and which functions in response to stress

BEHAVIOR: a physiological response made by an organism to internal or external stimuli

BIOPSYCHOLOGY: a branch of psychology that uses data from biology, endocrinology, genetics, and neuroscience in order to understand the mechanisms of behavior

ENDOCRINE SYSTEM: a series of ductless glands that secrete chemicals called hormones

ETHOLOGY: a science that studies animal behavior

HORMONE: a chemical messenger secreted by endocrine tissue that causes biochemical reactions

HYPOTHALAMUS: the area of the brain that interacts with the pituitary gland in executing control over the physiology of the body

PITUITARY: an endocrine gland located in the brain that controls several other endocrines and that cooperates with the hypothalamus of the nervous system in controlling physiology

Overview

A subdivision of biopsychology known as physiological psychology studies animal and human responses to internal and external stimuli. Much of the research in physiological psychology has focused on the role of the nervous system in determining behavior. As more was learned about nervous system activities and resulting behaviors, it was realized that the nervous system does not act independently of the endocrine system: The systems cooperate in providing the biological bases for behavior.

The endocrine system essentially consists of ductless glands that produce chemical substances called hormones. The hormones elicit physiological reactions, either locally or at some distant target site. When acting at a distance, the hormones travel to the site by way of the circulatory system.

Among most invertebrates, animals without backbones, endocrine glands are not in evidence. Specialized cells known as neurosecretory cells serve as endocrine tissue. The cells, which resemble the neuron or functional cell of the nervous system, are hormone producers. In invertebrate animals such as the hydra and planaria, the secretions (hormones) of the neurosecretory cells seem to influence growth and may be the underlying cause of the tremendous powers of regeneration possessed by the animals. There are indications that the development of sexuality, the laying of eggs, and the release of sperm may be under hormonal control. Attempts to establish the link between hormones and invertebrate behavior when the hormones are produced by neurosecretory cells have inherent problems. A common method of studying hormone influence involves removal of the secreting organ, which causes a hormone deficit. Changes in physiology and/or behavior are observed. Hormone is then provided to the animal to see if the original condition can be restored. Utilization of this method is complicated by the difficulty in removing all the functioning neurosecretory cells. In addition, the cells regenerate rapidly. This prevents an accurate assessment of the effects of hormone deficit.

Hormone effects are observable and measurable in the more developed invertebrates such as the *Arthropoda*. Studies carried out on insects and crustaceans indicate the presence of both neurosecretory cells and endocrine glands. Among the behaviors and activities which are controlled by the hormones released from either the cells or the glands are molting, sexual differentiation, sexual behavior, water balance, and diapause. Since arthropods are encased in an outer skeletal structure, it is necessary for the animals to shed their outer structure in order to grow. During the growth years, the animals go through cycles of shedding the outer skeleton or molting, growing, and reforming an outer coat. There is evidence that insects are under hormonal control when they enter a state of diapause, or arrested behavior in adverse times.

All vertebrates, animals with backbones, have a well-developed and highly organized endocrine system. The system consists of the following glands: the pituitary, the pineal, the thyroid, the thymus, the pancreas, a pair of adrenals (each adrenal actually acts as two glands; the adrenal cortex produces unique hormones and functions independently of the adrenal medulla), a pair of parathyroids, and a pair of ovaries or testes. Endocrine tissue in the gastrointestinal tract readies the system for the digestive process. During a pregnancy, the placental tissue assumes an endocrine function. Although the kidneys do not produce a hormone directly, they release an enzyme which converts a blood protein into a hormone that stimulates red blood cell production.

All vertebrates have a pituitary. The pituitary is a small, round organ found at the base of the brain. This major endocrine gland interacts with the hypothalamus of the nervous system. Together they control behavior. The hypothalamus is kept aware of physiological events in the body by monitoring the composition of the blood. In turn, the hypothalamus signals the pituitary by either nerve impulse or chemical messenger. The pituitary responds by releasing or ceasing to release hormones which will have a direct effect on physiology or will stimulate other endocrines to release their hormones in order to alter the physiological event and influence behavior. The endocrine system exerts its effects on a biochemical level.

The human endocrine system is typical of vertebrate endocrine systems and their effect on behavior, although certain hormones may have a more pronounced and obvious effect in other vertebrates. For example, melanocyte-stimulating hormone, which is generated by the anterior lobe of the pituitary, greatly increases skin pigmentation in amphibians. This creates a protective coloration. In humans, the darkening effect is not achieved unless excessive hormone is administered. The protective function is not apparent. There are enough similarities among human and animal endocrine functions and effects, however, to warrant the use of data from both ethology and human behavioral studies in determining the biological bases for behavior.

Applications

The influence of the endocrine system on behavior has been studied on many levels. Much of the work has been done on animals; laboratory rats have been the most frequently used subjects. There is, however, a growing body of information on hormonal effects on a variety of human behaviors, including reproductive and developmental behavior, reaction to stress, learning, and memory. Studies carried out in reproductive and developmental biology on both animal and human subjects have substantiated the belief that hormones influence mating behavior, developmental events including sexual differentiation, and female and male sexuality.

Castration experiments have linked the testes with a male mating behavior pattern in animals. The sexually active adult male animal aggressively seeks and attempts to mount the female whether she is receptive or not. The castrated male retains the ability to mount and impregnate a female but loses the aggressiveness and persistent pursuit of females. The male may assume the more submissive, female behavior and even engage in homosexual encounters. Normally, the release of reproductive hormones in the male is noncyclic, whereas in the female, it is cyclic. Castrated animals begin to exhibit the female, cyclic-pattern hormone release. The hormonal influence is confirmed by administering androgens (male hormones) to the castrated animals. Male mating behavior and the noncyclic release of hormones returns.

The presence of male hormones has an effect on the female cycle and sexual receptivity. Pheromones are substances secreted on the body of one individual which influence the behavior of another. These chemical messengers function during mate attraction, territoriality, and episodes of fear. Their existence and functions are well documented throughout the animal kingdom, especially among insects and mammals. In experiments using rats, it was shown that the pheromones act in conjunction with male hormones in bringing the female to a state of receptivity. The urine of noncastrated male rats contains androgens. When a male rat is introduced into a cage of sexually inactive females, the male sends off chemical signals by way of pheromones and the androgen-containing urine. The result is the accelerated onset of estrus, or sexual receptivity, on the part of the females. Castrated males produce pheromones but do not have androgens in the urine. When castrated males are introduced into a cage of inactive females, the estrous cycle is not affected.

Female mammals, with the exception of monkeys, apes, and humans, experience a reproductive cycle known as estrus. Under hormonal control, the female is receptive to the male once or twice a year, when her eggs are available for fertilization. This period of receptivity is known as the estrous phase, or heat. Research shows that the particular female hormone which induces estrus is progesterone.

The work done by researchers in developing contraceptives clarified the role of hormones in the functioning of the human female reproductive system. The system operates in a monthly cycle during which ovarian and uterine changes occur under hormonal control. These hormones do not affect the human female's receptivity, which is not limited to fertile periods.

Testosterone derivatives known as anabolic steroids are illegally used by some athletes in an attempt to increase muscularity, strength, and performance. While both sexes do experience the desired effects, long-term, high dosage usage has undesirable consequences. This is particularly true in the female, who begins to exhibit a deepening of the voice, a male body shape, and increased body and facial hair. Both males and females can become sterile. Psychotic behaviors such as depression and anger have been recorded.

Developmental biologists indicate that hormones exert their influence as early as six or seven weeks into embryonic development. At this point, undifferentiated tissue with the potential of developing into either a female or a male reproductive system will develop into a male system in the presence of testosterone, and into a female system in its absence. There is some evidence that the embryonic hormones have an effect on the developing brain, producing either a male or female brain. Functionally, this may account for the cyclic activity of female reproductive hormones and the noncyclic activity of the male. A few anatomical differences between male and female brains have been observed in both rats and humans. In the hypothalamus of the brain, there are cell bodies called nuclei. In rats and in humans, these nuclei are larger in males than in females.

Learning and memory can be experimentally affected by hormones. Experiments reveal that chemicals which resemble adrenocorticotropic hormone (ACTH) can extend the memory time of rats. Rats, stimulated by electric shock and provided with an avoidance possibility such as moving into another chamber of a cage or climbing a pole in the center of the cage, were administered ACTH-like molecules. The treated rats were able to remember the appropriate reaction to the stimulus for a longer period of time. In other experiments, rats in a maze were administered vasopressin, a posterior pituitary hormone, which increased their frequency in selecting the correct pathway through the maze.

The effect of vasopressin on human memory is not as clearly defined. There have been positive results with schizophrenic patients and patients with alcohol-induced amnesia. In these cases, memory has been enhanced to a limited degree. There is no solid evidence that learning and memory in humans will be greatly improved by the administration of vasopressin.

Areas such as eating disorders, psychotic behavior, hormone therapy, behavior modification, and biological clocks and rhythms challenge the physiological psychologist to further research to test hormonal influences.

Context

Curiosity about behavior, both animal and human, is of long standing. The suspicion that substances in the body contribute to behavior also has a long history. During the fifth century B.C., Hippocrates suggested, in his humoral theory, that personality was determined by four body fluids: phlegm, black bile, yellow bile, and blood. The dominance of one or another of the fluids was associated with a behavior pattern. A proportionate distribution of the fluids resulted in a balanced personality. This theory has contributed terms such as phlegmatic, sanguine, bilious, and good- or bad-humored to describe personality types and states of mind.

Aristotle (384-322 B.C.) is reported to have performed castration experiments on both fowl and men in order to alter behavior. He believed that something produced by the testes caused male behavior. Several nineteenth century researchers continued the study of the connection between the testes and male reproductive behavior. In 1849, Arnold Adolphe Berthold initiated a series of experiments on cockerels. He removed the testes from six birds and noted their loss of "male" behavior. Testes were transplanted into the abdomen of half the castrated birds. Successful transplantation restored the typical male crowing and combativeness.

During the late nineteenth and early twentieth centuries, sciences became more organized. Interest in behavior and its causes continued. The science of ethology, which focuses on animal behavior, came into existence. In the early 1900's, John B. Watson founded a branch of psychology that became known as behavior science. This area of psychology concentrated on human behavioral studies. Eventually, ethology and behavior science contributed to a new branch of psychology, biopsychology, which incorporates and applies data from neuroscience, genetics, endocrinology, and physiology in the quest for biological explanations of behavior. Biopsychology embraces several subdivisions. Physiological psychology focuses on nervous system and endocrine system research. Psychopharmacology specializes in the effects of drugs on the nervous system and ultimately on behavior. The development of therapeutic drugs is a goal of this discipline. The neuropsychologist studies the effects of brain damage on behavior. Psychophysiology differs from physiological psychology in that the psychophysiologist uses only human subjects while the physiological psychologist experiments on laboratory animals, especially rats.

Early research in physiological psychology focused on the nervous system, but it soon became evident that the endocrine system also influenced behavior and that the effects of the two systems were interrelated contributors to behavior. Hans Selye, a Canadian scientist, proposed a direct connection between the endocrine system and behavior. In 1946, he described physiological events that were triggered by stress.

This set of bodily changes became known as the general adaptation syndrome. The syndrome involved the mobilization of the autonomic nervous system, the adrenal glands, and the anterior lobe of the pituitary.

As research continued, data on the role of the endocrine system in determining behavior began to accumulate. Researchers continue to look to the endocrine system to provide clues about the causes of psychiatric diseases and the efficacy of hormone therapy in treating the diseases, as well as in altering behavior patterns.

Bibliography

Bioscience 33 (October, 1983). The entire issue is devoted to the effects of hormones on behavior. Includes an article on invertebrates in general, followed by articles on fish through primates. Written in nonesoteric language.

Brennan, James F. *History and Systems of Psychology.* Englewood Cliffs, N.J.: Prentice-Hall, 1982. Readable presentation of the history and development of psychology. Covers the highlights of the discipline from the time of ancient Greece up to the early 1980's. Good background material for those not well grounded in psychology, and interesting reading for those with a historical leaning.

Donovan, Bernard T. *Hormones and Human Behavior.* Cambridge, England: Cambridge University Press, 1985. An excellent compilation of the information available on hormones and behavior up to 1985. Uses technical language, but one who reads on a high school level and has had some exposure to science will find the book informative and interesting. Focuses on the pituitary, the gonads, and the adrenals, and their effect on human behavior.

Drickamer, Lee C., and Stephen H. Vessey. *Animal Behavior.* 3d ed. Dubuque, Iowa: Wm. C. Brown, 1991. Intended for undergraduate students who are interested in animal behavior. Of particular interest is chapter 10, which deals with hormones and behavior. Presents a clear explanation of the endocrine system and the mechanism of hormone action. Avoids highly technical language. The effect of hormones on behavior of invertebrates and vertebrates is well illustrated with many interesting examples from the animal world.

Highnam, Kenneth Charles, and Leonard Hill. *The Comparative Endocrinology of the Invertebrates.* New York: American Elsevier, 1969. The various types of invertebrate endocrine systems are described in this book. Although the book was published in 1969, it is a valuable source of information, especially on the insect and crustacean hormones. Technical language is used but is clearly explained in layperson's terms. Drawings and charts contribute to the understanding of the material.

Pinel, John P. J. *Biopsychology.* Boston: Allyn & Bacon, 1990. A textbook intended for use by the undergraduate college student. There are two chapters of particular interest. Chapter 1 defines the position of biopsychology within the larger field of psychology, delineates the subdivisions of biopsychology, and describes the type of research carried out in each area. An account of research involving the human reproductive hormones and their effects is found in chapter 10. Both chapters are interesting and well written. The author makes use of good examples, drawings, and charts.

Rosemary Scheirer

Cross-References

The Adrenal Gland, 136; Emotion: Mind-Body Processes, 907; General Adaptation Syndrome, 1068; Gonads, 1094; Hormones and Behavior, 1189; Memory: Animal Research, 1505; Neural and Hormonal Interaction, 1648; Pituitary Gland, 1829; Stress and the Endocrine System, 2445; The Thyroid Gland, 2571.

ENDORPHINS

Type of psychology: Biological bases of behavior
Field of study: Nervous system

Endorphins have been identified as pain relievers that are produced by verte-brates. Although occurring only in low concentrations and for short periods of time, they play a significant role in the response to pain and may have other important effects.

Principal terms
ENDOGENOUS SUBSTANCES: substances produced by the body in the course of normal physiological functioning
EXOGENOUS SUBSTANCES: substances not normally occurring in the body, present only when administered; exogenous substances include substances such as drugs or synthetic test compounds mimicking endogenous substances
NEUROTRANSMITTER: a substance released by the neuron that causes another nerve, muscle, or gland to respond to a given stimulus
OPIATES: a class of drugs that relieve pain; opiates include morphine, heroin, and several naturally occurring peptides
RECEPTORS: proteins on the surface of cells to which a specific chemical might bind, causing a specific cellular response; receptors are very specific for the chemical that they bind

Overview

The endorphins are a class of chemicals, found in the nervous system, which resemble morphine. The name "endorphin" is derived from "endogenous" (natu-rally occurring) and "morphine," because the substances are morphinelike.

Morphine was one of the first painkillers known to humankind. It is the active component of opium, and its effects have been well known for several centuries. Morphine is still widely used clinically for the treatment of pain. Scientists found in the 1970's that there are naturally occurring chemicals in the bodies of vertebrates that are capable of controlling pain, and several of them have been identified. Since they are typically short chains of amino acids, they are often referred to as opiate peptides.

Several endogenous opiates have been described: alpha, beta, gamma, and delta endorphins, as well as leucine enkephalin and methionine enkephalin. Of these, the beta endorphins and the enkephalins have been most widely studied. The endor-phins are composed of about thirty amino acids, while the enkephalins are made up of about five amino acids. Beta endorphin is more potent and lasts longer in the body than the enkephalins.

Beta endorphin is found in varying concentrations in the neurons in the brain, spinal cord, and gastrointestinal tract. Beta endorphins in the brain are released in response to unpleasant stimuli that are entering the brain; in the spinal cord, they are released in response to impulses that are relayed from the brain to peripheral muscles. Enkephalins are neurotransmitters of the brain and spinal cord that are weaker than endorphins but still considerably stronger and longer lasting than morphine.

The most widely studied effect of the endorphins is their ability to block painful stimuli (the analgesic effect). They have also been associated with many other physiological activities, including thermoregulation, appetite, memory, lipolysis, reproduction, and pleasure experiences. On the surface of target cells are proteins that serve as binding sites for a variety of chemicals. These receptors are typically very specific and bind only those chemicals with compatible size, shape, and chemical charge. There are receptors on cells in the nervous system that are specific for the opiate peptides; they are the same receptors that bind morphine.

It is believed that endorphins have their effect by binding to the receptors and thereby preventing the release of neurotransmitters from neurons. If no neurotransmitters are released, painful stimuli are prevented from being transmitted from the sensory receptors of the body to the cells of the spinal cord or the brain. This is the same mechanism of action that morphine possesses. In addition to the prevention of pain, the endorphins are said to produce a feeling of well-being in those persons with elevated endorphin levels.

It has been difficult to conduct studies on the effects of endorphins because of the low concentrations that have been found. Most research has been conducted in animals, in which cellular effects and injections into specific cells can be achieved. Animals, however, are unable to describe the feelings that are produced. In humans, endorphins have generally been studied through plasma levels in conditions in which changes in endorphin levels are expected.

Endorphins are released in humans in conditions of physical or psychological stress. The physical stress most closely associated with increases in plasma endorphin levels is aerobic exercise, especially running. Although the endorphin levels return to normal within thirty minutes to an hour, the endorphins are generally credited with the decreased sensitivity to pain in athletes who suffer physical injury. Endorphins are also believed to be the reason that runners experience a feeling of well-being after prolonged strenuous exercise.

The explanation for morphine addiction may also lie with the endorphins. Since morphine and the endorphins bind to the same receptors in cell membranes, the theory suggests that morphine, when available, occupies some of the receptor molecules and the endorphins occupy the rest. Adequate quantities of exogenous or endogenous painkillers are available to prevent pain. In patients to whom morphine is supplied, however, the circulating levels of enkephalins appear to decrease. Once the enkephalin levels fall, the receptor sites to which they had bound are no longer occupied, and the pain stimuli are able to reach the brain. This in turn signals a craving for more morphine to occupy the receptors which were previously occupied by the enkephalins.

Endorphins are also believed to be instrumental in the placebo effect. Patients who receive sugar in place of typical analgesics, and are told that they will feel better soon, often respond to the suggestion by experiencing an improvement in their condition. If the suggestion of pain relief could trigger the release of endorphins, it could explain the placebo effect.

Applications

The control of pain has long been a problem for the medical profession. The most effective pain relievers that are available are often habit forming. The ability to relieve pain requires ever-increasing doses of the painkillers, and withdrawal of the pain reducers can lead to unpleasant side effects for the patient. The discovery of the endorphins and enkephalins has provided hope that scientists will one day be able to control pain without the fear of addiction or the production of withdrawal symptoms when they are removed. This would require that scientists learn how to stimulate the production of opiates endogenously or be able to synthesize synthetic forms of the medications.

Studies have shown that animals under stress are better able to endure pain than those that are not under stress. Some of the ability to tolerate pain may be a result of the natural painkillers—the endogenously occurring opiates. This is also true in humans. Many instances have been described in which an individual has experienced severe stress and not felt the pain of an injury. For example, soldiers have described a feeling of detachment or curiosity when viewing their own serious injuries. Instances have been described in which they are not aware of the injury or, if they are aware, do not feel pain. Mood, too, may be a result of the endorphins and enkephalins. The soldiers describing their injuries without pain described a mood that is quite serene and accepting of the situation.

There are also correlates with more common experiences; one example is the athlete doing aerobic exercise. Continuous strenuous exercise leads to physiological changes very similar to stress reactions. It has been determined that intense exercise such as long-distance running can induce increases in the naturally occurring opiates. Runners tested after a long run have elevated levels of endorphins. The runners who exercise sufficiently to increase endorphin levels are less likely to experience pain than if they do not reach this intensity. Injuries are less bothersome and in some instances can be ignored.

Runners are also likely to experience a feeling of elation, the "runner's high" which some scientists attribute to the elevated levels of endorphins. Although the levels of endorphins remain elevated for only thirty minutes, the mood remains positive for far longer. Dedicated runners and others who regularly do aerobic exercise describe a sense of loss when they are unable to run or exercise. Some have suggested that this need to exercise resembles a form of exercise addiction, which could be explained as the withdrawal of endorphins.

Research on endorphins has not yet revealed ways that they could be used clinically, and the only known way to increase endorphin levels is by strenuous exercise. This may not be satisfactory for those who experience pain as a result of serious illness, but exercise has proved successful in the treatment of mildly depressed individuals.

Many known effects of endorphins and enkephalins appear to be related to their opiate properties. Scientists have sought other effects which would not involve analgesia. Although some of these effects have been observed in animals, correlations with humans have not yet been established. Hungry rats, for example, were more successful at running if they had received endorphins and enkephalins than if they had not. Rats also experienced increased grooming tendencies and increased sexual arousal after treatment with the opiate peptides.

Other animals also experienced changes in their behavior after administration of endogenous opiates. Young chicks that are isolated from their mother or from other young chicks would normally be expected to call for them extensively with loud vocalizations. After administration of endorphins, this behavior pattern was decreased. Goldfish tested with endorphins swam less and showed considerable immobility.

There is a good likelihood that other effects of the opiate peptides will be described in the future. There may be many types of behaviors that are effected by these substances in humans. Studies investigating this possibility await more information about the mechanisms involved in the release of endorphins and enkephalins, or the synthesis of similar compounds.

Context

During the early 1970's, the United States government declared a "war" on drugs. The federal government made money available to study the effects of drugs and the basis of drug addiction. The opiates, particularly heroin, were included in the target group.

It was theorized at that time that if the opiates were to have an effect on the brain, there must be opiate receptors. The opiate receptors were isolated in 1973 at The Johns Hopkins University School of Medicine by Solomon H. Snyder and Candice Pert. The presence of opiate receptors in humans suggested the existence of endogenously occurring opiates. Many laboratories in the United States and Europe were already trying to explain the structure and function of some very interesting substances that had been isolated from nervous and endocrine tissue.

The endogenous opiates were isolated and identified in 1973. They were present in very low quantities in various areas of the brain, in the synaptic membranes, and in the pituitary gland. The fact that they were present in such small quantities complicated efforts to determine in which tissues they would be likely to be found. The importance of the opiates comes not only from the influence of the exogenously administered opiates, but also from the endogenously produced opiates. The mechanism of addiction may be explained by the influence of both these substances on the opiate receptors.

The production of the endorphins and enkephalins is a major area of study. When scientists and physicians learn how to stimulate their production and release, they may be able to use this knowledge to control pain and stress. The ability to control pain would be a major advance for the medical community. By stimulating production of endorphins and enkephalins, physicians might be able to decrease the use of painkillers and thus reduce the risk of addiction. A treatment for those persons already addicted to opiates might also be a result of future research. Further, the fact that endorphins and enkephalins may be responsible for the placebo effect indicates that they may be involved in controlling how people "feel." The ability to create a feeling of well-being using substances produced naturally within the body is certainly a goal worth pursuing.

Bibliography

Goldberg, Jeff. *Anatomy of a Scientific Discovery.* New York: Bantam Books, 1988. An examination of the scientific rivalry that occurred between the scientists who were trying to isolate the first endogenous opiates. Contains some scientific discussions, but focuses on the personal relationships of the scientists. Enlightening to anyone interested in the endorphins and enkephalins or the workings of the scientific community.

Hucho, Ferdinand. *Neurochemistry Fundamentals and Concepts.* Deerfield Beach, Fla.: VCH Publishers, 1986. A basic book of neurochemistry that can be understood by anyone who has had high school chemistry. The chemical formula of the opiate peptides and the role of receptors is described.

Janov, Arthur. *Prisoners of Pain.* Garden City, N.Y.: Anchor Press, 1980. This discussion of pain does not include extensive information about the endorphins, but it describes the importance of pain in determining the behavior of animals, and the extent to which pain can be alleviated by substances such as opiates. Written for the layperson; accessible to all.

The Nervous System: Circuits of Communication. New York: Torstar Books, 1985. A well-written book which describes the nervous system in detail. Written for the student. Easy to understand and beautifully illustrated. Provides the background necessary for further research into the endorphins.

Restak, Richard. *The Brain.* New York: Bantam Books, 1984. Describes the brain and its functions. The experience of pain is described in some detail, and the role of the endorphins is included in this discussion. Written for the layperson.

Annette O'Connor

Cross-References

Biofeedback and Relaxation, 416; The Central and Peripheral Nervous Systems, 494; Neurons, 1661; Neurotransmitters, 1673; Pain, 1727; Pain Management, 1734; Stress and the Nervous System, 2452.

ENVIRONMENTAL PSYCHOLOGY

Type of psychology: Stress
Fields of study: Coping; stress and illness

Traditionally, environmental psychology has examined the relations between the physical (natural or artificial) environment or, more generally, the context, and human behavior and experience; it has proved valuable for understanding individual, social, and societal processes.

Principal terms
COGNITIVE MAP: the individual's internal or external representation of the spatial organization of an external environment
CONTEXT: the interrelated conditions in which something exists or occurs; a more specific term than "environment," but the two are often used synonymously
CROWDING: the individual's subjective perception of spatial restriction; distinguished from density, which is the actual number of persons per spatial area
ENVIRONMENT: the total set of circumstances by which one is surrounded, including physical, interpersonal, and sociocultural aspects
ENVIRONMENTAL COGNITION: the processes by which the individual "knows" the environment; includes a person's perception and appraisal of the environment
ENVIRONMENTAL STRESSOR: a condition in the environment that produces stress (bodily or mental tension), such as crowding, noise, toxic chemicals, or extreme temperatures
PERSONAL SPACE: the area surrounding a person's body into which intruders may not come without causing discomfort
PRIVACY: the selective control of access to one's self or to one's group
PROXEMICS: a field concerned with the ways individuals and groups deal with space as a limited resource
TERRITORIALITY: behavior associated with the ownership or occupation of a geographic place or area by an individual or group

Overview

Environmental psychology is concerned with the relationships between the physical environment—both natural and artificial—and human behavior and experiences; more specifically, it has traditionally dealt with contexts such as school and work settings. In its early stages, the field proved valuable for understanding the relationships between the physical environment and individual processes (such as the interpretation of information from the environment), social processes (such as the sharing and division of space), and societal processes (usually identified with key settings in society, such as school, work, home, and urban environments). The field has expanded to include considerations of formal theories attempting to explain person-environment relationships, and practical applications aimed at improving person-environment interactions—such as designing better environments and encouraging the management of natural resources through energy conservation and recycling.

Research examining the relations between the physical environment and individual processes has focused primarily on three areas. One encompasses environmental perception, or the ways people take in information from their environment, as well as environmental cognition—how people organize this information in their heads. Another area involves the ways people feel about and evaluate aspects of the physical environment. This includes both individual impressions, such as personal descriptions, preferences, and emotional responses (termed environmental appraisal), and collective impressions of places by expert groups (environmental assessment). A third area is the environmental aspects of personality, which looks at the ways characteristic patterns of behavior and experience influence people's transactions with the physical environment.

For example, studies have demonstrated that environmental perception is enhanced if the physical environment is novel, complex, surprising, or incongruous. Environmental cognition has been shown to be associated with life stage: In 1973, Roger A. Hart and Gary T. Moore demonstrated that, as children age, their mental organization of the physical environment (their cognitive map) becomes less egocentric, then more projective (thinking of settings from various physical vantage points), and finally more abstract (thinking of settings through the use of abstract concepts such as coordinates and directions). Research on person-oriented environmental appraisals and place- or policy-oriented environmental assessments has focused primarily on the scenic quality of natural settings such as river valleys but is expanding to include a variety of physical contexts—urban air quality and nursing homes, for example. Studies on environmental aspects of personality have indicated that traditional personality variables may explain some aspects of person-environment relationships. Compared with reserved individuals, outgoing individuals rated landscapes as more serene and beautiful. People with an internal sense of control over their lives have been shown to prefer buildings within the classical architectural style, while those believing their lives to be influenced by powerful others or by fate prefer the Romantic style.

Researchers in environmental psychology have extensively studied four areas in particular: personal space, territoriality, crowding, and privacy. These four areas make up what has come to be known as proxemics, a field concerned with the ways in which individuals and groups deal with space as a limited resource and structure their activities accordingly. Personal space is the area surrounding a person's body (as if there were invisible boundaries) into which intruders may not come without causing discomfort. This space has been shown to be larger for males, variable for disturbed individuals, smaller in situations of attraction or cooperation, and larger in situations involving stigma or unequal status. Studies of territoriality have typically shown that males are more territorial than females and that being within one's own territory is related to perceived control.

Research on crowding has distinguished between density (an objective measure on the number of individuals per unit area) and crowding, an individual's subjective perception of spatial restriction. Prolonged high indoor density acts as an environmental stressor, often impairing health (affecting blood pressure and other cardiac functions), performances of complex tasks, and social interaction (causing increased aggression, withdrawal, and lack of cooperation). Privacy refers to the selective control of access to one's self or one's group. Studies have shown that private preferences, expectations, values, and behaviors vary from person to person and from occasion to occasion.

Research on the relationships between the physical environment and societal processes has concentrated on living at home, learning in the classroom, and functioning in the workplace. Each of these environments involves many perceptions, activities, and attitudes. The home environment can include one's residence, neighborhood, and city; living there may include such varied activities as shopping, relaxing, waiting for the bus, deciding who really owns the bathroom, preparing for potential disasters, and moving.

Researchers have applied many of the individual and social processes described above in the specific contexts of the home, city, school, and workplace. For example, research has shown that neighborhood satisfaction is related to the absence of environmental stressors (such as noise, pollution, and ugliness), although some individuals seem able to adapt to at least some of these stressors. Climate has been shown, at the urban level, to influence prosocial and antisocial behavior slightly; high temperatures seem to increase aggression, while comfortable temperatures increase helping. Studies at schools have shown that classroom characteristics such as high noise and density levels may be associated with numerous difficulties, including decreased learning, participation, and classroom interaction, and may cause negative feelings about school.

Applications

Complementing the array of empirical studies are attempts at both theoretical and practical application. The theoretical applications have tried to provide integrative theories for the field—that is, for person-environment functioning more generally. A major theoretical point accepted by most investigators has been that the environment is composed not only of physical aspects but also of interpersonal (other people) and sociocultural (rules and customs) aspects.

To make sense of the field's varied theoretical applications, psychologists Irwin Altman and Barbara Rogoff (1987) have utilized the philosopher Stephen C. Pepper's four worldviews (general beliefs about the nature of the world and how reality is constructed) to organize theories of person-environment functioning. These four approaches are presented below. For each, a brief definition and an example of an empirical study are provided.

In formist, or trait, approaches to person-environment relations, the focus is on individuals or psychological processes as self-contained entities, with environments playing supplementary or secondary roles; for example, an investigator adhering to this type of approach might study how traditional personality characteristics (such as the locus of control) affect environmental appraisal. In mechanistic, or interactional, approaches, the focus is on person, group, and/or setting qualities as independently defined and operating entities influencing one another in causal fashions. Environmental factors, but sometimes person factors, are usually treated as causal influences on psychological functioning. For example, an investigator working from this type of approach might employ specific (operant) learning techniques to understand and then to decrease littering.

In organismic approaches, the emphasis is on dynamic and holistic systems, with complex reciprocal influences between person and environment components. For example, a researcher with this type of approach might study the development of individuals' cognitive maps across the life span. Finally, in contextual, or transactional, approaches, the focus is on the changing (temporal) relations among aspects of persons and of environments, which together compose holistic entities. An investigator might attempt to illustrate how descriptions of homes reflect inseparable confluences of psychological and environmental experiences.

Environmental psychology has also increasingly become concerned with practical applications such as optimizing person-environment relations. Such applications have included recommendations for the actual design of more fitting environments. For example, Barbara B. Brown and Irwin Altman have demonstrated that residential dwellings with real and symbolic barriers—communicating a strong sense of territoriality—are less likely to be burglarized than residences lacking such barriers; Harry Heft has reviewed the work on prolonged high indoor density on children and found it to be associated with difficulties in visual and auditory discrimination, object permanence, and language development (verbal imitation and reading). M. Powell Lawton designed a nursing home (characterized by single and double bedrooms, lighting improvements, and better-located staff offices) that successfully enhanced patients' perceptual and social transactions with the environment.

Further, research on environmental stress, at both the individual and societal levels, has generated intervention programs to decrease technological risk and to encourage the management and preservation of natural resources. For example, Jack Demick and his collaborators from Hiroshima University have analyzed cultural differences in the impact of governmental legislation; whereas the Japanese value adherence to legislation for the group as a whole, Americans value individuality and personal expression. These differences were then employed in the design of differential programs to enhance the use of automobile safety belts. Appeals to national pride were to be used in Japan, whereas freedom of choice—with accompanying reductions in insurance rates—was to be emphasized in the United States. Related programs have been instituted aimed at decreasing such environmental problems as air pollution, litter, and homelessness as well as at increasing such processes as energy conservation and recycling. Robert Gifford's *Environmental Psychology: Principles and Practice* (1987) reviews many of the major applied programs in these and related areas.

Context

Historically, the first stirrings of environmental psychology occurred in the 1940's. This was followed by increased activity in the 1950's, which grew significantly throughout the 1960's and into the 1970's. The movement in each of these decades is perhaps summarized best through the work of its pioneering researchers.

In the 1930's, psychologist Egon Brunswik (1903-1955), born in Budapest and trained in Vienna, emigrated to the United States. Initially focusing on the process of perception, he expanded his ideas to make three contributions to the field that was to become environmental psychology: He was one of the first to call for a more detailed analysis of the ways in which (physical) environmental factors affect behavior; he advocated the use of more varied environmental stimuli in psychological research than was typically the case; and he coined the term "environmental psychology" in 1934.

Even more contributory than Brunswik was psychologist Kurt Lewin (1890-1947). Born in Prussia and trained in Germany, he also emigrated to the United States. He was extremely influential for several reasons. First, his work on "field theory" in the 1940's was the first to give significant attention to the molar physical environment; his original notion that behavior is a joint function of the interaction between person and environment became a basic premise of modern psychology. Second, he influenced many students, among them Roger Barker and Herbert Wright. In the 1950's, Barker and Wright developed "ecological psychology," in which they studied "behavior settings," small ecological units enclosing everyday human behavior (such as the restaurant or the pharmacy) with both physical-spatial and social aspects. Ecological psychology is often credited as being the forerunner of environmental psychology.

Environmental psychology in its own right emerged full force in the 1960's as a problem-focused field, responding to practical questions posed by architects and planners about real-world design decisions. The shift from basic laboratory research to work on real-world applications was perhaps also expedited by changing societal realities related to the United States' involvement in the Vietnam War. This real-world focus was subsequently reinforced by environmental events such as the 1979 nuclear accident at Three Mile Island in Pennsylvania.

Theoretically, this movement into the real world and its accompanying focus on the real-life functioning of individuals have highlighted, for the field of psychology as a whole, the need to take the environmental context into account in all theories and research on human behavior and experience. While various subfields of psychology (such as developmental psychology and personality) have acknowledged the importance of context, environmental psychology as a subfield has strongly reinforced this idea by providing a unique perspective—the person in the context of the environment—on all psychological processes. It will continue to be a driving force behind psychology's renewed commitment to understanding individuals' real-world functioning in all of its complexity.

Bibliography

Downs, Roger M., and David Stea, eds. *Image and Environment: Cognitive Mapping and Spatial Behavior.* Chicago: Aldine, 1973. A landmark book in environmental psychology. Drawing on Kenneth Boulding's 1956 *The Image: Knowledge in Life and Society* (the image refers to a person's known or believed universe), these researchers focus on that part of the image called a "cognitive map," defined as an internal representation of the spatial organization of the external world. Provides the reader with a valuable backdrop for the field's extensive work on cognitive maps.

Gifford, Robert. *Environmental Psychology: Principles and Practice.* Boston: Allyn & Bacon, 1987. An excellent introductory textbook; slightly more sophisticated than its peers. A readable blend of theoretical and empirical work with an emphasis on practical application. An extensive bibliography is also provided. Can be understood by the high school or college student.

Hall, Edward Twitchell. *The Hidden Dimension.* Garden City, N.Y.: Doubleday, 1969. One of the best (relatively brief) introductions to the field of proxemics by one of its pioneers. Includes sections on crowding and social behavior, proxemics and culture, and proxemics and the future. Delightfully written and easily understood.

Holahan, Charles J. *Environmental Psychology.* New York: Random House, 1982. A beginning textbook by a leading researcher in the field. Particularly good coverage of topics such as environmental cognition, environmental stress, crowding, and privacy. The last chapter provides a unifying framework for the field; there is also an extensive bibliography. Can be understood by the high school or college student.

Proshansky, Harold M., William H. Ittelson, and Leanne G. Rivlin, eds. *Environmental Psychology: People and Their Physical Settings.* 2d ed. New York: Holt, Rinehart and Winston, 1976. An edited textbook with many outstanding selections from leaders in the field. The editors themselves established the first Ph.D. program in environmental psychology at the City University of New York in 1968; their introduction provides insights into the history and issues of the field.

Saegert, S., and G. H. Winkel. "Environmental Psychology." *Annual Review of Psychology* 41. Stanford, Calif.: Annual Reviews, 1990. Reviews developments in the field, presenting major theories of person-environment relations. Evaluates research with an eye toward future synthesis. Although a good overview, it is slightly technical in spots.

Stokols, Daniel, and Irwin Altman, eds. *Handbook of Environmental Psychology.* 2 vols. New York: John Wiley & Sons, 1987. Presents a wide array of chapters on environmental psychology, including theories, history, cross-cultural approaches, the field's relationship to child development, and numerous individual approaches to environmental psychology. A very comprehensive source. A must for anyone in the field; can be understood by the college student.

Wapner, S., and J. Demick. "Development of Experience and Action: Levels of Integration in Human Functioning." In *Theories of the Evolution of Knowing*, edited by Gary Greenberg and Ethel Tobach. Hillsdale, N.J.: Lawrence Erlbaum, 1990. A summary of a holistic/systems, developmental approach to person-in-environment functioning across the life span. Attempts to integrate organismic and transactional worldviews. Illustrates the relations among problem, theory, and method in psychology generally and in environmental psychology specifically. Reviews relevant environmental psychological research on life transitions and provides an extensive bibliography.

Jack Demick

Cross-References

Cognitive Maps, 566; Coping Strategies: An Overview, 706; Crowd Behavior, 737; Defense Reactions: Species-Specific, 775; Field Theory: Kurt Lewin, 1038; Health Psychology, 1139; Adaptation to Stress, 2390; Stress: Cognitive Appraisals, 2404; Effects of Stress, 2417; Stressors, 2471.

ESCAPE CONDITIONING

Type of psychology: Learning
Fields of study: Aversive conditioning; experimental methodologies

Escape conditioning is a procedure wherein a present and ongoing aversive condition or event is reduced or terminated by the actions of an organism. The organism learns the appropriate stimulus-terminating behavior and exhibits that behavior whenever the aversive stimulus is present. Much human behavior represents escape from aversive conditions.

> *Principal terms*
> AVERSIVE STIMULUS: anything that is obnoxious to a particular individual at some time and from which the person will actively seek to get away
> AVOIDANCE: behavior that results in the cancellation or postponement of the delivery of an aversive stimulus
> NEGATIVE REINFORCEMENT: the procedure whereby the probability of a response is increased by the contingent removal of an aversive stimulus
> POSITIVE REINFORCEMENT: the procedure whereby the probability of a response is increased by the response-contingent delivery of a stimulus
> PUNISHMENT: the procedure of decreasing the probability of a behavior by the response-contingent delivery of an aversive stimulus
> RATE: the dependent measure of the behavior; the frequency with which the behavior occurs

Overview

Escape conditioning is a procedure in which an aversive (unpleasant) stimulus is presented to a subject and the subject then reduces or terminates the stimulus by performing some action. For example, if people are suddenly exposed to a continuing loud noise, they can reduce the intensity of the sound by covering their ears or by turning down the volume. They have escaped an ongoing aversive situation. The point of escape conditioning is that a continuous and ongoing stimulus may prompt behaviors by the subject that reduce or terminate the stimulus. This escape action is therefore more likely to occur in the future whenever an aversive situation arises.

Removal of the aversive stimulus strengthens the escape response. This means that whenever some unpleasant condition arises in the future, a person will be more likely to make an escape response. Many everyday behaviors are of this type. For example, in order to stop the nagging from one's mother or spouse to clean the living room, a person will go ahead and do the cleaning. By cleaning in the presence of the actual nagging, this person has escaped, or terminated, the aversive stimulus; it stops once cleaning behavior starts. The conditioning that occurs is learning how to behave when a specific aversive stimulus occurs. After a number of experiences with aversive nagging, it may become the case that whenever mother or spouse comes into the room, cleaning begins without any nagging at all. The demanding person has been paired with nagging so often that his or her presence alone is enough to occasion escape (cleaning) behavior. A serious problem in this scenario is the probability of unauthorized escape responses. For example, instead of cleaning the living room, a person may simply leave the presence of the nagging individual or try to avoid the nagger altogether. This side effect is a serious drawback in using escape as a behavior management strategy.

Much human behavior occurs in order to reduce or terminate an ongoing aversive situation. Children finally stop playing and go eat dinner because of the discomfort of hunger. Employees do their work on the job to escape the ever-present threat of being fired. People put on sweaters to escape the cold, and they remove them when they get too warm.

Behavior that increases in probability as a result of the removal of a stimulus or condition is called escape behavior. The aversive condition must be present in order for an escape response to occur. If people put on their coats before going out into the cold, they are avoiding getting cold. They are not escaping the cold in this situation. Avoidance behavior occurs in the absence of the aversive stimulus, whereas escape can only happen when the aversive stimulus is already present. If people are in prison, they can only escape; it is too late to avoid. Prisoners might avoid further unpleasantness by obeying the prison rules. Escape, avoidance, and punishment are three separate types of aversive behavioral control procedures; that is, they are procedures that involve presenting or removing unpleasant conditions or events as opposed to positive reinforcement, which makes things better by the delivery of a desirable object or event.

Escape training is usually not the procedure of choice when dealing with human behavior modification. In the event of an accident, however, critical escape behaviors should be rapidly available. With a severe wound, for example, the behaviors that will stop the flow of blood (that is, escape hemorrhaging) are immediately necessary. The ongoing presence of an aversive stimulus (blood flow), together with the availability of an effective stimulus-terminating behavior (bandage), are the criteria for escape conditioning. In an intolerable social situation, the availability of appropriate escape behavior can also be very important.

One problem with escape training is that the trainer or teacher must initiate the aversive stimulus before the subject can make an escape response. It would not seem that one would want to make another person uncomfortable simply so that person could then escape the discomfort; in actuality, however, this is done all the time. A student or employee may be threatened that if a project is not completed correctly and on time, then bad things will happen. In order to escape this type of threat, the student or employee usually does whatever is necessary. Standing threats, such as those upholding laws and rules, make things uncomfortable for people. People can only escape the uncomfortable conditions by doing what the lawmakers want. Being put on the spot and asked to perform may engender a variety of escape responses. People can escape the induced anxiety or fear caused by the presence of a law enforcement officer by behaving as the rules dictate. One can escape obnoxious television commercials by changing channels. Escaping discomfort is a way of life.

To present an aversive stimulus so as to reduce the rate of the behavior that produces it is to punish. Punished behavior occurs less frequently in the future than it would if it had not been punished. Punishment is usually the presentation of an aversive stimulus immediately following the occurrence of an unwanted behavior. In the presence of a continuous aversive stimulus, on the other hand, subsequent behavior can lead to escape, or the termination of the aversive stimulus. In escape, the rate of the effective response will increase. If precautions are taken before the aversive stimulus is presented, then avoidance has occurred. For example, one might avoid exposure to the human immunodeficiency virus (HIV) or other sexually transmitted diseases by practicing safe sex. (No behavior can escape HIV once it is present.)

Escape, punishment, and avoidance are procedures for behavior control that employ aversive conditioning. They differ in the ways they are applied and the effects they have on behavior, as well as the side effects they produce, but they are all commonly used. Unwanted behavior can be reduced by punishment, and the individual can avoid further punishment by not performing the unwanted behavior. As a result of punishment, behavior is suppressed, whereas in an avoidance situation, the avoidance behavior increases in probability. Whenever good things follow a response, the probability of that response increases; this contingency is called reinforcement. Escape responses are directly followed by the termination of the aversive stimulus or event, a procedure called negative reinforcement. Positive reinforcement is the delivery of a stimulus that increases the rate of the response that produces it. Negative reinforcement is the removal of a stimulus that results in an increase in the response rate that escapes the aversive situation. Escape behavior is negatively reinforced because it results in the termination of the aversive stimulus, which then increases the probability of the effective response. Negative reinforcement is often confused with punishment, but the two are very different procedures and have very different results. All three aversive control procedures are effective, but the side effects have led to many of the problems society faces today. Murray Sidman has presented an excellent review and discussion of these problems in his book *Coercion and Its Fallout* (1989).

Applications

Conditioned (learned) escape behavior has been employed as a model in trying to account for some "abnormal" human behaviors. For example, if living conditions get too bad or uncomfortable, a person may drink, act "crazy," or use drugs to excess as a means of escape. The person may be physically unable to get away from an intolerable situation, so he or she tries to escape in other ways. This person may lie, steal, or try all sorts of chemicals as a means of terminating or reducing an ongoing aversive situation. He or she may even act appropriately; however, usually there are more wrong possibilities than right. There is even an informal model that attempts to account for change in institutional systems that is based on escape. This model suggests that nothing will change in an organization until the participants are in sufficient "pain." Only when enough discomfort is present will the individuals feeling the pain make efforts to do something to escape. That "something" may amount to changing the policies or procedures of the institution. In other words, it will be a response that reduces an uncomfortable situation.

"Coping" behavior is how a person goes about behaving in the presence of diffi- cult conditions. Learning appropriate coping skills, which often involves learning correct escape responses, provides socially acceptable escape behaviors. In terms of a disagreement with someone, the unpleasant situation may generate a form of es- cape response. One may merely stop talking and not contribute any further, and the argument stops. Thus, the participants have escaped the argument. A person in such a situation may actually leave the room or run away, thereby physically escaping the offending situation or person. Other coping responses may involve resorting to var- ious verbal tactics of persuasion, compromise, or logic. All of these can be consid- ered types of escape behaviors if they increase in probability and result in the termi- nation of an unpleasant situation.

When escape behaviors result in the removal of an ongoing aversive stimulus, the person behaving is said to be negatively reinforced. The likelihood of the same type of escape response recurring in the same or comparable aversive situation is in- creased. The termination of the unpleasant condition has strengthened the proba- bility of future escape responses. For example, in a laboratory situation, a rat may be placed on a grid floor that can be electrified. A lever is also available. When a continuous shock is presented, the rat can turn it off by pressing the lever. The rat learns quickly to remain near the lever. The instant the shock comes on, the rat presses the lever. Similarly, when a television commercial appears, a viewer may quickly operate the remote control and switch to another channel. The television watcher and the rat have each learned to escape aversive situations by pressing. These are appropriate escape behaviors, but one can, and does, also learn inappropriate or self-destructive escape responses. The abuse of drugs is an example of inadequate coping.

The immediate termination of an unpleasant situation contingent upon a response strengthens that response quickly. Organisms learn rapidly in an escape situation because the aversive stimulus usually generates a considerable amount of respond- ing, thus enhancing the probability of making the correct (or at least some effective) response. The effective parameters in escape learning include the intensity of the aversive stimulus, the "cost" of the escape response, and the amount of time the stimulus is off following an effective response.

A student may learn to escape responsibility, for example, by becoming assertive or by assigning someone else absolute blame. That is, the student may occasionally get out from under a constant threat by redirecting any accusation of inadequacy. When an aversive stimulus is presented (such as punishment, in the student's case), it also elicits aggression. If aggressive behavior, elicited by the presentation of an aversive stimulus, results in negative reinforcement, then the aggressor will tend to use aggression more often in the future; that is, aggressive behavior can be reinforced and therefore will have an increased probability of occurring again. Aggressive behavior may be strengthened by positive reinforcement as well, wherein good things follow the behavior and bad things cease. Hence an aggressive "personality" can be shaped.

Dealing with problem situations with aggression is almost always the wrong thing to do; it elicits aggression in return (counteraggression) or may lead to unhelpful and inappropriate escape behavior. If one lacks the good or necessary things in life, breaking and entering is not an appropriate escape response; but if one does not know any other escape or coping responses, then breaking the law may be the only (and paradoxically the appropriate) choice.

A curious phenomenon occurs as a result of being exposed to inescapable aversive stimuli. If a dog is placed in a chamber where there is no escape and shocked through the floor, later, when the dog can do something to escape the shock, it does nothing. This phenomenon was given the name "learned helplessness" by its discoverer, Martin E. P. Seligman (1975). What it says, in effect, is that if people are in a bad situation but can do nothing that will help, then subsequently, when they might be able to escape another bad situation, they seem helpless and do nothing. They appear to have learned that their efforts have no effect and that they are indeed helpless, so they do not even try. This finding has been replicated many times with human subjects (although the aversive stimulus was not foot shock). This learned helplessness model may account for the observation that some people do not seem even to try to improve or escape their unpleasant situations.

A person deprived of a job, and therefore money, might be seen as being in an aversive situation from which he or she tries to escape by job hunting. This person may also escape by some inappropriate activity as well, such as denial, self-deprecation, stealing, or other unlawful acts. A continuous physical pain also generates escape activities. Some of these pain-escape behaviors may be appropriate, such as seeking medical help; others, however, may be self-destructive, such as substance abuse or abusing other people.

Escape responses can also occur when it appears that only a positive situation has been in effect. Even though people may enjoy their work, they often plan for and go on vacations. This is another form of escape. Vacations, however, can be wearing, and people might long to get off the beach and be back at their jobs, escaping the boredom of doing nothing. People often do things to terminate situations in which they initially put themselves voluntarily because the conditions have subsequently become aversive. For example, sensory deprivation experiments did not last long, because total lack of sensory input is rather uncomfortable, and subjects would ask to get out of the situation and therefore escape.

Context

Escape conditioning is not an invention or discovery of experimental psychologists; it has been around as long as there have been behaving organisms. Even one-celled animals try to escape heat or chemicals that have become or are aversive. The scientific investigation of the functional relationships between environmental variables and escape behavior, however, is more recent. Escape conditioning as a subset of important relationships prompted a flurry of research activity in the 1960's and 1970's. What happened to slow this investigation was a growing reluctance by experimenters to make their subjects uncomfortable and the fact that much had been learned already. No legitimate researcher enjoys making subjects uncomfortable, but the topic was so important that such work had to be done. There is now a much more thorough understanding of how aversive events interact to develop both appropriate and inappropriate behaviors. Clearly, the use of nonhuman subjects in escape conditioning experiments is preferable to the use of humans, and the principles derived from such research have been found to be applicable to humans.

Researchers investigating aversive procedures have more often used the avoidance procedure than the escape procedure. In avoidance situations, the subject can respond in the absence of the aversive stimulus and thereby prevent the unpleasant condition altogether. If bills are paid on time, the utilities remain functional and there is no trouble. If they are not paid, however, one might experience all sorts of problems that might then be escaped. One intriguing question in avoidance research concerns what the reinforcer (or consequence) for an avoidance response actually is. A successful avoidance activity results in no bad thing happening, which often means that nothing happens. How can nothing be a reinforcer? How can no consequence strengthen a behavior? In escape conditioning, on the other hand, the aversive stimulus is present, the subject's response terminates that situation, and the offset of the shock (or whatever) is clearly the reinforcer. If the bank threatens to foreclose or repossess as a result of a client's failure to make payments, the client can escape the situation by paying what is owed. Paying prior to the due date would be an avoidance response in terms of foreclosure and an escape response in terms of the aversive threat.

It has been argued that negative reinforcement is simply another case of positive reinforcement. The offset of the aversive stimulus might be considered as easily the onset of a good stimulus situation. For example, if people in a cold room turn on a heater, have they escaped the cold, or are they being reinforced by the onset of heat? This controversy has not been settled and is not likely to be in the near future.

Some of the earliest systematic work on escape conditioning was reported by Edward L. Thorndike in 1911. He was a behavioral psychologist who used cats, among other species, as subjects in experiments on learning. Thorndike is well remembered for his expression of the law of effect. This law states that when good things follow a behavior, that behavior is more likely to occur in the future; when unpleasant things follow a behavior, that behavior is less likely to occur in the future. This general law of behavior has had great application in managing and accounting for behavior. Thorndike placed a cat in what he called a "puzzle box" and let the animal learn to escape. There was a lever in the box that, when operated, would release the door. The cat was deprived of food, but there was food right outside the box. The cat's correct operation of the lever to release the door increased in frequency over subsequent trials. Cats learned quickly to operate the lever and escape from the box. They did so in what could be called a "trial-and-success" fashion; that is, as each trial progressed, the successful behavior became more probable. The cat's escape response was selected from all possible behaviors by the consequences that followed. Another school of psychology, the Gestalt school, at the time (the early 1900's) was promoting an "insight" account of how animals solved problems. Followers of this school of thought argued that the cat came to "understand" the problem and to respond based upon an insightful analysis of the situation as a whole.

Bibliography

Dinsmoor, J. "Escape from Shock as a Conditioning Technique." In *Aversive Stimulation*, edited by Marshall R. Jones. Coral Gables, Fla.: University of Miami Press, 1968. This paper was presented at the Miami Symposium on the Prediction of Behavior, 1967. Presents an excellent description of the development of basic escape research in the laboratory and of the major variables involved.

Klein, Stephen B. *Learning*. 2d ed. New York: McGraw-Hill, 1991. General learning text with a section on escape and the critical factors involved. Also points out the ubiquitousness of adversity in people's lives and how this often leads to inappropriate escape behavior.

Seligman, Martin E. P. *Helplessness: On Depression, Development, and Death*. San Francisco: W. H. Freeman, 1975. Describes how a helplessness expectancy can be developed by unsuccessful experience and how such experience can then become involved in physical health.

Sidman, Murray. *Coercion and Its Fallout*. Boston: Authors Cooperative, 1989. Points out that coercion is everywhere in society and that the side effects of so much unpleasantness are disastrous. Also indicates how people can increase the use of noncoercive techniques of behavior management.

Staddon, J. E. R., and R. H. Ettinger. *Learning*. San Diego: Harcourt Brace Jovanovich, 1989. Behavioral-oriented text discusses escape and aversive control using different sources and examples than Klein's *Learning*. Places escape conditioning within the context of all operant behavior and illustrates how general principles of conditioning apply in this situation.

Carl D. Cheney

Cross-References

ETHOLOGY

Type of psychology: Origin and definition of psychology
Fields of study: Biological influences on learning; motivation theory

Ethology, the study of animal behavior, is concerned with the adaptive significance of behavior and the physiological, genetic, and psychological basis of behavioral responses in the animal kingdom; ethology emphasizes the importance of heredity and evolutionary factors in the study of behavior.

Principal terms
ADAPTATION: any heritable characteristic that presumably has developed as a result of natural selection and thus increases an animal's ability to survive and reproduce
CONDITIONING: the behavioral association that results from the reinforcement of a response with a stimulus
GENOTYPE: the genetic makeup of an individual
IMPRINTING: the innate behavioral attachment that a young animal forms with another individual (for example, its mother), with food, or with an object during a brief critical period shortly after birth
INNATE: a term describing any inborn characteristic or behavior that is determined and controlled largely by the genes
INSTINCT: any behavior that is determined entirely by the genes and is completely functional the first time it is performed
NATURAL SELECTION: the process of differential survival and reproduction which leads to heritable characteristics that are best suited for a particular environment
PHENOTYPE: the physical expression of an organism's genes (that is, any heritable characteristic)
STIMULUS: any environmental cue that can potentially modify an animal's behavior via its nervous system

Overview

Ethology, from the Greek *ethos* ("behavior or manner"), is the study of animal behavior. It is concerned primarily with the accurate description and rigorous experimental evaluation of animals' behavior under natural conditions. Unlike the field of behaviorism, which traditionally emphasized the sole importance of the environment on behavior, ethology also recognizes the genetic and physiological mechanisms that regulate behavioral processes. Ethologists operate under the primary assumption that much of behavior is hereditary and thus strongly influenced by the forces of natural selection.

In their search for a common, unifying explanation of behavioral processes, ethologists have sought to address three specific issues: the accurate, nonanthropomorphic description of behavior under natural conditions; the underlying mechanisms that regulate and control behavior; and the adaptive significance of various behavior patterns.

In its earliest stages, ethology was characterized by a highly descriptive approach. Early ethologists were concerned primarily with accurate and objective accounts of behavior. Behavior, however, unlike other aspects of an organism's biology (such as morphology or physiology), was a difficult and elusive thing to characterize, and thus required careful, unbiased approaches to understanding the ways in which animals responded to stimuli in their environment. Konrad Lorenz, one of the early founders of the field, insisted that the only way to study behavior was to make objective observations under completely natural field conditions. This approach, most evident in his classic studies on aggression and imprinting, greatly enhanced understanding of communication in the animal kingdom. In contrast to Lorenz's very subjective approach, Nikolaas Tinbergen and Karl von Frisch's rigorous field experiments were similar to those that later would characterize modern ethology.

The classic work of all three of these early ethologists helped demonstrate how an animal's sensory limitations and capabilities can shape its behavior. For example, in a series of classic learning experiments, von Frisch convincingly documented the unusual visual capabilities of the honeybee. He first trained honeybees to forage at small glass dishes of sugar water and then, by attaching different visual cues to each dish, provided the animals with an opportunity to learn where to forage through the simple process of association. From these elegant but simplistic experiments, he found that bees locate and remember foraging sites by the use of specific colors, ultraviolet cues, and polarized light, a discovery that revolutionized how humans view the sensory capabilities of animals.

With the classic work of Lorenz, Tinbergen, and von Frisch came an increasing appreciation for how physiological limitations define behavioral differences between species. This awareness eventually gave way to a mechanistic approach to behavior, in which ethologists sought to determine how internal factors such as physiology, development, and genetics regulate and control behavior. The physiologically oriented ethologists, for example, focused on the influence of neuronal pathways and sensory organs on behavior. They were concerned with topics such as the control of feeding in insects, echo location in bats, electric field detection in fishes, and infrared detection in snakes. Similarly, neurobiologists attempted to show how behavioral changes are linked to modifications in the function of nerves and neuronal pathways. By observing the response of individual nerves, neurobiologists can observe changes that occur in the nerves when an animal modifies its behavior in response to some stimulus. In a similar way, they can show how learning and behavior are affected when specific nerve fibers are experimentally cut or removed.

The third and perhaps most significant area in ethology is that which deals with the evolutionary (adaptive) significance of behavior. Since the seminal work of Charles Darwin, ethologists have maintained that a species' behavior is controlled largely by its genes. Darwin argued that an animal's behavior was no different than any other phenotypic characteristic (physical expression of the genes) in that it was heritable and therefore subject to the same kinds of selective processes that lead to evolutionary change among organisms. He considered instinctual (or innate) behavior a tremendous adaptation which frees some organisms from the risky and sometimes costly business of trial-and-error learning. At the same time, he recognized the adaptive plasticity that accompanies the more complex behaviors which involve various degrees of learning.

Both Lorenz and Tinbergen also recognized the importance of evolutionary questions in behavior, but Tinbergen was the first to put such hypotheses to rigorous experimental tests. In a classic experiment on the evolutionary significance of spines in sticklebacks, he tested predation rates by pike on several species of these fish. He found predation rates to be lowest on the three-spined stickleback (a conspicuous species with large horizontal spines), moderate on the more cryptic ten-spined stickleback (which possesses ten smaller vertical spines on its dorsal surface), and highest for unarmored minnows.

More recently, behavioral geneticists have shown that much of learning, and behavior in general, is intimately tied to mechanisms of heredity. The results of hybridization experiments and artificial breeding programs, as well as studies on human twins separated at birth, clearly demonstrate a strong genetic influence on behavior. In fact, it has been well documented that many animals (including both invertebrates and vertebrates) are genetically programmed (or have a genetic predisposition) to learn only specific kinds of behaviors. Such is the case for song learning in birds.

Thus, ethology places tremendous importance on the evolutionary history of an organism. It emphasizes the adaptive significance of the various types of behaviors, and it assumes that an animal's behavior is constrained largely by its genetic and evolutionary background.

Applications

The field of ethology has contributed markedly to the understanding of several psychological and behavioral phenomena. One such area that has been especially influenced by the work of ethologists is the learning process. Learning is defined as any modification in behavior (other than that caused by maturation, fatigue, or injury) that is directed by previous experience.

The early experiments of the behaviorist psychologists on conditioning led to the notion that all behavior is learned. Traditionally, behaviorists maintained that all complex behaviors are learned by means of either classical or operant conditioning. Classical conditioning, first demonstrated by the Russian psychologist Ivan Pavlov, is a form of associative learning in which an animal responds to an unrelated, novel stimulus after it is repeatedly paired with a more relevant stimulus. Operant conditioning, also a form of associative learning, occurs when an animal learns by manipulating some part of its environment (for example, the animal might ring a bell to receive a reward). This form of learning usually improves with experience and is therefore referred to as trial-and-error learning.

The primary objective of the approaches employed by the early behaviorists was to eliminate and control as many variables as possible, and thereby remove any uncertainty about the factors that may influence the learning process. These approaches were especially successful at identifying the external mechanisms responsible for learning. Such techniques focused only on the input (stimulus) and output (response) of an experiment, however, and consequently de-emphasized the importance of proximate mechanisms such as physiology and genetics. In addition, these approaches generally ignored the evolutionary considerations that ethologists considered so fundamental to the study of behavior.

In contrast, studies by the early ethologists suggested that much of behavior was dominated by innate processes that were constrained by physiological and genetic design of the organism. Lorenz and Tinbergen, for example, demonstrated that many behavioral responses in the animal kingdom are fixed or stereotyped (instinctive) and are often elicited by simple environmental stimuli. They referred to such responses as fixed action patterns and to the stimuli that triggered them as sign stimuli.

The egg-rolling behavior of the greylag goose is perhaps one of the most widely cited examples of this kind of innate behavior. When one of these ground-nesting birds notices an egg outside its nest, it stands, walks to the egg, extends its bill in a very characteristic manner, and proceeds to roll the egg back to the nest. Although at first glance this may seem to represent a simple learned response, Lorenz and Tinbergen found this to be a highly ritualized behavior that was initiated by a very specific environmental stimulus. Through a series of clever experiments, Tinbergen showed that this behavior could be elicited by an egglike object (a ball) or even any object with a convex surface (a bottle or can), and that objects larger than eggs caused a more vigorous (supernormal) response. He also found that once the behavior was initiated, it always ran to completion. In other words, even when the egg was removed, the goose would continue with the motions as if it were returning the egg to the nest.

This and countless other examples of very ritualized behaviors, such as the avoidance response of ducklings to hawk models, the imprinting of young vertebrates on their mothers, the aggressive displays of male stickleback fish to the red bellies of other males, and the various courtship displays of a wide range of species, led early ethologists to conclude that much of behavior is governed by instinct.

These opposing views of the ethologists and behaviorist psychologists eventually led to the misconception that learned behavior is governed entirely by the animal's environment, whereas instinct is completely controlled by the genes. It is now widely accepted, however, that nearly all forms of behavior and learning involve certain degrees of both processes. Countless studies, for example, have demonstrated that numerous animals are genetically programmed to learn only certain behaviors. In contrast, it has been shown that instinct need not be completely fixed, but instead can be modified with experience.

A second area of ethology that has received much attention from a variety of behavioral researchers and in some cases has sparked considerable controversy is sociobiology. In the early 1970's, Edward O. Wilson and Robert Trivers of Harvard University initiated a new area of behavioral research when they began their investigations on the evolutionary basis of social behavior in animals. Their attention focused on the evolutionary enigma presented by altruistic behaviors—acts that one organism performs (often at its own expense) to benefit another. Examples include alarm calls in the presence of a predator and nest-helping behavior. The most extreme cases of such behavior are found in those insect societies in which only a few individuals reproduce and all others work to maintain the colony. Through careful experimentation and observation, it was soon determined that such unselfish behaviors are always directed toward related individuals and that such behaviors probably evolve because they promote the survival of other individuals who also possess the genes for those same altruistic acts.

Although they initially sparked much debate, studies of the evolutionary basis for social behavior eventually strengthened the ethologists' long-held notion that much of behavior is coded in the genes.

Context

Although ethology had its beginnings with the work of Charles Darwin and other early naturalists, it was Karl von Frisch, Konrad Lorenz, and Nikolaas Tinbergen who conducted the first formal ethological studies and received a joint Nobel Prize for their pioneering work in 1973. Their approach represented a considerable departure from that of the behaviorist psychologists, and the differences between the two fields sparked a heated debate during the 1950's and 1960's, often referred to as the nature-versus-nurture controversy. While this debate eventually led to the decline and virtual demise of behaviorism, it also helped shape modern ethology into a rigorous biological discipline that now holds a compatible niche within the realm of psychology.

While the early ethologists argued that behaviorists treated their study organisms as "black boxes" and ignored the genetic, physiological, and evolutionary backgrounds of their subjects, the behaviorists leveled several criticisms in return. In addition to their disbelief in the genetic control of behavior, they were most critical of the methodological approaches employed by ethologists. In contrast with the rigorously controlled laboratory experiments of the psychologists, in which blind observers (observers unaware of the experimenters' hypotheses or experimental design) were often used to collect data, behaviorists held that early ethologists conducted nearly all their studies under natural conditions without any regard for experimental control. In addition, their observations were often highly subjective and almost never quantified. Even when attempts were made to quantify the behavior, they never involved the rigorous statistical and analytical techniques of the behaviorists.

Furthermore, although the early ethologists argued that much of behavior is shaped by evolution and constrained by an organism's physiological hardware, little evidence was initially available to support these contentions. Behaviorists, for example, held that ethologists often observed a behavior and casually assigned some adaptive significance to it without testing such evolutionary hypotheses.

These criticisms forced early ethologists to improve their approaches to data collection, experimental design, and data analysis, and as their approaches to the study of behavior were strengthened, so were their original hypotheses about the underlying control of behavior. Thus, as ethologists gained ground, behaviorism began to fall out of favor with most of the scientific community.

The basic views of early ethologists are still well preserved in all prominent areas of ethological research. In fact, the work of nearly all modern ethologists can best be characterized by two basic sets of questions which they seek to answer: the "how questions," concerning underlying proximate causes, and the "why questions," concerning ultimate causes (or evolutionary bases). The first of these is pursued by traditional ethologists and neurobiologists, while the latter is primarily the realm of behavioral ecologists. The fields of ethology and comparative psychology have begun to complement each other, and, increasingly, researchers from the two areas are merging their efforts on a diversity of research topics.

Bibliography

Alcock, John. *Animal Behavior: An Evolutionary Approach.* 4th ed. Sunderland, Mass.: Sinauer Associates, 1989. A clearly written, well-illustrated volume covering both the proximate mechanisms and the evolutionary basis of behavior. Two chapters deal with the sociobiology controversy and the evolution of human reproductive behavior. Especially helpful as an introduction to behavioral ecology.

Fisher, Arthur. "Sociobiology: A New Synthesis Comes of Age." *Mosaic* 22 (Spring, 1991): 2-9. This review article provides a comprehensive overview of the biological basis of behavior and the sociobiology controversy. Includes a thorough historical perspective. A well-written summary of major research in the field between 1965 and 1990.

Gould, James L. *Ethology: The Mechanisms and Evolution of Behavior.* New York: W. W. Norton, 1982. A well-illustrated text offering a complete introduction to the basic concepts of ethology. Early chapters include a complete review of the history of ethology and the debate between ethologists and psychologists. Provides detailed descriptions of various ethological experiments; three chapters are devoted entirely to human ethology.

Grier, James W. *Biology of Animal Behavior.* St. Louis: Times Mirror/Mosby, 1984. A college-level text providing an excellent treatment of the study of animal behavior. Clearly written, well illustrated; a good introduction for the layperson. Integrates information from a variety of disciplines including ethology, behavioral ecology, psychology, and neurobiology.

Krebs, J. R., and N. B. Davies. *An Introduction to Behavioral Ecology.* 2d ed. Oxford, England: Blackwell Scientific Publications, 1991. Intended as a basic overview of behavioral ecology for individuals outside the profession. Covers many aspects of foraging ecology, social behavior, and predator avoidance from an evolutionary perspective. Well referenced; includes many diagrams and data figures.

McFarland, David, ed. *The Oxford Companion to Animal Behavior.* Rev. and enl. ed. New York: Oxford University Press, 1987. Intended as a reference guide for both nonspecialists and people in the field. A comprehensive survey of behavior, written by a team of internationally known biologists, psychologists, and neurobiologists. Contains more than two hundred entries covering a variety of behavioral topics. A detailed index provides cross-references organized by both subject and species lists.

Manning, Aubrey. *An Introduction to Animal Behavior.* 3d ed. London: Edward Arnold, 1979. A concise introduction to many general aspects of animal behavior. Topics covered include learning, evolution and behavior, development of behavior, communication, conflict behavior, and social organization. Well researched, clearly written, and effectively illustrated.

Raven, Peter H. *Biology.* St. Louis: Times Mirror/Mosby, 1989. Chapter 56 of this general text on the science of biology offers an excellent introduction to the general concepts of ethology and animal behavior, with a strong emphasis on many basic ethological concepts in addition to the learning-versus-instinct debate and the sociobiology controversy. A concise summary, suggestions for additional reading, and review questions appear at the end of the chapter.

Michael A. Steele

Cross-References

Animal Experimentation, 252; Behaviorism: An Overview, 401; Emotion in Primates, 947; Habituation and Sensitization, 1132; Imprinting and Learning, 1262; Learning Defined, 1443; Reflexes, 2066.

EXISTENTIAL ANALYSIS AND THERAPY

Type of psychology: Personality
Field of study: Humanistic-phenomenological models

Existential analysis, derived from the insights of existential philosophy, offers a powerful portrait of the fundamental dilemmas of human living. It stresses the individual's freedom to make choices and responsibility to live life authentically according to those choices.

Principal terms

ABSURDITY: the sense that there is no inherent basis for conferring meaning to life

AUTHENTICITY: living in the recognition that one's life and choices are one's own responsibility

BEING-IN-THE-WORLD: a term indicating that individuals are situationally involved in a personal "world" rather than merely located in an objective environment

EXISTENTIAL ANALYSIS: analysis of one's existence as the network of relationships with others and the world in which one is actually living

INAUTHENTICITY: the suppression of responsibility for one's own life

Overview

Existential psychology was inspired by the original insights of the philosophy of existentialism. By examining situations of great horror (such as the concentration camps of the Nazis) and of great beauty or joy (such as a father seeing his little girl happily skipping down the sidewalk), existentialism posited that human existence is without absolutes: There are no limits either to human cruelty or to human love. Existentialism removes all presuppositions, abstractions, and universal rules. It attacks the conformity and complacency caused by the illusion that a human is only a predetermined cog in a completely ordered, mechanical universe.

Contemporary culture can be extremely alienating, with its huge bureaucratic and technological structures that do not recognize one's concrete existence. In spite of the pervasiveness of this alienation, existentialism holds that the possibility of existing as an authentic individual is never lost. Existentialism depicts the "absurdity" of the lack of pre-established systems of meaning, but it rejects the artificiality of schemes that try to account for meaning as somehow produced by systems "out there," beyond the individual. Instead, existentialism returns to concretely lived situations as the birthplace of whatever meaning may be found in life. In that sense, life is an adventure that unfolds as one lives it. As William Barrett has said, "life is not handed to us on a platter, but involves our own act of self-determination."

Mainstream psychology has not, for the most part, addressed this existentialist outlook. Instead, it borrowed from natural science the viewpoint that human life is essentially mechanistic and causally determined—that personal life can be reduced to a bundle of drives, stimuli, or biochemical reactions. The problem with those approaches, notes existential psychologist Rollo May, is that "the man disappears; we can no longer find 'the one' to whom this or that experience has happened." Thus, the crucial innovation offered by existential psychology is its aim to understand the personal, experienced reality of one's free and meaningful involvement in one's world. It does so by analyzing the experiential situations and concerns of persons as the most fundamental dimension of their existence. This approach has been especially evident in the areas of personality theory and psychotherapy. It is in those areas that psychologists are most directly confronted with real human problems and are therefore unable to settle for abstract laboratory experiments as a basis for knowledge.

Psychologists began to turn to existentialism in the 1940's. The pioneers of existential analysis were psychoanalysts originally influenced by the ideas of Sigmund Freud. As analysts, they already stood outside mainstream experimental psychology, and so were not as influenced by its presumptions. Furthermore, as therapists, their overriding purpose was to assist actual people who were experiencing real distress, anxiety, and conflict. Abstract theories and dogmas about stimuli and responses were more easily recognized as insufficient in that context, and an approach that focused on patients' actual existence was welcome.

The first practitioners were the Swiss psychiatrists Ludwig Binswanger and Medard Boss, whose early writings date from the late 1940's. They were inspired by the existential philosophy of Martin Heidegger's key book *Sein und Zeit* (1927; *Being and Time*, 1962) which had appeared in 1927. They believed that analysis needed to be broadened beyond the limits that Freud had established. In place of Freud's "psychoanalysis"—the aim of which was to understand an interior mental apparatus—they developed existential analysis, with the aim of understanding the person's existence—that is, the person's "being-in-the-world." This term, developed by Heidegger, was meant by its hyphens to indicate that the relation of person and world is not merely one of the person being located "in" the world (as a pencil is located in a drawer). Rather, the person is always "worlded" in the sense that one's existence is a network of meaningful involvements—relationships that are specifically and uniquely one's own. Heidegger had called this the "care" structure, and he saw it as the very core of what it means to be a human being: that people care, that the people, places, and things with which one is involved inevitably matter.

Being-in-the-world as involvement is revealed by how such basic dimensions of the world as time and space are actually experienced. Time is not lived as a clock would record it, in equal minutes and hours. Rather, some hours drag on and on, whereas others zip by, depending on one's involvements. Similarly, the space of a strange place looms different when it has become familiar. Even one's own body reflects this understanding of existence as being-in-the-world. A great variety of symptoms, from cold feet to high blood pressure, disclose one's involvements, as do gestures, both habitual and spontaneous.

Other continental European psychiatrists who advanced the development of existential psychology include Karl Jaspers, Eugene Minkowski, Henri Ey, Erwin Straus, Frederik Jacobus Buytendijk, and Viktor Frankl. In England, R. D. Laing, a brilliant young psychiatrist originally influenced by the British "object relations" school of psychoanalysis, developed an existential account of schizophrenic persons, beginning around 1960. He sought to show "that it was far more possible than is generally supposed to understand people diagnosed as psychotic." He proceeded to do so by examining their "existential context." In books such as *The Divided Self: An Existential Study in Sanity and Madness* (1965), Laing attempts to unravel the mystery of schizophrenic speaking and symptoms by revealing how their apparently nonsensical quality does have a sense when seen in terms of the person's own experience of the totality of his or her relationships and existence.

Existential analysis came to the United States at the end of the 1950's mainly through the influence of Rollo May, who introduced the writings of the European analysts. May provided both a very scholarly background to the approach and an examination of its role in psychotherapy. His later books, such as *Man's Search for Himself* (1953), *Psychology and the Human Dilemma* (1967), and *Love and Will* (1969), did much to popularize existential psychology in the United States without trivializing its philosophical depth.

Applications

Existential therapists, such as May, have generally argued that they are not seeking to establish a new type of therapy with new techniques. Rather, they have developed a different approach, one that can be used with any specific therapeutic system. They developed a different way for the therapist to "be present" for the patient or client. This distinctive way of being present is well illustrated in R. D. Laing's therapeutic work; it hinges upon the type of relationship that exists between the therapist and the patient. Laing points out the difference between two ways of relating to a patient: as a biochemical organism (and a diseased organism at that) or as a person. He cites, as an example, the difference between listening to another's speaking as evidence of certain neurological processes and trying to understand what the person is talking about. When a therapist sees a patient as an "it," the therapist cannot really understand that patient's desire, fear, hope, or despair. Seeing the patient as a person, however, implies seeing the patient "as responsible, as capable of choice, in short, as a self-acting agent."

This undiluted respect for the personhood of the patient is well exhibited in Laing's work with schizophrenic persons. In place of the usual medical model, Laing offered them a "hospital" in the original sense of that word: a place of refuge, of shelter and rest for a traveler. Their experience was respected there, however different it appeared. They were allowed to complete their journey through madness, accompanied by another person (Laing) who was always respectful that it was real.

Rollo May similarly asserts that "the central task and responsibility of the therapist is to seek to understand the patient as a being and as being-in-his-world." That understanding does not deny the validity of any psychodynamic insights; rather, it holds that any such dynamics "can be understood only in the context of the structure of existence of the person." Indeed, the very aim of existential therapy is to help the patient experience his or her existence as real. What makes it possible for the patient to change, says May, is ultimately this experience of being treated, in the moment, as the real person that the person is. That is why existential therapy emphasizes a sense of reality and concreteness above a set of techniques.

While each person's reality is unique, there are certain basic dilemmas that arise by virtue of one's being-in-the-world. Because existence is fundamentally a relationship with a world, the givens of existing provide what Irvin Yalom has called the "ultimate concerns of life." He has identified four: death, freedom, existential isolation, and meaninglessness. Yalom notes that the confrontation with any of these existential issues can become a serious conflict for a person. Specifically, to the extent that a person begins to become aware of these conflicts without yet facing them fully, that person will experience anxiety, and so will seek to defend against the experience by turning away from the underlying concern. The task of the existential therapist is to use that experience of anxiety as a clue to help patients find their way back to the ultimate concern and then, by fully facing it, discover the positive transformation it offers for authentic living. The first two of these ultimate concerns, death and freedom, can serve as illustrative examples.

The first of these conflicts is that one's life will end in death even though one wishes it could continue. Death therefore holds a terror that may leave one anxious. One may even try to evade any awareness of death, living as though one would live forever. For the existential therapist, however, this awareness of death can be used to propel the patient to live his or her life authentically. Because life's preciousness is most evident when one is aware that one will lose it, becoming authentically aware of one's mortality can give one a powerful commitment not to waste one's life. In that sense, the anxiety of trying to evade death can be turned around and transformed into a clue to help patients discover what it is that they would be most anxious about dying without having experienced.

The second of these conflicts has to do with freedom. Though it seems to be a positive value, realizing one's freedom fully can be terrifying, for it entails accepting responsibility for one's life. One is responsible for actualizing one's own true self. Experiences such as anxiety, guilt, and despair reveal the dilemma of trying to hide from oneself the fact that one was not willing to be true to oneself. They then provide the basic clue by which the patient can uncover the self.

Context

Existentialism arose in the mid-nineteenth century with Søren Kierkegaard. He opposed the Hegelian philosophy dominant during his time with the criticism that its formalism and abstractness omitted the individual. He insisted that the existing person was the most basic starting point for philosophy, that the authentic acceptance of being an individual is the basic task of one's life, and that "the purpose of life is to be the self which one truly is." Through analyses of such experiences as passion and commitment, Kierkegaard showed the important truths of subjective life.

At the beginning of the twentieth century, Edmund Husserl established phenomenology as a philosophical method by which to investigate actual experience. This provided a powerful boost to existentialism, especially evident in Heidegger's subsequent analysis of the "care structure" as the meaning of being human. The next developments in existentialism arose in France, during and immediately after World War II. In a country occupied by the Nazis for five years, people who worked in the French resistance movement came to know their own finitude up close. Death awaited around every corner; one never could know that this day was not the last. Such direct experience had a powerful impact on the French existential philosophers who participated in the resistance movement, of whom Jean-Paul Sartre, Albert Camus, Simone de Beauvoir, and Maurice Merleau-Ponty are the best known.

While Merleau-Ponty wrote books of particular relevance for a psychology of perception and behavior, it was Sartre who most fully depicted the foibles of human life that are relevant to the psychotherapist. In philosophical books such as *L'Être et le néant* (1943; *Being and Nothingness*, 1956), as well as in plays and novels, Sartre lucidly revealed the ways people dodge rather than face their own freedom and their own responsibility to choose. For him, this living as if one were not really free (inauthentic living) was "bad faith." Sartre contrasted his "existential analysis" of phenomena such as bad faith with the Freudian psychoanalysis of the unconscious. In doing so, he replaced Freud's conceptions of a theoretical construct (the unconscious) with descriptions of experiences of living inauthentically.

These developments in France led to a burst of expanded interest in existentialism throughout the 1950's, in both Europe and the United States. By the 1960's, many new books, journals, and even graduate programs began to emphasize existential philosophy and psychology. Graduate programs that focused on existential psychology appeared at Duquesne University, West Georgia College, and Sonoma State University.

Existentialism became one of the primary sources of inspiration for an alternative to the dominant psychoanalytic and behavioristic psychologies that began to gather momentum in the 1960's under the name "humanistic psychology." By offering the perspective that people's experiences of their own situations are vitally important to an understanding of their behavior, this view posed a central challenge to mainstream experimental psychology. This existential insight did not sway most psychologists, however; instead, the rise of cognitive psychology in the 1970's and 1980's established a new paradigm. It, too, offered the key notion that a person's involvement was crucial to understanding behavior, but cognitive psychology defined that involvement in terms of a computational model: The person "takes in" the world by "processing information." That model preserved the mechanistic assumption so important to mainstream psychology—the very assumption that existential psychology most decisively disputed. As a result, existential psychology remains a lively critic on psychology's periphery rather than being an equal partner with more traditional approaches.

Bibliography

Boss, Medard. *Psychoanalysis and Daseinsanalysis.* New York: Da Capo Press, 1982. This book is Boss's most clear and comprehensive presentation of his own approach to existential analysis. It offers a philosophically sophisticated critique of Freudian psychoanalysis with regard to neuroses and therapy and presents an alternative rooted in the existential insights of one's being-in-the-world.

Frankl, Viktor Emil. *Man's Search for Meaning.* Boston: Beacon Press, 1963. Includes Frankl's gripping account of his experience as a prisoner in a Nazi concentration camp during World War II and the insights he gained from it. Also presents Frankl's basic formulation of "logotherapy"—his original form of existential therapy, centered on the question of what it is that gives one's life meaning.

The Humanistic Psychologist 16, no. 1 (1988). This special issue, "Psychotherapy for Freedom," edited by Erik Craig, focuses on the existential approach to psychotherapy developed by Medard Boss known as daseinsanalysis. It features original articles by Boss and his colleagues at the Daseinsanalytic Institute in Switzerland, as well as pieces by Erik Craig and Martin Heidegger and an annotated bibliography of relevant readings on daseinsanalysis.

Laing, Ronald David. *The Divided Self: An Existential Study in Sanity and Madness.* New York: Penguin, 1965. This brilliant study of schizophrenia from an existential approach was a breakthrough for a totally new way of understanding the experience of the psychotic person. Though difficult for a general reader, the profound value of Laing's vision is worth the effort.

May, Rollo. *The Discovery of Being.* New York: W. W. Norton, 1983. This collection of May's essays offers a clear and easily grasped introduction to existential psychology. Though the emphasis is mostly on its relation to psychotherapy, the volume also covers some of the basic principles and background of the existential approach.

May, Rollo, Ernest Angel, and Henri F. Ellenberger, eds. *Existence.* New York: Basic Books, 1958. This famous volume was the first to introduce European existential psychology to American audiences. It includes the first English translations of articles by Binswanger, Minkowski, Straus, and others, as well as a now-classic introductory chapter by May that describes the significance of an existential approach to psychology and psychotherapy.

Review of Existential Psychology and Psychiatry 20, nos. 1-3 (1986-1987). These special issues of this journal, edited by Keith Hoeller and collectively entitled "Readings in Existential Psychology and Psychiatry," feature a collection of classic articles from the 1960's to the 1980's. Included are articles by Van Kaam, Frankl, Boss, Laing, Rogers, May, and others on such topics as existential psychotherapy, anxiety, guilt, freedom, imagination, myth, schizophrenia, suicide, the unconscious, and will.

Valle, Ronald S., and Steen Halling, eds. *Existential-Phenomenological Perspectives in Psychology.* New York: Plenum Press, 1989. Designed as an introduction to the field, this book examines, from an existential and phenomenological perspective, many of psychology's standard topics, such as learning, perception, psychotherapy, development, and research, as well as areas that traditional psychology overlooks, such as aesthetics, passion, forgiveness, and transpersonal experiences.

Van Kaam, Adrian L. *Existential Foundations of Psychology.* Pittsburgh: Duquesne University Press, 1966. Van Kaam's aim in this book is to provide a dialogue between traditional scientific psychology and the insights of existentialism. He sees psychology as needing to integrate the existential awareness that one's involvement in the world is necessarily from a personal perspective.

Yalom, Irvin D. *Existential Psychotherapy.* New York: Basic Books, 1980. A very well-written presentation of an existential understanding of psychological problems and therapy. Yalom grasps the basic conflicts of psychological life as flowing from "the individual's confrontation with the givens of existence," and he identifies these givens as death, freedom, existential isolation, and meaninglessness. For each theme, he presents the conflict and the way that existential therapy addresses it.

Christopher M. Aanstoos

Cross-References

Abnormality: Humanistic-Existential Models, 60; Gestalt Therapy, 1088; Humanism: An Overview, 1203; Person-Centered Therapy, 1777; Personality Theory: Major Issues, 1804; Self-Actualization, 2168; Social Psychological Models: Erich Fromm, 2318.

SOURCES OF EXPERIMENTAL BIAS

Type of psychology: Psychological methodologies
Field of study: Methodological issues

Sources of experimental bias can invalidate the results of psychological experimentation and cause erroneous conclusions to be drawn; with properly designed research, these sources can be controlled and more reliable information can be produced.

Principal terms

DEMAND CHARACTERISTICS: the cues and other information used by subjects to guide their behavior in a psychological study

DEPENDENT VARIABLE: the measured behavior that is of interest in a research study

DOUBLE-BLIND DESIGN: an experiment in which both the subject and observer are kept unaware of which subjects received the experimental treatment and which were part of the control group

EXPERIMENTER EFFECTS: biases introduced into a research study as a result of the expectations of the experimenter

EXTERNAL VALIDITY: the extent to which the results of a research study can be generalized to different populations, settings, or conditions

HAWTHORNE EFFECT: refers to changes in a person's behavior simply because of increased attention

INDEPENDENT VARIABLE: the factor that an experimenter selects or manipulates in order to assess its effect on behavior

INTERNAL VALIDITY: the degree to which conclusions about the cause-and-effect relationship between variables in an experiment are sound

PLACEBO: a substance that resembles a drug or other treatment but is inactive and causes no physical effect

RANDOM ASSIGNMENT: the most common technique to establish equivalent groups by balancing subject characteristics through the assigning of subjects to groups through some random process

Overview

Research psychologists attempt to answer questions about the nature of human behavior and mental functioning by employing various observational and experimental methodologies. In conducting these investigations, it is impossible to study everyone in the population; therefore, a subset of the population (referred to as a "sample") is selected, and the observations of the performance of the sample are used to make inferences about the population as a whole. If the sample is not drawn properly, or if the methodology employed is flawed, the results of the study will not reflect the true situation in the population, in which case the results are said to be biased.

There are various methodologies that can be employed in psychological research. For example, one can make in-depth observations of a single subject, as in a case study, or observe subjects in their normal surroundings, as in naturalistic observation. Psychologists also sometimes attempt to establish relationships between a set of circumstances or characteristics and some measurable behavior through a statistical procedure called correlation. Whereas all these methods can yield useful information, they are primarily descriptive and cannot provide an explanation of causal relationships. For this, it is necessary to design an experiment, which is the most powerful method of gaining information in psychology. The experiment provides the opportunity to investigate causal relationships, and it allows the researcher the ability to control major sources of bias.

Experiments involve the manipulation of one or more factors and the measurement of the effects that this manipulation has on behavior. The factors that the research manipulates are called independent variables, and the affected behaviors that are measured are called dependent variables. In experimental research, usually some statement, called a hypothesis, is made about the expected nature of the relationship between the independent and dependent variables, and the research study tests this hypothetical relationship.

There are always circumstances in an experiment besides the independent variable, however, that could be affecting the dependent variables (the measured behavior). These are usually called extraneous or confounding variables, and they can bias the results of an experiment.

The simplest example of this involves the use of two groups: an experimental group, which gets the treatment represented by the independent variable, and a control group, which does not get the treatment. The control group and the experimental group should be alike in every respect (except for the treatment of the independent variable), and the conditions under which they are studied should be as alike as possible. Therefore, the extraneous circumstances need to be controlled. If at the conclusion of the experiment there is a significant difference between the measured behavior of the experimental group and that of the control group, then it can be inferred that the difference was caused by the treatment.

The most frequently used method for equalizing the experimental and control groups on all variables is random selection of potential subjects from the population and then random assignment of subjects to the different conditions of the experiment. Randomization means that each subject has an equal likelihood of being included in each group of the experiment. Any deviation from the random assignment of subjects is a possible source of bias in the results of the research. Once the groups are equated through random selection and assignment, it is important to treat the groups in the same manner—anything done to the experimental group should also be done to the control group. Thus, if the experimental treatment involves taking a pill, the control group should also get a pill; if the experimental treatment involves an injection, the control group should also receive an injection. The treatment given to the control group will be something that does not produce any effect, such as a sugar pill or an injection of salt water. These are called placebo treatments; they are necessary because the behavior of a subject could be affected by merely anticipating effects after receiving some treatment. This source of bias is eliminated by the use of placebos.

In general, the expectations held by both the subjects and the experimenter can be a possible source of bias in an experiment. Cues and other information that subjects can use to guide their behavior in a psychological experiment are referred to as the demand characteristics of the experiment. If, for example, the subjects knew that they had been given alcohol as part of the study, their expectancies of certain effects could influence their behavior. In addition, subjects tend to want to please their experimenter, or to perform in a way that they think is expected of them. These demand characteristics lead to the introduction of bias by the subjects themselves.

The expectations of the experimenter can also be a source of bias, usually referred to as experimenter effects. Experimenters might unconsciously treat subjects in the experimental group differently from those in the control group, or their observations may be biased by knowing which treatment a subject has received. In general, the problems of demand characteristics or experimenter effects can never be completely eliminated, but their effects can be diminished by proper experimental design. The most effective design is called a double-blind design, in which neither the experimenter nor the subjects know which subjects are in the control group and which are in the experimental groups, and the subjects are not aware of the specific independent variable that is being studied. Another way that experimenter and subject bias is reduced in psychological research is through the principle of replication. Usually, the results of a single experiment are not thought to be established until that experiment has been done again (replicated) in a different laboratory under the supervision of other researchers.

Some major sources of experimental bias arise from threats to the internal and external validity of the research, which were first identified by researchers Donald Campbell and J. S. Stanley. Internal validity refers to how valid the statement is that change in the independent variable caused the observed change in the dependent variable. External validity refers to the degree to which the results of an experiment are generalizable to the population as a whole.

The primary threats to internal validity include the following six factors. One is history—the influence on the dependent variable of any event that occurs during the experimental period (other than the independent variable). Another is maturation—in long-term studies, the effects caused by the subjects simply growing older or more experienced. Selection may also cause problems—bias may be created whenever subjects are assigned by other than a random basis. Mortality (attrition), when subjects drop out of an experiment, is a problem if there is some systematic reason for their dropping out. Statistical regression may bias an experiment: If subjects are chosen on the basis of very high or very low scores on a particular test, their scores tend to move toward the mean on the second test, regardless of any experimental intervention (those who did poorly tend to do better, and those that did very well tend to do worse). Finally, testing can create bias: The very act of testing a group of subjects can in itself sometimes sensitize them and thereby change their behavior. It can also help to create demand characteristics by informing the subject of the experimenter's topic of interest.

As a general rule, the more tightly controlled the experiment, the less likely it is that any conclusions will suffer from threats to internal validity, but the more likely it is that they will suffer from threats to external validity. This is because a highly controlled laboratory experiment is an extremely artificial environment, and the results may not generalize to a real-world setting. Therefore, an experimenter often has to decide which is more important to his purpose—highly reliable results or highly generalizable results. All the sources of experimental bias mentioned above can cause the researcher to draw erroneous conclusions and can thereby invalidate the results of an experiment.

Applications

A well-known study that illustrates experimenter effects as a source of bias was conducted by psychologist Robert Rosenthal. The actual subjects he studied were his own laboratory assistants, who were studying the ability of rats to learn a maze. Some laboratory assistants were told that their rats had been bred to be particularly "maze-bright," while others were told that their rats were "maze-dull." The maze-bright rats learned the maze significantly faster than the maze-dull rats. In reality, both groups of rats were randomly drawn from the same population and had equal learning capabilities. Rosenthal concluded that these results were obtained because the assistants' knowledge of their rats "superior" or "inferior" maze-learning abilities caused them to bias or alter their training techniques subtly, which in turn affected the speed of the learning of the rats. In an applied setting, similar results were obtained when teachers were informed that their incoming classes were particularly bright or particularly dull. The "bright" students performed well above average, while the "dull" students performed in a below-average manner.

One of the most famous examples of the influence of subject bias on research results was a study conducted to increase worker productivity at the Hawthorne plant of the Western Electric Company in Cicero, Illinois. Industrial psychologists divided assembly-line workers into two groups, one working under increased levels of lighting and the other working under the normal lighting level. The results were increased productivity in both groups. Increased productivity was also found when new schedules of rest breaks were introduced and, curiously, also when lighting levels were *reduced*. In fact, whatever changes were made in the job environment led to an increase in productivity. It appeared that the subjects recognized the positive concern of the experimenters about their working conditions, and this recognition was the motivating factor in their increased productivity. This type of response by subjects is now referred to as the "Hawthorne effect."

An example of how the confounding effects of an extraneous variable can make the conclusion drawn from an experiment worthless is illustrated by the "Pepsi Challenge," which was a Pepsi advertising campaign. Subjects who said they were Coca-Cola drinkers were asked to taste two unidentified colas and state their preference. More than half of the subjects reportedly preferred the Pepsi. Officials of Coca-Cola decided to conduct their own replication of the Pepsi study. In the original research, Coke was always in a glass marked Q, and Pepsi was always in a glass marked M. The Coke researchers decided to test whether the preference for a particular letter could have created the Pepsi results. They also tested subjects with glasses marked Q and M, but this time Coke was in both glasses. More than 50 percent of their subjects still claimed to prefer the drink in the M glass. Thus, what looked like experimental evidence for preference for a particular cola was actually evidence for preference for one letter over another. This example not only illustrates the biasing effects that confounding variables can have but also shows the value of replication.

Threats to internal validity can be illustrated with a hypothetical educational experiment. Suppose one wished to study the effectiveness of a new intervention strategy for improving the educational achievement of slow learners. In this study, "educational achievement" is to be measured by scores on the Scholastic Aptitude Test (SAT). The experimental group that gets the new strategy is composed of students identified as slow learners by previous SAT scores. The group is given the new teaching method, then retested one year later. The treatment group increased its scores by a statistically significant amount, and the program is declared a success.

There were a number of potential threats to internal validity that could have biased the results of this study. There could be a problem with history, for example, since no control group was used, and some other circumstances during the year could have motivated the students. Testing could be a problem as well, in that the pretest could have been the first standardized test these children were exposed to, which could have increased their general test-taking skills. At the time of the second test, the testing environment and procedures would not have seemed so foreign. Also, they might have remembered specific items from the pretest and learned the answers over the year. If there were a high dropout rate from the treatment group, that could have been a problem in that the poorer students would have been the ones most likely to drop out, thereby increasing the average performance of the group simply by their absence. The biggest problem with the interpretation of the results, however, is the probable effect of statistical regression. The fact that these were low-achieving students identified by low SAT scores makes it highly likely that on taking a retest, their scores would be closer to the mean, and therefore higher.

Context

The identification and control of sources of experimental bias are extremely important for producing reliable information from psychological research. Psychology is much like any other science in that researchers, in order to understand human behavior, attempt to establish relationships between circumstances and behaviors and then fit these relationships into an orderly body of knowledge. The problem that is unique to psychology as a science is that the behavior of humans is much more variable than the subject matter of any of the other sciences, such as chemistry or physics. In addition to grappling with the great variability among humans, the psychological researcher also must deal with the variability in the behavior of a single subject from one experimental trial to another. This tremendous variability makes it much more difficult to reach definitive conclusions.

During the early 1900's, the movement in psychology known as behaviorism tried to remedy this problem by attempting to limit the scope of scientific psychology to only the most objective aspects of the human being—observable, measurable behavior. During this era, much of the research was also conducted on animals, since there is less variability among animals than among humans. Animals, for example, can be bred with similar genetic characteristics and raised in controlled, identical environments.

Psychology eventually tired of the limitations of behaviorism, however, and there was increasing interest in studying psychological constructs directly. Through the development of more sophisticated statistical techniques and the use of proper experimental design, it became possible to control variability to a great extent. This degree of experimental sophistication has helped psychologists first to identify, then to learn to control, sources of experimental bias. This has led to more reliable results from psychological research and to greater understanding of human psychological functioning.

An understanding of experimental bias, even by a nonscientist, can help to make one a better interpreter (or "consumer") of scientific information. People are constantly bombarded with information about the results of "scientific" studies in the newspapers, on television, and in other media. It is often important to "read between the lines" and ask critical questions before accepting these results. Knowing about experimenter bias should always lead one to question where a study was done, who provided the sponsorship, and whether or not the researchers had a vested interest in a particular outcome. (For example, studies conducted by researchers of the American Tobacco Institute often find different effects of tobacco smoke on health than does research conducted by the American Cancer Society.) Other questions should always be asked. Were subjects randomly selected? If performances were compared, are the groups equatable? If a causal relationship is inferred between two variables, are there other alternative explanations attributable to possible confounding factors?

By understanding the ways in which experimental bias can affect the conclusions reached, one can begin to develop the critical thinking skills that are necessary for gaining reliable knowledge in any field.

Bibliography

Baker, Therese L. *Doing Social Research.* New York: McGraw-Hill, 1988. This is a complete and understandable treatment of all areas of social research. There are thorough discussions of bias created from faulty sampling and obstacles to the validity of an experiment.

Campbell, Donald Thomas, and Julian C. Stanley. *Experimental and Quasi-experimental Design for Research*. Chicago: Rand McNally, 1966. Considered a classic in the field of experimental design in the social sciences. Campbell and Stanley originated the key concepts of internal and external validity, which have become the standards for use in analyzing research validity. This book is somewhat technical, but most advanced high school or college students should have no problem with it.

Martin, David W. *Doing Psychology Experiments*. 2d ed. Monterey, Calif.: Brooks/Cole, 1985. Martin writes with a humorous style, and this book is excellent as a first exposure to experimental methods. Light-hearted illustrations convey technical points in ways that are easily remembered.

Phillips, John L. *How to Think About Statistics*. 3d ed. New York: W. H. Freeman, 1988. An excellent introduction to the statistical principles underlying the logic of experimental design. Phillips stresses the kind of problem-solving skills necessary to become a good consumer of science information as well as to evaluate advertising claims, polls, economic forecasts, and other common issues.

Pyke, Sandra W., and Neil M. Agnew. *The Science Game*. 5th ed. Englewood Cliffs, N.J.: Prentice-Hall, 1991. Another well-written and popular introduction to all aspects of social science research. There is an extensive section on validity, with one of the most complete descriptions on threats to external validity that one will find. Also includes an in-depth discussion of sexual bias in social research.

Oliver W. Hill, Jr.

Cross-References

Complex Experimental Designs: Interactions, 625; Experimentation: Ethics and Subject Rights, 1013; Hypothesis Development and Testing, 1248; Psychological Experimentation: Independent, Dependent, and Control Variables, 1932; Quasi-Experimental Designs, 2024; Sampling, 2122; Survey Research: Questionnaires and Interviews, 2507; Within-Subject Experimental Designs, 2647.

EXPERIMENTATION: ETHICS AND SUBJECT RIGHTS

Type of psychology: Psychological methodologies
Fields of study: Experimental methodologies; methodological issues

One of the tasks of government is to protect people from exploitation and abuse, including potential abuse by unethical researchers. American society has instituted several levels of control over research, thus ensuring that experimental ethics reflect the ethics of society at large. Still, few ethical decisions are easy, and many remain controversial.

Principal terms

DEBRIEFING: discussing an experiment and its purpose with subjects afterward; this is required if the experiment used deception

DEMAND CHARACTERISTICS: aspects of the experimental setting that bring about behaviors in the subjects which they may not have shown in a nonexperimental setting

DOUBLE-BLIND STUDY: a study in which neither the experimenter nor the subjects know who is receiving treatment and who is not; this controls for subject and experimenter biases and expectations

INFORMED CONSENT: a written form explaining all potential risks of research participation to the potential subjects

INSTITUTIONAL REVIEW BOARD: a committee that reviews all human research proposals before they can be started; weeds out unethical procedures

MACROALLOCATION DECISIONS: decisions about which issues get priority attention and which go on the back burner; usually sociopolitical rather than individual decisions

PLACEBO CONDITION: a condition in which, as part of a double-blind study, a subject is not getting treatment but is part of a control group

Overview

A primary task of government is to protect people from exploitation. Scientists are sometimes in a position to take advantage of others and, unfortunately, have occasionally done so in the name of science. Hence, there is a role for government to regulate research to prevent exploitation of innocent people. On the other hand, excessive regulation can stifle innovation; if scientists are not allowed to try new (and perhaps risky) experimental techniques, science will not progress, and neither will human understanding of the world. This puts government in a bind: Since research topics, scientific methodology, and public attitudes are continuously changing, it would be impossible to write a single law or set of laws defining which research topics and methods are acceptable and which are not. As soon as such a law were written, it would be out of date or incomplete.

The United States Congress has decided to deal with this dilemma by letting local communities determine what research is and is not appropriate according to contemporary local standards. Today, each institution conducting research must have a committee called an institutional review board (IRB) consisting of a minimum of five members, all of whom belong to the local community. In order to ensure that the committee is kept up to date on current human research methodologies, the IRB membership must include at least one person who does, or has done, research using human subjects. The committee must also include at least one person who does research without using human subjects (for example, who specializes in animal research, theoretical modeling, or statistical analysis), who would be capable of suggesting alternative research methodologies if deemed necessary. A third member must be trained in ethics, such as a member of the local clergy, and at least one member must represent the general public and have no official or unofficial relationship with the institution where the research is taking place. (These latter two roles can be fulfilled by the same person.)

Each IRB is required to review written proposals for all local research on human subjects before that research can begin. It is the job of the IRB to ensure that unethical research is screened out before it starts. Government agencies which fund research projects will not consider a proposal until it has been approved by the local IRB, and, if research is conducted without IRB approval, the government can withhold all funds to that institution, even funds unrelated to the research.

The IRB review process requires that research proposals include a copy of the informed-consent contract. This contract allows potential subjects to see, in writing, a list of all possible physical or psychological risks which might occur as a result of participation in the project. People cannot be coerced or threatened into signing the form, and the form must also tell subjects that, if they agree to participate, they may quit at any time for any reason.

Occasionally, researchers use a procedure called deception, in which they tell the subjects that the study is about one thing when it really is about something else. Although it usually is considered unethical to lie to subjects, deception is sometimes necessary, because subjects may behave differently when they know what aspect of their behavior is being watched. (This is called a demand characteristic of the experimental setting.) More people will probably act helpful, for example, when they know that a study is about helpfulness. A researcher studying helpfulness thus might tell subjects that they are going to be involved in a study of, say, reading. Subjects are then asked to wait in a room until they are each called into the test room. When the first name is called, a person may get up and trip on his or her way out of the room. In actuality, the person who was called was really the experimenter's assistant (although none of the subjects knows that), and the real point of the research is to see how many of the subjects get up to help the person who fell down. In situations such as this, where demand characteristics would be likely, IRB's will allow deception to be used as long as the deception is not severe and the researchers debrief subjects at the end by explaining what was really occurring. After deception is used, experimenters must be careful to make sure that subjects do not leave the study feeling angry at having been "tricked"; ideally, they should leave feeling satisfaction for having contributed to science.

Researchers are also obliged to ensure that subjects can get help if they do experience any negative effects from their participation in the research. Ultimately, if a subject feels that he or she was somehow harmed or abused by the researcher or the research project, a civil suit can be filed in an attempt to claim compensation. Since subjects are explicitly told that they can drop out of a study at any time for any reason, however, such long-term negative feelings should be extremely rare.

Applications

Clinical psychology is perhaps the most difficult area in which to make ethical research decisions. One potential problem in clinical research that is not usually relevant for other research settings is that of getting truly informed consent from the subjects. The subjects of clinical research are selected specifically because they meet the criteria for some mental disorder. By making sure that subjects meet the relevant criteria, researchers ensure that their study results will be relevant to the population who suffers from the disorder; on the other hand, depending on the disorder being studied, it may be that the subjects are not capable of giving informed consent. How "informed" can a person be, for example, if he or she suffers from disordered thinking (as with schizophrenics) or dementia (as with Alzheimer's disease patients) or is otherwise mentally handicapped? In the cases of individuals who have been declared incompetent by the courts, a designated guardian can give informed consent for participation in a research study. There are also cases, however, of participants being legally competent, yet not truly understanding the consequences of what they read. Authority figures, including doctors and psychologists, can have a dramatic power over people; that power is likely to be even stronger for someone who is not in full control of his or her life, who has specifically sought help from others, and who is trusting that others have his or her best interests in mind.

Another concern about clinical research is the susceptibility of subjects to potential psychological damage. The typical response of research subjects is positive: They feel they are getting special attention and respond with healthy increases in self-esteem and well-being. A few, however, may end up feeling worse; for example, if they feel no immediate gain from the treatment, they may label themselves as "incurable" and give up, leading to a self-fulfilling prophecy.

A third concern in clinical research regards the use of control or placebo treatments. Good research designs always include both a treatment group and a control group. When there is no control group, any changes in the treatment group may be attributed to the treatment when in fact they may have been caused by the passage of time, or by the fact that subjects were getting special attention while in the study. Although control groups are necessary to ensure that research results are interpreted correctly, the dilemma that arises in clinical research is that it may be unethical to assign people to a control group if they need some kind of intervention. One way of dealing with this dilemma is to give all subjects some form of treatment and to compare the different treatment outcomes to one another rather than to a no-treatment group. This works well when there is already a known treatment with positive effects. Not only are there no subjects who are denied treatment; the new treatment can be tested to see if it is better than the old one, not only if it is better than nothing.

Sometimes, if there is no standard treatment for comparison, subjects assigned to the control group are put on a "waiting list" for the treatment; their progress without treatment is then compared with that of subjects who are getting treatment right away. To some extent, this mimics what happens in nonresearch settings, as people sometimes must wait for therapy, drug abuse counseling, and so on. On the other hand, in nonresearch settings, those who get assigned to waiting lists are likely to be those in less critical need, whereas in research, assignment to treatment and non-treatment groups must be random. Assigning the most critical cases to the treatment group would bias the study's outcome; yet assigning subjects randomly may be perceived as putting research needs ahead of clients' needs.

Another controversy surrounding psychological research has to do with what economists call macroallocation decisions. Researchers must decide which topics are most worthy of study. Society, too, must decide what kinds of topics its taxpayers want to support. Traditionally, psychology and other behavioral sciences have not received as much financial support from the government as have "harder" sciences such as molecular biology and physics. In addition, there are more sociopolitical and moral questions raised about the value of psychological research than about the research of other sciences.

An example of the impact of ethics and morals on macroallocation decisions regarding psychological research is the debate over government support for surveys of sexual behavior. Researchers argue that information about peoples' sexual behavior and attitudes is needed in order to address problems such as teenage pregnancy, sexual harassment, and the spread of acquired immune deficiency syndrome (AIDS). Many people believe, however, that asking questions about sexual behavior is an invasion of privacy; there is particular concern that adolescents would be asked to participate in such surveys without parental consent. Some people believe that government sponsorship of research on sexual behavior is a tacit stamp of approval of the behaviors addressed in the survey; they consider such studies to be propaganda which influences people's values and behavior as well as assessing it.

Ethical decisions about psychological research are made at all levels, from government to individual researchers and subjects. There may be no obvious right or wrong answers, but, at each level, the decisions that are made tend to reflect the ethical judgment of society; that is perhaps the best that can be hoped.

Context

Concern about potential abuse of research subjects arose in the 1960's, in response to publicity following a series of studies by Stanley Milgram at Yale University. Milgram was interested in finding out how physicians who had devoted their lives to helping people were so easily able to hurt and even kill others (in the name of science) in experiments in Nazi concentration camps.

In Milgram's now-famous experiment, each subject was paired with one of Milgram's colleagues but was told that this partner was another volunteer. Then each subject, both real and pretend, drew a slip of paper assigning him or her to the role of either "teacher" or "learner." Actually, both slips always said "teacher," but the assistants pretended that theirs said "learner"; this way, the real subjects were always assigned the role of teacher. Milgram then showed subjects an apparatus which supposedly delivered shocks; teachers, on one side of a partition, were instructed to deliver a shock to the learner on the other side whenever a mistake was made on a word-pairing task. The apparatus actually did not deliver shocks, but the learners pretended that it did; as the experiment continued, and the teachers were instructed to give larger and larger shocks, the learners gave more and more extreme responses. At a certain point, the learners started pounding on the partition, demanding to be released; eventually, they feigned a heart attack.

When Milgram designed this study, he asked psychiatrists and psychologists what percentage of people they thought would continue as teachers in this experiment; the typical response was about 0.1 percent. What Milgram found, however, was that two-thirds of people continued to deliver shocks to the learner even after the learner had apparently collapsed. The subjects were clearly upset; they repeatedly expressed concern that someone should check on the learner. Milgram would simply reply that although the shocks were painful, they would not cause permanent damage, and the teacher should continue. In spite of their concern and distress, most subjects obeyed.

Milgram's results revealed much about the power of authority; subjects obeyed the authority figure (Milgram) even against their own moral judgment. These results help explain the abominable behavior of Nazi physicians, as well as other acts of violence committed by normal people who were simply doing what they were told.

Ironically, although Milgram's study was so valuable, he was accused of abusing his own subjects by "forcing" them to continue the experiment even when they were clearly upset. Critics also claimed that Milgram's study might have permanently damaged his subjects' self-esteem. Although interviews with the subjects showed that this was not true—they generally reported learning much about themselves and about human nature—media discussions and reenactments of the study led the public to believe that many of Milgram's subjects had been permanently harmed. Thus began the discussion of experimental ethics which ultimately led to the system of regulation in force today.

Bibliography

American Psychological Association Council of Representatives. "Ethical Principles of Psychologists." *American Psychologist* 36, no. 6 (1981): 633-638. This is the actual text of the ten ethical principles of the American Psychological Association. Number nine is on research with human participants. An annotated casebook is also available from the APA, but unfortunately it does not give examples for principle number nine.

Beauchamp, Tom L., Ruth R. Faden, R. Jay Wallace, Jr., and Le Roy Walters, eds. *Ethical Issues in Social Science Research.* Baltimore: The Johns Hopkins University Press, 1982. This excellent four-hundred-page book delves into the controversies surrounding the costs and benefits of social science research (macroallocation issues are covered in parts 1 and 2), as well as the more concrete issues of informed consent, deception, and confidentiality (parts 3 and 4). Part 5 addresses controversies over government regulation of research. A selected bibliography is provided for each chapter. In-depth and thorough, yet very readable.

Bower, Robert T., and Priscilla de Gasparis. *Ethics in Social Research: Protecting the Interests of Human Subjects.* New York: Praeger, 1978. Provides a fairly technical, seventy-page synopsis of ethical issues in research; a ten-page appendix summarizing the ethical codes of the major social science professional organizations (does not give actual texts or full citations); a five-page appendix listing public-interest groups active in the protection of subject rights; and a lengthy annotated bibliography.

Katz, Jay. *Experimentation with Human Beings.* New York: Russell Sage Foundation, 1972. Although this volume was inspired by abuses in medical research, it is extremely thorough in coverage of social and psychological issues in human experimentation, and includes many examples of psychological studies. Follows the format of a law school text, but remains accessible to the general reader.

Levine, Carol, and Robert M. Veatch, eds. *Cases in Bioethics.* Hastings-on-Hudson, N.Y.: The Hastings Center, 1982. This casebook includes a chapter on human-subjects research. Although the casebook is primarily on biomedical issues, three of the four cases presented in chapter 5 concern psychological research. Commentaries illustrate the complexity of the issues and encourage readers to make their own evaluations.

Milgram, Stanley, and Thomas H. Murray. "Can Deception in Research Be Justified?" In *Taking Sides: Clashing Views on Controversial Psychological Issues,* edited by Joseph Rubinstein and Brent Slife. 5th ed. Guilford, Conn.: Dushkin, 1988. Each chapter includes two commentaries from different sides of controversial issues. Chapter 1 addresses the issue of deception. Milgram gives his side of the story of his controversial experiment. Murray addresses the example of studies on helping behavior.

Linda Mealey

Cross-References

Animal Experimentation, 252; Sources of Experimental Bias, 1006; Field Experimentation, 1031; Observational Methods in Psychology, 1700; Psychological Experimentation: Independent, Dependent, and Control Variables, 1932; Survey Research: Questionnaires and Interviews, 2507.

THE FACIAL FEEDBACK THEORY OF EMOTION

Type of psychology: Emotion
Field of study: Social perception and cognition

The facial feedback theory of emotion concerns the relationship between emotional experience and facial expression. In general, the theory argues that emotional experience (feelings) can be managed by producing different or opposite facial expressions. It also suggests that people do not experience emotions directly; instead, they infer or "read" their emotions from the expressions that appear on their faces.

Principal terms
EMOTIONAL EXPERIENCE: the perception of, and the physiological and psychological sensations associated with, feelings or emotions
EXPRESSIVE BEHAVIOR: any behavior that consistently occurs with and is thought to be associated with a particular emotion and that communicates that experience to others
FACIAL EXPRESSIONS: characteristic arrangements of the facial muscles, such as smiling or frowning, that convey specific emotional experiences
SELF-PERCEPTION PROCESSES: cognitive processes through which people infer their feelings or attitudes from their own behaviors and the situations in which those behaviors take place
SELF-REGULATORY MECHANISMS: a set of loosely related processes through which an organism becomes aware of and alters internal (either physiological or psychological) events

Overview

The purpose of expressive behavior has been the subject of vigorous debate among psychologists. Why do people make facial expressions? They may be simply the outward manifestation and unavoidable consequence of emotional experiences. They may be intended to communicate a person's feelings to others. They may serve some other, more subtle, function, such as telling people what their own feelings are. The purpose of facial expressions has been a topic of interest to writers, poets, philosophers, and social scientists for centuries. Some scientists have suggested that facial expressions are simply the external manifestations of internal emotional states (sometimes referred to as "affective" states). Others claim that facial expressions are designed to communicate information about how people are feeling to other people. Still others have argued that facial expressions are the "data" on which people base decisions about the emotions they themselves may be experiencing. This latter idea is the foundation of the facial feedback theories of emotion.

In the early 1970's, psychologists first confirmed Charles Darwin's speculations that a set of basic human facial expressions is innate and constant across cultures.

Since then, researchers have sought to understand the function and significance of facial expressions in the production and experience of emotion. This search has led to the formulation of theories about the role of facial expressions in emotional experience, of which the facial feedback theories are one subset. Although there are several variants of the central theme, all facial feedback theories share three defining characteristics. First, all hold that the experience of naturally occurring emotions (such as anger or fear) can be managed by producing different or opposite facial expressions. In other words, if a person feels sad and "puts on a happy face," the experience of sadness will be reduced. Second, all these theories argue that, in the absence of a naturally occurring emotion, self-generated facial expressions can produce their corresponding internal emotional states. In other words, even though a person may not feel sad, smiling will make that person feel happy. Finally, all the theories share a belief that internal emotional states are not experienced directly, but are instead mediated by some sort of mechanism involving feedback from the skin or the muscles of the face (hence the term "feedback" in the name). Put simply, this means that the specific configuration of people's facial muscles tells them that they are experiencing a particular emotion. If people's faces display smiles, the particular arrangement of the muscles involved in smiling "tells" them that they are happy.

An example that was first offered by William James may help clarify how facial (and other bodily) feedback is thought to lead to emotional experience. Suppose a woman encounters a growling bear in the woods. Upon noticing the bear, her heartbeat increases, her body secretes adrenaline (epinephrine), her face tenses in fear, and she runs away. Does she first notice she is afraid and then respond by fleeing from the bear, or does she flee first and then decide that she must have been afraid because she made a terrified facial expression? The latter idea explains the woman's behavior in terms of a feedback theory of emotional experience.

Because they seem to suggest a process that is at odds with most people's intuitions, facial feedback theories have had a long and controversial history in social psychology. Their origins can be traced at least as far back as Charles Darwin and William James, and some social scientists have noted that the ideas embodied in facial feedback theories can be found in the writings of Homer and Shakespeare. In *The Expression of the Emotions in Man and Animals* (1872), Darwin claimed that freely expressing an emotion would intensify its experience, whereas repressing or dampening the expression of an emotion would tend to reduce its effects. James echoed a similar idea in the second volume of *The Principles of Psychology* (1890). James's ideas, coupled with similar ideas offered independently by Danish physician Carl Lange, led to one of the earliest feedback theories, the James-Lange theory. More recently, psychologist Silvan Tomkins and social psychologists Carroll Izard, James Laird, John Lanzetta, and their colleagues have each proposed similar theories implicating facial expressions in the experience of emotions. Although they all differ in regard to the exact mechanism through which facial expressions produce or manage emotional experiences, all are collectively referred to as facial feedback theories. For example, the idea that facial expressions are emotions (or that being aware of one's facial expression is essentially the same as being aware of an emotion) is attributable to Tomkins. He argued that sensory receptors in the skin of the face provide information on the status of facial expressions that trigger emotional experiences from memory. The somewhat different idea that facial expressions are used (through self-perception processes) to infer an emotional state is based on the work of Laird. Laird argued that when people are unsure of what emotion they may be experiencing, they use attributional and self-perception processes to work backward, deciding that "if I am smiling, I must be happy."

Applications

Numerous social psychological experiments have supported the role of facial expressions in the production and regulation of emotions as predicted by the facial feedback theories. Recall that one of the propositions of the facial feedback theories is that in the presence of naturally occurring emotions such as disgust or delight, generating an opposite facial expression should have the effect of reducing the intensity of the original emotional experience. In contrast, exaggerating a spontaneous facial expression should have the effect of enhancing the intensity of the original emotional experience. Psychologist Robert Kraut examined this proposition in an experiment in which subjects sniffed a set of substances with characteristically unpleasant, neutral, and pleasant odors. Subjects then rated how pleasant each odor was. The substances Kraut used ranged from pyridine and butyric acid (both of which have a disgusting odor) through water (a neutral odor) to vanilla, wintergreen, and tangerine (all of which are very pleasant smelling to most people). In addition to smelling and rating the odors spontaneously, the subjects were sometimes instructed to pose a facial expression of delight or disgust when sniffing the odors, irrespective of the odor's actual pleasantness. Kraut found a strong effect for posing the different facial expressions. Consistent with the first proposition of facial feedback theories, when subjects posed a delighted expression, they rated all the odors as more pleasant smelling than when they rated the odors after reacting to them spontaneously. In contrast, and consistent with the facial feedback hypothesis, when subjects posed a disgusted expression, they rated all the odors as less pleasant smelling than when they rated the odors after reacting to them spontaneously. The results of Kraut's experiment suggest that the proverbial wisdom of "putting on a happy face" when a person feels sad may contain more than a little truth.

A second proposition of the facial feedback theories is that in the absence of naturally occurring emotions, generating a facial expression should have the effect of producing the corresponding emotional experience. In an early experiment, James Laird examined just this sort of proposition. He covertly manipulated college students' facial muscles to produce a frown while attaching electrodes to their faces. In other words, as part of an experiment in which brain-wave recordings were supposedly being made, Laird told subjects to contract or relax various facial muscles. These instructions had the net effect of producing a frown without subjects knowing that they were frowning. These subjects subsequently reported that they felt angry.

Other students' facial muscles were arranged into smiles. These subjects reported feeling happy and rated cartoons to be funnier than did control subjects. These studies have been criticized, however, because subjects might have been aware that their faces were being arranged into frowns and smiles and may have been responding to experimental demand characteristics.

In a different study, social psychologists Fritz Strack, Lenny Martin, and Sabina Stepper had subjects rate cartoons while holding a pen in their mouths. Some of these subjects clenched the end of a pen in their teeth, which models the facial muscle actions of smiling. Other subjects pursed the end of a pen in their lips, which models the facial muscle actions of frowning. According to these psychologists, these tasks model smiling and frowning more subtly than Laird's manipulations did. Consistent with facial feedback theory predictions, Strack and his colleagues found that the induced smilers rated the cartoons funnier than did the induced frowners.

Although facial feedback theories are concerned primarily with the effects of facial expressions on emotional experience, many of them acknowledge that facial expressions are not the only bodily cues that can produce or manage emotional experiences. For example, psychologists have found that people's physical posture (slumping versus sitting erect) affected their performance on a task. Similarly, a number of studies have shown that biofeedback techniques can be used to reduce anxiety and stress. When using biofeedback, a person concentrates his or her attention on some internal event, such as breathing rate, pulse rate, or heartbeat, and consciously tries to manage the event. With practice, biofeedback techniques have produced some surprising results.

Perhaps one of the most exciting potential applications for facial feedback theories is in clinical therapy settings. Carroll Izard has suggested that manipulation of facial expression can be used in a manner similar to biofeedback to help people cope with and overcome adverse emotional responses to situations and events. Although this application has not yet been put to the test, it could well become an important technique for use with such psychological problems as phobias, anxiety disorders, panic disorders, and depression.

Context

Facial feedback theories of emotion are, as they have been since they were first suggested, surrounded by controversy. Facial feedback theories have received considerable attention from psychologists and psychophysiologists. They have attracted staunch supporters as well as vehement critics. Part of the controversy may be attributable to the theories' counter-intuitive nature; they seem to fly in the face of common sense. On the other hand, proverbial wisdom suggests that at least some aspects of facial feedback theories make intuitive sense. Another part of the controversy has resulted from the difficulty of demonstrating the phenomenon in the laboratory. Although numerous studies have supported the facial feedback hypothesis, many have also failed to support it. In fact, two summaries of research related to facial feedback theories reached opposite conclusions concerning how well the available research has actually supported the theories.

As facial feedback research approaches its fourth decade, a number of questions about the role of facial expressions (and other bodily movements) in the production and regulation of emotional experience remain unanswered. For example, what is the exact mechanism through which facial (and bodily) expressions produce and regulate emotion? Is it sensory feedback from the facial muscles and skin, unmediated by thinking, that affects emotional experience, as William James, Charles Darwin, Silvan Tomkins, and Carroll Izard have suggested? Is it sensory feedback mediated by self-perception processes, as James Laird has proposed? Is it caused by some other, as yet unspecified, mechanism? These questions will be important focuses of future research on the facial feedback theories.

In addition, a number of newer approaches to and formulations of facial feedback theories have been offered. One of the most intriguing is psychologist Robert Zajonc and colleagues' vascular theory of facial efference. According to this formulation, facial expressions produce their effects on emotion not through sensory feedback from the muscles and skin but through changes in the volume of blood that reaches the brain. Expanding on a model originally proposed by Israel Waynbaum at the beginning of the twentieth century, Zajonc proposes that the facial muscles regulate the amount of blood that reaches and helps cool the brain. He and his colleagues have shown, for example, that changes in brain temperature are related to changes in emotional experience and that changes in facial expressions affect brain temperature. This seemingly improbable theory has received some experimental support and promises to maintain interest in facial feedback theories. Along more practical lines, Carroll Izard's suggestions for using facial feedback as a therapeutic tool may provide an alternative technique for managing specific psychological problems. Because of the interest in human self-regulatory mechanisms within social psychology, facial feedback theories and their successors will undoubtedly receive additional theoretical and empirical attention. The future holds considerable promise for advances in understanding the true relationship between facial expressions and the emotions they represent.

Bibliography

Buck, Ross. *The Communication of Emotion.* New York: Guilford Press, 1984. Presents the views of a critic of facial feedback theories and argues that facial expression is simply the automatic and unavoidable output from emotional experience. Intended for advanced college students, graduate students, and professionals.

Darwin, Charles. *The Expression of the Emotions in Man and Animals.* Chicago: University of Chicago Press, 1965. This is a classic text (first published in 1872) that presents Darwin's evolutionary approach to emotional expression, including ideas that led to later formulations of facial feedback theories.

Ekman, Paul, ed. *Darwin and Facial Expression: A Century of Research in Review.* New York: Academic Press, 1972. This book, edited by a leading researcher on facial expression, surveys the research that has been generated as a result of Darwin's 1872 treatise. Includes a review of Ekman's work on the universality of emotional expression. Most suitable for college students and graduate students.

Ekman, Paul, Wallace Friesen, and Phoebe Ellsworth. *Emotion in the Human Face.* New York: Pergamon Press, 1972. This book reviews and discusses a variety of issues related to emotion and human facial expression. Includes a review of Ekman's work on the universality of emotional expression.

Fiske, Susan T., and Shelley E. Taylor. *Social Cognition.* 2d ed. New York: McGraw-Hill, 1991. A comprehensive textbook on social cognition that contains a brief but excellent summary of research and theory related to the facial feedback hypothesis. Reviews a number of the formulations of theories related to emotion and facial expression, including Robert Zajonc and his colleagues' vascular theory of facial efference.

Izard, Carroll E. *The Face of Emotion.* New York: Appleton-Century-Crofts, 1971.

_____. "Facial Expressions and the Regulation of Emotions." *Journal of Personality and Social Psychology* 58, no. 3 (1990): 487-498.

_____. *Human Emotions.* New York: Plenum Press, 1977.

_____. *Patterns of Emotion: A New Analysis of Anxiety and Depression.* New York: Academic Press, 1972. The three books and journal article above present Izard's approach to the facial feedback hypothesis and his application of facial feedback principles to clinical therapy. Offering detailed and broad overviews and reviews of topics related to emotion and to facial feedback theories, these works describe major theories and research in detail and provide a useful context with which to understand the importance of emotion and facial expression in everyday life.

Tomkins, Silvan Solomon. *The Positive Affects.* Vol. 1 in *Affect, Imagery, Consciousness.* New York: Springer, 1962. This book presents possibly the most radical variant of the facial feedback theories. Tomkins argues that facial expression itself *is* emotional experience. Suitable for advanced college students and graduate students.

John H. Fleming

Cross-References

The Autonomic Nervous System, 362; Emotion: Cognitive and Physiological Interaction, 881; Emotion: Cultural Variations, 887; Emotion: Definition and Assessment, 893; Emotion: Neurophysiology and Neuroanatomy, 914; Emotion and Attribution Theory, 921; Emotion and Stress, 941; Emotional Expression, 954; Nonverbal Communication, 1681; Self-Perception Theory, 2193.

FEMINIST PSYCHOTHERAPY

Type of psychology: Psychotherapy
Fields of study: Evaluating psychotherapy; models of abnormality; psychodynamic
  therapies

Feminist psychotherapy integrates feminist philosophy with principles of counseling and therapy. It promotes consciousness-raising and awareness, fosters egalitarian therapist-client relationships, focuses on the ways in which personal problems are influenced by social forces and sexism, encourages individuals to acknowledge and act on their strengths, and emphasizes the importance of both personal change and social change.

> *Principal terms*
>
> CONSCIOUSNESS-RAISING: increasing awareness of sexism and its impact
>   on personal lives and choices
> EQUALITY: a mutually defined, egalitarian balance of personal power in
>   therapeutic and interpersonal relationships
> FEMINIST ANALYSIS: the examination of the way in which inequality,
>   injustice, or oppression devalues women and/or limits their potential,
>   both individually and collectively
> GENDER BIAS: behaviors, theories, practices, or attitudes that reinforce
>   inequality between men and women; it may involve ascribing
>   different standards of behavior or mental health to men and women
> GENDER-ROLE ANALYSIS: a technique for examining one's restrictive
>   gender-role behaviors and their origins; analysis is linked to
>   implementation of behavioral changes
> INFORMED CHOICE: the provision of information about therapy and what
>   it can accomplish so that clients can make informed decisions; the
>   development of clear agreements or contracts with clients
> THE PERSONAL IS POLITICAL: the idea that personal problems are related
>   to social problems and issues of all women; personal issues have
>   implications for political and social change

Overview

The dictionary definition of a feminist is a person who advocates political, social, and economic equality between women and men. Feminist therapy is much more difficult to define, because interpretations of feminist therapy depend upon the particular feminist philosophy and therapeutic orientation that a therapist adopts. At the most basic level, feminist psychotherapy involves the integration of feminist principles with psychotherapeutic practices, but the nature of this combination takes many forms. A wide range of psychotherapies may be employed or combined in feminist psychotherapy, excluding those that are gender biased.

An assumption underlying feminist psychotherapy is that personal behavior and social expectations are interwoven in an intricate, complex manner. Problems are shaped by social and cultural environments that limit choices or encourage individuals to see themselves in restricted ways. Psychological conflicts are not viewed as personal deficits; they often arise from efforts to cope with or survive unjust or oppressive environmental conditions. When problems are viewed solely as internal conflicts or symptoms that need to be removed, women learn to feel responsible for and guilty for pain that is promoted or reinforced by inequality or gender-role expectations. The personal is considered political in the sense that personal change should be connected to social change that allows all people to meet their goals effectively.

Feminist psychotherapists are often critical of the standard diagnostic criteria adopted by psychiatry and psychology and outlined in the American Psychiatric Association's *Diagnostic and Statistical Manual of Mental Disorders* (rev. 3d ed., 1987, DSM-III-R). They believe that these categories have strong judgmental qualities and are based on a medical model which implies that psychological problems are lodged primarily within the person; such categorization may lead to blaming victims rather than solving the social problems that contribute to these personal problems.

The therapist-client relationship is based on egalitarian values. Therapists inform clients about their orientation and goals, and attempt to demystify the counseling experience. Clients are encouraged to take on the attitude of a consumer and to ask questions of the therapist to ensure that they receive what they need. Although feminist therapists work toward equalizing the balance of power, they also recognize that because of their professional skills and the special status given to helping professionals, the relationship will not be fully equal. Clients are seen as their own best experts, as competent and powerful, and as capable of making productive choices.

The goals of feminist psychotherapy emphasize the importance of healthy self-chosen change, rather than adjustment to status-quo definitions of mental health. Consciousness-raising about sexism in society is a central feature of feminist therapy, and clients are encouraged to understand the role of socialization and culture in shaping their lives. Because women are frequently socialized to define themselves according to expectations of significant others, feminist therapy emphasizes the importance of self-nurturing behaviors and defining one's own identity. In addition, since women are frequently taught to use covert, indirect forms of influence and communication in relationships, special emphasis is placed on learning direct, constructive, assertive forms of expression. Finally, it is hoped that as clients meet personal goals, they will become interested in working toward social change that will benefit all women and thus, indirectly, all people.

Although many forms of therapy can be integrated with feminist therapy, certain techniques are associated with feminist psychotherapy. Through gender-role analysis, clients are encouraged to examine their own gender-role behaviors and attitudes and choose alternatives to behaviors that are not productive for them. Gender-role analysis helps persons to identify how they learned from their culture the behaviors and emotions that are expected of them as "normal" women or men and to consider other ways of fulfilling their full potential as competent persons. In addition, feminist analysis, or social analysis, is used to convey information about the sociocultural barriers that limit the development of women. This analysis may focus on the ways in which job discrimination, sexual harassment, stereotypes, or poverty may contribute to personal problems, and it helps clients understand the ways in which the environment limits their potential. Insight about these power structures decreases their damaging effects, because clients recognize that they are not to blame for many problems they experience. In feminist analysis, clients are encouraged to separate internal causes of problems from external ones. When clients are able to distinguish between these factors, they feel greater freedom and commitment to make active, constructive changes within their own lives and within their environments.

The expression of anger and therapist self-disclosure are two additional techniques. The recognition of sexism and oppression in society may lead to intense anger, and the healthy expression of emotion within a safe, mutual relationship is considered essential. Because women are frequently socialized to express only "soft" emotions, they may not have a vocabulary with which to express anger or may fear its destructive qualities. Techniques that help individuals express strong emotion in healthy, constructive ways contribute to their confidence. Finally, appropriate self-disclosure on the part of the therapist is an important tool because it decreases a client's feelings of aloneness and models the healthy expression about issues and feelings. The human qualities of the therapist help motivate and empower the client.

Applications

Feminist psychotherapy provides an alternative to traditional psychotherapy. The differences between a feminist approach and a traditional approach to problems can be illustrated by the discussion of depression in women. From a traditional perspective, depression is often viewed as resulting from biological vulnerabilities, faulty thinking patterns, skills deficits, or a depressive personality style. Psychotherapy focuses on removing the symptom and alleviating suffering so that the client can readjust to her living environment. A feminist perspective does not ignore personal factors and vulnerabilities, but it goes beyond them to examine the ways in which depression is associated with women's limited access to power and with other environmental factors.

The American Psychological Association National Task Force on Women and Depression reported in 1990 that women are twice as likely as men to experience depression and that the interpersonal violence, poverty, and discrimination that women face contribute to these higher rates. Multiple roles, inequities in division of labor at home, the presence of young children in the home, and the expectations that women should define themselves in terms of others contribute to suppressed anger and frustration and may lead to depression. In feminist therapy, the therapist and client collaborate in identifying and understanding these factors, practice healthy ways of expressing suppressed emotion, focus on ways the client can define herself on her own terms, and establish ways of altering the environment so that the client can reach her potential.

Therapy for survivors of violence, such as rape, battering, or incest, is an important application of feminist psychotherapy. Gender-biased attitudes that were based on Sigmund Freud's view of women have promoted psychological myths and encouraged blaming the victim by suggesting that women are inherently masochistic and gain pleasure through experiencing pain. Other cultural attitudes contribute to notions that women's own personal flaws lead to abuse, that sexual violence is caused by women's seductiveness, that women precipitate battering incidents through verbal provocation, and that women tend to remain in violent relationships. Many survivors of violence, having absorbed these negative cultural myths, struggle with low self-esteem and suffer in secrecy. Feminist therapists help clients talk about and deal with intense feelings of shame and guilt that are fostered by myths about sexual and interpersonal violence. They validate women's experiences and acknowledge the painful circumstances, such as poverty or limited resources, that contribute to their pain. Feminist psychotherapists help women place blame outside themselves and deal with anger that must be expressed toward perpetrators and a social system that condones violence against women. Providing support and a safe physical environment are also crucial components of feminist intervention. Finally, many survivors of violence experience further healing and empowerment by becoming involved in helping other women. They may become advocates on behalf of other women, engage in political efforts to establish new programs, or become involved in peer-counseling activities in a crisis center.

Group work is another component of feminist therapy. Groups enable individuals to decrease their isolation from other women, construct mutual support systems, and validate one another's strengths. When group members share experiences, the similarities of their concerns are often striking, and they become aware that broader social issues are often mistakenly identified as individual problems. Groups help counter the negative aspects of socialization that encourage women to adopt passive roles; they provide a safe environment in which members can practice new skills, develop confidence, and make new choices. The original feminist therapy groups were modeled after the consciousness-raising groups of the 1970's. Specialized feminist therapy groups deal with many issues, such as eating disorders, self-esteem concerns, or incest and abuse issues.

Feminist therapy not only is a distinct entity, but also seeks to transform mainstream psychological practice. For example, because of the efforts of feminist psychologists, the American Psychological Association adopted the "Principles Concerning the Counseling and Therapy of Women." This document recommends that counselors and therapists become knowledgeable and seek training about women's issues, utilize skills that will facilitate women's development, and work toward eliminating gender bias within institutions and individuals. Feminist therapists continue to work toward heightening the sensitivity of all therapists to women's concerns.

Context

Feminist psychotherapy emerged during the women's movement of the 1970's in response to traditional mental health practices that contributed to an unequal, oppressive environment for women. Phyllis Chesler, in *Women and Madness* (1972), charged that women were diagnosed for both underconforming and overconforming to gender-role stereotypes, and that the higher treatment and hospitalization rates of women were related to sexist mental health practices. Feminists within the mental health field noted that the goals, psychological theories, and practices of psychotherapists were based on masculine criteria of psychological health, encouraged hierarchical relationships between therapists and clients, and promoted adjustment to traditional, stereotyped roles for women. Feminist psychotherapy became a method for counteracting these negative influences.

The consciousness-raising groups associated with the feminist movement also influenced feminist psychotherapy. Women reported therapeutic benefits of consciousness-raising, including increased feelings of self-esteem and autonomy, awareness of commonalities between women, an expanded ability to express strong feelings such as anger, and an awareness of the ways in which sociopolitical forces influence the female experience. Feminist psychotherapists incorporated many elements of consciousness-raising groups into their work, and the group practice of feminist therapy has remained important.

Feminist psychotherapy began as a strong reaction against traditional therapy rather than as a particular form of therapy; however, feminist therapists have also transformed mainstream therapies by applying a feminist perspective. Feminist therapists are also developing personality theories that value women on their own terms, rather than viewing them as diverging from the male norm. During the early 1970's, the feminist movement and feminist therapy did not adequately consider the needs of women of color and the combined impact of racism and sexism. Subsequent efforts have focused on acknowledging the diversity of women's lives and increasing the sensitivity of feminist practices to these complexities. Feminist therapy has also been extended to counseling with men and emphasizes the importance of integrating relationship and achievement needs, increasing the capacity for intimacy, creating mutual, collaborative relationships, and learning noncoercive problem-solving methods.

Bibliography

Brodsky, Annette M., and Rachel T. Hare-Mustin. *Women and Psychotherapy.* New York: Guilford Press, 1980. Chapters summarize research issues on gender and gender-role stereotyping, describe disorders of high prevalence in women's lives, and propose a variety of therapeutic approaches for intervening in women's lives.

Chesler, Phyllis. *Women and Madness.* Garden City, N.Y.: Doubleday, 1972. One of the original, classic documentations of the way in which sexism has operated within mental health systems and contributed to unequal treatment of women.

Dutton-Douglas, Mary Ann, and Lenore E. A. Walker. *Feminist Psychotherapies.* Norwood, N.J.: Ablex, 1988. Includes chapters on the integration of feminist philosophy and mainstream therapy systems, feminist psychotherapy with special populations, feminist therapy with men, and future directions.

Franks, Violet, and Esther D. Rothblum, eds. *The Stereotyping of Women: Its Effects on Mental Health.* New York: Springer, 1983. Describes ways in which gender-role stereotypes contribute to disorders such as depression, agoraphobia, weight and communication problems, sexual dysfunction, and violence against women.

Greenspan, Miriam. *A New Approach to Women and Therapy.* New York: McGraw-Hill, 1983. A highly readable account of the ways in which mental health systems and mainstream therapies discriminate against women. Describes feminist therapy, compares it to humanistic therapy, and provides case studies.

Johnson, Karen, and Tom Ferguson. *Trusting Ourselves: The Sourcebook on Psychology for Women.* New York: Atlantic Monthly Press, 1990. Discusses common psychological concerns of women, such as self-esteem, depression, anxiety, sexuality, alcohol, body image, and violence. Highly readable, written for a lay audience. Includes a consumer guide to seeking psychological help.

McGrath, Ellen, ed. *Women and Depression: Risk Factors and Treatment Issues.* Washington, D.C.: American Psychological Association, 1990. Report of the APA Task Force on Women and Depression. Includes discussions of gender differences, women's status, the influence of victimization and poverty, and treatment considerations.

Rosewater, Lynne Bravo, and Lenore E. A. Walker, eds. *Handbook of Feminist Therapy: Women's Issues in Psychotherapy.* New York: Springer, 1985. Includes brief chapters dealing with feminist philosophy, techniques, special populations, and ethics. Includes the American Psychological Association's "Principles Concerning the Counseling and Therapy of Women."

Carolyn Zerbe Enns

Cross-References

Abnormality: Sociocultural Models, 82; Depression: Theoretical Explanations, 789; Psychology of Women: Karen Horney, 1950; Psychology of Women: Sigmund Freud, 1956; Psychotherapeutic Effectiveness, 1989; Psychotherapy: Historical Approaches to Treatment, 2002.

FIELD EXPERIMENTATION

Type of psychology: Psychological methodologies
Fields of study: Descriptive methodologies; experimental methodologies

Field experimentation comprises a variety of techniques to study people or other organisms within their natural environments; typically it involves observing, recording, tracking, and interviewing subjects to produce an in-depth study written as a narrative.

Principal terms

COVERT RESEARCH: a type of field research in which subjects are unaware of the true identity of the researcher

FIELD NOTES: the recorded behaviors and observations which make up the data of the field study

HAWTHORNE EFFECT: a phenomenon that occurs when a subject's behavior changes after finding out he or she is being studied

INDUCTIVE RESEARCH: the process of constructing general principles from a body of data

LABORATORY RESEARCH: research in which phenomena are studied in an artificial setting with rigorous procedures in place to control for outside influences

NATURALISTIC OBSERVATION: a technique in which subjects are studied in the environment where they live, with little or no intervention on the part of the researcher

NONPARTICIPANT OBSERVER: a field technique in which the researcher passively observes the behavior of the subjects, trying not to get involved in the setting

PARTICIPANT OBSERVER: a field technique in which the researcher actively participates with the subjects being studied

Overview

As an alternative to studying behavior in the sometimes restricted and sterile confines of the laboratory, scientists can turn to field experimentation as a method of finding out how people or other organisms interact with their natural environment. As the term "field experimentation" implies, genuine science is being conducted; however, the place and context of the research involves the places where the subjects normally live, work, and play. Instead of removing subjects from their normal surroundings and placing them into artificial situations, a field researcher attempts to study behaviors as they occur spontaneously in the real world.

Studying people in their natural environments can yield a number of advantages over more traditional laboratory research methods. For example, it has been found that when subjects are aware that they are being studied, their actions sometimes differ from their actions when they are unaware that they are being observed. This phenomenon is known as the Hawthorne effect. A field study can avoid the Hawthorne effect by enabling the researcher to go "undercover" and study the subjects without them being aware that a study is going on. A field study helps ensure that genuine, rather than contrived, behaviors will emerge.

Another advantage of the field experimentation method is that it lends itself to the study of complex behaviors, such as relationships among family members, that would be too difficult to simulate in a laboratory setting. Another important strength is that the researcher can maintain the interaction between the subject and the setting in which the subject lives or works. Under this set of circumstances, the field study is the method most preferred. In addition, there are some instances where time does not allow the researcher to bring the phenomena under study into the laboratory. Such instances include those associated with natural disasters or national calamities. For example, a researcher might want to study the psychological reactions of people who have lost their homes in a hurricane. Since it would be imperative to begin collecting data immediately, taking the time to develop a comprehensive survey or identify and eventually test the important variables in a more controlled setting would jeopardize the data collection of this dynamic, rapidly changing situation.

Conducting a field experiment does not come without its share of disadvantages. First, there are many topics worthy of study that are too difficult to stage outside the well-controlled confines of a laboratory. Studying memory loss or the processes involved in solving a complex algebra problem are examples of these kinds of variables. Second, some researchers argue that because so many uncontrolled outside influences are present in a field study, it is difficult, if not impossible, to understand causal relationships among the behaviors which are being studied. Third, field research is particularly susceptible to the biases of the researcher while the data is being collected. Since data collection is typically less standardized and formal than other methodologies, it is possible that the researcher may be unaware that observations which support the researcher's hypothesis may be recorded and given more attention than behaviors which go contrary to the researcher's beliefs. Some of the research published by anthropologist Margaret Mead during the 1920's, for example, has been called into question by other researchers who have reached different conclusions.

Field experimentation usually entails going into a naturalistic setting to collect data which can be used to generate research questions. The researcher will take such information, begin to organize it, and try to draw some general conclusions from it. This process, referred to as "inductive research," occurs when data are first collected and then used to formulate general principles. Thus, field research differs from many other kinds of research methodologies. Field research begins with a broad theory, then sets out to test specific aspects of the theory to see if the data support it.

As mentioned earlier, field experimentation represents a variety of strategies for studying behavior. One specific technique involves a researcher who goes into the field and chooses to identify herself or himself to the subjects; the researcher also becomes actively involved in the group's activities. The researcher has become a "participant observer." An example of this method would be a person who wanted to study a violent inner-city gang. The researcher might approach the gang's leadership, then identify himself or herself and give reasons for studying the group. The researcher would also participate in the gang's meetings and other activities. (Perhaps a better approach, in this situation, would be to do everything described except participating in the group's activities, especially if the gang's activities were illegal or harmful to others.) A researcher who revealed his or her true identity to the group, yet chose to play a passive, inactive role from a distance, would be considered a "nonparticipant observer."

An equally important field study technique involves concealing the identity of the researcher from the group that is being studied. In a classic study by John Howard Griffin described in the book *Black Like Me* (1962), Griffin colored his skin to take on the appearance of a black man. He then traveled throughout the South, documenting his experiences, especially those involving race discrimination. This kind of activity is called covert research.

Conducting research in the field does not prevent the researcher from manipulating or altering the environment. In fact, it is a rather common occurrence for the "field" to be contrived. For example, a study on altruism might be designed for field experimentation. A scenario would be designed to discover what kind of person would come to the assistance of someone in need. The "need" could be helping to fix a flat tire or helping a lost child find his or her mother. In either case, since both occur infrequently in the real world and would be difficult to study, the setting would need to be staged. The ability to stage events opens the possibility of studying a variety of phenomena in a convenient context.

Applications

There are basically five steps that need to be completed in field experimentation. First, an appropriate field must be selected. This is a crucial decision, because the quality of the research hinges on the vitality of the data collected. Second, specific methods and techniques (for example, nonparticipant observation) must be developed to ensure that the behaviors the experimenter wants to observe can occur. In addition, an attempt must be made to try to eliminate outside influences that might bias the research. Third, the data must be collected. Fourth, the data are organized, analyzed, and interpreted. The fifth and final step is to report the study within an appropriate format—which might be either a journal article or a book. In order to show how these steps are implemented and how field experimentation can contribute to scientific knowledge, two examples will be explored in detail.

In his article "The Pace of Life," published in *American Scientist* (1990), Robert Levine attempts to understand how different cultures perceive time. In his opinion, attitudes toward time could affect a society's pace of life and ultimately might lead to detrimental health problems for its members. Levine chose to collect data from the largest city in six different countries: Japan, Taiwan, Indonesia, Italy, England,

and the United States. To gauge the general pace of life, he chose to study three unique indicators: the accuracy of outdoor bank clocks, the average time it took pedestrians to walk a distance of 100 feet (about 30.5 meters), and the time needed for a postal clerk to complete a transaction that entailed selling stamps and returning some change. Notice that none of these measures relies on the subjective evaluations of the pace of life by the person collecting the data. Levine preferred these particular "objective" measures over a survey approach, which might have required subjects to respond to how they "feel" about the pace of life. He was more interested in direct measures of behavior as indicators of pace.

Standardized techniques were employed while collecting the data to ensure that the pace-of-life indicators would be measured fairly. For example, walking speed would not be measured if it were raining outside. Levine chose a covert approach, since he did not want subjects to be aware that they were in a study, thus eliminating any Hawthorne effect. In addition, both participant and nonparticipant observations were made. Measuring walking speed some distance away from a subject would be an example of a nonparticipant observer. On the other hand, the purchasing of stamps on the part of the experimenter was an example of the participant observer technique.

The data were collected primarily by Levine's students, who visited the countries. The data were then analyzed via basic statistical procedures. The study revealed that Japan had the fastest pace of life of the six countries, scoring the highest on all three measures. The United States came in with the second-fastest pace, followed by England. Indonesia was last, having the slowest walkers and the most inaccurate clocks.

Levine extended this research by looking at associations between the pace of life and both psychological and physical health. He found that the tempo of a society is significantly related to the prevalence of heart disease. In fact, the time-related variables often turn out to be better predictors of heart disease than psychological measures which identify high-energy behaviors in individuals. He concluded that a person who chooses to live in a fast-paced city should take necessary precautions to keep from becoming a time-urgent person. Living in a busy and stressful city can lead to unhealthy behaviors such as smoking and poor eating habits.

In another field study, David Rosenhan studied mental health professionals' ability to distinguish the "sane" from the "insane." Rosenhan later published the research in the article "On Being Sane in Insane Places" in *Science* (1973). He sent eight psychologically stable individuals to twelve different mental institutions to find out if they would be admitted as patients. Each "pseudopatient" went to an institution under an assumed name and a false occupation; this was necessary because three of the pseudopatients were psychologists and one was a psychiatrist, and they might be treated differently from other patients. The pseudopatients told the admitting staff that they had been hearing voices that appeared to say the words "hollow," "empty," and "thud." All pseudopatients were admitted and diagnosed as "schizophrenic" or "manic-depressive." From the moment the pseudopatients gained entrance into the institutions, they began to act in a completely normal manner.

Rosenhan's stud; used both covert and participant observation techniques to collect the data. Field notes concerning the behavior of staff members were taken on a daily basis. Although Rosenhan was shocked that all of his assistants (as well as himself) were admitted, he was even more dismayed that the pseudopatients' "insanity" was never questioned by the staff. When the pseudopatients were observed writing their field notes, it was interpreted by many of the staff members as paranoid and secretive behavior.

The pseudopatients were released from the hospital anywhere from seven to fifty-two days later. Field studies, as this example indicates, can be filled with risks. None of the pseudopatients truly expected to be admitted, let alone having to stay an average of nineteen days in the hospital before the mental health professionals declared them well enough to be released. Rosenhan's study was significant because it underscores the problem of distinguishing the normal from the abnormal with conventional diagnostic procedures. Rosenhan applied the results of this study to the broader issue of psychological labels. He pointed out that categorizing an individual with a particular mental illness can be misleading, and in many instances harmful. Rosenhan's pseudopatients were discharged with the label "schizophrenia in remission"—that is, according to the mental health workers, they had been relieved of their insanity, although perhaps only temporarily.

Context

Royce Singleton, Jr., Bruce Straits, Margaret Straits, and Ronald McAllister, in their book *Approaches to Social Research* (1988), make the point that field experimentation procedures were used long before the techniques were recognized by the scientific community. The authors also state there is a general consensus that anthropologists—followed shortly thereafter by sociologists—first developed and then legitimized this approach to research. Franz Boas and Robert Park were among the early pioneers of field research during the late nineteenth century and the beginning of the twentieth century. Boas was noted for his research in cultural anthropology. He emphasized the importance of circumventing one's Western cultural biases by living in other cultures for an extended time and acquiring their perspective. On the other hand, Park, who taught for a number of years at the University of Chicago, was influential in encouraging students to use the city as an alternative laboratory—studying people where they lived.

Field experimentation grew out of a need to seek answers to questions that could not be brought into a laboratory setting. Studying foreign cultures, complex social relationships, and secretive sects are examples of the kinds of phenomena that lend themselves to this method. Laboratory research might be seen as a hindrance to understanding dynamic human behavior. An alternative method needed to be found, and field research filled this vacuum.

Early in its development, field experimentation used data-collection procedures that almost entirely consisted of informal notes. A long narrative describing a sequence of behaviors would not have been uncommon. There has been a gradual move toward the use of more "objective" techniques such as standardized rating scales, behavioral checklists, and structured surveys. These methods were created in order to quantify better the observations being made. Once the behaviors could be quantified (that is, once specific behaviors could be assigned numbers), they could be subjected to the same statistical analyses used by laboratory experimenters. This improved approach to data collection helped field experimentation methods play a significant role in the social and behavioral sciences.

Bibliography

Baker, Therese L. *Doing Social Research.* New York: McGraw-Hill, 1988. Gives the reader a general introduction to field research, observational studies, data collection methods, survey research, sampling techniques, and other topics that will help the reader distinguish good field experiments from those that are poorly constructed.

Berg, Bruce Lawrence. *Qualitative Research Methods for the Social Sciences.* Boston: Allyn & Bacon, 1989. Discusses a field strategy used by anthropologists and sociologists to study groups of people. In addition, discusses the ethical issues that arise while conducting such research. The dangers of covert research are discussed; the book also provides the guidelines established by the National Research Act.

Griffin, John Howard. *Black Like Me.* New York: New American Library, 1962. This excellent book is a narrative of the author's experiences traveling around the United States and observing how people react to him after he has taken on the appearance of a black man. This monumental field study, which contributed to the understanding of social prejudice, provides the reader with an excellent example of the significance and need for conducting field research.

Levine, Robert V. "The Pace of Life." *American Scientist* 78 (September/October, 1990): 450-459. Levine describes his research on cross-cultural perspectives of time. Also describes research done within different regions of the United States.

McCall, George J., and J. L. Simmons. *Issues in Participant Observation: A Text and Reader.* Reading, Mass.: Addison-Wesley, 1969. This text provides a more in-depth discussion of how to get inside a group as a participant observer and conduct observational field research. Provides a number of examples from the literature to help understand how this research is conducted.

Rosenhan, David Leonard. "On Being Sane in Insane Places." *Science* 179 (January 19, 1973): 250-258. Rosenhan describes his research on psychiatric facilities after he and his associates assumed the identity of psychiatric patients. An interesting and provocative example of field research, this paper also raises the question of the dangers of conducting covert research and the dangers inherent in psychological labels.

Singleton, Royce, Jr., Bruce C. Straits, M. M. Straits, and Ronald J. McAllister. *Approaches to Social Research.* New York: Oxford University Press, 1988. This well-written text discusses various aspects of field experimentation such as selecting a research setting, gathering information, how to get into the field, and when a field study should be adopted. The chapter on "Experimentation" can be used to contrast "true" experiments with field studies.

Bryan C. Auday

Cross-References

Case-Study Methodologies, 481; Data Description: Descriptive Statistics, 751; Sources of Experimental Bias, 1006; Experimentation: Ethics and Subject Rights, 1013; Hypothesis Development and Testing, 1248; Observational Methods in Psychology, 1700; Survey Research: Questionnaires and Interviews, 2507.

FIELD THEORY: KURT LEWIN

Type of psychology: Personality
Fields of study: Motivation theory; personality theory; social perception and
 cognition

Kurt Lewin's field theory maintains that behavior is a function of the life space, or psychological reality, of the individual. Individuals are motivated to reduce tensions that arise in this life space. Lewin's theory can be used to understand a wide range of everyday behavior and to suggest strategies for addressing social problems such as the reduction of prejudice and the resolution of social conflicts.

Principal terms
> LIFE SPACE: the psychological reality of the individual; the totality of all
> psychological facts and social forces that influence an individual at a
> given time
> LOCOMOTION: behavior and change in the life space
> QUASI-STATIONARY EQUILIBRIUM: a position in which all opposing forces
> are equal in strength
> REGION OF LIFE SPACE: any major part of the life space that can be
> distinguished from other parts and is separated by more or less
> permeable boundaries
> TENSION: a psychological state produced by opposing forces in the life
> space

Overview

Kurt Lewin was a theorist of everyday life. His field theory attempts to explain life's everyday behavior, such as how a waiter remembers an order, what determines the morale and productivity of a work group, what causes intergroup prejudice, how a child encounters a new environment, or why people eat the foods that they do.

For Lewin, what determines everyday behavior is the "life space" of the individual. The life space represents the psychological reality of the individual; it is the totality of all psychological facts and social forces that influence an individual at a given time and place. For example, the life space of a child entering a novel domain is, for the most part, undifferentiated, and thus results in exploration on the part of the child. On the other hand, the life space of an employee at work may be well-differentiated and populated with demands from the employer to produce more goods, from coworkers to follow a production norm, and from home for more income. There might, additionally, be physical needs to slow down.

The life space is usually divided into two parts: person and environment. These parts can be differentiated further into regions. A region is any major part of the life space that can be distinguished from other parts and is separated by more or less permeable boundaries. For example, regions differentiated within the person might consist of needs, goals, hopes, and aspirations of the individual, whereas the differentiation of the environment might consist of profession, family, friendships, social norms, and taboos.

Locomotion, or behavior and change in the life space, is determined by the differentiation of regions in the life space and the forces for change emanating from each region. Often, in any given life space, there are opposing or conflicting forces. For example, the boss may want to increase productivity as much as possible, whereas coworkers may seek to limit production to levels obtainable by all workers. According to Lewin, these tensions, or opposing social forces, provide the motivation for behavior and change in the life space. Tension can be resolved by any number of activities, including reconfiguring the life space either physically (for example, getting a new job) or mentally (for example, devaluing either the boss's or coworkers' opinions); performing a substitute task that symbolically reduces tension (for example, performing different tasks of value to the boss); or finding the "quasi-stationary equilibrium," or position where all opposing forces are equal in strength (for example, performing at a level between boss's and coworkers' recommendations).

It is useful to compare Lewin's field theory with the two other major theories of the time: behaviorism and psychoanalysis. Lewin's field theory can be summarized by the equation $B = f(P,E)$, or, "Behavior is a function of person and environment." In other words, behavior is function of the life space of a total environment as perceived by the individual. In psychoanalytic thought, behavior is a function of the history of the individual. For example, past childhood experience is supposed to have a direct impact on current psychological processes. In contrast, Lewin's theory is ahistorical. Although the individual's past may influence that person's approach and construal of the psychological field, its influence is only indirect, as behavior is a function of the current and immediate life space.

Lewin's field theory differs from behaviorism on at least two key dimensions. First, Lewin emphasized the subjectivity of the psychological field. To predict and understand behavior successfully, a therapist needs to describe the situation from the viewpoint of the individual whose behavior is under consideration, not from the viewpoint of an observer. Second, Lewin's theory emphasizes that behavior must be understood as a function of the life space or situation as a whole. In other words, behavior is motivated by the multitude of often-interdependent forces affecting an individual, as opposed to one or two salient rewards or reinforcers that may be present.

Applications

Kurt Lewin's field theory has had many applications, particularly in the area of social change. Lewin's approach to solving social problems was to specify, first, in as much detail as possible, the life space of the individual involved. Next, he would identify the social forces affecting the individual. Finally, Lewin would experiment with changing these social forces or adding new ones to enact social change. Two applications of field theory performed by Lewin and his associates serve as good examples. One deals with changing food preferences, and the other with the reduction of intergroup conflicts and prejudice.

During World War II, there was a shortage of high-protein meats in the United States. As part of the war effort, Lewin was assigned the task of convincing Americans to eat sweetbreads—certain organ meats, which many Americans find unappetizing—to maintain protein levels. Lewin began by first describing the consumption channel, or how food reaches a family's table. At the time, housewives obtained food from either a garden or a grocery store and then moved it to the table by purchasing it, transporting it home, storing it in an icebox or pantry, and then preparing it. At each step, Lewin identified forces that prevented the gatekeeper—in this case, the housewife—from serving sweetbreads. Such forces might have included the belief that family members will not eat sweetbreads, inexperience with the selection and preparation of sweetbreads, inherently distasteful aspects of the food, and so on.

In attempting to remove and redirect these forces, Lewin experimented with two approaches, one successful and the other not. In the unsuccessful case, Lewin presented housewives with a lecture detailing the problems of nutrition during the war and stating ways of overcoming obstacles in serving sweetbreads; he discussed ways to prepare sweetbreads, provided recipes, and indicated that other women had successfully served sweetbreads for their families with little complaint. Only 3 percent of the housewives hearing this lecture served sweetbreads. From Lewin's perspective, such a lecture was ineffective because it did not involve the audience and arouse the level of tension needed to produce change. Lewin's second method was a group discussion. The housewives were asked to discuss how they could persuade "housewives like themselves" to serve sweetbreads. This led to a discussion of the obstacles that the housewife might encounter, along with ways of overcoming these obstacles (just as in the lecture). Such a discussion was effective because it created tension for the housewife: "I just told everyone why they should and how they could eat sweetbreads, and I am not currently serving them myself." After this group discussion, 32 percent (an almost elevenfold increase) of the housewives involved served sweetbreads.

Lewin approached the problem of intergroup conflict and racial prejudice by describing the life space of the members of the conflicting parties. For example, Lewin saw the life space of many minority group members (such as religious and racial minorities) as full of obstacles and barriers which restrict movement in the life space. The life space of the majority member often consigned the minority member to a small and rigidly bounded region (for example, a ghetto). By isolating minority group members, majority group members can develop unrealistic perceptions or stereotypes of the out-group. Such life spaces are very likely to result in intergroup conflict.

The field theory analysis of racial prejudice suggests that one way to reduce intergroup conflict is to remove obstacles and increase the permeability of the intergroup barriers. In the later part of his career, Lewin established the Commission on Community Interrelations as a vehicle for discovering ways of removing intergroup barriers. Lewin and his colleagues discovered some of the following successful techniques for promoting intergroup harmony: enacting laws that immediately removed barriers such as racial quotas limiting the number of Jews who could attend certain universities; immediate hiring of blacks as sales personnel, thereby increasing the permeability of intergroup boundaries by making contact between group members more likely; responding directly to racial slurs with a calm appeal based on American traditions and democracy to provide a countervailing force to the slur; promoting meetings of warring groups in a friendly atmosphere as a means of breaking down group boundaries; and immediate integration of housing as a successful way of promoting racial harmony.

Context

Field theory was born on the battlefields of World War I. Kurt Lewin served as a soldier in the German army. His first published article was entitled "The War Landscape," and it described the battlefield in terms of life space. The soldier's needs determined how the landscape was to be perceived. When the soldier was miles from the front, the peaceful landscape seemed to stretch endlessly on all sides without direction. As the war front approached, the landscape took on direction, and peaceful things such as rocks and trees became elements of battle, such as weapons and places to hide.

After the war, Lewin took an academic appointment at the Psychological Institute of Berlin, where he served on the faculty with Gestalt psychologists Wolfgang Köhler and Max Wertheimer. While at the institute, Lewin further developed his field theory and conducted the first program of experimental social psychological research exploring topics such as memory for interrupted tasks, level of aspiration, and anger. His work derived as much from field theory as it did from his curiosity about the social world. For example, research on memory for interrupted tasks began when he and his students wondered why a waiter could remember their rather lengthy order but would forget it immediately after the food was served. In field theory terms, noncompleted tasks (such as the waiter's recall before delivering the order and other interrupted tasks) were recalled better because they maintain a tension for completion compared to completed tasks, for which this tension is resolved.

As the Nazi Party rose to power in Germany, Lewin correctly perceived that his own Jewish life space and that of his family were becoming progressively more threatened and intolerable. As did many Jewish intellectuals of the time, Lewin emigrated to the United States; he obtained a number of visiting appointments until he established the Center for Group Dynamics at the Massachusetts Institute of Technology. Lewin's American research was much more applied, and it concentrated particularly on social problems such as prejudice and intergroup conflict—perhaps as a result of his own experience of prejudice as a Jew in Germany.

Before his early death in 1947, Lewin helped train the first generation of American students interested in experimental social psychology, including such notables as Leon Festinger, Harold Kelley, Stanley Schachter, and Morton Deutsch. It has been estimated that more than half of all living social psychologists can directly trace their intellectual roots to Kurt Lewin. Today, first-, second-, third-, and even fourth-generation Lewinian social psychologists continue to carry on his research legacy by investigating topics of long-standing interest to Lewin such as prejudice, achievement, organizational behavior, social cognition, and the reduction of cognitive tensions or dissonance, and by attempting to explain how individuals construe their environments and how those environments affect behavior.

Bibliography

De Rivera, Joseph, comp. *Field Theory as Human-Science: Contributions of Lewin's Berlin Group.* New York: Gardner Press, 1976. An English translation of research conducted by Lewin and his students when Lewin was at the University of Berlin.

Lewin, Kurt. *A Dynamic Theory of Personality.* New York: McGraw-Hill, 1935. Lewin's first major English work, consisting of a translation of many of his first papers published in Germany.

_____. "Group Decision and Social Change." In *Readings in Social Psychology*, edited by Theodore M. Newcomb and Eugene L. Hartley. New York: Henry Holt, 1947. Describes how Lewin changed food preferences during World War II, providing an excellent example of how to apply field theory to practical problems.

_____. *Resolving Social Conflicts.* New York: Harper, 1948. Collects Lewin's major papers discussing practical problems of modern society such as prejudice and group conflict. Provides excellent examples of how to apply field theory to social problems.

Marrow, Alfred Jay. *The Practical Theorist: The Life and Work of Kurt Lewin.* New York: Basic Books, 1969. This definitive biography of Lewin, written by one of his students, describes the life of Lewin and provides a glimpse of the personality behind field theory.

Patnoe, Shelley. *A Narrative History of Experimental Social Psychology: The Lewin Tradition.* New York: Springer-Verlag, 1988. This volume contains a series of interviews with modern social psychologists and discusses the impact of Lewin on their research and theories.

Weiner, Bernard. *Theories of Motivation.* Chicago: Markham, 1972. A textbook that provides a detailed summary of Lewin's field theory and compares it with other theories of motivation.

Anthony R. Pratkanis
Marlene E. Turner

Cross-References

Achievement Motivation, 96; Cognitive Dissonance Theory, 560; Cooperation, Competition, and Negotiation, 689; Group Decision Making, 1114; Groups: Nature and Function, 1125; Motivation: Cognitive Theories, 1606; Thought Structures, 2565.

FOREBRAIN STRUCTURES

Type of psychology: Biological bases of behavior
Fields of study: Nervous system; thought

The forebrain is the forward portion of the brain, and it consists of portions of the cerebrum, the olfactory bulbs, the thalamus, and the hypothalamus. This portion of the brain affects consciousness, appetite, and emotions.

Principal terms
> CEREBRUM: the largest and uppermost portion of the brain, affecting both sensory and motor functions
> DIENCEPHALON: a portion of the forebrain which includes the thalamus and hypothalamus
> GYRUS: a convolution of the brain in regions where the cortex is infolded
> HYPOTHALAMUS: a portion of the forebrain below the thalamus which influences body drives such as hunger, sex, and anger
> OLFACTORY BULB: a region of the forebrain associated with the sense of smell
> SENSORY NERVES: nerves that carry signals from the periphery of the body to the brain or spinal cord
> TELENCEPHALON: a portion of the forebrain which includes the cerebrum and olfactory bulbs
> THALAMUS: a portion of the diencephalon, located at the base of the forebrain, which receives sensory information from the body and relays these signals to the appropriate regions of the cerebrum

Overview

The brain of vertebrate animals (that is, those with backbones) consists of three divisions: the forebrain, midbrain, and hindbrain. In mammals such as humans and other primates, the forebrain has evolved into a prominent structure dominated by the cerebrum. When one visualizes the brain, it is the image of the cerebrum, with its two convoluted hemispheres, that one imagines.

The forebrain is the largest portion of the human brain. Actually consisting of the entire upper portion of the brain, the forebrain controls a person's thoughts and memory, the ability to think and reason, and the conscious movement of a person's muscles. The regions of the forebrain are generally subdivided into three functional areas: the thalamus and the hypothalamus, referred to as the diencephalon; the cerebral hemispheres, or cerebrum; and the olfactory bulbs, found as swellings near the lower front of each half of the cerebrum. The cerebrum and olfactory bulbs are considered the region called the telencephalon.

The "thinking center" of the forebrain resides in the large area of the cerebrum. The cerebrum is physically divided into two halves, or hemispheres. The outer, gray area of the cerebrum is the cortex, which consists of a layer of neurons, or nerve cells. Fibers from these cells reach into the inner, white matter of the cerebrum. These nerve fibers then carry nerve impulses both to and from the various regions of the brain for processing.

Though all vertebrates possess the cerebrum, development and function differ markedly among these animals. In less-evolved organisms, other, older portions of the brain perform many of the functions associated with the human cerebrum. For example, frogs which have had their cerebrum removed show little change in most behaviors. Cats which have undergone removal of their cerebrum continue to meow, eat, and move, though in a more sluggish manner. Massive cerebral damage in humans, as observed following accidents, results in blindness and paralysis.

The increase in cerebral function through the course of evolution is paralleled by the increase in cerebral size. Among fish, for example, the mid- and hindbrain regions dominate the brain. The forebrain, dominated by the olfactory bulbs, receives information from a single sense, smell. The midbrain is the major center of control. As animals evolved in complexity, the forebrain region increased in size, acquiring many of the functions previously associated with the other portions of the brain. The midbrain was relegated to a role as reflex center. Among mammals, the forebrain— more specifically, the cerebrum—has become the dominant area within the brain.

The result of the enormous expansion of the cerebral cortex is a region of immense complexity. The cortex is estimated to contain some 70 percent of the total number of neurons in the central nervous system (that is, the brain and spinal cord). Reflecting its relatively recent appearance on the evolutionary scale, this region of the forebrain is often referred to as the neocortex.

The cerebrum in humans is functionally divided into four lobes: frontal, occipital, parietal, and temporal. The frontal lobe regulates voluntary movement, including movement associated with speech. The occipital lobe, in the rear of the cerebrum, receives sensory input from the eyes. The parietal lobe lies just to the rear of the frontal lobe and is separated from that region by a central fissure, or cleft. It is within this region that sensory input from skin receptors is analyzed. Finally, the temporal lobes are found in the region of the temples, and they serve to process information related to sound and smell. Each of these regions is present in both hemispheres of the cerebrum.

The thalamus (actually thalami, since they are paired structures) is the region at the base of the forebrain. The structures contain a densely packed mass of nerve cells often referred to as the brain's relay station. Sensory input from outside the brain passes through the thalamus, where it is translated into sensations of pain, temperature, or touch. By integrating the enormous quantity of sensory information to which the body is exposed, sending the signals to appropriate regions of the cerebrum, the thalamus plays a role in the association of impulses with both pleasant and unpleasant feelings. The thalamus also participates in arousal mechanisms of the body, allowing a person to awaken from sleep. It is also through the thalamus that signals from the cerebrum are distributed to the cerebellum, a region of the brain which controls coordination. For example, children often play a game of not stepping on the cracks of the sidewalk. In this case, sensory information from the cerebrum is relayed through the thalamus to the cerebellum, from which balance is maintained.

Below the thalamus is the region called the hypothalamus. The hypothalamus is concerned with maintaining the internal environment of the body, or homeostasis. Among the conditions regulated by this region are body temperature, blood pressure, heart rate, and appetite. Certain aspects of behavior also come under the control of this region. Stimulation of the hypothalamus can result in violent behavior or rage, sexual arousal, and even fear.

Applications

The dominant area of the human brain is the cerebral cortex, the thin layer of gray matter which overlies each of the cerebral hemispheres. About two-thirds of this area is composed of fissures, or convolutions. It is within the cerebral cortex that numerous behavioral functions are controlled: thought and mental capacities, perception and behavioral reactions. The precentral area, for example, has received particular attention, since electrical stimulation of this region results in contraction of specific voluntary muscles. Stimulation of the frontal area, on the other hand, will affect respiratory reactions.

The frontal area of the forebrain, particularly the region associated with the thalamus, has been associated with certain behavioral psychoses, such as uncontrollable rage. Isolation or removal of this region, as in the surgical operation called a prefrontal lobotomy, has at times been used in the treatment of these types of psychoses.

Association of particular regions of the forebrain with defined behaviors is often the result of damage to these regions. When a particular region is damaged, behavioral anomalies may develop. For example, through reinforcement, monkeys can be taught to distinguish between patterns. If the task is modified such that the objects are removed from view for a period prior to the time at which the monkey may choose (a delay), the task becomes more difficult. Even with this modification, however, the monkey remains able to pick the preferred choice consistently. If a specific region on the frontal lobe is damaged, performance of the delay test is impaired. That this region of the forebrain is specific for the delay test can be demonstrated by damage to a different area of the lobe. In this case, the monkey may find it more difficult to recognize complex patterns but will show no impairment in the delay test.

More humane methods than these have been developed for studying the association of regions of the forebrain with behavior. Otfrid Foerster and Wilder Penfield, for example, studied behavioral responses in conscious patients who were undergoing brain surgery. By stimulating various regions of the forebrain with electrodes, they were able to map specific functions. As pointed out by Norman Geschwind, the application of their procedure had two benefits. First, they were able to map regions of the brain. In addition, by associating specific regions with defined functions, neurosurgeons were able to avoid areas of the brain where damage might result in significant behavioral changes.

By continuing Foerster and Penfield's work, researchers have determined that the cerebral cortex is divided into two general regions which regulate sensory and motor activities. The motor area lies forward of the central fissure (which, as described earlier, also serves to separate the frontal lobe from the parietal); the sensory area lies behind the fissure. Specific sensory and motor areas are located in the convolutions, called gyri. As pointed out by Robert Wallace, the motor gyri allow a person significant control of the tongue, face, and fingers. People exert little conscious control of the genitals.

Among the most interesting specialized regions of the forebrain are those associated with speech. In the 1860's, Paul Broca discovered that damage to a particular region near the frontal lobe resulted in aphasia, or inability to articulate speech. Speech becomes slow and labored, and often cannot be expressed as a sentence. This region has since been called Broca's area. Broca also discovered that aphasia is caused by damage on the left side of the brain only. Similar damage on the right side generally does not result in aphasia. Indeed, most cases of aphasia which result from brain damage involve the left hemisphere of the region. Ironically, though patients with damage to Broca's area cannot speak, often they remain capable of singing.

In 1874, another form of aphasia was described by Carl Wernicke. In the case of Wernicke's aphasia, speech is grammatically normal, but the words used in a sentence are often nonsensical or inappropriate. This form of aphasia was associated with another region of the forebrain, in the temporal lobe. This region is now called Wernicke's area. Wernicke suggested that speech first arises in Wernicke's area, creating a nerve impulse which then travels through Broca's area, from which it is then vocalized.

The thalamus, located at the base of the forebrain, serves to channel incoming messages to the appropriate regions of the cerebrum. Among these tasks are those associated with consciousness. A class of nerve cells which run through the thalamus and into other regions of the forebrain is particularly important in this regard. These nerves have been termed the reticular activating system (RAS). The system seems particularly important in events surrounding arousal, activating regions of the brain when stimulated. Defects in the RAS result in problems associated not only with arousal but also with attention and concentration.

Context

Since the brain plays a central role in the function of the body, pathologies or changes in electrical or chemical properties of the brain result in a wide variety of physiological or behavioral disorders. The structure and complexity of the brain lend themselves to this problem. During the mid-nineteenth century, it became clear that damage to specific regions of the brain, whether from injury, atrophy, or hemorrhage, resulted in specific behavioral changes. These studies, in turn, resulted in the association of these regions of the brain, including the forebrain, with certain behavioral characteristics.

For example, in 1861, the French neurologist Paul Broca had been treating a surgical patient who for ten years had been unable to articulate speech. Following the patient's death, Broca carried out an autopsy and discovered an anomaly in a region of the forebrain which he described as the motor center for speech. This region of the forebrain became known as Broca's area. Broca termed the condition aphemia, which was later changed to aphasia.

Perhaps the most prominent of the nineteenth century neurophysiologists was Sir Charles Sherrington. From his first study in 1884 until his retirement from Oxford in 1936, Sherrington published more than three hundred papers dealing with his mapping of the central nervous system. His work during the early twentieth century defined specific areas of the forebrain with respect to sensory and motor functions.

Broca is also credited with recognizing the role of the limbic system, which he originally referred to as the large limbic lobe. Later, this region was associated specifically with certain emotions or feelings such as anger, fear, or sexual arousal. Control of the functions within this region remains poorly understood. The region represents an area of research yet to be carried out.

The control of behavioral processes results from development of specific neural pathways within particular areas of the brain. Patterns of behavior develop from the early years of life, as children learn the appropriate responses to stimuli such as hunger, thirst, or fear. It is one thing to map the specific areas of the forebrain which recognize these stimuli. It is quite another to understand the neural network which results in memory, and ultimately an appropriate response, to these stimuli. The operation of these networks remains another area open to research for the future.

Finally, the role of biological or chemical agents as the cause of behavioral disorders remains to be elucidated more fully. The cause of a variety of presenile dementias, including Alzheimer's disease, remains to be established. Toxic psychoses, such as those that occurred among nineteenth century hatmakers, who were exposed daily to mercury, remain a problem. One need only witness the tragic cases of lead poisoning among children that still occur. Treatment of these disorders is often only palliative, as the damage is irreversible.

Bibliography

Changeux, Jean-Pierre. *Neuronal Man: The Biology of Mind.* New York: Pantheon, 1985. A general text directed to a nontechnical audience. Provides an easily understood outline of the nervous system in general and the brain in particular.

Cotman, Carl W., and James L. McGaugh. *Behavioral Neuroscience: An Introduction.* New York: Academic Press, 1980. A textbook for an undergraduate course; an excellent introduction to the subject. Chapters include general introductions to the nervous system, followed by more complete analyses of specific regions of the brain and of the regulation of behaviors by these regions.

Geschwind, Norman. "Specializations of the Human Brain." *Scientific American*

241 (September, 1979): 180-182+. An excellent discussion of the roles played by specific regions of the brain in behavior. Emphasis is placed on the role of the forebrain. This particular issue was completely devoted to the development and function of the brain.

Nauta, Walle, and Michael Feirtag. "The Organization of the Brain." *Scientific American* 241 (September, 1979): 88-90+. An excellent, though technical, discussion of the major regions of the brain. Emphasis is placed on the role played by the cerebral cortex. The role of neuronal networks is outlined in some depth.

Sagan, Carl. *The Dragons of Eden: Speculations on the Evolution of Human Intelligence.* New York: Random House, 1977. Written by a well-known astronomer, the book provides an easily understood description of the development of the brain through the course of evolution. The connection between development of forebrain structures and various behaviors is presented in the informal manner associated with this popular speaker.

Symposium on the Neural Basis of Behavior. *The Neural Basis of Behavior.* Edited by Alexander L. Beckman. New York: SP Medical & Scientific Books, 1982. Based on a 1979 symposium devoted to the neural basis of behavior. A specialized publication, but does provide a good background and history of various neural problems.

Wallace, Robert A., Gerald P. Sanders, and Robert J. Ferl. *Biology: The Science of Life.* 3d ed. New York: HarperCollins, 1991. A general biology text with excellent chapters outlining the structure and function of the brain. Though this is a college text, the material is written in a manner that can be easily understood by the nonexpert. Illustrations are plentiful and clear.

Richard Adler

Cross-References

Brain Specialization, 455; Brain-Stem Structures, 461; The Central and Peripheral Nervous Systems, 494; The Cerebral Cortex, 500; Hindbrain Structures, 1175; Split-Brain Studies, 2355.

FORGETTING AND FORGETFULNESS

Type of psychology: Memory
Field of study: Cognitive processes

Forgetting is one of the many puzzling aspects of memory, and various theories have tried to explain it in different ways; among the proposed theories are the concepts of memory decay, interference, and purposeful forgetting.

Principal terms

BIT: a very small amount of data or information, such as a number, letter, or name
CHUNK: an amount of information or data
DECAY: the loss of memory traces over time
ENCODING: the learning of new material or information
INFORMATION-PROCESSING MODEL: the idea that people learn new information by performing various operations on it; the analogy is to a computer's operation
RETRIEVAL: the remembering or recalling of previously learned information or material

Overview

Although everyone has forgotten something at some point in their lives, some people seem to have better memories than others. There are several theories concerning why people forget and why some people seem to be forgetful or "absent-minded." Nevertheless, it is not really known why some people forget and others have very good memories.

One theory on forgetting holds that "forgotten" material was never learned in the first place. Another possibility is that very little importance was attached to the material learned and forgotten. Sometimes people are overwhelmed by the sheer amount of information they must learn and are simply incapable of remembering the massive amount of material. Another theory about forgetting suggests that material is never really forgotten; rather, one cannot find the key to retrieve the information from the brain's filing system—its long-term memory. Nearly everyone has experienced the "tip-of-the-tongue" phenomenon (one sees someone at a party, for example, and cannot quite remember the person's name). Sometimes concentration aids memory retrieval; often association helps the process. Psychologists have also noted primacy and recency effects regarding memory; that is, one remembers what is learned first and what is learned last most efficiently. Material that is presented in the middle tends to be more easily forgotten. Aging seems to affect the retrieval process, but the reasons are not completely understood; brain deterioration and diminished care, concern, or motivation are all possible factors.

Sometimes interference can affect one's ability to remember. If one is taking classes at nine, ten, and eleven in the morning, for example, one may have difficulty remembering material because the information from each of the three classes interferes with that of the other classes; this will be especially true if the subject matter is similar. This same process can affect memories of everything from motion pictures seen to events in one's own life. The greater the number of similar films or events (such as dinners in the same type of restaurant) there have been, the more interference there may be. There are two types of interference, retroactive and proactive interference. In proactive interference, occurrences that come before an event or learning situation interfere with one's ability to learn or remember; in retroactive interference, the occurrence that interferes with remembering comes after the event or learning situation.

One's mental state, according to many psychologists, has much to do with one's ability to learn, retain, and recall information. If one is suffering from grief or loss, one's ability to remember will be severely impaired. Children who are abused often have difficulties learning and remembering, since they are preoccupied with the worries and concerns caused by their traumatic home situation. People suffering from depression also may have problems remembering. Counseling or therapy will sometimes alleviate a person's emotional concerns and therefore result in better recall. Emotional problems that may be helped in this way include depression, anxiety, and fear of failure.

There has been debate among psychologists as to whether information stored in long-term memory is stored there permanently. Some memory theorists believe that a decay or fading factor is at work when one forgets information. That is, memory traces naturally fade away and are lost simply because of the passage of time. If one is a freshman in college, one may remember many members of one's senior class in high school very well. In another ten years, however, one may be less able to remember one's classmates and may have forgotten some of those with whom one had only superficial friendships. In twenty years, more information will fade unless one actively tries to rehearse or review the people who were in the class. For example, if one takes out one's high school yearbook every June for twenty years and reminisces about the people in it, one will better be able to recall the names at a twenty-fifth high school reunion.

Some theorists believe that if one can link or associate people, places, or events with other things, one may be able to recall past people or events more effectively. This theory holds that people's minds normally tend to associate one thing with another. These "associationistic" theories are based on the idea that bonds are formed in the brain between places or bits of information. If the bonds are inadequately or poorly formed, then forgetting may occur; bonds must periodically be re-formed to guard against forgetting.

The psychoanalytic (or Freudian) perspective on forgetting emphasizes the idea that people "forget" events that are emotionally traumatic. This is motivated, or purposeful, forgetting; the Freudian term for it is "repression." An example would be a woman who, as a six-year-old girl, had been sexually molested by her father or another relative and who has since forgotten the incident. Interestingly, repression has been known to occur in both victims and perpetrators of violent crimes.

Applications

Two different types of tests are used to assess memory and learning; one type tests recognition, while the other tests recall. A multiple-choice test assesses the first type of memory, because in this type of test one needs to recognize the correct answer when one sees it. An essay examination tests recall—all the responsibility is on the learner to recall as much relevant information as he or she can.

Research on memory and forgetting can be applied in both academic and non-academic settings. There are a number of things one can do to aid learning and protect against forgetting. Overlearning is one tactic that ensures that one has learned material and will remember it later. In this technique, a student repeats the material by rehearsing it in his or her head to ensure later recall. If one needs to learn a formula, one may repeat it over and over—perhaps writing it a hundred times. This can be tedious, which undoubtedly spurred the search for other options to learn and remember more effectively. Constant review is another strategy. In spaced practice, students study materials to be learned for one hour each night before the test. These students seem to remember the material better than those who spent eight hours studying the material the night before the test. (That type of study—"cramming"— is called massed practice.) For some students, cramming does work, but the material is easily forgotten following its use immediately after the cramming session. Cramming also creates anxiety and fatigue, which may interfere with optimal performance. It is important to eat and sleep well the night before a test.

Some students with poor organizational skills need to expend extra effort to organize the material they have learned. They may employ index cards, for example, to help group and link relevant materials. Mnemonics are memory tricks or devices that help one recall information. The poem that begins "Thirty days have September, April, June, and November," for example, helps one remember the number of days in each month. The word "homes" is frequently used as an acronym for the names of the Great Lakes—Huron, Ontario, Michigan, Erie, and Superior.

Note taking is one way to minimize forgetting; reviewing notes can help one prepare for an examination. For this to be most effective, however, one must be able to discriminate between useful and unimportant information at the time of writing the material down. The same holds true for underlining or highlighting material in books or notes. Taping lectures for later review is particularly useful in cases where a lecturer speaks very rapidly, making effective note taking difficult. Tapes are also effective and important aids in learning a foreign language. One advantage is that material can be reviewed in the car or while using a portable cassette player.

Concentration is an important part of learning and remembering, and people do not often spend enough time concentrating intensely. It has been said that thirty minutes of concentrated, uninterrupted study is better than two hours of haphazard study. The minimizing of outside stimuli is also important; one should study in a quiet place with few distractions. Studying in the same place (and at the same time) every night is also thought to be important for optimal results. Learning should also be active in order to minimize forgetting. Making decisions regarding material to be learned is a useful tool for facilitating learning; one may ask oneself questions about topics or subjects in order to learn or review. Students should be prompted to think about their own learning styles and to allot the necessary time to learn a given amount of material. Many people have their own preferred learning style. Some people learn better by seeing data and information; others assimilate information better by hearing it. Ideally, one should find and maximize one's preferred mode. There are tests designed to determine one's preferred mode of learning.

If one is trying to assimilate too much information in too short a time, one may experience "information overload." Students taking summer classes in which a semester's worth of information is compressed into a few weeks experience this, as may those taking eighteen or more hours of classes in a semester. This may also affect someone beginning a new job that involves mastering a large amount of information or technical material. Material that is meaningful to the learner has been found to be easier to remember and recall.

Context

The mysteries of remembering and forgetting have certainly fascinated humankind for hundreds, even thousands, of years. In the late nineteenth century, memory was one of the areas of interest to early psychologists such as Hermann Ebbinghaus and William James. Ebbinghaus conducted an experiment in 1885 in which he tested his own memory; he graphed a "forgetting curve," illustrating how much information on a particular list he forgot over time. William James wrote about the "tip-of-the-tongue" phenomenon in 1890, evocatively describing the "gap" that exists in the place of a name one is trying to recall as "intensely active" and containing the "wraith of the name" beckoning within it.

Research on memory has explored many avenues; among them are memory losses that are attributable to physical or physiological causes. Head injuries, for example, can cause difficulties remembering certain information after an accident. In cases of brain tumor, when certain parts of the brain are removed, aspects of memory may be irreparably lost. Alcoholics who drink heavily for many years frequently encounter difficulties remembering; this condition is sometimes termed Korsakoff syndrome. Those who use drugs may also experience memory impairment; actual brain damage may occur in such cases. Older people with Alzheimer's disease or other types of dementia have trouble remembering. Strokes or internal injuries can also cause memory loss, as can epilepsy; during an epileptic seizure, oxygen is not getting to the brain, a condition that may result in brain damage and memory loss.

It is not known exactly how people learn or why they remember or forget. Some psychologists posit that the brain's chemical makeup and activity (particularly involving those substances known as neurotransmitters) are central to learning and remembering; others contend that the brain's electrical activity is crucial in determining one's memory. If there is either a chemical or an electrical abnormality in the brain, people may have difficulties learning or recalling information and events that have been learned.

With newer methodologies for brain scanning, including such noninvasive procedures as nuclear magnetic resonance (NMR) imaging, positron emission tomography (PET) scanning, and computerized axial tomography (CAT) scanning, researchers may be better able to probe various physiological reasons for forgetting. With more and more data available to be learned, research on memory and forgetting will continue to be imperative. Teachers must teach students how to learn and remember, and students must participate actively in the learning process as well as employ many of the available tactics for aiding recall.

Bibliography

Graham, Kenneth G., and H. Alan Robinson. *Study Skills Handbook*. Newark, Del.: International Reading Association, 1984. A very practical handbook which includes many of the principles set forth by Frank Robinson (who developed the "survey, question, read, recite, and review," or SQ3R, study method). Helps to teach study skills, thereby increasing memory and helping to prevent forgetting.

Hayes, John R. *The Complete Problem Solver*. Philadelphia: Franklin Institute Press, 1981. The title of this book is somewhat deceiving: Although it does discuss problem solving, it emphasizes the role of memory in problem solving, teaches how to use memory effectively, and links memory to learning strategies.

Kail, Robert V. *The Development of Memory in Children*. 3d ed. New York: W. H. Freeman, 1990. A theoretical book dealing with issues regarding children's memory. This text discusses how children develop the capacity to remember. Good reference book on how memory develops.

Loftus, Geoffrey R., and Elizabeth F. Loftus. *Human Memory: The Processing of Information*. Hillsdale, N.J.: Lawrence Erlbaum, 1976. One of the best single books on memory available. Covers learning, remembering and forgetting, and a number of other topics regarding memory.

Lorayne, Harry, and Jerry Lucas. *The Memory Book*. New York: Stein & Day, 1974. This is a popular "mass market" book on memory written by two memory experts. They teach various devices to help people remember faces, names, and so on. Readable and enjoyable, even amusing in places.

Stern, Leonard. *The Structures and Strategies of Human Memory*. Homewood, Ill.: Dorsey Press, 1985. This book is a good overview of memory and the applications of memory in life. Discusses long-term memory, a topic many researchers tend to avoid or downplay because of assessment problems. Contains a very systematic review of much of the research in a wide diversity of topics. A good reference book for the serious investigator of human memory in all of its complexities.

Michael F. Shaughnessy

Cross-References

FUNCTIONALISM

Type of psychology: Origin and definition of psychology
Fields of study: Descriptive methodologies; experimental methodologies; methodological issues

Functionalism, an early school of psychology, had a relatively brief but significant history as a distinctly American approach to the subject matter of psychology. Considered the psychology of modern urban America, functionalism formed a bridge between the mentalism of the first school of psychology (structuralism) and behaviorism, the dominant school in the first half of the twentieth century.

Principal terms

BEHAVIORISM: a school of psychology that emphasizes overt observable behavior rather than mental processes as the proper object of study for psychology

FUNCTIONALISM: an early school of American psychology that argued for the study of the human mind from the standpoint of understanding consciousness in terms of its purpose rather than its elements

MENTALISM: the idea that the mind or mental processes should be studied by psychology

NATURAL SELECTION: Darwin's concept that adaptation to an environment is aided by possession of certain characteristics that some members of the species have

PRAGMATISM: a philosophical position that provided the framework of functionalism by proposing that the value of something lies in its usefulness

STRUCTURALISM: the first school of psychology which focused on studying the elements or structure of normal adult consciousness

ZEITGEIST: a German word that means the flavor of the times or the social, political, and intellectual climate of a period of history

Overview

Functionalism was the name given to a particular way of approaching psychological questions that was important in the latter nineteenth and early twentieth centuries. It has been called the first American school of psychology, and it proposed a very different definition of what scientific psychology should study from that of the original school of scientific psychology, structuralism.

As the name implies, the subject matter of interest had to do with purpose or function. Earlier scientific psychology was interested in the contents or structure of human consciousness. In addition, this school—the structuralists, as they became known—insisted that psychology was to limit itself to the normal adult mind and did not have any application outside laboratory research. With the rise of functionalism, the content and methods of psychology would change in fundamental ways.

In one way, the functionalists and the structuralists had something in common. Both defined psychology as the study of the mind, especially consciousness; however, their concerns with consciousness took very different paths. As previously mentioned, the school of structuralism wanted to discover what it could about how the normal human mind was structured, or what its elements were. Those who became identified with functionalism were interested in human consciousness from the perspective of the purpose it served in helping humans adapt to their environment. As a result of this particular concern with function and adaptation, this school broadened psychology from a pure laboratory science to one with potential applications to a number of human and societal problems. Movement into applied areas led naturally to a need to understand special populations. The functionalists were interested in studying not only normal adults but also children, lower-order animals, and those individuals considered abnormal or to be suffering from some form of mental illness. The rise of functionalistic thinking in psychology also marked the beginning of a shift in influence from Europe, especially Germany, where scientific psychology began in 1879, to the United States.

Strictly speaking, functionalism as a school of psychology came into existence as a result of the most ardent of structuralists, Edward Bradford Titchener (1867-1927). In 1898, Titchener published an article in the journal *Philosophical Review* entitled "Postulates of a Structural Psychology." In this article, he distinguished between a structural approach to psychology and a functional one. Although his arguments for a structural approach and against the functional one fell on deaf ears, his labels for the two approaches did not.

Titchener was referring to ideas about psychology that existed before he wrote the article that gave functionalism its particular name. His was merely a label for a direction that some who identified themselves with psychology were taking. To understand better how and why functionalism developed, it is helpful to divide its development into two time periods. The first period can really be called "prefunctionalism," as the people significant during its early development were not actually a part of a systematic approach to psychology, but were more important for their influence on the intellectual climate of the developing science of psychology. Of particular importance to an understanding of what this school was and how it came to be is the groundwork for functionalism laid by William James, G. Stanley Hall, Hugo Münsterberg, James McKeen Cattell, and John Dewey. The careers of James Rowland Angell, Harvey Carr, and Robert Sessions Woodworth at the University of Chicago and Columbia University will be the focus for examining the development of functionalism as a more distinct school of psychology.

Any history of psychology must include a discussion of the contributions made by William James (1842-1910). Volumes have been written about James, as he was truly one of America's most distinguished thinkers. Given the opportunity for both an excellent education and extensive travel by virtue of his family's wealth, James developed into a scholar who influenced more than one field. His original pursuits included the study of art and medicine, but philosophy and psychology soon became his major areas of interest.

Much of James's strength as an important early American psychologist and as an intellectual forerunner to functionalism was in his ability as a writer. Even though James's most important work for psychology, *The Principles of Psychology* (1890), was published more than a hundred years ago, it remains a very readable and useful source on psychological questions and concerns. Through this text, which went through a number of editions, his smaller adaptation, *Psychology: The Briefer Course* (1892), as well as a number of other psychological writings, James significantly altered the direction of the new science of psychology. Some historians argue that it would be more accurate to say that James revolutionized psychology.

It would not be possible to describe or even outline all James's psychological thinking in this overview of functionalism; however, it might be useful to take a brief look at a few of his major concepts, as they are representative of his functional thinking. James was familiar with the basic ideas and methods being espoused by the structuralists, having read works by Wilhelm Wundt, the head of the German school responsible for the position of psychology as the science of the mind that sought to search for its elements and its structure. James was not impressed with this approach.

His opposition to this elemental approach can be seen in his famous concept of the stream of consciousness. In essence, James used the metaphor of a stream for both describing consciousness and illustrating why psychology from the structuralist perspective was doomed. In this idea, the roots of the functional approach to psychology can also easily be seen. Five aspects of the stream of consciousness were presented by James. He said that consciousness was personal; continuous, and not divisible for investigation or analysis; in a state of constant change; selective; and functional. In all of these, his challenge to the study of the elements of the mind can be seen. In the last of these, his legacy to the school of functionalism is readily apparent.

James was interested in a number of other facets of human behavior that paved the way for the direction psychology was to take under the influence of functionalism. Among these areas were those of habit and instinct, the perception of self, emotions, free will and religious experience, and pragmatism. The latter of these concerns has a special role in the development of functionalism. Pragmatism is a philosophical position which contends that the best criterion for judging the value of something, including an idea or theory, is its usefulness. Pragmatism was the underlying philosophical position of functionalism and remains a truly American contribution to the fields of both psychology and philosophy. It can be said that James made functionalism as a school of psychology possible, although he himself predates its major impact on the discipline. By looking at human behavior in the context of evolution or function, James expanded both the subject matter and research techniques of the developing science of psychology.

In 1892, Hugo Münsterberg, a onetime assistant to Wundt, accepted William James's offer to become the Harvard University psychology laboratory's new director. James, never a real experimentalist, had tired of the responsibility and sought Münsterberg as his replacement. From that position, Münsterberg began a career not only as an experimenter but also as an applied psychologist, something not really known up to that time. In his desire to use psychological knowledge in formulating solutions to a wide array of problems, Münsterberg fostered thinking that was to culminate in the functionalist approach. A number of specialities in psychology, such as clinical and industrial psychology, owe their existence partly to Hugo Münsterberg and his purposive or functional approach to psychology.

Two other early figures in American psychology should be mentioned, as they both contributed to the intellectual climate that bore functionalism. G. Stanley Hall and James McKeen Cattell both embodied the spirit and attitude of the functional approach to psychology. Hall is known for his variety of interests, such as child and adolescent psychology, and for his efforts at organizing and making psychology an institutionalized discipline through the development of psychological journals such as the *American Journal of Psychology* and the creation of the American Psychological Association (APA) in 1892. Cattell, a student of both Hall and Wundt, is best known for his work in psychological testing, epitomized by his creation of the Psychological Corporation, a business founded for the selling of psychology through psychometric tests—a functionalistic idea if there ever was one.

Some historians of psychology mark 1896 as the birth year of functionalism as a distinct school of psychology because of the publication that year of the article "The Reflex Arc Concept in Psychology" by John Dewey in *Psychological Review*. Dewey, a person much better known as a philosopher and educator, argued against the elemental thinking found in the structuralist school and for viewing all behavior in terms of its function.

The characteristics that distinguish functionalism as a school emerged in the forefront of American psychology shortly after Dewey's 1896 article, but they were being overtaken by the new school of psychology, behaviorism, by 1913. As a school, functionalism was neither highly systematized nor long lived. Functionalists were characterized by their opposition to the elemental approach of the structuralists and by their interest in the purpose, rather than contents, of the mind. In addition, a bent toward pragmatism produced a view of psychology as a practical rather than a pure science. As a result of these views, the functionalists expanded psychology in terms of both subject matter and methods of research that were considered acceptable. Behavior as well as mental processes was now a fair target for the psychologist's aim.

The history of functionalism is largely found in the history of psychology as it was studied at the University of Chicago. Under the twenty-five-year leadership of James Rowland Angell, this institution led the way in developing functionalistic thought. After Angell left Chicago in 1921 to become president of Yale University, functionalism at this school was in the hands of his former student Harvey Carr.

Carr, who wrote *Psychology: A Study of Mental Activity* (1925), focused on learning as the major means by which organisms adapt to the environment. This continued to move functionalism toward experimentation and animal research. Functionalism was also found at Columbia University, first under Cattell, and later under Robert Sessions Woodworth. Woodworth's major concern was motivation, or why people do what they do.

With the death of Edward Bradford Titchener in 1927, structuralism as a school of psychology also ceased to exist. The fate of functionalism, on the other hand, was not tied to any one person. Often criticized for being more an attitude than a systematic school of psychology, functionalism continues up to present conceptions of psychology. It has not existed as an identifiable school, however, since the rise of behaviorism, which became the dominant force in American psychology for several decades. Focusing on function, maintaining openness to an array of methods, and especially pursuing applied areas of psychology remain strongly entrenched in the discipline; these are all functionalistic ideas.

Applications

One of the hallmarks of American psychology has been its dedication to finding uses for its knowledge. A significant number of people who identify themselves with psychology are actively engaged in its application. The field of clinical psychology, for example, which is concerned with the diagnosis and treatment of abnormal behaviors and mental states, has more people specializing in it than does any other area of psychology. Other applied areas, such as various types of counseling, educational and industrial/organizational psychology, and health, also make up a significant part of the psychologist population. Almost every state has a board of examiners, similar to a medical board, to regulate the practice of psychology.

Functionalism, as an early school of American psychology, played a role in the development of the applied side of psychology. While functionalism was not as formal a school as was structuralism, it did lay the groundwork for mainstream American psychology. In the numerous applied areas of psychology existing today, the functionalists' open, expansive attitude toward the discipline can be seen. Functionalism's concern with understanding the adaptive value of psychological functions led to a natural tolerance for those interested in determining how the findings of psychology as a science could be used to solve real-world problems.

Many of the early psychologists historically associated with functionalism had an interest in using their knowledge in applied areas. One such individual was James McKeen Cattell. With his interest in mental testing, Cattell founded the Psychological Corporation. This organization was in the business of developing and selling psychological tests. While no longer associated with the Cattell family, the company continues to be one of the major distributors of psychological tests. The work of Hugo Münsterberg is another example of the influence of functionalism on the application of psychology. Originally hired by William James to run the psychological laboratory at Harvard University, he made a name for himself by pioneering the use of psychology in business and industry and in the legal system. The contemporary specializations of industrial/organizational and forensic psychology owe their origins largely to Münsterberg.

While functionalism no longer exists as a school of psychology, it continues to live in the legacy it left to American psychology. Perhaps the most significant aspect of this heritage is the idea that psychology can and should apply its knowledge and theory to addressing the improvement of the human condition.

Context

One of the major intellectual and scientific forces that moved some psychologists in the direction of concern for function was Charles Darwin's revolutionizing theory of evolution. Although Darwin was not the first thinker to propose an evolutionary viewpoint or theory with regard to biological organisms and their development, the publication of his *On the Origin of Species by Means of Natural Selection* (1859) created an intellectual and scientific storm that has still not abated. Darwin's theory essentially proposed that more offspring of a species are produced than can be supported by the environment, that certain individual differences among the offspring exist, and that some of these differences are more advantageous than others, thus increasing certain offsprings' probability of survival over that of others. This is Darwin's idea of natural selection.

William James, John Dewey, James McKeen Cattell, and G. Stanley Hall were all heavily influenced in their psychological thought by the concepts of evolution, especially natural selection and adaptation to an environment. The fact that functionalism sought to understand human consciousness from the standpoint of how it aided in adapting and adjusting to the environment is testament to the influence of evolutionary theory on this school. Darwin's theory also led naturally to questions of development and to the necessity of studying lower-order animals, children, and people who showed less-than-adequate adaptation, such as abnormal individuals. These approaches are readily identified as hallmarks of functionalism.

Science is a human and thus a social enterprise. Therefore, it is important to look to the social and historical context, or Zeitgeist. Zeitgeist is a German word that is generally translated to mean the flavor or influence of a particular historical time. It is helpful to look at functionalism as a product of an American approach to psychological questions.

Scientific psychology is generally agreed to have begun in 1879 with the founding of Wilhelm Wundt's psychological laboratory at the University of Leipzig. Structuralism grew out of this laboratory and his influence. Many students from all over the world came to Leipzig and studied under Wundt's direction; many were from the United States. They returned to found programs and laboratories in psychology in a variety of American universities. Although trained in a psychology of mentalism or structure, these American academics were also influenced by American culture, which placed significant value on the practical, the pragmatic, and the useful. Functionalism's applied concerns attest this cultural influence. In addition, American optimism and general democratic political structure favored a psychology that focused on adaptation and change.

Bibliography

Boring, Edwin G. *A History of Experimental Psychology.* Englewood Cliffs, N.J.: Prentice-Hall, 1950. A classic text in the history of psychology, this book will give the reader a good idea as to how functionalism was being viewed shortly after its absorption into behaviorally dominated American psychology.

Brennan, James F. *History and Systems of Psychology.* 3d ed. Englewood Cliffs, N.J.: Prentice-Hall, 1991. Chapter 12 presents a good overview of the rise of functionalism. Particularly useful is the list of primary sources at the end of the chapter.

James, William. *Principles of Psychology.* 2 vols. New York: Dove, 1890. Although more than a hundred years old, James's classic text on psychological issues remains both readable and illuminating. His functionalistic thinking is evident.

Leahey, Thomas H. *A History of Modern Psychology.* Englewood Cliffs, N.J.: Prentice-Hall, 1991. A very readable textbook that contains two chapters (4 and 5) specifically related to functionalism and its antecedents. Also discusses some European functional ideas.

Murphy, Gardner. *Historical Introduction to Modern Psychology.* Rev. ed. New York: Harcourt Brace, 1950. In a concise way, presents the major differences between the schools of structuralism and functionalism.

Sahakian, William S., ed. *History of Psychology: A Source Book in Systematic Psychology.* Itasca, Ill.: F. E. Peacock, 1968. Contains samples of the writings of people whose thinking developed psychology. Includes some of William James's most influential works as well as those of others important to functionalism such as Dewey, Angell, and Carr.

John P. Hall

Cross-References

Behaviorism: An Overview, 401; Ethology, 992; Psychology: Fields of Specialization, 1939; Psychology Defined, 1945; Structuralism, 2477.

GENDER-IDENTITY FORMATION

Type of psychology: Developmental psychology
Fields of study: Cognitive development; infancy and childhood

Gender-identity formation refers to the complex processes through which young children come to incorporate their gender into their behavior, attitudes, and self-understanding. This includes the development of an inner sense of one's femaleness or maleness; the acquisition of knowledge about cultural expectations for females and males; and the development of attitudes, interests, and behavior that reflect these expectations.

Principal terms
GENDER CONSTANCY: the understanding that gender is a permanent
    characteristic of the self and other people
GENDER IDENTITY: a child's accurate labeling of himself or herself by
    gender; also, a person's inner sense of femaleness or maleness
GENDER SCHEMA: a general knowledge framework that organizes
    information and guides perceptions related to males and females
SEX ROLE: the set of expectations about a person's attitudes and behavior
    that is culturally assigned based on one's gender
SEX-ROLE SOCIALIZATION: the process of teaching children to conform to
    gender-linked social rules and expectations
SEX TYPING: the process of acquiring traits, attitudes, and behaviors seen
    culturally as appropriate for members of one's gender; gender-role
    acquisition

Overview

The first question that is usually asked about a newborn baby is whether it is a boy or a girl. The single fact of the child's gender has enormous implications for the course of his or her entire life. Gender-identity formation refers to the complex processes through which children incorporate the biological and social fact of their gender into their behavior, attitudes, and self-understanding.

This area includes ideas about two major interrelated processes: gender-identity development and sex typing. The term "gender-identity development," used in its narrower sense, refers to the process through which children come to label themselves cognitively as boys or girls and to have an inner sense of themselves as male or female. "Sex typing," also called gender-role acquisition, refers to the processes through which children learn what is expected of members of their gender and come to exhibit primarily those personality traits, behaviors, interests, and attitudes.

Social-learning theorists such as Walter Mischel have described mechanisms of learning through which children come to exhibit sex-typed behavior. Boys and girls often behave differently because they are rewarded and punished for different behaviors. In other words, they receive different conditioning. In addition, children's behavior becomes sex typed because children observe other males and females regularly behaving differently according to their gender, and they imitate or model this behavior.

Parents are especially important in the process of learning one's gender role, both as models for gender-appropriate behavior and as sources of rewards or reinforcement. Because parents become associated with positive experiences (such as being fed and comforted) early in life, children learn to look to them and other adults for rewards. Parents and other adults such as teachers often react differentially to gender-typed behaviors, rewarding gender-appropriate behavior (for example, giving praise or attention) and punishing gender-inappropriate behavior (for example, frowning, ignoring, or reprimanding).

As children become more involved with their peers (children their own age) they begin to influence one another's behavior, often strongly reinforcing traditional gender roles. The fact that children are usually given different toys and different areas in which to play based on their gender is also important. Girls are given opportunities to learn different behaviors from those of boys (for example, girls learn nurturing behavior through playing with dolls) because they are exposed to different experiences.

Using what is called a cognitive developmental perspective, Lawrence Kohlberg described developmental changes in children's understanding of gender concepts. These changes parallel the broad developmental changes in the way children's thinking is organized, first described by Jean Piaget and Barbel Inhelder. Children mature naturally through stages of more and more complex cognitive organization. In the area of understanding gender, the first stage is the acquisition of a rudimentary gender identity, the ability to categorize oneself correctly as a boy or a girl.

Children are able to apply gender labels to themselves correctly by about age three. At this stage, young children base gender labeling on differences in easily observable characteristics such as hairstyle and clothing, and they do not grasp the importance of genital differences in determining gender. As children's thinking about the physical world becomes more complex, so does their understanding of gender. Gradually, by about age seven, children enter a second stage and acquire the concept known as gender constancy.

Gender constancy refers to the understanding that gender is a stable characteristic that cannot change over time and that is not altered by superficial physical transformations such as wearing a dress or cutting one's hair. As children come to see gender as a stable, important characteristic of themselves and other people, they begin to use the concept consistently to organize social information. They learn societal expectations for members of each gender by watching the actions of the people around them.

Kohlberg proposed that children use their developing knowledge of cultural gender expectations to teach themselves to adopt culturally defined gender roles (self-socialization). He argued that children acquire a strong motive to conform to gender roles because of their need for self-consistency and self-esteem. A young boy says to himself, "I am a boy, not a girl; I want to do boy things, play with boy toys, and wear boy clothes."

Children hold more rigid gender stereotypes before they acquire gender constancy (ages two through seven); once gender constancy is achieved, they become more flexible in their adherence to gender roles. As children enter adolescence, their thinking about the world again enters a new stage of development, becoming even more complex and less rigid. As a result, they may be able to achieve what Joseph Pleck has called "sex-role transcendence" and to choose their interests and behaviors somewhat independent of cultural gender-role expectations.

Gender-schema theory is a way of explaining gender-identity formation, which is closely related to the cognitive developmental approach. The concept of a schema or a general knowledge framework comes from the field of cognitive psychology. Sandra Bem proposed that each person develops a set of gender-linked associations, or a gender schema, as part of a personal knowledge structure. This gender schema filters and interprets new information, and as a result, people have a basic predisposition to process information on the basis of gender. People tend to dichotomize objects and attributes on the basis of gender, even including things such as colors, which have no relevance to biological sex.

Bem proposed that sex typing develops as children learn the content of society's gender schema and as they begin to link that schema to their self-concept or view of themselves. Individuals vary in the degree to which the gender schema is central to their self-concept; it is central to the self-concept of highly sex-typed individuals (traditionally masculine males or traditionally feminine females).

Applications

Ideas about gender-identity formation have important implications for child rearing and education. Most parents want to help their child identify with and feel positive about his or her own gender. Those few children who fail to develop a clear inner sense of themselves as male or female that is consistent with their biological sex may have significant social adjustment difficulties; they are sometimes given psychological treatment for a condition called "gender-identity disorder." Adults who continue to have a gender identity that is inconsistent with their biological sex desire surgery and hormonal treatments to change their sex. This rare condition is called transsexualism, and it is more common among biological males than females. Although many people have interests, personality characteristics, or sexual preferences commonly associated with the other gender, they are not transsexuals; their inner sense of their gender is consistent with their biological sex.

Often, parents and educators want to help children avoid becoming strongly sex typed. They do not want children's options for activities, interests, and aspirations to be limited to those traditionally associated with their gender. Adopting strongly sex-typed interests may be especially problematic for girls, because the traditional female role and the qualities associated with it (that is, emotionality, nurturance, and dependence) tend to be devalued in American culture. Traditionally masculine interests and behaviors are usually tolerated in girls before puberty; it is all right to be a tomboy. Traditionally feminine interests and behaviors, however, tend to be vigorously discouraged in boys; it is not acceptable to be a sissy.

Considerable research has focused on whether and how socializing agents, including parents, teachers, peers, and media such as children's books and television, reinforce gender stereotypes and teach children to exhibit sex-typed behaviors. Researchers have been concerned both with how gender roles are modeled for children and with how sex-typed behavior is rewarded. A study by Lisa Serbin and her colleagues is an example. These researchers observed teachers' interactions with children in a preschool setting and recorded their observations in a standardized way. They found that teachers gave more attention to girls when they were physically close to them than when they were farther away; however, teachers' attention to boys did not vary with the child's proximity. This finding suggests that teachers reinforce girls more than boys for "dependent" behavior without necessarily meaning to do so.

Parents often report that they try to treat their children the same regardless of their gender. Many of the most powerful influences parents exert result from behaviors of which they are probably unaware. Research studies have shown that parents consistently interact differently with male and female children in areas such as engaging in gross motor play (for example, running, jumping, throwing), encouraging children's sex-typed play (particularly, discouraging doll-play among boys), demanding effort and giving help with problem-solving tasks, and allowing children to have independence and freedom from supervision.

Children's peers have been shown to play an important role in sex-role socialization. Particularly in early childhood, when children's gender concepts tend to be far more rigid than those of adults, peers may be the source of misinformation (for example, "girls can't be doctors; girls have to be nurses") and of strong sanctions against behavior that is inconsistent with one's gender role.

Laboratory studies have shown that exposure to gender stereotypes in books and on television tends to have a measurable effect on children's sex-typed behavior. For example, children are more likely to play with a "gender-inappropriate" toy after reading a story in which a child of their gender played with that toy. In addition, these media may be important in the development of a child's gender schema because they provide a rich network of information and associations related to gender. Extensive studies of the gender-related content of children's books and children's television were conducted in the 1970's, and this led to reform efforts by some textbook publishers and television producers.

One influential study by a group called Women on Words and Images analyzed the contents of 134 grade-school readers and found gender-stereotypic portrayals of male and female characters, gender-stereotypic themes, and male dominance to be the rule. Boys outnumbered girls as major characters by five to two; in 2,760 stories examined, only three mothers were shown working outside the home. Systematic studies of children's television have produced similar results.

Context

Psychologists have been interested in gender-identity formation since the work of Sigmund Freud and other early theorists in the beginning of the twentieth century. Since the early 1970's, however, there has been a major shift in thinking about this topic, largely as a result of the women's movement. Early work in this area considered sex typing to be a healthy and desirable goal for children. Since the 1970's, much research has been based on the assumption that rigid adherence to traditional gender roles is restrictive and undesirable.

Freud's theory of psychosexual development was the first to attempt to explain gender-identity formation. Freud believed that sex-typed behavior results primarily from girls identifying with (wanting to be like) their mothers and boys identifying with their fathers; however, he believed that during infancy both boys and girls form strong sexual feelings for their mothers and identify with them. Thus, Freud tried to explain how boys come to identify with their fathers and how girls transfer their sexual feelings to their fathers.

Freud believed that the discovery that girls and women do not have penises leads the three- to five-year-old boy to develop great fear that he will lose his own penis (castration anxiety). As a result, the boy begins to identify with his father out of fear that the father will take away the penis. He gives up his identification with his mother and suppresses his sexual feelings toward her. For a little girl, the same discovery leads to penis envy and to blaming the mother for her lack of this desired organ. Because of her disappointment, she transfers her sexual feelings from her mother to her father, and she fantasizes that her father will give her a penis substitute—a baby.

Freud's theory was an important inspiration for much of the work done on gender identity prior to the late 1960's. Since that time, however, developmental psychologists have not often used Freud's theory because most of its concepts rely on the idea of unconscious forces that cannot be evaluated scientifically.

Freud's idea that "anatomy is destiny"—that profound psychological differences between the sexes are inevitable—has met with strong criticism with the rise of the women's movement. The issue of the relative importance of biological, genetic factors (or "nature") compared with experiential, social factors (or "nurture") in gender-identity formation has been a major source of controversy in psychology. Most psychologists acknowledge a role for both nature and nurture in forming differences in the behavior of boys and girls. Psychologists are interested in understanding how inborn capacities (such as cognitive organization) interact with environmental experiences in forming a person's identity as a male or a female.

The twentieth century has experienced a great upheaval in thinking about gender roles, and this has been mirrored by changes in psychological research and theory about gender. The growing scientific understanding of gender identity may help to form future societal attitudes as well as being formed by them.

Bibliography

Bem, Sandra L. "Gender Schema Theory and Its Implications for Child Development: Raising Gender-Aschematic Children in a Gender-Schematic Society." *Signs* 8, no. 4 (1983): 598-616. Introduction to gender-schema for nonpsychologists. Provides an in-depth discussion of this approach to gender-identity formation and compares it to other major psychological theories. Bem also suggests practical applications of her perspective to child rearing.

Brooks-Gunn, Jeanne, and Wendy Schempp Matthews. *He and She: How Children Develop Their Sex-Role Identity.* Englewood Cliffs, N.J.: Prentice-Hall, 1979. Provides a clear, thorough description of children's sex-role development for parents, educators, and students. Also provides research evidence and anecdotal examples describing sex-role acquisition from the prenatal period through adolescence. A good, usable reference for high school students.

Hughes, Fergus, and Lloyd Noppe. "Gender Roles and Gender Differences." In *Human Development Across the Life Span.* St. Paul, Minn.: West, 1985. Presents an overview of gender-identity formation across the entire life span, including information about gender roles in old age. Provides extensive information about gender from a developmental perspective. Easily accessible to beginning college students.

Huston, A. C. "Sex-Typing." In *Handbook of Child Psychology*, edited by Paul H. Mussen. Vol. 4, edited by E. Mavis Hetherington. 4th ed. New York: John Wiley & Sons, 1983. Relatively technical, but provides a masterful organization and in-depth analysis of theory and research relevant to sex typing. Also includes a long and thorough bibliography.

Lott, Bernice E. *Women's Lives: Themes and Variations in Gender Learning.* Monterey, Calif.: Brooks/Cole, 1987. Frequently used textbook for college classes on the psychology of women. Chapters 3 and 4 present an accessible, entertaining account of gender-identity formation from a social-learning perspective, integrating research evidence. Other chapters explore implications of gender-role acquisition for women in adult life. Helpful for those who are interested in gender-related topics in psychology.

Ruble, D. N. "Sex-Role Development." In *Developmental Psychology: An Advanced Textbook*, edited by Marc H. Bornstein and Michael E. Lamb. Hillsdale, N.J.: Lawrence Erlbaum, 1984. Presents a comprehensive discussion of gender-identity formation and related issues in developmental psychology. Includes research evidence for sex differences in behavior and biological, social, and cognitive factors in sex-role development. Clearly written, scholarly in tone, and presupposes some prior familiarity with the field.

Lesley A. Slavin

Cross-References

Cognitive Ability: Gender Differences, 540; Development: Theoretical Issues, 804; Hormones and Behavior, 1189; Personality Theory: Major Issues, 1804; Psychoanalytic Psychology and Personality: Sigmund Freud, 1912; Sexism, 2240.

GENERAL ADAPTATION SYNDROME

Type of psychology: Stress
Field of study: Critical issues in stress

General adaptation syndrome (GAS) is the name given to the manifestations of the state of stress in a body. Stress is the most active specific conditioning factor in the human organism. Psychosomatic medicine virtually had its beginnings with the discovery of the GAS.

Principal terms

ADAPTATION: the adjustment of an organism to new conditions

ADRENAL GLANDS: two endocrine (hormonal) glands, each located on the top of one kidney, which secrete glucocorticoid and mineralocorticoid hormones as well as auxiliary sex hormones and epinephrine

ALARM REACTION: the first stage of the general adaptation syndrome, in which the adrenals release large amounts of their hormones into the blood circulation

CONDITIONING FACTORS: agents or situations which themselves have no independent effects, but can modify the response to a particular stimulus

GLUCOCORTICOIDS: the antiinflammatory hormones cortisol and cortisone, secreted by the adrenal cortex and having a role in sugar metabolism

LYMPHATIC TISSUE: the lymph vessels, lymph nodes, spleen, thymus, and tonsils

MINERALOCORTICOIDS: the proinflammatory hormones aldosterone and desoxycorticosterone, secreted by the adrenal cortex and having a role in salt metabolism

STAGE OF EXHAUSTION: the third stage of the GAS, in which the body is rapidly deteriorating

STAGE OF RESISTANCE: the second stage of the GAS, in which the tissues return to their normal state and the secretion of hormones is only slightly above normal

THYMUS GLAND: a gland located in the front of the chest which is large at birth and shrinks after puberty; it aids the maturation of white blood cells, which defend the body against foreign matter

Overview

Stress is the rate of wear and tear, in particular the strain on the nervous system, in an organism. It is the sum of all adaptive reactions in the body, and it manifests itself by a specific syndrome which consists of all the nonspecifically induced changes within the individual.

Adaptive reactions, or adaptation, are the process by which the organism adjusts itself to changed circumstances. A syndrome is a group of symptoms usually appearing together in a disease. Nonspecific changes are those that involve many organs of the body and can be induced by a variety of causal factors. Nevertheless, the form in which these changes appear is quite specific: It is the general adaptation syndrome (GAS), first described by Hans Selye in the 1950's. The explanation of this seeming contradiction lies in the fact that stress produces two kinds of changes: one that is nonspecifically caused and appears in a nonspecific form, called the primary change; and one that, although nonspecifically caused, is specific in form, the secondary change called GAS.

The GAS is composed of three stages. The first is the alarm reaction, in which the body arms itself for the defense against an aggression (such as a bacterial or viral infection, physical damage, or a strong nervous stimulus) but has had no time yet to adjust itself to the new condition. The second is the stage of resistance, in which the body succeeds in adapting itself to the condition. The third is the stage of exhaustion, in which the body's resistance is breaking down with the loss of its adaptive response, a development that can lead to death.

There are three main signs of the first (alarm reaction) stage: an enlargement of the cortex (outer layer) of the adrenal glands; a degeneration of the thymus gland (located in the front of the chest, and playing an important role in defense against infections) and the lymphatic system (the vessels that carry the lymph, or white blood, and the lymph nodes, including the spleen and tonsils); and the appearance of gastrointestinal (stomach and gut) ulcers.

In the second (resistance) stage, the body is at its highest level of adaptation, above the normal range, and the body organs return to their normal state. The adrenals, which in the first stage completely discharged their hormones, now again accumulate large amounts of them. In the last (exhaustion) stage, the adrenals again loose their secretions, and the other organs degenerate even more; the body's resistance drops to below-normal levels. Although the third stage can lead to death, this is not necessarily the outcome. Often a person undergoes all three stages only to recuperate at the end. A marathon runner goes through all stages of GAS and, although completely exhausted at the end of the race, regains strength after only a few hours of rest.

The adrenal glands have an important role in GAS. These are two little glands, each sitting on top of one of the kidneys. The gland is composed of an outer part, or cortex, and a core, or medulla. The cortex is subdivided into layers, one of which manufactures the so-called mineralocorticoids, aldosterone and desoxycorticosterone (DOCA), which have a role in electrolyte (salt) metabolism and have a proinflammatory effect in the body; the second layer secretes the glucocorticoids, cortisol and cortisone, which play a role in sugar metabolism and have an antiinflammatory effect. Now, inflammation is a local defense mechanism of the body; the antiinflammatory hormones suppress this defensive weapon. They also promote the spread of infections and the formation of gastrointestinal ulcers. In spite of this apparent antagonism between the two types of cortical hormones, their effects are absolutely necessary for the body to resist aggression. If the adrenal glands are damaged to a degree that they can no longer produce these hormones, then, without treatment, death is inevitable. In contrast, the hormones secreted by the medullary part of the adrenal gland, epinephrine (also known as adrenaline) and norepinephrine, are not absolutely necessary for survival because they are produced also by nerve endings in other parts of the body.

Any agent that attacks the body will induce, besides specific effects, nonspecific ones as well. These are direct effects, such as a burn wound, and indirect effects, which are of two kinds: one that triggers the proinflammatory mechanism, inducing it to fight the damage, and one that triggers the antiinflammatory mechanism, which limits the extent of the damage. The system is actually a bit more complex than this; another component, the so-called conditioning factors, must be taken into account.

Conditioning factors are agents or situations which themselves have no independent effects; however, they can modify the response to a particular stimulus. There are external and internal conditioning factors. The external ones comprise, for example, geographical, social, and nutritional factors, whereas the internal conditioning factors are those determined by genetics and previous experiences.

Based on this information, the sequence of events that occur when a stressor (a stress inducer) acts on an individual may be summarized as follows: The brain senses the stimulus and sends messages to the adrenal medulla, inducing it to release epinephrine, and to the pituitary gland, inducing it to release adrenocorticotropic hormone (ACTH). Epinephrine has two effects: It acts on the pituitary gland increasing the secretion of ACTH. It also acts on most of the body tissues, increasing their rate of activity: The heart rate, breathing rate, and blood pressure are increased, as well as the blood sugar level. All these changes prepare the organism to "fight or flee." ACTH, in the meantime, reaches the adrenal cortex and induces the secretion of antiinflammatory hormones. Simultaneously, proinflammatory hormones are released. Both types act on the tissues affected directly by the stressor, and also have a systemic effect on the whole body, inducing the GAS. The particular type and degree of response is modulated by the conditioning factors.

Applications

Disease could be defined as the alteration, as a result of a changed environment, of the structure and function of tissues that interferes with their ability to survive. To produce a disease, two types of factors are necessary: environmental, that is, external factors; and the response of the organism, that is, internal factors. The discovery that stress elicits a specific response, the general adaptation syndrome, made it possible to apply exact measurements to the state of stress and its consequences (stress-induced diseases). Although the GAS has a defensive purpose in the body because it promotes adaptation to new conditions, an excess of adaptive hormones can induce untoward symptoms, that is, cause disease. This aspect of stress, that adaptive reactions can themselves become harmful, is one of the most important characteristics of the phenomenon. It made physicians realize that there are many diseases which are not caused by specific agents such as microorganisms, toxic chemicals, or injuries, but rather by the response of tissues to these aggressors (stressors). One type of such diseases is an allergy such as hay fever or hives. It was found that the inflammation of the nasal passages, eyes, or skin is caused by the tissues reacting against chemicals contained in pollen or in some foods. The body fights these reactions with glucocorticoids (antiinflammatory hormones) secreted by the adrenal cortex. This discovery, that adrenal glucocorticoids have antiinflammatory and antiallergic effects, was immediately applied in clinical medicine to treat very grave diseases such as arthritis and asthma. The glucocorticoids proved to be lifesaving in these cases.

As the phenomenon of stress is primarily produced by a strain on the nervous system, it seemed reasonable to look into the role of the GAS in nervous and mental diseases. It became clear that what is called maladaptation can be the cause of a nervous breakdown or even outright mental disease. This led physicians to search for the connection between psychic maladjustments and bodily diseases. The result was the foundation of the medical specialty called psychosomatic medicine. It is now known that what is called "executive disease"—that is, gastrointestinal ulcers and high blood pressure, sometimes accompanied by a nervous breakdown—is induced by the inability to adjust to a new situation, or by an exceptionally heavy workload, or by fear of responsibility and inability to make decisions. Psychosomatic medicine attempts to elucidate how maladaptation causes disease as well as how it influences aging and the degenerative diseases of old age, in particular, coronary heart disease and cancer. It is known that chronological age is not the same as physiological age. That is, a fifty-year-old person, from the point of view of tissue integrity and function, may be much older than a seventy-year-old person whose tissues are still in good functioning order. The underlying causes of these individual differences are based in individuals' differential response to stressful situations.

As an outgrowth of the study of stress and the GAS, two subfields of research opened up: the psychology of stress, and psychophysiology. The study of stress psychology implies that human behavior is affected by biological mechanisms which appear to be a common heritage of all mammals. The aim of the study would be to enable people to control their emotions and, thus, their behavior. This would be of obvious benefit in the rehabilitation of persons who came in conflict with the law because of their violent behavior and, possibly, would allow society to reduce violent crimes. Psychophysiology, which was founded as a separate branch of psychology in 1960, studies psychological or behavioral variables with their respective physiological responses. For example, one of the major preoccupations of psychophysiology is the study of biofeedback, or the control by a subject of his or her own heart rate or brain function. There is great interest in biofeedback studies, because it is hoped that psychosomatic disturbances could be treated successfully by this technique. In 1949, researchers studied two groups of patients: one group which had recurring head and neck pains, and another which complained of cardiovascular (heart) symptoms. When the researchers administered painful stimuli to the two groups, each reported an increased intensity in its particular symptoms, although they had been well before the test. The researchers concluded that psychosomatic disorders are caused by the exaggerated response of a particular physiological system, characteristic for the individual. This phenomenon has been named "symptom specificity."

Context

In ancient Greece, the father of medicine, Hippocrates, taught that in every diseased body there is a natural force that fights the disease from within. Later, in eighteenth century England, John Hunter stated that every injury has the tendency to produce the means for a cure. That is, the concept of being sick includes a battle between the aggressor and the defense mechanisms of the body. Rufus of Ephesus, a Greek physician, around the year A.D. 100 discovered that high fever had a beneficial effect upon the progression of many illnesses. This fact was rediscovered by a Viennese psychiatrist, Julius Wagner von Jauregg, who tried to alleviate the mental disease of patients in the last stage of syphilis. In 1883, he observed that the symptoms improved markedly when the patients contracted typhoid fever. Subsequently, he introduced the treatment with malaria and achieved spectacular results, but without knowing the reason for the cure. The great French physiologist Claude Bernard, in the nineteenth century, taught that a characteristic of living organisms is their ability to maintain a constant internal environment in spite of significant fluctuations in the external conditions in which they live. Walter B. Cannon, at Harvard University, gave this phenomenon the name "homeostasis." He also coined the term "emergency reaction" to describe the immediate functional changes occurring in the body as a consequence of stressful stimuli. When the homeostatic mechanisms of the body fail to maintain the constancy of the internal medium, disease and eventually death ensue. Although all these findings converged in the treatment of disease by nonspecific means, it was a Viennese physician who formulated a scientific theory of the "syndrome of being sick," or, in other words, the concept of stress and of the general adaptation syndrome.

Hans Selye (1907-1982), who was born in Vienna but immigrated to Canada, discovered in 1936 that the physical response to stress could cause disease and even death. He detected the effects of stress when he injected ovarian extracts into laboratory rats. He found that the extract induced an enlargement of the adrenal cortex, the shrinkage of the thymus gland, and gastric ulcers. Selye realized that it was the stress caused by the impurities in the extract that induced the characteristic changes. He extrapolated his findings to humans and stated that stress could initiate disease and cause death. In 1950, he published *The Physiology and Pathology of Exposure to Stress*, in which he gave a detailed description of the GAS concept. In the beginning, the medical establishment was reluctant to accept the idea that hormones could have a role in the causation of nonspecific aspects of disease; until that time, hormones were only known to act on specific target tissues. They caused disease either by too little or too much of a particular hormone. For example, a lack of growth hormone resulted in dwarfism, whereas too much of the same created a giant. Selye, however, postulated general hormonal effects that transcended their known immediate action on target tissues. Another, unjustified, criticism of his theory was that he attributed too great a role to the hormonal system, neglecting the part played by the nervous system. These criticisms did not hold up in the long run, and Selye's teachings on stress and the GAS were in the end accepted by medical and physiological researchers.

Bibliography

Allen, Roger J. *Human Stress: Its Nature and Control.* Minneapolis: Burgess, 1983. A well-written account of the broad concept of stress, with good chapters on the general adaptation syndrome and on the psychophysiology of the stress response (that is, the mind-body link). The work is divided into three parts: the nature of stress; the causes and effects of stress; and stress control, which includes the psychophysiological subjects of meditation, relaxation, and biofeedback. Addressed to the general public; includes very good reference lists after each chapter, in addition to an index and illustrations.

Cox, Tom. *Stress.* London: Macmillan, 1978. In two hundred pages, in an easily understood language, explains for the layperson the nature of stress. Discusses the physiological (GAS) and psychological responses to stress. Contains some line drawings which complement the text, and includes a short index and bibliography.

Dobson, Clifford B. *Stress, the Hidden Adversary.* Lancaster, England: MTP Press, 1982. Addresses a college audience. Covers the physiological and psychological responses to stress, physical and behavioral effects of stress, stress and medical disorders, and the control of stress. Includes a very good index, references after each chapter, and good line drawings which enhance the text.

Gross, Nancy E. *Living with Stress.* New York: McGraw-Hill, 1958. Very easy reading. Relates the story of stress, explains the concept, and gives advice on how to cope with stress in daily life. In a foreword, Hans Selye says that the author succeeds in conveying the essence of what has been learned about stress (although much has been learned since this 1958 book). Lacks references, but includes an index and a glossary.

Kerner, Fred. *Stress and Your Heart.* New York: Hawthorn Books, 1961. Gives a good overview of the effects of stress on the heart; succeeds in outlining, for the layperson, the essentials of the relationship between stress and heart disease. Augmented by an appendix containing an appreciation and a curriculum vitae of Hans Selye, the discoverer of the general adaptation syndrome. Includes an index and a glossary, but no illustrations.

Knight, Edwin. *Living with Stress.* Caufield East, Victoria, Australia: Edward Arnold, 1987. In a humorous style, complemented by cartoons, this work describes for the general public the nature of stress and its symptoms. Also discusses stress and physical illness, as well as the management of stress with relaxation techniques. Contains an index and a bibliography.

Levi, Lennart. *Stress: Sources, Management, and Prevention.* New York: Liveright, 1967. A relatively short work covering the problems of body and mind, stress as a cause of disease, and psychosomatic treatments. In a foreword, Selye writes: "[Levi] has attacked some of the cardinal aspects of the relationship between body and psyche. . . . [He has] the talent of combining technical competence with the gift of explaining the findings in an entertaining style." Includes an index, bibliography, glossary, some photographic illustrations, and line drawings.

McQuade, Walter, and Ann Aikman. *Stress: What It Is, What It Can Do to Your Health, How To Fight Back.* New York: E. P. Dutton, 1974. In a nontechnical style, deals with the effects of stress on the cardiovascular, digestive, musculoskeletal, and immune systems. Also discusses the way in which the mind and body handle stress, and the means by which the response to stress can be altered. No illustrations, but the book contains an index and a bibliography.

Selye, Hans. *The Stress of Life.* Rev. ed. New York: McGraw-Hill, 1978. The discoverer of the general adaptation syndrome provides in this work a lucid, comprehensible, nontechnical description of the stress concept and the stress response (GAS). The book is divided into five parts, covering the evolution of the stress concept; the means through which the body can defend itself against stress; the diseases of adaptation; the contribution of the study of stress to understanding the theory of life; and the application of the knowledge of stress to medicine to ensure better health. Includes an index and a glossary; the text is complemented by illustrations (photographs and line drawings).

_____. *Stress Without Distress.* New York: New American Library, 1975. A relatively short work in which the father of the stress response advises how to use stress as a positive force to achieve a rewarding life-style. The first part of the book covers in layperson's terms the same material as *The Stress of Life*, that is, the general adaptation syndrome; the second part has a more philosophical approach. Includes some line drawings, an index, and a bibliography.

René R. Roth

Cross-References

Hormones and Behavior, 1189; Adaptation to Stress, 2390; Stress: Behavioral and Psychological Responses, 2397; The Concept of Stress, 2411; Effects of Stress, 2417; Stress: Physiological Responses, 2425; Theories of Stress, 2432; Stress and the Endocrine System, 2445; Stress and the Nervous System, 2452; Stress-Related Diseases, 2464.

GENERATIVITY IN ADULTHOOD: ERIKSON

Type of psychology: Developmental psychology
Field of study: Adulthood

Generativity describes the task of Erik Erikson's seventh stage of the life cycle, which occurs at about age forty. Individuals who have achieved generativity show a concern for the next generation and engage in activities that will leave the world a better place for others. Those who ignore the needs of others and focus on their own needs experience stagnation and meaninglessness.

Principal terms

GENERATIVITY: the need to take care of future generations through the experiences of caring, nurturing, and education

ID: the powerful basic drives (such as the need to express anger) that motivate individuals to behave with little awareness of the reasons for their behavior

IDENTITY: the establishment of a distinctive personality based on the foundation laid in childhood and the expectations associated with reaching adulthood

MIDLIFE TRANSITION: a stage occurring around the age of forty marked by physical changes associated with aging as well as thoughts about death

SELF-ABSORPTION: the inability to show concern for the well-being of others; synonymous with stagnation

SELF-CENTEREDNESS: an attitude in which an individual views the world from his or her own perspective, with a focus on what he or she can get from the world

STAGNATION: a preoccupation with self that may lead to feelings of insecurity and a failure to take responsibility for one's life

SUPEREGO: the collection of moral behaviors learned from parents, teachers, and other authority figures that, without awareness, affect the decisions a person makes

UNCONSCIOUS MOTIVES: forces underlying behavior of which individuals are usually unaware; they are probably the result of the desires of the id and/or the superego

Overview

Caring, nurturing, and educating form the basis for generativity. The need to give something to or leave something for the next generation helps give meaning and purpose to the middle-aged adult. The failure to find effective ways of assisting the next generation may lead to a sense of uselessness and stagnation.

According to Erik Erikson, individuals go through a series of stages as they grow into adulthood and approach their death. By the time adults reach their forties, they have passed through six stages of development centered on the individual's interaction with his or her environment. The seventh stage of the life cycle is called the generativity-versus-stagnation stage. The stage begins at about age forty and lasts ten to thirty years.

The generativity-versus-stagnation stage is characterized by a need to begin a review of one's life, with the focus of that review centering on the care received as a child and the care given to the generation to come. Individuals in this stage are busy with careers, parenting, and the care of their own parents. In a work entitled *Vital Involvement in Old Age* (1986), Erik Erikson, his wife Joan Erikson, and their co-author Helen Kivnick indicate that individuals in the middle-adulthood period of development have a responsibility for the "maintenance of the world." They must give birth to, rear, and mentor the people who will survive them. They must see to it that social institutions such as schools and governments are strong, and they have an obligation to make others aware of the importance of preserving natural resources and leaving the environment intact for the next generation.

If individuals relinquish their responsibilities to care for the next generation, they are likely to feel stagnated. The stagnated person may eventually experience despair and a sense of meaninglessness. Individuals who do not develop a sense of concern for the next generation are often self-indulgent. They want to take from the world and the people around them what they think they deserve, rather than return what they have gained in wisdom and resources in an effort to preserve the world. The self-indulgent adult will often seek intimate relationships but will not bring to those relationships enough care and concern. Consequently, the self-indulgent adult will fail to find the intimacy he or she seeks or will develop a false sense of intimacy, usually with another person who is unable to convey genuine concern for others.

The stagnated person conveys a sense of self-centeredness. Often, these individuals are obsessed with cleanliness and order. They are rigid and unable to tolerate a change in plans or a new approach to solving problems. They pamper themselves and find little comfort in sharing with others.

Though it might appear that an individual who has reached middle age must either have a caring, giving personality or must be selfish and unconcerned about the welfare of others, it is the case that most people between the ages of forty and sixty have moments of genuine concern for others as well as moments of extreme selfishness. No caring person has achieved generativity without moments of stagnation. Caring individuals may get angry at the many needs put before them. They may, at times, resent the efforts they have put into child rearing, education, or providing for the next generation. There may be times when caring parents, teachers, or artists grow bitter because their efforts go unrewarded or, worse yet, unnoticed. Truly caring persons use these moments of selfishness to evaluate their motives and check their priorities. They often emerge with purer motives and a stronger need to make the world a better place without expecting so much in return. They then move into the next stage of development, integrity versus despair, with a good sense of purpose and meaningfulness.

Finally, it is important to note that not all manifestations of generativity occur through parenting and grandparenting. An individual's concern for the next generation may come through the world of work or through the world of ideas. Erikson has noted that this type of generativity is accompanied by a sense of playfulness and is present in the most creative individuals. People such as Albert Einstein, Mahatma Gandhi, and George Bernard Shaw showed their generativity through their creative and often ingenious approaches to ideas and to the people those ideas touch. What these creative people share is their deep and genuine concern for others. The teacher, the compassionate politician, and the environmental activist also share this concern for others and for the world people share, and in doing so express their generativity.

The generativity-versus-stagnation stage of the life cycle is characterized by the struggle between giving of oneself to the next generation and stealing moments of selfishness in which one keeps one's resources for oneself. The adult who success-fully reaches a balance between the need to serve others and the need to serve the self will enter the final stage of development with few regrets.

Applications

Erikson first introduced the concept of generativity in his book *Childhood and Society* (1950). Though first introduced as an approach to understanding continuing development through adulthood, Erikson's ideas have been used by therapists as well as research scientists in a variety of situations to explain a variety of behaviors.

Therapists concerned about the psychological trauma associated with the midlife transition rely heavily on Erikson's theory of adult development to help clients un-derstand and overcome many of their fears and reservations about reaching the mid-point of their lives. Marriage and family counselors often guide their clients through the difficult process of acknowledging that their lives are half over by helping them see where they have come and what they have done to ensure a better life for their children and for the rest of the next generation.

Those individuals seeking counseling during their forties and fifties are often con-cerned that their lives are meaningless. Therapists, using Erikson's ideas about the need to give something to future generations, can guide their clients toward giving back some of what they have learned from their lives thus far. This giving may take many forms and may include monetary gifts to charities, educational trust funds, or children and grandchildren. The gift of time can be given through established volun-teer programs such as Retired Seniors Volunteer Programs, Foster Grandparents, VISTA, or the Peace Corps. Time can be spent serving the needs of local charities or schools. Letters to politicians and other types of political involvement may often help persons who suffer from a lack of meaning find purpose and direction in their lives.

Thus, the therapist confronted with a client who appears apathetic and direction-less may rely heavily on the ideas of Erikson to lead the client away from the slow-moving, stale life of self-centeredness to the more exciting, creative world of gener-ativity. In so doing, the therapist may be paving the way for the next stage of the life cycle, in which individuals review their life in an attempt to make peace with themselves before they die. Those individuals who can identify how and where they have created a better world for the next generation will find the integrity they seek and avoid the despair of a life not given to the service of others.

Many other therapeutic applications of Erikson's work are possible. One particularly interesting application involves work with incest victims. According to Sebastian Mudry in an article published in 1986 in the *Journal for Specialists in Group Work*, incest victims have many developmental crises to resolve. Those who reach the generativity-versus-stagnation stage may be able to help the next generation by sharing their experiences with others. They may become professionally trained therapists specializing in the treatment of incest victims. They will most likely work hard to ensure that their own children do not become incest victims. They may volunteer to help other incest victims learn to cope with their victimization. If, however, they are unable to resolve the crisis present during the generativity stage of adult development, they may turn toward nurturing themselves at the expense of others. They may focus on self-preservation, refusing to share with others the many insights they have to offer because of their life experiences. On the other hand, incest victims who have successfully resolved the generativity-versus-stagnation crisis are likely to discover a way to nurture themselves in appropriately selfish ways while simultaneously giving of themselves to others without giving themselves away.

Clearly, the need to achieve some sense of generativity is important, and a failure to do so may send an individual to a therapist for assistance. Therapeutic intervention, however, is not the only use for Erikson's theory. Research scientists, in an effort to determine how well individuals have resolved the conflicts important in each of Erikson's stages of the life cycle, have developed a series of questionnaires. The most commonly used measure is called the Self-Description Questionnaire, developed by Robert Boyd in 1970. Individuals are asked to say whether they are like or not like a person who would make a statement such as "I express the belief that adults should leave teenagers to work out their own problems." While most teenagers would like most adults to agree with such statements, the adult who is concerned about the next generation would most likely say he or she was not like someone who would make such a statement. Those same adults would, however, probably agree with statements such as "I express enjoyment in working with and guiding the development of young people."

Scores on the Self-Description Questionnaire can be used in a variety of ways. Organizations seeking volunteers or employees to work with youth in programs such as the Boy Scouts or Campfire Girls, or as parole officers, might want to screen applicants using the questionnaire before offering them positions.

In a direct application to the Self-Description Questionnaire, the measure has been modified to be used with low-literate adults as a tool to assist in the development of individually tailored educational programs. Robert Boyd and Larry Martin, in an article published in *Adult Education Quarterly* (1984), suggest that teachers of adult students administer the questionnaires to determine why adult learners have returned to school. They argue that understanding the motivation of the students may help create a more enjoyable learning environment. They also suggest that teachers use the questionnaire to identify their own motives for being teachers.

Context

The roots of Erikson's theory of development across the life span are deep and complex. According to Robert Coles, author of *Erik H. Erikson: The Growth of His Work* (1970), the philosopher Søren Kierkegaard had a tremendous influence on Erikson's thinking. Of particular importance were Kierkegaard's ideas about the mind. He claimed that the mind is a battleground in which the selfish desires of the individual fight against the need to survive with other individuals and eventually face a judgmental God who expects selflessness. Clearly, Erikson's work reflects pieces of Kierkegaard's thinking.

Though the philosopher's influence was substantial, the work of Sigmund Freud was instrumental in the development of Erikson's theory. From Freud's theory, Erikson retained the idea of unconscious motives for behavior and the important interplay between one's selfish desires (represented by the id) and one's moral conscience (represented by the superego). Erikson enhanced Freud's work by introducing the need to be aware of the environmental and cultural climate in which an individual develops. He also argued that the culture can determine what needs are most important to the id, as well as the values that will be incorporated into the superego.

The foundations for the proposal of the generativity-versus-stagnation stage of the life cycle can be found in Erikson's extensive observations of American Indian culture as well as veterans returning from World War II. After the war, American society was in need of a review of its goals and what kind of world it was leaving for the next generation. In the postwar nuclear age, Erikson's ideas about leaving the world a better place developed and helped shape a generation of young thinkers who devoured his book *Childhood and Society*. In the book, they found permission to question the direction in which American society was heading and affirmation of the need to attend to one's place in the world order.

The ideas about development set forth in Erikson's work were quietly revolutionary. He was the first to propose that development is a lifelong process culminating only in death. He was the first to incorporate the needs of and important influence of the culture into a theory of development. He was one of the first to expand Freud's clinical observational techniques to normal individuals and to those from a variety of economic and ethnic backgrounds.

Despite these important contributions, Erikson's theory, like most theories of personality, is difficult to test using the well-established methods of science. Some success at defining and measuring identity (Erikson's fifth stage of development) has been achieved. Such accomplishments suggest that future work with each of the remaining seven stages will be fruitful. Therapists and scientists alike are beginning to put Erikson's notion of generativity to the test. The importance of resolving the crisis that occurs during middle adulthood is likely to continue to attract the attention of therapists. In addition, research scientists depend on theories to explain their observations. Erikson's developmental theory provides a fertile ground for testing new ideas and explaining findings, and is likely to continue to be one of the most important theories of adult development, if for no other reason than that it was the first.

Bibliography

Elkind, David. "Erik Erikson's Eight Ages of Man." In *Readings in Human Development: Contemporary Perspectives*, edited by David Elkind and D. C. Hetzel. New York: Harper & Row, 1977. In an easy-to-read, conversational style, Elkind presents the eight stages of Erikson's developmental theory. Intermingles descriptions of Erikson's theory with pieces of his life story in a manner that brings his work to life. An excellent starting point for a basic understanding of Erikson's developmental theory that also provides good insight into Erikson himself.

Erikson, Erik H. *Childhood and Society.* New York: W. W. Norton, 1950. Lays the foundation for and explains Erikson's theory of development. Erikson's psychological training, his artistic background, and his excellent command of the language are evident throughout the book. The clinical method of study is described and then applied to children and to Native Americans. The concept of the ego is developed and explored through biography and literature as well as clinical case histories. Well written; should be read by anyone with an interest in personality or development.

Evans, Richard I. *Dialogue with Erik Erikson.* New York: Harper & Row, 1967. As the title suggests, this work is the result of several hours of conversation with Erikson, conducted for a film series of discussions with major personality theorists. Has appeal for the novice reader, who will discover Erikson's warmth and humanness in the dialogue. Also has appeal for those familiar with Erikson's theories in that it helps put his ideas into the context of the human condition. Discusses at length the eight stages of development, as well as Erikson's ideas on the application of his theories in the therapeutic environment. Some readers may find the question-and-answer format difficult to follow, but their efforts will be worth the insights they gain from reading the book.

Green, Michael. *Theories of Human Development: A Comparative Approach.* Englewood Cliffs, N.J.: Prentice-Hall, 1989. A must read for anyone who wants to put Erikson's ideas in the broader context of developmental theories. From the chart comparing seven theorists on sixteen characteristics, to the final chapter on the compatibility of the theories, the author encourages a critical comparison of ideas about development. The eight stages of development are described, as are the influences of culture and history on the development of individuals. The book is a textbook designed for courses in development; most readers will find it well written, easy to read, and complete with summaries and thought-provoking questions about human development. Highly recommended for those contemplating future study of developmental theories.

Schlein, Stephen, ed. *A Way of Looking at Things: Selected Papers from 1930 to 1980, Erik H. Erikson.* New York: W. W. Norton, 1987. The selected papers of Erikson chosen for this work reflect five decades of thought about development and the human condition. Works included are among the best from Erikson's writings and are organized topically, adding to readability. The chapter entitled "The Human Life Cycle" eloquently describes and provides examples of each of Erikson's proposed developmental stages, complete with graphs and charts to assist the reader in comprehending the theory. Difficult reading for the novice, but well worth the effort. Of special interest are the sketches by Erikson distributed throughout the book.

Lori L. Temple

Cross-References
Career Selection, Development, and Change, 474; Ego Psychology: Erik Erikson, 867; Identity Crises: Erikson, 1255; Integrity: Erikson, 1321; Intimacy in Adulthood: Erikson, 1363; Midlife Crises, 1575; Psychoanalytic Psychology: An Overview, 1905; Trust, Autonomy, Initiative, and Industry: Erikson, 2591.

GESTALT LAWS OF ORGANIZATION

Type of psychology: Sensation and perception
Fields of study: Cognitive processes; vision

The Gestalt laws of organization outline the way in which individuals organize their perceptions into meaningful, coherent configurations; the Gestalt perspective on which these laws are based has contributed significantly to the psychology of perception and to the study of specific issues in problem solving, social relations, and development.

Principal terms
ELEMENTISM: the theory that perception may be understood through the analysis of the simple elements of what is perceived, without reference to how those elements are put together
GESTALT: a German word for which there is no precise translation but which is generally used to refer to form, whole, or configuration
INSIGHT: a novel solution to a problem, not based on previous experience
LAW OF CLOSURE: the Gestalt principle holding that the gaps in a figure will be mentally "filled in" by the perceiver, creating a complete, whole figure
LAW OF CONTINUITY: the Gestalt principle holding that smooth, continuous patterns will be perceived as units, whereas discontinuous patterns will not
LAW OF PROXIMITY: the Gestalt principle holding that stimuli that are near to one another will be perceived as elements of a single perceptual unit
LAW OF SIMILARITY: the Gestalt principle holding that stimuli that are similar will be perceived as elements of a single perceptual unit
PERCEPTUAL CONSTANCY: the tendency to perceive figures as constant and stable in terms of shape, color, size, or brightness
PRAGNANZ: a German word referring to the "goodness" of a perceived figure, generally in terms of its simplicity and symmetry

Overview

The Gestalt laws of organization, formulated by psychologists of the Gestalt school between 1910 and 1940, are principles that outline the way in which individuals organize their perceptions of the world around them. The first Gestalt psychologists, Max Wertheimer (1880-1943), Wolfgang Köhler (1887-1967), and Kurt Koffka (1886-1941), emphasized that analysis of the elements of perceived figures was insufficient for the understanding of perception. They wanted to understand the way in which the mind organized the elements of figures into integrated configurations, or "wholes," which they termed Gestalts. Wertheimer, the founder of Gestalt psychology, introduced the Gestalt perspective into experimental psychology with his studies of the "phi phenomenon." Wertheimer showed that turning two lamps on and off alternately against a dark background induced the perception of motion: Subjects "saw" light "jumping" from one lamp to the other and back again, even though there was in fact no motion but only two stationary, flashing lights.

This illustrates the basic axiom of Gestalt psychology, which holds that the whole may differ from the sum of the parts. Wertheimer's subjects actually saw two lights being sequentially turned on and off, but they mentally organized these elements into the very different picture of a single light leaping from point to point. Clearly, perception of the light's motion was not inherent in the stimulus elements, the two stationary lamps. Instead, the perception of motion emerged from the mental reorganization of the stimulus elements. The Gestalt psychologists found similar types of perceptual organization in a variety of experimental situations, and they ultimately refined the principles involved into the four basic Gestalt laws of organization: the laws of proximity, similarity, closure, and continuity. These laws govern the perceptual organization of perceived stimuli, called "figures," once these have been perceptually distinguished from their surroundings, termed their "ground."

The law of proximity holds that items which are close together tend to be perceived as parts of the same unit. Consider the following:

XXXXXX

Most human beings will see this as a single perceptual unit, or figure, composed of six *X*'s in a row. Grouped differently, however,

XX XX XX

these basic elements become three units of two *X*'s each. This relatively simple reorganization of the elements of this figure in terms of proximity, their nearness to one another, leads to a new interpretation of what is perceived.

The law of similarity is illustrated by the following:

XXOOXX

The elements of this figure are spaced exactly as they were in the first simple figure of six *X*'s in a row. Yet most people see this figure as a set of three units of two elements each, rather than as a single unit of six elements: The *O*'s in the middle are similar to each other but not to the *X*'s which surround them, and so are seen as a separate organized unit. This demonstrates the law of similarity: Elements that are similar to one another tend to be grouped into perceptual units.

Consider the opening words of the Gettysburg Address, as typed below:

Four sc ore and se ven years a go, our fa thers . . .

The words are easy to recognize for most readers, even though there are gaps in the words "score," "seven," "ago," and "fathers." Virtually no one attempts to read "se" and "ven," or "sc" and "ore," as separate words. The gaps are "closed" perceptually, enabling the reader to perceive the words as whole units in spite of the gaps, and in some cases not to notice the gaps at all. This is the law of closure: Irrelevant gaps in perceived figures tend not to be noticed, and imperfect figures are generally perceived as integrated wholes in spite of the gaps.

The law of continuity, also called the law of good continuation, holds that continuous contours tend to be perceived as units. If one is looking at a winding river, it is easy to tell that it is a single river, a unit, because the banks form continuous boundaries and because the bright continuous surface of the water contrasts with the duller continuous surfaces of the ground on both sides. Yet when the river flows through swampy country and begins to overflow its banks to form connecting pools and marshes, it becomes more difficult to see what is river and what is overflow, pond, or marshy ground: The continuity of the banks and of the bright and dull surfaces is lost, and the river loses its identity as a single perceptual "figure."

The organization of a figure according to these four laws contributes to the *Pragnanz* of that figure, its perceptual "goodness." "Good" figures are generally simple, complete, and symmetrical. If the elements of a figure are similar to one another, are arranged in proximity to one another, and have few discontinuities and few gaps requiring closure, the figure will be relatively easy to perceive and will therefore possess greater *Pragnanz* than a figure which is not well organized in terms of these Gestalt laws. The concept of *Pragnanz* was further refined by the psychologist Julian Hochberg into the minimum principle, which holds that the organization perceived in a given figure is that which keeps changes and discontinuities to a minimum. In other words, perceptual situations tend to be interpreted in terms of the simplest and most stable figures that the stimulus elements and their organization will allow. The question of stability is of paramount importance in perception. If the perceptual world were unstable—if, for example, the trees that stand outside the window could suddenly appear to turn pink instead of green, or were to appear to alternate rapidly between a height of several inches and several thousand feet—it would be impossible to cope with the world; no organism could function in such a chaotic environment. Fortunately, the essential characteristics of stimuli, including trees, buildings, people, and objects, are perceived as constant and stable: Figures tend to retain the same apparent brightness, shape, color, size, and other characteristics as they are viewed against their grounds. These "perceptual constancies" were considered in some detail by the Gestalt psychologists, and, together with the four basic laws of organization and the principle of *Pragnanz*, help to explain how the perceptual world is maintained and interpreted in stable, constant, and systematic terms.

Applications

The principles described by the Gestalt laws of organization apply directly to everyday perception. For example, the laws of similarity and proximity become evident in every football game. At the beginning of any given play, the players of each team are close together (proximity), and are wearing the same color uniforms (similarity). The "figure" comprising the entire game situation is easily processed. As play begins, however, the organization of the teams in terms of proximity is lost: The two teams become mingled, and the primary cue as to which players are on which team comes from the similarity of their uniforms. Also, the players are in motion, which requires the perceiver to process the constant shifts in their relative positions. Consequently, *Pragnanz*, "goodness," is lost from the "figure," and the entire game situation becomes more difficult to perceive and process.

The law of closure is seen, together with the law of continuity, whenever an individual drives through an intersection. The street on which one is driving is perceived as a closed, single, continuous unit, rather than as two separate streets separated by the "gap" presented by the cross street. The fact that drivers are able to process an intersection as a simple situation of two crossed streets rather than as a complex affair of four separate streets ending at the same point contributes significantly to the ease of driving.

The best example of the law of continuity lies in its application to camouflage. Camouflage does not simply consist in being the same color as one's environment; one must also form a continuous Gestalt pattern with the elements of the environment. This is the reason for the blotchy clothing worn by hunters and soldiers. If one wishes to hide among forest leaves, a pattern of leaves dyed into one's clothing helps to form a continuous pattern with the pattern of leaves in the background. If the background consists of bare tree trunks, then vertical wavy lines are typically the appropriate camouflage: The individual's clothing can form lines of good continuation with the wavy, vertical patterns of bark against which it is seen. The idea of camouflage is to diminish *Pragnanz* and to make it difficult to distinguish the figure from the ground.

The basic principles of Gestalt psychology have applications outside the psychology of perception as well. The Gestalt psychologists held that in problem solving as well as perception, the whole may differ from the sum of its parts. Both Köhler and Wertheimer conducted studies of problem solving, the former in chimpanzees and the latter in human beings including Galileo Galilei and Albert Einstein. The Gestalt investigators found that problem solving is not merely a passive association of the elements of a given problem into correct solutions, as had been previously thought. Instead, solutions resulted from insight, the reconfiguration of problem elements into new, meaningful solutions. This view of problem solving was vigorously challenged and continues to be debated. Yet there is abundant evidence of the importance of insight in problem solving, and the Gestalt idea that the solution to a problem results from the novel reconfiguration of problem elements rather than from simple passive associations forms the basis of many modern treatments of problem solving. For example, the later Gestalt psychologist Kurt Lewin's approach to group dynamics focused on the creative reconfiguration of elements of the social world into new solutions to the problems inherent in dealing with other people in settings such as families, workplaces, and communities. Lewin's work led directly to the "leadership institutes" and "sensitivity training" found in industrial and counseling settings.

Context

Prior to the beginning of the Gestalt school, most psychologists believed that perception could best be understood through an elementistic approach, through analyzing the basic components of what subjects perceived. The majority of psychologists held a similarly elementistic view of learning and problem solving. The Gestalt perspective arose in part as a reaction to these dominant views in psychology, incurring anger and rejection from many in the field. The Gestalt school ceased to be a dominant force in experimental psychology by 1950, partly because the mechanisms underlying the laws of organization and various concepts in problem solving were not adequately specified. Yet Gestalt research into the laws of organization and related issues form a significant legacy in psychology. Later theories of perception have built heavily on Gestalt concepts, and the findings of the school have led directly to the rejection of elementistic theories and the adoption of more sophisticated views of perception, learning, and problem solving.

Other areas of psychology have also received a significant inheritance from the Gestaltists, especially from the concept that the whole may differ from the sum of the parts. It is now generally understood that the behaviors and responses of organisms may not be simple results of the stimuli that were initially presented, but may emerge from novel configurations of organism, experience, and behavior. For example, it is recognized in developmental psychology that language is not merely acquired by the passive association of words and phrases as these are learned. Rather, language emerges as a result of the active organization of linguistic elements by the child, whose ability to engage in such organization increases with maturation. In social psychology, it has been repeatedly shown that the behavior of groups may be very different from the behavior of individuals; for example, people may behave more violently and make less intelligent decisions in groups, because of the diffusion of responsibility among group members and because of various forms of social pressure. The behavior of a group of people arises from the way in which the individuals involved come together and from the processes involved in social affiliation, rather than as a simple result of the behavioral tendencies of group members as individuals.

The Gestalt perspective, and research into the Gestalt laws of organization, have contributed to the rejection of elementistic ideas in the psychology of perception, learning, and problem solving, and have provided a basis for study in many other areas. The legacy of the Gestalt school for modern psychology is significant and substantial.

Bibliography

Ericsson, K. A., and H. A. Simon. "Sources of Evidence on Cognition: A Historical Overview." In *Cognitive Assessment*, edited by Thomas V. Merluzzi, Carol R.

Glass, and Myles Genest. New York: Guilford Press, 1981. Examines the role of Gestalt theory in the development of modern cognitive science, set against the contributions of other schools of psychological thought. Accessible primarily to advanced students or those with some background in perceptual or cognitive psychology.

Hochberg, Julian E. *Perception.* 2d ed. Englewood Cliffs, N.J.: Prentice-Hall, 1978. Gives a comprehensive treatment of Gestalt principles and other areas of perceptual psychology. Explores the contributions of Gestalt theory and principles to modern theories in perception. Accessible to the college student or advanced high school student.

Koffka, Kurt. *Principles of Gestalt Psychology.* New York: Harcourt, Brace, 1935. Exhaustive account of Gestalt theory and experiments on perception by one of the school's cofounders. Extremely comprehensive, and useful for an understanding of Gestalt methodology as well as theory and findings. Accessible to the serious college student or other advanced reader.

Köhler, Wolfgang. *Gestalt Psychology.* New York: New American Library, 1947. The classic popular exposition of Gestalt theory, written by one of the school's cofounders. Provides an accessible, comprehensive treatment of the theory and the laws of organization.

Wertheimer, Max. *Productive Thinking.* Chicago: University of Chicago Press, 1982. Classic account of Max Wertheimer's original studies and observations of problem solving. Beautifully written, this book is easily read by college or high school students and contains accounts of Gestalt approaches to problems ranging from simple geometry to Einstein's development of the theory of relativity.

Wertheimer, Michael. "Gestalt Psychology." In *A Brief History of Psychology.* 3d ed. New York: Holt, Rinehart, and Winston, 1987. Wertheimer provides a concise but clearly written overview of the basic principles of Gestalt psychology, the intellectual antecedents of the theory, and its place within experimental psychology. A superb work on the subject, easily understood by the college student and quite accessible to the high school student.

Matthew J. Sharps

Cross-References

Motion Perception, 1600; Pattern Recognition as a Cognitive Process, 1747; Pattern Vision, 1752; Perceptual Constancies, 1771; Problem-Solving Stages, 1873; Sensation and Perception Defined, 2207; Visual Illusions, 2622; Visual Neural Processing, 2629.

GESTALT THERAPY

Type of psychology: Psychotherapy
Field of study: Humanistic therapies

> *Gestalt therapy, founded by Fritz Perls, is an outgrowth of the existential-humanistic approach to psychotherapy. It focuses on nonverbal behaviors, dreams, and current thoughts and emotions; as clients become more aware of denied feelings, their innate healing powers are activated.*

Principal terms

DREAMWORK: the Gestalt process of determining the meaning of one's dreams by role-playing the various parts of the dream

EMPTY-CHAIR TECHNIQUE: a Gestalt procedure in which one discusses an interpersonal conflict by addressing an empty chair as though the other person were seated in it

EXISTENTIAL-HUMANISTIC PSYCHOTHERAPY: an approach to psychotherapy that stresses one's freedom to make choices, responsibility, and the innate goodness of human beings

HERE AND NOW: a term used in Gestalt therapy that refers to allowing the client to focus only on present thoughts and feelings

HOT SEAT: a term used in Gestalt group therapy for the situation in which one of the clients sits in front of the therapist

Overview

Gestalt therapy emerged during the 1960's as a powerful alternative to the main two available therapeutic techniques, psychoanalysis and behavioral therapy. This approach to therapy, founded by Frederick (Fritz) Perls, attempts to integrate clients' thoughts, feelings, and actions into a unified whole; *Gestalt*, in fact, is the German word for "whole." Gestalt therapists believe that emotional problems as well as some of the dissatisfactions experienced by ordinary individuals are attributable to a lack of recognizing and understanding one's feelings. The fast pace of technological society and the general loss of purpose in individuals' lives has led to a numbing of emotions. Gestaltists believe that many people deny or lose parts of themselves when they are faced with the overwhelming task of coping in society; for example, a person may deny anger toward a loved one.

The role for the Gestalt therapist is to help the client become more aware of the split-off emotions. The therapist takes an active role by requiring the patient to talk about current experiences and feelings. The patient is neither allowed to look for explanations or problems from the past nor expected to talk about future plans. Gestaltists believe that anxiety is the result of an excessive focus on the future. The client is expected to attend to current feelings and experiences—to stay in the "here and now."

Gestalt therapy arose from the existential-humanistic school of psychology. Prior schools had portrayed individuals rather pessimistically, believing that human beings are relatively evil creatures whose actions are determined by forces outside their control (such as instincts or the environment). People were seen as adaptive hedonists trying to receive the greatest amount of pleasure for the least amount of effort. The existential-humanistic school of psychology portrays individuals more optimistically, believing people innately strive to achieve their fullest human potential. Failure to do so is not the result of an evil nature but rather the fault of obstacles on this path to perfection. Gestalt therapists agree with the existential-humanistic focus on individual responsibility. One freely chooses one's actions and therefore is responsible for them. There is no provision for blaming a past situation or one's current environment. Gestalt therapists encourage independence and uniqueness in their clients. They push them to be themselves rather than adopting the "shoulds" and "oughts" recommended by society. Perls emphasized this focus on independence and responsibility by stating that the process of maturation is moving from environmental support to self-support.

Probably the greatest contribution of the Gestalt style of therapy has been the techniques developed to increase individual self-awareness. These techniques are consistent with the belief that emotional problems stem from avoidance of or failure to recognize one's feelings. The Gestalt therapist is very active and confrontational during the therapy session (in fact, in a group setting, talking to the therapist is called taking the "hot seat") and frequently interprets and questions the client's statements. The goal is a genuine relationship between two individuals, free of normal social conventions, in which a free exchange of thoughts and feelings can take place.

In one technique of Gestalt therapy, called the "dreamwork," the client reports a recent dream. The Gestalt school believes that the events in a dream represent fragmented and denied parts of the personality. Rather than search for explanations in one's childhood, as in the approach of dream analysis originated by Sigmund Freud, clients are encouraged to bring the dream into the present by acting out different parts of the dream. Rather than say "There was a train in my dream," they are required to act out the part of the train. They might say "I am a train. I am very powerful and useful as long as I stay on track." This moves the focus of the dream into the here and now.

Another therapeutic technique used by Gestalt therapists involves a focus on and exaggeration of nonverbal behaviors. Gestaltists believe that much denied information is accessible through body language. For example, a client may state that she is happy and content in a relationship, while she is scowling and keeping her arms and legs crossed in a tight and tense fashion. Gestalt therapists help their clients become aware of these feelings by getting them to exaggerate their actions. A man who is talking about his wife while clenching his hand in a fist and tapping it on the table may be told to clench his fist tighter and bang it hard on the table. This exaggeration of nonverbal behavior would be to make him acutely aware of his anger toward his wife.

Another well-known procedure developed by the Gestalt school of psychotherapy is the "empty-chair technique." This strategy is employed to bring past conflicts into the here and now, where feelings can be reexperienced. The client often will relate to the therapist a disagreement with some significant other. Rather than ask for details of the encounter (a procedure that keeps the focus in the past), the therapist will encourage the client to address an empty chair in the office as though that person were sitting in it. The client must role-play the relevant situation. The therapist may also get the client to play the part of the significant other in the empty chair. This switching back and forth of chairs and roles is a powerful technique to foster empathy, understanding, and a clarification of feelings. This technique can be used not only for conflicts between individuals but also for discrepant feelings within one person.

Applications

The Gestalt approach to psychotherapy is best explained by examples. A student once reported a dream in which she remembered a gum wrapper being dropped outside a nearby church. Rather than search for a meaning of the dream's symbols in her childhood, her friend, a clinical psychologist, asked her to become the elements in the dream. She initially chose the gum wrapper. She stated that as a gum wrapper she concealed something very good and appealing and that most people took the good part from inside her and then threw her away. She stated that she felt like trash littered on a beautiful lawn and that eventually some caring person would come and throw her away.

The student then began to play the role of the church in the dream. She stated that as a church she was a beautiful building constructed from caring hands. She indicated that good things happened inside her but that she was used too infrequently. Many people were afraid or disliked coming to her, she said, and most of the time she was empty inside. The student was surprised as she completed this description of the dream. She talked about the similarity of her explanations of the two elements in the dream. When asked if she felt this way, she stated that this idea at first surprised her somewhat; however, as she continued to elaborate, she became more aware of her feelings of emptiness and loneliness. She had become aware of denied aspects of her emotions.

Gestalt therapy's active focus on nonverbal behavior and denied portions of the personality often can be quite dramatic. The judicious use of these techniques may allow insights into dynamics that are not available through ordinary interpersonal interactions. In one case, a family was being seen by co-therapists in family therapy. The family consisted of a mother, father, son, and daughter. The son was the identified troublemaker in the family, and he demonstrated a wide range of symptoms that caused the family much pain and suffering. During the course of therapy, it became apparent that the mother was an unwitting co-conspirator in these troubles. She often would rescue her son from his precarious and often dangerous situation and restore matters to normal. This served the function of ensuring her role as a "good mother," while providing the son with the reassurance that he was loved by her.

Whenever she threatened not to rescue him, he accused her of not caring for him. She inevitably crumbled and provided for his needs. The father and daughter had their own alliance in the family and, although they complained, they did not interfere in this dysfunctional family pattern that frequently ended in severe problems.

The two therapists hypothesized the pathological nature of this interaction and periodically attempted to present it to the family; however, the pattern was so important and so entrenched in the family's style of interaction that any mention of it led to vehement protests and denials that it was an issue of importance. During a therapy session, one of the therapists noticed the pattern in which the family members usually seated themselves. The mother and son sat close to each other on one side of the therapy room, while the father and daughter sat near each other across from them. The two therapists sat across from each other on the other sides of the room. One therapist, taking a cue from the Gestalt emphasis on the importance of nonverbal behaviors, moved his chair and sat in the small space between the mother and son. A stunned silence ensued. The mother and son began to show agitation, while the father and daughter, from across the room, became increasingly amused at the nature of this interaction. The therapists elicited the reactions and analyses of the family to this new seating arrangement. The mother and son continued to display uncertainty and bewilderment, while the father and daughter immediately identified that someone had dared to come between "Mom and her boy." This led to a more open discussion of the pathological nature of the family interactions. The father and daughter could see that they had allowed this damaging pattern to continue. The mother and son, while not quite as open to this discovery because of the threatening nature of the disclosure, could not deny the emotions that were aroused from someone physically invading their territory. The insights that resulted from this simple Gestalt technique moved therapy along much faster than had previous verbal interactions. It demonstrates the Gestalt tenet that a focus on nonverbal patterns of communication may allow clients to become aware of previously denied aspects of their personalities.

Context

Gestalt therapy emerged during a period of increased popularity for the existential-humanistic position in psychology. This approach, sometimes known as the "third force" in psychology, came from opposition to the earlier forces of psychoanalysis and behaviorism. Existential-humanistic proponents objected to the pessimistic psychoanalytic view of humans as vile creatures held captive by primitive, unconscious desires. They also differed from the environmental determinism set forth by the behavioral school that people are simply products of past punishments and rewards. The existential-humanistic therapists focused on the human freedom to choose one's actions (regardless of unconscious desires and past consequences), the relative goodness of the human species, and people's innate desire to reach their fullest potential. This approach fit well with the period of great social upheaval and change following World War II.

The Gestalt approach often is compared to the client-centered (or person-centered) therapy of Carl Rogers. Both types of psychotherapy endorse the basic assumptions of the existential-humanistic school; however, they differ considerably in their approach and techniques. In client-centered therapy, the client is encouraged to express his or her thoughts and feelings about a situation. The therapist remains relatively passive, giving minimal verbal prompts or paraphrasing the client's statements. The client is responsible for the direction and content of the therapy session; the therapist provides only a clarification of unclear statements or feelings. The idea behind this approach is that the therapist is providing an atmosphere of unconditional acceptance in which the client can explore his or her emotional issues. Eventually, the client's innate curative ability will take over. The Gestalt therapist, in contrast, is much more confrontational in interpreting statements and asking questions. The Gestalt approach places a greater emphasis on the interpretation of nonverbal behaviors and the usefulness of dreams. Although different in technique, both approaches point to the freedom to choose, the innate goodness of the client, and the strength of the therapeutic relationship as curative factors.

The influence of the Gestalt approach to psychotherapy diminished with the death of Fritz Perls in 1970. He was the emotional and spiritual leader of the group, and his charisma was not replaced easily. Gestalt therapy is not considered a mainstream psychotherapy; however, it does have numerous enthusiastic followers. The greatest contribution of the Gestalt orientation has been the techniques developed to assist clients in becoming more aware of hidden thoughts and emotions. Therapists from a wide variety of orientations have adapted and applied these procedures within their own theoretical framework. The impact of dreamwork, the hot seat, nonverbal interpretations, and the empty-chair techniques seems to have outlasted the theory from which they came.

Bibliography

Davison, G. C., and J. M. Neale. *Abnormal Psychology.* 5th ed. New York: John Wiley & Sons, 1990. A frequently used textbook in the field of abnormal psychology. It gives an interesting overview of Gestalt therapy practice as well as an explanation of how these techniques may be applied to abnormal behaviors. The authors present a balanced critique of Gestalt therapy and of how it fits with the existential-humanistic approach to abnormality.

Ivey, Allen E., and Lynn Simek-Downing. *Counseling and Psychotherapy: Skills, Theories, and Practice.* 2d ed. Englewood Cliffs, N.J.: Prentice-Hall, 1980. This popular textbook on psychotherapy gives a brief overview of Gestalt therapy. It includes examples of Gestalt therapists working with clients and analyzes each statement in terms of type of approach (confrontation, question, or empathy).

Perls, Frederick S. *The Gestalt Approach and Eye Witness to Therapy.* Ben Lomond, Calif.: Science & Behavior Books, 1973. Two short books printed in one volume. *The Gestalt Approach* was Perls's last attempt to rework Gestalt therapy and is one of his most complete attempts to do so. *Eye Witness to Therapy* is a collection of verbatim therapy transcripts. They are easily readable and present excellent examples of practical applications of Gestalt theories.

_____. *Gestalt Therapy Verbatim.* Toronto: Bantam Books, 1959. This book is easy to read and contains a good balance of theory and case examples. Many of the examples come from group dreamwork seminars and portray the Gestalt approach to dream analysis.

_____. *In and Out the Garbage Pail.* Toronto: Bantam Books, 1969. This is a humorous and free-floating autobiography by the founder of Gestalt therapy. Often entertaining, Perls uses his memories and experiences to illuminate principles of his theory.

Brett L. Beck

Cross-References

Abnormality: Humanistic-Existential Models, 60; Dream Analysis, 830; Existential Analysis and Therapy, 999; Group Therapy, 1120; Humanism: An Overview, 1203; Person-Centered Therapy, 1777; Self-Actualization, 2168.

GONADS

Type of psychology: Biological bases of behavior
Field of study: Endocrine system

The gonads are the mammalian male testes and female ovaries, which secrete sex hormones. These hormones determine sex differences in reproductive structures and functions and have been strongly implicated in the expression of sexual, aggressive, and maternal behaviors.

Principal terms

ACTIVATIONAL EFFECTS: the effects of sex hormone secretion on the behavior of an adult mammal, such as causing sexual desire

ADRENOGENITAL SYNDROME: a condition in which the female embryo has been exposed to excessive androgens, resulting in masculinization of the external genitalia

ANDROGEN INSENSITIVITY SYNDROME: a condition caused in the developing male embryo in which androgen receptors are not functional and the sexual organs become female in structure

ANDROGENIZATION: exposure of the developing embryo to male sex hormones

ANDROGENS: male sex hormones secreted by the testes; testosterone, the primary mammalian male androgen, is responsible for the development and maturation of male sexual structures and sexual behaviors

ESTRADIOL: the primary sex hormone of mammalian females, which is responsible for the menstrual cycle and for development of secondary sex characteristics; secreted by the corpus luteum

H-Y ANTIGEN: a protein on the Y chromosome of the male that activates the development of primordial gonads into testes

ORGANIZATIONAL EFFECTS: the effects of sex hormones on the differentiation in the developing embryo of primordial gonads, internal reproductive structures, and external genitalia

PROGESTERONE: a female sex hormone secreted by the corpus luteum of the ovary; maintains the lining of the uterus during pregnancy and the second half of the menstrual cycle

TURNER'S SYNDROME: a condition in which a fetus has only one X sex chromosome, with no second female X or male Y; causes the development of female structures

Overview

The gonads are endocrine glands that secrete sex hormones in all mammalian species. In males, the gonads are the testes, which secrete sex hormones called androgens; in the female, the gonads are the ovaries, which secrete estradiol and progesterone. These sex hormones, which are released into the bloodstream, have effects on the formation of both internal and external reproductive organs during prenatal development; later, they have important behavioral effects, particularly in the expression of sexual behaviors. They are also implicated in maternal and aggressive behaviors.

In the prenatal period (that is, before birth), as the embryo is developing, the gonads are the first sex organs to differentiate into male and female organs. Prior to the seventh week of human gestation, the gonads are identical for the two sexes. If the embryo is genetically male, the gonads differentiate into male testes at the seventh or eighth week of development. If the embryo is female, the gonads differentiate into ovaries. This differentiation is controlled by a protein called the H-Y antigen, which is present only if the embryo has a Y chromosome and is therefore a genetic male. When the H-Y antigen is present, it will stimulate receptors on the surface of the gonads to become testes. If it is absent, ovaries will automatically develop.

Once the sexual differentiation of the gonads has occurred, a sequence of events takes place which will determine the sexual dimorphism of both the internal and the external reproductive organs, and therefore the gender of the individual. This is known as the organizational effect of the gonads. If the gonads have differentiated into testes, the testes will begin to secrete androgens, primarily testosterone, which have a masculinizing effect and cause the development of the internal male structures such as the prostate, the vas deferens, and the epididymis. If there is an absence of androgens, the female uterus, Fallopian tubes, and the inner two-thirds of the vagina will develop instead. A genetic disorder called Turner's syndrome illustrates how the absence of androgens results in the development of female structures. In this disorder, the individual has only one X chromosome, which prevents the development of ovaries, and no Y chromosome to create H-Y antigen; therefore, there are no testes to secrete androgens. This individual's other internal sexual organs are normal female structures.

The external or visible genitalia develop in much the same way, governed by the presence or absence of androgens. The embryos of both sexes begin with undifferentiated genitals that are capable of becoming characteristically male or female, depending on androgen exposure. If there is androgen exposure, the primordial phallus will differentiate into the glans or head of the penis, the genital swelling will become the scrotum (into which the testes will eventually descend from the abdominal cavity), and the genital tubercle will differentiate into the shaft or main body of the penis. If there is no androgen exposure, then the primordial phallus will become the clitoris, the genital swelling will become the labia majora, and the genital tubercle will become the labia minora and the outer one-third of the vagina. Again, regardless of the genetic sex of the embryo, the absence of stimulation of primordial genital tissue by androgens will result in female structures. The presence of androgens is required for masculine development. In the above example of Turner's syndrome, the external genitalia are those of a normal female even though she lacks ovaries.

At birth, the infant has his or her primary sex characteristics: testes or ovaries and both internal and external sexual organs characteristic of males or females. It is not until puberty that an individual's gonadal hormones begin to determine further development. Puberty begins with the secretion of hormones by the hypothalamus and the pituitary of the brain; they travel via the bloodstream to the testes or ovaries, causing the production of the gonadal hormones that will direct the development of sexual maturation. These hormones will direct the emergence of secondary sexual characteristics. The ovaries begin to produce estradiol, while the testes secrete testosterone. Estradiol causes enlargement of the breasts, growth in the lining of the uterus, widening of the hips, changes in the deposition of fat, and maturation of the female genitalia. Testosterone is responsible for growth of facial hair, deepening of the voice, masculine muscular development, and growth of the male genitalia.

Estradiol secretion in the female is also responsible for the onset of the first menstrual cycle. The cycle begins when an ovarian follicle is stimulated by hormones from the pituitary and thereby matures. It then secretes estradiol, which causes growth in the lining of the uterus in preparation for implantation of a fertilized ovum. It also causes ovulation, in which the follicle ruptures, releasing an ovum. During the second half of the cycle, the follicle itself becomes the corpus luteum, which produces both estradiol and progesterone. The latter hormone is responsible for maintaining the lining of the uterus during pregnancy. If the ovum is not fertilized, both estradiol and progesterone production decrease and the uterine lining is sloughed off in menstruation.

Applications

The influence of gonadal hormones has been studied in relation to the activation of sexual, maternal, and aggressive behaviors. The effects of gonadal hormones on behavior can be subdivided into organizational and activational influences, with the former occurring during prenatal development and the latter occurring after puberty.

Psychologists have studied the ways in which prenatal exposure or insensitivity to androgens organize sexual behavior. In the adrenogenital syndrome, the adrenal glands secrete unusually high levels of androgens, to which the developing embryo is exposed. If the embryo is male, normal development will occur. If the exposed embryo is female, masculinization will occur, with enlargement of the clitoris and possibly fused labia. Researchers at The Johns Hopkins University studied thirty young women with adrenogenital syndrome to determine whether androgenization affected their sexual orientation—that is, the gender of their preferred sexual partners. The women described themselves as homosexual or bisexual at approximately four times the rate that occurs naturally in random populations of women. This hints that exposure of the developing female fetus to androgens may affect sexual orientation, possibly by altering the organization of the brain in ways that are not yet understood. A similar finding has occurred in primate research. When androgens were injected into monkeys pregnant with female fetuses, these androgenized infants became significantly different from their nonandrogenized peers in displaying more malelike behaviors, such as engaging in attempted mountings of other females.

The failure of male fetuses to be androgenized properly occurs in the androgen insensitivity syndrome. These genetically male individuals will develop female genitalia and, if reared as females, will easily assume feminine sexual identities and overwhelmingly prefer male sexual partners. There is some possibility, then, that prenatal androgenization encourages a preference for female sexual partners, while lack of such exposure results in a preference for male sexual partners, regardless of genetic sex. It should be remembered, however, that this remains quite speculative and conclusive research has not yet been conducted.

The activational effects of gonadal hormones on adult sexual behavior has also been of interest to psychologists. While estradiol and progesterone strongly influence the sexual behaviors of lower animals, these hormones do not seem to influence human female sexual behavior. For example, while both estrogen and progesterone levels fluctuate considerably over the menstrual cycle, women can become aroused at any time in the cycle and are not more easily aroused when these hormones are especially high or low. Further, when a woman's ovaries are surgically removed or cease to produce hormones after menopause, sexual activity and interest is not affected.

There is some evidence that androgens, either present in small amounts secreted by the adrenal glands or ingested in the form of synthetic male hormones, will cause greater sexual desire in females and more frequent instigation of sexual activity but will have no effect on an already-established sexual orientation. The influence of androgens on male animals is direct: All male mammals respond to the presence of testosterone with increased sexual desire. Without testosterone, sperm production and copulatory ability cease.

Much aggressive behavior among animals takes place within the context of reproductive behavior. It comes as no surprise, then, that aggressive behaviors in both sexes are also strongly influenced by gonadal hormones, particularly androgens. Offensive attacks and competitive behaviors between males, as well as interfemale aggressiveness and maternal aggression, are increased by exposure to androgens in most mammals.

One of the most stable behavioral differences between males and females is aggression; males display higher levels of aggression at all ages and in all forms. Because this sex difference has been observed in toddlers, before strong socialization influences have had their impact, it is speculated that prenatal exposure to androgens is partly responsible for these behavioral differences. This same relationship holds for all other mammalian species: the greater the prenatal androgenization, the more aggressive the subsequent behavior.

The relationship between aggressive behavior and testosterone levels has been studied in a variety of ways. One avenue of research has been to examine the testosterone levels of males who display different levels of aggressive behavior. For example, the testosterone levels of male prisoners with a history of violent crime have been compared with the frequency of their violent behavior while incarcerated. No relationship between the androgen levels and current aggressive expression has been found; however, androgen levels have been positively correlated with the frequency of these prisoners' aggressive behaviors in adolescence. Perhaps by adulthood, learning had intervened to modulate this relationship, with some high-testosterone males able to exert control over their aggressive impulses while some men with lower testosterone levels learn to vent their aggressiveness.

With regard to the effects of gonadal hormones on maternal behavior, the findings are clear in most lower animals. In laboratory rats, for example, sequences of progesterone followed by estradiol will facilitate nest-building behaviors. No such relationship, however, seems to hold for humans. It seems that maternal behavior is determined largely by learning and by an early bonding between mother and infant and that caretaking behaviors are not influenced by hormonal activation.

Context

Research concerning the effects of gonadal hormones on behavior is one of the many avenues of investigation into the development of gender identity, an individual's sense of being a man or a woman. There are many determinants of such identity: one's genetic makeup, prenatal sex hormone exposure, one's internal and external genitalia, the gender to which one is assigned at birth, and socialization—learning about culturally appropriate gender behaviors through interaction with parents and peers. Most often, all these determinants are consistent with one another, and the individual develops a clear, stable sense of gender identity.

Future research concerning gonadal hormones will continue in two major directions: the effects of gonadal hormones on the sexual differentiation of the brain and the interaction between sex hormones and adult sexual behaviors. Most research on sexual differentiation of the brain has been conducted with nonhuman species. For example, it has been found that testosterone "masculinizes" the brains of birds to produce typical male birdsong and produces male or female sexual behaviors in laboratory animals. The way in which this masculinization occurs is somewhat paradoxical: Inside the brain of the male embryo, testosterone is converted to estrogen, the hormone that actually produces the masculinization. In females, on the other hand, a protein exists in the neurons of the brain that prevents estrogen from effecting such masculinization.

In humans, it is known that the absence of prenatal androgen exposure sets the brain in a female pattern, which causes the pituitary to function in a cyclical manner, thus creating the menstrual cycle. Some interesting initial research with humans suggests that, as a result of prenatal hormone exposure, there is greater lateralization of male brains than of female brains. Therefore, there is more specialization of the two cerebral hemispheres in males and more crossover of functions across the two hemispheres in females. This notice remains speculative and will be subject to considerable scrutiny.

Research interest will continue to be directed toward discovering the role of gonadal hormones in adult sexual behavior. As mentioned previously, one of the newer areas of study concerns the question of prenatal hormonal determinants of sexual orientation (homosexual or heterosexual partner preferences). Studies will also continue to be focused on the age-old question of sexual motivation in general to determine the levels and kinds of sex hormones that either enhance or depress sexual interest.

Bibliography

Beyer, Carlos, ed. *Endocrine Control of Sexual Behavior.* New York: Raven Press, 1979. This is a superb collection of review articles concerning hormonal influences on the sexual behavior of mammals. Particularly helpful in describing the methodology of such analysis.

Drickamer, Lee C., and Stephen H. Vessey. *Animal Behavior: Concepts, Processes, and Methods.* 2d ed. Boston: Prindle, Weber and Schmidt, 1986. An excellent, detailed text that describes the various physiological determinants of animal behavior. Includes chapters on sexual, reproductive, and aggressive behaviors.

Graham, Robert B. *Physiological Psychology.* Belmont, Calif.: Wadsworth, 1990. A comprehensive presentation of the major aspects of the physiological determination of behavior in all mammalian species. The chapter devoted to sexuality and reproduction covers most of the effects of gonadal hormones in detail.

Money, John, and Anke A. Ehrhardt. *Man and Woman, Boy and Girl.* Baltimore: The Johns Hopkins University Press, 1972. This is an accessible text which describes genetic and hormonal anomalies in fetal development and the consequences of these conditions on gender-identity development.

Unger, Rhoda Kesler. *Female and Male: Psychological Perspectives.* New York: Harper & Row, 1979. This classic test concerning the psychology of sex differences has two chapters which focus on the interaction between sex hormones and the development of gender identity, both prenatally and at puberty.

Barbara E. Brackney

Cross-References

GRAMMAR AND SPEECH

Type of psychology: Language
Field of study: Descriptive methodologies

Grammar and speech are the building blocks of the human communication systems known as languages. The study of language structure has enhanced growth in a number of areas in psychology, including language acquisition, the biological basis for language, and the relationship between language and thought.

Principal terms
CRITICAL PERIOD: a limited period of time during which a particular behavior may be acquired
GENERATIVE GRAMMAR: a grammar that projects the structure of a potentially infinite number of sentences, including both those already produced and those yet to be uttered
MORPHEME: the smallest part of a word that has a discernible meaning
MORPHOLOGY: the rules in a given language that govern how morphemes can be combined to form words
PHONOLOGY: the specifications for a given language of which speech sounds may occur and how they may be combined and of the pitch and stress patterns that accompany words and sentences
SUFFIX: a morpheme that attaches to the ends of words
SYNTAX: the rules in a given language that determine which sequences of words constitute possible phrases and which sequences do not

Overview

Human beings everywhere, despite differences in geography, culture, and ethnicity, have a capacity for language, a system of communication primarily involving a patterned, rule-governed sequence of oral sounds. The rules that human beings implicitly use to produce and understand such communication are collectively known as grammar, and the vocalizations that serve as the vehicle of the communication are called speech.

When most people think of grammar, they usually think of a set of arbitrary rules learned in school about correct and incorrect ways of speaking or writing. Indeed, such rules do constitute a grammar of sorts, one that prescribes standards of appropriate style. Grammar, however, has a wider and more important meaning, because without a grammar no language is possible. In fact, every speaker of a language knows the rules of the grammar of that language without being explicitly taught. Grammar, in its most important sense, is the set of rules that each language has and that each native speaker of that language knows even before going to school; it determines what the basic building blocks of the language are (the words, morphemes, sounds) and specifies the rules for combining those basic elements into meaningful utterances. Grammar is simply the structure of that unique human behavior called language.

Language scientists generally subdivide language into a set of structural subsystems, each of which has its own set of rules, or regular patterns. When discovered, these rules can be seen to operate in every utterance of that language. Each of these subsystems—syntax, morphology, and phonology—therefore is a grammar, although the term "grammar" itself in its everyday use is usually associated only with syntax.

The syntax of a language is the set of rules which govern how meaningful elements, the words, are combined into the permissible sequences known as sentences. Syntax also dictates how sentences can be combined with other sentences to form more complex utterances and how elements within sentences can be rearranged to change the focus of a sentence without changing its meaning. For example, speakers of English know that the sequence of words "the dog chased the cat" means that an instigator of an action, a dog, behaved in such a way to affect the second participant mentioned in the string of words, the cat. Moreover, they know that the word "the" must precede and never follow words such as "cat" and "dog." Finally, they know that the sequence "the cat was chased by the dog" is merely a paraphrase, a restatement, of the original string and not a contradiction of it.

The morphology of a language, the second subsystem, defines the basic set of elements which operate in the formation of words. Each of these basic elements is called a morpheme. Many morphemes may be words in a language, but some morphemes are less than an entire word. For example, the English suffix -*s* attached to a word such as "cup" states that there is more than one cup; it is apparent to any speaker of English that this suffix (ending) is considerably less than a word. Nevertheless, the -*s* is a meaningful element in the English language and constitutes a morpheme, or minimal meaningful unit, of the language. The way words are constructed is rule-governed and is therefore a kind of grammar; for example, the -*s* that signals "more than one" is always attached to the end of the word, not to the beginning of it, and it cannot be inserted in the middle. This fact about English is predictable. If English speakers encounter a new word which designates some object, they know that talking about more than one of these objects usually requires the addition of the -*s* suffix to the new word. This implicit knowledge is a kind of grammar known as morphology.

The third important structural subsystem of language is phonology, or the sound system of a language. Each of the world's languages uses only some of the vocal sounds that human beings are capable of producing, and this limited set is further constrained regarding what sounds may follow one another at the beginnings, middles, and ends of words. For example, the English language has both /t/ and /l/ as sounds which may. be used in words, and though /l/ may follow /t/ in the middle of words such as "antler" and "butler," there are no English words beginning with this sequence of sounds, nor are there likely to be any. The sequence *tl* simply does not occur at the beginning of English words, although there is no physiological reason that it cannot. Human beings are perfectly capable of producing such a sound combination. It is the grammar of the sound system of English—its phonology—which prohibits such a possibility.

These subsystems of language are found in every one of the world's languages, even though the particulars of each subsystem and its importance are unique for each language. As an example, languages such as modern-day English can be compared to classical Latin, the ancestor language of French, Italian, and Spanish. In English, the ordering of words is of paramount importance. A sentence such as "The boy loved the girl" has only one meaning, and changing the sequencing of words would drastically change that meaning. That is, if the words "boy" and "girl" were interchanged, the resulting sentence, "The girl loved the boy," would mean something entirely different. The initiator of the state of love is now the girl, not the boy. Thus, in English, the critical information of who is doing what to whom is given in the syntax, in the ordering of words. In Latin, on the other hand, although there is surely word sequencing, since words can only be expressed one at a time, the word order—the syntax—does not indicate relationships as it does in English. Instead, the matter of who is doing what to whom is given by morphology, by suffixes attached to the ends of words. The sentence "The boy loved the girl" could be expressed by any of the following: "puer puellam amabat," "puellam puer amabat," "amabat puer puellam," "puellam amabat puer," and so on. That is, the arrangement of words has little effect on meaning; the endings on the words tell speakers of Latin who does what. The *-m* at the end of the word for "girl" signals that the girl is affected by the action and is not the initiator of it. These facts about the two languages show that word order is more important to English than it is to Latin and that endings on words are more important to Latin, even though English continues to make use of endings to some degree (the *-ed* on "love" indicates, for example, that an action or state occurred at some past time).

The fact that all languages have a grammar, a predictable pattern underlying every utterance, allows human languages to be unique among all the communication systems found in nature. Most important, grammar allows people to talk about new things, about events that occurred in the past, about events that might possibly occur in the future, and even about things that can never be. A grammar allows people to produce an infinite number of possible sentences because words can be combined and recombined in many ways to generate many different meanings. This possibility makes language qualitatively different from the songs and calls of birds, which are rigidly structured to allow only a limited number of meanings; from the dance of bees, which has the single function of indicating the location of nectar; and even from the gestures of the apes, which can indicate only a limited set of communications.

Applications

The complexity and variation in systems of grammar have led to a number of speculations about the nature of the human mind in particular, about the relationship between language and thought, and about how such complex systems could be achieved by human children before they are capable of logical thought. The first of these two areas, also known as linguistic relativity, is discussed in a separate entry in this volume. The second, the possibility that at base all languages are essentially the same because they are constructed by human beings who have an innate capacity for language, has been proposed by linguist Noam Chomsky, the founder of the field of syntactic inquiry known as generative grammar.

Examining the complexity of the syntax of English, Chomsky suggested that the capacity for language must be innate, that human beings have an inborn language acquisition device which enables them to determine the grammar of the language spoken by the people who rear them. Chomsky explained that much of what young children hear must be full of errors and false starts, and yet before age five, most children speak their native language with a high degree of accuracy. He suggested that the language acquisition device must act as a kind of analyzer which assigns a structure to the incoming stream of speech. The resulting analysis then becomes the foundation of the grammar that permits children to produce new, original sentences of the language they hear all around them.

This speculation fueled much research during the 1960's and 1970's, and the result is that most language scientists—linguists and psychologists alike—agree that indeed the capacity for language acquisition is innate; the actual nature of the innate capacity, however, remains uncertain. Research has generally found that parents and other caregivers tend to be extremely careful in the kinds of speech they address to children; that is, they tend to speak without the errors and the false starts Chomsky had supposed. Moreover, they tend to pause and change the pitch of their voices at precisely those places in an utterance where the grammar would assign an important boundary. In many ways, then, the speech addressed to children seems an ideal teaching device, and so Chomsky's hypothesis that children formulate a grammar on the basis of fragmentary and poorly structured input has been disconfirmed. It has also been found, however, that even very young infants tend to prefer the sound of human voices to other sounds and are capable of telling the difference between very similar but distinct speech sounds. Thus, it is clear that human beings are predisposed to acquire language.

Other evidence also supports the notion that there is a biological predisposition to language. In his book *Biological Foundations of Language* (1967), Eric Lenneberg proposed that there is a critical period for language acquisition, an age beyond which the acquisition of a first language would not be possible. That is, Lenneberg contended that a child deprived of the opportunity to acquire a language—any language at all—would never be able to do so if the deprivation continued past the onset of puberty. Supporting evidence for this hypothesis suggested a discontinuity in language abilities at adolescence. Children who suffer trauma to the parts of the brain where language is processed, for example, tend to recover if the injury occurs before puberty but typically do not recover their language abilities if the injury occurs in their midteen years. In addition, children who are exposed to a second language during childhood apparently acquire that language with little difficulty when compared with adults facing the same task. This too seems to support a critical period for language acquisition. Moreover, case studies of feral children raised without language by nurturing animals such as wolves have indicated that these children failed to acquire language when introduced into civilization.

These kinds of evidence provide only partial (and debatable) support for the critical-period hypothesis. For example, no two injuries are exactly alike, so the successful recovery of one patient from a brain injury compared to the failure of another may stem from a number of causes. The facility of children compared to the difficulty for adults with respect to second-language acquisition may result from children's lack of self-consciousness. Finally, children raised by wolves during the last several centuries may have been abandoned by their parents because they had some apparent disability; perhaps the children lacked the cognitive or speech skills necessary to acquire language.

In 1970, however, a thirteen-year-old girl suffering from severe neglect was found. The child of a psychotic father and an abused and half-blind mother, "Genie," as she came to be called, had been locked in a darkened room since infancy and deprived of all genuine human contact. She was absolutely devoid of any language skills, although her hearing was found to be normal. Since medical records indicated normal development during infancy, save for a hip defect, and since she was clearly past puberty, Genie provided a test case for the critical-period hypothesis.

Removed from her abusive environment and given the attention of caring adults, Genie made remarkable progress. At first, she seemed able to acquire language after all, and reports of her linguistic achievements were thought to herald the demise of the critical-period hypothesis. It soon became evident, however, that although Genie was making excellent progress with social and cognitive skills, her development of syntax and morphology lagged far behind. She was able to acquire a vocabulary of some size—a word list—but she failed to put words together in the ways that were typical of children acquiring language during the usual developmental period. She also had difficulty with those English morphemes that show relationship among elements in a sentence. In short, although Genie could understand words and word meanings, she was having considerable difficulty mastering grammar. Genie's case provides partial support for the critical-period hypothesis; after puberty, parts of language may still be acquired, but a full elaboration of the grammatical patterns that underlie a language will not be achieved. The importance of the early childhood years to the acquisition of language skills is clearly demonstrated by this case.

Genie's progress with language acquisition—or lack of it—could not be mapped without a knowledge of the parts of language, an understanding of syntax and morphology. Similarly, the accomplishments of young children with respect to language acquisition could not be appreciated without a knowledge of the structures underlying grammar and speech. The field of language acquisition is an entire area of study which crucially depends on knowledge of the structure of language. To study acquisition requires a knowledge of what is being acquired.

A third area which depends on an understanding of grammar and speech is the machine recognition and production of speech. This project requires a knowledge of the units of linguistic analysis, the physical properties of these units, and the rules which relate units to one another. In short, it requires as complete an understanding as possible of syntax, morphology, and phonology, the structural subsystems of language.

Context

Although interest in language is as old as language itself, prior to the nineteenth century investigations were philosophical and speculative. Questions about language were likely to concern the origins of language or the identity of the oldest language. During the early part of the nineteenth century, newly discovered relationships between languages fueled interest in a field of study now called comparative and historical linguistics, which attempted to ascertain which languages derived from the same prehistoric ancestor language. Late in that century, however, interest began to turn away from the comparison of languages and toward an investigation of languages on their own terms. In the early part of the twentieth century, the scientific study of language was encouraged by the great American linguists Edward Sapir and Leonard Bloomfield.

Both Sapir and Bloomfield were spurred on by the study of the indigenous languages of America, the languages spoken by the peoples often called American Indians. These languages were unwritten, so recording them involved a detailed investigation of their phonology, morphology, and syntax. The languages of Europe were also subjected to this new, rigorous scientific study, now called linguistics.

At first, scientific linguistics dealt mainly with phonology and morphology and studied syntax only as an afterthought. The publication of Noam Chomsky's *Syntactic Structures* (1957), however, revolutionized the field. This small book redistributed the rankings among the various subfields of language by showing the formal relationships among apparently diverse structures in syntax; what had previously been backgrounded in the study of language, the syntax, was now seen as the central focus of linguistic inquiry. In fact, syntax became so important within linguistics that Chomsky and his colleagues argued for an autonomous syntax, a system of structural relations that has an existence apart from sound and meaning. During the 1970's and 1980's, many linguists abandoned this notion and opted instead for a pragmatic analysis of language, a description based on how particular words, syntactic structures, phonological features, and other patterns of discourse such as overlaps and interruptions among participants in a conversation are used to achieve certain effects in the real world. This approach has the effect of integrating the subsystems of language so that the focus is on the basic circumstance of communication: people talking.

Bibliography

Crystal, David. *What Is Linguistics?* London: Edward Arnold, 1968. A brief, eminently readable introduction to the areas of study covered in linguistics. Assumes no prior knowledge, yet manages to dispel in a lively, engaging style some major misconceptions people tend to have about language and to explain what sorts of inquiries are linguistically relevant. Also discusses the applications of linguistic knowledge to other areas, such as language teaching and speech pathology.

Hall, Robert Anderson. *Linguistics and Your Language.* Garden City, N.Y.: Doubleday, 1960. An introduction to linguistics aimed at the general reader. Clearly explains linguistic terminology. Covers the debate between prescriptivism and descriptivism, and discusses matters of sound, form, meaning, and system in language, as well as historical change and regional differences.

Laird, Charlton Grant. *The Miracle of Language.* Greenwich, Conn.: Fawcett, 1953. A well-written introduction to the study of language. Examines word, grammar, and speech from a historical perspective. Discusses the antecedents of modern English words, sounds, and structures, and tries to dispel notions of good and "bad" grammar.

Lyons, John. *Noam Chomsky.* New York: Viking Press, 1970. Anyone who wishes to understand the foundations of Chomsky's theory of generative grammar should start with this book. Lyons places Chomsky's work in the context of modern linguistics and provides an introduction to the thought of one of the most influential linguistic thinkers of the twentieth century. Since Chomsky's own books tend to be quite abstract and difficult, Lyons aids the general reader in gaining a foothold in difficult terrain, with the additional advantage that Chomsky read, commented on, and corrected the manuscript. Thus, the book avoids as much as possible any distortion or misinterpretation of Chomsky's work.

Sapir, Edward. *Language: An Introduction to the Study of Speech.* New York: Harcourt Brace, 1921. The classic introduction to language. Probably the most eminent linguist of the twentieth century, Sapir provides his own viewpoint on language, drawing from his vast knowledge of many of the world's languages. He demonstrates how all languages share some common features and yet differ markedly in their structures; what can be rendered in a single word in one language may require an entire proposition in another. Much of the foundation for theories of linguistic relativity can be found in this slim volume, along with much of the justification for the universality of language structures. Required reading for all those interested in language study.

Marilyn N. Silva

Cross-References

Artificial Intelligence, 299; Language: The Developmental Sequence, 1387; Language Acquisition Theories, 1394; Language and Cognition, 1401; Language in Primates, 1407; Linguistic Relativity Theory, 1450; Linguistic Structure: Phonemes and Morphemes, 1457; Psycholinguistics, 1918.

GRANDPARENTHOOD

Type of psychology: Developmental psychology
Fields of study: Adulthood; aging

Since the 1970's, there has been a new interest in clarifying the nature and importance of grandparenthood. The connection between grandparent and grandchild has been described as "vital," and empirical research has attempted to define the values and satisfactions of the role of grandparent.

Principal terms

COMPONENTS OF GRANDPARENTING: as described by Helen Kivnick, these include the meaning of the grandparent role, the behaviors involved, and the satisfaction experienced

GRANDPARENTS' MOVEMENT: the development of efforts to spotlight the importance of grandparents via grants for research, the enactment of legislation, and the creation of programs to bring the generations together

MODERNIZATION OF GRANDPARENTHOOD: changes to the role of grandparent in contemporary society, often including a reduction of the importance of the grandparent

NORMATIVE TIME: the average or expected time for an event to occur; for becoming a grandparent, it has been said to be between forty-five and sixty years of age

PSYCHOSOCIAL STAGES: the eight stages in Erik Erikson's model of human development from infancy to old age; old age involves resolving the "crisis" of integrity versus despair

Overview

Studies by demographers attest the rapid increase of the over-sixty population and the fact that there are more grandparents living now than ever before. Life expectancy for men is approaching seventy-five; for women it is approaching eighty. Politicians have become aware of this fact; when Grandparents' Day was proposed in Congress in 1978 as the first Sunday after Labor Day, fewer than ten representatives dared vote against it.

Life-span textbooks in the area of developmental psychology make their readers aware that later adulthood is one of the most meaningful periods in the family life cycle. It is frequently when the "launching" of the adult child takes place. Often the "empty nest" is portrayed as a time of loneliness and depression, when, in fact, it is in some ways more satisfying than any of the earlier stages of married life. Much of this satisfaction can derive from the interest with which grandparents watch their grandchildren develop. Grandparenting has a fulfilling function and offers grandparents a unique type of immortality.

Historically, there has been an ambiguity in defining the role of the grandparent. Much is written about changing styles of grandparenting and about its variation among cultures and subcultures. Questions arise about a possible gap between contemporary and traditional roles. One author refers to it as the "modernization" of grandparenthood. It is generally agreed among those researching American grandparenting that there is considerable disparity of viewpoints concerning what constitutes fulfillment of the grandparenting role. These viewpoints range from seeing grandparenthood as a meaningless, unimportant role on the one hand to that of Lillian Troll (1983) on the other, who characterizes grandparents as "the family watchdogs," ever on the lookout for trouble and ready to provide assistance if a family crisis occurs.

The delineation of this ambiguity in roles has occurred in certain areas. A sampling of these includes the issue of authority. Parents vary in their flexibility to release authority over their child to the child's grandparent. Other areas are gift-giving and indulgence, financial support, frequency of visits, offering suggestions on child rearing, and baby-sitting. The continuing lack of definition is one of several primary reasons for the subject of grandparenthood to have emerged as a legitimate topic for psychological investigation. Andrew J. Cherlin and Frank F. Furstenberg, Jr., in 1986, noted that such studies "until recently were a mere footnote in the social scientific literature on the family." They further state that articles prior to 1960 on the topic referred to grandparents as "isolated, cut off from kin, a social problem." They were often characterized in the psychoanalytic literature as sources of potential harm because of their meddlesome behavior. This review of the literature whetted the appetite of Cherlin and Furstenberg. Their book entitled *The New American Grandparent* (1986) is a result of what was probably the first representative nationwide study of American grandparents. As sociologists of the family, they present grandparents as often trying to balance their adult needs for autonomy and independence with their needs for intimacy and strong sentimental ties.

A stream of thought continuously present in the literature is the theme of the fundamental reciprocal value of a positive relationship between grandparents and grandchildren. It is especially noticeable during family crises such as divorce or times of dire economic need. Single parents often rely heavily on their parents to come to the rescue in child rearing. Many popular titles emphasize the importance of grandparents as sources of wisdom, care, and emotional support. One such book is entitled *Grandparents: Then God Created Grandparents and It Was Very Good* (1976). Its author, Charlie Shedd, is a minister and family counselor. He speculates that the most important grandparenting role is that of providing companionship. Myron and Mary Madden edited a book entitled *For Grandparents: Wonders and Worries* (1980), emphasizing how grandparents provide a sense of family history. Arthur Kornhaber and Kenneth J. Woodward, who coauthored a book on grandparenting, characterize grandparents as the "vital connection." Kornhaber faults the nuclear family as a "new social contract" that destroys the emotional bonds between grandparents and grandchildren. These writers agree that with the existing sharp increases in broken families and working mothers, grandparents are needed more than ever.

This underscoring of the value of grandparenthood has kept researchers curious and looking for persistent details to the "vital connection" that can be studied scientifically. The basic design has been the interview and the clinical interview. The questionnaires for such interviews have to be refined so that both children and grandparents are able to express themselves freely. As an example of this, social psychologist Nicholas Zill, in 1976, supervised interviews with a randomly selected, nationally representative sample of children between the ages of seven and eleven. The intent of the study was to learn about their well-being—their health, happiness, and problems. As a follow-up, Zill, along with Furstenberg (1981), studied the families from the 1976 study whose families had been disrupted by then or were in serious difficulty. A randomly selected subsample of children from maritally stable homes was also interviewed. At this time, the psychologists told their interviewees that they would like to interview their grandparents (this included both groups—the disrupted families and the maritally stable ones). They were able to get addresses and telephone numbers of this nationally representative group of grandparents. In 1983, Cherlin and Furstenberg, armed with their information, conducted 510 telephone interviews (since they were scattered from coast to coast) with grandparents of children they had studied in 1981.

The telephone interviewers of the 510 grandparents found them to be mostly very interested in or enthusiastic about speaking at length about their families. Only 4 percent were indifferent or reluctant. Such studies, new as regards grandparenting, are designed to lend a greater and more systematic insight into the grandparenting roles that contribute to the well-being of both the grandchildren and the grandparents.

Applications

Despite the fact that empirical work in the area of grandparenthood is at worst preliminary and at best descriptive, there are aspects of grandparenthood that studies are revealing to be fundamental. Lillian E. Troll (1983) makes one of these very clear in her statements about the contingencies of grandparenting. The "timing" contingency, she states, is crucial. For example, people generally make a decision to become parents, but rarely do people make a decision to become grandparents. One's becoming a grandparent is decided by someone else, no matter how eager or how reluctant one may be to have that title. Timing, then, is one of the contingencies that determines the positive or negative character of grandparenting. If one's children make one a grandparent too early, it may be seen as an indictment of one's own parenting. There is an "expected time" for grandparenthood; the implication is that it can be too early, on time, or too late. Troll notes Bernice Neugarten's finding that the expected time, or "normative time," is between ages forty-five and sixty. Earlier is too early and later is too late in American middle-class society for grandparenting to be optimal.

Troll hastens to add that there are many other contingencies to consider other than timing, but she gives a poignant personal example of a timing problem. She states that when she acquired the title "grandmother," she had returned to the university to complete her dissertation, with an academic job waiting in the wings. Her children were "finding themselves," she had separated from her husband, and her father was dying; the timing, therefore, of her grandparenthood—too early—caused it to be of minimal importance. Her sister, on the other hand, had not found a niche outside the home when she became a grandmother; her first year was spent sewing baby clothes, writing letters to her daughter (the baby's mother), and waiting for new photographs.

Other contingencies are the health and vigor of the grandparents; their job status (employed, nonemployed, or retired); the existence of other family (one grandmother studied had forty grandchildren); personality, which often shifts to either a doting grandparent or an assertive one, contrary to the person's previous parenting style; and social responsibilities. Troll's belief is that social responsibilities often change— not to disengagement from the family but to entering into the family more completely.

The essential components of grandparenting are described by Helen Q. Kivnick (1985). They are the meaning of the role, the behaviors characterizing the role, and the degree of satisfaction experienced in the role. Kivnick also isolated empirically five dimensions of grandparenthood: centrality, valued elder, immortality through clan, reinvolvement with personal past, and indulgence. She viewed the meaning of grandparenthood as comprising all five dimensions, although one or more of these may be dominant. For example, seventy-four-year-old Mr. Goodman placed the highest emphasis on "valued elder" as a grandparenthood dimension. He looked forward to passing along his Hebrew blessing as well as sharing attendance at synagogue and other involvement with religion. His only child, a son, however, married a Catholic woman. Rather than accept their daughter-in-law as a loving partner to their son, the elder Goodmans have continued to hope the marriage will break up. The older couple is not particularly welcome in their son's home, and their daughter-in-law offers them little access to their grandchildren. Such a situation leads to continuous disappointment, and Mr. Goodman's experience as a grandparent does not include being a valued elder.

The second component, grandparenting behaviors, has been the easiest for researchers to observe, describe, and measure. Some behaviors that have been studied are troublemaker, surrogate caregiver, formal, fun-seeking, and friendly mutuality. Erik Erikson's writings emphasized the "significant other" concept, in which the person rewards and punishes, and teaches explicitly in concepts and implicitly in behavior. The grandparent who mediates, litigates, rewards, and cherishes can be a significant other.

Kivnick's third component is that of degree of satisfaction experienced in the grandparenting role. The example of Mr. Goodman illustrates this component. Part of her study involved the mental health of grandparents as it relates to their grandparenting. She learned that grandparent behavior is not associated with mental health as much as it is with meaning or with satisfaction. The dimension of indulgence may also illustrate the satisfaction component. Grandparents may notice grandchildren's need of shorts, T-shirts, or pajamas, for example, and may take grandchildren a toy or book or treat them at their favorite fast-food restaurant. If the grandparents' religious heritage has been passed to their children, they may achieve satisfaction at seeing it transmitted to the grandchildren. These satisfactions automatically involve Kivnick's dimensions of centrality, valued elder, immortality through clan, and reinvolvement with personal past.

Much of the research makes reference to the "new American grandparent," sometimes referred to as "contemporary" or "modernized." Kornhaber believes that, as many families become isolated and weakened, the United States is becoming a society of surrogates: surrogate grandchildren, surrogate parents, and surrogate grandparents. It is crucial, he contends, that the three-dimensional family be kept intact, since "every time a child is born, a grandparent is born, and a new three-generational family is formed." His research has shown that the grandparent-grandchild bond is second in emotional importance only to the parent-child bond. He calls for the repeal of what he calls the new social contract, characterized as narcissistic rather than altruistic, committed to individuality and independence instead of family, and committed to a materialistic and acquisitive philosophy that emphasizes personal pleasure.

The "grandparents' movement" has established the role of grandparents as important and necessary. It has validated the fundamental value of the three-generational family system and its emotional attachments. In Kornhaber's research, hundreds of children revealed in their own words and drawings what loving grandparents mean to them and how they suffer when their grandparents ignore or abandon them. Cherlin and Furstenberg's research through their telephone interviews categorized grandparents as belonging to three groups: detached, passive, and active. The active group, being the largest, was in turn determined to be supportive, authoritative (or parent-like), and influential (living closer and visiting often). Roughly half the grandparents were active, while one-fourth were detached and one-fourth were passive. The general view by most research sociologists and psychologists is that if grandparents select a detached or passive role, it will be at considerable emotional cost both to the grandchild and to the grandparent.

Context

Minimal attention was paid to the subject of grandparenting in social scientific research prior to the 1970's. Since then, there has been a notable rediscovery of grandparents, largely attributable to the increase of divorce and remarriage in the 1960's and 1970's. They often stepped in to provide valuable service and assistance in times of need. Much of what "knowledge" had existed about grandparenthood was based on speculation and was composed of stereotypes about grandparents. In order to uproot such stereotypical thought, some hard work had to be begun. This took the form of systematic research as well as work on the part of legislators at local, state, and national levels. One of the leading researchers to emerge has been

Lillian E. Troll, who has been critical of much of the existing literature as incomplete, ambiguous, contradictory, and tentative. She is noteworthy, along with Vern L. Bengston, for moving the study of grandparenthood into the arena of a systematic and cumulative building of knowledge.

Legislators went to work for grandparents because the growing number of adults age sixty and above makes this segment of society important politically. State and federal legislators became aware of the increasing proportion of aging voters; an act of Congress established Grandparents' Day in 1978. The Foundation for Grandparenting in Mount Kisco, New York, was established in the early 1980's to encourage natural grandparenting. Since 1982, legal statutes have emerged for protecting grandparents' rights to see their grandchildren following a parental divorce. There are at least forty states that have statutes addressing various rights of grandparents.

A number of social programs have been initiated over the past twenty years to bring the generations together. These include Volunteers in Service to America (VISTA), the Retired Senior Volunteer Program (RSVP), Senior Companions, the Foster Grandparent Program, and the Senior Community Service programs. There is a new emphasis on making grandparenthood an explicit part of schools, hospitals, community centers, museums, religious institutions, and social service organizations; such programs are designed to provide the young with the presence of older adults.

Erikson's eight-stage formulation of the human life cycle proposes that an essential component of psychosocial old age is the renewal of an age-appropriate balance for all seven earlier tensions. This psychosocial old age culminates in what he termed the crisis of integrity versus despair. The positive resolution in old age of all previous crises of the life cycle is the integrated (whole) individual. Grandparenthood may now be a situation in which the individual participates for several decades. Its importance may be extreme, merely for maintaining good mental health—fostering an integrated old age as opposed to one of despair.

Bibliography

Bengston, Vern L., and Joan F. Robertson, eds. *Grandparenthood.* Beverly Hills, Calif.: Sage, 1985. The chapters in this volume represent a significant effort to pull together much of the available research and thinking about grandparenting. Provides much information about and insight into intergenerational relations and needs. The authors should serve as models for researchers who wish to expand on this aspect of family life and American society as a whole.

Cherlin, Andrew J., and Frank F. Furstenberg, Jr. *The New American Grandparent.* New York: Basic Books, 1986. A groundbreaking book based on the first representative nationwide study of American grandparents. Presents a sometimes troubling portrait of grandparenthood characterized by strong sentimental ties and loose bonds of obligation. Today's grandparents often have the economic resources, vigor, and mobility to live apart from the family, but at the cost of intimacy, substance, and sentiment.

Kivnick, Helen Q. "Grandparenthood and Mental Health: Meaning, Behavior, and

Satisfaction." In *Grandparenthood*, edited by Vern L. Bengston and Joan F. Robertson. Beverly Hills, Calif.: Sage, 1985. Kivnick addresses grandparenthood in terms of three interrelated components: meaning, behavior, and satisfaction. The mental health of grandparents relates more to meaning and satisfaction than to behavior. Levels of dimensional importance are likely to shift as the individual ages and life circumstances change.

Kornhaber, Arthur, and Kenneth L. Woodward. *Grandparents/Grandchildren: The Vital Connection.* Garden City, N.Y.: Anchor Press, 1981. The authors explain the "vital connection" that links these generations to each other and expose what they call the "new social contract" that is destroying the emotional bonds between grandparents and grandchildren. For the first time, hundreds of children reveal in their own words and drawings what loving grandparents mean to them and how they suffer when grandparents ignore or abandon them.

Troll, Lillian E. "Grandparents: The Family Watchdogs." In *Family Relationships in Later Life*, edited by Timothy H. Brubaker. Beverly Hills, Calif.: Sage, 1983. Troll raises the question, "Why is there a heightened interest in grandparenting at this point in time?" Her answers point to the importance of families in the lives of Americans, contrary to the prevailing myths that the family is dying. Her portrayal of grandparents is that of "family watchdogs," ever on the lookout for trouble and ready to provide assistance if a family crisis occurs.

F. Wayne Reno

Cross-References

Ageism, 156; Aging: Cognitive Changes, 180; Generativity in Adulthood: Erikson, 1075; Integrity: Erikson, 1321; Retirement, 2109.

GROUP DECISION MAKING

Type of psychology: Social psychology
Field of study: Group processes

Group decision making is one of the oldest areas of inquiry in social psychology. Research has shown that groups have profound effects on the behavior of their individual members; the decisions that people make in groups can be quite different from those that they make on their own.

Principal terms

CHOICE SHIFT: the difference between the decision of a group and the average decision of group members as individuals

GROUP CONFIDENCE: the group members' collective belief about the quality of their group decision

HETEROGENEITY: variety in a group; important differences among members regarding perspectives, values, or areas of expertise

INFORMATIONAL INFLUENCE: a change in a person's decision as a result of arguments, logic, reasoning, and information presented by others

NORMATIVE INFLUENCE: a change in a person's decision as the result of the decisions of others

PROCESS LOSS: the failure of a group to perform at the level of its best member

SOCIAL DECISION SCHEME: a rule describing the process by which a group transforms a set of individual choices into a single group choice

Overview

Important societal, business, medical, legal, and personal decisions are often made by more than one person. Psychologists in the field of group decision making have attempted to describe the processes through which such decisions are made. The process in which a set of individual group members' decisions becomes transformed into a single group decision can be described by a "social decision scheme." Research by James H. Davis and his colleagues at the University of Illinois has shown the conditions under which groups use various rules, such as adopting the preference of the majority or that of the member who has the best answer.

The nature of the decision problem facing a group must be considered in an evaluation of the group's decision process. Psychologist Ivan Steiner pioneered the analysis of the group's task in his book *Group Process and Productivity* (1972). Steiner identified three characteristics of group tasks that should be considered in analyzing group decision making. The first is the ability to subdivide the task into subtasks that members can perform individually. For example, a group can plan a meal by making one member responsible for selecting a meat dish, another for choosing a vegetarian entrée, another for choosing desserts, and so forth. Other tasks, in which division of labor is not feasible, are said to be "unitary." In general, the more important the decision, the more difficult it is to divide it among group members. Yet it is often precisely because a decision task is important that it is given to a group rather than an individual. Therefore, even if some aspect of the task (such as gathering information) can be done individually, final responsibility for the decision rests with a set of people.

Another variable in group tasks is the nature of the goal. In many cases, there is no "best" or "right" decision; the process is simply a matter of determining the group preference. Other decision tasks are called "optimizing" by Steiner because it is assumed that some optimal decision exists. The group's task is to find it. Most important group decision tasks are not only unitary but also optimizing. Finally, Steiner noted that the rules governing the group's decision-making activities were a critical feature of the task. If the group members are not constrained to particular procedures, the task is "discretionary."

Important insights about decision process and quality in unitary, optimizing, and discretionary tasks have been gained by comparing the decision-making behavior of individuals acting alone to that of persons in groups. It is apparent that the way people behave in groups is different from the way they behave alone. As a consequence, decisions made in groups can differ radically from those made by the same persons acting alone. It is not uncommon for group decisions to be more extreme than an average of members' individual decisions.

Such a "choice shift" can lead to group decisions that are better than—or not as good as—the average member's decision. The average group member's judgment or choice provides one standard against which group decision quality can be compared. Another is the quality of the best individual member's decision. Steiner called any decrease in quality from the decision of the best member, acting alone, to the group decision "process loss." Reviews of group decision research typically conclude that an average group performs above the level of its average member but below that of its best member. It is possible, however, for groups to reach better decisions than can any of their members alone.

Social psychologists recognize two types of influence that can cause group decisions to differ from those of individual group members: normative and informational. Normative influence comes merely from knowledge of the positions of others. One may come to doubt the quality of the alternative that one has selected simply by learning that everyone else believes that another alternative is superior. Confidence in a belief is difficult to maintain in the face of others who are in consensus about a contrary belief. The second type of influence, informational influence, results from logic or argument concerning the relative merits of various choice alternatives. Both types of influence usually operate in group decision making. Through normative or informational influence, individual group members can shift their positions.

Since groups usually make decisions under conditions of uncertainty, it can be difficult to evaluate the actual quality of a group decision. For this reason, the study of "group confidence" has become increasingly important. In general, groups exhibit greater confidence about the quality of their decisions than do individuals. This can be a desirable outcome if commitment to the group decision is necessary. As Irving Janis has shown in his analyses of political and managerial decision making, however, groups can be highly confident even while making disastrous decisions. Proper evaluation of group decision quality and confidence requires an ability to evaluate objectively the decision outcome. This has been done in a number of laboratory studies.

Applications

Experiments on group judgment by Janet A. Sniezek and her colleagues show how different group and individual decision making can be. These studies examine two aspects of group performance in judgment tasks. The first, accuracy, refers to the proximity of the consensus group judgment of some unknown value to the actual value. The other performance measure is one of confidence. Results show that consensus group judgments are typically far more accurate, and somewhat more confident, than the independent judgments of comparable individuals.

Two factors appear to be related to an increase in judgment accuracy in groups. One is the tendency of some groups to develop group judgments that are quite different from the members' individual judgments. A representative study asked students to judge various risks by estimating the annual frequency of deaths in the United States from each of several causes. A minority of group judgments were either higher or lower than all the members' individual estimates. For example, individual members' estimates for a given cause of death were 300, 500, and 650, but the consensus of these persons as a group was 200. This phenomenon is often associated with great gains in group judgment accuracy, but unfortunately, such radical shifts in judgment as a result of grouping can also lead to extreme process loss. Some groups become far more inaccurate than their average members by going out of the range of individual estimates.

The second factor that is related to improvements in the accuracy of group judgment is heterogeneity within the group. On the whole, groups that begin with a wide variety of judgments improve more in comparison to their average members than groups that begin with more homogeneity. This supports the creation of groups with members from different ethnic, racial, religious, or educational backgrounds. Such differences are likely to promote heterogeneity, because the members of the group will have different sources of information and varying perspectives. Groups that lack sufficient heterogeneity face the danger of merely averaging their individual contributions. The result of averaging is to fail to improve appreciably in comparison to the level of quality of the average member.

There have been many efforts to identify procedures that are better than discretionary procedures in improving the quality of group decisions for optimizing tasks. Many group techniques have been developed in an attempt to eliminate factors that are thought to contribute to process loss. The most popular techniques are designed to alter group discussion. Some inhibit normative influence by restricting the extent to which group members can reveal their preferences. Instead, group discussion is limited—at least initially—to a thorough evaluation of all options.

Other techniques for enhancing group decision making are designed to suppress the extent to which members are influenced by irrelevant factors. For example, status effects can operate in groups, causing the person with the highest status to exert a greater influence on the group decision than other members. This is undesirable if the high-status person's judgments are no more accurate—or even less accurate— than those of other group members. Other factors that have been shown to be irrelevant include the amount of participation in group discussion and self-confidence. Perhaps the most well-known technique developed to maximize informational influence and minimize irrelevant influences is the Delphi technique. This procedure prevents any potential problems of noninformational influence by not allowing face-to-face interaction. Instead, group members are given periodic anonymous feedback about the current positions of other group members. Often, group members provide information and logic to support their positions. More advanced technology, such as that available with computerized group decision support systems, has greatly expanded the ability to control group decision-making processes.

In addition to the goal of improving the quality of group decision making, some theorists have stressed the importance of increasing group members' satisfaction with their decisions. This objective remains somewhat controversial, since it is not always the case that people are more satisfied with better decisions and less satisfied with inferior ones. Ironically, people appear to be most satisfied when given the opportunity for group discussion—though this is precisely what is often eliminated in the hope of improving group decision quality.

Nevertheless, high group confidence can be an important end in itself. Presumably, groups with more confidence in their decisions are more committed to implementing them successfully. The increasing use of groups for decision making in organizations is based in part on this principle. Confidence in decision making can be increased by encouraging the participation of employees from various segments and levels of the organization. With such participative decision making, not only is confidence increased, but the number of organizational members who support the decision is increased as well.

Context

Historically, scientific interest in group phenomena in general has been linked to social movements. Group research seems to thrive in the "we" decades, compared with the "me" decades. Interest specifically in group decision making, however, has tended to be stimulated by political and economic events.

Irving Janis carefully analyzed decision making by groups in President John F. Kennedy's administration. He diagnosed numerous problems regarding the way in which the Bay of Pigs crisis was handled during group meetings. Collectively, the symptoms represent "groupthink," a narrow-minded approach to decision making that is caused primarily by a strong attachment of the group to its prevailing viewpoints. Janis shows how Kennedy altered the group decision process to accommodate and stimulate diverse perspectives during meetings about the Cuban Missile Crisis.

For many reasons, the study of decision making by groups is likely to become increasingly important to psychologists. As a result of the collectivist nature of most cultures, psychology will need to become less individualistic as it grows in non-Western societies and as social psychology expands to encompass more cultures. In addition, the growing interdependence of nations means that more and more global decisions will be made by groups of leaders, not by individual leaders.

Events within the United States can also be expected to create further demand for scientific investigation of group decision making. American organizations are using groups to a larger extent than ever before. For example, the group meeting is the most common approach to forecasting within organizations. The movement toward group decision making has been influenced in part by the apparent success of groups in Japanese firms. The desire to provide greater representation of workers in decisions should result in the increased use of groups for decision making.

While group decision-making research and applications are encouraged by national and global changes, these are not sufficient to bring about a genuine revolution in the making of decisions. There also needs to be an increase in the capacity to use groups. Here, too, it is reasonable to expect developments that support the use of groups in decision making. Major advances in communications allow more people to participate in the decision process in a timely fashion. They also have the potential for creating techniques that lead to higher-quality decision making than can be provided by traditional meetings.

Bibliography

Davis, James H. "Social Interaction as a Combinatorial Process in Group Decision." In *Group Decision Making*, edited by H. Brandstatter, James H. Davis, and Gisela Stocker-Kreichgauer. London: Academic Press, 1982. Emphasizes models of group process. Good presentation of the social decision scheme approach, particularly as it has been applied in research on jury decision making.

Guzzo, Richard A., ed. *Improving Group Decision Making in Organizations.* New York: Academic Press, 1982. A collection of articles by group decision researchers. Despite its title, it is not a how-to book but rather an exploration of research paradigms that have potential applications to the improvement of decision making by groups. Topics include coalition formation, group remembering, and social judgment analysis.

Hastie, Reid. "Experimental Evidence on Group Accuracy." In *Decision Research*, edited by B. Grofman and G. Owen. Vol. 2. Greenwich, Conn.: JAI Press, 1986. A review of research on the quality of decisions made by groups. Strong emphasis on literature pertaining to decision making by juries. Also includes discussion of data on confidence.

Janis, Irving Lester. *Victims of Groupthink.* Boston: Houghton Mifflin, 1972. An illustration of the factors that can lead groups to make poor decisions with great confidence; includes dramatic examples based on historical incidents. Appropriate for a general audience.

McGrath, Joseph Edward. *Groups: Interaction and Performance.* Englewood Cliffs, N.J.: Prentice-Hall, 1984. Thorough and thoughtful integration of research on group performance. Includes numerous figures and research reports, as well as balanced discussions of ongoing and past debates. Appropriate as a text or reference book.

Sniezek, Janet A., and Rebecca A. Henry. "Accuracy and Confidence in Group Judgment." *Organizational Behavior and Human Decision Processes* 43 (February 1, 1989): 1-28. A research article showing how group and individual judgment accuracy and confidence can be compared. Technical, but the figures and main results can be appreciated by the student.

Steiner, Ivan Dale. *Group Process and Productivity.* New York: Academic Press, 1972. A classic work that will remain important in the group decision-making literature. Analyzes the components of successful group performance and the processes required to get there. Scholarly rather than entertaining.

Janet A. Sniezek

Cross-References

Consumer Psychology: Decisions, 669; Cooperation, Competition, and Negotiation, 689; Crowd Behavior, 737; Decision Making as a Cognitive Process, 769; Groups: Nature and Function, 1125; Theories of Intergroup Relations, 1356; Leadership, 1419.

GROUP THERAPY

Type of psychology: Psychotherapy
Field of study: Group and family therapies

Group therapy allows individuals to enter into the therapeutic process with others who have the same or similar problems. This gives an individual much more freedom of expression and the support of others from within the group.

Principal terms
DISCLOSURE: the point at which a member of a group will share private feelings and concerns
GROUP DYNAMIC: the commonality of purpose that unites a group of people and their desire to succeed
GROUP LEADER: a qualified and trained therapist whose work is to lead the group through the therapeutic process
SESSION: the time span allotted to and agreed on by the group as an acceptable time in which to complete the necessary therapy
THERAPEUTIC PROCESS: the various stages of understanding through which an individual will pass during a therapy session

Overview

Society to a greater or lesser degree always forms itself into some kinds of groupings, whether they are for economic stability, religious expression, educational endeavor, or simply a sense of belonging. Within the field of psychotherapy, many theories and practices have been developed that deal with specific problems facing individuals as they try to relate to their environment as a whole and to become valuable members of society. Available approaches range from psychoanalysis to the more recently formulated transpersonal therapy. Taking advantage of the natural tendency for people to form groups, therapists, since the years following World War II, have developed various forms of group therapy. Therapy groups, although they do not form "naturally," are most frequently composed of people with similar problems.

Among the different types of group counseling available are those that focus on preventative and developmental aspects of living. Preventative group counseling deals with enhancing the individual's understanding of a specific aspect of life. These aspects range from simple job-seeking skills to more complex studies of career changes in midlife. Developmental groups are composed of well-adjusted people who seek to enhance their social and emotional skills through personal growth and transformation. Conversely, group therapy is concerned with remedial help. The majority of people entering group therapy are aware that they have dysfunctional components in their life; they are seeking group work as a possible way of resolving those problems. The size of most groups ranges from four to twelve participants. Sometimes all the members in the group belong to one family, and the group becomes a specialized one with the emphasis being on family therapy. Treating the problems of one family member in the larger context of the whole family has proved successful.

There are as many approaches to therapy as there are therapists; thus, the direction that any given group takes will be dependent on the group leader. Group leadership is probably the one factor that is vital in enabling a group to succeed in reaching both individual and group goals. Often there will be two therapists involved with the one group, the second therapist sometimes being an intern or trainee.

There are definite advantages, both economic and therapeutic, to group therapy. The economic burden of paying for therapy does not fall solely on one person's shoulders; moreover, the therapist can use his or her time economically, helping a larger number of people. More important, group work may be much more beneficial than individual therapy for certain people. Often the group setting will produce conditions similar to those the member faces in real life and can thus offer an opportunity to face and correct the problem.

In group therapy, a "session" consists of a number of meetings; the number is specific and is usually determined at the beginning by the group leader. Flexibility is a key concept in counseling, however, and if a group requires more time and all the participants agree, then the number of sessions can usually be extended. Therapists have generally come to accept five stages as being necessary for a group to complete a therapy session. These five stages do not have definite boundaries; indeed, if a group experiences problems at any stage, it may return to earlier stages.

Orientation is a necessary first step in establishing a sense of well-being and trust among the group's members. A therapy group does not choose its own members; it is a random and arbitrary gathering of different people. Each member will critically assess the group as to whether this group will benefit them significantly. One way for participants to discover the sincerity of the membership of the group is to reveal something of the problem which brought them to the group in the first place, without going into a full disclosure. An individual can then assess from the responses of the other members of the group whether they are going to be empathetic or critical. After the orientation stage comes the transitional stage, in which more self-revelation is required on the part of the individual members. This is usually an anxious time for members of the therapy group. Yet despite this anxiety, each member must make a commitment to the group and must further define the problem that has brought him or her to the group in the first place.

When the transitional stage has proved successful, the group will be able to begin the third stage, which involves a greater sense of cohesiveness and openness. This sense of belonging is a necessary and important aspect of group therapy. Without this feeling, the subsequent work of resolving problems cannot be fully addressed. By this time, each member of the group will have disclosed some very personal and troubling part of their lives. Once a group cohesiveness has been achieved, the fourth stage—actually wanting to work on certain behavior-modifying skills—becomes dominant. At this point in the therapeutic continuum, the group leader will play a less significant role in what is said or the direction taken. This seeming withdrawal on the part of the leader allows the group participants to take the primary role in creating changes that will affect them on a permanent basis.

As with all therapeutic methods and procedures, regardless of school or persuasion, a completion or summation stage is vital. The personal commitment to the group must be seen in the larger context of life and one's need to become a part of the greater fabric of living. By consciously creating a finale to the therapy sessions, members avoid being limited in their personal growth through dependence on the group. This symbolic act of stepping away from the group reaffirms all that the group work achieved during the third and fourth stages of the therapeutic process.

Applications

Group work offers participants an opportunity to express their feelings and fears in the hope that behavioral change will take place. Group therapy only takes on significance and meaning when the individual members of the group want to change their old behavioral patterns and learn a new behavioral repertoire. Most individuals come from a background where they have experienced difficulties with other members of their immediate family. Whether the problem has been a spousal difficulty or a parental problem, those who enter into therapy are desperately looking for answers. The very fact that there is more than one person within the group who can understand and sympathize with another's problem begins the process of acceptance and change.

A group will very quickly become close, intimate, and in some ways self-guarding and self-preserving. Through continually meeting with one another in an intense emotional environment, members begin to look upon the group as a very important part of their life. When one member does not come to a meeting, it can create anxiety in others, for the group works as a whole; for one person not to be present undermines the confidence of those who already lack self-esteem. There are also those who come to group meetings and express very little in the way of what is actually bothering them. While even coming into the therapeutic process is one large step, to disclose anything about themselves is too painful. For those who remain aloof and detached, believing that they are the best judge of their own problems, the group experience will be a superficial one.

According to Irvin D. Yalom, therapy is "an emotional and a corrective experience." The corrective aspect of therapy takes on a new meaning when placed in a group setting. There is general agreement that a person who seeks help from a therapist will eventually reveal what is truly troubling him or her. This may take weeks or even months of talking—generally talking around the problem. This is equally true of group participants. Since many difficulties experienced by the participants will be of an interpersonal nature, the group acts as a perfect setting for creating the conditions in which those behavioral problems will manifest. One major advantage that the group therapist has over a therapist involved in individual therapy is that the conditions that trigger the response can also be observed.

For those people who believe that their particular problem inhibits them from caring or even thinking about others, particularly the narcissistic or schizoid personality, seeing the distress of others in the group often evokes strong sympathy and caring. The ability to be able to offer some kind of help to another person often acts as a catalyst for a person to see that there is an opportunity to become a whole and useful member of the greater community. For all of its limitations, the group reflects, to some degree, the actual real-life situations that each of its members experiences each day.

The acknowledgment of another member's life predicament creates a cohesiveness among the members of the group, as each participant grapples with his or her own problems and with those of the others in the group. As each member becomes supportive of all other members, a climate of trust and understanding comes into being. This is a prerequisite for all group discovery, and it eventually leads to the defining of problems and thus to seeking help for particular problems shared by members. When the individual members of a group begin to care and respond to the needs of the other members, a meaningful relationship exists that allows healing to take place. Compassion, tempered by understanding and acceptance, will eventually prove the ingredients of success for participating members.

Context

Immediately after World War II, the demand for therapeutic help was so great that the only way to cope with the need was to create therapeutic groups. Group therapy did not boast any one particular founder at that time, although among the first counseling theorists to embrace group therapy actively were Joseph Pratt, Alfred Adler, Jacob Moreno, Trigant Burrow, and Cody Marsh. Psychoanalysis, so firmly placed within the schools for individual psychotherapy, nevertheless became one of the first therapeutic approaches to be applied to group therapy. Gestalt therapy and transactional analysis have proved extremely successful when applied to the group dynamic. Fritz Perls was quick to apply his theories to group therapy work, although he usually worked with one member of the group at a time. Gestalt group therapists aim as part of their treatment to try and break down the numerous denial systems which, once overcome, will bring the individual to a new and more unified understanding of life. Eric Berne, the founder of transactional analysis, has postulated that the group setting is the ideal therapeutic setting.

Group therapy has certainly not been fully accepted in all quarters of the therapeutic professions. Advocates of group therapy have attempted to show, through research and studies, that group therapy is equally effective as individual therapy, but this claim has not settled all arguments. In fact, what has been shown is that if the group leader shows the necessary warmth, understanding, and empathy with the members, then success is generally assured. If the group leader is more on the offensive, however—even taking on an attacking position—then the effects are anything but positive.

Group therapy continues to play an important role within the field of professional care. Perhaps what has been lacking and will need to be reassessed is not so much whether the theories work but whether the participants gain as much as they can from group work. There has been a general lack of systematized study and research into the effectiveness of group therapy, especially as far as feedback from the participants of the group therapy experience is concerned. This reluctance on the part of psychologists and counselors to assess more closely the type of therapy that is being offered will change as participants of group work expect a greater degree of accountability from the professionals who serve them.

Bibliography

Corey, Gerald, and Marianne Schneider Corey. *Groups: Process and Practice.* 2d ed. Monterey, Calif.: Brooks/Cole, 1982. This book is primarily concerned with identifying the main therapeutic stages and assessing the important role that the group leader plays in the process.

Donigian, Jeremiah, and Richard Malnati. *Critical Incidents in Group Therapy.* Monterey, Calif.: Brooks/Cole, 1987. Six incidents are chosen by the authors and are presented to therapists from six different therapeutic approaches. Client-centered therapy, Gestalt therapy, individual psychology, reality therapy, rational-emotive therapy, and transactional analysis approaches are then applied to the same incidents.

Peterson, Vincent, and Bernard Nisenholz. "Group Work." In *Orientation to Counseling.* 2d ed. Needham Heights, Mass.: Allyn & Bacon, 1990. This chapter gives a very concise yet broad survey of group work as it relates to the general field of counseling and counseling theory. Acts as a good introduction to the field.

Rogers, Carl Ransom. *On Becoming a Person.* Boston: Houghton Mifflin, 1961. Carl Rogers' influence on group work is acknowledged by all in the field. Rogers was mostly involved with encounter groups, but the theories and approaches spoken about in his book form the basis of much of group therapy practice today.

Yalom, Irvin D. *The Theory and Practice of Group Psychotherapy.* New York: Basic Books, 1985. Yalom's book is a comprehensive work on group therapy. The entire subject of group therapy, from method to application, is covered both from a theoretical viewpoint as well as from the experiential perspective. Actual cases are used as examples of what happens during a group therapy session, making this work indispensable.

Richard G. Cormack

Cross-References

Behavioral Family Therapy, 394; Community Psychology, 618; Couples Therapy, 718; Group Decision Making, 1114; Person-Centered Therapy, 1777; Psychotherapeutic Goals and Techniques, 1996; Self-Actualization, 2168; Strategic Family Therapy, 2382.

GROUPS: NATURE AND FUNCTION

Type of psychology: Social psychology
Field of study: Group processes

The structure and function of groups has stimulated a large quantity of research over the years. What groups are, how groups form, and the positive and negative effects of groups on individuals are the primary areas of research that have provided insights into social behavior.

Principal terms

DEINDIVIDUATION: an individual's loss of self-awareness, resulting in a breakdown in the capacity to self-regulate

DENSITY: the topographical dimension of amount of space per person in a group; changing the number of people affects social density, whereas changing the size of the room affects spatial density

GROUP FORMATION: a series of stages that groups experience in their development; the stages have been termed forming, storming, norming, performing, and adjourning

IDENTITY: a sense or definition of one's self

INTERPERSONAL DISTANCE: the physical proximity between individuals

SELF-ATTENTION: an individual's increased self-awareness, resulting in the capacity to self-regulate

SOCIAL SUPPORT: the physical and psychological comfort given to an individual by relatives and friends

Overview

In any newspaper, one is likely to find several captivating stories that highlight the powerful negative influence that groups can exert on individuals. For example, one may recall the tragic violence exhibited by British sports fans at the international soccer matches in Belgium in the spring of 1985. One may also consider the one-man crime wave of Fred Postlewaite. For twenty years, Postlewaite engaged in a cross-country vandalism spree against the Sigma Alpha Epsilon college fraternity, which had rejected him in his youth.

There are equally dramatic instances of the powerful positive influences of groups. When the Spy Run Creek in Fort Wayne, Indiana, began to flood its banks a few years ago, a group of the community's youths voluntarily participated in efforts to hold back its rising waters. There was also the rescue of four-year-old Michelle de Jesus, who had fallen from a subway platform into the path of an onrushing train. Everett Sanderson, a bystander, leapt down onto the tracks and flung the child into the crowd above. After he failed in his attempt to jump back to the platform, he was pulled up to safety at the last instant by bystanders.

These real-life events are noteworthy because they illustrate the universality of groups and the various ways that groups influence individual behavior. Although everyone can attest the prevalence of groups and the power that they can wield over individuals, several characteristics of groups are not as well defined. Several questions remain as to what groups are, how groups form, what groups look like, and the disadvantages and advantages of group membership. In spite of these questions, psychologists have come to understand many aspects of groups and the ways in which they influence individual behavior.

The members of Congress who compose the House of Representatives of the United States are a group. The urban committee deciding how to allocate budgetary resources for unwed mothers in a particular city is a group. The members of a carpool sharing a ride to the train station everyday are a group. The family seated around the dinner table at home in the evening is a group. The acting troupe performing *Hamlet* is a group. There are other examples of groups, however, that may be a little less obvious. All the unwed mothers in an urban area might be considered a group. A line of people waiting to buy tickets to a Broadway show might be thought of as a group. People eating dinner at the same time in a diner might even be considered a group. The people in the audience who are watching an acting troupe perform could behave as a group.

There are several ways in which people come to join the groups to which they belong. Some groups people are born into. Several types of groupings are influenced in large part by birth: family, socioeconomic status, class, race, and religion. Other groups are formed largely by happenstance. Consider the constellation of factors that go into the determination of the membership of a line of the same people waiting for the 8:05 ferry every day. Some groups, however, are determined more clearly by intentional, goal-oriented factors. For example, a group of people at work who share a common concern for well-being, health, and fitness may decide to form an exercise and nutrition group. Students interested in bringing in a musical band might decide to form a committee to organize bake sales, car washes, and fund drives in order to raise the money needed to achieve this goal. Finally, group memberships are sometimes created or changed as an effort toward self-definition or self-validation. For example, one can try to change one's religion, political orientation, professional associations, friendships, or family in an effort to enhance how one feels about oneself—or how others feel about one. An individual searching for a positive self-definition may join a country club, for example, to benefit from the social status acquired from such group membership.

Almost regardless of the underlying reason for someone's membership in a given group, the work of Bruce Tuckman suggests that groups seem to progress through a relatively consistent series of stages or phases in their development. Forming refers to a phase of coming together and orientation. Group members become acquainted with one another and define the requirements of group membership as well as the tasks to be performed. Storming refers to a phase of polarization and conflict. During this phase, group members deal with disagreements, compete for attractive positions within the group, and may become dissatisfied with other group members or the group as a whole. Norming refers to a phase when conflicts are solved and group members arrive at agreements regarding definitions of tasks and the requirements of group membership. Performing refers to the phase when group members concentrate on achieving their major task and strive toward shared goals. Finally, for some groups, adjourning refers to the disbanding or dissolution of the group after task completion.

For example, consider a special task force created to search for a missing child. During the forming stage, the members of this group will volunteer, or be appointed, into the group. Although the general goals and definition of the group may have been set up with the decision to implement such a task force, a storming phase would occur that would lead the group members into the sometimes difficult task of defining specific procedures of operation, responsibilities of particular task force members, a functional hierarchy, and so on. The norming phase would represent the resolution of the polarizations that emerged during the storming phase, as the committee proceeded to establish an agenda, a decision structure, and a means of implementing decisions. During the performing phase, the task force would actually perform the tasks agreed upon during the norming phase. Having finished its task, the group would then be adjourned.

When considering the basic structure and function of groups, the topography of a group refers to the physical features of the group. This includes such things as the size of the group, the composition of the group, and the relationships between the various members of the groups. These topographical features of groups have been the focus of countless studies.

One obvious physical feature that could vary from one group to another is size. Some scholars have categorized group types in terms of size. For example, some researchers have found it useful to distinguish between small primary groups (from two to twenty group members), small nonprimary groups (from three to a hundred members), large groups (one thousand to ten thousand members), and largest groups (ten thousand-plus members). While such classifications may be interesting, the realities of everyday groups are typically more modest than such grand schemes would suggest. In a large number of settings, naturally occurring, free-forming groups typically range in size from two to seven persons, with a mean of about three. There are certainly exceptions to this rule of thumb; for example, most audiences watching theater troupes are considerably larger than three people. Nevertheless, most of the groups in which people interact on a day-to-day basis are relatively small. The size of a group tends to set the stage for many other topographical features of group life.

Applications

The number of relationships possible in a group, according to James H. S. Bosard, is a direct consequence of the size of the group: the larger the group, the larger the number of possible relationships the individual might find within the group. It is possible to express the precise mathematical function relating the number of possible relationships between individuals in a group and group size (N): This function is represented by the formula $(N^2 - N)/2$. For example, if the group is made of Tom and Dick, there is only one possible relationship between members of the group (Tom-Dick). If the group is made up of the three people Tom, Dick, and Harry, there are three possible relationships (Tom-Dick, Tom-Harry, and Dick-Harry). If the group is made up of seven people, there are twenty-one possible relationships between individuals; if there are ten people in the group, there are forty-five possible relationships between individuals.

Thus, groups have the potential to become increasingly complex as the number of people in the group increases. There are many possible consequences of this increasing complexity. For one thing, it becomes increasingly harder to pay an equal amount of attention to everyone in the group as it increases in size. Brian Mullen and colleagues state that the person in the group who talks the most is paid the most attention, and in turn is most likely to emerge as the leader of the group; this effect (sometimes referred to as the "blabbermouth" theory of leadership) increases as the size of the group increases. It also becomes increasingly more difficult to get to know everyone in the group and to spend an equal amount of time with everyone in the group as the group increases in size.

People in groups may tend toward a convenient simplification of this inevitable complexity. Scholars have long recognized the tendency for group members to divide other group members into groups of "us" and "them" rather than to perceive each person as a distinct entity. Groups can often be divided into perceptually distinct, smaller groups. For example, a committee might sometimes be composed predominantly of elderly members, with only one or a few young members. The general tendency is for people to focus their attention on the smaller group. The reason for this is that the smaller group seems to "stand out" as a perceptual figure against the background of the larger group. Thus, the youthful member of an otherwise elderly committee is likely to attract a disproportionate amount of attention from the committee members.

Not only will the members of the larger group pay more attention to the smaller group, but the members of the smaller group will do so as well. Thus, the members of the smaller group will become more self-attentive, more aware of themselves and their behavior. On the other hand, the members of the larger group become less self-attentive, or, as Ed Diener contends, more deindividuated—less aware of themselves and their behavior. For example, the singular female of a group of mechanical engineers that is predominantly male will quickly stand out. The male mechanical engineers may tend to think of that one distinct individual in terms of her status as a female. Moreover, the lone female may become more sensitive than usual about her behavioral transgressions of the norms guiding sexual roles in the presence of an all-male working environment.

Thus, group composition has been demonstrated to predict the extent to which people pay attention to, and are aware of, themselves and specific facets of themselves, and a variety of social behaviors including participation in religious groups, bystander intervention in emergencies, worker productivity, stuttering in front of an audience, and conformity.

For example, an analysis of the participation of congregation members in their religious groups documented the powerful effect of group composition on behavior of group members. As the size of the congregation increased relative to the number of ministers, the congregation members were less likely to participate in the group (in terms of things such as attending worship services, becoming lay ministers, or "inquiring for Christ"). In this instance, becoming "lost in the crowd" impaired the normal self-regulation behaviors necessary for participation. Alternatively, analysis of the behavior of stutterers in front of an audience also documented the powerful effects of group composition on the behavior of group members. As the size of the audience increased relative to the number of stutterers speaking, the verbal disfluencies (stuttering and stammering) of the speakers increased. In this instance, becoming the center of attention exaggerated the normal self-regulation behaviors necessary for speech, to the point of interfering with those behaviors. The point is that group composition's effects of making the individual lost in the crowd or the center of attention are not inherently good or bad. They may produce either positive or negative effects, depending on the context.

Another facet of the topography of the group that is related to group size is density. Density refers to the amount of space per person in the group (the less space per person, the higher the density). Consider a room of a given size: Doubling the number of people in the group will decrease by one-half the amount of space available for each member of the group. Alternatively, halving the number of people in the group will double the amount of space available per person. Thus, in a room of a given size, density is directly linked to the size of the group. This particular approach to density is called social density, because it involves a change in density by manipulation of the social dimension (group size). One could also manipulate the physical dimension (room size), rendering a change in what is called spatial density. Thus, halving the size of the room will halve the amount of space available to each group member. Density has been demonstrated to influence a variety of social behaviors. People have been found to report feeling more anxious, more aggressive, more unpleasant, and, understandably, more crowded as a function of density. For example, an analysis of the effects of "tripling" in college dormitories illustrates these types of effects. As a cost-cutting measure, colleges and universities will often house three students in a dormitory room that was initially constructed for two (hence, tripling). Tripling has been demonstrated to lead to an increase in arguments among the roommates, increased visits to the student health center, decreased grades, and increased overall dissatisfaction.

Context

Groups exert sometimes dramatic, sometimes subtle influences on behavior. These influences are sometimes beneficial and sometimes detrimental. An understanding of the effect of groups on the individual sets the stage for a deeper understanding of many facets of social life. One of the reasons for the formation or joining of groups is the definition of the self. On a commonly used questionnaire that requires a person to respond twenty times to the question "Who am I?", people tend to respond with references to some sort of group membership, be it family, occupation, hobby, school, ethnic, religious, or neighborhood. Groups help establish one's identity, both for one's own benefit and for the benefit of others with whom one interacts.

Belonging to groups has its price, however; as discussed at length by Christian Buys, one's very membership in a group may carry with it hidden costs, risks, or sacrifices. A more complete understanding of groups requires a consideration of this aspect of membership in a group. Attaining certain types of rewards may be incompatible with belonging to a group. For example, the goal of completing a difficult and complicated task may be facilitated by belonging to a group of coworkers who bring the varied skills and knowledge required for successful task completion. Yet one group member's goal of always being the center of attention, or of needing to feel special and unique, may have to be subverted if the group is to perform the task for which it formed. What the individual wants or needs may sometimes be displaced by what the group needs.

Moreover, groups and the deindividuation they foster break down the individual's ability to self-regulate. Research has demonstrated the state of deindividuation to increase the (simulated) electric shocks people will deliver to other people in experiments, to increase the use of profanity, and to increase stealing among Halloween trick-or-treaters. The paradigm illustration of the negative effects of deindividuation is the lynch mob. An analysis of newspaper accounts, conducted by Brian Mullen, of lynch mob atrocities committed in the United States over a sixty-year period showed that the savagery and atrocity of the mob toward its victim(s) increased as the size of the mob increased relative to the number of its victims.

Yet as discussed by Lynn Anderson, just as there are costs involved in belonging to a group, there are also benefits that accrue from group membership. Although the negative aspects of group membership may capture one's attention more forcefully, the positive aspects are no less common or important. A complete understanding of the purpose of groups requires a consideration of the positive side of belonging to a group. A considerable amount of evidence in recent years has documented the physiological, attitudinal, and health effects of social support systems. For example, people who belong to a varied and tight social support network have been found to be in better physical health and to be better able to resist stress than those lacking such support. As examples, one might consider the effects of such popular support groups as Alcoholics Anonymous and Mothers Against Drunk Driving as well as less popular support groups that deal with specific issues such as loss and bereavement. These groups provide the imperative psychological function of allowing their members a new avenue with which to cope with their problems.

Perhaps the most notable effects of the group on self-definition and identity are observed when these taken-for-granted benefits are taken away. The woman who has defined herself in terms of her marital status can find her identity cast adrift after a divorce. Similarly, foreign-exchange students often report a similar dislocation or disorientation of identity immediately upon their return home. After months or years of trying to establish a new identity based on new friends, new social contexts, or new groups, that new identity is now inappropriate and out of place in their old social context.

Bibliography

Brown, Rupert. *Group Processes: Dynamics Within and Between Groups.* New York: Basil Blackwell, 1988. This is a very readable treatment of theories and research on group processes, with a particular emphasis on British and European contributions. A variety of compelling and relevant social issues are covered, such as social conformity, crowd behavior, group productivity, and ethnic prejudice.

Canetti, Elias. *Crowds and Power.* New York: Viking Press, 1962. This is a classic historical discussion of the effects of crowds on individuals and societies. Such avenues of group behavior are described as open and closed crowds, invisible crowds, baiting crowds, and feast crowds.

Forsyth, Donalson R. *An Introduction to Group Dynamics.* Monterey, Calif.: Brooks/Cole, 1983. This thorough volume provides access to a wide-ranging review of evidence regarding all aspects of group processes.

Mullen, Brian, and George R. Goethals, eds. *Theories of Group Behavior.* New York: Springer-Verlag, 1987. This comprehensive edited volume considers several theories of group behavior in order to expand fully on this phenomenon. Classic as well as contemporary and controversial theories are described by several of the social psychologists who originally formulated the accounts.

Turner, John C., Michael A. Hogg, et al. *Rediscovering the Social Group: A Self-Categorization Theory.* Oxford, England: Basil Blackwell, 1987. A sophisticated in-depth treatment of a new theory of behavior in groups. This theoretical approach integrates a vast amount of data and sets the stage for further research in group behavior.

Tara Anthony
Brian Mullen

Cross-References

Affiliation and Friendship, 142; Cooperation, Competition, and Negotiation, 689; Crowd Behavior, 737; Group Decision Making, 1114; Leadership, 1419; Social Identity Theory, 2297.

HABITUATION AND SENSITIZATION

Type of psychology: Learning
Field of study: Biological influences on learning

Habituation is a decrease in behavioral response that results from repeated presentation of a stimulus, whereas sensitization is a heightened behavioral response that results from a stronger stimulus. These two processes differ physiologically, and are the most fundamental and widespread forms of learning in the animal kingdom.

Principal terms
ADAPTATION: a heritable characteristic that presumably has developed as a result of natural selection and thus increases an animal's ability to survive and reproduce
INNATE: a term describing any inborn characteristic or behavior that is determined and controlled largely by the genes
LEARNING: a modification in behavior that involves changes in the nervous system that are not caused by fatigue, maturation, or injury
NEURON: a single nerve cell responsible for transmission of a nervous impulse
NEUROTRANSMITTER: a chemical released at the terminal end of one neuron that moves across the synapse and stimulates or inhibits another neuron
STIMULUS: an environmental cue that can potentially modify an animal's behavior via its nervous system
SYNAPSE: the junction between two neurons over which a nervous impulse is chemically transduced

Overview

Habituation and sensitization are the two most fundamental and widespread forms of learning in the animal kingdom. According to ethologists, learning is any modification in behavior that results from previous experience and in some way involves the nervous system, and is not caused by development, fatigue, or injury. More advanced forms of learning include association, perceptual or programmed learning, and insight; the two simplest (nonassociative) forms are habituation and sensitization. These two processes can be characterized as behavioral modifications that result from repeated presentation of simple environmental stimuli.

Habituation is a decrease in response to repeated presentation of a stimulus. One of the most widely cited examples of this kind of learning involves the startle response exhibited by young nestling birds in response to potential predators such as hawks. A young duck, for example, will exhibit an innate startle response whenever a hawk-shaped model or silhouette is passed overhead. With repeated presentation of the model, however, the intensity of the bird's response will decline as the animal becomes habituated, or learns that the stimulus bears no immediate significance.

Common throughout the animal kingdom and even among some groups of protozoans, habituation is important for preventing repeated responses to irrelevant environmental stimuli that could otherwise overwhelm an organism's senses and interfere with other critical tasks. In the case of a young nestling bird, there is a clear advantage to an alarm response in the presence of a potential predator; however, a continued fixed response would result in an unnecessary expenditure of energy and distraction from other important activities such as feeding.

In identifying a habituation response, it is necessary to distinguish between true habituation and sensory adaptation and fatigue. These latter two phenomena involve a waning in responsiveness that is caused by temporary insensitivity of sense organs or muscle fatigue, and thus are not considered forms of learning. In contrast, habituation results in a drop in responsiveness even though the nervous system is fully capable of detecting a signal and eliciting a muscle response.

In contrast to habituation, sensitization is the heightened sensitivity (or hypersensitivity) that results from initial or repeated exposure to a strong stimulus. Examples of sensitization include the increased sensitivity of humans to soft sounds following exposure to a loud startling noise, such as a gunshot, or the increased responsiveness and sensitivity of a laboratory animal to mild (usually irrelevant) tactile stimulation after an electric shock. Sensitization increases an organism's awareness and responsiveness to a variety of environmental stimuli, thereby preparing it for potentially dangerous situations.

At first glance, habituation and sensitization seem to be opposite behavioral responses—one simply a decrease in responsiveness and the other an increase—but in fact, they are physiologically different processes, each with its own set of unique characteristics.

At the physiological level, the two responses are determined by contrasting neurological processes that take place in different parts of the nervous system. Habituation is thought to take place primarily in the reflex arc (or SR) system, which consists of short neuronal circuits between sense organs and muscles. In contrast, sensitization is assumed to occur in the state system, or that part of the nervous system that regulates an organism's state of responsiveness. The SR system controls specific responses, whereas the state system determines an organism's general level of readiness to respond. The interaction between habituation and sensitization and these systems determines the exact outcome of a response. At the cellular level, habituated sensory neurons produce fewer neurotransmitters on the postsynaptic membrane, and sensitized neurons are stimulated by other neurons to increase neurotransmitter production and hence, responsiveness of the nerves. Thus, while their ultimate neurological effects are somewhat opposite, the mechanisms by which such effects are achieved are quite different.

Other important differences between habituation and sensitization include contrasting recovery times, opposite patterns of stimuli specificity, and differences in responsiveness to stimuli intensity. Sensitization is generally characterized by a short-term or spontaneous recovery, as are some cases of habituation. In certain situations, however, recovery from habituation may take several days and even then result in incomplete or less intensive responses.

In comparison to sensitization, habituation is usually elicited by very specific sign stimuli such as certain colors, shapes, or sounds. Thus, even after complete habituation to one stimulus, the organism will still respond fully to a second stimulus. Sensitization, on the other hand, can be characterized as a more generalized response, one in which a single stimulus will result in complete sensitization to a variety of stimuli. Such fundamental differences between these two learning processes reflect differences in their function and survival value. It is a clear advantage to an organism to increase its general awareness to a variety of stimuli (such as occurs in sensitization) once it is alarmed. A similar generalized pattern of habituation, however, would shut down the organism's sensitivity to many important stimuli and possibly put the organism in danger.

A final important difference between habituation and sensitization is the manner in which the two processes are affected by stimulus strength. Habituation is more likely to occur if the repeated stimulus is weak, and sensitization will occur when the stimulus is strong.

These various characteristics have important survival implications, especially for species that rely on stereotypic responses to avoid predation and other life-threatening situations. They ensure that the response is elicited in a timely fashion, that the animal is returned to a normal state in a relatively short period of time, and that the animal is not overwhelmed with sensory input.

Applications

Habituation and sensitization have been studied in a variety of contexts and in a number of organisms, from simple protozoans (such as stentor) to human subjects. Such studies have focused on the adaptive significance of these simple learning processes, their neurological control, and the range of behavioral responses that result from interaction between these two forms of learning.

One particular organism in which the neurological basis of habituation and sensitization has been extensively studied is the marine slug *Aplysia*. Eric Kendel and his associates at Columbia University have shown that when the mantle of this organism is prodded, the slug quickly withdraws its gills into a central cavity; but after repeated prodding, it learns to ignore the stimulus (that is, it becomes habituated). Conversely, when the slug is stimulated with an electric shock, its sensitivity to prodding increases greatly, and it withdraws its gills in response to even the slightest tactile stimulation (that is, it becomes sensitized).

Because *Aplysia* possesses only a few, large neurons, it is an excellent organism in which to study the physiological basis of learning. Capitalizing on this unique system, Kendel and his colleagues have been able to establish the neurological changes that accompany simple forms of learning. In the case of habituation, they have shown that repeated stimulation interferes with calcium ion channels in the nerve, which, under normal circumstances, causes synaptic vesicles to release neurotransmitters, which in turn relay a nervous impulse between two neurons. Thus, habituation results in a blocking of the chemical signals between nerves and thereby prevents gill withdrawal.

When *Aplysia* is stimulated (or sensitized) by an electric shock, an interneuron (a closed nerve circuit contained within one part of the nervous system) stimulates the sensory neuron by opening calcium ion channels, increasing neurotransmitter production and promoting gill withdrawal. Thus, the proximate neurological changes that take place during sensitization and habituation are nearly opposite, but they are achieved by very different neurological circuits.

A second area in which habituation and sensitization responses have been the subject of extensive investigation is the sucking reflex exhibited by human infants. When the cheek or lips of a young child are touched with a nipple or finger, they will automatically begin sucking. In a study designed to explore how various stimuli affect this reflex, it was shown that babies respond much more vigorously to a bottle nipple than to the end of a piece of rubber tubing. In addition, repeated presentation of a bottle nipple causes an increase in sucking response, whereas repeated stimulation with rubber tubing causes a decline in sucking. The sensitized or elevated response to a rubber nipple is a result of activation of the state system, which increases the baby's awareness and readiness to respond. Sensitization, however, does not occur when the baby is stimulated with rubber tubing, and instead the child habituates to this stimulus.

In addition to influencing these simple innate behaviors such as sucking reflexes and withdrawal responses, habituation is believed to be responsible for a number of more complex emotional reactions in humans. Explanations for the effects of habituation on emotions are derived primarily from the opponent process theory of motivation.

The opponent process theory holds that each emotional stimulation (or primary process) initiated by an environmental stimulus is opposed by an internal process in the organism. The emotional changes that actually occur in the organism are predicted to result from the net effect of these two processes. The opponent process detracts from the primary process, and summation of the two yields a particular emotional response. It is hypothesized that when the organism is repeatedly stimulated, the primary process is unaffected but the opponent process is strengthened, which results in a net reduction in the overall emotional response. In other words, repeated presentation of an emotion-arousing stimulus results in habituation in the emotional response, primarily as a result of the elevated opponent response.

An increase in drug tolerance, which results from repeated usage of a drug, is best explained by this kind of habituation. Habitual users of alcohol, caffeine, nicotine, and various opiate derivatives must consume greater quantities of such drugs each time they are ingested in order to achieve the same emotional stimulation. Thus, with repeated usage, there is a decline in the overall emotional response. This decline in the euphoric effects of a drug is primarily the result of an increase in the opponent process, which can be characterized as the negative effects of the drug. This is presumably why habitual users experience more severe physiological problems (for example, headaches or delirium tremens) upon termination of a drug.

Similar patterns of habituation have also been suggested to explain the human emotional responses associated with love and attachment, and the extreme feelings of euphoria derived from various thrill-seeking activities such as skydiving. Thus, while habituation and sensitization are simple forms of learning, they may be involved in a variety of more complex behaviors and emotions as well.

Context

Studies of habituation and sensitization have been especially helpful in clarifying the physiological and genetic mechanisms that control various forms of learning. Such investigations have also shown that habituation and sensitization are widespread phenomena with tremendous adaptive significance throughout the animal kingdom.

Ethologists, in marked contrast with psychologists (especially behaviorist psychologists), have historically emphasized the importance of underlying physiological mechanisms in regulation of various behavioral phenomena. Traditionally, they argued that many forms of behavior are not only genetically determined, or innate, but further constrained by the physiological hardware of the organism. They held that psychologists completely ignored these factors by focusing on only the input and output of experiments. Psychologists, on the other hand, have maintained that nearly all forms of behavior are influenced in some way by learning. These contrasting views, which developed largely as a result of different experimental approaches, eventually gave way to a more modern and unified picture of behavior.

One area of research that greatly facilitated this unification was the study of habituation and sensitization. By discovering the chemical and neurological changes that take place during these simple forms of learning, neurobiologists succeeded in demonstrating how the physiological environment is modified during the learning process and that such modifications are remarkably similar throughout the animal kingdom. Thus, it became quite clear that an understanding of proximate physiological mechanisms was central to the study of behavior and learning.

In addition, other studies on sensitization and habituation helped establish the generality of these processes among various groups of animals. They showed that simple forms of learning can occur in nearly all major animal phyla, and that these learning processes often result in modification of simple innate behaviors as well as a variety of more complex responses. From these and other studies, it was soon evident that learning and instinct are not mutually exclusive events, but two processes that work together to provide animals with maximum flexibility to their environment. The kind of learning that occurs during habituation and sensitization allows animals to modify simple, fixed behaviors in response to repeated exposure to environmental stimuli. Habituation allows an organism to filter irrelevant background stimuli and prevent sensory overload and interference of normal activities critical to its survival. Sensitization helps increase an organism's awareness to stimuli in the face of potentially dangerous situations.

These two forms of learning represent important behavioral adaptations with tremendous generality in the animal kingdom. Even in humans, a variety of seemingly complex behaviors can be attributed to interactions between sensitization and habituation, and the simple neurological changes that accompany them.

Bibliography

Domjan, Michael, and Barbara Burkhard. *Principles of Learning and Behavior.* Monterey, Calif.: Brooks/Cole, 1982. Provides a complete treatment of the psychological basis and mechanisms of learning. Chapter 3 is devoted entirely to habituation and sensitization, and it provides several specific examples of these processes in both human and animal subjects. Includes many original data tables and graphs, and a thorough review of the literature.

Grier, James W. *Biology of Animal Behavior.* St. Louis: Times Mirror/Mosby, 1984. This college-level text provides comprehensive treatment of the study of animal behavior. Clearly written and well illustrated; should provide a good introduction for the layperson. Integrates information from a variety of disciplines including ethology, behavioral ecology, psychology, and neurobiology. Six chapters are devoted to the physiological control of behavior, and one chapter deals entirely with learning and memory.

McFarland, David, ed. *The Oxford Companion to Animal Behavior.* Rev. and enl. ed. New York: Oxford University Press, 1987. Intended as a reference guide, this comprehensive survey of behavior was written by a team of internationally known biologists, psychologists, and neurobiologists, and contains more than two hundred entries covering a variety of topics. Provides a detailed summary of various forms of learning, including habituation and sensitization. The index provides cross-references organized by both subject and species lists.

Manning, Aubrey. *An Introduction to Animal Behavior.* 3d ed. Reading, Mass.: Addison-Wesley, 1979. A concise handbook offering a light introduction to many general aspects of animal behavior and learning. Provides a discussion on stimulus filtering, an entire chapter on the physiological basis of behavior and motivation, and a complete summary of various forms of learning. Well researched, clearly written, and effectively illustrated.

Raven, Peter H. *Biology.* St. Louis: Times Mirror/Mosby, 1989. Chapter 56 of this general text on the science of biology offers an excellent first introduction to the general concepts of ethology and animal behavior. Includes a brief summary of learning and detailed coverage of habituation, sensitization, and conditioning in *Aplysia.* A concise summary, suggestions for additional reading, and review questions appear at the end of the chapter.

Shepherd, Gordon Murray. *Neurobiology.* Oxford, England: Oxford University Press, 1983. This somewhat advanced college-level volume on neurobiology offers an in-depth account of the physiological basis of learning and memory. A portion of chapter 30 is devoted specifically to the neurological changes associated with habituation and sensitization. Detailed diagrams, data summaries, and complete literature reviews are provided.

Michael A. Steele

Cross-References

Ethology, 992; Learning Defined, 1443; Motivation: Opponent Process Theory, 1611; Neurotransmitters, 1673; Reflexes, 2066.

HEALTH PSYCHOLOGY

Type of psychology: Stress
Fields of study: Coping; critical issues in stress; stress and illness

Health psychology examines psychological components of health, illness, and health care systems. It encompasses the maintenance and promotion of health, the treatment and prevention of illness, the growth of health care services, and the development of health policy.

Principal terms

BIOMEDICAL MODEL: an approach that assumes illness or disease is biological in nature, so that diagnosis and treatment focus on the body

BIOPSYCHOSOCIAL MODEL: a perspective in which health status is dependent upon a combination of biological, psychological, and social factors

DISPOSITIONAL OPTIMISM: a general expectation that positive outcomes will occur in the future

PATHOGENIC FOCUS: a view that emphasizes the causes of illness and disease

PERCEPTION OF CONTROL: the belief that one can influence outcomes

PSYCHOSOCIAL VARIABLES: the internal mental states and external situational factors influencing one's physical state and/or behavior

SALUTOGENIC FOCUS: a view that seeks to understand the origins of health by attending to factors promoting health and well-being

SOCIAL SUPPORT: the relationships with other people that provide emotional, informational, or tangible resources that affect one's health

Overview

Health psychology is concerned with the psychological components of promoting and maintaining health, treating and preventing illnesses, improving health care services, and developing health care policy. Health psychology seeks to generate new knowledge about people's health beliefs and practices, and to apply existing knowledge to improve health and well-being. Psychologists interested in health psychology generally adhere to the belief that health cannot be understood exclusively by focusing on the physical condition of the body. The psychological side—the state of the mind—must be considered as well.

The relationship between mind and body, and its impact on health, is best understood by utilizing what has been labeled the biopsychosocial model. This model assumes that one's health state is based on the often complicated interactions of three sets of factors: biological factors, psychological factors, and social factors.

Biological factors include genetic or inherited influences that may predispose some individuals to be more susceptible than average to certain maladies such as heart disease. Examples of psychological factors could include the amount of stress perceived in a work place, a personality trait such as optimism, or the degree of belief in control over one's own health. Support and empathy one receives from family, friends, or colleagues constitute social factors. Such social support can come in the form of emotional, informational, or even tangible resources.

Thus, the biopsychosocial model assumes that health is based on more than only the absence of illness; it is also physical, social, and mental well-being. Indeed, this model highlights the role of psychosocial variables. Psychosocial variables can be internal mental states, such as depression, or external situational factors, such as the aforementioned social support one receives. The important point is that psychosocial factors should be examined in combination with, not independent of, biological influences.

While this model's biological aspects are readily accepted as important to understanding health, the psychosocial components are controversial in some areas in which the biomedical model is heavily relied upon. This more traditional model assumes that disease or illness is exclusively biological in nature, so that diagnosis and subsequent treatment are focused on the state of the body as distinct from the mind. The controversy concerning the biopsychosocial model is relatively minor, however, because there is a recognition among many researchers and health professionals that psychosocial variables often add more to knowledge concerning health, illness, and disease than do biological factors alone.

The rise in interest concerning psychosocial variables specifically, and health psychology generally, can be attributed in part to the changing conditions of health problems. Because of the relatively high standard of living in the United States, most of the primary health problems are no longer major infectious diseases, such as polio, smallpox, or rubella. (Acquired immune deficiency syndrome, AIDS, is one major exception.) The threat of these acute diseases has been successfully eliminated through vaccination programs, which has resulted in a doubled life expectancy within the last century. This increased life span, however, coupled with American affluence, has a price. A collection of more chronic diseases, including cancer, heart disease, and stroke, now are the major health problems faced in the United States. Unlike infectious diseases, these threats cannot be treated through vaccination because they are largely caused by people's life-styles.

The intriguing aspect of these modern life-style diseases is that they are largely preventable. Ironically, most people are probably aware of ways they could reduce their susceptibility to these diseases, yet they choose not to change their life-styles. In order to decrease the risk of lung cancer, for example, people should simply not smoke. Heart disease can be controlled by a sensible diet and a reasonable amount of exercise. Alcohol consumption should be moderate, and nonmedicinal drugs should be avoided altogether. Making people aware of the origins of these life-style diseases is no longer the key problem. It has been replaced by the problem of how to alter negative behaviors affecting health.

Some advances in dealing with the problems of life-style and behavior have been made. There has been a downward trend in smoking; more people are exercising than ever before; and healthier foods are being consumed. Yet resistance still exists; finding ways to alter health behaviors is one of the major contributions health psychologists can provide, one which relies on an understanding of biological as well as psychosocial factors in health.

The changing nature of illness, whether it is related to behavior or biology, must be understood in relation to broader issues in health psychology, such as the expansion and development of adequate health care services. It has been estimated that more than $500 billion per year is spent by Americans on health-related expenses. On an individual level, this is an average of more than 10 percent of one's total income, supporting everything from health care workers' jobs to medical research. The health care industry, then, is a major economic force that comes in contact with practically every citizen. Health psychology can address the effects that this industry has on people both within and outside it, as well as make recommendations concerning future directions for health care.

Applications

Because health psychology encompasses both basic and applied elements, researchers work in both laboratory and field settings. Given the variety of research efforts that potentially fall within the bounds of health psychology, only a brief review of representative pieces of research is possible. This review will be highly selective, focusing on two studies that explicitly link psychosocial variables to health-related issues: recovery following coronary artery bypass surgery, and adjustment to a nursing care facility.

Heart disease is an important topic within health psychology because it accounts for more deaths annually in the United States than all other diseases combined. Each year, many persons require lifesaving cardiac surgery to increase blood flow to the heart, thereby decreasing the risk of subsequent heart attack. The surgery itself, however, can be a stressful experience. It is useful for medical professionals to be able to predict which patients will cope better with the coronary artery bypass operation and show more rapid rates of recovery.

Michael F. Scheier and Charles S. Carver have argued that a personality trait they call "dispositional optimism" can lead to more effective coping with a threatening event such as heart surgery. Dispositional optimism refers to a person's general belief that positive outcomes will occur in the future. If individuals can envision good things happening in the future, then these expectations might allow them both to cope effectively with and to recover more quickly from the surgery. Pessimists, those who anticipate relatively negative outcomes, might show a slower rate of recovery and poorer adjustment to the surgery.

In an article published in the *Journal of Personality and Social Psychology* (1989), Scheier, Carver, and their colleagues assessed the optimism of a group of middle-aged men one day prior to their coronary artery bypass surgeries. As expected, the optimists showed earlier signs of physical recovery following surgery, such as walking around their hospital rooms, than did the pessimists. They were also judged by the medical staff to have demonstrated faster recovery rates. After six months, optimists were more likely to have resumed their normal routines of work, exercise, and social activity, and to have done so more quickly than the pessimists.

Clearly, a more optimistic orientation can lead some people to deal effectively with adverse health problems. It may be that dispositional optimism promotes a reliance on useful coping strategies, such as making future plans or setting goals. In turn, these strategies affect one's adjustment to the physical illness. Further research has shown that optimism leads people to seek social support and to focus on the positive aspects of stressful events. As a psychosocial variable, then, dispositional optimism has important implications for adjusting to physical problems related to disease.

Other psychosocial variables are relevant to adequate adjustment to health problems posed by particular environments. While the majority of older adults are not institutionalized in nursing homes, many are forced to live out their lives in nursing care facilities because of health or economic difficulties. Such facilities provide adequate shelter and health care, but they frequently operate under fixed financial resources which limit the individualized activities and freedoms enjoyed by their residents.

Writing in the *Journal of Personality and Social Psychology* (1976), Ellen J. Langer and Judith Rodin argued that such institutional environments unwittingly reduce morale and health by gradually taking away the patients' perceptions of control over daily events. As a psychosocial variable, the perception of control is the belief that one can influence outcomes. Nursing home residents may lack such perceptions of control, because almost no aspect of their environment is their responsibility. Practically all decisions, from hygiene to entertainment, are made for them by staff members.

Langer and Rodin reasoned that by creating opportunities for institutionalized patients to perceive even relatively small amounts of control, their health and well-being might improve. To test this idea, these researchers gave one floor of patients in a nursing home plants to care for and then asked them to make some decisions regarding participation in recreational activities in the facility. Patients on a comparison floor also received plants, but were told that the nursing staff would be responsible for their care. This group also participated in the same recreational activities but made no decisions about them. Several weeks later, staff observations and comments made by the patients showed that those individuals who perceived control were more physically active and had a stronger sense of well-being. One year later, those patients who were made to feel responsible for events in their environment were still physically and psychologically healthier, even exhibiting a lower mortality rate than those who did not perceive control.

Perceived control is only one psychosocial variable that can be linked to environmental effects on health and well-being, just as the elderly represent only one group who may benefit from interventions of this sort. Based on these results, however, a few conclusions can be drawn. Perceived control can be engendered in fairly simple ways with profound effects on people's physical and mental states. The adverse effects of some environments, such as institutions that care for patients with chronic health problems, can be reduced. Finally, some health interventions can be implemented in a cost-effective manner. Many applications of the biopsychosocial model are clearly possible.

Context

The belief that a sound mind leads to a sound body is by no means novel. The medical and psychological communities have long operated under the assumption that mental and physical states affect one another, though active cooperation between professionals in these two groups was limited. Psychiatry, for example, served as one of the bridges for communication between these groups. Within psychology itself, there have always been scholars whose research focused on health and medical issues, although they tended to identify themselves with areas such as clinical, social, or physiological psychology.

In the late 1970's, there was growing recognition that a distinct subdiscipline of psychology relating to health matters was coalescing. Various names for this subdiscipline, such as behavioral medicine, medical psychology, and behavioral health, became more common, as did specialized journals, texts, symposia, and organizations. A division of health psychology became an official part of the American Psychological Association in 1978. Health psychology has since become more formalized, articulating its goals, defining its scientific and professional orientations, and evaluating the training needs of students drawn to it. One prominent health psychologist, Shelley E. Taylor, has described the field as a "maturing discipline."

Because philosophers have always speculated about the association between mind and body, the philosophical roots of health psychology can be located in antiquity and traced forward to modern times. Psychology's interest and experimental approaches are a more recent development. From the 1930's to the 1950's, researchers such as Flanders Dunbar and Harold Wolff attempted to link personality variables and psychosocial stressors to specific diseases. In the early 1960's, Stanley Schachter and Jerome E. Singer examined the role of cognitive and physiological processes in the perception of emotional states. In related work during the same period, Richard S. Lazarus pioneered the study of stress and coping. The 1970's and 1980's led to the study of topics such as the Type A, or coronary-prone, personality; of commonsense ideas about illness; and of the perception of physical symptoms. Given its prominence as a health threat, AIDS will undoubtedly continue to receive increasing attention from researchers.

Because of this growing interest in health threats, health psychology may increasingly adopt a salutogenic rather than a pathogenic focus. A salutogenic focus seeks to understand the origins of health by attending to those factors which promote people's health and psychological well-being. Healthy people often stay healthy, and researchers attempt to uncover the aspects of healthy life-styles that may aid individuals suffering from illness or disease. In contrast, a pathogenic focus highlights the causes of illness and disease, and is less prevention-oriented. This is not to say that the cause of illness is a secondary concern. Rather, the onset of illness should be understood in relation to behaviors and psychological factors that maintain good health.

Health psychology promises to continue as an important arena for interdisciplinary research on health. Basic and applied approaches to understanding health will develop by examining the interplay of biological, psychological, and social factors. As a growing subdiscipline of the field of psychology, health psychology will yield intriguing insights regarding the relationship between mind and body.

Bibliography

Antonovsky, Aaron. *Unraveling the Mystery of Health: How People Manage Stress and Stay Well.* San Francisco, Calif.: Jossey-Bass, 1987. This work, which advocates the salutogenic view of health and illness, is written by a medical sociologist. Following up on ideas begun in an earlier book, Antonovsky elaborates on the implications of the "sense of coherence concept," an enduring confidence that events, both within and outside the individual, are predictable and will work out well.

Gatchel, Robert J., Andrew Baum, and David S. Krantz. *An Introduction to Health Psychology.* 2d ed. New York: Random House, 1989. A comprehensive overview of health psychology, giving equal emphasis to both biological and psychological points of view. Includes a chapter on psychological immunology, cancer, and AIDS. Recommended readings are noted at the end of every chapter.

Peterson, Christopher, and Lisa M. Bossio. *Health and Optimism.* New York: Free Press, 1991. A very readable and enjoyable introduction to recent research on positive thinking and physical health. Optimism is contrasted with pessimism and explored in biological, emotional, behavioral, and interpersonal contexts. Notes at the book's end provide rich detail and further reading. For readers at all levels.

Rodin, Judith, and P. Salovey. "Health Psychology." In *Annual Review of Psychology* 40. Stanford, Calif.: Annual Reviews, 1989. Summarizes the recent literature in health psychology, with a strong emphasis on health models, and discusses the often complex interactions among relevant variables. The latter include personality traits, cognitive factors, and environmental and cultural influences. Specific behaviors, both health-promoting and damaging, are also discussed.

Stone, George C., ed. *Health Psychology: A Discipline and a Profession.* Chicago: University of Chicago Press, 1987. A collection of content-specific chapters written to summarize the field's first decade and to set an agenda for the next. Describes the field's history and knowledge base; targets population groups for study, including children, women, minorities, and the elderly; covers training and professional issues.

Taylor, Shelley E. *Health Psychology.* 2d ed. New York: McGraw-Hill, 1991. Written by an active researcher in the field, this engaging text provides substantive coverage of health psychology. A novel quality is its separate chapters on health-enhancing and health-compromising behaviors. Includes detailed sections on stress and coping, patients in treatment settings, and the management of chronic and terminal illnesses.

Dana S. Dunn

Cross-References

HEARING: LOUDNESS, PITCH, AND FREQUENCY

Type of psychology: Sensation and perception
Field of study: Auditory, chemical, cutaneous, and body senses

What a person hears depends on sound waves made by vibrating objects; these sound waves convey information about the characteristics of the sound source. This information enters a person's mind via the relationship of the frequency components of the sound wave and their amplitude to the experience of pitch, loudness, and timbre.

Principal terms

AMPLITUDE: the peak deviation of the movement of a vibrating object from the rest state or the ambient state of the medium through which vibration is conducted

FREQUENCY: the number of complete, back-and-forth, movement or pressure changes (cycles) from the rest or ambient state each second; measured in units called hertz

FUNDAMENTAL: the lowest frequency in a harmonic series of overtones; the overtones are integer multiples of the fundamental

LOUDNESS: the strength of a sound as heard, related to sound pressure level but affected by frequency

OVERTONE: one of several sine waves simultaneously generated by most sound sources; these pure tones are all integer multiples of the fundamental

PITCH: the highness or lowness of a sound as heard, related to frequency but affected by loudness

PSYCHOPHYSICS: the study of the relationship between physical units of a stimulus, such as amplitude, and its sensory, experienced qualities, such as loudness

SOUND PRESSURE LEVEL (SPL): the pressure at the peak amplitude of the sound wave, normally expressed in decibels

SPECTRUM ANALYSIS: the ability of a system, such as hearing, to decompose a complex wave into its sine-wave components and their respective amplitudes

TUNING: the selective response of sensory systems such as hearing to different stimuli, providing strong sensation to some and weak or no sensation to others

Overview

Pure tones, or simple sound waves, have three basic attributes: amplitude, frequency, and phase. Sound waves are conducted through the elastic medium of air by compression and rarefaction of air molecules. The amplitude of a sound wave can thus be considered in several ways. The peak of the wave represents the point of maximum compression of air molecules; the trough, the point of greatest rarefaction (partial vacuum). The difference between either value and the general atmospheric pressure may be taken as the amplitude of the sound wave. Thus, when sound waves impinge upon objects, these objects are placed under varying pressure. The maximum variation of this pressure from the background atmospheric pressure (either up or down) is another measure of amplitude and is called the sound pressure level, or SPL. (The velocity of local back-and-forth movements of air molecules is also a measure of wave amplitude, but it is less relevant to the following discussion.)

It is the pressure of the sound wave, conducted to receptors in the inner ear, that ultimately leads to the perception of sound. Other factors being equal, the greater the amplitude of the wave, the greater the perceived loudness of the sound. Here, amplitude refers to physical units of SPL, typically the decibel, while loudness refers to how subjectively intense the sound is heard to be. The decibel measure of sound pressure is twenty times the common logarithm of the ratio of the SPL being measured to a value representing the SPL at the absolute threshold of hearing for a 1,000-hertz tone. The reason for the use of the decibel scale to measure sound wave amplitude is twofold. First, the range of sound pressures that correspond with the sounds that can be heard is so large that a logarithmic measure is needed to depict it. Second, the ear's ability to respond to both extremely weak and extremely strong sounds is based on its having a roughly linear response to the ratio of SPLs to which it is responding. Thus, for example, two sounds that are 10 decibels apart in SPL will appear to have the same difference in loudness regardless if they are, respectively, 10 and 20 decibels or 60 and 70 decibels.

The frequency of a pure tone refers to how many times per second the sound source vibrates back and forth through one full cycle of movement (360 degrees of phase angle). This corresponds to the number of full waves per second conducted through an elastic medium (usually air) and to the ensuing number of waves per second created in the ear. Frequency is measured in units called hertz, named for the nineteenth century German physicist closely associated with the study of electrical wave theory, Heinrich Hertz. Everyone is familiar with the way that a "creaking" door, when moved slowly, produces a series of clicks (pulses). Move that door faster and the clicks fuse into the creaking sound; faster still and the creak often becomes a perceptible tone with the definite quality of pitch. This illustrates that the pitch of a sound or musical tone corresponds with the frequency of the sound wave. The higher the frequency, the higher the pitch of the sound. As with loudness, pitch refers to a subjective phenomenon; frequency refers to its physical correlate. As next discussed, there may be many frequencies that cannot be heard at all (and thus have no pitch) or, if heard, may not produce the sensation of pitch. For example, the meaning of pitch as the musical tone is limited to frequencies below about 5,000 hertz and above 20 hertz. While frequencies outside this range can be heard, they lack the subjective quality of pitch.

One of the most basic and important facts of sensation and perception is that the sensory systems of all organisms are tuned. That is, they do not respond equally to all physical signals that they are capable of receiving. In the case of hearing, very weak signals of certain frequencies may be readily detected, while intense signals of other frequencies may be responded to feebly if at all. A person can typically hear frequencies between 20 and 20,000 hertz, but those frequencies between 1,000 and 4,000 hertz are detectable at the lowest amplitudes (people are best tuned and therefore most sensitive to them). As the frequency of a sound wave differs from the best-detected frequencies, either below or above, it requires a greater sound pressure level to be heard equally well.

Applications

The general relationship between the amplitude and frequency of sound waves and the loudness and pitch of the sensation of sound is relatively straightforward, but pitch is not perfectly correlated with frequency, nor is loudness with intensity; there are important exceptions. In the real world, people are seldom dealing with pure tones (individual sine waves). Vibrating objects, including musical instruments and the vocal apparatuses of humans and many animals, create sound waves made up of several individual frequencies, called complex tones. The series of frequencies in naturally occurring complex tones usually begins with the strongest tone, called the fundamental, and then adds tones that are each integer multiples of the fundamental. This mix of frequencies gives sounds their characteristic quality, called timbre. A brilliant German physicist of the nineteenth century, Hermann von Helmholtz, believed that the pitch of a complex tone was set by the fundamental frequency because it was typically the strongest in the harmonic series. If one carefully listens to the sound of an inexpensive, small television or radio, however, one can often hear the fundamental tone of many musical notes that are too low to be reproduced by the set's loudspeaker. This phenomenon, called the missing fundamental, is both pleasing and fortuitous: One seems to be getting more than one has paid for. Nevertheless, it invalidates Helmholtz's theory. It now appears that the perceived pitch of a complex wave is derived from the common size of the increments between perceptible harmonics. Thus, a tone with a fundamental of 32 hertz, too low for all but the best sound systems to reproduce, can have harmonics at 64, 96, 128, 160, and 192 hertz and even higher. The auditory system thus seems able to extract information about the size—in this case 32 hertz—of the harmonic step, called the periodicity of the sound wave.

The perception of pitch is determined not only by the specific characteristics of the complex wave but by the wave's intensity as well. In 1935, the experimental psychologist and psychophysicist S. S. Stevens presented subjects with two tones, one right after the other. There was a small difference in frequency between the tones. Stevens had his subjects adjust the intensity of one of the tones until they both appeared to have the same pitch. This research yielded a set of curves that showed how the perception of pitch is influenced by intensity. In general, when low tones become more intense, they sound lower in pitch; however, when high tones become more intense, they sound higher pitched. Fortunately for people's enjoyment of music, this effect is much more pronounced for pure tones than for complex tones. The reason for this effect may be that, as discussed above, complex tones are more solidly represented in the auditory system as a result of the redundant information supplied by their periodicity.

This is not the only way that the processing of frequency information is influenced by intensity. As discussed above, the ear is better tuned to some frequencies than to others. This makes the tones that are responded to more efficiently sound louder. Yet this relationship itself changes as the intensity of the sound wave changes. People tend to respond equally to strong sounds of a broader range of frequencies. As sound intensity becomes weak, the ear becomes relatively less sensitive to the low and high extremes of the range of hearing. This effect tends to change the character of the perceived sound, making it thinner, lacking in the solidity of the low-pitched tones and the brilliance of the high-pitched tones. Fortunately, the relationship between intensity and frequency selectivity has been well studied and is the same for most people. This finding has been incorporated into many sound systems by the inclusion of a "loudness" control (a modification of the so-called volume control). The purpose of the loudness control option is to raise automatically the relative intensity of the low and high frequencies as the loudness setting is lowered. If done precisely enough, this will compensate for the falling off of the ear's sensitivity to these tones as they become weaker. The effect is often more realistic sound reproduction at lower sound levels. On sets without a loudness control, one may experiment with this effect by raising the bass and treble control settings for quiet listening. Those people with multiband frequency "equalizers" will find this experimentation even more intriguing to carry out.

Context

People essentially live in a subjective world of sensations, perceptions, and ideas—not an objective, physical world. There are thus two ways to consider natural phenomena: the subjective view, from inside the self; and the objective view, from, as much as is ever possible, outside the self and in the world. Sounds people hear correspond to physical vibrations, and the relationship between physical states such as frequency and amplitude and their psychological counterparts is called psychophysics.

Psychophysical research tries to show relationships between subjective and objective states, rather than reducing one to the other. The subjective quality of music, for example, can never be captured by or reduced to the study of amplitude, frequency, or even quantitative psychological scaling of pitch. Understanding the way that conscious properties such as loudness and pitch are related to their physical counterparts, however, is a valuable model for making conscious states more objective. This same rationale applies to all the senses. In this way, one can realize that hearing is just an exquisitely sensitive form of touch, responding to the frequency and amplitude of delicate pressure waves. Color corresponds to the wavelengths of light, and brightness to the amplitude of the wave (in terms of number of photons). Pain caused by a physical stimulus seems to involve free nerve endings, although many pains seem poorly connected to specific stimuli. The nature of smell and taste is still the subject of much research concerning the way chemical molecules affect receptors and how the pattern of such stimulation compares to conscious states.

Studying the relationship between sensory quality and physical stimulation provides a reminder that people are selectively tuned to external stimuli, and that this selectivity helps define their world. Indeed, many psychological processes, such as learning, motivation, cognition, and personality, involve the specification of how a person uniquely defines and responds to stimuli that are salient to him or her. Thus, the problem of defining the stimulus is in many ways the central problem for psychology. Historically, it was one of the fundamental issues for the first school of psychology, structuralism. It remains the common aspect of many diverse fields of psychological research.

Bibliography

Coren, Stanley. *Sensation and Perception.* 3d ed. San Diego: Harcourt Brace Jovanovich, 1989. A particularly comprehensive and well-written survey of sensory processes. The section on audition contains many felicitous examples that make a complex topic accessible. Other chapters place the study of sound waves and hearing in the context of general sensory processes.

Deutsch, Diana, ed. *The Psychology of Music.* New York: Academic Press, 1982. A unique collection of monographs written by experts in their respective fields. Although intended for the professional, there is no other source as comprehensive in terms of physics, psychoacoustics, and the psychology of music, both its structure and performance. Much is readable by the nonexpert.

Gulick, Walter Lawrence. *Hearing: Physiology and Psychophysics.* New York: Oxford University Press, 1971. A classic. Beautifully written so as to present difficult topics comprehensively but accessibly. All topics basic to the sense of hearing are included. Further reading should start here.

Tobias, Jerry V., ed. *Foundations of Modern Auditory Theory.* 2 vols. New York: Academic Press, 1972. Although not primarily intended for the general reader, this is an extremely valuable reference work. Edited intensively so that most chapters are accessible to the nonspecialist. Most questions not adequately answered by the other entries in this bibliography should be answered here.

Van Bergeijk, Willem André Maria, John R. Pierce, and Edward E. David, Jr. *Waves and the Ear.* Garden City, N.Y.: Anchor Press, 1960. A very good introduction to wave theory and hearing. Key research is simply and clearly presented with excellent figures and examples. Physiology and applications are also covered.

John Santelli

Cross-References

HEARING AND SOUND WAVES

Type of psychology: Sensation and perception
Field of study: Auditory, chemical, cutaneous, and body senses

Hearing, like vision and the sense of smell, lets people know about things and events in the distance. Hearing is dependent on sound waves—the movement of air molecules caused by a vibrating object's elasticity and mass.

Principal terms
  AMPLITUDE: the peak deviation from the rest state of the movement of a vibrating object, or the ambient state of the medium through which vibration is conducted
  FREQUENCY: the number of complete back-and-forth movements or pressure changes (cycles) from the rest or ambient state each second; measured in units called hertz
  FUNDAMENTAL: the lowest frequency in a harmonic series of overtones; the overtones are integer multiples of the fundamental
  LOUDNESS: the strength of a sound as heard, related to sound pressure level but also affected by frequency
  PITCH: the highness or lowness of a sound as heard, related to frequency but also affected by loudness
  PURE TONE: a sound produced by a vibration of a single frequency, the amplitude of which changes over time as a sinusoidal function (sine wave)
  TIMBRE: the sound quality produced by the respective amplitude and frequency of the overtones, or underlying sine waves that make up a complex wave
  WAVELENGTH: the distance traveled by the wave front in the time given by one cycle (the period of the wave); has an inverse relation to frequency

Overview

Most things produce sound waves by vibrating. All vibrations are similar in that they result from the basic physical properties of elasticity and inertia. Take a rubber band and stretch it between thumb and forefinger. Pluck one strand and consider what happens. Stretched into elastic tension and released, the band accelerates as the elastic force stored in it by a pluck is changed to kinetic energy (movement). The elastic tension of the strand is fully spent and its velocity highest when it is at its midpoint of flight, where it was before it was plucked. The strand's inertia (tendency to keep moving) then carries it almost as far as did the pluck but in the opposite direction, until this kinetic energy is stored again as potential energy in the elastic tension of the restretched strand. The process repeats itself rapidly many times until all the energy imparted to the strand has been lost, partly because of friction in the rubber and air molecules and, more importantly, through the transfer of kinetic energy to air molecules. It is this movement of air molecules that is the physical stimulus for the sound that one hears. Thus, objects' elasticity and mass allow them to produce sound waves when energized. This is how musical instruments and the vocal apparatuses of animals, including humans, work.

Sound waves move over distances through an elastic medium such as air in the following way. Consider as an example a violin string. Like a rubber band, it moves back and forth—but virtually continuously, as it is being continually replucked by the bow. The vibrating string moves in air. Although originally distributed evenly, the gas molecules in the air are compressed when the string moves one way against them and then are placed in a partial vacuum (a region of lower density of molecules) by the motion of the string in the opposite direction. The compressed particles push against the molecules immediately down the line, compressing them. Then, their elastic energy transferred, the particles return to fill the space created initially by the opposite movement of the string. The just-compressed molecules now push against their neighbors before returning to fill the space created by their predecessors' reverse motion. It can thus be seen that there are two kinds of particle motion involved in a sound wave: a back-and-forth oscillation of compressed and rarefied air that remains essentially in place and a linear, continuous, outward movement of successive waves. The acoustic waves move outward from the vibrating object like waves in the ocean.

Recognizing that pressure wave fronts traveling in air are like waves in the ocean may provide the clearest example of what is meant by the amplitude of the wave. When a water wave reaches a barrier, it exerts a pressure against that obstruction proportional to its amplitude (think of the force of waves against a jetty). The height (or depth) of a wave, measured from the zero reference of the average water level, is the wave's amplitude. In air, an acoustic wave's amplitude is the maximum amount of compression (or rarefaction) of air molecules compared to the atmospheric pressure. When this pressure wave reaches an object, it also exerts a force, although vastly weaker. Since the amplitude of a wave may be equated with the pressure created against objects in its path, such as a human eardrum, the strength of a sound wave is referred to as its sound pressure level.

Note that the amplitude of a wave determines how rapidly air molecules move back and forth in a very small space. A large wave will require that the particles move at a higher average velocity to complete a large back-and-forth displacement compared to a smaller one. The waves themselves, however, move at the same speed for all sounds. This is called the speed of sound and is, in air at room temperature, approximately 335 meters per second. A sound wave's wavelength may be seen as the distance a wave travels in the time taken to complete one cycle (or the distance between any two points representing one full cycle of the wave).

The mass and elasticity of a vibrating object also determine how fast it vibrates. This rate of vibration determines the frequency of the sound wave, or how many times per second the air molecules move through one back-and-forth cycle. This value of cycles per second is expressed in units called hertz. The range of audible sound wave frequencies is roughly 20 to 20,000 hertz.

Finally, consider again the way in which objects vibrate. Their rate of movement back and forth is not linear. It is fastest at the vibration's midpoint and slows down until the motion actually reverses and then accelerates again to maximum velocity at the midpoint. To picture this, affix a small object near the rim of a rotating phonograph turntable and view its shadow on the wall by positioning a light at the level of the turntable. The mathematical function that describes these changes, and thus the changes in pressure or displacement over time that form the sound wave, is the sine function of an angle rotated through 360 degrees. The simplest sound wave (one that has only a single frequency) is a pure tone or sine wave. The instantaneous amplitude (the point in its 360-degree cycle) of such a wave is described by the phase angle of the wave. Thus, the peak of a wave is at 90 degrees, and its trough occurs at 270 degrees.

Applications

When sound waves reach the ear, they are funneled by the outer ear to the eardrum. The eardrum is elastic and is pushed by the sound wave's compression and "pulled" by its rarefaction. It then transfers, by a specialized lever and hydraulic system, the energy derived from the sound wave to a complex receptor mechanism located in the inner ear. This receptor system sends signals to the brain which tell it about the sound wave and which a person hears as sound.

In everyday life, however, pure tones are seldom heard because vibrating objects rarely move only as a single piece. They normally have several integer subdivisions of themselves simultaneously vibrating at integer multiples, called harmonics, of their lowest frequency of vibration, called the fundamental. Each harmonic is produced at its own amplitude, determined by the physical characteristics of the sound source. In addition to the vibrating material, which includes the elastic column of air in a wind instrument or organ pipe, the overall size and shape of the source also serve to increase, reduce, or even eliminate selectively specific harmonics by the effect of resonance. Thus, normal sounds, even from a single source, are complex waves made of several simultaneously occurring sine waves of different frequencies, amplitudes, and phase relationships. Sounds from several sources interact still further. Looking at a "picture" of sound on an oscilloscope screen or closely examining the grooves in a phonograph record shows that sound is highly irregular, quite unlike the perfect undulations of a sine wave. Nevertheless, all vibrating objects emit sine waves—but many of them at the same time.

The complexity of a sound wave—how many and which harmonics it contains—determines its timbre, or quality. Typically, it is the fundamental (lowest) frequency that gives the sound its characteristic pitch. Many different types of musical instruments, or many different singers, can produce the same note, but one can readily distinguish the sound of one from another by their characteristic timbre.

How the auditory system allows people to hear timbre is one of the astonishing properties of hearing. To begin to understand this process, individually strike three or four keys on a keyboard instrument that form a chord (every other white key will do). It is easy to tell them apart. Now strike two together, then three, then four. It is easy to keep track of each note, even though together they form a harmonious chord. This would not be possible if one could hear only the complex sum of the underlying tones. Instead, one's auditory system is able to extract each fundamental tone from the complex wave. This ability is based on the ability of the ear to analyze complex waves into their sine wave components, the possibility of which was formally established by the nineteenth century French mathematician and physicist Jean Fourier and applied to hearing by his German contemporary, the physicist Georg Ohm.

This principle is applied in a common piece of modern sound-reproduction electronics: the real-time spectrum analyzer. Many home and automotive sound systems have versions of this device. It displays the relative amplitude of several bands of frequencies, often at octave separation, as a constantly changing set of columns of light, each column representing a range of frequencies and the height of each illuminated column indicating the amplitude of the frequencies measured by that column. Imagine the ear performing the same function but on a vastly finer scale, using thousands of very finely tuned frequency detectors. Much of what a person hears, then, corresponds and is limited to the output of these individual detectors. It is as if what one hears is logically equivalent to what one would see if one had such an elaborate, multichannelled analyzer in one's electronic sound system.

The ear is a remarkable sound wave analyzer. Because the ears are separated by the width of a solid skull, a sound wave originating off to one side arrives at each ear at a slightly different time (phase) and at a slightly different amplitude (weaker in the ear away from the sound source). The auditory system uses this information, along with appropriate head movements, to localize where the sound wave originates and let the listener direct attention appropriately. The ability of the auditory system to note extremely small differences in the timing of sound waves reaching the ear is the basis of multichannel sound reproduction. When the listener is surrounded with multiple sound sources, a realistic or even spectacular sense of ambience may be created.

The ability to analyze and locate sounds is more than equaled by the ear's incredible sensitivity and dynamic (amplitude) range. A person can hear sound waves whose pressure moves the eardrum only slightly more than the width of a hydrogen molecule (the proverbial pin dropping). The sound of a rock band, or loud sounds played through earphones, however, can be more than one million times greater. Because of the need to respond to such a large dynamic range, the ear responds in a roughly logarithmic way, with the perceived loudness of a sound increasing linearly as the sound wave's amplitude leaps ahead exponentially (by ratios). Thus, a logarithmic unit, the decibel, is used to express values along this large linear range. Sustained exposure to high-amplitude sound waves can permanently damage the delicate receptor cells of the inner ear. This is another reminder that the sound wave is a physical pressure and can produce tissue damage, as can any sufficient impact.

Context

Plato was one of the first thinkers to be struck by the fact that humans live in a subjective world of sensations, perceptions, and ideas, rather than in a "real" world of objective physical phenomena. Psychology's preoccupation with "knowing one's self" is really an outgrowth of philosophy's attempt to understand this strikingly problematic gap between the subjective view from inside the self and the objective view from, as much as is ever possible, outside the self and in the world.

It was not until the seventeenth century that scientists realized that sounds that are heard correspond to physical vibrations, and not until late in the nineteenth century that the brilliant German physicist Hermann von Helmholtz developed a theory of how complex waves are analyzed into individual signals. Research into the relationship between physical states and their psychological counterparts was an important part of nineteenth century German science and became known as psychophysics. Psychophysics then became a major part of the research program of the first experimental psychology laboratory, established in 1879 by the "father" of modern psychology, Wilhelm Wundt. Along with the psychophysicists Ernst Weber and Gustav Fechner, Wundt argued that lawful relationships between physical stimulation and subjective sensation showed that the scientific study of the mind was feasible.

People are often struck by the complexity of psychophysical research, but it is important to remember its roots. While the subjective beauty of great instrumental music and song can never be reduced to "nothing but vibrations," people still gain valuable self-awareness by recognizing how such personal sensory experience fits into the larger, objective scheme of things. This same rationale applies to all sensory modalities, but it even goes beyond the senses. Somewhat metaphorically, personality, values, interests, and psychological adjustment all can be understood as the way people are uniquely tuned to, select, and respond to external stimuli. Understanding the way sound waves are related to hearing provides a valuable model for psychology's concern for making the subjective more objective.

Bibliography

Coren, Stanley. *Sensation and Perception.* 3d ed. San Diego: Harcourt Brace Jovanovich, 1989. A particularly comprehensive and well-written survey of sensory processes. The section on audition contains many felicitous examples that make a complex topic accessible. Other chapters place the study of sound waves and hearing into a valuable general perspective.

Deutsch, Diana, ed. *The Perception of Music.* New York: Academic Press, 1982. A unique collection of monographs written by experts in their respective fields. Extremely comprehensive in terms of physics, psychoacoustics, and the psychology of music, both its structure and performance. Intended for the professional, but much is readable by the nonexpert.

Gulick, W. Lawrence. *Hearing: Physiology and Psychophysics.* New York: Oxford University Press, 1971. A classic. Beautifully written so as to present difficult topics comprehensively but accessibly. All topics basic to the sense of hearing are included; further reading should start here.

Tobias, Jerry V., ed. *Foundations of Modern Auditory Theory.* 2 vols. New York: Academic Press, 1972. Although not primarily intended for the general reader, this is an extremely valuable reference work. Edited intensively so that most chapters are accessible to the nonspecialist. Most questions not adequately answered by the other entries in this bibliography should be answered here.

Van Bergeijk, Willem André Maria, John R. Pierce, and Edward E. David, Jr. *Waves and the Ear.* Garden City, N.Y.: Anchor Press, 1960. Specifically written for the general reader and high school student. A very good introduction to wave theory and hearing. Key research is simply and clearly presented with excellent figures and examples. Physiology and applications are also covered.

John Santelli

Cross-References

The Auditory System, 344; Hearing: Loudness, Pitch, and Frequency, 1146; Hearing Loss, 1157; Sensation and Perception Defined, 2207; Sensory Modalities and Stimuli, 2214; Sound Localization, 2335; Speech Perception, 2348.

HEARING LOSS

Type of psychology: Sensation and perception
Field of study: Auditory, chemical, cutaneous, and body senses

Hearing loss (deafness) is caused by a group of hereditary or acquired malfunctions of the auditory system that make it difficult or impossible to hear sounds. Total deafness from birth makes it difficult to learn spoken language; acquired deafness is also a severe problem. At any point in life, hearing loss causes sensory deprivation and may produce psychological problems.

Principal terms
ADVENTITIOUS DEAFNESS: deafness acquired after birth, through accident or disease
AUDITORY NERVE: the so-called eighth cranial nerve, connecting the inner ear and the hearing center of the brain
COCHLEA: the snail-shell-shaped portion of the inner ear that contains the nerve connections to the auditory nerve
CONGENITAL DEAFNESS: deafness existing at birth as a result of genetic causes
NEUROSIS: any functional disorder of the mind or the emotions occurring without obvious brain damage and involving anxiety, phobic responses, or other abnormal behavior symptoms
OSSICLE: any of the three bones of the middle ear (the hammer, anvil, and stirrup) that are involved in conduction of sound into the inner ear
OTORHINOLARYNGOLOGIST: a physician who specializes in the treatment of diseases of the ear, nose, and throat
OTOTOXIC: a substance that causes damage to the ear
PSYCHOSIS: a severe mental disorder, with or without brain damage, characterized by deterioration of normal intellectual and social functioning and withdrawal from reality

Overview

Hearing loss, often called deafness, afflicts up to eighteen million Americans. Only a small percentage of these people are totally unable to hear; however, the impact on life of even mild hearing loss is quite serious because the ability to hear sounds is so very important to people's understanding of the world around them. Before discussing deafness, it is useful to describe the mechanics of sound perception in the auditory system, which consists of the ears and the auditory nerve that carries sound to the brain.

Each ear is composed of three parts: an outer, middle, and inner ear. The outer ear begins with an external sound-catching auricle attached to the head (this is thought of as "the ear" by most people). The auricle carries sound into the second outer ear component, the tubular external auditory canal that enters the head. This canal contains, at its end, an eardrum that lies against one end of the middle ear, a small cavity in the bone of the skull.

Sound enters the auricle, passes through the external ear canal, and causes the eardrum to vibrate. This makes three small, attached bones—the hammer, anvil, and stirrup—in the middle ear vibrate also. These bones (ossicles) transmit sound sequentially across the middle ear, until the vibration reaches the oval window of the ear. Here, the fluid-filled inner ear—or bony labyrinth—connects the middle ear to the auditory nerve via the snail-shell-shaped cochlea. The cochlea is divided into vestibular, tympanic, and cochlear canals. The first two canals receive sound waves from the middle ear, and the cochlear canal contains the organ of Corti, filled with thousands of fibers of differing lengths.

When sound waves make organ of Corti fibers vibrate, the low-pitched ones interact with long fibers and the high-pitched ones interact with short fibers. The variation of fiber length in human ears enables most people to distinguish many sounds, ranging from those caused by waves vibrating fifteen times a second (low pitch) to those attributable to waves vibrating twenty thousand times a second (very high pitch). Fiber vibration stimulates the auditory nerve to carry sound to the brain; loud sounds cause vibration of more fibers than soft sounds.

It can be shown with implanted electrodes that the cochlea acts like a microphone, changing audible sounds to electrical impulses. Such studies also indicate that low tones are picked up at the cochlear apex, while high tones are picked up at its base. The main hearing mechanism theories are resonance theory, which bases sound differentiation on position of cochlear stimulation; frequency (or telephone) theory, proposing direct translation of individual sound waves into nerve impulses; and resonance-volley theory, which proposes that the perception of low-pitched and high-pitched sounds depends upon telephone and resonance-theory concepts, respectively.

Health problems causing auditory-system malfunction produce hearing loss—deafness—at various levels. This deafness is divided into two main types: conductive deafness and nerve (sensorineural) deafness. Conductive deafness is caused by problems in the outer or middle ear. Major causes include otitis media and otosclerosis. The very common otitis media is middle-ear infection that usually begins with a cold or an allergy attack. Situations leading to the disease cause the nasal secretions to block the eustachian tube that normally maintains needed equal pressure on both sides of the eardrum. The blockage presses the eardrum up against the ossicles, preventing normal ossicle motion and diminishing hearing. In contrast, otosclerosis is a hereditary disease in which decalcified bone surrounding the middle ear is replaced by abnormal bone growths that immobilize the stirrup bone. This problem decreases hearing progressively, beginning at adolescence and steadily worsening.

Nerve deafness is damage to the inner ear, the auditory nerve, or the hearing center of the brain. One aspect of such deafness is related to exposure to loud noise. Best known are explosions or close proximity to gunshots, which cause deafness by breaking off portions of the organ of Corti. Continual listening to loud music can also, in time, cause permanent hearing loss that worsens without pain or any other warning. Tumors of the auditory nerve, encephalitis, loss of nerve cells with age (presbycusis), or use of some therapeutic drugs (for example, streptomycin) can also cause nerve deafness.

Hearing impairment, whether temporary or permanent, is unpleasant and can cause psychological problems. Although some hearing-impaired people are born with the problem (congenital deafness), hearing loss can develop at almost any time in life (adventitious deafness). Regardless of the time of onset, such impairment can be devastating because spoken language, which must be heard, pervades all aspects of human life. Hearing-impaired people (especially the congenitally deaf) possess diminished communication capacities. Educational achievements, intellectual functions, and maintaining a good quality of life all involve great struggles to overcome this hardship. Often deaf people are introverted, and some may develop depression. The commonly held presumption that the other senses of hearing-impaired people "sharpen" in a useful trade-off is simply not true.

Applications

The problems of the congenitally deaf and victims of adventitious hearing loss are quite different; however, all such people, to quote John Chalmers Ballantyne, author of *Deafness* (1984), have the "handicap of the silent world, the difficulty of communicating with the hearing and speaking world." These problems may begin in the cradle, where much of a baby's security comes from the soothing sound of a mother's voice. Such support is not possible for the deaf baby, and visual or tactile comforting may not wholly replace it.

In their school years, deaf children are disadvantaged, whether they are educated in a normal school and made very aware of their handicap or placed in special schools for the deaf, feeling more comfortable but not being encouraged to adapt to the hearing society in which they must eventually function. In contrast, a person suffering from adventitious hearing loss knows how to speak but, suddenly cut off from the hearing world, has other problems, including sudden loss of self-esteem. Consequently, treatment of hearing loss will vary but must include successful correction of the disease involved and rehabilitation to whatever extent is needed.

Many types of deafness can be treated medically by prudent use of a wide variety of appropriate surgical techniques. For example, perforated eardrums can be repaired via myringoplasty. Similarly, stapedectomy can repair the ravages of otosclerosis. Here, the stirrup ossicle is removed, and a pistonlike prosthesis that connects appropriately to the anvil bone is used to replace it. Cochlear implants are also utilized to restore hearing by direct electrical stimulation of the auditory nerve.

Valuable nonsurgical treatment of hearing impairment includes use of hearing aids, worn by millions of the hearing impaired. Because most conductive hearing losses are surgically correctable, hearing aids are usually acoustical devices aimed at the correction of nerve deafness. They may be worn on the body, in eyeglasses, or placed within the outer ear. The choice of hearing aid type is often cosmetic, rather than based upon performance, as all types operate with similar efficiency.

The sound pickup of a hearing aid may be from the front or back of the user; in some cases, signals from two microphones feed acoustic signals into the "better" ear of an individual. It is also important that the hearing-aid consumer be aware that simple provision of a hearing aid is not sufficient to produce normal hearing. Auditory training by a bona fide hearing therapist is an essential component of effective hearing-aid use. Without it, a hearing-impaired patient may experience great frustration and incomplete success in hearing at a desired level.

A variety of other special-education techniques are also used to teach deaf people to communicate by nonaural methods, including sign language. In addition, social counseling and the efforts of psychologists and psychiatrists can be quite useful for treatment of psychological problems that may stem from sensory deprivation and other problems that accompany hearing loss.

In a great many cases, the best treatment is prevention. Some useful techniques are immunization for viral diseases, control of allergies, and early medical intervention for upper-respiratory infections and earaches. The sensible control of infection with appropriate antibiotics is valuable. It is important to remember, however, that several antibiotics (for example, kanamycin and neomycin) and other medications can be ototoxic—detrimental to the hearing apparatus. In addition, routine hearing screening should be carried out wherever possible, on people of all ages. In the case of small children, who may not be aware of potential problems, periodic screening at the pediatrician's office or an appropriate clinic should be a routine practice. Adolescents and adults should have any persistent hearing problem (for example, earache, ringing in the ears, or pressure pain) checked out quickly, before it can become serious. After the confirmation of a problem by a physician, appropriate follow-up with a specialist such as an otorhinolaryngologist is advisable.

Yet another valuable aspect of prevention of hearing loss is the avoidance of excessively loud and continuous noises. This includes amplified rock music as well as noises that occur in the workplace. It cannot be overemphasized that excessively loud music can be a cause of serious hearing impairment. In addition, many problems arise from job-related noise, so techniques and devices that protect the worker have been developed in many instances. Strict federal regulations govern permissible noise levels in the workplace. Therefore, an individual exposed to suspected excess noise on the job should explore its potential dangers, understand federal regulation, and seek advice from the company safety office or the appropriate federal regulatory agency, where necessary.

Context

Hearing loss (or deafness) is much more likely to occur later than earlier in life. It can attack at any time, however, and such acquired (adventitious) hearing loss occurs in young children, in adolescents, and in adults of all ages. Often, adventitious hearing loss has disastrous psychological and economic effects on the afflicted person.

In children, adolescents, and young adults, most hearing loss can be avoided through frequent, thorough medical examinations followed immediately by prompt corrective action where needed. Many older people become deaf as their lives progress and the sensorineural components of the auditory system wear out. They, too, can be helped by hearing aids, by good medical treatment, and by the use of psychological counseling.

In addition, the congenitally deaf can be aided by appropriate medical and psychological counseling and by special-education programs. Such an approach helps them to enter the work force at levels more commensurate with their innate intellectual abilities, prevents them from becoming maladjusted, and removes them from public assistance programs. Dealing with deafness in young, congenitally deaf persons is particularly important because it helps prevent the development of many problems, including psychoses, that may otherwise occur and greatly improves the quality of their lives.

As better understanding of the auditory system has developed, more effective methods for the prevention, diagnosis, and treatment of various aspects of hearing loss have developed in a parallel fashion. These include immunization and antibiotic therapies against the communicable diseases that can cause hearing loss; much better diagnostic techniques, including the use of the professional audiologist; improved diagnosis and treatment in hospitals, ear clinics, and schools; diversified surgery; the better use of hearing aids; and special-education techniques.

The best treatments for widespread hearing loss are viewed by most experts as including prevention by avoiding noise and other environmental challenges that can produce it, obtaining quick treatment for observed auditory problems, and early impairment identification and cure. It is hoped that ongoing research will continue to increase the avenues for the prevention of hearing loss and identify additional methods for the handling of all forms of deafness.

Bibliography

Ballantyne, John Chalmers. *Deafness.* 4th ed. Edinburgh, Scotland: Churchill Livingstone, 1984. This expert book provides "a general account couched in simple terms, of deafness and its relief." Provides a solid description of the auditory system. Covers the diagnosis of deafness and explains its causes. Includes a description of hearing aids and their use, and explores rehabilitation of the deaf.

Bess, Fred H., and Larry E. Humes. *Audiology: The Fundamentals.* Baltimore: Williams & Wilkins, 1990. A valuable book designed for students of audiology. Notable for its clear, simple language, abundant related vignettes, and many literature references. Topics of major interest include the nature of sound, the structure and function of the auditory system, the assessment of auditory function, and useful management strategies for the hearing impaired.

Bolton, Brian, ed. *Psychology of Deafness for Rehabilitation Counselors.* Baltimore: University Park Press, 1976. Provides useful information on problems associated with deafness and their treatment. Topics include various aspects of the intellectual and vocational development of the hearing impaired, their academic achievement, the psychiatry of deafness, and consequences of intervention and rehabilitation programs.

Bradford, Larry J., and William G. Hardy. *Hearing and Hearing Impairment.* New York: Grune & Stratton, 1979. Covers hearing impairment, the sciences of hearing and hearing impairment, programs and practices with the hearing impaired, mental health and hearing impairment, the hearing impaired and society, and aid delivery systems. Many valuable references and diagrams are also included.

Daniloff, Raymond, Gordon Schuckers, and Lawrence Feth. *The Physiology of Speech and Hearing: An Introduction.* Englewood Cliffs, N.J.: Prentice-Hall, 1980. This introductory book does a thorough job, using clear, simple language. Most relevant here is the chapter entitled "Audition: The Sense of Hearing." Chapters providing overviews of speech and hearing, basic neuroscience, and acoustics are also quite useful.

Feldman, Alan S., and Charles T. Grimes, eds. *Hearing Conservation in Industry.* Baltimore: Williams & Wilkins, 1985. Covers many useful topics including the effects of noise on hearing, federal noise regulations, hearing protection devices, workers compensation, legal issues, and noise exposure standards. The persistent reader will get an excellent overview, obtain many technical details, and find an abundant source of references on many issues.

Smith, Karl U. "Human Hearing." In *McGraw-Hill Encyclopedia of Science and Technology.* 6th ed. New York: McGraw-Hill, 1987. This detailed review article on the human auditory system touches many bases. Examples are sound properties; detection and discrimination; and the basis for hearing, including theory and experimental aspects, neurological function, and integration with other body senses. Several useful cross-references are also included.

Sanford S. Singer

Cross-References

The Auditory System, 344; Hearing: Loudness, Pitch, and Frequency, 1146; Hearing and Sound Waves, 1151; Sound Localization, 2335; Speech Perception, 2348.

HELPING: BYSTANDER INTERVENTION

Type of psychology: Social psychology
Fields of study: Group processes; prosocial behavior

The study of the psychology of bystander intervention has led to an understanding of the processes that often prevent witnesses to an incident from offering needed assistance, even if an emergency is involved; such events may have tragic consequences, and knowledge of the dynamics of these situations may sometimes keep them from occurring.

Principal terms

AUDIENCE INHIBITION: a tendency to be hesitant to act in front of others
BYSTANDER EFFECT: the tendency to be less likely to help when other people are present; also referred to as the social inhibition of helping
CONFEDERATE: in a social psychological experiment, a person who is "part of the act" and is instructed to behave in a certain way
DIFFUSION OF RESPONSIBILITY: the tendency to share the obligation to help in an emergency with the other people present
SOCIAL INFLUENCE: as applied to bystander intervention, the process whereby each bystander is led by the inaction of others to conclude that no emergency is really occurring

Overview

In early 1964, Kitty Genovese was stabbed to death in front of her New York City apartment building as she returned from work around 3:30 A.M. The assault was particularly brutal, actually consisting of three separate attacks stretching over a period of more than a half hour. Perhaps most shocking about this tragedy, however, was a troubling fact that emerged in the police department's subsequent investigation: Thirty-eight of the woman's neighbors had witnessed the incident without intervening. No one had even called the police during the episode.

This case was only one of several similar occurrences that took place in the mid-1960's, attracting considerable attention and prompting much commentary. The remarks of newspaper columnists, magazine writers, and the like focused on such notions as "alienation," "apathy," "indifference," and "lack of concern for our fellow humans." Bibb Latané and John Darley, social psychologists who at the time were professors at universities in New York City, reasoned that ascribing personality characteristics such as these to bystanders who fail to help is not the key to understanding how onlookers can remain inactive while another individual is victimized. Rather, one must look to the situation itself to uncover the powerful social forces that inhibit helping.

Latané and Darley thus embarked on a program of research that culminated in their classic 1970 book *The Unresponsive Bystander: Why Doesn't He Help?* They began their analysis of the "bystander effect" by recognizing that there are usually several good reasons that one should not necessarily expect bystanders to offer help in an emergency. For example, most people are not prepared to deal with emergencies, which tend to happen quickly and without warning. In addition, direct intervention may involve real physical danger, as in the Genovese incident. Finally, becoming involved in such situations may lead to court appearances or other legal consequences.

Latané and Darley also proposed a model describing a sequence of cognitive events that must occur before a bystander will offer assistance in an emergency. First, a bystander must notice the event; second, he or she must interpret that event as an emergency; third, the bystander must decide that it is his or her responsibility to do something. At this point, two steps in the process still remain: The bystander must decide exactly what to do; then he or she must successfully implement that decision. It is important to recognize that a negative outcome at any of these steps in the decision-making process will prevent helping. In the light of the cognitive process just described and the other reasons that people fail to intervene in emergencies, it is perhaps surprising, Latané and Darley suggested, that bystanders ever help.

Remarkably (and ironically), one situational factor is primarily responsible for the social inhibition of helping: the presence of other people. Latané and Darley proposed three social psychological processes to explain precisely how the presence of others inhibits helping. Each of these operates within the decision-making framework described earlier, and all three appear to be necessary to account completely for the bystander effect.

The first of these processes is audience inhibition, which refers to people's general reluctance to do things in front of others. When people are aware that their behavior is on public display and are concerned about what other people think, they may be hesitant to offer help for fear of appearing incompetent. Furthermore, a bystander who decides to offer help will be embarrassed if it turns out that he or she has misinterpreted the situation when it is not really an emergency. For example, how might a person feel if he or she stepped out of the crowd to administer CPR to a man lying unconscious on the ground, only to roll him over and realize that he is merely intoxicated? Risks of this sort are greater the larger the number of other people present.

The second process, social influence, frequently contributes to the social inhibition of helping by leading bystanders to misinterpret the event. Emergencies are often ambiguous, and a person confronted with ambiguity will look to the behavior of other people for clues about how to behave. While the person is attempting to appraise the reactions of other people, he or she will probably attempt to remain calm. That person, then, is likely to see a group of others doing exactly the same: appearing calm and doing nothing while trying to figure out whether a true emergency is taking place. Each person will be fooled by the inaction of everyone else into thinking that the situation is less serious than it really is and that not intervening is the appropriate course of action. The ultimate result is a sort of group behavioral paralysis, and the victim goes without help.

The final process, the most powerful of the three, was probably the main force at work in the Genovese incident (social influence was probably not involved, since witnesses remained isolated from one another in their own apartments). This phenomenon, known as diffusion of responsibility, occurs when an individual knows that others are available to help. While a lone bystander at an emergency bears the total responsibility for helping, those in a group share the responsibility equally with the others present. Thus, the larger the number of other witnesses, the smaller is each individual's obligation to act. As a result, individuals in groups are likely to assume that someone else will intervene.

Applications

Latané and Darley tested their ideas in a number of ingenious experiments, several of which are considered classic examples of social psychological research. In one of these, Columbia University students arrived individually at a laboratory to take part in a study that they believed would involve an interview. Each subject was sent to a waiting room to complete a preliminary questionnaire. Some of them found two other people already seated in the room, while others sat down alone.

Soon after the subject began working on the questionnaire, smoke began filling the room through a wall vent. The smoke could hardly be ignored; within four minutes the room contained enough smoke to interfere with vision and breathing. Latané and Darley were primarily interested in how frequently subjects simply got up and left the room to report the emergency. Most (75 percent) of the subjects who were waiting alone reported the smoke, but those in groups were far less likely to do so. Groups consisting of three naïve subjects reported it only 38 percent of the time; when the subject waited (unknowingly, of course) with two confederates who were instructed to do nothing, only 10 percent responded.

Observations of the unresponsive subjects supported the researchers' notion that the social influence process in groups would inhibit helping by leading people to misinterpret the situation. Interviews with these participants revealed that they had produced a variety of explanations for the smoke: air conditioning vapor, steam, smog, and even "truth gas." In other words, lone subjects for the most part behaved responsibly, but those in groups were generally led by the inaction of others to conclude almost anything but the obvious—that a legitimate emergency was taking place. It is important to realize that social influence, as demonstrated in this experiment, is most potent when bystanders in groups do not communicate with one another; such was the case in this experiment, and such tends to be the case with analogous groups in real life. Simply talking to the others present can clarify what really is happening, thus eliminating the bystander effect.

A second classic study demonstrates the power of the diffusion-of-responsibility process. In this experiment, college students thought they were participating in a group discussion about the difficulties of adjusting to college. In order to reduce the discomfort that could be associated with discussing personal matters, each subject was ushered to a private cubicle from which he or she would communicate with other group members through an intercom system. In each case, however, there was only one actual subject; the other "group members" had been previously tape recorded. Thus, Latané and Darley were able to manipulate the size of the group as perceived by the subject.

Each "member" of the group talked for two minutes, with the actual subject speaking last. A second round then began, and the first "group member" to speak began suffering a frighteningly severe epileptic seizure, choking and pleading for help. Since the subject had no idea where the other "group members" were located, the only available course of helping action was to leave the cubicle and report the emergency to the person in charge.

On the basis of the diffusion-of-responsibility concept, Latané and Darley expected that the likelihood of helping would decrease as the perceived size of the group increased. When the subject was part of a two-person group (only him or her and the victim, thus making the subject the only person available to help), 85 percent of the participants reported the seizure. When the subject believed that he or she was in a group of three, 62 percent responded. Only 31 percent of those who thought they were in a six-person group offered help. Without question, the responsibility for acting in this emergency was perceived to be divided among everyone believed to be available to help.

The circumstances of this experiment correspond directly to those of the Kitty Genovese murder. Most important, the subjects in this study were not in a face-to-face group, just as the witnesses to the Genovese murder were isolated in their own apartments; consequently, social influence could not lead to a misinterpretation of the event (which was not ambiguous anyway). In short, simply knowing that others are available to respond acts as a powerful deterrent to helping. It is also significant that this experiment demonstrated that bystanders who fail to intervene are usually not the least bit apathetic or indifferent. Rather, the typical unresponsive subject showed clear signs of distress over the plight of the victim; nevertheless, the belief that others were present still tended to suppress intervention.

Diffusion of responsibility is a very common social force and is not at all restricted to situations as serious as those that have been discussed here. Anyone who has failed to work as hard as possible on a group task, heard a doorbell go unanswered at a party, or experienced a telephone ringing seven or eight times even though the entire family is at home has probably fallen victim to the same process.

Context

The work of Latané and Darley attracted much attention and acclaim. From a methodological standpoint, their experiments are still regarded as some of social psychology's most clever and intriguing. Their findings, however, were even more remarkable: Demonstrating consistently the social inhibition of helping, they destroyed the common belief in "safety in numbers." This research also provides a powerful illustration of one of the major lessons of social psychology—that situational forces affecting behavior can be overpowering, eliminating at least temporarily the influence of personality. The work of Latané and Darley showed convincingly that a person cannot rely on human nature, kindness, or any other dispositional quality if he or she should become the victim of an emergency.

This program of research also provided the impetus for much work on helping that has been conducted by other investigators. Various kinds of precipitating incidents were examined, as were differences between experiments conducted in laboratories and those performed in natural settings. Other studies investigated the effects of a wide range of different characteristics of the subjects, victims, and other bystanders involved. It was discovered, for example, that people are more likely to offer assistance when someone else has already modeled helping behavior and if the victim is particularly needy, deserving, or somehow similar to the helper; certain transitory mood states, such as happiness and guilt, were also found to increase helping. The research findings mentioned here are only a sample, as helping behavior continued to be a popular topic among social psychologists throughout the 1970's.

Despite the large assortment of factors investigated, many of these other studies included a manipulation of the variable that had been the principal concern of Latané and Darley: group size. Two major articles published by Latané and his colleagues in 1981 reviewed nearly one hundred different instances of research comparing helping by individuals in groups with that by lone bystanders. They found, almost without exception in these studies, that people were less likely to help in groups than when they were alone, suggesting that the bystander effect is perhaps as consistent and predictable as any within the domain of social psychology.

Although incidents such as the murder of Kitty Genovese do not occur every day, it is important to recognize that scores of them have been reported over the years, and they continue to occur regularly. Unfortunately, the understanding provided by the research has not led to strategies for avoiding these tragedies. (Considering the ability of situational forces to override personality influences, one should not be too surprised by this.) There is, however, one bit of hope: At least one study has demonstrated that students who have learned about the bystander effect in a psychology class are more likely to intervene in an emergency than those who have not been exposed to that material.

Bibliography

Batson, C. D. "Prosocial Motivation: Is It Ever Truly Altruistic?" In *Advances in Experimental Social Psychology*, edited by Leonard Berkowitz. San Diego: Academic Press, 1987. A very thorough examination of what happens psychologically within the person who helps, with a special focus on the role of empathy in determining the helping response. This chapter is somewhat high-level, but it does convey the flavor of this area of research.

Cialdini, Robert B. *Influence: Science and Practice.* 2d ed. Glenview, Ill.: Scott, Foresman, 1988. An extremely interesting book dealing generally with the issue of social influence. Contains an excellent chapter analyzing the bystander effect, with emphasis on the role of other people in helping to define a social situation. Cialdini presents some provocative examples and offers advice about how to prevent oneself from becoming a victim.

Latané, Bibb, and John M. Darley. *The Unresponsive Bystander: Why Doesn't He Help?* New York: Appleton-Century-Crofts, 1970. The classic source on bystander intervention in emergencies, detailing all of Latané and Darley's original research on the problem. The clever methodology of many of their experiments and their engaging writing style make this a fascinating and readable book.

Latané, Bibb, S. A. Nida, and D. W. Wilson. "The Effects of Group Size on Helping Behavior." In *Altruism and Helping Behavior: Social, Personality, and Developmental Perspectives*, edited by J. Phillipe Rushton and Richard M. Sorrentino. Hillsdale, N.J.: Lawrence Erlbaum, 1981. Reviews the research examining the relationship between group size and helping, including a discussion of the methodological problems involved. Contains not only a good summary of Latané and Darley's original theoretical ideas but also some subsequent developments, such as Latané's general model of group behavior known as social impact theory.

Macaulay, Jaqueline, and Leonard Berkowitz, eds. *Altruism and Helping Behavior: Social Psychological Studies of Some Antecedents and Consequences.* New York: Academic Press, 1970. A classic volume reporting much of the earliest work on the social psychology of helping. Not all the chapters deal directly with bystander intervention, but the book does contain two separate chapters by Latané and Darley that provide excellent summaries of much of their original work.

Rushton, J. Phillipe, and Richard M. Sorrentino, eds. *Altruism and Helping Behavior: Social, Personality, and Developmental Perspectives.* Hillsdale, N.J.: Lawrence Erlbaum, 1981. Presents a range of articles reflecting the different directions established in the study of helping behavior following the initial exploration of bystander intervention in emergencies. Some of the chapters deal not with bystander intervention per se but with helping or altruism in the broader sense (such as how altruism is learned).

Staub, Ervin. "Helping a Distressed Person: Social, Personality, and Stimulus Determinants." In *Advances in Experimental Social Psychology*, edited by Leonard Berkowitz. New York: Academic Press, 1974. Another important and frequently cited chapter from an earlier point in the history of research in this area. Although social psychologists rarely take issue with Latané and Darley's analysis of bystander intervention, Staub offers a somewhat different perspective, placing more emphasis on personality influences. He also presents some interesting research with children.

Steve A. Nida

Cross-References

HELPING: THEORETICAL PERSPECTIVES

Type of psychology: Social psychology
Field of study: Prosocial behavior

Theories of helping behavior have attempted to explain why people offer physical and psychological assistance to others in both emergency and nonemergency situations. These theories have considered the roles of physiological arousal, judgments of costs and rewards, mood states, and attributions of responsibility in influencing helping behavior.

Principal terms

ATTRIBUTIONS OF RESPONSIBILITY: inferences or judgments of who or what is responsible for a given event

BEHAVIORAL STANDARDS: rules or expectations of ideal behavior; similar to norms

NET COSTS: costs or negative outcomes associated with engaging in a behavior (for example, effort, embarrassment, possible injury) minus rewards or positive outcomes associated with engaging in the behavior (for example, admiration from others, feelings of accomplishment, monetary compensation)

NORM OF RECIPROCITY: a shared belief that one should treat others as one would like them to treat oneself and help people who have not harmed one

NORM OF SOCIAL RESPONSIBILITY: a shared belief that one should help those who are in need, especially those who are dependent on one, such as children

SELF-FOCUSED ATTENTION: attention or consciousness focused on the self, as opposed to other aspects of the external environment; often associated with attempts to follow behavioral standards or norms

Overview

Helping behaviors can take a variety of forms. Some, such as carrying a book for a friend, require little effort. Others, such as jumping into a frozen lake to rescue a drowning stranger, are life-threatening. To explain helping behavior, researchers have studied many variables and developed theories to organize them and account for their interrelationships.

In 1981, Jane Allyn Piliavin, John Dovidio, Samuel Gaertner, and Russell Clark introduced the "arousal cost-reward" model. This model assumes that witnessing the need or distress of another person is physiologically arousing. When one attributes the source of one's arousal to another person's distress, the arousal is sometimes experienced as emotionally unpleasant, and one becomes motivated to reduce it.

According to the arousal cost-reward model, a person will choose to engage in the arousal-decreasing response associated with the fewest net costs. Net costs are based on two types of rewards and costs associated with the helping situation: costs for not helping and rewards and costs for helping. Costs for not helping occur when no assistance is given and may include experiences such as feeling troubled because someone in need is continuing to suffer or receiving criticism from others for being callous. Costs for helping are direct negative outcomes that the potential helper might experience after offering help, such as loss of time, embarrassment, or injury. Helping, however, can also be associated with positive outcomes such as praise, gratitude, and feelings of self-worth.

Piliavin and her colleagues suggest that both types of costs influence the decision to help. When net costs are low, as the costs for not helping increase, helping in the form of direct intervention becomes more likely. If net costs for helping are high, however, direct intervention is unlikely regardless of potential costs for not helping. In this latter situation, a person may give indirect assistance (for example, call someone else to help). Alternatively, the person may deny responsibility for helping, reinterpret the situation as one in which help is not needed, or try to leave the scene altogether.

Philip Brickman and his colleagues argue that when one sees a person in need, one makes attributions about how responsible that person is for the problem he or she faces and also about how much responsibility the person should take for its solution. These attributions in turn influence one's judgment about who one thinks is best suited to deliver help, and, if one decides to offer it oneself, they influence its form. One may be most likely to offer direct assistance if one attributes little responsibility to that person for solving the problem—as when a child is lost in a shopping mall. In contrast, if one judges a person as responsible for solving his or her problem, as when a friend has a nasty boss, one may offer encouragement and moral support but not directly intervene. Thus, who one thinks should provide the remedy—oneself, experts, or the person who needs the help—depends on attributions that one makes about responsibility.

One's mood may also influence one's decision to help someone who is in need. In general, people experiencing a positive mood, such as happiness, are more likely to offer help than are those in neutral moods. Using quantitative procedures for summarizing the results of thirty-four experimental studies, Michael Carlson, Ventura Charlin, and Norman Miller concluded that the best general explanation for why positive moods increase helpfulness is that they heighten sensitivity to positive reinforcement or good outcomes. This sensitivity includes both thinking more about good outcomes for oneself and increased thought about the goodness of behaving prosocially. This general summary incorporates many explanations that have been proposed for the relation between positive moods and helping, among them the mood maintenance and social outlook explanations.

Mood maintenance argues that one behaves more helpfully when happy because doing so prolongs one's good mood. The social outlook explanation points instead to the fact that positive moods are often the consequences of another person's behavior (for example, being given a compliment). Such actions by others trigger thoughts about human kindness, cooperativeness, and goodness. These thoughts, if still present when someone asks for help, make a person more likely to respond positively.

The effects of bad moods on helpfulness are more complex. Carlson and Miller also quantitatively summarized the effects found in forty-four studies concerned with the impact of various mood-lowering events on helpfulness. These studies included such diverse procedures for inducing negative moods as having subjects repeat depressing phrases, view unpleasant slides, imagine sad experiences, and fail at a task. Two factors can apparently account for most of the findings on negative moods and helping. The first is whether the target of the mood-lowering event is the self or someone else; the second is whether the self or an outside force is responsible for the mood-lowering event. When one is responsible for imposing a mood-lowering event on another person, and therefore feels guilty, helping is very likely. When one is responsible for an event that lowers one's own mood (as when one engages in self-harm) or when one witnesses another person impose a mood-lowering event on someone else (that is, when one experiences empathy), a positive response to a subsequent request for help is more likely, but not as much so as in the first case. In contrast, when someone else is responsible for one's own negative mood—when one has been victimized—one's helpfulness tends to be inhibited.

Applications

The explanations discussed above can be applied to a wide range of helping situations—reactions to both physical and psychological distress, situations in which helping appears to be determined by a rational consideration of costs and rewards, and situations in which the help offered seemingly is irrational and very costly.

One of the studies on which the arousal: cost-reward model was based suggests how consideration of costs and rewards might affect the decision to offer direct physical assistance. In this study, a man feigned collapse on the floor of a New York subway a few minutes after boarding the train and remained there until help was given. In some cases, the man smelled of alcohol and carried an alcohol bottle wrapped in a paper bag, giving the impression that drunkenness had caused his fall. In other instances, the man carried a cane, suggesting that he had fallen because of a physical impairment. Although many people offered assistance in both conditions, more people helped the man with the cane than the man who appeared to be drunk.

The different amounts of assistance in the two conditions may result from differences in perceived net costs. Potential helpers may have expected greater costs when the man looked drunk than when he appeared to be disabled. Helping a drunk may require more effort and be more unpleasant then helping someone with a physical impairment. It may also be less intrinsically and extrinsically rewarding than helping someone with a physical impairment. Finally, costs for not helping may be lower in the case of the drunk than for the man with the cane. The drunk may be perceived as "only drunk" and therefore not really needy. Thus, the finding that more people helped the man with the cane is consistent with the hypothesis that helping increases as the net costs associated with the helping response decrease.

Although considerations of costs and rewards are important, it would be unrealistic to think that helping only occurs when net costs are low. People may engage in very costly helping behaviors when physiological arousal is especially high, such as in clear, unambiguous emergencies. The actions of an unknown passenger aboard an airplane that had crashed into a frozen river illustrate this point. As a helicopter attempted to pull people out of the water to safety, this passenger repeatedly handed the lowered life ring to other, more seriously injured passengers, even though these acts of heroism eventually cost him his life.

Much research on helpfulness has asked, When do people help? It is also important, however, to look at what type of help is given and how the person in need is expected to react to offers of assistance. The Brickman model, involving attributions of responsibility for the problem and its solution, does this; it also looks at more everyday forms of helping. According to Brickman, if one attributes responsibility for both the problem and its solution to the person in need, one is applying the moral model of helping. With this orientation, one may have the tendency to view the person in need as lazy and undeserving of help. In the subway example, people may not have helped the fallen drunk because they made such attributions. Although people who apply the moral model may not give direct assistance, they may sometimes support and encourage the person's own effort to overcome the problem.

If one sees people as responsible for their problem but not for its solution, then one is applying the enlightenment model. Criminals are held responsible for violating the law but are jailed because they are judged incapable of reforming themselves, and jail is believed to be rehabilitating. Discipline from those in authority is seen as the appropriate helping response, and submission to it is expected from the person receiving the "assistance."

The medical model applies when the person is seen as responsible for neither the problem nor its solution. This orientation is often taken toward the ill. Such situations call for an expert whose recommendations are to be accepted and fulfilled.

In the final combination of attributions of responsibility for a problem and its solution, the compensatory model, the person is not held responsible for having caused the problem. The problem may be judged to be caused by factors beyond the person's control, such as when an earthquake occurs. In this model, however, the person is held responsible for solving the problem. Helpers may provide useful resources but are not expected to take the initiative for a solution. In the case of an earthquake, the government may offer low-interest loans for rebuilding, but victims must decide whether to apply for one and rebuild their homes.

Context

Concern with helping behavior has its roots in early philosophy. Thinkers such as Aristotle, Socrates, Niccolò Machiavelli, and Thomas Hobbes debated whether humans are by nature good or bad, selfish or selfless. Most empirical psychological research on the topic, however, was only initiated after the 1950's. This was probably not coincidental. Many people were concerned with the atrocities of World War II and, in the United States, with rising crime rates. In response, psychologists not only began to investigate human cruelty but also gave increased attention to what could be done to offset it and promote positive behavior instead. Similarly, the emergence of the Civil Rights movement, with its emphasis on cooperation and harmony, probably further propelled the study of prosocial behavior.

Early studies of helping behavior examined situational variables that influence the decision to help someone who is in physical distress. The arousal cost-reward model and the subway experiment characterize this type of work. Also important during this period were Alvin Gouldner's theorizing on the norm of reciprocity and subsequent empirical investigation of the norms governing helping behavior, such as Leonard Berkowitz's work in the 1960's. As social psychologists explored situational variables that influence helping, developmental psychologists examined the emergence of positive social behavior in children. Some, such as Jean Piaget and Lawrence Kohlberg, postulated distinct stages of moral development. Others focused on how helpful models influenced children's subsequent behavior.

While research continues in all these areas, new questions also attract interest. Studies of people's responses to others' physical distress have now been complemented by research on how people respond to someone in psychological distress. Similarly, researchers have extended their interests in the potential helper to examine how the person in need of help is affected by seeking and receiving it.

Also important in understanding helping behavior has been the study of personality and how individuals differ in their tendency to help. Some of this work is related to research on norms, in that it looks at whether people develop a personal set of rules or standards which govern their helping behavior. Another approach, adopted by Margaret Clark and Judson Mills, has looked at how the relationship between the help requester and the help giver influences helpfulness. Research on helping now incorporates many different influences on the helping process, from individual to social to developmental factors. In the process, the applicability of the research findings has grown and has given rise to a broader understanding of the types of helping behavior that may occur, when they may occur, who might engage in them, and why.

Bibliography

Clark, Margaret S., ed. *Prosocial Behavior.* Newbury Park, Calif.: Sage Publications, 1991. Focuses on the broader area of positive social behaviors and therefore includes discussions of altruism as well as chapters on helping. Two chapters deal with the development of prosocial behavior. Also noteworthy is a chapter that covers aspects of help-seeking behavior. A chapter on moods and one on the arousal cost-reward model are included as well.

Derlega, Valerian J., and Janusz Grzelak, eds. *Cooperation and Helping Behavior: Theories and Research.* New York: Academic Press, 1982. The first chapter provides a nontechnical discussion of the similarities and differences between the related issues of helping and cooperation, while also serving as an introduction to later chapters. Chapters on helping discuss the arousal cost-reward model and extend the model to show how help seekers may be influenced by cost/reward considerations.

Piliavin, Jane Allyn, John F. Dovidio, Samuel L. Gaertner, and Russell Clark. *Emergency Intervention.* New York: Academic Press, 1981. Explores the processes that lead people to offer help to others. The development of the arousal cost-reward model is traced through the discussion of the particular research on which it is based, including the subway study reviewed here.

Rushton, J. Philippe, and Richard M. Sorrentino, eds. *Altruism and Helping Behavior: Social, Personality, and Developmental Perspectives.* Hillsdale, N.J.: Lawrence Erlbaum, 1981. Covers, as the title implies, three main areas. Under developmental issues, varied topics such as the influence of television and the role of genetics (sociobiology) are covered. Also includes a discussion of moods and a model of how norms may influence helping.

Staub, Ervin, Daniel Bar-Tal, Jerzy Karylowski, and Janusz Reykowski, eds. *Development and Maintenance of Prosocial Behavior: International Perspectives on Prosocial Behavior.* New York: Plenum Press, 1984. This set of twenty-four chapters from various researchers focuses not only on helping but also on other positive behaviors such as cooperation, generosity, and kindness. Covers a range of topics, from developmental aspects of prosocial behavior to the effects of help seeking and help receiving to applications of knowledge about helping behavior. A unique aspect of this book is its consideration of research done in many different countries.

Tiffany A. Ito
Norman Miller

Cross-References

Aggression: Definitions and Theoretical Explanations, 162; Altruism, Cooperation, and Empathy, 228; Crowd Behavior, 737; Helping: Bystander Intervention, 1163; Moral Development, 1594; Social Perception: Others, 2311.

HINDBRAIN STRUCTURES

Type of psychology: Biological bases of behavior
Field of study: Nervous system

The hindbrain is a developmentally defined portion of the brain that contains the pons, medulla, and cerebellum; although many portions of the hindbrain are involved in relaying information from higher brain regions to other parts of the brain and body, some areas generate activity that is important for motor control, arousal, sleep, and motor learning.

Principal terms
AROUSAL: an increased state of excitation in the nervous system, possibly caused by heightened activity in the cerebral cortex induced by hindbrain input
FIBER PATHWAYS: a collection of axons from a number of neurons that forms a bundle as it courses through the brain; the white matter of the brain
FOREBRAIN: a developmentally defined division of the brain that contains structures such as the cerebral hemispheres, the thalamus, and the hypothalamus
HINDBRAIN: a developmentally defined division of the brain that contains the pons, medulla, and cerebellum
MOTOR LEARNING: simple types of learning that involve modification of the motor system; classical (Pavlovian) conditioning of skeletal muscle responses is an example
MOTOR SYSTEM: that portion of the nervous system concerned with generating and executing muscle movements
NUCLEI: a collection of a number of neuron cell bodies that usually share a common function; the gray matter of the brain
SENSORY SYSTEM: that portion of the nervous system concerned with transmitting and registering information from stimuli found in the environment or generated by other parts of the body

Overview

Over the years, anatomists have found it convenient to subdivide the vertebrate brain into three general regions: the forebrain (or prosencephalon), the midbrain (or mesencephalon), and the hindbrain (or rhombencephalon). The subdivisions were created on the basis of how the vertebrate brain develops early in life. In very young embryos, the central nervous system resembles a tube with walls made of nerve cells (called neurons) and a fluid-filled interior. Within a few weeks after conception, the head region of the tube enlarges and begins to show three distinct regions that anatomists have designated, from front to back, the forebrain, the midbrain, and the hindbrain. Within six to seven weeks after conception, the forebrain and hindbrain show signs of subdividing further. Regions of the forebrain eventually develop into a number of structures such as the cerebral hemispheres, the thalamus, and the hypothalamus. The hindbrain forms two major subdivisions, which are referred to as the metencephalon and myelencephalon. Eventually, the metencephalon region develops into the cerebellum and pons, while the myelencephalon develops into the medulla.

Much attention and research has been focused over the years on the role of forebrain structures in behavior. The major reason for this attention is that the forebrain contains the cerebral hemispheres (cerebral cortex), a large, prominent feature of the human brain. Moreover, complex behavioral functions such as problem solving, speech, and perception have been thought to be generated solely by activity in the cerebral cortex. Because these relatively complex processes are generally thought to be uniquely human, they have been of interest to a variety of researchers, including cognitive psychologists, neuropsychologists, and neuroscientists.

Conversely, the hindbrain has typically been thought to be involved in more basic, maintenance functions. The cerebellum, for example, has long been known to be part of the brain's motor system (that part of the brain that participates in the production of movements). Through its interactions with motor areas of the cerebral cortex and other portions of the motor system, the cerebellum is thought to play major roles in providing feedback control of movement and integrating the activities of the sensory system and motor system. The medulla contains a number of groups of neurons called cranial nerve nuclei that provide relay or interface points between the brain and other parts of the body such as the stomach, heart, and mouth region. In addition to the cranial nerve nuclei, the medulla contains other clusters of neurons that monitor and control basic bodily functions such as respiration and heart rate as well as neurons that provide input to the cerebral cortex regarding levels of general arousal. All neural pathways that descend from higher brain regions to the other portions of the body, as well as all ascending paths, course through the medulla.

A general hierarchical scheme of information processing in the vertebrate brain, based partially on functional differences between brain areas, has been developed. The forebrain is typically thought to be the central brain region where high-level perceptual and cognitive analysis takes place, where complex motor functions occur, where sensory information is integrated, and where emotional and motivational information is processed. The hindbrain is generally believed to be involved in processing and relaying information that originates in the higher brain regions either by acting as a simple conduit for fibers ascending to or descending from other parts of the nervous system or by providing target neurons that receive input from higher levels. An example of this hierarchical arrangement is the primate motor system. Large neurons in the motor area of the frontal cortex have long been known to be involved in controlling precise movements of the digits and hands of primates. These neurons send long output fibers (called axons) through the midbrain and hindbrain areas to make contact directly with neurons in the spinal cord that control the muscles of the hand.

Hence, the hindbrain in this example acts as a simple conduit for descending motor pathways that are projecting to the spinal cord. Other neurons from the cerebral cortex make contact with neurons in the hindbrain. For example, neurons that control the musculature of the face and neck as well as neurons that project to trunk muscles are located in the hindbrain. The motor neurons located in the cerebral cortex innervate these hindbrain neurons, thus allowing activity generated in the forebrain to activate the muscles of the face and neck.

Although the common perception of brain function is that forebrain regions always "control" or "regulate" lower brain regions such as the hindbrain, this characterization is not entirely accurate. There are instances in which hindbrain activity influences forebrain activity during movement. The cerebellum receives extensive descending input from the forebrain. Much of the output of the cerebellum is not simply routed to the periphery but rather projects back upward to the forebrain, where it modifies the activity of motor cortex neurons. Examples such as these have made it clear that, in addition to executing commands issued by the forebrain (either as a conduit for descending pathways or as a location of relay neurons), the hindbrain makes substantial contributions to the generation and modification of behavior.

Applications

One hindbrain structure that has been studied extensively for its involvement in behavior is the cerebellum. The cerebellum is located on the dorsal (back) surface of the hindbrain immediately above the medulla. Although the cerebellum is present in all vertebrates, in mammals it is greatly expanded, especially its lateral regions. The cerebellum has two general regions, a cortical region and a deep nuclear region. It is attached to the brain stem via a set of fiber pathways that make up a large part of the pons. Like that of the cerebral cortex, the outer surface of the cerebellum is highly convoluted, with many regions buried in deep fissures. Activity generated in the cerebellar cortex is projected to the deep nuclei, which in turn send output to several other brain regions.

The predominant function of the cerebellum is motor control. It receives input from a variety of sensory structures (including information from skin, joints, and muscle receptors), input from the inner ear concerned with equilibrium (the vestibular system), auditory information, and visual information. Most of the cerebellar outputs are directed toward brain regions involved in the control of movement. The relationship between the cerebellum and the motor regions of the cerebral cortex exemplifies how the cerebellum is involved in motor control. Edward Evarts and his colleagues demonstrated that neurons in both the cerebellum and cerebral cortex discharged when an animal made a voluntary movement (such as pushing a lever). A closer examination of when the neurons began discharging in the two structures revealed that the cerebellar cells increased their activity before cells in the cerebral cortex did. It is now well known that an intricate relationship between the cerebellum and the sensorimotor areas of the cerebral cortex exists; the system can be described as a massive loop of motor control. Fibers from the deep cerebellar nuclei ascend toward the forebrain and terminate in a specific brain structure called the thalamus. This large nucleus then projects to motor areas of the cerebral cortex in a very specific fashion: A precise area-to-area projection from the cerebellum to the cerebral cortex is created. The motor cortex, in turn, sends descending projections to the pons, which then relays the input into the cerebellum. In this system, activity generated in the cerebellum can affect activity in the cerebral cortex and vice versa.

Another series of experiments, by Richard F. Thompson and his colleagues, has suggested that the cerebellum may be important for simple forms of motor learning, such as classical conditioning. One example of this form of learning is classical eyelid conditioning in rabbits. Before training, an air puff directed at the eye produces a rather discrete eyeblink. If a tone is presented 0.5 to 2.0 seconds before the air puff, the rabbits eventually learn that the tone signals the impending air puff and close their eyes in anticipation of the puff. Thompson and his coworkers discovered that very small lesions (smaller than 1 cubic millimeter) placed in the deep cerebellar nuclei permanently abolished the conditioned eyeblink response. Other studies have extended these results to show that these lesions prevent initial learning of the response when delivered before training, abolish conditioned eyelid responses in rats and cats, disrupt classical leg flexion conditioning, and abolish conditioning when other conditioning stimuli are used (such as lights and mild electric shocks). Furthermore, neurons in the deep cerebellar nuclei discharge in a pattern of activity that appears to produce the classically conditioned response. These studies suggest that the cerebellum may be involved in more than simply modifying motor commands generated in the forebrain. Activity in the cerebellum may actually be altered during motor learning situations, thus providing the neural substrates of a simple form of learning.

The second major region of the vertebrate hindbrain includes the pons and medulla. In most mammals, the medulla is a continuation of the spinal cord at its rostral end, and it continues upward until the pons. The medulla resembles the spinal cord in its tubelike appearance; it contains a number of readily identifiable clusters of neurons (medullary nuclei) and all ascending and descending fiber tracts linking the brain stem and spinal cord with higher brain regions. The pons is an upward continuation of the medulla and borders the midbrain. A number of nuclei and fiber tracts are located in the pons, including the massive pontine nuclei, which serve as a relay point for information descending from the cerebral cortex to the cerebellum and other nervous system sites.

The medulla and pons contain a number of cell groups that are involved in behavior. The dorsal-column nuclei serve as a relay point for fibers ascending from the spinal cord to the cerebral cortex. These fibers carry sensory information from touch and pressure detectors located in the periphery of the body. A number of cranial nerve nuclei are also located in the medulla. These include several motor nuclei that send neural input to muscles and several sensory nuclei that relay sensory information from other regions of the body to the brain. An example of cranial nerve nuclei is the vagus nerve nuclei, which have both sensory and motor components. The vagus nerve nuclei serve as relay points for sensory information coming to the central nervous system from many internal organs, such as the stomach, thus providing a means to signal the status of a variety of internal states (such as aspects of hunger). The motor component of the vagus nuclei relays information to muscles of the throat and many internal organs such as the heart, blood vessels, and tear glands. This system allows the brain to control the function of a number of internal organs. A number of other cranial nerve nuclei are found in the pons. Other clusters of cells can be found in this region, including a group of cells that control rhythmic diaphragm movement through feedback control during respiration. The reticular formation and the raphe system are also located in the pons and medulla. These regions of the hindbrain project somewhat diffusely to many regions of the forebrain and are thought to be involved in regulating arousal and sleep. It is believed that the diffuse pattern of projections from the reticular formation to the forebrain allows any strong stimulus that activates the hindbrain reticular formation to activate large areas of the cerebral cortex, thus altering general arousal level.

Because the cranial nerve nuclei and regions such as the respiration control area have been found in the medulla and pons, this area of the hindbrain has generally been recognized as having an important role in a variety of "automatic" behaviors that are important for the immediate survival of the animal. In addition to providing a means of communication with other body areas, these hindbrain regions receive input from higher brain areas and send ascending output to the higher areas. In short, these hindbrain regions provide an interface between higher brain regions and body regions outside the central nervous system. There are neural connections, however, within and between hindbrain structures. It is therefore possible for these structures to coordinate, through interactions that take place solely at the hindbrain level, complex behavioral responses to changes in the environment.

Context

Over the years, attempts have been made to determine which functions the hindbrain and lower nervous system areas could perform when higher brain areas were removed. For example, Sir Charles Sherrington, a British physiologist, and his co-workers summarized in 1906 that some simple behaviors could be generated by the spinal cord after it had been surgically isolated from the rest of the central nervous system. These behaviors included flexion (withdrawal) reflexes as well as a primitive scratching reflex. Both Wilder Penfield and Phillip Bard and their colleagues studied the behavior of low-decerebrate vertebrates (animals with all nervous-system tissue above the hindbrain removed). Although these animals had no thermoregulatory ability, they could swallow food. Lightly touching the animals resulted in a movement to a crouched position, and they could walk (unsteadily) when stimulated more strongly. A number of simple affective behaviors could also be elicited with stimulation, including tail-lashing, growling, biting, and hissing, and the animals were capable of exhibiting primitive sleep/waking cycles. The most characteristic behavior seen in the low-decerebrate animals was called "exaggerated standing" or "decerebrate rigidity." This condition is marked by a high level of tone in those muscles used to hold up the body (the antigravity muscles) and is thought to be caused by an imbalance in the postural system's inhibitory and excitatory inputs to the antigravity muscles. In brief, studies of low-decerebrate animals have indicated a role of the hindbrain in generating many simple reflexes (such as those used in swallowing and respiration) as well as providing mechanisms for postural support.

Since the 1960's, most research concerning the role of the hindbrain in behavior has concentrated on the cerebellum. Mostly through the efforts of researchers such as Sir John Eccles, Masao Ito, and Rudolfo Llinas, much is known about the anatomy and physiology of the cerebellum. Its role in modulating motor-related activity in the cerebral cortex and its role in processing vestibular information have been well documented over the years. During the 1980's, work by Thompson and his colleagues focused attention on possible changes in neural activity in the cerebellum that may form the basis of motor learning. These experiments suggest that the cerebellum may be involved in more than passively processing movement-related activity that originates in other brain regions. Rather, these experiments suggest that learning processes may occur within the cerebellum and that it is capable of projecting these changes to other portions of the nervous system to generate new or altered behaviors.

Studies of the involvement of the hindbrain in behavior have suggested that it has two general behavioral functions. First, the hindbrain contains several groups of neurons, such as the cranial nerve nuclei, that provide an interface between regions of the central nervous system, such as the forebrain, and other parts of the body (including other parts of the nervous system, such as motor areas). Second, the hindbrain contains some populations of neurons, such as those in the cerebellum, that may play a central role in generating behaviors such as those involved in motor learning. This latter hindbrain function should provide an interesting direction of study for years to come.

Bibliography

Kalat, James. *Biological Psychology.* 3d ed. Belmont, Calif.: Wadsworth, 1984. Kalat's textbook provides a relatively easy-to-read summary of the field of biological psychology. The chapter on daily rhythms of activity and sleep provides a good summary of how the hindbrain influences forebrain structures in regulating activity levels.

Kolb, Bryan, and Ian Q. Wishaw. *Fundamentals of Human Neuropsychology.* 3d ed. New York: W. H. Freeman, 1990. Kolb and Wishaw's book provides an in-depth treatment of several topics in the field of human neuropsychology. They present a general theory of brain organization and function that is chiefly based on observing behaviors in animals that have progressively larger portions of the nervous system intact.

Nauta, W. J. H., and M. Fiertag. "The Organization of the Brain." In *The Brain.* San Francisco: W. H. Freeman, 1979. This article provides a succinct yet comprehensive overview of how the brain is organized. In addition to the excellent text, the figures that appear in this paper greatly assist the reader in understanding basic connectivity within the brain.

Rosenzweig, Mark R., and Arnold L. Leiman. *Physiological Psychology.* 2d ed. New York: Random House, 1989. This textbook provides a fourfold approach for studying physiological psychology: descriptive, comparative/evolutionary, developmental, and biologically mechanistic. The chapters on brain development and the cranial nerve nuclei should contribute to the reader's understanding of the hindbrain's involvement in behavior.

Thompson, Richard F. *The Brain: An Introduction to Neuroscience.* New York: W. H. Freeman, 1985. This well-written text provides a clear introduction to many areas of neuroscience research. The section on motor control systems provides an excellent overview of how the hindbrain and the cerebral cortex interact during movement generation and execution.

Joseph E. Steinmetz

Cross-References

The Autonomic Nervous System, 362; Brain-Stem Structures, 461; The Central and Peripheral Nervous Systems, 494; Forebrain Structures, 1043; Reflexes, 2066; Reticular Formation, 2103.

HOMOSEXUALITY

Type of psychology: Motivation
Fields of study: Attitudes and behavior; interpersonal relations; physical motives

Sexuality is one of the most complex and individual attributes of the human psyche. There are four types of theories with regard to the development of sexual orientation, but none seems sufficient to explain the huge diversity to be found in sexual expression across ages and cultures.

Principal terms
ANDROGYNY: the expression of both traditionally feminine and
traditionally masculine attributes
GAY: a term that is usually, but not exclusively, used to describe a
homosexual male who is open about his sexual orientation
HOMOPHOBIA: a fear of, prejudice against, or hatred toward homosexuals,
usually based upon irrational stereotyping
HOMOSEXUAL: a person who is attracted to members of the same sex;
of or relating to sexual activity with a member of the same sex
LESBIAN: a female homosexual; often used in association with the term
"gay," which usually refers to males
PEDOPHILE: an adult who is sexually aroused by children; about
90 percent of pedophiles are males with a heterosexual orientation
TRANSSEXUAL: someone who feels like he or she is trapped in the body
of a member of the wrong sex; sometimes gender-change surgery
is sought
TRANSVESTITE: a person who, for fun or sexual arousal, often dresses
and acts like a member of the opposite sex (going "in drag"); most
are heterosexual males

Overview

Theories on the origin and development of homosexual orientation can be categorized into four groups: psychoanalytic, biological, social learning, and sociobiological theories. Psychoanalytic theories are based on the Freudian model of "psychosexual stages" of development, developed by Austrian psychiatrist Sigmund Freud. According to this model, every child goes through several stages, including the "phallic stage," during which he or she learns to identify with his or her same-sex parent. For boys, this is supposed to be particularly difficult, since it requires redefining the strong bond that they have had with their mother since birth. According to Freudian theorists, homosexuality is an outcome of the failure to resolve this developmental crisis: If a boy's father is absent or "weak," and his mother is domineering or overprotective, the boy may never come to identify with his father; for a girl, having a "cold" or rejecting mother could prevent her from identifying with the female role.

Research has found that homosexuals are, in fact, more likely to feel an inability to relate to their same-sex parent than heterosexuals are and to report that the same-sex parent was "cold" or "distant" during their childhood. Some studies have suggested, however, that this psychological distance between parent and offspring is found mostly in families with children who show cross-gender behaviors when very young and that the distancing is more likely to be a result of preexisting differences in the child than a cause of later differences.

Biological theories have suggested that homosexuality is genetic, a result of unusual hormone levels, or is a result of prenatal maternal effects on the developing fetus. Although there may be genes which predispose a person to become homosexual under certain circumstances, there are no specific genes for homosexuality. Similarly, there are no consistent differences between levels of hormones in homosexual and heterosexual adults. The possibility remains that subtle fluctuations of hormones during critical periods of fetal development may influence brain structures which regulate sexual arousal and attraction.

Social-learning models suggest that homosexual orientation develops as a response to pleasurable homosexual experiences during childhood and adolescence, perhaps coupled with unpleasant heterosexual experiences. Many boys have homosexual experiences as part of their normal sexual experimentation while growing up. According to the model, some boys will find these experiences more pleasurable or successful than their experiments with heterosexuality and will continue to seek homosexual interactions. Why only certain boys find their homosexual experiences more pleasurable than their heterosexual experiences could be related to a variety of factors, including age, family dynamics, the child's social skills, and personality. Young girls are less likely to have early homosexual experiences but may be "turned off" from heterosexuality by experiences such as rape, abuse, or assault.

Sociobiological models are all based on the assumption that common behaviors must have evolved because they were somehow beneficial, or related to something beneficial, which helped the individuals who performed them to pass their genes to the next generation. From this perspective, homosexuality seems incongruous, but since it is so common, researchers have tried to find out how homosexual behavior might in fact increase a person's ability to pass on genes to subsequent generations. Theorists have come up with three possible explanations—the parental manipulation model, the kin selection model, and the by-product model.

The parental manipulation model suggests that homosexuals do not directly pass on more of their genes than heterosexuals, but that their parents do. According to this model, parents subconsciously manipulate their child's development to make him or her less likely to start a family; in this way, the adult child is able to contribute time, energy, and income to brothers, sisters, nieces, and nephews. In the end, the parents have "sacrificed" one child's reproduction in exchange for more grandchildren—or, at least, for more indulged, more evolutionarily competitive grandchildren.

The kin selection model is similar, but in it, the homosexual individual is not manipulated but is sacrificing his or her own reproduction willingly (although subconsciously) in exchange for more nieces and nephews (that is, more relatives' genes in subsequent generations). According to this model, individuals who are willing to make this sacrifice (no matter how subconscious) are either those who are not likely to be very successful in heterosexual interactions (and are thus not actually making much of a sacrifice) or those who have a particular attribute that makes them especially good at helping their families. As an analogy, theorists point out how, through much of human history, reproductive sacrifice in the form of joining a religious order often provided income, protection, or status for other family members.

The by-product model suggests that homosexuality is an inevitable outcome of evolved sex differences. According to this model, the facts that, overall, men have a higher sex drive than women and that, historically, most societies have allowed polygyny (where one man has more than one wife) will result in many unmated males who still have an urge to satisfy their high sex drive. Thus, men will become (or will at least act) homosexual when male partners are easier to find than females. This model is the one most likely to explain "facultative homosexuality," that is, homosexual behavior by people who consider themselves basically heterosexual.

Applications

Prior to the gay liberation movement, homosexuality was classified as a mental disorder. In the 1970's, however, when psychiatrists were revising the American Psychiatric Association's *Diagnostic and Statistical Manual of Mental Disorders* (DSM), they removed homosexuality from the list of illnesses. The third edition of the manual (DSM-III), published in 1980, reflected this change. Homosexuality is not associated with disordered thinking or impaired abilities in any way. Therefore, counseling or therapy for the purpose of changing sexual orientation is not recommended. Even when sought, such therapy is rarely successful. On the other hand, many gays, especially adolescents, find benefit from counseling in order to find information, support, and ways to cope with their sexuality.

For men, sexual orientation seems to be fixed at an early age; most gay men feel as though they were "always" homosexual, just as most heterosexual men feel they were "always" heterosexual. In women, however, sexual orientation is less likely to be fixed early; some women change from a heterosexual to homosexual orientation (or vice versa) in adulthood. In such cases, sexual orientation is better seen as a choice than as an acting out of something preexisting in the psyche, and often such changes are made after a woman has left an unhealthy or abusive relationship or has experienced some other sort of emotional or psychological awakening that changes her outlook on life. In these cases, counseling for the sake of changing sexual orientation per se is not recommended, but it may be appropriate for the woman to seek help dealing with the other changes or events in her life. Most women in this circumstance find that a same-sex, even lesbian, therapist is most helpful, since she will be more likely to empathize with her client.

Many women who change sexual orientation in mid-life already have children, and many who are lesbian from adolescence choose to have children (by artificial insemination or by having intercourse with a male friend). Often, such women have found a lack of support for their parenting and sometimes even experience legal problems retaining custody rights of their children. Gay men, too, have had difficulty retaining parental rights or becoming foster or adoptive parents.

Psychological research shows, however, that homosexuals are as good at parenting as heterosexuals and that they are as effective at providing role models. Homosexuals are more likely than heterosexuals to model androgyny—the expression of both traditionally masculine and traditionally feminine attributes—for their children. Some research has shown that an androgynous approach is more healthy and more successful in American society than sticking to traditionally defined roles. For example, sometimes women need to be assertive on the job or in relationships, whereas traditionally men were assertive and women were passive. Similarly, men are less likely to experience stress-related mental and physical health problems if they learn to express their emotions, something only women were traditionally supposed to do.

Neither modeling androgyny nor modeling homosexuality is likely to cause a child to become homosexual, and children reared by homosexual parents are no more likely to become homosexual than children reared by heterosexual parents. Similarly, modeling of androgyny or homosexuality by teachers does not influence the development of homosexuality in children and adolescents. Having an openly homosexual teacher may be a stimulus for a gay child to discover and explore his or her sexuality, but it does not create that sexuality.

Other variations in adult sexual expression, sometimes associated with, or confused with, homosexuality, are transvestism and transsexuality. Transvestism occurs when a person enjoys, or gets sexually excited by, dressing as a member of the opposite sex. Some gay men enjoy cross-dressing, and others enjoy acting feminine. The majority of homosexuals, however, do not do either; most transvestites are heterosexual. Transsexuality is different from both homosexuality and transvestism; it is categorized by a feeling that one is trapped in the body of the wrong sex. Transsexuality, unlike homosexuality or transvestism, is considered a mental disorder; it is officially a form of gender dysphoria—gender confusion. Transsexuals may feel as though they are engaging in homosexual activity if they have sexual relations with a member of the opposite sex. Some transsexuals decide to cross-dress and live as a member of the opposite sex. They may have hormone treatments and surgery to change legally into a member of the opposite sex. Transsexuality, unlike homosexuality or transvestism, is very rare.

Context

The word "homosexual" is usually used in everyday language as a noun, referring to someone who is sexually attracted to, and has sexual relations with, members of the same sex. As a noun, however, the word is misleading, since few people who call themselves homosexual have never engaged in heterosexual activity; similarly, many people who call themselves heterosexual have at some time engaged in some sort of homosexual activity. Therefore, many sex researchers (sexologists) use a seven-point scale first devised for the Alfred Kinsey surveys in the 1940's, ranging from 0 (exclusively heterosexual) to 6 (exclusively homosexual). Others prefer to use the words "heterosexual" and "homosexual" as adjectives describing behaviors rather than as nouns.

Homosexual behavior has been documented in every society that sexologists have studied; in many societies it has been institutionalized. For example, the ancient Greeks believed that women were spiritually beneath men and that male-male love was the highest form. In Melanesian societies, homosexual activity was thought to be necessary for young boys to mature into virile, heterosexual adults. Homosexuality as an overall preference or orientation is harder to study, but it is thought that between 5 and 10 percent of adult males, and between 2 and 4 percent of females, have a predominantly homosexual orientation.

In Western, Judeo-Christian culture, homosexual behavior has long been considered taboo or sinful. Thus, in the United States and other predominantly Christian cultures, homosexuality has been frowned upon, and homosexuals have been ostracized, being seen as perverted, unnatural, or sick. In 1974, however, the American Psychiatric Association determined that homosexuality was not indicative of mental illness. In contrast to early twentieth century studies of homosexuals, who were either psychiatric patients or prison inmates, later studies of a representative cross-section of people showed that individuals with a homosexual orientation are no more likely to suffer from mental illness than those with a heterosexual orientation.

In spite of these scientific data, many heterosexuals (especially males) still harbor negative feelings about homosexuality. This phenomenon is called homophobia. Some of this fear, disgust, and hatred is attributable to the incorrect belief that many homosexuals are child molesters. In fact, more than 90 percent of pedophiles are heterosexual. Another source of homophobia is the fear of acquired immune deficiency syndrome (AIDS). This deadly sexually transmitted disease is more easily transmitted through anal intercourse than through vaginal intercourse and thus has spread more rapidly among homosexuals than heterosexuals. Education about "safe sex" practices, however, has dramatically reduced transmission rates in homosexual communities.

Sexologists have not been able to avoid the political controversies surrounding their field—making the study of a difficult subject even harder. Research will continue, but no one should expect fast and simple explanations. Sexuality, perhaps more than any other attribute of the human psyche, is personal and individual. Questions about sexual orientation, sexual development, and sexual behavior are all complex; it will take a long time to unravel the answers.

Bibliography

Bell, Alan P., and Martin Weinberg. *Homosexualities: A Study of Diversity Among Men and Women.* New York: Simon & Schuster, 1978. This official Kinsey Institute publication presents the methods and results of the most extensive sex survey to focus specifically on homosexual behavior. Presents descriptions of homosexual feelings, partnerships, and life-styles, based on intensive interviews with more than fifteen hundred men and women.

Bell, Alan P., Martin S. Weinberg, and Sue Kiefer Hammersmith. *Sexual Preference: Its Development in Men and Women.* Bloomington: Indiana University Press, 1981. In a follow-up to Bell and Weinberg's first book (described above), this volume compares the childhood and adolescent experiences of male and female homosexual and heterosexual adults. Organized in a question-and-answer format, this book explores possible explanations for homosexual versus heterosexual development.

Blumstein, Philip W., and Pepper Schwartz. *American Couples: Money, Work, Sex.* New York: William Morrow, 1983. Part 1 presents statistical data on the life-styles and interpersonal relationships of more than five thousand married, heterosexual cohabiting, homosexual, and lesbian couples. Part 2 presents interviews with selected couples from each of the four groups, along with a follow-up study on each several years later. Many user-friendly charts for comparison.

Koertge, Noretta, ed. *Nature and Causes of Homosexuality: A Philosophic and Scientific Inquiry.* New York: Haworth Press, 1981. This volume is the third in an ongoing monograph series entitled "Research on Homosexuality," each volume of which was originally published as an issue of the *Journal of Homosexuality.* All volumes are valuable, although somewhat technical. This one is a good place to start; others cover law, psychotherapy, literature, alcoholism, anthropology, historical perspectives, social sex roles, bisexuality, and homophobia.

McNaught, Brian. *A Disturbed Peace: Selected Writings of an Irish Catholic Homosexual.* Washington, D.C.: Dignity, 1981. A very personal viewpoint from an advocate of gay rights. The publisher, Dignity, is an organization of gay Catholics (and their friends and relatives) who feel rejected by their church but who still feel a need to exercise both their religion and their sexual feelings.

Marmor, Judd, ed. *Homosexual Behavior: A Modern Appraisal.* New York: Basic Books, 1980. For those interested in a clinical perspective on homosexuality, this is the book. It puts the early twentieth century psychoanalytic viewpoint in context after presenting late twentieth century information from both the biological and social sciences. Collectively, the contributors' expertise is quite vast.

Tripp, C. A. *The Homosexual Matrix.* New York: McGraw-Hill, 1975. For those who want to sit down and read for pleasure as well as for information. Tripp covers fact, culture, and mythology, both historical and modern. A good representative of the "gay liberation" era books on homosexuality, most of the text is as valid as when it was written (though it clearly does not cover post-AIDS changes in homosexual culture and behavior).

Whitham, Frederick L. "Culturally Invariable Properties of Male Homosexuality: Tentative Conclusions from Cross-Cultural Research." *Archives of Sexual Behavior* 12 (1983): 40. Unlike much of the cross-cultural literature on homosexuality, this article focuses specifically on cross-cultural prevalence and attributes of those with a homosexual orientation, rather than on the institutionalized and ritual forms of homosexual behavior found in many non-Western cultures.

Linda Mealey

Cross-References

Adolescence: Sexuality, 130; Attraction Theories, 332; Gender-Identity Formation, 1062; Love, 1486; Physical Development: Environmental versus Genetic Determinants, 1823; Psychosexual Development, 1969; Sex Hormones and Motivation, 2234; Sexual Behavior Patterns, 2246; Sexual Variants and Paraphilias, 2259.

HORMONES AND BEHAVIOR

Type of psychology: Biological bases of behavior
Fields of study: Auditory, chemical, cutaneous, and body senses; endocrine system

Hormones are chemical messengers, usually of protein or steroid content, that are produced in certain body tissues and that target specific genes in the cells of other body tissues, thereby affecting the development and function of these tissues and the entire organism. By controlling portions of the central nervous system (the brain and spinal cord) and various metabolic activities, hormones can affect behavior.

Principal terms

ADRENAL GLAND: an endocrine gland located above each kidney that produces and secretes hormones and neurotransmitters which accelerate body metabolic activities, such as the fight-or-flight response

ENDOCRINE GLAND: a small organ within the body that lacks ducts (channels) and that must secrete its hormones directly into the bloodstream for transport to target body tissue cells

GENE: a small segment of a chromosome whose DNA nucleotide sequence encodes a specific protein; each cell's chromosomes contain tens of thousands of genes

HORMONE: a chemical messenger, usually composed of protein or steroids, that is produced and secreted by an endocrine gland and that targets specific genes in certain body tissue cells

HYPOPHYSIS: the pituitary gland, a principal control center in the endocrine system that secretes at least eight major hormones that affect body physiology and behavior

HYPOTHALAMUS: a critical brain region located just above the hypophysis and brain stem that controls many physiological cycles, including heart rate and all endocrine system hormones

NEUROTRANSMITTER: a hormone that is secreted by some endocrine glands and by all neurons for information transfer from cell to cell

PHEROMONE: a hormone whose target is nervous system neurons in another individual, thereby affecting that individual's behavior

PINEAL GLAND: a light-sensitive endocrine gland that is located toward the back of the brain and that controls reproductive cycles in many mammalian species

STEROID: a substance, derived from cholesterol, that is a major component of some hormone structures, especially reproductive hormones and adrenal cortex hormones

Overview

Cell-to-cell communication among the trillions of cells that make up multicellular animals relies primarily upon the specialized tissues of the nervous and endocrine systems. These two systems are intricately connected, with the former having evolved from the latter during the past five hundred million years of animal life. The endocrine system consists of specialized ductless glands located throughout the animal body that produce and secrete hormones directly into the bloodstream. Hormones are chemical messengers that usually are composed of protein or steroid subunits. The bloodstream transports the hormones to various target body tissues, where the hormones contact cell membranes and trigger a sequence of enzyme reactions which ultimately result in the activation or inactivation of genes located on chromosomes in the cell nucleus.

A gene is a segment of a chromosome that is composed of deoxyribonucleic acid (DNA). The DNA nucleotide sequence of the gene encodes a molecule of messenger ribonucleic acid (RNA), which, in turn, encodes a specific protein for the given gene. If the control sequence of a gene is activated, then RNA and protein will be produced. If the control sequence of a gene is inactivated, then RNA and protein will not be produced. Hormones target the genes in specific cells to start or stop the manufacture of certain proteins. Within cells and the entire organism, proteins perform important functions. Therefore, hormones control the production of proteins by genes and, as a result, control many activities of the entire animal.

The nervous system, which has evolved to become more elaborate than the endocrine system in vertebrate animals, consists of billions of neurons (nerve cells) which conduct electrical impulses throughout the body. Neurons transmit information, contract and relax muscles, and detect pressures, temperature, and pain. Neuron networks are most dense in the brain (where there are one hundred billion neurons) and spinal cord, where much of the electrical information is centralized, relayed, and analyzed. Neurons must communicate electrical information across the gaps, or synapses, which separate them. To accomplish this goal, the transmitting neuron releases hormones called neurotransmitters, which diffuse across the synapse to the receiving neuron, in so doing instructing the receiving neuron to continue or stop the conduction of the electrical message. There are many different types of neurotransmitters, just as there are many different types of regular hormones.

The link between the nervous and endocrine systems lies in two structures which are located between the cerebrum and the brain stem. These two glands are the hypothalamus and the hypophysis (the pituitary gland). Electrical impulses from neurons in the cerebral cortex may activate the hypothalamus to release hormones that activate the hypophysis to release its hormones, which in turn activate or inactivate other endocrine glands throughout the body. These glands include the thyroid, parathyroids, thymus, pancreas, adrenals, and reproductive organs. This entire system operates by negative feedback homeostasis so that, once information is transferred and specific bodily functions are achieved, nervous or hormonal signals travel back to the hypothalamus to terminate any further action.

Animal behavior occurs as a result of the actions of the nervous and endocrine systems. There is a complex interplay among these two body systems, the environment, and an individual's genetic makeup in terms of the cause-and-effect, stimulus-response events that constitute behavior. An animal receives external information via its special senses (eyes, ears, nose, mouth) and somatic senses (touch, pain, temperature, pressure). This external information travels along sensory neurons toward the brain and spinal cord, where the information is analyzed and a motor response to the external stimulus is initiated. Some of these motor responses will be directed toward the sense organs, locomotory muscles, and organs such as the heart and intestines. Other impulses will be directed toward the hypothalamus, which controls body cycles such as all endocrine system hormones, heart rate, sleep-wake cycles, and hunger.

When the hypothalamus releases the hormone corticoliberin, the pituitary gland (the hypophysis) releases the hormones thyrotropin (which activates the thyroid gland), prolactin (which stimulates milk production in the female breast), and growth hormone (which triggers growth in children and metabolic changes in adults). When the thyroid gland is activated, hormones such as thyroxine and triiodothyronine are released to accelerate cellular metabolism, an event which may occur in certain situations (such as stress or fight-or-flight encounters).

If the pituitary gland releases adrenocorticotropic hormone (ACTH), the adrenal glands will be activated to release their hormones. The adrenal cortex produces and secretes a variety of hormones, such as aldosterone, which regulates the blood-salt balance directly and blood pressure indirectly; cortisol, which accelerates body metabolism; and androgens, or sex hormones. All of these are steroid hormones, which are involved in rapidly preparing the body for strenuous performance. Even more pronounced are the effects of the adrenal medulla, which produces and secretes the hormone neurotransmitters epinephrine and norepinephrine; these two hormones accelerate heart, muscle, and nerve action as well as stimulate the release of fat and sugar into the bloodstream for quick energy, all of which are extremely important for spontaneous activity such as fighting with or fleeing from enemies. The control of sugar storage and release from the liver by the pancreatic hormones insulin and glucagon also are important in this process.

Among the most powerful behavior-influencing hormones are the pituitary gonadotropins luteinizing hormone (LH) and follicle-stimulating hormone (FSH). These two hormones target the reproductive organs of both males and females and stimulate these organs to initiate sexual development and the production of sexual steroid hormones—estrogen and progesterone in females, testosterone in males. These sex hormones are responsible not only for the maturation of the reproductive organs but also for secondary sexual characteristics such as male aggressive behavior and female nesting behavior. The pineal gland, located in the posterior cerebrum, releases the hormone melatonin, which regulates the body's circadian rhythms and possibly sexual cycles as well.

Pheromones are hormones released from the reproductive organs and skin glands. These hormones target the sense organs of other individuals and affect the behavior of these individuals. Sex pheromones, for example, attract males to females and vice versa. Other pheromones enable a male to mark his territory and to detect the intrusion of competitor males into his territory. Others enable an infant to imprint upon its mother. Such hormones number in the hundreds, but only a few dozen have been studied in detail.

Applications

The study of hormones and their effects upon individual and group behaviors is of immense interest to psychologists. Hormones represent the biochemical control signals for much of animal and human behaviors. Understanding how hormones precisely affect individuals, both psychologically and physiologically, could be of great value in comprehending many different human behaviors, in treating abnormal behaviors, and in helping individuals to cope psychologically with disease and stress. The hormonal control of behavior in humans and in many other animal species has been extensively studied, although much research remains to be performed. Hormones have been clearly linked to reproductive behavior, sex-specific behavioral characteristics, territoriality and mating behaviors, physiological responses to certain external stimuli, and stress.

The most extensive research involving hormonal effects on behavior has been conducted on reproductive behavior. Reproductive patterns vary from species to species in occurrence, repetition of occurrence, and behaviors associated with courtship, mating, and caring for young. The achievement of reproductive maturity and reproductive readiness in a given species is subject to that species' circadian rhythm, a phenomenon which is regulated by hormones released from the hypothalamus, hypophysis, and pineal gland. These three endocrine glands are influenced primarily by the twenty-four-hour Earth rotation (via day-night cycles) period and the twenty-eight-day lunar cycle. Furthermore, genetically programmed hormonal changes at specific times during one's life cycle also play a major role in the occurrence of reproductive behaviors.

In female vertebrates, luteinizing hormone, follicle-stimulating hormone, and estrogen are responsible for the maturation of the ovaries, the completion of meiosis (chromosome halving) and release of eggs for fertilization, and secondary sexual characteristics. The secondary sexual characteristics involve physiological and closely related behavioral changes. In bird species, these changes include the construction of a nest and receptivity to dominant males during courtship rituals. In mammals, these same hormones are involved in female receptivity to dominant males during courtship. Physiological changes in mammals include the deposition of fat in various body regions, such as the breasts and buttocks, and increased vascularization (more blood vessel growth) in the skin. Females of most mammal and bird species go into heat, or estrus, one or several times per year, based on hormonally regulated changes in reproductive organs. Human females follow a lunar menstrual cycle in which luteinizing hormone, follicle-stimulating hormone, estrogen, and progesterone oscillate in production rates. These hormonal variations influence female body temperature and behavior accordingly.

Male sexual behavior is controlled predominantly by testosterone produced in the testicles and male androgens produced in the adrenal cortex. These steroid hormones cause muscle build-up, increased hair, and aggressive behavior. In a number of mammal and bird species, elevation of sex steroids causes increased coloration, which serves both as an attractant for females and as an antagonistic signal to competitor males. The aggressive behavior which is stimulated by the male sex steroid hormones thus plays a dual role in courtship/mating rituals and in territorial behavior, two phenomena which are tightly linked in determining the biological success of the individual.

Pheromones released by males serve as territorial markers, as is evidenced by most mammalian males spraying urine on objects in their own territory. Exchanges of pheromones between males and females are important stimulants for courtship and mating. In some species, the release of pheromones—or even the sight of a potential mate—will trigger hormonally controlled ovulation in the female. Furthermore, in several species, such as elephant seals and lions, the takeover of a harem by a new dominant male, a process that usually involves the murder of the previous male's offspring, stimulates the harem females to ovulate. The diversity of reproductive behaviors that are regulated by hormones seems to be almost as great as the number of species.

The fight-or-flight response is a hormonally controlled situation in which the body must pool all of its available resources within a relatively short time span. The detection of danger by any of the special senses (sight, smell, hearing) triggers the hypothalamus to activate the pituitary gland to release adrenocorticotropic hormone, which causes the adrenal gland to release its highly motivating hormones and neurotransmitters. Many body systems are subsequently affected, especially the heart and circulatory system, the central nervous system, the digestive system, and even the immune system. One reason the fight-or-flight response is of major interest to psychologists is its linkage to stress.

Stress is overexcitation of the nervous and endocrine systems. It is caused by the body's repeated exposure to danger, excessive physical exertion, or environmental pressures that psychologically affect the individual. Stress is a major problem for humans in a fast-paced technological society. The physiological and behavioral manifestations of stress are very evident. There is considerable evidence that stress is associated with heart disease, cancer, weakened immune systems, asthma, allergies, accelerated aging, susceptibility to infections, learning disorders, behavioral abnormalities, insanity, and violent crime. The demands that are placed upon individuals in fast-paced, overpopulated societies are so great that many people physiologically exhibit a near-continuous fight-or-flight response. This response, in which the body prepares for maximum physical exertion in a short time span, is the physiological basis of stress. It is not intended to be maintained for long periods of time; if it is not relieved, irreparable effects begin to accumulate throughout the body, particularly within the nervous system. Medical psychologists seek to understand the hormonal basis of physiological stress in order to treat stress-prone individuals.

The ultimate goal of all these studies is to arrive at an understanding of the physiological basis of behavior and to develop treatments for behavioral abnormalities. Hormones can be synthetically manufactured in the laboratory. Their mass production could provide solutions to many psychological problems such as stress, deviant behavior, and sexual dysfunction. Synthetic hormones already are being used as birth control mechanisms aimed at fooling the female body's own reproductive hormonal systems.

Context

The activities of all living organisms are functionally dependent upon the biochemical reactions that make up life itself. Since the evolution of the first eukaryotic cells more than one billion years ago, hormones have been utilized in cell-to-cell communication. In vertebrate animals (fish, amphibians, reptiles, birds, and mammals), endocrine systems have evolved into highly complicated nervous systems. These nervous systems are even very evident in the invertebrate arthropods (crustaceans, spiders, and so on), especially among the social insects, such as ants. The endocrine and nervous systems are intricately interconnected in the control of animal physiology and behavior.

Psychologists are interested in the chemical basis of human behavior and therefore are interested in human and mammalian hormones. Such hormones control a variety of behaviors such as maternal imprinting (in which an infant and mother bond to each other), courtship and mating, territoriality, and physiological responses to stress and danger. Animal behaviorists and psychologists study the connection between hormones and behavior in humans, primates, and other closely related mammalian species. They identify similarities in behaviors and hormones among a variety of species. They also recognize the occurrence of abnormal behaviors, such as antisocial behavior and sexual deviance, and possible hormonal imbalances that contribute to these behavioral anomalies.

Among the endocrine glands that are specifically involved in the regulation of animal behavior are the dominant hypothalamus and hypophysis (pituitary), the pineal gland, the adrenal glands, and the reproductive organs (such as the ovaries in females and testicles in males). Hormones produced and secreted from these endocrine glands both trigger specific behaviors and respond to external stimuli. External stimuli are relayed to the central nervous system, then to the hypothalamus, then to the other endocrine glands. Among these behavior-inducing hormones are the hypothalamic releasing factors that activate or inactivate the pituitary gland, the pituitary gonadotropins (luteinizing hormone and follicle-stimulating hormone), the ovarian steroids estrogen and progesterone, the testicular steroid testosterone, the adrenal neurotransmitters (such as epinephrine) and steroids (such as aldosterone), and the ubiquitous pheromones.

While the biochemistry of these hormones and their effects upon various behaviors have been established in considerable detail, there are numerous behaviors that are very probably under hormonal influence that have yet to be critically analyzed.

Among these are many subtle pheromones that affect one's interactions with other people, imprinting pheromones that trigger attraction and bonding between individuals, and hormones that link together a variety of bodily functions such as stress. These hormones may number in the hundreds, and they represent a challenging avenue for further research. Unraveling the relationships between hormones and behavior can enable researchers to gain a greater understanding of the human mind and its link to the rest of the body and to other individuals. These studies offer potential treatments for behavioral abnormalities and for mental disturbances created by the physiologically disruptive effects of drug use, a major problem in American society. They also offer great promise in the alleviation of stress, another major social and medical problem.

Bibliography

Alberts, Bruce, et al. *Molecular Biology of the Cell.* New York: Garland, 1983. This outstanding introduction to molecular biology, written by leading scientists in the field, is of great value both to the layperson and to the research scientist. Chapter 13, "Chemical Signaling Between Cells," is a clear, exhaustive survey of hormone structure, function, and physiology in terms of production sites and target tissues. A list of major human hormones and their effects is provided.

Beck, William S., Karel F. Liem, and George Gaylord Simpson. *Life: An Introduction to Biology.* 3d ed. New York: HarperCollins, 1991. This introduction to basic biology for the beginning student is an exhaustive survey of all avenues of the subject. The book is beautifully illustrated and very well organized. Chapter 28, "Chemical Coordination," describes the principal human hormones and their effects upon the body. Chapter 32, "Behavior," describes various mechanisms of animal behavior, including the role of hormones in influencing behavior.

Manning, Aubrey. *An Introduction to Animal Behavior.* 3d ed. Reading, Mass.: Addison-Wesley, 1979. Manning's concise, thorough survey of animal behavior theory and research employs hundreds of experimental studies to describe major aspects of the subject. Chapter 2, "The Development of Behavior," discusses the roles of hormones in animal development and social behavior. Chapter 4, "Motivation," is an extensive study of animal drives and motivations as influenced by hormones, pheromones, and environmental stimuli.

Marler, Peter, and William J. Hamilton III. *Mechanisms of Animal Behavior.* New York: John Wiley & Sons, 1966. Marler and Hamilton's work is a thorough survey of animal behavior research that incorporates the detailed experiments of hundreds of scientists. They clearly present all major types of behaviors, in organisms from insects to humans. Chapter 3, "Reproduction: Hormones and Behavior," discusses the roles of the sex steroid hormones in courtship, mating, and territoriality for many diverse species. Other chapters emphasize the roles of hormones in many types of animal behaviors.

Raven, Peter H., and George B. Johnson. *Biology.* St. Louis: Times Mirror/Mosby, 1989. Raven and Johnson's book is an introductory survey of biology for the beginning student. It contains beautiful illustrations and photographs. Chapter 48, "Hormones," describes the endocrine systems of human and mammals, the major hormones produced by each endocrine gland, and the effects of these hormones upon the body. Chapter 56, "Behavior," describes various aspects of animal behavior, including the control of some of these behaviors by hormones.

Stryer, Lubert. *Biochemistry.* 2d ed. San Francisco: W. H. Freeman, 1981. Stryer's outstanding introductory biochemistry book is aimed at advanced students, although much of it is easily understandable to the layperson, with its excellent diagrams and illustrations. Chapter 35, "Hormone Action," represents a thorough study of human and mammalian hormones, their sites of production, their target tissues, their mechanisms of action, and their effects upon the body.

Wallace, Robert A., Gerald P. Sanders, and Robert J. Ferl. *Biology: The Science of Life.* 3d ed. New York: HarperCollins, 1991. Wallace, Sanders, and Ferl's introduction to biology for the beginning student exhausts the subject, but it does so by providing a wealth of information, constructive diagrams, and beautiful photographs. Chapter 37, "Hormonal Control," discusses human hormones and their effects upon the body. Chapters 44, "The Development and Structure of Animal Behavior," and 45, "Adaptiveness of Behavior," describe various animal behaviors and hormonal/pheromonal effects upon some of these behaviors.

Zubay, Geoffrey L. *Biochemistry.* Reading, Mass.: Addison-Wesley, 1983. Zubay's introduction to biochemistry is intended for advanced biology students, although portions of it are understandable to the layperson. Chapter 29, "Hormone Action," contains a lengthy discussion of major mammalian hormones and their effects upon the body. Molecular structures and clarifying diagrams highlight much of the text.

David Wason Hollar, Jr.

Cross-References

The Adrenal Gland, 136; Emotion: Neurophysiology and Neuroanatomy, 914; The Endocrine System, 966; Gonads, 1094; Neural and Hormonal Interaction, 1648; The Pituitary Gland, 1829; Sex Hormones and Motivation, 2234; Smell and Taste, 2290; Stress and the Endocrine System, 2445; The Thyroid Gland, 2571.

HUMAN RESOURCE TRAINING AND DEVELOPMENT

Type of psychology: Motivation
Fields of study: Cognitive learning; social motives

Human resource training and development programs provide employees with the knowledge and skills they need to perform their jobs successfully. In an increasingly technical and complex world, training and development programs are vital for organizational survival.

Principal terms

APPRENTICESHIPS: long-term on-the-job training programs typically used in the skilled trades

COMPUTER-AIDED INSTRUCTION (CAI): the use of computers to support programmed instruction

JOB ANALYSIS: a technique used to define the specific knowledge, skills, and aptitudes a worker needs to perform a job

MODELING: a teaching technique in which employees learn a skill by watching someone perform the skill

PROGRAMMED INSTRUCTION: self-paced training programs characterized by many small, increasingly difficult lessons separated by frequent tests

ROLE PLAYING: a training technique in which a learner has the opportunity to take on the perspective and perform the behaviors of another person

TRANSFER OF TRAINING: the degree to which skills learned in training transfer to an actual job

Overview

The term "human resources" implies that human abilities and potential, such as aptitudes, knowledge, and skills, are as important to a company's survival as are monetary and natural resources. In order to help employees perform their jobs as well as they can, companies develop training and development programs.

Virtually every employee must go through some form of training program. Some programs are designed for newly hired or recently promoted employees who need training to perform their jobs. Other programs are designed to help employees improve their performance in their existing jobs. Although the terms are used interchangeably in this discussion, the former type of program is often referred to as a "training program" and the latter as a "development program."

There are three phases to a training or development program. During the first phase, managers determine training needs. One of the best ways to determine these needs is with job analysis. Job analysis is a process that details the exact nature and sequencing of the tasks which make up a job. Job analysis also determines performance standards for each task and specifies the corresponding knowledge, skills, and aptitudes (potential) required to meet these standards. Ideally, job analysis is used as the basis for recruiting and selecting employees. Managers like to hire employees who already have the ability to perform the job; however, most employees enter an organization with strong aptitudes but only general knowledge and skills. Consequently, during the second phase of training, a method of training is designed that will turn aptitudes into specific forms of task-related knowledge and skills.

A long history of training and educational research suggests a number of guidelines for designing effective training programs. First, training is most effective if employees have strong intellectual potential and are highly motivated to learn. Second, trainees should be given active participation in training, including the opportunity to practice the skills learned in training. Practice will usually be most effective if workers are given frequent, short practice sessions (a method called "distributed practice") rather than infrequent, long practice sessions (called "massed practice"). Third, trainees should be given continuous feedback concerning their performance. Feedback allows the trainee to monitor and adjust performance to meet training and personal standards.

One of the greatest concerns for trainers is to make certain that skills developed in training will transfer to the job. Problems with transfer vary greatly with the type of training program. In general, transfer of training will be facilitated if the content of the training program is concrete and behavioral, rather than abstract and theoretical. In addition, transfer is improved if the training environment is similar to the job environment. For example, a manager listening to a lecture on leadership at a local community college will have more difficulty transferring the skills learned in the classroom than will a mechanic receiving individual instruction and on-the-job training.

Once training needs have been analyzed and a training program has been implemented, the effectiveness of the training program must be measured. During the third phase of training, managers attempt to determine the degree to which employees have acquired the knowledge and skills presented in the training program. Some form of testing usually serves this goal. In addition, managers attempt to measure the degree to which training has influenced productivity. In order to do this, managers must have a performance evaluation program in place. Like the selection system and the training program, the performance evaluation system should be based on job analysis. Ideally, a third goal of the evaluation phase of training should be to examine whether the benefits of training, in terms of productivity and job satisfaction, warrant the cost of training. A common problem with training programs is that managers do not check the effectiveness of programs.

Training and development is an integral part of a larger human resource system which includes selection, performance evaluation, and promotion. Because employee retention and promotion can be considerably influenced by training, training and development programs are subject to equal employment opportunity (EEO) legislation. This legislation ensures that the criteria used to select employees for training programs, as well as the criteria used to evaluate employees once in training programs, are related to performance on the job. When managers fail to examine the effectiveness of their training program, they cannot tell whether they are complying with EEO legislation. EEO legislation also ensures that if minority group members do not perform as well as majority group members in training, then minorities must be given the opportunity for additional training or a longer training period. Minorities are given the additional time based on the assumption that their life experiences may not have provided them with the opportunity to develop the basic skills which would, in turn, allow them to acquire the training material as fast as majority group members.

Applications

The most common form of training is on-the-job training. In on-the-job training, newly hired employees are put to work immediately and are given instruction from an experienced worker or a supervisor. On-the-job training is popular because it is inexpensive and transfer of training is excellent. This type of training program is most successful for simple jobs not requiring high levels of knowledge and skill. On-the-job-training is often used for food service, clerical, janitorial, assembly, and retail sales jobs. Problems with on-the-job training arise when formal training programs are not established, and the individuals chosen to act as trainers are either uninterested in training or are unskilled in training techniques. A potential drawback of on-the-job training is that untrained workers are slow and tend to make mistakes.

An apprenticeship is a form of long-term training in which an employee often receives both on-the-job training and classroom instruction. Apprenticeships are one of the oldest forms of training and are typically used in unionized skilled trades such as masonry, painting, and plumbing. Apprenticeships last between two and five years, depending on the trade. During this time, the apprentice works under the supervision of a skilled worker, or "journeyman." Once a worker completes the training, he or she may join a trade union and thereby secure a position in the company. Apprenticeships are excellent programs for training employees to perform highly complex jobs. Apprenticeships offer all the benefits of on-the-job training and reduce the likelihood that training will be carried out in a haphazard fashion. Critics of apprenticeship programs, however, claim that some apprenticeships are artificially long and are used to keep employee wages low.

While on-the-job training and apprenticeship programs allow employers to utilize trainees immediately, some jobs require employees to obtain considerable skill before they can perform the job. For example, it would be unwise to allow an airline pilot to begin training by piloting an airplane filled with passengers. Where employees are required to perform tasks requiring high levels of skill, and the costs of mistakes are very high, simulator training is often used. In simulator training, a working model or reproduction of the work environment is created. Trainees are allowed to learn and practice skills on the simulator before they start their actual jobs. Simulators have been created for jobs as varied as pilots, mechanics, police officers, nuclear power plant controllers, and nurses. The advantage of simulator training is that trainees can train at a comfortable pace. Further, training on simulators is less expensive than training in the actual work environment. For example, flight-simulator training can be done for a fraction of the cost of operating a plane. An additional benefit of simulator training is that simulators can be used to train employees to respond to unusual or emergency situations with virtually no cost to the company for employee errors. A potential disadvantage of simulator training is the high cost of developing and maintaining a simulator.

The simulator training programs described above are used for technically oriented jobs held by nonmanagerial employees. Simulator training can also be used for managers. Two popular managerial simulations are in-basket exercises and business games. Here, managers are put in a hypothetical business setting and asked to respond as they would on the job. The simulation may last a number of days and involve letter and memo writing, telephone calls, scheduling, budgeting, purchases, and meetings.

Programmed instruction is a self-instructed and self-paced training method. Training material is printed in a workbook and presented in small units or chapters. A self-administered test follows each unit and provides the trainee with feedback concerning how well the material has been learned. If the trainee fails the test, he or she rereads the material. If the trainee passes the test, he or she moves on to the next unit. Each successive unit is more difficult. Programmed instruction has been used for such topics as safety training, blueprint reading, organizational policies, and sales skills. The advantage of programmed instruction is that trainees proceed at their own pace. Further, because training and tests are self-administered, employees do not feel much evaluation pressure. In addition, when units are short and tests are frequent, learners get immediate feedback concerning their performance. Computers have increasingly replaced the function of the workbook. Computer-assisted instruction is useful because the computer can monitor the trainee's performance and provide more information in areas where the trainee is having trouble. A potential drawback of programmed instruction is that employees may react to the impersonal nature of training. Further, if the employees are not committed to the program, they can find it easier to cheat.

The training programs described above are primarily used for technical training. Interpersonal skills training programs teach employees how to be effective leaders and productive group members. These programs are based on the assumption that an employee can learn how to be a good group participant or a good leader by learning specific behaviors. Many of the interpersonal skills programs involve modeling and role playing. For example, videotapes of managerial scenarios are used to demonstrate techniques a manager might use to encourage an employee. After the manager has seen the model, he or she might play the role of the encouraging manager and thus be given an opportunity to practice leader behaviors. An advantage of role playing is that people get the opportunity to see the world from the perspective of the individual who normally fills the role. Consequently, role playing is a useful tool in helping members of a group in conflict. Role playing allows group members to see the world from the perspective of the adversary.

Context

Over the last two hundred years, there have been dramatic changes in both the nature of jobs and the composition of the work force. Consequently, there have also been dramatic changes in the scope and importance of training. The history of formal employment training dates back thousands of years. Training programs were essential for jobs in the military, church, and skilled trades. Prior to the Industrial Revolution, however, only a small percentage of the population had jobs that required formal training. Training for the masses is a relatively new concept. At the beginning of the Industrial Revolution, the vast majority of workers lived in rural areas and worked on small farms. Training was simple and was done within the family. During the Industrial Revolution, the population started to migrate to the cities, seeking jobs in factories. Employers became responsible for training. While early factory work was often grueling, the jobs themselves were relatively easy to learn. In fact, jobs required so little training that children were often employed as factory workers.

Since the Industrial Revolution began, manufacturing processes have become increasingly technical and complex. Now, many jobs in manufacturing require not only lengthy on-the-job training but also a college degree. In addition, technology is changing at an ever-increasing pace. This means that employees must spend considerable time updating their knowledge and skills.

Just as manufacturing has become more complex, so has the process of managing an organization. Alfred Chandler, a business historian, suggests that one of the most important changes since the Industrial Revolution has been the rise of the "professional" manager. Chandler suggests that management used to be performed by company owners, and managerial skills were specific to each company. Today, managers work for company owners and are trained in universities. Because management functions are so similar across organizations, managers can take their skills to a wide variety of companies and industries.

In contrast to the increasingly technical nature of jobs, there has been an alarming increase in the number of illiterate and poorly trained entrants into the work force. There has also been an increase in the number of job applicants who do not speak English. In response to these problems, many companies have begun to provide remedial training in reading, writing, and mathematics. Companies are thus taking the role of public schools by providing basic education. Training and development programs will continue to be essential to organizational survival. As the managerial and technological worlds become more complex, and as the number of highly skilled entrants into the work force declines, companies will need to focus on both remedial training for new employees and updating the knowledge and skills of older employees.

Bibliography

Bandura, Albert. *Social Learning Theory.* Englewood Cliffs, N.J.: Prentice-Hall, 1977.
Describes the ways people learn by observing others' behavior, thus describing

the conditions under which modeling is an effective training technique. Social learning theory is one of the most widely studied theories in psychology.

Craig, Robert L., ed. *Training and Development Handbook: A Guide to Human Resource Development.* 3d ed. New York: McGraw-Hill, 1987. Well-respected authors in training and development contribute chapters. This book is useful for both academics and practitioners.

Landy, Frank J., and Don A. Trumbo. "Personnel Training and Development: Concepts, Models, and Techniques." In *Psychology of Work Behavior.* Pacific Grove, Calif.: Brooks/Cole, 1989. This chapter provides a good overview of training and development programs. Similar textbooks on either industrial/organizational psychology or human resource management will also have chapters on training and development.

Latham, Gary P. "Human Resource Training and Development." In *Annual Review of Psychology* 39. Stanford, Calif.: Annual Reviews, 1988. A review of academic research on training and development. Topics include training history, identifying training needs, evaluating training programs, training programs in other cultures, and leadership training. New updates are published every few years.

Wexley, K. N., and Gary P. Latham. *Developing and Training Human Resources in Organizations.* New York: HarperCollins, 1991. Provides an overview of training methods. The book is well written and includes many examples of actual training programs. A useful tool for students, educators, and trainers.

Daniel Sachau

Cross-References

HUMANISM: AN OVERVIEW

Type of psychology: Origin and definition of psychology
Fields of study: Humanistic therapies; humanistic-phenomenological models

Humanistic psychology attempts to understand a person's experience precisely as it is lived. By respecting the reality of a person's own experiential viewpoint, humanistic psychologists can examine the actual meanings a situation has for the person; in doing so, humanistic psychology develops a comprehensive understanding of human nature and of psychological life in general.

Principal terms
EXISTENCE: in humanistic psychology, one's irreducible being in a world that is carved out by one's personal involvements
EXISTENTIALISM: a philosophy originating in Europe that takes one's existence as the starting point for an understanding of being human
HUMAN SCIENCE: as distinct from natural science, an approach to psychological research that aims at understanding human experiencing through a qualitative analysis of descriptions of situations
INTENTIONALITY: the phenomenological notion that consciousness is fundamentally relational; a way of being engaged with a personally meaningful world
PERSON-CENTERED THERAPY: a humanistic form of psychotherapy developed by Carl Rogers; a nondirective therapy whose goal is to enable clients to actualize their real selves
PHENOMENOLOGY: a philosophy that seeks to make explicit the essential structures of any phenomenon that appears for intentional consciousness
SELF-ACTUALIZATION: the humanistic notion that people have a natural tendency, if unblocked, to fulfill their own unique possibilities for growth

Overview

Humanism became influential in psychology through a loosely knit movement that began in the 1950's and became a significant force in the 1960's. Known as humanistic psychology, it is not one branch of psychology, focused on a particular content area, but a unique approach to all of psychology's content areas. Because humanistic psychology was not created around the work of one founder, it has avoided becoming dogmatic, but it suffers the corresponding disadvantage of having no unanimously inclusive doctrines. Nevertheless, humanistic psychology does offer a distinctive approach to psychological life, based on respect for the specifically "human" quality of human existence. Fidelity to the full meaning of being human requires understanding human psychological life on its own terms, as it actually presents itself, rather than on models borrowed from other fields of inquiry. In contrast, traditional psychology assembled its foundational concepts about human existence during the nineteenth century from such disciplines as physiology, biology, chemistry, and physics. These natural sciences share a common assumption about their subject matter—namely, that it is "matter," objective things that are completely determined by the causal impacts of other things in mechanical and lawful ways that can be explained, measured, predicted, and controlled.

Humanistic psychology arose to counter that position. It argues that the natural science model distorts, trivializes, and mostly neglects the real subject matter— human existence. When love is reduced to a biological drive and insight to a conditioned response, humanistic psychologists protest, psychology has lost contact with the real humanness of its subject matter. Their alternative approach includes four essential features.

First, integral to humanistic psychology is its appreciation of the person as a whole. Such a holistic emphasis holds that people cannot be reduced to "parts" (whether labeled processes, instincts, drives, conditioned responses, or whatever), since the meaning of any part can only be understood in relation to the whole person. For example, a humanistic psychology of thinking also takes into account the thinker's feelings and motives, since it is the person as a whole who thinks, not only the brain or an information-processing system. Even the most seemingly isolated physiological events cannot be fully comprehended apart from the person's total existence. A study of women recently widowed, for example, showed that their bodies' immune systems weakened in the year after their husbands' deaths. This subtle yet profound way of embodying grief is best understood when the human body is grasped as a "bodying forth" of a whole existence and personal history.

A second essential feature of humanistic psychology concerns its notion of consciousness, which is informed by the phenomenological concept of intentionality. Consciousness is seen as "intending" an object, meaning not the everyday sense of intending as a deliberate choice but rather that consciousness is always consciousness of something. Whereas traditional psychologies conceive of consciousness as a machine, a brain, or a container, or dismiss it altogether, the concept of intentionality means that consciousness is fundamentally relational: It is an encountering and dwelling in one's world. For example, to be conscious of the room means to be intertwined with it. To be immersed in a memory means to be there, in that remembered scene. This communion is reciprocal in the sense that the objects of consciousness are also implicated in this relation. It is neither objective stimulation nor variables that ordinary consciousness intends, but a meaningful world, intended through one's own way of being with it. For example, a student driver is conscious of other cars as looming too close, whereas the consciousness of the race car driver intends the spaces through which he or she could drive the car.

Third, this notion of consciousness leads to humanistic psychology's recognition of the irreducible reality of the person's own experience as the core of his or her psychological life. Rather than preconceiving a person's behavior from an outside point of view, humanistic psychology seeks to clarify its significance by understanding the behaving person's own viewpoint. In other words, behavior is seen as an expression of a person's involvement in a situation. For example, a man walking across a snow-covered frozen lake could not be said to be brave (or foolhardy) if he experienced it as a field instead.

A fourth essential constituent is a vision of human freedom. For humanistic psychology, a person unfolds his or her existence over time by responsibly owning and becoming who he or she is. This does not mean that the self is whatever a person wants to be. On the contrary, one's own choice is to be the self that one authentically is. This choice, because one is free to make it or not, is also the source of anxiety, as people confront their own ultimate responsibility for what they will make of their lives. Terms such as self-actualization and self-realization depict this most crucial obligation of being human. Selfhood, in other words, is not simply what one has been given by environmental or genetic sources. It is, rather, a possibility to be owned and lived by transcending the given. Instead of determining the course of psychological life, the givens of one's existence must be freely engaged in the process of one's own authentic self-becoming.

Applications

Within psychology, the humanistic approach's most important applications have been in the areas of psychotherapy, personality theory, and research methods. Rollo May aptly described the humanistic idea of psychotherapy as being to help patients experience their existence as real. Carl Rogers' person-centered therapy depicts the humanistic purpose: to assist clients in unblocking and experiencing their own self-actualizing tendencies. This is accomplished by nonjudgmentally clarifying and mirroring back to clients their own spontaneous expressions of self with genuine empathy and unconditional positive regard.

A second area of major application has been personality theory. Among the many who have contributed in this regard are Gordon Allport, Henry Murray, Charlotte Buhler, and James Bugental. The three most famous are Rogers, May, and Abraham Maslow. They see personality as a tendency of self-actualizing: of "becoming" (May), of realizing one's possibilities for "full humanness" (Maslow), of being "fully functioning" (Rogers). They emphasize that the personality is oriented toward growth, thus being dynamic rather than static, yet recognize that this process is unfinished and far from automatic. Rogers noted that "incongruence" between one's self-concept and one's actual self blocks actualizing tendencies. If a person experiences positive regard from significant others, such as parents, as being conditional (for example, "I love you because you never get angry" or "I'll love you if you always agree with me"), the effort to meet these conditions results in an "incongruence" between one's self-concept and the self one actually is being.

May stressed that to become self-actualized, one must be aware of oneself. Facing one's own being requires risk and commitment, based on one's capacities for love and will, courage and care. This "central distinguishing characteristic," the human capacity for self-awareness, can, however, be blocked. People may evade the insecurity of this risk by not facing themselves, but the resulting deadening leads to boredom and a trivialization of life.

Maslow specified his conception of self-actualization in the context of his theory of motivation. He described a hierarchy of motives, extending from "deficiency needs" (physiological needs and safety) to "being needs" (belongingness, love, self-esteem, and self-actualization). He considered "growth motivation" an inherent tendency of people to fulfill ever higher motives on this hierarchy.

A third application of the humanistic approach has been innovative methods for psychological research. Known as human science, these methods can be used to study human experience as it is actually lived in the world. Human science research is phenomenologically based, and it utilizes data gathered by interviews and written descriptions, which are then analyzed qualitatively. The aim is not to reduce experience to the traditional operationally defined variables, but to understand the essential structure of the person's actually lived experience. The leading figure in these innovations has been Amedeo Giorgi, at Duquesne University.

Humanistic innovations have been widely applied beyond psychology, in such areas as medicine, politics, feminism, law, religion, social action, international relations, and ecology. For example, former United States president Jimmy Carter used Rogers' techniques (in consultation with Rogers) during the successful Camp David peace talks he facilitated between Anwar Sadat of Egypt and Menachem Begin of Israel. The three areas in which humanistic psychology has had the widest impact are business management, education, and personal growth. In each, humanistic innovations derive from its basic point that the fully functioning person is one whose striving for self-actualization is unblocked.

Within management, humanistic psychology was an early contributor to the emerging field of organizational development. Rogers' person-centered approach was a key influence on the development of the human-relations training for business managers conducted by the National Training Laboratory. In *Eupsychian Management: A Journal* (1965), Maslow provided a humanistic theory of management. He proposed that employees could be most productive if, through more democratic boss-worker relationships, they were given the opportunity to grow in terms of self-actualization and reach their highest human potential. (This book was translated into Japanese and was influential in the development of the managerial style now so characteristic of Japanese business.) Maslow's motivation hierarchy also was the basis for Douglas McGregor's well-known contrast between "theory X" (a traditional authoritarian managerial approach) and "theory Y" (a humanistic one proposing a more participative managerial style).

As humanistic psychology became more prevalent, it also had an impact on the adjoining field of education. Both Rogers and Maslow were severe critics of the prevailing system of education, in which education had been reduced to the acquisition of skills, as if it were merely technical training. Disgusted by the extrinsic focus of education, they promoted the view that educators needed to foster students' intrinsic or natural sense of wonder, creativity, capacity for self-understanding, and growth toward their own self-actualization. Rogers' *Freedom to Learn: A View of What Education Might Become* (1969) became an influential summary of those views.

Beyond the professional fields of business and education, humanistic psychology affected the larger society most directly through its having spawned the human potential movement. In many "growth centers" (Esalen, in California, being the most prominent), a wide assortment of services are offered. These include such techniques as sensitivity training, encounter groups, sensory awareness, and meditation. The length of time involved varies but is usually of a short duration, such as a weekend or a week. The aim is not treatment for psychologically disturbed persons, but a means of facilitating personal growth.

Context

Humanistic psychology's roots include European psychology and philosophy. Among the psychological ancestors are Kurt Goldstein's organismic theory, Karen Horney's self theory, and Erich Fromm's social analyses. Its philosophical heritage includes existentialism and phenomenology. Fearing the eclipse of the human in a world dominated by science, existentialism began with the recognition that "[i]t is important . . . to hold fast to what it means to be a human being," as originally stated by Søren Kierkegaard in 1846. Beginning in the early twentieth century, Edmund Husserl, phenomenology's founder, articulated the key notion of the intentionality of consciousness. Husserl also fashioned a distinction between the natural sciences and the human sciences (made earlier by Wilhelm Dilthey) into a powerful critique of psychology's traditional scientific foundations. Later philosophers, particularly Martin Heidegger, Jean-Paul Sartre, and Maurice Merleau-Ponty joined existentialism and phenomenology into a compelling philosophy of existence.

Existential phenomenology first affected the work of European psychologists, especially R. D. Laing, Jan Hendrik van den Berg, Viktor Frankl, Erwin Straus, Ludwig Binswanger, and Medard Boss. In the United States, May was influential in importing these European currents through his edited book of translated readings, *Existence: A New Dimension in Psychiatry and Psychology* (1958). Also, Duquesne University was a pioneer with its 1959 establishment of a graduate program devoted to existential phenomenological psychology. In the 1960's, graduate programs in humanistic psychology were established at Sonoma State University, Saybrook Institute, and West Georgia College.

Much of the early organizational work was done by Maslow, who, with Tony Sutich, launched the *Journal of Humanistic Psychology* in 1961. In 1963, Maslow, Sutich, and Bugental inaugurated the Association for Humanistic Psychology. Within psychology's main organization, the American Psychological Association, the Division of Humanistic Psychology was established in 1971 in response to a petition by its members. It now also publishes a journal, *The Humanistic Psychologist.*

With the rapid pace of such developments, by the end of the 1960's humanistic psychologists saw themselves as a "third force": an alternative to behaviorism and psychoanalysis, the two dominant traditions in American psychology at that time. A naïve optimism characterized their sense of the future; humanistic psychology has not succeeded in supplanting those traditions. What happened instead was the rise of cognitive psychology as the main challenger for dominance. Like humanistic psychology, the cognitive approach was formed during the 1950's to dispute traditional psychology's narrow focus on behavior as an objective, observable event, but it offered a more conventional alternative. While returning to the mind as a topic of psychology, it did so while retaining the traditional mechanistic view of mental life. In comparison, humanistic psychology's more fundamental proposal that psychology set aside its mechanistic assumption altogether continues to cast it in the role of a less palatable alternative for most psychologists.

In other ways, however, the humanistic approach has been a victim of its own successes beyond psychology. Its applications to psychotherapy, management, and education are now so commonly known they are scarcely recognized anymore as "humanistic." It appears that, for now at least, humanistic psychology has found greater integration beyond psychology than within it.

Bibliography

Bugental, James F. T. *Intimate Journeys: Stories from Life-Changing Therapy.* San Francisco: Jossey-Bass, 1990. A personal tour of the struggles, defeats, and triumphs of one humanistic psychotherapist, Bugental himself.

Giorgi, Amedeo. *Psychology as a Human Science.* New York: Harper & Row, 1970. This scholarly book provides a fine summary of a human science approach to psychology and carefully distinguishes it from a natural science approach. Giorgi also describes a phenomenological foundation for human science psychology.

Kinget, G. Marian. *On Becoming Human.* New York: Harcourt Brace Jovanovich, 1975. This readable book answers the question "What is human about a human being?" by describing seventeen key characteristics of uniquely human existence. Topics include time, death, symbols, reflective consciousness, creativity, ethics, freedom, and beauty.

Maslow, Abraham H. *Toward a Psychology of Being.* 2d ed. New York: Van Nostrand Reinhold, 1968. Maslow's study of human nature and the conditions and blocks to self-actualization. Topics include growth, motivation, cognition, creativeness, and values.

May, Rollo. *Psychology and the Human Dilemma.* Princeton, N.J.: Van Nostrand, 1967. May's accessible yet probing analysis of humans' paradoxical capacity to experience themselves as both subject and object. Topics include meaning, anxiety, freedom, responsibility, values, psychotherapy, science, and the social responsibilities of psychologists.

Pollio, Howard R. *Behavior and Existence: An Introduction to Empirical Humanistic Psychology.* Monterey, Calif.: Brooks/Cole, 1982. This book is the most coherent introductory textbook on general psychology from a humanistic standpoint. It covers the usual survey of psychology topics (such as learning, thinking, perceiving, and remembering) from a humanistic approach.

Rogers, Carl. *On Becoming a Person.* Boston: Houghton Mifflin, 1961. Rogers' most widely read book, providing his views of person-centered psychotherapy, including its key characteristics and how to research its effectiveness. Also includes Rogers' philosophy of persons, analyses of education, families, personal growth, creativity, relationships, and the fully functioning person.

Valle, Ronald S., and Steen Halling, eds. *Existential-Phenomenological Perspectives in Psychology: Exploring the Breadth of Human Experience.* New York: Plenum Press, 1989. A widely ranging collection of topics, many centrally important to psychology, each approached phenomenologically in original and creative ways. Topics include social psychology, assessment, perception, learning, child development, emotion, and many others, including transpersonal psychology.

Van den Berg, Jan Hendrik. *A Different Existence.* Pittsburgh: Duquesne University Press, 1972. A remarkably easy introduction to some major themes of phenomenological psychology. Within the framework of a case study of a disturbed patient, van den Berg examines such forms of experiencing as "world," "others," "time," and "body."

Christopher M. Aanstoos

Cross-References

Abnormality: Humanistic-Existential Models, 60; Existential Analysis and Therapy, 999; Gestalt Therapy, 1088; Humanistic Trait Models: Gordon Allport, 1210; Person-Centered Therapy, 1777; Personology: Henry A. Murray, 1810; Play Therapy, 1835; Self-Actualization, 2168.

HUMANISTIC TRAIT MODELS: GORDON ALLPORT

Type of psychology: Personality
Fields of study: Humanistic-phenomenological models; personality theory

The humanistic trait model of Gordon Allport explains how a person's unique personal characteristics provide a pattern and direction to personality. It reveals the limitations of psychological theories that focus only on general rules of human behavior and provides insight into how to conduct in-depth study of individual dispositions.

Principal terms
CARDINAL DISPOSITION: a single, outstanding characteristic that dominates a person's life; few individuals are characterized by a cardinal disposition
CENTRAL DISPOSITIONS: five to ten distinctive and descriptive characteristics that provide direction and focus to a person's life
COMMON TRAITS: characteristics that are shared by many people and facilitate comparisons between people; they may not shed light on the unique personality
FUNCTIONAL AUTONOMY: the concept that many adult motives are independent in purpose from their childhood origins
IDIOGRAPHIC OR MORPHOGENIC STUDY: study of the unique patterns of the individual through methods such as case studies, autobiographies, and tests that examine patterns of behavior within a single person
NOMOTHETIC STUDY: research approaches that compare groups of people in order to identify general principles; the dominant method of personality research
PERSONAL DISPOSITIONS: the unique traits that are peculiar to the person and not shared with others or comparable to others; contrasted with common traits
PROPRIUM: the unifying personal core of personality; consisting of behaviors and characteristics that are considered important and central to one's self-identity; there are eight specific aspects
SECONDARY DISPOSITIONS: specific, focused tendencies that are not as crucial or as consistently displayed as central dispositions but that occur with some regularity
VALUE ORIENTATION: a unifying philosophy that provides meaning to one's life and that is organized around theoretical, economic, aesthetic, social, political, or religious values

Overview
The humanistic trait model of Gordon Allport (1897-1967) was based on his pro-

found belief in the uniqueness of every personality, as well as his conviction that the person's individuality is displayed through dominant personal characteristics that provide continuity and direction to a person's life. He saw personality as dynamic, growing, changing, and based on one's personal perception of the world. Like other humanists, Allport believed that people are essentially proactive, or forward moving; they are motivated by the future and seek tension and change rather than sameness. In addition, each individual possesses a set of personal dispositions that define the person and provide a pattern to behavior.

Allport's approach is different from those of other trait theorists, who have typically sought to categorize personalities according to a basic set of universal, essential characteristics. Allport referred to such characteristics as common traits. Instead of focusing on common traits that allow for comparisons between many people, Allport believed that each person is defined by a different set of characteristics. Based on his research, he estimated that there are four thousand to five thousand traits and eighteen thousand trait names.

Most personality theorists view adulthood as an extension of the basic motives present in childhood. Consistent with his belief that personality is always evolving, Allport believed that the motivations of adulthood are often independent of the motivations of childhood, and he referred to this concept as functional autonomy. For example, a person who plays a musical instrument during childhood years because of parental pressure may play the same instrument for relaxation or enjoyment as an adult. Although not all motives are functionally autonomous, many adult activities represent a break from childhood and are based on varied and self-sustaining motives.

According to this perspective, personality is based on concrete human motives that are represented by personal traits or dispositions. Human traits are seen as guiding human behavior, but they must also account for wide variability within a person's conduct from situation to situation. As a result, Allport distinguished between different types and levels of traits or dispositions. Common traits represent those elements of personality that are useful for comparing most people within a specific culture, but they cannot provide a complete profile of any individual person. In contrast, personal dispositions represent the true personality, are unique to the person, and represent subtle differences among persons.

Three kinds of personal dispositions exist: cardinal dispositions, central dispositions, and secondary dispositions. When a person's life is dominated by a single, fundamental, outstanding characteristic, the quality is referred to as a cardinal disposition. For example, Adolf Hitler's cruelty and Ebenezer Scrooge's miserliness are examples of cardinal dispositions. Central dispositions represent the five to ten important qualities of a person that would typically be discussed and described in a thorough letter of recommendation. Finally, secondary dispositions are characteristics that are more numerous, less consistently displayed, and less important than central dispositions.

Allport referred to the unifying core of personality, or those aspects of the self that a person considers central to self-identity, as the proprium. During the first three to four years of life, three aspects of the proprium emerge. The sense of a bodily self involves awareness of body sensations. Self-identity represents the child's knowledge of an inner sameness or continuity over time, and self-esteem reflects personal efforts to maintain pride and avoid embarrassment. Self-extension emerges between the fourth and sixth year of life; this refers to the child's concept of that which is "mine," and it forms the foundation for later self-extensions such as career and love of country. The self-image, which also emerges between ages four to six, represents an awareness of personal goals and abilities, as well as the "good" and "bad" parts of the self. The ability to see the self as a rational, coping being emerges between ages six and twelve and represents the ability to place one's inner needs within the context of outer reality. Propriate striving often begins in adolescence and focuses on the person's ability to form long-term goals and purposes. Finally, the self as knower represents the subjective self and one's ability to reflect on aspects of the proprium.

Applications

From this humanistic trait framework, human personality can only be fully understood through the examination of personal characteristics within a single individual. The emphasis on individuality has significant implications for the measurement of personality and research methods in psychology. Most psychological research deals with standardized measurements and large numbers of people, and it attempts to make generalizations about characteristics that people hold in common. Allport referred to this approach as nomothetic. He contrasted the study of groups and general laws with idiographic research, or approaches for studying the single person. Idiographic research, which is sometimes referred to as morphogenic research, includes diverse methods such as autobiographies, interviews, dreams, and verbatim recordings.

One of Allport's famous studies of the individual appears in *Letters from Jenny* (1965), a description of an older woman's personality that is based on the analysis of approximately three hundred letters that she wrote to her son and his wife. Through the use of personal structure analysis, statistical analysis, and the reactions of various trained judges, Allport and his colleagues identified eight clusters of characteristics, including the following: artistic, self-centered, aggressive, and sentimental. Through revealing the central dispositions of a single individual, this study provided increased insight about all people. It also demonstrated that objective, scientific practices can be applied to the study of one person at a time.

Gordon Allport preferred personality measures designed to examine the pattern of characteristics important to a person and that allow for comparison of the strengths of specific characteristics within the person rather than with other persons. The *Study of Values* (3d ed., 1960), which was developed by Allport, Philip Vernon, and Gardner Lindzey, measures a person's preference for the six value systems of theoretical, economic, social, political, aesthetic, and religious orientations. After rank ordering forty-five items, the individual receives feedback about the relative importance of the six orientations within himself or herself. Consistent with the emphasis on uniqueness, the scale does not facilitate comparisons between people. Although the language of this scale is somewhat outdated, it is still used for value clarification and the exploration of career and life-style goals.

Allport's research also focused on attitudes that are influenced by group participation, such as religious values and prejudice. Through the study of churchgoers' attitudes, he distinguished between extrinsic religion, or a conventional, self-serving approach, and intrinsic religion, which is based on internalized beliefs and efforts to act upon religious beliefs. Allport and his colleagues found that extrinsic churchgoers were more prejudiced than intrinsic religious churchgoers; however, churchgoers who strongly endorsed both extrinsic and intrinsic religion were even more prejudiced than either extrinsic or intrinsic religious church attenders. Allport also examined cultural, family, historical, and situational factors that influence prejudice.

Context

Gordon Allport provided theoretical and research alternatives at a time when a variety of competing approaches, including humanistic, psychoanalytic, and behavioral perspectives, were seeking preeminence in psychology. Allport found many existing theories to be limiting, overly narrow, and inadequate for describing the wide variations in human personality. As a result, he proposed an eclectic approach to theory that combined the strengths of various other perspectives. Instead of emphasizing a single approach, Allport thought that personality can be both growth-oriented and proactive, as well as reactive and based on instinctual processes. Through an eclectic approach, he hoped that the understanding of personality would become more complete.

Allport was also concerned that many of the existing theories of his time, especially psychoanalytic theories, virtually ignored the healthy personality. In contrast to Freud, Allport strongly emphasized conscious aspects of personality and believed that healthy adults are generally aware of their motivations. Unlike Freud's notion that people are motivated to reduce the tension of instinctual drives, he believed that people seek the kind of tension that allows them to grow, develop goals, and act in innovative ways.

Like humanistic theorists Carl Rogers and Abraham Maslow, Allport identified vital characteristics of mature persons. His list of the characteristics of mature persons overlaps substantially with Maslow's enumeration of the qualities of self-actualizing persons and Rogers' definitions of the "person of tomorrow." Allport's list includes extension of the sense of self (identifying with events and persons outside oneself), emotional security, realistic perception, insight and humor, and a unifying philosophy of life.

Allport developed his theory at a time when other trait approaches that were based on nomothetic study were gaining prominence. Whereas Allport emphasized individual uniqueness, Raymond Cattell identified twenty-three source traits, or building blocks of personality, and Hans Eysenck identified three primary dimensions of extroversion, neuroticism, and psychoticism. Within the nomothetic tradition, more recent researchers have reexamined earlier nomothetic trait theories and have identified five primary common dimensions of personality: surgency (active/dominant persons versus passive/submissive persons), agreeableness (one's warmth or coldness), conscientiousness (one's level of responsibility or undependability), emotional stability (unpredictability versus stability), and culture (one's intellectual understanding of the world). Allport would have found these efforts to identify basic dimensions of personality to have limited usefulness for defining and understanding individual personality styles.

Recent criticisms of trait approaches that emphasize universal characteristics of people indicate that these approaches underestimate the role of situations and human variability and change across different contexts. Furthermore, those approaches that focus on general traits provide summaries and demonstrate trends about behavior, but do not provide explanations for behavior.

The awareness that general trait approaches are inadequate for predicting behavior across situations has led to a resurgence of interest in the types of idiographic research methods proposed by Allport. Approaches to personality have increasingly acknowledged the complexity of human beings and the reality that individuals are influenced by a wide array of features that are often contradictory and inconsistent. Allport's emphasis on the scientific study of unique aspects of personality provided both the inspiration and a general method for examining the singular, diverse variables that define human beings.

Bibliography

Allport, Gordon W. "An Autobiography." In *A History of Psychology in Autobiography.* Vol. 5. Edited by Edwin Garrigues Boring and Gardner Lindzey. New York: Appleton-Century-Crofts, 1967. Allport provides an interesting account of his life, including an encounter with Sigmund Freud.

_____. *Becoming: Basic Considerations for a Psychology of Personality.* New Haven, Conn.: Yale University Press, 1955. A short, straightforward, clear statement of Allport's basic assumptions about personality. Allport attempts to provide the basic foundation for a complete personality theory and emphasizes the importance for both open-mindedness and eclecticism in the study of personality.

_____. *The Nature of Prejudice.* Cambridge, Mass.: Addison-Wesley, 1954. An extensive review of Allport's theoretical perspective on prejudice. Includes definitions of prejudice and discussions of how individuals perceive and think about group differences, sociocultural influences on prejudice, how prejudice is acquired and maintained, the personality of the prejudiced person, and methods for reducing prejudice.

_____. *Pattern and Growth in Personality.* New York: Holt, Rinehart and

Winston, 1961. This textbook is the most complete account of Gordon Allport's personality theory. It includes extensive descriptions of Allport's approach to personality and individuality, personality development, the structure of the personality, the characteristics of the mature personality, and methods of personality assessment.

——————. *Personality and Social Encounter.* Boston: Beacon Press, 1960. A collection of Allport's essays that are scholarly but not overly technical. They are organized into five parts that focus on basic assumptions about personality, personality structure and motivation, personality problems, group tensions associated with prejudice and religion, and social issues and personality.

Allport, Gordon W., Philip E. Vernon, and Gardner Lindzey. *Study of Values.* 3d ed. Boston: Houghton Mifflin, 1960. A scale that measures a person's preference for six value orientations: religious, theoretical, economic, aesthetic, social, political values. The personal ordering of these values provides a framework for reflecting upon and understanding the values that make up one's philosophy of life. Language is outdated and gender-biased, but the book represents one application of Allport's work.

Evans, Richard I. *Gordon Allport: The Man and His Ideas.* New York: E. P. Dutton, 1971. This book is based on a series of dialogues with Allport that focus on his unique contributions and his vision of the future of personality psychology. Also includes a discussion and evaluation of Allport's ideas by three distinguished psychologists who studied under his direction.

Maddi, Salvatore R., and Paul T. Costa. *Humanism in Personology: Allport, Maslow, and Murray.* Chicago: Aldine-Atherton, 1972. This volume compares the work of Allport with the contributions of two other humanistic personality theorists. Although the theories of these three differ substantially, they share an emphasis on human uniqueness, a faith in human capabilities, and a view of people as proactive, complex, and oriented toward the future.

Masterson, Jenny (Gove), pseudonym. *Letters from Jenny.* Edited and interpreted by Gordon W. Allport. New York: Harcourt, Brace & World, 1965. An example of idiographic or morphogenic study of the personality. After studying 301 letters from an older woman to her son and his wife, Allport grouped her characteristics into eight clusters that correspond to the number of central dispositions that he proposed make up important elements of personality.

Peterson, Christopher. *Personality.* San Diego: Harcourt Brace Jovanovich, 1988. This text on personality contains three chapters that summarize, compare, and evaluate various trait approaches along the following dimensions: theory, research, and applications. Describes major criticisms of trait approaches and discusses the practical implications of trait theories.

Carolyn Zerbe Enns

Cross-References

Existential Analysis and Therapy, 999; Gestalt Therapy, 1088; Humanism: An Overview, 1203; Personality Interviewing Strategies, 1797; Psychoanalytic Psychology and Personality: Sigmund Freud, 1912; Religion and Psychology, 2090; Self-Actualization, 2168.

HUNGER: BIOLOGICAL BASES

Type of psychology: Motivation
Fields of study: Motivation theory; nervous system; physical motives

Research into the biological bases of hunger examines the underlying nutritional, hormonal, and neural factors that govern the feelings of hunger and satiety; it provides insight into the basic mechanisms of meal initiation and satisfaction, as well as probable causes and treatments of eating disorders.

Principal terms

ANOREXIA NERVOSA: an eating disorder characterized by obsessive-compulsive concern for thinness by dieting; often combined with extreme exercising, and sometimes part of a binge-purge cycle

BINGING: the uncontrolled consumption of food; in the obsessive extreme, and when combined with purging, called bulimia

CARBOHYDRATE: a major nutrient made of carbon, hydrogen, and oxygen; sugars and starches are carbohydrates

CENTRAL FACTORS: factors having to do with the control of hunger by the central nervous system, especially, but not exclusively, in the hypothalamus

CENTRAL NERVOUS SYSTEM: the brain and spinal cord

HOMEOSTASIS: the process of maintaining a physiological variable (for example, blood glucose) at an equilibrium, or reference, level

HYPOTHALAMUS: a part of the brain that acts as a regulator for hormones and nutrients and for basic drives such as hunger

NEUROTRANSMITTER: a chemical communicator released by nerve cells when signaling other nerve cells; acts to stimulate or inhibit the "listening" cells

NOREPINEPHRINE: a neurotransmitter system that links the brain stem autonomic centers with the hypothalamus in the control of hunger

PERIPHERAL FACTORS: factors having to do with the control of hunger by organs of the gut, including the stomach and liver, as well as by autonomic nerves

Overview

The biological bases of hunger include all the central and peripheral factors—nutrients, hormones, and neural systems—that participate in the initiation, duration, and cessation of a meal. They may even include such purely "psychological" factors as learning or depression, especially when these are considered within the context of their effects on or causes in the nervous system. The major focus in biopsychology, however, has centered on the direct control of the behavior of eating.

Explanations of eating behavior are derived from two primary positions, one with a focus on the central nervous system and the other on peripheral mechanisms of the gut. Investigation of the central control of eating is best exemplified in the ongoing research of psychologist Sarah Leibowitz. When she began her work in the early 1970's, Leibowitz had been interested in the discovery in 1960 by Sebastian Grossman that the neurotransmitter norepinephrine played a major role in stimulating the behavior of eating. Although Grossman had found norepinephrine to be especially active in regions of the hypothalamus in the floor of the brain, Leibowitz was able to pinpoint the critical neural system with great accuracy.

Injecting small amounts of norepinephrine through a fine tube, or cannula, implanted within the brain of experimental animals, Leibowitz found that the paraventricular nucleus (PVN), a small group of cells immediately adjacent to the central duct for cerebrospinal fluid, was the principal site of norepinephrine's control of hunger. Norepinephrine in the PVN stimulated eating even in animals that were still full from their last meal, thus suggesting that hunger was in the head (central factors) and not in the stomach (peripheral factors).

Later, Leibowitz and her colleagues showed that satiety, the feeling that a meal is over, may also be in the head and not in the fullness of the stomach. If serotonin, another neurotransmitter, was injected into the PVN, the food intake of animals that were presumably hungry from being deprived of food for several hours was sharply reduced. Leibowitz has continued to elucidate the neural circuits that connect the PVN with the brain stem, where neural information about the taste of food is integrated with visceral information about the fullness of the stomach and the amounts of nutrients in the bloodstream.

Central factors research may seem to minimize the importance of peripheral factors, but in fact the signaling of nutrient status by the stomach and liver plays a major role in the control of food intake. Though Walter Cannon's research idea in the 1930's that stomach contractions, or hunger "pangs," activated hunger was later shown to be false—hunger pangs are merely a correlate and not a cause of hunger—more recent investigations show the importance of the gastrointestinal tract. When the nutrient glucose, a simple sugar found in most carbohydrate foods, is infused slowly into the otherwise empty duodenum, which is situated between the stomach and the small intestine, animals no longer feel the strong need to eat, even when their stomachs are also empty.

The liver, too, is important in this peripheral control of food intake. Infusion of glucose into the hepatic-portal venous system that leads to the liver depresses the desire to consume a simple sugar solution; however, the control of food intake by the liver is far stronger when the glucose reaches the liver after first going through the process of alimentation: digestion in the gut. Thus, the gastrointestinal tract and the liver work together in the periphery to control food intake. Moreover, glucose in particular is stronger in shutting off the desire for more glucose than it is for a meal of mixed nutrients. This research, conducted in psychologist Donald Novin's laboratory, shows that nutrient sensors in the periphery may act to control the desire for foods that differ in nutrient content.

Homeostasis is a self-regulatory process that controls the level of a physiological variable such as glucose. The idea that blood levels of glucose may be controlled by a feeding system selective for nutrients has received considerable support in work by Arthur Campfield, who devised an ingenious instrument to measure moment-to-moment blood glucose levels in experimental animals that were free to eat. He found that a drop in blood glucose immediately preceded a meal. If additional glucose was infused into the system to prevent this premeal decline, the meal was delayed. The body thus seems to engage in glucostasis: a homeostasis for glucose.

Working with others in Leibowitz's laboratory, psychologist Michael Chafetz showed how glucostasis may be tied to central factors. The group found that drugs that lower blood glucose by releasing insulin from the islets in the pancreas activate the central norepinephrine system that makes an animal want to eat, as well as a peripheral hormonal system that elevates blood glucose. Moreover, animals want to eat carbohydrates, which will restore blood glucose, as opposed to proteins or fats, which will not.

Besides glucose, other nutrients may be controlled by individual feeding systems. These include fats, proteins, salt, iron, zinc, and vitamins. Nutrients essential to survival but not manufactured in the body typically have receptors in the brain that may signal a hunger when the body lacks these nutrients. The desire to eat certain foods may thus depend upon the stimulation of particular feeding systems, acting to keep nutrients in balance.

Applications

As the biological bases of hunger become better understood, clinicians have more powerful tools to treat eating disorders, as well as psychological disorders that involve eating behavior. For example, the urge to binge, or overeat in an uncontrolled way, especially on carbohydrate-rich foods, has been explained in two ways, one involving peripheral factors and one central. Both explanations have led to useful clinical applications.

The peripheral factors explanation comes from psychologist Paula Geiselman. Working in Novin's laboratory, she had been studying how infusions of glucose into the duodenum of experimental animals curtailed the desire to eat. Her work fit neatly into the body of evidence outlined above showing a regulatory system for hunger and glucose. While experimenting with the rate of infusions, however, she discovered that fast infusions had the opposite effect from slow ones: They increased the animal's hunger for sugar solutions.

In the context of a well-established homeostasis for glucose, this was quite surprising. Geiselman realized, though, that her finding explained why some people have trouble controlling what they eat. If a candy bar is consumed on an empty stomach, the rapid infusion of sugar into the gastrointestinal tract can stimulate more hunger rather than satisfy it, as the snacker seeks to do. Additional sweet food is then consumed in a vicious binging cycle that is outside the bounds of normal homeostatic regulation. In order to break this cycle, the snacker is advised to consume fruit instead of candy, because the fiber in fruit delays the passage of its sugar content through the duodenum.

Central factors research from the Massachusetts Institute of Technology laboratories of Judith and Richard Wurtman provides another explanation for carbohydrate binging. This research examined the chain of physiological events that takes place after a meal (or snack) of carbohydrates. Once digested, carbohydrates produce a rapid rise in blood sugar, which stimulates the release of insulin from the pancreas. Insulin facilitates the entry of blood sugar and amino acids (the building blocks of protein) into tissues that use them for energy or protein formation. This action of insulin cleanses the blood of amino acids, except for tryptophan, an amino acid that is used by the brain to manufacture the neurotransmitter serotonin. Because tryptophan usually competes with these other amino acids for entry into the brain, it now enters the brain at a faster rate, which allows the brain to make more serotonin. In short, a carbohydrate meal, through this chain of events, can boost the brain's amount of serotonin.

Recall that serotonin, when infused into the PVN of the hypothalamus, depresses food intake. The Wurtmans showed that drugs that mimic the action of serotonin also depress food intake, especially intake of carbohydrates. In an ingenious experiment with a computerized vending machine that recorded whether volunteers chose carbohydrate-rich or protein-rich snacks, the Wurtmans found that people mostly wanted to snack on carbohydrates: sugars or starches. If the volunteers had taken a drug that mimics the activity of serotonin, they no longer wanted a snack. The drug, by mimicking the natural end result of carbohydrate intake, had depressed the desire for more carbohydrates. People who binge, however, may have some physiological error in the chain of events leading to the serotonin signal for shutting off carbohydrate desire. They keep eating carbohydrates because their brains cannot tell them to stop.

The drugs that mimic serotonin activity and curtail carbohydrate intake are also used as clinical antidepressants. One of these drugs, Prozac, is a widely used antidepressant. Additional research from the Wurtmans' laboratory has shown that obese carbohydrate cravers tend to score higher on a depression rating scale, indicating that carbohydrate craving may be linked to depression for similar neurochemical reasons: A person who is depressed and who craves carbohydrates has low serotonin activity in the brain. Antidepressant drugs, by stimulating serotonin, alleviate depression and curtail snacking.

As Judith Wurtman has proposed, obese carbohydrate cravers may be snacking as a way of self-medicating to alleviate their own depression. By trying to get a charge of brain serotonin through a carbohydrate snack, they are using carbohydrates as antidepressants (antidepressant drugs would do the same thing without extra calories). The trouble is, in their systems, the carbohydrates do not provide enough boost to brain serotonin to shut off the craving or the depression, which keeps them going back for more. The development of antidepressants that effectively boost brain serotonin has been quite helpful in alleviating both depression and the uncontrolled binging in obese carbohydrate cravers.

Other research on central factors has been similarly useful in identifying drugs that may soon be helpful in treating disorders such as anorexia nervosa, which is characterized by excessive concern over food intake and body image. Research in the Leibowitz laboratory has identified several substances that may prove worthy in these cases. Some of these drugs act directly through the norepinephrine feeding system in the brain, while a drug called neuropeptide Y, which is more potent in stimulating feeding than any other drug tested on experimental animals, may be less direct. A challenge remains in modeling the disease in animals before the drugs can be used on humans.

Context

The modern history of the biological bases of hunger derives in large part from the work of Claude Bernard, a French physiologist who established the principle of physiological regulation, or homeostasis, in the mid-1800's. It was not until the 1930's, however, that this principle gained a behavioral component through the research of Curt Richter in the United States.

Richter's early research, which is still actively cited today, established the tie between food selection and the underlying regulation of the nutrients contained in the foods selected. His work proved that animals can maintain themselves on a "cafeteria diet" of pure nutrients, and can compensate for physiological deficits by eating more of the deficient nutrient. This early work gave impetus to hundreds of laboratory and field studies showing behavioral "hungers" for specific nutrients, as well as the ability of animals to select an optimal diet in the wild.

The understanding of specific hunger regulation also led to studies of the brain's role in food behavior. In the 1940's and 1950's, the discoveries that paved the way to the focus on the hypothalamus were made, but by then researchers had consolidated their interests from specific hungers to the more general psychological abstraction of "hunger." Several studies over the next twenty to thirty years showed how animals would become more or less hungry when nutrients or neurotransmitters interacted with hypothalamic function. The studies began to conflict, however; some found an increase in food intake, and others found a decrease after one given manipulation. It soon became clear that Richter had been right all along: There was no simple regulation of a general "hunger." In the 1980's, scientists began investigating specific nutrient hungers again.

This work is leading to an understanding of how different neural systems control specific nutrient hungers. There is some knowledge of how carbohydrate and salt intakes are regulated; research that will give rise to an understanding of the behavioral control of other nutrients, such as protein, fats, vitamins, and minerals, is progressing. Research on nutrient hungers lies at the interface between psychology and neuroscience. It helps psychologists understand the more general principles of motivation by showing them how a specific motivated entity is controlled. In particular, research on hunger motivation increases insight into thirst and sex motives by showing when and how behavior contributes to the overall physiological regulation. This research contributes to neuroscience in clarifying how neural systems control behavior, leading to a more general understanding of the brain.

Bibliography

Chafetz, Michael D. *Nutrition and Neurotransmitters: The Nutrient Bases of Behavior.* Englewood Cliffs, N.J.: Prentice-Hall, 1990. Shows how neurotransmitters and nutrients interact to control food behavior. The means by which other "nonfood" behaviors (for example, learning and memory) are impacted by nutrients are also considered. The reader can safely skip the chapter and sections on neuroanatomy while focusing on the behavioral control of nutrients.

Crisp, A. H. *Anorexia Nervosa: Let Me Be.* London: Academic Press, 1980. A comprehensive and readable account of a major eating disorder by an important writer in the field. Includes both biological and psychological components of the illness, and has insightful discussions of patients' behavior, psychological status, and families.

Denton, Derek A. *The Hunger for Salt.* New York: Springer-Verlag, 1982. This comprehensive book provides an anthropological, physiological, and medical analysis of the control of a single nutrient. Much of the historical and case data will provide fascinating reading for the general reader. The medical and scientific data is also accessible to the motivated reader.

Kalat, James W. *Introduction to Psychology.* 2d ed. Belmont, Calif.: Wadsworth, 1986. The sections on hunger and motivation were written by an author (Kalat) whose own work in the field provided many important contributions. His writing style is literate and readable; he strove to write with informed clarity.

Wurtman, Judith. *The Carbohydrate Craver's Diet.* New York: Ballantine, 1983. Translates the scientific data on carbohydrate regulation from the Wurtman laboratory into a readable presentation. The diet-book format also provides useful advice for those who need to implement this information. Especially helpful for getting a feel for the impact of science on daily life.

Michael D. Chafetz

Cross-References

Drive Theory, 843; Hunger: Psychological Bases, 1223; Hunger Regulation, 1229; Motivational Constructs, 1616; Neural and Hormonal Interaction, 1648; Neurotransmitters, 1673; Smell and Taste, 2290; Thirst, 2547.

HUNGER: PSYCHOLOGICAL BASES

Type of psychology: Motivation
Field of study: Physical motives

The psychological bases of hunger play an important role in the external and internal mediating forces that can affect and modify the physiological aspects of hunger.

Principal terms

APPETITE: a desire for food
HOMEOSTASIS: the balance or equilibrium of the internal systems
HYPOTHALAMUS: a group of neuron cell bodies that control the endocrine system and are responsible for the regulation of drives such as hunger, thirst, sex, and aggression
PRIMARY MOTIVES: motives that arise from innate, biological needs and that must be met for survival
SATIETY: feelings of fullness and satisfaction
SET POINT: an organism's personal homeostatic level for a particular body weight, which results from factors such as early feeding experiences and heredity

Overview

Primary motives are generated by innate biological needs that must be met for survival. These motives include hunger, thirst, and sleep. Hunger, like thirst, the need for sleep, and other physiological drives, has been studied extensively, yet there is still uncertainty as to exactly how hunger works. A large body of research about the physiological analysis of hunger has led to the identification of important differences between physical hunger and psychological hunger.

Physical hunger theories assumed that the body's physiological mechanisms and systems produce hunger as a need and that when this need is satisfied, the hunger drive is, for the time being, reduced. Psychologists have developed models and theories of hunger by analyzing its boundaries and restraint or regulation. The early findings on hunger regulation mechanisms emphasized the biological state of the individual and the control of an individual over the hunger drive. If a person experiences hunger, consumption of food will continue until it is terminated by internal cues. This is referred to as regulation.

The individual learns to avoid hunger by reacting to the internal cues of satiety or fullness. The satiety boundary is characterized by feelings of fullness ranging from satisfaction to uncomfortable bloating. The normal eater learns to avoid transgression far or often into this latter zone. Beyond the reaction to internal cues is a zone of indifference, in which the body is not subject to biological cues. Instead, hunger is influenced by social, cognitive, and psychological cues. These cues may be external and/or internalized but do not rely on satiety cues for restraint.

Eating past the point of satiety is referred to as counterregulation or, more commonly, as binge eating or compulsive eating. Because the inhibitors of hunger restraint are not physiological in this zone, the restraint and dietary boundaries are cognitively determined. The physical hunger mechanisms may send signals, but quite ordinary ideas such as "being hungry" and "not being hungry" must be interpreted or received by the individual. The person must learn to distinguish between bodily sensations that indicate the need for food and the feelings that accompany this need, such as anxiety, boredom, loneliness, or depression.

Thus, there are both internal cues and external cues that define hunger and lead an individual to know when to eat and how much to eat. External cues as a motive for eating have been studied extensively, particularly in research on obesity and eating disorders such as binge behavior and compulsive overeating. External cues include enticing smells, locations such as restaurants or other kinds of social settings, and the social environment—what other people are doing. When external cues prevail, a person does not have to be hungry in order to feel hungry.

The awareness of hunger begins very early in life. Those infants who are fed on demand, whose cries of hunger determine the times at which they are fed, are taught soon after they can feed themselves that their eating must conform to family rules about when, what, and how much to eat in order to satisfy their hunger. Infants fed on a schedule learn even earlier to conform to external constraints and regulations regarding hunger. Throughout life, responding to hunger by feeding oneself is nourishing both physiologically and psychologically. Beginning in infancy, the sequences of getting hungry and being fed establish the foundations of the relationship between the physiological need or drive and the psychological components of feelings such as affiliation, interaction, calm, and security when hunger is satisfied.

In preschool and early school years, when children are integrating themselves into their social world, food acceptance and cultural practices are learned. Prior to the peer group and school environment, the family and media are usually the main vehicles of cultural socialization of the hunger drive. According to social learning theory, these agents will play an important role in the child's learning to interpret his or her level of hunger and in subsequent eating patterns, both directly and indirectly. The modeling behavior of children is also related to hunger learning.

Experiences of hunger and satiety play a central role in a person's relationship to hunger awareness, eating, and food. Some dispositions that influence hunger and eating behavior are long-term (fairly stable and enduring), while other habits and attitudes may fluctuate. There are numerous explanations that theorize about the relation between the hunger drive and other factors such as genetic inheritance and activity level.

A strictly physiological analysis of hunger claims that an individual's responses to hunger are caused by the brain's regulation of body weight. If the body goes below its predetermined "set point," internal hunger cues are initiated to signal the need for food consumption. External restraints, such as attempts to live up to ideal cultural thinness standards, also affect behavior and may result in restrained eating in order to maintain a body weight below the body's defined set point.

The idea of a body set point is actually rooted in the nineteenth century work of physiologist Claude Bernard, a pioneer in research based on the concept of homeostasis, or system balance in the body. Homeostasis has since played a fundamental role in many subsequent investigations regarding the physiology of hunger and the regulatory systems involved in hunger satisfaction. Inherent in the set-point theory is the concept of motivation, meaning that an organism is driven physiologically and behaviorally toward maintenance of homeostasis and the body's set point, and will adapt to accommodate the systems involved in maintenance.

In addition, there appear to be two anatomically and behaviorally distinct centers located in the hypothalamus, one regulating hunger and the other regulating satiety. The area of the hypothalamus responsible for stimulating eating behavior is the lateral hypothalamus. The ventromedial hypothalamus is the area responsible for signaling the organism to stop eating. The lateral hypothalamus is responsible for establishing a set point for body weight.

In comparing hunger and satiety sensation differences, increased hunger and disturbed satiety appear to be two different and quite separate mechanisms. Imbalance or dysfunction of either the hunger mechanism or the satiety sensation can lead to obesity, overeating, binge eating, and other eating disorders. It appears that the way hunger is experienced accounts, in part, for its recognition. Whether hunger is experienced in context with other drives or becomes a compulsive force that dominates all other drives in life is a complex issue. The prevalence of eating disorders and the multitude of variables associated with hunger drives and regulation have provided psychologists with an opportunity to examine the ways in which hunger might take on different meanings. To a person who is anorexic, for example, hunger may be a positive feeling—a state of being "high" and thus a goal to seek. To others, hunger may produce feelings of anxiety, insecurity, or anger. In this case, a person might eat before feeling hunger to prevent the feelings from arising. People's ability to experience hunger in different ways provides psychologists with two types of hunger, which are commonly referred to as hunger and appetite.

Hunger and appetite are not the same. Actual physical need is the basis of true hunger, while appetite can be triggered by thought, feeling, or sensation. Physical need can be separate from psychological need, although they may feel the same to the person who is not conscious of the difference. Compulsive eaters are often unable to recognize the difference between "real" hunger and psychological hunger, or appetite. While psychological hunger can be equally as motivating a need as stomach hunger, because appetite (or mouth hunger) is emotionally, cognitively, and psychologically based, it cannot be fed in the same way. Stomach hunger can be satisfied by eating, whereas "feeding" mouth hunger must involve other activities and behaviors, since food does not ultimately seem to satisfy the mouth type of hunger.

Applications

Studies of hunger have pointed to marked changes in psychological functioning caused by hunger, with the exact change depending largely on the type and extent of the deficiency. Some of these effects were demonstrated in a pioneering study of semistarvation carried out during World War II. Researchers found that during periods of semistarvation, subjects showed dramatic personality and behavioral changes. They became irritable, unsociable, and increasingly unable to concentrate on anything but food. Among other psychological changes were apathy, loss of pride in personal appearance, and feelings of inadequacy. By the end of the experiment, there was a marked reduction or disappearance of interest in sex, and the predominant mood of the subjects was one of gloom and depression. Hunger and food dominated thought, conversation, and daydreams and had become the dominant influence in the behavior of the subjects.

Another approach to increasing understanding of hunger and its psychological components is to examine hunger in its cultural context. In American culture, the experience of hunger is inextricably tied to weight, eating, body image, self-concept, social definitions of fatness and thinness, and other factors which take the issue of hunger far beyond the physiological facts. Historian Hillel Schwartz has traced the American cultural preoccupation with hunger, eating, and diet by examining the cultural fit between shared fictions about the body and their psychological, social, and cultural consequences. Hunger becomes a broader social issue when viewed in the context of the culture's history of obsession with diet, weight control, and body image. The personal experience of hunger is affected by the social and historical context.

Eating disorders such as anorexia, bulimia, and compulsive overeating provide evidence of the complex relationship between the physiological and psychological components of hunger. Obesity has also been examined using medical and psychological models. The etiology of hunger's relationship to eating disorders has provided insight, if not consensus, by investigating the roles of hereditary factors, social learning, family systems, and multigenerational transmission in hunger as well as the socially learned eating patterns, food preferences, and cultural ideals that can mediate the hunger drive. Body image, eating restraint, and eating attitudes have been assessed by various methods. The focus of much of the research on hunger beyond the early animal experiments has been eating disorders. The findings confirm that hunger is more than a physiological need and is affected by a multitude of variables.

Context

Early scientific interest in hunger research was dominated by medical models, which identified the physiological mechanisms and systems involved. One of the earliest attempts to understand the sensation of hunger was an experiment conducted in 1912, in which a subject swallowed a balloon and then inflated it in his stomach. His stomach contractions and subjective reports of hunger feelings could then be simultaneously recorded. When the recordings were compared to the voluntary key presses that the subject made each time he experienced the feeling of hunger, the researchers concluded that it was the stomach movements that caused the sensation of hunger. It was later found, however, that an empty stomach is relatively inactive and that the stomach contractions experienced by the subject were an experimental artifact caused by the mere presence of the balloon in the stomach.

Further evidence for the lack of connection between stomach stimuli and feelings of hunger was provided in animal experiments which resulted in differentiating two areas of the hypothalamus responsible for stimulating eating behavior and signaling satiety—the "start eating" and "stop eating" centers.

Psychologist Stanley Schachter and his colleagues began to explore the psychological issues involved in hunger by emphasizing the external, nonphysiological factors involved. In a series of experiments in which normal-weight and overweight individuals were provided with a variety of external eating cues, Schachter found that overweight subjects were more attentive to the passage of time in determining when to eat and were more excited by the taste and sight of food than were normal-weight persons. More recently, the growth of the field of social psychology has provided yet a different perspective on hunger, one that accounts for the situational and environment factors which influence the physiological and psychological states. For example, psychologists have examined extreme hunger and deprivation in case studies from historical episodes such as war, concentration camps, and famine in light of the more recent interest in the identification and treatment of eating disorders.

There does not appear to be a consistent or ongoing effort to develop an interdisciplinary approach to the study of hunger. Because hunger is such a complex drive, isolating the factors associated with it poses a challenge to the standard research methodologies of psychology such as the case study, experiment, observation, and survey. Each methodology has its shortcomings, but together the methodologies have produced findings which clearly demonstrate that hunger is a physiological drive embedded in a psychological, social, and cultural context.

Viewing hunger as a multidimensional behavior has led to an awareness of hunger and its implications in a broader context. Changing dysfunctional attitudes, feelings, thoughts, and behaviors concerning hunger has not always been seen as a choice. Through continued psychological research into the topic of hunger—and increasing individual and group participation in efforts to understand, control, and change behaviors associated with hunger—new insights continue to emerge that will no doubt cast new light on this important and not yet completely understood topic.

Bibliography

Arenson, Gloria. *A Substance Called Food.* 2d ed. Blue Ridge Summit, Pa.: Tab Books, 1989. Presents a variety of perspectives on eating: the psychological, the physiological, and the transpersonal. Particularly useful in providing self-help advice and treatment modalities. Examines the compulsiveness of food addiction and sees behavior modification as a means of addressing the addictive behavior.

Hirschmann, Jane R., and Carol H. Munter. *Overcoming Overeating: Living Free in a World of Food.* Reading, Mass.: Addison-Wesley, 1988. Reviews the psychological bases for compulsive eating and provides alternative strategies to persons who have an addictive relationship with food. Presents convincing arguments against dieting and proposes that self-acceptance, physical activity, and health are more appropriate long-term solutions to the problem of overeating.

Nisbett, Richard E. "Hunger, Obesity, and the Ventromedial Hypothalamus." *Psychological Review* 79, no. 6 (1972): 433-453. Based on research which differentiated the two areas of the hypothalamus that involve hunger: the "start eating" and "stop eating" mechanisms. Explains the idea of "set point," or the body mechanism which regulates homeostasis. This article is a classic in the field of hunger because it explains the physiological location of hunger and the important role of the hypothalamus.

Schachter, Stanley, and Larry P. Gross. "Manipulated Time and Eating Behavior." *Journal of Personality and Social Psychology* 10, no. 2 (1968): 98-106. Schachter's experiments provide the basis for attention to, and recognition of the importance of, external, nonphysiological factors affecting hunger. This article was one of the first to address the psychological components of hunger by examining the external triggers to eating.

Schwartz, Hillel. *Never Satisfied: A Cultural History of Diets, Fantasies, and Fat.* New York: Free Press, 1986. Schwartz, a historian, looks at diets and eating from the perspective of American social and cultural history. Begins with the first weight watchers, in the early nineteenth century; examines how "shared fictions" about the body fit with various reducing methods and fads in different eras.

Robin Franck

Cross-References

Addictive Personality and Behaviors, 102; Anorexia Nervosa and Bulimia Nervosa, 259; Drive Theory, 843; Hunger: Biological Bases, 1217; Hunger Regulation, 1229; Obesity, 1688.

HUNGER REGULATION

Type of psychology: Motivation
Field of study: Physical motives

The regulation of hunger involves both physiological and psychological components; culture and socialization play an important role in hunger regulation.

Principal terms
APPETITE: a desire for food
BINGE: an episode of uncontrolled eating
DEPRIVATION: the act of taking away or withholding
EATING DISORDERS: afflictions resulting from dysfunctional relationships to hunger, food, and eating
EXTERNAL CUES: cues to eating that lie outside the individual
HUNGER: a physiological need for food
INTERNAL CUES: cues to eating that come from within the body
SATIETY: a feeling of fullness and satisfaction

Overview

Scientific interest in the regulation of hunger was long centered on the stomach, but more recent research in this area has explored the role of the brain in hunger regulation. The brain is now considered, in effect, the first part of the digestive system. Hunger regulation seems to be centered in the hypothalamus, where research has shown that one area seems to stimulate eating and another area creates feelings of satiation or satisfaction. When the hypothalamus signals hunger, a human may respond in a number of ways. The internal regulators in the brain that tell humans to eat can be overridden by personal, social, and cultural attitudes. Feelings of revulsion about certain foods may cause people to starve themselves rather than eat a food that their culture has labeled inedible.

The reason humans eat or do not eat is not solely explicable in terms of a full or empty stomach or of any one mechanism operating in isolation—such as the level of sugar in the blood, the emptiness or fullness of fat cells, or a need for caloric energy. Moreover, even if a combination of mechanisms does send humans in search of food, no single part of the brain dictates that they will eat the food. In the final analysis, how humans regulate their hunger depends upon the interactions among numerous physiological, psychological, and environmental variables.

Although there are numerous theories regarding hunger regulation, they seem to share the common feature of treating the regulation of hunger as a psychobiological process—that is, a process whereby psychological factors interact with biological processes. Humans are one of the few species that enjoy the "privilege" of eating when not hungry and, conversely, of not eating when hungry. This means in theory that people should be hungry when the body has used up its available supply of nutrients; people should not feel hunger if the nutrient supply is adequate. If this were the case, hunger regulation mechanisms would reside solely in the physiological realm.

In reality, however, even if one's physical hunger needs have been met, psychological hunger can still be experienced. A wide variety of circumstances and conditions contribute to this type of hunger, such as feelings of boredom, loneliness, anger, anxiety, or depression. Coming in contact with tempting foods may fuel psychological hunger, as may the belief that one has not had enough to eat. Not having encountered a sufficient range of taste and textures to satisfy is another possible trigger of psychological hunger. Thus, the regulation of hunger must include the examination of psychological components of hunger as well as the body's regulatory mechanisms.

It is evident that children have a self-regulatory mechanism that responds to internal cues for food consumption and hunger regulation. Self-regulation of food intake and hunger has been demonstrated in infants and young children, although it is unclear exactly when hunger awareness and food regulation mechanisms for hunger and satiety actually develop. Hunger is not solely innate knowledge. Learning is necessary for the organization of hunger experiences into recognizable patterns and for its regulation. What is learned becomes incorporated into the child's behavior. Inappropriate responses to infant-initiated hunger and satiety cues by the caregiver will cause the infant to ignore internal hunger and satiety cues and instead learn to regulate hunger and food consumption by responding to external cues. For example, during infant feedings, pauses may occur. The feeder may terminate feeding and the infant will not be satisfied. The opposite may also occur; if the infant is internally satiated and stops feeding, the feeder may force-feed past satiation. Thus, the infant learns that self-initiated actions are unsuccessful and may show less initiative in future feedings.

In the same way that eating responses to internal and external hunger cues are learned, eating cues are learned. It is possible to confuse various internal sensations, such as anxiety, with hunger and therefore to learn inappropriate means—such as eating—to attempt to gratify them. Thus it is necessary to learn how to interpret one's own internal hunger cues, satiety levels, and emotional sensations appropriately and to learn appropriate means to gratify them.

Early childhood autonomy struggles also play a role in hunger regulation. In the struggle for independence, food may be used as a weapon or tool by the parent who restricts food consumption or who forces child food consumption. The child may refuse to eat or, conversely, may become obsessed with obtaining food and eating. Autonomy battles may cause the child further to lose sight of his or her own hunger and satiety cues, resulting in eating that becomes associated with external cues. Later in life, the child may not know when and if he or she is hungry.

External cue theories state that people may ignore or be unaware of physiological hunger and satiety cues and may instead regulate food consumption by external cues such as sight, smell, taste, social setting, and availability of food. In fact, many persons with eating disorders display externally controlled eating behaviors. Hunger regulation is also affected by eating attitudes, which include feelings about food and body-image perceptions and attitudes that accompany eating situations. Feelings about food are beliefs associated with such judgments as "good" and "bad," "fattening," and so on. How prevalent food feelings are varies widely among children and adults. Restricting or regulating hunger by dieting causes an increased preoccupation with food feelings, and thoughts of food can become obsessive. Eating disorders such as the diet-binge-purge pattern and compulsive overeating or undereating often show a pattern of intense food preoccupation.

Children may learn to regulate their hunger in order to meet the expectations of parents. Dieting and compulsive overeating have been found to be related to the child's perceived failure to meet parental expectations. Adults may learn to regulate their hunger in order to meet the expectations of spouse, family, or friends. To differentiate among various patterns of psychological reactions and hunger regulation requires analysis of factors intrinsically interwoven with the whole development process. Attitudes and psychological problems that will affect hunger regulation may develop in childhood, adolescence, or adulthood. Feelings of not being in control, failing to organize discriminating awareness of the signals of bodily urges (in particular, awareness of hunger as a signal of nutritional need), and lack of conviction of emotional and interpersonal effectiveness are common among those with eating disorders.

Hunger regulation is also related to the family system. Disturbances in family relationships and autonomy and self-identity development issues may impact hunger-regulation mechanisms. Women who struggle with hunger regulation and who manifest eating disorders often lack self-identity and are reported to be insecure, anxious, and depressed.

Applications

The desire to regulate hunger has resulted in a wide variety of approaches and techniques, including professional diet centers, programs, and clinics; self-help books and magazines; diet clubs and support groups; self-help classes; and "diet doctors." Many people have benefited from psychotherapy in an effort to understand and control their hunger regulation mechanisms. Group therapy is one of the most successful forms of psychotherapy for food abusers. Types of group therapy vary greatly and include leaderless support groups, nonprofessional self-help groups such as Overeaters Anonymous, and groups led by professional therapists.

Advantages of group support for hunger regulation include the realization that one is not alone. An often-heard expression in group therapy is "I always thought I was the only person who ever felt this way." Other advantages include group support for risk taking, feedback from different perspectives, and a group laboratory for experimenting with new social behaviors. Witnessing others struggling to resolve life issues can provide powerful motivation to change. Self-help and therapy groups also offer friendship and acceptance. Creative arts therapies are other forms of psychotherapy used by persons seeking to understand and control their hunger regulation mechanisms. Creative therapy may involve art, music, dance, poetry, dreams, and other creative processes. These are experiential activities, and the process is sometimes nonverbal.

A more common experience for those who have faced the issue of hunger regulation is dieting. Despite the high failure rate of diets and weight-loss programs, the "diet mentality" is often associated with hunger regulation. Robert Schwartz studied the elements of the diet mentality, which is based on the assumption that fat is bad and thin is good. Dieting often sets up a vicious cycle of failure, which deflates self-esteem, thus contributing to shame and guilt, and to another diet. The diet mentality is self-defeating. Another key element to the diet mentality is the mechanism of self-deprivation that comes from not being allowed to indulge in certain foods and the accompanying social restrictions and isolation that dieting creates. Dieting treats the symptom rather than the cause of overeating.

Numerous approaches to hunger regulation share a condemnation of the diet mentality. Overcoming overeating; understanding, controlling, and recovering from addictive eating; and being "thin-within" are approaches based on addressing hunger regulation from a psychological perspective rather than a physiological one. These approaches share an emphasis on the emotional and feeling components of hunger regulation. They encourage the development of skills to differentiate between stomach hunger and mind hunger—that is, between hunger and appetite—and thereby to learn to recognize satiety as well as the reasons for hunger.

Behavior modification consists of a variety of techniques that attempt to apply the findings and methods of experimental psychology to human behavior. Interest in applying behavioral modification to hunger regulation developed as a result of the research on external cues and environmental factors that control the food intake of individuals. By emphasizing specific training in "stimulus control," behavior modification helps the individual to manage the environmental determinants of eating.

The first step in most behavior modification programs is to help the patient identify and monitor activities that are contributing to the specific behavior. In the case of an individual who overeats, this could involve identifying such behaviors as frequent ingestion of sweets, late evening snacking, eating huge meals, or eating in response to social demands. Because most people have more than one stimulus for eating behavior, the individual then observes situational stimuli: those that arise from the environment in which eating usually takes place. Once the stimuli are identified, new behaviors can be substituted—in effect, behavior can be modified.

Context

Hunger regulation is an age-old topic, going back at least to the time of Socrates, who warned his forum to beware of those foods that tempt one to eat when one is not hungry. Psychologists have traditionally made a sharp distinction between motivation based on personal strivings and motivation deriving from the maintenance of the organism as a biological system. Early research into hunger regulation was predominantly physiologically based, whereas later investigations have explored the psychological, social, and cultural components of regulating hunger.

Psychologists and psychiatrists have applied the techniques of behavior modification to the topic of hunger regulation. Behavior modification, behavior therapy, and experimental analysis of behavior are all techniques which attempt to apply the data and methods of experimental psychology to human behavior. The underlying philosophy is based on the principles of learning, with the assumption that if a behavior is learned, it can be retrained; if it is not learned behavior, it can be shaped.

Behavior modification in the treatment of hunger regulation is directed at both the control of ingestive behavior (when, why, where, and how much) and the control of the activity and energy expenditure of the individual. The idea that modifications in eating behavior and activity may ultimately become permanent provides the possibility for long-term alterations of the body's mechanisms for maintaining equilibrium.

The role of psychotherapy in controlling primary drives usually involves a multifaceted approach, with both physiological and psychological aspects; both have therapeutic significance. The discoveries of the marked influence of social factors on eating disorders and the use of various psychotherapy techniques to treat these disorders is an example of the growth of applied psychology.

Bibliography

Bruch, Hilde. *The Golden Cage: The Enigma of Anorexia Nervosa.* New York: Vintage Books, 1979. The author is one of the best-known practitioners treating anorexia nervosa. A valuable book, based on detailed case histories from her practice, that give insight into the disease's possible causes, its effects, and the methods of treatment that have worked. Helpful in understanding the external cues involved with hunger regulation.

Hirschmann, Jane R., and Carol H. Munter. *Overcoming Overeating: Living Free in a World of Food.* Reading, Mass.: Addison-Wesley, 1988. Reviews the psychological bases for compulsive eating and provides alternative strategies for persons who have an addictive relationship with food. Especially useful for the compulsive dieter, because it examines whether dieting actually produces the desired goal of slimness, attractiveness, and happiness.

LeBow, Michael D. *Weight Control: The Behavioural Strategies.* New York: John Wiley & Sons, 1981. Exhaustive compendium of behavioral control methods used to control eating and weight. Contains the facts about weight and dieting by describing various research studies and their conclusions. The book is aimed at the long-term, repeated pattern dieter as well as the binge eater.

Schwartz, Hillel. *Never Satisfied.* New York: Collier-Macmillan, 1986. Presents a cultural history of diets, fantasies, and fat by explaining the cultural fit between shared fictions about the body and the reducing methods of each era, beginning with the first American weight watchers in the early 1800's. Particularly helpful in examining hunger from a sociological perspective.

Schwartz, Robert. *Diets Don't Work.* Oakland, Calif.: Breakthru Publishing, 1982.

Practical "how-to" guide to dismantling the diet mentality. This book is a good, basic, and sensible guide for taking stock of the self-defeating weight-loss attitudes and behaviors prevalent in temporary diets versus long-term attitudinal and behavior strategies for permanent weight control.

Stuart, Richard B. *Act Thin, Stay Thin*. New York: W. W. Norton, 1977. Particularly useful in examining the moods behind the urge to eat. Written by the psychological director of Weight Watchers, an international weight-loss program. Written for those who are chronic dieters; contains ways to lose the preoccupation with food that many compulsive eaters have.

Robin Franck

Cross-References

Anorexia Nervosa and Bulimia Nervosa, 259; Drive Theory, 843; Hunger: Biological Bases, 1217; Hunger: Psychological Bases, 1223; Obesity, 1688; Thirst, 2547.

HYPERACTIVITY

Type of psychology: Psychopathology
Field of study: Childhood and adolescent disorders

Hyperactivity (known as attention-deficit hyperactivity disorder) is one of the most common disorders of childhood and adolescence, but it is also one of the most disturbing and debilitating disorders that a child or adolescent can experience. Research into this disorder has identified its primary causes; however, it remains a difficult disorder to treat effectively.

Principal terms

ETIOLOGY: the factors that are thought to cause or contribute to a particular disorder

IMPULSIVITY: excitability, poor self-control, and inability to delay gratification or to inhibit urges; examples include difficulty waiting, blurting out answers, and interrupting others

INATTENTION: difficulty in sustaining attention, distractibility; examples include poor concentration and distraction by unimportant stimuli, such as a passing vehicle

OVERACTIVITY: excessive levels of vocal or motor activity, such as restlessness, fidgeting, and unnecessary movements

PREVALENCE: the percentage of a population that has a particular disorder at a given time

TREATMENT: the attempt to ameliorate or treat the symptoms of a disorder; treatments can include medication, cognitive-behavioral therapy, and parent training, among others

Overview

Attention-deficit hyperactivity disorder (ADHD), better known as "hyperactivity," is one of the most extensively studied behavior disorders of childhood. It is estimated that there are more than ten thousand individual studies of this disorder, as well as numerous books and other writings. There are a number of reasons why this disorder is of such interest to researchers and clinicians. The two primary reasons are, first, that ADHD is a relatively common disorder of childhood, and second, there are numerous problems associated with ADHD, including lower levels of intellectual and academic performance and higher levels of aggressive and defiant behavior.

In national and international studies of childhood emotional and behavioral disorders, ADHD has been found to be relatively common among children. Although prevalence estimates range from 1 percent to 20 percent, most researchers agree that between 3 percent and 5 percent of children could be diagnosed as having ADHD. In order to be diagnosed as having ADHD, a child needs to show more than hyperactivity alone. The revised third edition of the *Diagnostic and Statistical Manual of Men-*

tal Disorders (DSM-III-R), which was published by the American Psychiatric Association in 1987, describes the diagnostic criteria for ADHD. In order to receive the diagnosis of ADHD according to DSM-III-R, a child must show abnormally high levels of eight out of fourteen listed behaviors when compared with peers of the same age. The behaviors fall roughly into three categories: inattention (such as having difficulty sustaining attention in play activities or tasks), impulsivity (such as having difficulty waiting one's turn in a game), and overactivity (such as difficulty remaining still or seated when asked). Although many of these behaviors are quite common for most children at some point in their lives, the important point to consider in the diagnosis of ADHD is that these behaviors must be in excess of the levels of behaviors most frequently exhibited for children of that age. Additionally, it is expected that these behaviors have been excessive for at least six months and that the problem behaviors were present by the time the child was seven years old.

Boys tend to outnumber girls in the diagnosis of ADHD. It is estimated that, of children diagnosed as having ADHD, boys outnumber girls six to one. This estimate may be somewhat high, however, since the ratio is reported to be three to one in samples of children who have not been referred for therapy. It may be that boys are disproportionately referred for therapy. ADHD boys tend to be more aggressive and antisocial than ADHD girls, and therefore boys may be more frequently referred for therapy than girls even when similar levels of ADHD behavior occur.

There are a number of additional problems associated with ADHD, including the greater likelihood of ADHD boys exhibiting aggressive and antisocial behavior. Although many ADHD children do not show any associated problems, many ADHD children show deficits in both intellectual and behavioral functioning. For example, a number of studies have found that ADHD children score an average of seven to fifteen points below normal children on standardized intelligence tests. It may be, however, that this poorer performance reflects poor test-taking skills or inattention during the test rather than actual impairment in intellectual functioning. Additionally, ADHD children tend to have difficulty with academic performance and scholastic achievement. It is assumed that this poor academic performance is a result of inattention and impulsiveness in the classrooom. When ADHD children are given medication to control their inattention and impulsiveness, their academic productivity has been shown to improve.

ADHD children have also been shown to have a high number of associated emotional and behavioral difficulties. As mentioned earlier, ADHD boys tend to show higher levels of aggressive and antisocial behavior than ADHD girls and normal children. Additionally, it is estimated that 11 percent of ADHD children have at least three other psychiatric disorders, 32 percent have at least two other disorders, and 44 percent have at least one other disorder. Many of these problems are related to depression and anxiety, although many ADHD children also have severe problems with temper tantrums, stubbornness, and defiant behavior. It is also estimated that up to 50 percent of ADHD children have impaired social relations; that is, they do not get along with other children. In general, there are many problems associated with ADHD, and this may be part of the reason that researchers have been so intrigued by this disorder.

Researchers must understand a disorder before they can attempt to treat it. There are a variety of theories on the etiology of ADHD, but most researchers now believe that there are multiple factors that influence its development. It appears that many children may have a biological predisposition toward ADHD; in other words, they may have a greater likelihood of developing ADHD as a result of genetic factors. This predisposition is exacerbated by a variety of factors, such as complications during pregnancy, neurological disease, exposure to toxins, family adversity, and inconsistent parental discipline. Although a very popular belief is that food additives or sugar can cause ADHD, there has been almost no scientific support for these claims. Since so many factors have been found to be associated with the development of ADHD, it is not surprising that numerous treatments have been developed for the amelioration of ADHD symptoms. Although numerous treatment methods have been developed and studied, ADHD remains a difficult disorder to treat effectively.

Applications

Treatments of ADHD can be broken down into roughly two categories: medication; and behavioral or cognitive-behavioral treatment with the individual ADHD child, parents, or teachers. It should be noted that traditional psychotherapy and play therapy have not been found to be effective in the treatment of ADHD. Stimulant medications have been used in the treatment of ADHD since 1937. The most commonly prescribed stimulant medications are methylphenidate (Ritalin), pemoline (Cylert), and dextroamphetamine (Dexedrine). Behavioral improvements caused by stimulant medications include impulse control and improved attending behavior. Overall, approximately 75 percent of ADHD children on stimulant medication show behavioral improvement, and 25 percent show either no improvement or decreased behavioral functioning. The findings related to academic performance are mixed. It appears that stimulant medications can help the ADHD child with school productivity and accuracy, but not with overall academic achievement. In addition, although ADHD children tend to show improvement while they are on a stimulant medication, there are rarely any long-term benefits to the use of stimulant medications. In general, stimulant medication can be seen as only a short-term management tool.

Antidepressant medications (such as imipramine and desipramine) have also been used with ADHD children. These medications are sometimes used when stimulant medication is not appropriate (for example, if the child has motor or vocal tics). Antidepressant medications, however, like stimulant medications, appear to provide only short-term improvement in ADHD symptoms. Overall, the use or nonuse of medications in the treatment of ADHD should be carefully evaluated by a qualified physician (such as a psychiatrist). If the child is started on medication for ADHD, the safety and appropriateness of the medication must be monitored continually throughout its use.

Behavioral and cognitive-behavioral treatments have been used with ADHD children themselves, with parents, and with teachers. Most of these techniques attempt to provide the child with a consistent environment in which on-task behavior is rewarded (for example, the teacher praises the child for raising his or her hand and not shouting out an answer), and in which off-task behavior is either ignored or punished (for example, the parent has the child sit alone in a chair near an empty wall, a "time-out chair," after the child impulsively throws a book across the room). In addition, cognitive-behavioral treatments try to teach ADHD children to internalize their own self-control by learning to "stop and think" before they act.

One example of a cognitive-behavioral treatment, which was developed by Philip Kendall and Lauren Braswell, is intended to teach the child to learn five "steps" that can be applied to academic tasks as well as social interactions. The five problem-solving steps that children are to repeat to themselves each time they encounter a new situation are the following: Ask "What am I supposed to do?"; ask "What are my choices?"; concentrate and focus in; make a choice; ask "How did I do?" (If I did well, I can congratulate myself; if I did poorly, I should try to go more slowly next time.) In each therapy session, the child is given twenty plastic chips at the beginning of the session. The child loses a chip each time he or she does not use one of the steps, goes too fast, or gives an incorrect answer. At the end of the session, the child can use the chips to purchase a small prize; chips can also be stored in a "bank" in order to purchase an even larger prize in the following sessions. This treatment approach combines the use of cognitive strategies (the child learns self-instructional steps) and behavioral techniques (the child loses a desired object, a chip, for impulsive behavior).

Overall, behavioral and cognitive-behavioral treatments have been found to be relatively effective in the settings in which they are used and at the time they are being instituted. Like the effects of medication, however, the effects of behavioral and cognitive-behavioral therapies tend not to be long-lasting. There is some evidence to suggest that the combination of medication and behavior therapy can increase the effectiveness of treatment. In the long run, however, no treatment of ADHD has been found to be truly effective.

Context

Children who might now be diagnosed as having ADHD have been written about and discussed in scientific publications since the mid-1800's. Attention to ADHD began in the United States after an encephalitis epidemic in 1917. Because the damage to the central nervous system caused by the disease led to poor attention, impulsivity, and overactivity in children who survived, researchers began to look for signs of brain injury in other children who had similar behavioral profiles. By the 1950's, researchers began to refer to this disorder as "minimal brain damage," which was then changed to "minimal brain dysfunction" (MBD). By the 1960's, however, the use of the term MBD was severely criticized because of its overinclusiveness and nonspecificity. Researchers began to use terms that more specifically characterized children's problems, such as "hyperkinesis" and "hyperactivity."

The *Diagnostic and Statistical Manual of Mental Disorders* (DSM), published by the American Psychiatric Association, is the primary diagnostic manual used in the United States. In 1968, DSM-II presented the diagnosis of "Hyperkinetic Reaction of Childhood" to characterize children who were overactive and restless. By 1980, when DSM-III was published, researchers had begun to focus on the deficits of attention in these children, so two diagnostic categories were established: "Attention Deficit Disorder with Hyperactivity (ADD with H)" and "Attention Deficit Disorder without Hyperactivity (ADD without H)." After the publication of DSM-III, many researchers argued that there were no empirical data to support the existence of the ADD without H diagnosis. In other words, it was difficult to find any children who were inattentive and impulsive but who were not hyperactive. For this reason, in 1987, when DSM-III-R was published, the only diagnostic category for these children was "Attention-deficit Hyperactivity Disorder (ADHD)."

The next version of this diagnostic manual, DSM-IV, will undoubtedly revise this diagnosis, as has every other edition of the manual. It is expected that the diagnostic category may be altered in a variety of ways. Some manifestation of ADD without H may reappear. There is increasing empirical support for the existence of ADD without H as a separate clinical syndrome. There may also be more discussion of gender differences in ADHD. Some researchers believe that the definition of ADHD for boys should be different from the definition for girls, given that normal boys and normal girls have very different levels of activity and aggressiveness. There may also be an increased focus on ADHD symptoms in older adolescents and adults. There is growing awareness that ADHD symptoms do not disappear as a result of a child getting older, so research has begun focusing on how to define ADHD in older adolescents and adults.

While the diagnostic definition and specific terminology of ADHD will undoubtedly change throughout the years, the interest in and commitment to this disorder will likely continue. Children and adults with ADHD, as well as the people around them, have difficult lives to lead. The research community is committed to finding better explanations of the etiology and treatment of this common disorder.

Bibliography

Barkley, Russell A. "Attention-Deficit Hyperactivity Disorder." In *Treatment of Childhood Disorders*, edited by E. J. Mash and R. A. Barkley. New York: Guilford Press, 1989. This chapter provides a thorough discussion of different treatments for ADHD children, including stimulant medication, antidepressant medication, behavior therapy, parent training, teacher training, and cognitive-behavioral therapy. Each treatment modality is discussed in a fair and objective manner, and empirical research is provided to support the conclusions given.

_____. *Attention-Deficit Hyperactivity Disorder: A Handbook for Diagnosis and Treatment.* New York: Guilford Press, 1990. Provides comprehensive discussion of nearly all aspects of ADHD, including assessment, diagnosis, and treatment. Also notable for a thorough discussion of ADHD in older adolescents and adults. This excellent and comprehensive book is written by one of the leading researchers in the investigation of ADHD.

Campbell, Susan B. "The Socialization and Social Development of Hyperactive Children." In *Handbook of Developmental Psychopathology*, edited by M. Lewis and S. M. Miller. New York: Plenum Press, 1990. A succinct overview of the social climate surrounding children with ADHD. This chapter covers such topics as child-rearing practices, sibling conflict, family climate, parental psychopathology, and peer relationships of ADHD children.

Kendall, Philip C., and Lauren Braswell. *Cognitive-Behavioral Therapy for Impulsive Children*. New York: Guilford Press, 1984. Presents a comprehensive, step-by-step discussion of a popular cognitive-behavioral treatment for ADHD children. The authors provide a thorough rationale for this therapy and provide research data to support the efficacy of the therapy. Practical applications of this therapy are discussed.

Rapport, Mark D. "Attention Deficit Disorder with Hyperactivity." In *Child Behavior Therapy Casebook*, edited by M. Hersen and C. G. Last. New York: Plenum Press, 1988. Presents an in-depth case study of an eight-year-old boy who was referred for treatment of ADHD. This chapter provides a thorough discussion of the way in which a child is evaluated and treated for ADHD. In this case study, the boy is treated with stimulant medication and behavior therapy techniques. A comprehensive evaluation of the treatment effects is provided, and special attention is given to continuous monitoring of the boy's behavioral and academic performance.

Vicky Phares

Cross-References

Abnormality: Behavioral Models, 33; Abnormality: Biomedical Models, 39; Abnormality Defined, 89; Cognitive Behavior Therapy, 546; Psychoactive Drug Therapy, 1891; Psychological Diagnosis and Classification: DSM-III-R, 1925.

HYPNOSIS

Type of psychology: Consciousness
Field of study: Cognitive processes

Hypnosis is a trancelike altered state of consciousness in which the hypnotizable subject is typically more responsive to suggestions than is a waking subject. Hypnosis research has provided psychology with a number of useful theoretical insights into human cognition, as well as practical benefits in controlling pain and treating behavior disorders such as obesity, smoking, and sexual dysfunction.

Principal terms
> HYPNOTIC ANALGESIA: the use of hypnotic procedures to reduce or eliminate present pain
> HYPNOTIC ANESTHESIA: the use of hypnotic procedures for preventing the occurrence of future pain
> HYPNOTIC DISSOCIATION: a hypnotic state in which thoughts, feelings, and perceptions are separated or dissociated from conscious awareness
> HYPNOTIC HYPERMNESIA: the use of hypnosis to enhance recall of past events
> HYPNOTIC SUSCEPTIBILITY: a subject's measured level of responsiveness to hypnotic suggestions on standardized scales
> SOMNAMBULISM: an older term for hypnosis, which is now used as the scientific term for sleepwalking

Overview

Hypnosis derives its name from the Greek term *hypnos,* which translates into English as "sleep." Hypnosis was so named by the Scottish physician James Braid (1795-1860), who noted the sleeplike features of the somnambulistic trance. Though hypnosis may appear to be a sleeplike state, several differences exist between hypnosis and sleep. First, hypnotic subjects will respond to suggestions from the hypnotist. Second, hypnotizable subjects exhibit a phenomenon known as waking hypnosis, in which they will open their eyes and behave as if awake yet continue to be in hypnosis. Last, brain-wave recordings in hypnosis reveal primarily an alpha pattern characteristic of a relaxed state, while those in sleep reveal theta and delta activity.

If hypnosis is not a sleeplike state, how can it be characterized? Since two major theoretical views exist on hypnosis, the answer to that question is quite complex. From one perspective, hypnosis is an altered state of consciousness involving a trance state that is usually accompanied by heightened suggestibility. The primary feature of the hypnotic trance is the loss or suspension of a normal reality-testing orientation. Subjects become so absorbed in the hypnotist's words that they subjectively create the reality of those suggestions and limit their awareness of the environment to a very narrow range of external stimuli. Other qualitative dimensions of the hypnotic trance include a loss of volition, a sense of unreality, a diminished sense of identity, and physical relaxation.

A view of hypnosis as a trance state or an altered state of consciousness is represented by the neo-dissociation theory, which was reported by Ernest Hilgard in 1973. He was conducting studies on the anesthetic properties of hypnosis. Hilgard produced cold pressor pain in his subjects by placing one of their arms into a circulating pool of ice water, which resulted in reports of intolerable pain in approximately one minute. In contrast, when hypnotic subjects were given suggestions for limb anesthesia, they reported low levels of pain or the complete absence of pain. Yet if subjects were told to write down their experience, they reported the presence of pain. These results suggested a discrepancy between the subjects' oral and written reports of pain. Hilgard dubbed this phenomenon the "hidden observer" effect, because it was as though a hidden observer, who saw and felt everything, were present in the brain. According to Hilgard, the hidden observer effect suggests that the perceiver experiences pain at two levels. One level is experienced in immediate awareness and is subject to the effects of hypnotic analgesia and anesthesia. Subjects report a diminution in pain when this level of awareness is blocked by suggestions for pain relief. The second level of pain is dissociated from immediate awareness and maintains constant vigilance to detect the presence of pain. It is at the second level that the hidden observer operates in the brain. Since Hilgard's theory implies cognitive control of a stimulus event, it suggests that a trance or altered state of consciousness is operating during hypnosis.

The second major theoretical perspective emphasizes the importance of the social context in which hypnosis occurs, and it has been referred to as the social psychological theory. From this viewpoint, hypnotized subjects are not in a trance or an altered state of consciousness. Rather, they meet the implicit and explicit demand characteristics of hypnosis by enacting the role of a hypnotic subject. In other words, subjects simulate hypnotic behavior in response to their own preconceived notions and motivations, as well as those expectations conveyed by the hypnotist. T. R. Sarbin and W. C. Coe, in 1972, proposed several variables that influence hypnotic role enactment. These include the location of individual participants in their proper roles, perceived congruence between self and role, accuracy of role expectations, possession of role-relevant skills, and the influence of the audience. If these factors are positive for the subject, hypnotic role enactment may be convincingly demonstrated to the audience and the subject.

While both theories may explain hypnotic behavior, it is clear that not all subjects are simulating hypnosis to enact the role of a hypnotized subject. Measurements of hypnotic responsiveness indicate that hypnosis significantly increases suggestibility beyond that found in a waking state. If subjects were merely simulating hypnosis, why would hypnotic suggestibility exceed waking suggestibility? Clearly, hypnosis involves more than motivation to enact the role of a hypnotized subject.

Measurements of hypnotic responsiveness are typically undertaken with two scales: the Harvard Group Scale of Hypnotic Susceptibility, Form A (HGSHS:A), and the

Stanford Hypnotic Susceptibility Scale, Form C (SHSS:C). The HGSHS:A is used primarily as a screening device for large groups. Most of its suggestions are motor in nature, although some cognitive ones are included. The SHSS:C is usually administered to individuals and includes both cognitive and motor suggestions. Generally, the SHSS:C is considered to be a better measure of hypnotic susceptibility. Both scales include a sample of twelve total suggestions, with high hypnotizables defined as 9 to 12 on each scale, mediums as 4 to 8, and lows as 0 to 3.

Exactly what makes some people more hypnotizable than others is not entirely clear. Surprisingly, personality traits are not reliably correlated with hypnotic susceptibility. Instead, the following three cognitive variables seem to be more strongly related to hypnotic susceptibility: imaginative involvement, concentrated attention, and suspension of reality testing. In general, the higher a person scores on these three variables, the more hypnotizable that person tends to be. One thing is certain: There is no correlation between hypnotic susceptibility and strength of will. Although hypnosis reduces inhibitions and increases compliance to suggestions the subject considers to be acceptable, hypnotized subjects cannot be forced to perform morally reprehensible acts.

Applications

Among forms of altered consciousness, hypnosis may have the greatest practical utility. Hypnosis has been used in pain control, to treat behavior disorders, and to recover lost memories or enhance existing memories of eyewitnesses.

The use of hypnotic anesthesia has a long history, beginning with an alleged surgical amputation performed by the British physician W. S. Ward in 1842. Ward's report was strongly criticized at the time, but evidence suggests that it was legitimate. Another early report of hypnotic anesthesia use was provided by the nineteenth century Scottish physician James Esdaile, who was practicing in India at the time. Esdaile performed more than thirteen hundred operations on hypnotized subjects in the 1840's. Many of those surgeries involved the removal of scrotal tumors, which resulted in a recovery rate of only 50 percent for unanesthetized patients. With the use of hypnotic anesthesia, however, the mortality rate dropped to 5 percent. Esdaile's findings were also criticized by the British scientific community on the rather dubious and racist grounds that "native" assistants hypnotized the patients and that the patients actually liked to undergo operations.

The effectiveness of hypnotic anesthesia and analgesia has been examined in a number of well-controlled laboratory studies. Using cold pressor pain, Ernest and Josephine Hilgard (1983) demonstrated that hypnotic analgesia significantly reduces verbal reports of pain and increases pain tolerance levels as compared with a normal waking state. Reports of pain relief were correlated with hypnotic susceptibility levels; high hypnotizables tended to benefit more from hypnotic analgesia than did low hypnotizables.

Based on laboratory findings, three clinical procedures have been developed for using hypnosis to control pain. The first procedure involves giving the patient a direct suggestion that the painful body part is getting numb and can no longer feel any pain. If the patient requires a more concrete suggestion, the hypnotist may suggest that a local anesthetic is being injected into the shoulder. A second procedure is to alter the experience of pain by giving suggestions for its displacement to a less sensitive region of the body and/or by converting the pain into a less aversive experience. With diffuse pain, the patient may be told that the pain is diminishing in size to a small spot; then a transfer of the pain to a less sensitive body region, where it can be converted into a tingling sensation, is suggested. Finally, therapists use hypnotic anesthesia to direct attention away from the pain and its source. For example, the patient may be told that the painful body part no longer exists. Alternatively, age regression to an earlier and happier experience may be employed, or the therapist may engage the patient in hypnotic fantasies. The latter two approaches presumably distract the patient's attention away from the pain.

A second major field of application for hypnosis has been in the treatment of behavior disorders. Hypnotherapy has been used to treat a variety of behavior disorders, including smoking and obesity, both of which involve poor habit control. The use of hypnotherapy to alter bad habits may be successful because the strength of the habit is not in full force in an altered state of consciousness. In a normal waking state, the habit exerts its dominance over the patient's behavior and may be difficult to reshape or modify. In addition, the highly concentrated state of attention in hypnosis may allow patients to direct all of their resources to the task of altering the negative habit.

Hypnotherapy, in the treatment of smoking and obesity, seems to be more effective with several treatment sessions or with procedures for reinforcing the hypnotic suggestions on a daily basis. For example, H. E. Stanton (1975) combined the following hypnotic procedures to treat overweight patients: direct suggestions to reduce food intake, ego-enhancing suggestions to improve self-esteem, self-hypnosis to reinforce the therapist's suggestions, and hypnosis audiotapes to provide additional support following the completion of formal treatment. The combined use of these hypnotic procedures resulted in marked weight loss among patients who completed the therapeutic process.

Although repeated hypnotherapy sessions appear to be most effective for treating behavior disorders, even one session may be useful. Harold Spiegel (1970) used a competing-response hypnotic technique for the treatment of smoking. Subjects were told that cigarette smoke is a toxin to the body, that life is not possible without the body, and that life is possible only if one protects and treats the body well. The adverse effects of smoking were then placed in competition with the life process. The subjects could choose smoking, thereby threatening their life, or they could choose to enhance life by abandoning the smoking habit. Although subjects were only exposed to one hypnotic session, 20 percent quit smoking. With a total of five hypnotic sessions, Harold Crasilneck and James Hall (1970) reported a success rate of 75 percent. Many subjects do subsequently begin smoking again, but with a greater number of therapy sessions, the rate of recidivism declines.

Finally, hypnosis has been used to enhance recall of past events, which is termed hypnotic hypermnesia. A sensational real-world example of hypnotic hypermnesia was reported in Chowchilla, California, in 1976. This incident involved the kidnapping of a group of children who were on a field trip. The bus, with all occupants aboard, was buried underground and kept there until a ransom was paid. The case was cracked by law enforcement officials when the bus driver was able to recall under hypnosis the license plate of the car driven by the kidnappers. He was not able to do so in a normal waking state.

Hypnosis has been extremely valuable in everyday applications. Not only has it been helpful for controlling pain and smoking, losing weight, and improving recall, but it has also been used to induce amnesia for traumatic events, to treat emotional disturbances, to help remove skin growths, and to treat impotence and frigidity.

Context

Franz Anton Mesmer (1734-1815), an Austrian physician, is generally credited with the discovery of hypnosis. In his medical practice, Mesmer was sometimes confronted with patients who reported symptoms of physical illness but did not manifest any underlying physical pathology. To treat these seemingly incurable patients, Mesmer would pass magnets over the patients' bodies. In many cases, the patient would go into what Mesmer described as a "crisis," with trembling, twitching, intense pain at body regions associated with symptoms, and sometimes convulsions. After completion of the magnetic therapy, most patients would report a relief of symptoms. Eventually, Mesmer discovered that a cure could be wrought by simply passing his hands over the patient, usually accompanied by soft, soothing words.

One of Mesmer's students, Armand-Marie Jacques de Chastenet, the marquis de Puységur, disliked the rather violent and painful magnetic "crises" elicited in patients. While treating a young male patient, Puységur discovered that a peaceful, sleeplike state, resembling sleepwalking and talking in sleep, could be spontaneously induced. Because of its resemblance to these phenomena, he coined the term "artificial somnambulism." Puységur later reproduced this trance state by suggesting it overtly.

It was left to the nineteenth century Scottish physician James Braid to incorporate artificial somnambulism into the mainstream of science. Braid made three important contributions. First, he scientifically demonstrated the existence of many somnambulistic phenomena and published his results. Second, Braid convinced the scientific establishment that the main effects of hypnosis were a function of the subject's hypnotic susceptibility level, and not attributable to the power of the magnetizer. Finally, Braid provided magnetic and somnambulistic phenomena with a new, more scientific-sounding name. He coined the term "neuro-hypnology," which was shortened, first to "hypnology," and later to the modern term, "hypnosis."

In the twentieth century, Ernest Hilgard and his colleagues were instrumental in obtaining psychological recognition for hypnosis, especially as an altered state and as a method for controlling pain. Since the 1960's, hypnosis has been integrated into mainstream psychology, enjoying greater acceptance than ever before in areas such as cognitive and clinical psychology. The dissociative processes in hypnosis and the mechanisms by which hypnosis enhances cognitive functioning are especially important in cognitive psychology. In clinical psychology, hypnosis offers a host of practical applications for treating clients. Clinicians are also interested in the parallels between hypnotic dissociation and dissociative disorders, such as multiple personalities.

Future research will continue to examine the controversy that surrounds the fundamental nature of hypnosis—whether it induces a trance state or is simply role modeling, an instance of simulation. This controversy continues to rage, with no apparent end in sight to the heated debate. Additional research will also be needed to understand why some people are hypnotizable and others are not. Some cognitive and physiological correlates of hypnotizability have been discovered, but such correlations are only moderate in magnitude. Research into potential clinical applications of hypnosis will continue to be a central focus. Hypnotherapy is only in its infancy, and will require much research to provide it with a solid scientific foundation. Finally, exploring the range of hypnotic effects on psychological and behavioral processes will continue to be a central concern among researchers. Only tightly controlled laboratory investigations will yield answers to questions such as what perceptual and cognitive processes are affected by hypnosis, how, and why.

Bibliography

Bowers, Kenneth S. *Hypnosis for the Seriously Curious.* Monterey, Calif.: Brooks/ Cole, 1976. Explores the full range of hypnotic theories and phenomena, as well as practical applications of hypnosis research. Does a thorough job of exploring the controversy surrounding the true nature of hypnosis, providing convincing empirical support for the trance theory. Bowers has provided the most comprehensible treatment of hypnosis for high school and college students.

Hilgard, Ernest Ropiequet, and Josephine Rohrs Hilgard. *Hypnosis in the Relief of Pain.* Rev. ed. Los Altos, Calif.: William Kaufmann, 1983. Provides a comprehensive review of the Hilgards' own research on hypnotic anesthesia and analgesia, as well as the research of others. Examines the physiological and psychological bases of pain, and explores laboratory and clinical methods of controlling pain with hypnosis. Highly recommended for college students and advanced high school students.

Hilgard, Josephine Rohrs. *Personality and Hypnosis: A Study of Imaginative Involvement.* 2d ed. Chicago: University of Chicago Press, 1979. Josephine Hilgard reviews her own extensive research on the role of imaginative involvement in hypnotic susceptibility and in the personality development of both hypnotizable and nonhypnotizable people. Written in nontechnical language; recommended for junior high, high school, and college students, as well as interested adults.

Sheehan, Peter W., and Kevin M. McConkey. *Hypnosis and Experience: The Exploration of Phenomena and Process.* Hillsdale, N.J.: Lawrence Erlbaum, 1982.

An advanced treatise on hypnosis, focusing on the experiential analysis of hypnotic phenomena, such as ideomotor responses, age regression, hypnotic dreams and hallucinations, and posthypnotic amnesia. Because of its technical nature, recommended only for serious, advanced students.

Spanos, Nicholas P., and John F. Chaves, eds. *Hypnosis: The Cognitive-Behavioral Approach.* Buffalo, N.Y.: Prometheus Books, 1989. An extremely thorough review of the cognitive-behavioral approach, which includes the social learning theory of hypnosis. Highly technical; intended to be a review text for professional hypnosis researchers. It may be of some value, however, to serious, advanced college students.

Wallace, Benjamin. *Applied Hypnosis: An Overview.* Chicago: Nelson-Hall, 1979. A nontechnical, introductory book focusing on applications of hypnosis, but not limited exclusively to practical concerns. Highly recommended as a brief overview of hypnosis for junior high and high school students, as well as interested adults.

Wallace, Benjamin, and Leslie E. Fisher. *Consciousness and Behavior.* 3d ed. Boston: Allyn & Bacon, 1991. A general textbook on consciousness containing an excellent, updated chapter on hypnosis. The chapter reviews theories and the history of hypnosis, describes ways of assessing hypnotic susceptibility, reviews research on basic hypnotic phenomena, and discusses practical applications of hypnosis. Highly recommended for high school and college students, as well as interested adults.

Richard P. Atkinson

Cross-References

Altered States of Consciousness, 220; Amnesia, Fugue, and Multiple Personality, 234; Attention, 313; Automaticity, 356; Levels of Consciousness, 663; Observational Learning, 1694; Pain Management, 1734.

HYPOTHESIS DEVELOPMENT AND TESTING

Type of psychology: Psychological methodologies
Field of study: Methodological issues

A useful strategy for answering questions about behavior is to propose several possible answers (hypotheses), generate predictions based on these hypotheses, and collect information (data) to determine which hypothesis appears to have produced a correct prediction.

Principal terms
> EXPERIMENT: a set of controlled conditions used to test hypotheses, which contains at least one experimental group and one or more comparison, or control, groups
> FALSIFIABILITY: the stating of a prediction in such a way that it may be shown to be false
> HYPOTHESIS: a tentative explanation for something, generated as a possible answer to a research question
> PREDICTION: a statement of the evidence that would lead to acceptance of a hypothesis
> SPECIFICITY: a criterion for a hypothesis which is satisfied when predictions are unlikely to be confirmed unless the hypothesis is true
> TESTABILITY: a characteristic of a hypothesis allowing the researcher to decide on the basis of evidence whether the prediction has been confirmed

Overview

All psychological research begins with observations of behavior, either informal everyday observations or formal observations based on prior psychological research. Such observations frequently lead to questions. For example, many people drink beverages containing caffeine throughout the day. When asked why, these people say that it helps them stay alert. Does caffeine really help people stay alert?

For every question one can ask, there are many possible answers. Caffeine might affect alertness at all dosages. It might only affect alertness at certain dosages, or only in some situations. On the other hand, caffeine might decrease, not increase, alertness. Finally, one should not discount the possibility that caffeine has no effect on alertness and that the reported effects are "placebo effects"—that is, they might be caused by expectations about caffeine and not by caffeine itself.

In the language of science, the possible answers to questions are called hypotheses, and the procedure scientists employ to choose among these hypotheses is called hypothesis testing. Hypothesis testing, when used correctly, is a powerful tool for advancing knowledge because it provides a procedure for retaining hypotheses that are probably true and rejecting those that are probably false.

Scientists test hypotheses by making predictions and collecting information. A prediction is a statement of the evidence that would lead the scientist to accept a particular hypothesis. The hypothesis that caffeine maintains alertness leads to the prediction that people who ingest a measured dose of caffeine a given time before engaging in a task that requires alertness will perform better than people who do not ingest caffeine. An experiment could be conducted to test this hypothesis.

Hypothesis tests are only as good as the predictions generated. Good predictions tell the researcher what evidence to collect. To be a good test of the hypothesis, predictions must have three characteristics. The predictions must follow as a logical consequence from the hypothesis and the assumptions the researcher makes about the test situation. The hypothesis and its corresponding prediction must be testable, in the sense that the researcher could decide from the data whether a given prediction has been confirmed. Finally, it should be unlikely that a given prediction is confirmed unless the hypothesis upon which it is based is correct.

If the prediction were not logically related to the hypothesis, a confirmation by the data would reveal nothing about the truth of the hypothesis. This logical relationship is complicated by the fact that rarely is it the case that a prediction can be generated solely from the hypothesis. In order to generate a prediction, a number of additional assumptions are usually required: It takes a certain amount of time for caffeine to enter the system and affect behavior. Any behavioral effects will not be evident until the dosage reaches a certain level. The time it takes to detect the occurrence of a new object on a computer screen is a valid measure of alertness.

Although the prediction may logically follow from the hypothesis, it will not be confirmed if any of the assumptions are incorrect. Unfortunately, there is no foolproof way to avoid this problem. Researchers must carefully consider all assumptions they make.

The condition of testability means that it must be possible to decide on the basis of evidence whether the prediction has been confirmed. Testable predictions are falsifiable; that is, certain experimental outcomes would lead the researcher to conclude that the prediction and the hypothesis are incorrect. A prediction that is not potentially falsifiable is worthless. If a researcher cannot conceive of data that would lead him or her to disconfirm a prediction, the prediction cannot be tested; all data would lead to confirmation.

The third condition, that it should be unlikely for a given prediction to be confirmed unless the hypothesis upon which it is based is correct, is met when the hypothesis leads to a very specific prediction. Specificity is a characteristic of the hypothesis; if the hypothesis is specific, it should lead to a specific prediction. Hypotheses that meet the criterion of specificity tend to require fewer additional assumptions. Unfortunately, such hypotheses are rare in psychological research. Because of this lack of specificity, a single experiment rarely provides a definitive test of a hypothesis. As knowledge about behavior increases, the ability of psychologists to generate and test such hypotheses will no doubt improve.

Hypotheses are tested by comparing predictions to data. If the data confirm the prediction, then the researcher can continue to consider the hypothesis as a reasonable explanation for the phenomenon under investigation and a possible answer to the research question. If subjects react faster to new objects after ingesting caffeine, the investigator would conclude that caffeine affects alertness in this situation. If the data do not confirm the prediction, however, then the investigator would conclude that the hypothesis does not provide a correct explanation of the phenomenon and is not a correct answer to the research question. If subjects given caffeine perform similarly to those not given caffeine, then the researcher would conclude that caffeine does not have much, if any, effect on alertness in this experimental situation.

A useful strategy for testing hypotheses is to generate two hypotheses and attempt to show that if one is false, the other must be true. This can be accomplished if the hypotheses selected are mutually exclusive (they both cannot be true) and exhaustive (they are the only logical possibilities). When two hypotheses satisfy these conditions, demonstrating the truth or falseness of one of these hypotheses determines the status of the other: If one is probably true, the other must be probably false, and vice versa.

The conclusion drawn from a hypothesis test is that the hypothesis is either probably true or probably false—"probably" because it is possible that the wrong conclusion has been reached. The success of any hypothesis test depends on the logical connections between the hypothesis, assumptions, and prediction. Even when this connection is sound, however, different results might occur if the experiment were repeated again. Repeating the experiment and obtaining similar results increases the researcher's confidence in the data.

It is typically the case that a given experiment will not answer the research question unambiguously. By performing additional experiments with a variety of dosages, times, and tasks, researchers should discover the range of conditions under which caffeine affects alertness. Testing one hypothesis typically leads to more questions, and the cycle of asking questions, generating hypotheses, making predictions, collecting data, and drawing conclusions is repeated. Each round of hypothesis tests increases knowledge about the phenomenon in question.

Applications

An excellent example of hypothesis testing was described by Bibb Latané and John M. Darley in their 1970 book, *The Unresponsive Bystander: Why Doesn't He Help?* Latané and Darley became interested in this topic from reading newspaper accounts of people assaulted in the presence of bystanders who did little to assist the victims. The most famous of these was the murder of Kitty Genovese in the presence of thirty-eight neighbors who witnessed this event from their apartment windows; none of them intervened or even called the police. Latané and Darley asked the question, What determines in a particular situation whether one person will help another?

One of their hypotheses was that the number of people present is an important factor affecting how likely it is that someone will react to a dangerous situation.

They also hypothesized that what a person does also depends on the behavior of other people at the scene. Latané and Darley predicted that people would be more likely to respond to an emergency when alone than when in the presence of others. They also predicted that what others who are present do affects a person's behavior.

To test this hypothesis, Latané and Darley solicited the participation of male college students to complete a questionnaire. Students went to a room in a university building where they worked on the task alone, along with two confederates of the experimenters, or with two other people who were also naïve subjects. After several minutes, smoke was introduced into the room through a small vent in the wall. The response measures were whether subjects would seek assistance, and, if they did, how long it took them to do so. If subjects did not respond after six minutes of sitting in a room that was filling with smoke, someone came in to get them.

The predictions and experiments to test them were based on the above hypotheses and on assumptions about how subjects would view the test situation. Darley and Latané assumed that subjects would believe the emergency in the experiment was real and not contrived, and that subjects would perceive the situation as potentially dangerous.

Their predictions were confirmed by the data. Subjects were most likely to report the smoke when alone. When there were two passive confederates who acted nonchalant in the presence of the smoke, subjects were least likely to respond. Being in a group of three naïve subjects also inhibited responding, but not as much as when the other two people ignored the apparent danger.

The results of this experiment appear to provide rather convincing evidence for the correctness of Latané and Darley's hypotheses; however, the assumption that subjects would view the smoke as potentially dangerous is suspect. Postexperimental interviews revealed that some subjects did not perceive the smoke as potentially dangerous. Furthermore, the results of this experiment suggested additional questions to Latané and Darley: "Does the inhibitory effect of other people depend on the fact that in a three-person group, the subject is in a minority? What would happen if only one other person were present? Does the effect depend on the fact that the other people were strangers to the subject? What would happen if the subject were tested with a close friend?"

These questions were addressed in subsequent experiments. In each case, hypotheses were generated and predictions were derived and tested. Care was taken to make the dangerous situation as unambiguous as possible and not give away the fact that it was contrived. The general results confirmed Latané and Darley's predictions and validated their hypotheses about bystander apathy.

For more than eighty years, psychologists have studied people's accuracy at describing events they have witnessed (eyewitness testimony). The history of this work is recounted by Gary Wells and Elizabeth Loftus in their edited volume *Eyewitness Testimony: Psychological Perspectives* (1984). Considerable evidence, collected in a wide variety of settings, demonstrates that people's recollections of an event can be influenced by postevent experiences such as interviews by the police and attorneys, or by viewing mug shots. This raises an interesting question: When people's recollection of an event is changed by postevent information, is the underlying memory changed, or is the original memory still intact but rendered temporarily inaccessible? In other words, does reporting of the event change following postevent experiences because the memory has changed, or because the new information blocks the ability to recall the event as originally experienced?

This is an example of an interesting question to which no satisfactory answer has yet been obtained—but not for lack of trying. The question suggests two mutually exclusive and exhaustive hypotheses: The underlying memory is changed by the postevent experience, so that what the person reports is not what he or she originally saw or heard; or the postevent experience has created a new memory that is in competition with the existing, original memory, and the new memory simply overwhelms the old memory. Both hypotheses lead to the prediction that postevent experiences will affect what a subject reports, but the second hypothesis leads to the additional prediction that the original memory can be teased out into the open under the right circumstances. The problem is how to do this in a convincing manner.

David Hall, Elizabeth Loftus, and James Tousignant reviewed the research on this question. They note that it is difficult, if not impossible, to disprove the hypothesis that both memories coexist. In some studies, what appear to be original memories seem to have been recovered, but not always. The question as asked assumes an either-or situation (either the original unaltered memory still exists or it does not). Unfortunately, this question cannot be answered unambiguously with present knowledge and technology. On the other hand, the question, Under what conditions are recollections (as opposed to memories) changed? can be answered, because it leads to a number of testable predictions based on hypotheses about these conditions.

Clearly, not all questions lead to testable hypotheses and falsifiable predictions. When data support more than one hypothesis, or if the data are likely to occur even if the hypotheses are false, hypotheses have not been adequately tested. The hypotheses about the status of the original memory are an excellent illustration of this. Knowledge of the effects of postevent experiences was advanced by asking the more limited question which led to testable hypotheses. Scientific understanding advances when people ask the right question.

Context

Laboratory experimentation, with its tight control over the variables that affect behavior, is the best way to test hypotheses. By randomly assigning subjects to conditions and isolating the variables of interest through various control procedures, researchers are afforded the opportunity to arrange situations in which one hypothesis will be confirmed to the exclusion of all other hypotheses. Unfortunately, laboratory experimentation is not always an appropriate way to test hypotheses.

When laboratory experimentation is neither possible nor appropriate, researchers can use field experiments, in which experimental methods are used in a natural setting. The inability to control the field setting, however, makes it more difficult to exclude some explanations for the data. Thus, the advantages and disadvantages of field experimentation must be weighed against those of the laboratory. The earliest research of Latané and Darley on bystander apathy involved field experimentation; however, they found it inadequate for rigorous hypothesis testing and moved their research to the laboratory.

Surveys and questionnaires can provide answers to some kinds of questions that experiments cannot: Do certain characteristics distinguish people with different attitudes or opinions on an issue? How many people have such and such an attitude or such and such an opinion? Do certain attitudes or opinions tend to occur together? Predictions can be made and tested with carefully designed surveys and questionnaires.

Archival data and case studies can be extremely useful sources for generating questions and hypotheses, but they are poor techniques for testing hypotheses. Both archival research and case studies can indicate relationships among various factors or events. Whether these relationships are causal or accidental cannot be determined by these methodologies; therefore, the only question that can be answered from archival data and case studies is whether certain relationships have been observed. An experiment is necessary in order to ascertain whether there is a causal connection.

Statistical significance tests are often part of hypothesis testing. Statistical hypotheses parallel research hypotheses; statistical hypotheses are about aspects of populations, while research hypotheses are about the subject of inquiry. Deciding which statistical hypothesis to accept tells the researcher which research hypothesis to accept. The logic of hypothesis testing in general applies to statistical significance tests.

Knowledge is advanced when research questions can be answered. Hypothesis testing, when used correctly, is a powerful method for sorting among possible answers to find the best one. For this reason, it is frequently employed by psychologists in their research.

Bibliography

Giere, Ronald N. *Understanding Scientific Reasoning*. New York: Holt, Rinehart and Winston, 1979. This readable book presents scientific reasoning from the point of view of a philosopher of science, with many examples from all areas of science, including psychology. Chapter 6, on testing theoretical hypotheses, and Chapter 12, on causal hypotheses, provide several detailed examples of evaluating data.

Hall, David, Elizabeth Loftus, and James Tousignant. "Postevent Information and Changes in Recollection for a Natural Event." In *Eyewitness Testimony: Psychological Perspectives*, edited by Gary L. Wells and Elizabeth F. Loftus. Cambridge, England: Cambridge University Press, 1984. Discusses the hypotheses pertaining to the effects of postevent information on original memories, and why these hypotheses cannot be tested. Illustrates how questions about the conditions under which recollections change may be answered.

Latané, Bibb, and John M. Darley. *The Unresponsive Bystander: Why Doesn't He Help?* East Norwalk, Conn.: Appleton-Century-Crofts, 1970. Latané and Darley describe why and how they performed their now-classic set of experiments on bystander apathy, clearly laying out for the reader their observations, questions, hypotheses, assumptions, predictions, experimental procedures, and conclusions.
Moore, K. D. *A Field Guide to Inductive Arguments.* 2d ed. Dubuque, Iowa: Kendall-Hunt, 1989. An excellent workbook for learning how to analyze arguments and evaluate evidence. Chapter 4, on hypothetical evidence, provides several interesting exercises on how to generate and test hypotheses.
Stanovich, Keith E. *How to Think Straight About Psychology.* 2d ed. Glenview, Ill.: Scott, Foresman, 1989. Stanovich tries to undermine the misconceptions that many people have about the contributions of psychology to the scientific study of human behavior. Examples of hypothesis testing abound throughout the book.

Jerome Frieman

Cross-References

Animal Experimentation, 252; Case-Study Methodologies, 481; Data Description: Inferential Statistics, 757; Field Experimentation, 1031; Psychological Experimentation: Independent, Dependent, and Control Variables, 1932; The Scientific Method in Psychology, 2148; Statistical Significance Tests, 2375; Survey Research: Questionnaires and Interviews, 2507.

IDENTITY CRISES: ERIKSON

Type of psychology: Developmental psychology
Fields of study: Adolescence; adulthood

Identity crises are the internal and external conflicts faced by the adolescent/ young adult when choosing an occupation and coming to terms with a basic ideology. Development of a personal identity is a central component of psychosocial maturity.

Principal terms

IDENTITY: a configuration of occupational, sexual, and ideological commitments; according to Erikson, the positive pole of the fifth stage of psychosocial development

IDENTITY CONFUSION/DIFFUSION: an incomplete or inadequate sense of self, which can range from a state of occasional uncertainty to a psychotic state

IDENTITY STATUS: a description of one's self-structure based on evidence of exploration of alternatives and commitments to a career and a basic set of values

NEGATIVE IDENTITY: a self-structure that reflects a deviant life-style such as that taken on by a delinquent

PSYCHOSOCIAL MATURITY: the completion of development in those areas that include both psychological and social aspects, such as identity and sexuality

PSYCHOSOCIAL MORATORIUM: a period during which the adolescent is free from responsibilities and obligations in order to explore the meaning of life

Overview

Identity crises are an integral phase in human development. According to Erik Erikson, successful resolution of the identity crisis is contingent on the earlier resolution of the crises associated with infancy and childhood, such as trust, autonomy, initiative, and industry. Further, the extent to which the conflict surrounding identity is resolved will influence how the individual will cope with the crises of adulthood.

According to Erikson's model of the human life cycle, an identity crisis is one of the psychosocial conflicts faced by the adolescent. In Erikson's model, which was published in the 1960's, each age period is defined by a certain type of psychosocial crisis. Adolescence is the life stage during which acquiring an identity presents a major conflict. Failure to resolve the conflict results in identity confusion/diffusion— that is, an inadequate sense of self.

Identity implies an existential position, according to James Marcia (1980), who construes identity as a self-structure composed of one's personal history, belief system, and competencies. One's perception of uniqueness is directly related to the development of this self-structure. A somewhat similar position has been taken by Jane Kroger (1989), who views the identity crisis as a problem of self-definition. The resulting identity is a balance between self and others. Erikson defines identity as the belief that one's past experiences and identity will be confirmed in the future—as exemplified in the choice of a career. Identity is a composite of one's sexuality, physical makeup, vocation, and belief system. Identity is the pulling together of who one is and who one can become, which involves compositing one's past, present, and future. It is a synthesis of earlier identifications. Successfully resolving the identity crisis is contingent on the interactions that the adolescent/young adult has with others. Erikson contends that interacting with others provides the needed feedback about who one is and who one ought to be. These interactions with others enable the adolescent/young adult to gain a perspective of self that includes an evaluation of his or her physical and social self. Identity acquisition is cognitive as well as social.

From Erikson's perspective, as discussed by James Cote and Charles Levine (1987), four conditions are necessary for an identity crisis: Puberty has been reached; the requisite cognitive development is present; physical growth is nearing adult stature; and societal influences are guiding the person toward an integration and resynthesis of identity. The dialectics of society and personality, implicit in the last condition, are given the most attention by Erikson, according to Cote and Levine, because the other three conditions are part of normative development. Developmental level of the individual and societal pressures combine to elicit an identity crisis; but Cote and Levine note that timing of this crisis is contingent on factors such as ethnicity, gender, socioeconomic status, and subculture, as well as personality factors (for example, authoritarianism or neuroticism) and socialization practices. The severity of the identity crisis is determined by the extent to which one's identity portrayal is interfered with by the uncertainty inherent in moving toward self-definition and unexpected events.

An integral part of the identity crisis is the psychological moratorium, a time during which society permits the individual to work on crisis resolution. During this moratorium, the adolescent/young adult has the opportunity to examine societal roles, career possibilities, and values, free from the expectation of commitments and long-term responsibilities. Although some individuals choose to remain in a moratorium indefinitely, Erikson contends that there is an absolute end to the recognizable moratorium. At its completion, the adolescent/young adult should have attained the necessary restructuring of self and identifications so that he or she can find a place in society which fits this identity.

Based on Erikson's writings, Cote and Levine identify two types of institutionalized moratoria: the technological moratorium, which is highly structured, and the humanistic moratorium, which is less highly structured. The technological moratorium is the product of the educational system, which is charged by society with socializing youth to fit in adult society. Individuals in this moratorium option experience less difficulty in resolving the identity crisis because they move into occupations and societal roles for which they have been prepared with significantly less intrapsychic trauma in accepting an ideology. The school takes an active role in easing this transition by providing vocational and academic counseling for students, facilitating scheduling so that students can gain work experience while enrolled in school, and encouraging early decison making as to a future career.

The identity crisis for individuals in the humanistic moratorium is more stressful, painful, and of longer duration than for those in the technological moratorium. The focal concern of the adolescent/young adult in the humanistic moratorium is humanistic values, which are largely missing from the technological moratorium. There is more variability in this concern for humanistic values, which is reflected in the moratorium that is chosen and the commitments that are made. These conditions elicit an alternation between progressive and regressive states, with the individual making commitments at one time and disengaging at another. The character Holden Caulfield in J. D. Salinger's classic novel *The Catcher in the Rye* (1951) is an example of this type of identity problem. More extreme identity confusion is found among individuals in this moratorium. According to Cote and Levine, social support is often lacking, which hinders formation of a stable identity. Family and community support is especially important for these individuals. Yet these are the adolescents/young adults who, because their life-style departs from the societal mold, are often ostracized and denied support. Individuals may promote a cause of some type. Those who choose a humanistic moratorium are more likely to be intellectual, artistic, antiestablishment, and ideologically nonconforming. After a time, some of these individuals accept technological values and roles.

Individuals whose identity seeking is not influenced by technological or humanistic moratoria face a rather different situation. Some remain in a constant state of flux in which choices are avoided and commitments are lacking. Others take on a negative identity by accepting a deviant life-style and value system (for example, delinquency or gang membership). In this instance, the negative elements of an identity outweigh the positive elements. This type of identity crisis resolution occurs in an environment which precludes normative identity development (for example, excessively demanding parents, absence of an adequate role model).

Applications

Erikson's writings on identity crises have been responsible for an extensive literature, consisting of conceptual as well as empirical articles. Perhaps the most widely used application is Marcia's identity status paradigm, in which he has conceptualized and operationalized Erikson's theory of identity development in terms of several statuses which result from exploration and commitment. More than one hundred empirical studies have been generated from this paradigm, according to a review by Cote and Levine (1988). The identity status paradigm provides a methodological procedure for determining identity statuses based on resolution of an identity crisis, and the presence of commitments to an occupation and an ideology.

According to the Marcia paradigm, an ego identity can be one of several statuses consisting of achievement, foreclosure, moratorium, or diffusion. An achievement status indicates resolution of the identity crisis and firm commitments to an occupation and an ideology. In a foreclosure status, one has formed commitments, but has not experienced a crisis. The moratorium status denotes that an identity crisis is currently being experienced, and no commitments have been made. The diffusion status implies the absence of a crisis, and no commitments. Much of the research has focused on identifying the personality characteristics associated with each of these statuses. Other studies have examined the interactional patterns as well as information-processing and problem-solving strategies. Achievement and moratorium statuses seek out, process, and evaluate information in their decision making. Foreclosures have more rigid belief systems and conform to normative standards held by significant others, while those in the diffusion status delay decision making. Significant differences have been found among the statuses in terms of their capacity for intimacy, with diffusions scoring lowest, followed by foreclosures. Achievement and moratorium statuses have a greater capacity for intimacy.

Two areas of research that continue to attract attention are parental socialization patterns associated with crisis resolution, and identity crises in females. The findings to date reveal distinctive parental patterns associated with each status. Positive but somewhat ambivalent relationships between parents and the adolescent/young adult are reported for achievement status. Moratorium-status adolescents/young adults also seem to have ambivalent relationships with their parents, but they are less conforming. Males in this status tend to experience difficulty in separating from their mother. Foreclosures view their parents as highly accepting and encouraging. Parental pressure for conformity to family values is very evident. Diffusion-status adolescents report much parental rejection and detachment from parents, especially from the father. In general, the data from family studies show that the same-sex parent is an important figure in identity resolution.

The interest in female identity has arisen because different criteria have been used to identify identity status based on the Marcia paradigm. Attitudes toward premarital sexual relations is a major content area in status determination. The research in general shows that achievement and foreclosure statuses are very similar in females, as are the moratorium and diffusion statuses. This pattern is not found for males. It has been argued by some that the focal concerns of females, in addition to concerns with occupation and ideology, involve interpersonal relationships more than do the concerns of males. Therefore, in forming a self-structure, females may examine the world outside for self-evaluation and acceptance in addition to the internal examination of self which typically occurs in males. The effect of an external focus on identity resolution in females is unknown, but this type of focus is likely to prolong the identity crisis. Further, it is still necessary to determine the areas in which choices and commitments are made for females.

The concept of negative identity has been used frequently in clinical settings to explain antisocial acts and delinquency in youth, as well as gang-related behavior. Randall Jones and Barbara Hartman (1988) found that the use of substances (for example, cigarettes, alcohol, and other drugs) was higher and more likely in youths of identity-diffusion status. Erikson and others have argued that troubled youths find that elements of a negative identity provide them with a sense of some mastery over a situation for which a positive approach has been continually denied them. In the examples cited, deviant behavior provided this sense of mastery and an identity.

Context

The identity crisis is the major conflict faced by the adolescent. Erikson's theorizing about the identity crisis made a major contribution to the adolescent literature. Marcia's reconceptualization of ego identity facilitated identity research and clinical assessment by providing a methodological approach for determining identity development and the psychological concomitants of identity. As a result, the study of identity and the awareness of the psychological impact on the individual has become a major research area, and has provided a basis for clinical intervention.

The concept of identity crises originated with Erikson, based on the clinical experiences which he used to develop a theory of ego identity development. Explication of this theory appeared in his writings during the 1950's and 1960's. Erikson's theory of the human life cycle places identity resolution as the major crisis faced by the adolescent. The success of this resolution is determined by the satisfactory resolution of crises in the stages preceding adolescence.

Identity formation is a major topic in most textbooks on adolescence, and is a focal concern of practitioners who treat adolescents with psychological adjustment problems. Until the appearance of Erikson's writings, the field of adolescence was mostly a discussion of physical and sexual development. His focus on psychosocial development, especially the emergence of a self-structure, increased immeasurably the understanding of adolescent development and the problems faced by the adolescent growing up in Western society. As Cote and Levine have noted, identity is a multidimensional construct, consisting of sociological perspectives, specifically the social environment in which the individual interacts, as well as psychological processes. Thus, a supportive social environment is critical to crisis resolution. The absence of this supportive environment has frequently been cited as an explanation for identity problems and the acquisition of a negative identity.

It is important to realize that identity has a temporal element as well as a lifelong duration. That is, identity as a personality characteristic undergoes transformations throughout the life cycle. While crisis resolution may be achieved during adolescence/young adulthood, this self-structure is not permanent. Crises can reemerge during the life span. The midlife crises of middle adulthood, written about frequently in the popular press, are often viewed as a manifestation of the earlier identity crisis experienced during adolescence/young adulthood.

A future role for identity crises is difficult to forecast. The psychological moratorium will continue to be an important process. Given the constant change in American society, the moratorium options available for youth may be more restricted, or more ambiguous and less stable. This scenario is more probable for humanistic moratoria as society moves toward more institutional structure in the form of schools taking on increased responsibility for the socialization of children and youth. The provision of child care before and after school is one example of the school's increased role. The erosion which has occurred in family structure presents another problem for identity crisis resolution.

Bibliography

Cote, James E., and Charles Levine. "A Critical Examination of the Ego Identity Status Paradigm." *Developmental Review* 8 (June, 1988): 147-184. Critiques the Marcia identity-status paradigm and notes several areas of divergence from Erikson's conceptualization theory of identity. Advances the argument for an interdisciplinary approach to understanding identity, and identifies several questions about identity crises that need to be considered.

_____. "A Formulation of Erikson's Theory of Ego Identity Formation." *Developmental Review* 7 (December, 1987): 209-218. A comprehensive review of Erikson's theory of ego identity and the role of psychological moratoria in the resolution of identity crises. Discusses Erikson's concepts of value orientation stages and the ego-superego conflict over personality control. Offers criticisms of Erikson's work, and suggests cautions for the researcher.

Erikson, Erik Homburger. *Childhood and Society.* 2d ed. New York: W. W. Norton, 1963. A presentation of case histories based on Erikson's clinical experiences, as well as a discussion of Erikson's life-cycle model of human development. One section of the book is devoted to an examination of youth and identity. Clinical studies are used to illustrate the problems youth face in identity resolution.

_____. *Identity, Youth, and Crisis.* New York: W. W. Norton, 1968. A theoretical discussion of ego identity formation and identity confusion, with special attention given to issues such as womanhood, and race and identity. Erikson relies heavily on his vast clinical experiences to illustrate the concepts that he discusses. The life cycle as it applies to identity is examined from an epigenetic perspective.

Kroger, Jane. *Identity in Adolescence.* London: Routledge & Kegan Paul, 1989. A presentation of identity development as conceptualized by Erikson and others. Each approach is criticized, and the empirical findings generated by the approach are summarized. The first chapter of the book is devoted to an overview of identity from a developmental and sociocultural perspective. The final chapter presents an integration of what is known about identity.

Marcia, James E. "Identity in Adolescence." In *Handbooks of Adolescent Psychology,* edited by Joseph Adelson. New York: John Wiley & Sons, 1980. A discussion of the identity statuses developed by Marcia, based on a paradigm derived from Erikson's conceptualization of ego identity. Reviews the research literature on personality characteristics, patterns of interaction, developmental studies, identity in women, and other directions in identity research. Ends with a discussion of a general ego-developmental approach to identity.

Joseph C. LaVoie

Cross-References

IMPRINTING AND LEARNING

Type of psychology: Learning
Fields of study: Biological influences on learning; endocrine system

Imprinting is an endogenous, or inborn, animal behavior by which young mammals and birds learn specific, visible physical patterns to associate with important concepts such as the identification of one's mother, navigation routes, and danger. The phenomenon, which relies primarily upon visual cues and hormonal scents, is of high survival value for the species possessing it.

Principal terms
CONDITIONING: a type of learning in which an animal understands a
concept by associating it with some object or by the administration
of rewards and/or punishments
CRITICAL PERIOD: a specific time period during an animal's development
during which a certain type of learning such as imprinting must
occur if it is to be successfully incorporated into the animal's psyche
ENDOGENOUS BEHAVIOR: an innate, or inborn, behavior that is established
by the animal's inherited genetic code (DNA) and that
is not influenced by the animal's experiences or environment
ETHOLOGY: the study of animal behavior, psychology, and biology and
the theories describing such behaviors
EXOGENOUS BEHAVIOR: a behavior that an animal acquires by learning,
experience, and direct contact with its environment
IMPRINTING: a type of endogenous animal behavior by which a young
individual mentally "photographs" a pattern and associates that
pattern with a specific concept; the phenomenon occurs primarily
in mammals and birds
PHEROMONE: a hormone or other chemical that is produced and released
from the tissues of one individual and targets tissues in another
individual, usually with a consciously or unconsciously detectable
scent
PLASTICITY: a phenomenon of neuronal growth in the cerebral cortex of
higher vertebrate animals that is associated with an animal's memory,
learning capacity, and intelligence
VISUAL CUES: specific visible physical objects or patterns that an animal
learns to associate with certain concepts
VOCAL CUES: specific sounds, frequency, and language that an animal
learns to associate with certain concepts

Overview

Imprinting is an important type of behavior by which an animal learns specific concepts and identifies certain objects or individuals that are essential for survival. Imprinting events almost always occur very early in the life of an animal, during critical periods or time frames when the animal is most sensitive to environmental cues and influences. The phenomenon occurs in a variety of species, but it is most pronounced in the homeothermic (warm-blooded) and socially oriented higher vertebrate species, especially mammals and birds.

Imprinting is learned behavior. Most learned behavior falls within the domain of exogenous behavior, or behavior that an animal obtains by its experiences with fellow conspecifics (members of the same species) and the environment. Imprinting, however, is predominantly, if not exclusively, an endogenous behavior, which is a behavior that is genetically encoded within the individual. An individual is born with the capacity to imprint. The animal's cellular biochemistry and physiology will determine when in its development that it will imprint. The only environmental influence of any consequence in imprinting is the object of the imprint during the critical period. Ethologists, scientists who study animal behavior, debate the extent of endogenous and exogenous influences upon animal behavior. Most behaviors involve a combination of both, although one type may be more pronounced than the other.

The capacity for an animal to imprint is genetically determined and, therefore, is inherited. This type of behavior is to the animal's advantage for critical situations that must be correctly handled the first time. Such behaviors include the identification of one's parents (especially one's mother), the ability to navigate, the ability to identify danger, and even the tendency to perform the language of one's own species. Imprinting behaviors generally are of high survival value and hence must be programmed into the individual via the genes. Biological research has failed to identify many of the genes that are responsible for imprinting behaviors, although the hormonal basis of imprinting is well understood. Most imprinting studies have focused upon the environmental signals and developmental state of the individual during the occurrence of imprinting.

These studies have involved mammals and birds, warm-blooded species that have high social bonding, which seems to be a prerequisite for imprinting. The most famous imprinting studies were performed by the animal behaviorists and Nobel laureates Konrad Lorenz and Nikolaas Tinbergen. They and their many colleagues have detailed analyses of imprinting in a variety of species, in particular waterfowl such as geese and ducks. The maternal imprinting behavior of the newborn gosling or duckling upon the first moving object that it sees is the most striking example of imprinting behavior.

The maternal imprint is the means by which a newborn identifies its mother and the mother identifies its young. In birds, the newborn chick follows the first moving object that it sees, an object that should be its mother. The critical imprinting period is within a few hours after hatching. The chick visually will lock in on its moving mother and follow it wherever it goes until the chick reaches adulthood. The act of imprinting not only allows for the identification of one's parents but also serves as a trigger for all subsequent social events with members of one's own species. As has been established in numerous experiments, a newborn gosling that first sees a female duck will imprint on the duck and follow it endlessly. Upon reaching adulthood, the grown goose, which has been raised in the social environment of ducks, will attempt to behave as a duck, even to the point of mating. Newborn goslings, ducklings, and chicks can easily imprint on humans.

In mammals, imprinting relies not only upon visual cues but also on physical contact and smell. Newborn infants imprint upon their mothers, and vice versa, by direct contact, sight, and smell during the critical period, which usually occurs within twenty hours following birth. The newborn and its mother must come into direct contact with each other's skin and become familiarized with each other's smell. The latter phenomenon involves the release of special hormones called pheromones from each individual's body. Pheromones trigger a biochemical response in the body of the recipient individual, in this case leading to a locked identification pattern for the other involved individual. If direct contact between mother and infant is not maintained during the critical imprinting period, then the mother may reject the infant because she is unfamiliar with its scent. In such a case, the infant's life would be in jeopardy unless it were claimed by a substitute mother. Even in this situation, the failure to imprint would trigger subsequent psychological trauma in the infant, possibly leading to aberrant social behavior in later life.

Although maternal imprinting in mammal and bird species represents the best-documented studies of imprinting behavior, imprinting may be involved in other types of learned behavior. In migratory bird species, ethologists have attempted to explain how bird populations navigate from their summer nesting sites to their wintering sites and back every year without error. Different species manage to navigate in different fashions. The indigo bunting, however, navigates via the patterns of stars in the sky at night. Indigo bunting chicks imprint upon the celestial star patterns for their summer nesting site during a specific critical period, a fact that was determined by the rearrangement of planetarium stars for chicks by some nefarious research scientists.

Further research studies on birds also implicate imprinting in danger recognition and identification of one's species-specific call or song. Young birds of many species identify predatory birds (for example, hawks, falcons, and owls) by the outline of the predator's body during flight or attack and by special markings on the predator's body. Experiments also have demonstrated that unhatched birds can hear their mother's call or song; birds may imprint on their own species' call or song before they hatch. These studies reiterate the fact that imprinting is associated with a critical period during early development in which survival-related behaviors must become firmly established.

Applications

Imprinting is of considerable interest to psychologists because of its role in the learning process for humans. Humans imprint in much the same fashion as other mammals. The extended lifetime, long childhood, and great capacity for learning and intelligence make imprinting in humans an important area of study. Active research on imprinting is continually being conducted with humans, primates, cetaceans (such as dolphins, whales, and seals), and many other mammals, as well as with a large variety of bird species. Comparisons among the behaviors of these many species yield considerable similarities in the mechanisms of imprinting. These similarities underscore the importance of imprinting events in the life, survival, and socialization of the individual.

With humans, maternal imprinting occurs much as in other mammals. The infant and its mother must be in direct contact during the hours following birth. During this critical period, there is an exchange of pheromones between mother and infant, an exchange that, to a large extent, will bond the two. Such bonding immediately following birth can occur between infant and father in the same manner. Many psychologists stress the importance of both parents being present at the time of a child's delivery and making contact with the child during the critical hours of the first day following birth. Familiarization is important not only for the child but for the parents as well because all three are imprinting upon one another.

Failure of maternal or paternal imprinting during the critical period following birth can have drastic consequences in humans. The necessary, and poorly understood, biochemical changes that occur in the bodies of a child and parent during the critical period will not occur if there is no direct contact and, therefore, no transfer of imprinting pheromones. Consequently, familiarization and acceptance between the involved individuals may not occur, even if intense contact is maintained after the end of the critical period. The psychological impact upon the child and upon the parents may be profound, perhaps not immediately, but in later years. Studies on this problem are extremely limited because of the difficulty of tracing cause-and-effect relationships over many years when many behaviors are involved. There is some evidence, however, which indicates that failure to imprint may be associated with such things as learning disabilities, child-parent conflicts, and abnormal adolescent behavior. Nevertheless, other cases of imprinting failure seem to have no effect, as can be seen in tens of thousands of adopted children. The success or failure of maternal imprinting in humans is a subject of considerable importance in terms of how maternal imprinting affects human behavior and social interactions in later life.

Different human cultures maintain distinct methods of child rearing. In some cultures, children are reared by family servants or relatives from birth onward, not by the actual mother. Some cultures wrap infants very tightly so that they can barely move; other cultures are more permissive. Child and adolescent psychology focuses attention upon early life experiences that could have great influence upon later social behavior. The success or failure of imprinting, along with other early childhood experiences, may be a factor in later social behaviors such as competitiveness, interaction with individuals of the opposite sex, mating, and maintenance of a stable family structure. Even criminal behavior and psychological abnormalities may be traceable to such early childhood events.

Imprinting studies with mammal and bird species are much easier, because the researcher has the freedom to conduct controlled experiments that test many different variables, thereby identifying the factors that influence an individual animal's ability to imprint. For bird species, a famous experiment is the moving ball experiment. A newly hatched chick is isolated in a chamber within which a suspended ball revolves around the center of the chamber. The researcher can test not only movement as an imprinting trigger but also other variables, such as critical imprinting time after hatching, color as an imprinting factor, and variations in the shape of the ball as imprinting factors. Other experiments involve switching eggs between different species (for example, placing a duck egg among geese eggs).

For mammals, imprinting has been observed in many species, such as humans, chimpanzees, gorillas, dolphins, elephant seals, wolves, and cattle. In most of these species, the failure of a mother to contact her newborn almost always results in her rejection of the child. In species such as elephant seals, smell is the primary means by which a mother identifies its pups. Maternal imprinting is of critical importance in a mammalian child's subsequent social development. Replacement of a newborn monkey's natural mother with a "doll" substitute leads to irreparable damage; the infant is socially and sexually repressed in its later life encounters with other monkeys. These and other studies establish imprinting as a required learning behavior for the successful survival and socialization of all birds and mammals.

Context

Animal behaviorists and psychologists attempt to identify the key factors that are responsible for imprinting in mammalian and avian species. Numerous factors, including vocal and visual cues, probably are involved, although the strongest two factors appear to be direct skin contact and the exchange of pheromones that are detectable by smell. The maternal imprinting behavior is the most intensively studied imprinting phenomenon, though imprinting appears to occur in diverse behaviors such as mating, migratory navigation, and certain forms of communication.

Imprinting attracts the interest of psychologists because it occurs at critical periods in an individual's life; because subsequent developmental, social, and behavioral events hinge upon what happens during the imprinting event; and because imprinting occurs at the genetic or biochemical level. Biochemically, imprinting relies upon the production and release of pheromones, molecules that have a specific structure and that can be manufactured in the laboratory. The identification and mass production of these pheromones could possibly produce treatments for some behavioral abnormalities.

As an endogenous (instinctive) form of learning, imprinting relies upon the highly complex nervous and endocrine systems of birds and mammals. It also appears limited to social behavior, a major characteristic of these species. The complex nervous systems involve a highly developed brain, vocal communication, well-developed eyes, and a keen sense of smell. The endocrine systems of these species produce a variety of hormones, including the pheromones that are involved in imprinting, mating, and territoriality. Understanding the nervous and endocrine regulation of behavior at all levels is of major interest to biological and psychological researchers. Such studies may prove to be fruitful in the discovery of the origin and nature of animal consciousness.

Imprinting may be contrasted with exogenous forms of learning. These other learning types include conditioning, in which individuals learn by repeated exposure to a stimulus, by association of the concept stimulus with apparently unrelated phenomena and objects, or by a system of reward and punishment administered by parents. Other exogenous learning forms include habituation (getting used to something) and trial and error. All learned behaviors are a combination of endogenous and exogenous factors.

Imprinting occurs at critical time periods during an individual's life, especially during early childhood. Maternal imprinting usually occurs between ten and thirty hours after birth or hatching for most species, with optimum imprinting occurring around twenty hours after birth. The imprinting event serves as a lock onto a specific behavior pattern and triggers subsequent behavioral events, including social interactions and sexual behavior. It is important for the individual that the imprinting events occur properly, or subsequent developmental and behavioral events could be affected drastically.

Bibliography

Beck, William S., Karel F. Liem, and George Gaylord Simpson. *Life: An Introduction to Biology.* 3d ed. New York: HarperCollins, 1991. Introduction to biology for the beginning student. Contains a clear text, many strong diagrams and illustrations, and beautiful photographs. Contains a thorough discussion of animal behavior, famous experiments, and various types of animal learning, including imprinting, and describes the studies of Konrad Lorenz and others.

Klopfer, Peter H., and Jack P. Hailman. *An Introduction to Animal Behavior: Ethology's First Century.* Englewood Cliffs, N.J.: Prentice-Hall, 1967. An excellent and well-organized introduction to the history of animal behavior research. Presents major themes and models, and cites many important studies. Chapters 3 and 12 discuss instinctive and learned aspects of behavioral development.

Manning, Aubrey. *An Introduction to Animal Behavior.* Reading, Mass.: Addison-Wesley, 1979. Concise, detailed, and thorough presentation of animal behavior research. Encompasses all major behavioral theories and supporting experiments. Includes a good discussion of imprinting studies, particularly with reference to maternal imprinting, and describes the biological bases behind imprinting and other behaviors.

Marler, Peter, and William J. Hamilton III. *Mechanisms of Animal Behavior.* New York: John Wiley & Sons, 1966. A detailed and comprehensive introduction to animal behavior, theories of behavior, and behavior research. Cites hundreds of case studies. Discusses imprinting, including maternal and sexual imprinting, and the biological bases behind imprinting behavior. Several chapters deal with imprinting-related phenomena.

Raven, Peter H., and George B. Johnson. *Biology.* 2d ed. St. Louis: Times Mirror/ Mosby, 1989. A strong presentation of all aspects of biology for the beginning student. Includes excellent diagrams and illustrations. Summarizes the major theories and classic experiments of animal behavior research, including imprinting studies.

Wallace, Robert A., Gerald P. Sanders, and Robert J. Ferl. *Biology: The Science of Life.* 3d ed. New York: HarperCollins, 1991. An outstanding book for beginning students that describes all major concepts in biology with great clarity, using numerous examples, good illustrations, and beautiful photographs. Discusses behavioral research, including studies of maternal imprinting.

Wilson, Edward Osborne. *Sociobiology: The New Synthesis.* Cambridge, Mass.: The Belknap Press of Harvard University Press, 1975. An incredibly comprehensive study of sociobiology, a perspective which maintains that animal behavior is a driving force in animal species evolution. The author, a prominent entomologist, is the leading proponent of this controversial theory, which he defends with hundreds of case studies. Describes the biological basis of behavior during all stages of animal development.

David Wason Hollar, Jr.

Cross-References

Defense Reactions; Species-Specific, 775; Ethology, 992; Hormones and Behavior, 1189; Instinct Theory, 1309; Preparedness and Learning, 1866; Taste Aversion and Learning Theory, 2520.

INCENTIVE MOTIVATION

Type of psychology: Motivation
Field of study: Motivation theory

Incentive motivation is a determinant of behavior from without, in contrast to drive motivation, which is a determinant from within. Both jointly determine the quality and quantity of behavior. Each motivation can energize behavior alone, however, and the relative importance of each differs for different behaviors.

Principal terms

ACHIEVEMENT MOTIVATION: the tendency for people to strive for goals of certain difficulties because of the relative attractiveness of success and repulsiveness of failure

ANTICIPATORY GOAL RESPONSES: responses that are elicited before an animal reaches a goal; along with related sensory consequences, they are the source of incentive motivation

BRAIN REWARD MECHANISM: the rewarding effect of various stimuli, such as food, cocaine, and intracranial self-stimulation, as related to dopamine activity in the brain

CRESPI EFFECT: observable elation or depression responses caused by a change in the amount of a reward

EXPECTANCY THEORY: a behavior theory in which expected outcome determines the amount of energy expended in work

INTRACRANIAL SELF-STIMULATION (ICSS): a situation in which a research animal repeatedly performs an activity that delivers pleasurable electrical stimulation to its brain

Overview

Motivation refers to a group of variables that determine what behavior—and how strong and how persistent a behavior—is to occur. Motivation is different from learning. Learning variables are the conditions under which a new association is formed. An association is the potential for a certain behavior; however, it does not become behavior until motivation is introduced. Thus, motivation is necessary to convert a behavioral potential into a behavioral manifestation. Motivation turns a behavior on and off.

"Incentive motivation" is an attracting force, while "drive motivation" is an expelling force. Incentive is said to "pull," and drive to "push," an individual toward a goal. The attracting force originates from the reward object in the goal and is based on expectation of the goal object in certain locations in the environment. The expelling force originates from within organisms as a need, which is related to disturbances in homeostasis in the body. The two forces jointly determine behavior in a familiar environment. In a novel environment which the organism is encountering for the first time, however, there is not yet an expectation; no incentive motivation is yet formed, and drive is the only force to cause behavior. The organism can be expected to manifest various responses until the goal-oriented responses emerge.

Once the organism achieves the goal, the reward stimuli elicit consummatory responses. Before the organism reaches the goal, the stimuli which antedate the goal would elicit responses; these are termed anticipatory goal responses. The anticipatory responses are based upon the associational experience between the goal stimuli, the goal responses, and the situational stimuli present prior to reaching the goal. The anticipatory responses and their stimulus consequences provide the force of incentive motivation. Incentive refers to the expected amount of reward given certain behavior.

Though drive motivation and incentive motivation jointly determine behaviors, the importance of each differs for different behaviors. For example, bar-pressing behavior for drinking water by an animal in a Skinner box normally needs both drive motivation, induced by water deprivation, and the incentive motivation of a past experience of getting water. Under special conditions, however, the animal will press the bar to drink water even without being water-deprived. In this case, drinking is no longer related to drive. This type of drinking is called nonhomeostatic drinking. Drinking a sweet solution, such as one containing sugar or saccharin, does not require any deprivation, so the behavior to get sweet solutions is based upon incentive motivation alone. Under normal conditions, sexual behavior is elicited by external stimuli, so sexual drive is actually incentive motivation elicited from without.

Two experiments will illustrate how the concept of incentive motivation may be applied to explain behavior. Carl J. Warden of Columbia University conducted a study which is regarded as a classic. A rat was placed in the start box of a short runway, and a reward (food) was placed in its goal box at the other end. The food-deprived animal had to cross an electrified grid on the runway to reach the goal. When the animal reached the goal, it was repeatedly brought back to the start box. The number of times the animal would cross the grid in a twenty-minute period was recorded. It was found that the longer the food deprivation, the more times the animal crossed the grid, for up to about three days without food (then the number decreased). The animal crossed only about two times with no food deprivation; however, the number increased to about seventeen at three days of food deprivation, then decreased to about seven at eight days without food. When the animal was water-deprived, the animal crossed the grid about twenty times to the goal box containing water at one day without water. When the reward was an infant rat, a mother rat crossed about twenty times. A male rat crossed about thirteen times to a female rat after being sex-deprived (without female companion) for one day. A female rat in heat crossed thirteen times to a male rat. Even without any object in the goal box, the animal crossed about six times; Warden attributed this to a "novelty" reward. The reward variable in this experiment was the goal object, which was manipulated to fit the source of the drive induced by deprivation or hormonal state (as in an estrous female). The rat, placed in the start box, was induced by the goal

The second study, conducted by Leo P. Crespi, established the concept of incentive motivation as an anticipatory response. He trained rats in a runway with different amounts of food and found that the animals reached different levels of performance. The speed of running was a function of the amount of reward: The more the food in the goal box, the faster the animal would run. There were three groups of rats. Group one was given 256 food pellets (about a full day's ration) in the goal box; the animals would run at slightly over a meter per second after twenty training trials. Group two was given sixteen pellets, and their speed was about 76 centimeters (2.5 feet) per second. Group three was given only one pellet, and the speed was about 15 centimeters (6 inches) per second.

When the speed became stable, Crespi shifted the amount of food. The rats in all groups were now given sixteen pellets. The postshift speed eventually, but not immediately, settled to near that of the group originally given sixteen pellets. An interesting transitional effect of so-called incentive contrast was observed. Immediately after the shift from the 256-pellet reward to the sixteen-pellet reward, the animal's speed was much lower than the group continuously given the sixteen-pellet reward. Following the shift from the one-pellet to the sixteen-pellet reward, however, the animal's speed was higher than the group continuously given the sixteen-pellet reward. Crespi called these the elation effect and the depression effect, or the positive contrast effect and the negative contrast effect, respectively. Clark Hull and K. W. Spencer, two of the most influential theorists of motivation and learning, interpreted the "Crespi effect" as evidence of anticipatory responses. They theorized that the goal response had become conditioned to the runway stimuli such that the fractional goal responses were elicited. Since the responses occurred prior to the goal responses, they were anticipatory in nature. The fractional goal responses, along with their stimulus consequence, constitute the "incentive motivation" that would energize a learned associative potential to make it into a behavior.

Incentive motivation has been manipulated in many other ways. Besides the amount of reward, it can be manipulated by the delay of reward presentation, the quality of the reward, and various partial reinforcement schedules. In relation to the delay variable, the sooner the reward presentation follows the responses, the more effective it is in energizing behavior, although the relationship is not linear. In the case of partial reinforcement, when the subject received a reward only part of the time, behavior was shown to be more resistant to extinction than when reward was delivered every time following a response; that is, following withdrawal of the reward, the behavior lasted longer when the reward was given only part of the time than when the reward was given every time following the response. The quality of the reward variable could be changed by, for example, giving a monkey a banana as a reward after it had been steadily given raisins. As mentioned earlier, in Warden's experiment, the various objects (water, food, male rat, female rat, or rat pup) placed in the goal box belong to the quality variable of incentive. Another incentive variable is how much effort a subject must exert to obtain a reward, such as climbing a slope to get to the goal versus running a horizontal path.

Applications

The term "reinforcer" usually indicates any stimulus which would result in increasing the probability or magnitude of a response upon its presentation following that response. When the response has reached its maximum strength, however, a reinforcer can no longer increase it; nevertheless, it has a maintenance effect. Without it the response would soon cease. A reward reinforces and maintains a response. It is believed that the rewarding effects are mediated by the brain; the mechanism which serves as the substrate of the effects has been studied.

In a breakthrough experiment in this line of study, in 1954, James Olds and Peter Milner published a paper reporting that a rat would press a bar repeatedly to stimulate certain areas of its brain. (If the bar press resulted in stimulation of certain other areas of the brain, the rat would not repeat the bar press.) Thus, this particular brain electrical stimulation has a rewarding effect. The phenomenon is termed intracranial self-stimulation (ICSS or ICS). The rewarding effect is so powerful that the hungry animal would rather press the bar to stimulate its brain than eat. It has also been shown that animals will press a bar to self-inject cocaine, amphetamine, morphine, and many other drugs. The rewarding effect is so powerful that if rats or monkeys are given access to a bar that allows continuous self-administration of cocaine, they often die of an overdose. It is now known that the neurotransmitter involved in this rewarding effect, as well as in the rewarding effect of food, is dopamine, acting at the nucleus accumbens, a part of the limbic system in the brain. Addictions and drug-directed behaviors can be understood better because of studies related to the brain reward mechanism. Whether incentive motivation is mediated by the same brain mechanism can also be studied.

In humans, achievement motivation can be measured in order to predict what a subject would choose to do given tasks of different difficulty as well as how persevering the subject will be when he or she encounters failure. Achievement motivation is related to past experiences of rewards and failures to obtain a reward, so it becomes an incentive motivation of anticipating either success or failure to obtain a reward. Fear of failure is a negative motivational force; that is, it contributes negatively to achievement motivation. Those people with a strong fear of failure will choose easy tasks to ensure success, and upon failure they will give up quickly.

Unless an individual anticipates or believes that the effort will lead to some desired outcome, the person will not expend much effort. Expectancy theory states that how much effort a person will expend depends upon the expected outcome of the effort. If the expected outcome is positively correlated to the effort, the person will work as hard as he or she can. In a classroom setting, effort can be evaluated from a student's attendance, note-taking, and discussions with classmates or teachers. The expected outcome would be to get a particular grade, as well as perhaps to obtain a scholarship, make the dean's list, get a certain job, gain admission to graduate school, or gain respect from peers and parents. Unless the effort is perceived to be related to the outcome, little effort will be expended.

If one is expecting a big reward, one would work harder than if the reward were small. An Olympic gold medal is worth harder work than a school gold medal is. Anyone can affect other people's behavior with proper incentive; it can be manipulated to promote learning in students and promote productivity in industry. The way incentive is used to promote productivity distinguishes the free enterprise system based on a market economy from a socialist society of controlled economy which is not based on market force. In a socialist economy, one's reward is not based on the amount of one's economic contribution; it is based on the degree of socialistic behavior. One's political background, in terms of family, loyalty to the party, and "political consciousness," are the things that matter most. It is difficult or impossible to predict, under this kind of reward situation, what kinds of activities will be reinforced and maintained. The expected outcome of an individual's effort or behavior is the incentive motivation; teachers and managers must understand it to promote desired learning and production. For example, an employee will be motivated to perform certain tasks well by a pay raise only when he or she perceives the relationship between the effort and the raise. A student will be motivated to study only when he or she sees the relationship between the effort and the outcome.

Context

The concepts of incentive, reward, and reinforcement originated with the concept of pleasure, or hedonism. The assumption that a major motivation of behavior is the pursuit of pleasure has a long history. Epicurus, a fourth century B.C. Greek philosopher, asserted that pleasure is good and wholesome and that human life should maximize it. Later, Christian philosophers asserted that pleasure is bad and that if a behavior leads to pleasure it is most likely bad as well. John Locke, a seventeenth century British philosopher, asserted that behavior is based on maximizing anticipated pleasure. Whether a behavior would indeed lead to pleasure was another matter. Thus, Locke's concept of hedonism became a behavioral principle. Modern incentive motivation, based upon anticipation of reward, has the same tone as Locke's behavioral principle. Both traditions involve the concepts of incentive and of reinforcement being a generator of behaviors.

There is a danger of circularity in this line of thought. For example, one may explain behavior in terms of it resulting in obtaining a reward, then explain or define reward in terms of behavior. There is no new understanding to be gained in such circular reasoning. Fortunately, there is an independent definition of the rewarding effect, in terms of the brain mechanism of reward. If this mechanism is related to pleasure, there could also be a definition of pleasure independent of behavior. Pleasure and reward are the motivating force, and anticipation of them is termed incentive motivation. Because it attracts people toward their sources, by manipulating the sources, the behavior can be predictably altered.

Bibliography

Bolles, Robert C. *Theory of Motivation.* 2d ed. New York: Harper & Row, 1975. An authoritative book by a productive psychological theoretician; incentive motivation is detailed in several sections.

Crespi, Leo P. "Quantitative Variation of Incentive and Performance in the White Rat." *American Journal of Psychology* 55, no. 4 (1942): 467-517. The anticipatory nature of incentive motivation was first demonstrated in this paper. It is termed the Crespi effect, which includes the elation and depression effects following the incentive contrast.

Hellriegel, Don, John W. Slocum, Jr., and Richard W. Woodman. *Organizational Behavior.* 5th ed. St. Paul, Minn.: West, 1989. A popular text in industrial psychology and personnel management. How to motivate workers with various incentive systems is explained with examples; incentive motivation can be applied in industry to promote productivity.

Liebman, Jeffrey M., and Steven J. Cooper, eds. *The Neuropharmacological Basis of Reward.* Oxford, England: Oxford University Press, 1989. Summarizes studies in the area of brain mechanisms of rewarding effects, an area of great interest to many studying incentive motivation.

Logan, Frank A., and Douglas P. Ferraro. *Systematic Analyses of Learning and Motivation.* New York: John Wiley & Sons, 1978. Logan is a well-known researcher in the area of incentive. This book summarizes the relationship between learning and motivation.

Olds, James, and Peter Milner. "Positive Reinforcement Produced by Electrical Stimulation of Septal Area and Other Regions of Rat Brain." *Journal of Comparative and Physiological Psychology* 47 (1954): 419-427. Reports a breakthrough in the area of studying the brain mechanisms involved in the rewarding effects.

Warden, Carl John. *Animal Motivation: Experimental Studies on the Albino Rat.* New York: Columbia University Press, 1931. This is the first research attempting to compare different sources of drive using various reward substances.

Sigmund Hsiao

Cross-References

INDIVIDUAL PSYCHOLOGY: ALFRED ADLER

Type of psychology: Personality
Fields of study: Personality theory; psychodynamic and neoanalytic models

Individual psychology is the personality theory that was developed by Alfred Adler after he broke from Freudian psychoanalytical ideas. Adler emphasized the impor-tance of childhood inferiority feelings and stressed psychosocial rather than psycho-sexual development.

Principal terms

COMPENSATION: a defense mechanism for overcoming feelings of inferiority by trying harder to excel

INFERIORITY: a feeling of being less strong, knowledgeable, talented, and privileged than others that is universal for all people; the unique way an individual copes with this is the key to his or her style of life

MASCULINE PROTEST: the denying of inferiority feeling through rebelliousness, violence, or maintaining a tough exterior

PRIVATE LOGIC: an individual's techniques for coping with the feeling of inferiority by unconsciously redefining himself or herself in a way not compatible with social interest

SOCIAL INTEREST: a communal feeling which is engendered by fulfilling contacts with friends, family, and career; it overcomes feelings of inferiority

STYLE OF LIFE: an individual's unique and holistic way of coping with life

Overview

Individual psychology is the name of the school of personality theory and psycho-therapy developed by Alfred Adler (1870-1937), a Viennese general-practice physi-cian turned psychiatrist. The term "individual" has a dual implication: It implies uniqueness (each personality exists in a person whose distinctiveness must be appre-ciated); also, the personality is an indivisible unit that cannot be broken down into separate traits, drives, or habits which could be analyzed as if they had an existence apart from the whole.

The essence of a person's uniqueness is his or her style of life: a unified system which provides the principles that guide everyday behavior and gives the individual a perspective with which to perceive the self and the world. The style of life is fairly stable after about age six, and it represents the individual's attempt to explain and cope with the great problem of human existence: the feeling of inferiority.

All people develop a feeling of inferiority. First of all, they are born children in an adult world and realize that they have smaller and weaker bodies, less knowledge, and virtually no privileges. Then people start to compare themselves and realize that there are other people their own age who are better athletes, better scholars, more popular, more artistically talented, wealthier, more socially privileged, more physically attractive, or simply luckier. If one allows the perception of one's own self-worth to be influenced by such subjective comparisons, then one's self-esteem will be lowered by an inferiority complex.

Adler believed that since one's style of life was largely determined early in life, certain childhood conditions made individuals more vulnerable to feelings of inferiority. For example, children born into poverty or into ethnic groups subjected to prejudice may develop a heightened sense of inferiority. Those children with real disabilities (learning or physical disabilities, for example) would also be more susceptible to devaluing their own worth, especially when others are excessively critical or mocking.

Adler looked inside the family for the most powerful influences on a child's developing style of life. Parents who treat a child harshly (through physical, verbal, or sexual abuse) would certainly foster feelings of inferiority in that child. Similarly, parents who neglect or abandon their children contribute to the problem. (Adler believed that such children, instead of directing their rage outward against such parents, turn it inward and say, "There must be something wrong with me, or they would not treat me this way.") Surprisingly, Adler also believed that those parents who pamper their children frustrate the development of positive self-esteem, for such youngsters conclude that they must be very weak and ineffectual in order to require such constant protection and service. When such pampered children go out into the larger world and are not the recipients of constant attention and favors, their previous training has not prepared them for this; they rapidly develop inferior feelings.

The impact of the family on the formulation of one's style of life also includes the influence of siblings. Adler was the first to note that a child's birth order contributed to personality. Oldest children tend to be more serious and success-oriented, because they spend more time with their parents and identify more closely with them. When the younger children come along, the oldest child naturally falls into a leadership role. Youngest children are more likely to have greater social skills and be creative and rebellious. Regardless of birth order, intense sibling rivalries and comparisons can easily damage the esteem of children.

Adler was not fatalistic in discussing the possible impact on style of life of these congenital and environmental forces; he held that it is neither heredity nor environment which determines personality, but rather the way that individuals interpret heredity and environment. These furnish only the building blocks out of which the individual fashions a work of art: the style of life. People have (and make) choices, and this determines their own development; some people, however, have been trained by life to make better choices than others.

All individuals have the capacity to compensate for feelings of inferiority. Many great athletes were frail children and worked hard to develop their physical strength and skills. Great painters overcame weak eyesight; great musicians overcame poor hearing. Given proper encouragement, people are capable of great accomplishments.

The healthy, normal course of development is for individuals to overcome their feeling of inferiority and develop social interest. This involves a feeling of community, or humanistic identification, and a concern with the well-being of others, not only one's own private feelings. Social interest is reflected in and reinforced by cooperative and constructive interactions with others. It starts in childhood, when the youngster has nurturing and encouraging contacts with parents, teachers, and peers.

Later, the three main pillars of social interest are friends, family, and career. Having friends helps one to overcome inferiority, because it allows one to be important in the eyes of someone else. Friends tell one their problems, so one does not feel that one is the only person who has self-doubt and frustration. Starting one's own family reduces inferiority feeling in much the same way. One feels loved by spouse and children, and one is very important to them. Having an occupation allows one to develop a sense of mastery and accomplishment and provides some service to others or to society at large. Therefore, those people who have difficulty establishing and maintaining friendships, succeeding as a spouse or parent, or finding a fulfilling career will have less opportunity to develop a healthy social interest and will have a greater susceptibility to lingering feelings of inferiority.

The alternatives to developing social interest as a way of escaping from feelings of inferiority are either to wallow in them or to explain them away with private logic. Such individuals retreat from meaningful interpersonal relationships and challenging work because it might threaten their precariously balanced self-esteem. Private logic convinces these individuals to seek a sham sense of superiority or notoriety in some way that lacks social interest.

One such approach in private logic is what Adler termed masculine protest (because Western patriarchal culture has encouraged such behavior in males and discouraged it in females). The formula is to be rebellious, defiant, even violent. Underlying all sadism, for example, is an attempt to deny weakness. The gangster wants more than money, the rapist more than sex: They need a feeling of power in order to cover up an unresolved inferiority feeling. The prostitute wants more than money; she needs to have the power to attract and manipulate men, even though she herself may be totally dependent on her pimp or on drugs.

Applications

Adler's theory, like Freud's psychoanalysis and B. F. Skinner's radical behaviorism, is a flexible and powerful tool for understanding and guiding human behavior. The first and foremost applications of individual psychology have been in the areas of child rearing, education, and guidance. Because the first six years of life are formative, the contact that children have during this time with parents, teachers, siblings, and peers will influence that child's later decisions in the direction of social interest or private logic. Adlerians recommend that parents and teachers be firm and fair, and above all, encouraging. One should tell children that they can overcome their disabilities and praise every progress toward accomplishment and social interest. One should avoid excessive punishments, for this will only convince children that others are against them and that they must withdraw into private logic.

After World War I, the new Social Democratic government of Austria gave Adler the task of developing a system of youth guidance clinics throughout the nation. Each child age six to fourteen was screened, then counseled, if necessary. In the 1920's, the rates of crime and mental disorders among young people declined dramatically.

A second example of the applicability of Adler's theory would be at the other end of the life cycle: old age. Late life is a period in which the incidence of mental disorder, especially depression, increases. This can be understood in terms of diminished opportunity to sustain social interest and increased sources of inferiority feeling.

Recall that social interest has three pillars: career, friends, and family. Traditionally, one retires from one's career at about age sixty-five. Elders who do not develop satisfying new activities (especially those activities which involve a sense of accomplishment and contribution to others) adjust poorly to retirement and tend to become depressed. Old friends die or move into retirement communities. Sometimes it is harder to see and talk with old friends because of the difficulty of driving or using public transportation as one ages, or because one or one's friends become hard of hearing or experience a stroke that impairs speech. By far the greatest interpersonal loss of later life is the loss of a spouse. When adult children move away in pursuit of their own lives, this may also give an elder the perception of being abandoned.

Conditions that can rekindle old feelings of inferiority abound in later life. Real physical inferiorities arise. The average elder reports at least two of the following chronic conditions: impaired vision, impaired hearing, a heart condition, stroke, or arthritis. The United States is a youth- and body-oriented culture that worships physical attractiveness, not wrinkles and fat. Some elders, especially those who have had the burdens of long-term illness, feel inferior because of their reduced financial resources.

A third area of application is social psychology, especially the study of prejudice. Gordon Allport suggested that those people who exhibit racial or religious prejudice are typically people who feel inferior themselves: They are trying to feel better about themselves by at least feeling superior to someone else. Typically, prejudice against African Americans has been greatest among whites of low socioeconomic status. Prejudice against new immigrants has been greatest among the more poorly skilled domestic workers. Another example of prejudice would be social class distinctions. The middle class feels inferior (in terms of wealth and privilege) to the upper class. Therefore, the middle class responds by using its private logic to demean the justification of wealth: "The rich are rich because their ancestors were robber barons or because they themselves were junk bond traders in the 1980's." The middle class feels superior to the lower class, however, and again uses private logic to justify and legitimize that class distinction: "The poor are poor because they are lazy and irresponsible." In order to solidify its own identity as hardworking and responsible, the middle class develops a perception of the poor that is more derogatory than an objective analysis would permit.

The most telling application of the theory of individual psychology to prejudice occurred in the first part of the twentieth century in Germany. The rise of Nazi anti-Semitism can be associated with the humiliating German defeat in World War I and with the deplorable economic conditions brought about by hyperinflation and depression. Adolf Hitler first blamed the Jews for the "November treason" which stabbed the German army in the back. (This private logic allowed the German people to believe that their defeated army would have achieved an all-out victory at the front had it not been for the Jewish traitors back in Berlin.) All the problems of capitalism and social inequality were laid at the feet of Jewish financiers, and every fear of rabble-rousing Communists was associated with Jewish radicals. Since everything bad, weak, cowardly, or exploitive was labeled "Jewish," the Germans could believe that they themselves were everything good. The result of the institutionalization of this private logic in the Third Reich led to one of the most blatant examples of masculine protest that humankind has witnessed: World War II and the Holocaust.

A fourth application is associated with management and sales. Management applies interpersonal relations to subordinates; sales applies interpersonal relations to prospective customers. Adler's formula for effective interpersonal relations is simple: Do not make the other person feel inferior. Treat workers with respect. Act as if they are intelligent, competent, wise, and motivated. Give subordinates the opportunity and the encouragement to do a good job, so that they can nurture their own social interest by having a feeling of accomplishment and contribution. Mary Kay Ash, the cosmetics magnate, said that she treated each of her employees and distributors as if each were wearing a sign saying "make me feel important." A similar strategy should apply to customers.

Context

The idea of the inferiority complex bears some similarity to the writings of many previous thinkers. Nineteenth century French psychologist Pierre Janet came closest by developing a theory of perceived insufficiency as a root of all neurosis. American psychologist William James spoke of an innate craving to be appreciated. Adler's emphasis on the individual's capacity of striving for compensation and on masculine protest has parallels in the writings of philosopher Friedrich Nietzsche.

Yet the optimistic, simplified, psychosocial approach of Alfred Adler can only be understood as a reaction to the pessimistic, esoteric, psychosexual approach of Sigmund Freud. Adler was a respected general practitioner in Vienna. He heard his first lecture on psychoanalysis in 1899 and was fascinated, although he never regarded himself as a pupil or disciple of Freud. He was invited to join the Vienna Psychoanalytic Society, and did so in 1902, but he was never psychoanalyzed himself. By the end of the decade, he had become president of the society and editor of its journal. As Adler's own theories developed, and as he voiced them within the psychoanalytic association, Freud became increasingly defensive.

Adler came to criticize several underpinnings of psychoanalytic theory. For example, he suggested that the Oedipus complex was merely the reaction of a pampered child, not a universal complex. Adler saw dysfunctional sexual attitudes and practices as a symptom of underlying neurosis, not as its underlying cause. When Adler would not recant his heresy, the Vienna Psychoanalytic Society was split into a Freudian majority and an Adlerian minority. For a brief period, the Adlerians retained the term "psychoanalysis," only later defining their school as individual psychology.

Freud's influence on Adler can be seen in the emphasis on the importance of early childhood and on the ideas that the motives that underlie neurosis are outside conscious awareness (private logic) and that is it only through insight into these motives that cure can be attained. It is largely in Adler's reaction against Freud, however, that Adler truly defined himself. He saw Freud as offering a mechanistic system in which individuals merely react according to instincts and their early childhood environment; Adler believed that individuals have choices about their futures. He saw Freud as emphasizing universal themes that are rigidly repeated in each patient; Adler believed that people fashion their unique styles of life. Adler saw Freud as being focused on the intrapsychic; Adler emphasized the interpersonal, social field.

While Freud's personality theory has been the best remembered, Adler's has been the most rediscovered. In the 1940's, holistic theorists such as Kurt Lewin and Kurt Goldstein reiterated Adler's emphasis on the individual's subjective and comprehensive approach to perceptions. In the 1960's, humanistic theorists such as Abraham Maslow and Carl Rogers rediscovered his emphasis on individuals overcoming the conditions of their childhood and striving toward a self-actualization and potential to love. In the 1980's, cognitive theorists such as Albert Ellis, Aaron Beck, and Martin E. P. Seligman emphasized how individuals perceive and understand their situation as the central element underlying psychopathology.

An evaluation of individual psychology must necessarily include some enumeration of its weaknesses as well as its strengths. The positives are obvious: The theory is easy to comprehend, optimistic about human nature, and applicable to the understanding of a wide variety of issues. The weaknesses would be the other side of those very strengths. If a theory is so easy to comprehend, is it not then simplistic— or merely a reformulation of common sense? This may explain why so many other theorists "rediscovered" Adler's ideas throughout the twentieth century. If a theory is so optimistic about human potential, can it present a balanced view of human nature? If a theory is flexible and broad enough as to be able to explain so much, can it be precise enough to explain anything with any depth? Although everything in individual psychology fits together as a unified whole, it is not always clear what the lines of reasoning are. Does excessive inferiority feeling preclude the formulation of social interest, or does social interest assuage inferiority feeling? Does inferiority feeling engender private logic, or does private logic sustain inferiority feeling? At different times, Adler and Adlerians seem to argue both sides of these questions. The Achilles heel of individual psychology (and of psychoanalysis) is prediction. If a given child is in a situation that heightens feelings of inferiority, will that child overcompensate effectively and develop social interest as an adult, or will private logic take over—if it does, will it be in the form of self-brooding or masculine protest?

Although the fuzziness of Adlerian concepts will preclude individual psychology from being a major force in academic psychology, it is safe to predict that future theorists will again rediscover many of Alfred Adler's concepts.

Bibliography

Adler, Alfred. *The Individual Psychology of Alfred Adler.* Edited by Heinz L. and Rowena L. Ansbacher. New York: Basic Books, 1956.

──────────. *Superiority and Social Interest.* Edited by Heinz L. and Rowena R. Ansbacher. Evanston, Ill.: Northwestern University Press, 1964. There is no standard edition or comprehensive collection of Adler's writings. He wrote many books, but unlike Sigmund Freud or Carl Jung, he essentially said the same thing over and over (especially after 1913, when his theory congealed). Any of Adler's later books will give a good sense of his theory. The above two edited works by the Ansbachers take representative excerpts from Adler's numerous books and, together with editorial comments, give a good picture of the development of Adler's thought.

Bottome, Phyllis. *Alfred Adler: A Biography.* New York: G. P. Putnam's Sons, 1939. This classic biography was written only two years after Adler's death. It gives much insight into the man and his theory, but the book is a bit too laudatory.

Dreikurs, Rudolf. *Fundamentals of Adlerian Psychology.* New York: Greenberg, 1950. The author was an Adlerian disciple who became the leader of the Adlerian movement in the United States after World War II. His simple style and straightforward advice are very much in keeping with the style of Adler himself. Dreikurs' own expertise was in the area of child development.

Mosak, Harold H. *Alfred Adler: His Influence on Psychology Today.* Park Ridge, N.J.: Noyes Press, 1973. This edited volume covers Adlerian applications to understanding education, social issues, and the humanities, as well as discussing the clinical aspects of the theory.

Mosak, Harold H., and Birdie Mosak. *A Bibliography of Adlerian Psychology.* Washington, D.C.: Hemisphere, 1975. This is a very comprehensive bibliography covering individual psychology up through the early 1970's. Even articles appearing in newsletters are included. It is organized by author's last name but has a subject index.

Stepansky, Paul E. *In Freud's Shadow: Adler in Context.* New York: Analytic Press, 1983. This is one of the more recent biographies of Adler. It does an excellent job of considering Adler's sociohistorical context and his interpersonal struggles with Freud. True Adlerians will maintain that this book does not do Adler justice.

T. L. Brink

Cross-References

INDUSTRIAL AND ORGANIZATIONAL PSYCHOLOGY

Type of psychology: Social psychology
Fields of study: Group processes; motivation theory; social perception and cognition

Industrial and organizational psychology applies psychological research methods and theories to issues of importance in work organizations. From its beginnings as psychology applied to a few personnel topics, it has expanded to deal with almost all aspects of work, changing as they have.

Principal terms

EXPERIMENTATION: a research technique in which the scientist changes one aspect of a situation to assess the impact on another aspect—for example, increasing illumination to see if fatigue is lessened

FAIRNESS IN WORK SETTINGS: the basing of decisions about workers' hiring, salary, promotion, and so on entirely on work-relevant considerations and not on race, sex, age, or other personal characteristics

FIELD RESEARCH: an approach in which evidence is gathered in a "natural" setting, such as the workplace; by contrast, laboratory research involves an artificial, contrived setting

INDUSTRIAL PSYCHOLOGY: the original label for what is now called industrial and organizational psychology; since about 1970, it has referred to activities such as recruiting, selecting, placing, and evaluating individual employees

ORGANIZATIONAL PSYCHOLOGY: the label for activities such as motivating and leading employees, influencing job satisfaction and morale, and so on, generally at the group level

SCIENTIFIC METHOD: an approach to gaining knowledge that involves proposing a hypothesis, rejecting or accepting it on the basis of evidence gathered, and sharing what was learned with others

Overview

Industrial and organizational psychology (often shortened to I/O psychology) is a somewhat deceptive title for the field. Even when industrial psychology alone was used to label it, practitioners were involved with issues and activities far beyond solving industrial problems—for example, designing procedures for selecting sales people, advertising methods, and reducing accidents on public transportation. "Organizational" suggests the application of knowledge to organizations, but the intended meaning is closer to "the study of forces that influence how people and their activities at work are organized."

In colleges and universities, I/O psychology is a long-recognized discipline. Graduate programs leading to the M.A. and, more commonly, Ph.D. degrees in this field are most typically offered within psychology departments, sometimes in collaboration with departments of business; occasionally they are offered by business departments alone. In most cases, students working toward graduate degrees in I/O psychology first study a wide range of psychological topics, then study in even greater detail those that make up the I/O specialty. The study of research methods, statistical tools for evaluating findings, motivation, personality, and so on forms a base from which psychological testing, interviewing, job analysis, and performance evaluation are studied in depth.

Industrial and organizational psychology borrowed much from many other areas of psychology during its growth and has retained the strong research orientation common to them, along with many of the research methods each has developed and many of the findings that each has generated. Bringing psychological methods to work settings where experts from many other disciplines are studying some of the same problems results in conflicts, but it also produces a richness of information beyond the scope of any one of the disciplines.

In most cases, the most feasible approach to data collection for I/O psychologists is field research. Systematic observation of ongoing work can often give a psychologist some needed information without much disturbing the workers involved. Generally, they will be told that data are being gathered, but when the known presence of an observer likely would change what is being studied, unobtrusive methods might be used. Information from hidden cameras, or observations from researchers pretending to be workers and actually engaging in whatever must be done, can be used when justified.

Again studying within the actual work setting, I/O psychologists may sometimes take advantage of natural experiments, situations in which a change not deliberately introduced may be studied for its effect on some important outcome. If, for example, very extreme, unseasonable temperatures resulted in uncontrollably high, or low, temperatures in an office setting, a psychologist could assess the effects on employee discomfort, absenteeism, or productivity.

Still studying within the actual work setting, an I/O psychologist may arrange a quasi-experiment, a situation in which the researcher changes some factor to assess its effect while having only partial control over other factors that might influence that change. For example, the psychologist might study the effects of different work schedules by assigning one schedule to one department of a company, a second schedule to a second department, and a third schedule to a third department. The departments, the people, and the differences in the work itself would prevent the strategy from being a true experiment, but it still could produce some useful data.

An experiment, as psychology and other sciences define it, is difficult to arrange within work settings, but it may be worth the effort to evaluate information gathered by other methods. In the simplest form of experiment, the researcher randomly assigns the people studied into two groups and, while holding constant all other factors that might influence the experiment's outcome, presents some condition (known as an independent variable) to one group of subjects (the experimental group) and withholds it from another (the control group). Finally, the researcher measures the outcome (the dependent variable) for both groups.

Carrying out a true experiment almost always requires taking the people involved away from their typical activities into a setting obviously designed for study (usually called the laboratory, even though it may bear little resemblance to a laboratory of, say, a chemist). The need to establish a new, artificial setting and the need to pull workers away from their work to gather information are both troublesome, as is the risk that what is learned in the laboratory setting may not hold true back in the natural work setting.

Correlational methods, borrowed from psychometrics, complement the observational and experimental techniques just described. Correlation is a mathematical technique for comparing the similarity of two sets of data (literally, to determine their co-relation). An important example of the I/O psychologist's seeking information on relationships is found in the process of hiring-test validation, answering the question of to what extent test scores and eventual work performance are correlated. To establish validity, a researcher must demonstrate a substantial relationship between scores and performance, evidence that the test is measuring what is intended.

Applications

Industrial and organizational psychology, as the term implies, focuses on two broad areas; Linda Jewell and Marc Siegall, in their *Contemporary Industrial/Organizational Psychology* (2d ed., 1990), demonstrate this by their arrangement of topics. Industrial topics include testing, job analysis and evaluation, recruiting, selecting and placing applicants, employee training and socialization, evaluating employee job performance, job design, working conditions, health and safety, and motivation. Organizational topics include a company's social system and communication, groups within organizations, leadership, and organizational change and development. Topics of overlap of the two areas include absenteeism, turnover, job commitment, job satisfaction, employee development, and quality of work life.

Testing in I/O psychology most often is done to assess peoples' aptitudes or abilities as a basis for making selection, placement, or promotion decisions about them. It may also be used for other purposes—for example, to judge the quality of training programs. Tests used range from ones of general aptitude (IQ, or intelligence quotient, tests) through tests of specific aptitudes, interests, and personality, although use of IQ and personality tests remains controversial. Aptitude for success in academically related activity (as might be related to one's IQ) is often of only modest importance in work settings, but the folk wisdom "the best person is the most intelligent person" can lead to giving IQ tests routinely to applicants. Personality is a troublesome concept within psychology. Tests of it can be useful to clinicians working with mental health issues but are rarely useful as bases for employment-related decisions. When outcomes from personality testing are specific enough to be useful—for example, when they reveal serious personality problems—the same information is usually obtainable from reviews of work history or from interviews.

Along with other procedures related to making decisions about people in work settings, testing is often targeted as being unfair to some groups—for example, African Americans or women. If the use of a particular test results in decision making that even suggests unfair discrimination, companies must have available solid evidence that this is not the case if they choose to continue using the test.

Job analysis determines what tasks must be carried out in a job. It serves as the major basis for deciding what skills successful job applicants must have or what training to provide unskilled applicants. Evaluating job performances of individual employees must be based on what they should be doing, revealed by job analysis. Their dismissal, retention, promotion, and wage increases may all be related to job analysis information. It is also a basis for job evaluation, the determining of what is appropriate pay for the job, although evaluation often must also be based on the availability of applicants, average wages in a geographic area, and other factors.

Recruiting, selecting, and placing refer to sequential steps in filling positions. Although some companies can let prospective employees come to them, many prefer actively to seek applicants. Recruiting may involve little more than announcing that a position is open or as much as sending trained representatives to find promising people and encourage them to apply for work. At least two considerations make vigorous recruiting attractive. First, it is often possible for companies to reduce training costs greatly by finding already-proficient applicants. Second, when minority-group employees are needed to achieve fair balance in an organization, recruiting can often focus on, for example, African Americans or women.

Although training may be unnecessary if a company is able to hire already-skilled people, training is generally advantageous after hiring and periodically over a worker's tenure. Promotion may be based on success in training, or training may follow promotion based on other considerations. Although "training" suggests the development or enhancement of job skills, it often also includes socialization, the bringing of new employees into the "family" of the company and the teaching of values, goals, and expectations that extend beyond carrying out a specific work assignment.

Job design, working conditions, health and safety, and motivation are usually given separate chapters in texts, but often in work settings they must be considered as a set. For example, if a job, as designed, forces or even encourages workers to put their health or safety at risk, their working conditions are unsatisfactory, and when they recognize the nature of the situation, their motivation is likely to be impaired.

When industrial psychologists of the early twentieth century recommended hiring or promotion, designed training, or carried out any other of their responsibilities, they had only to satisfy their employers' demands. Since the late 1960's, industrial/organizational psychologists have also had to satisfy legal and ethical requirements pertaining to a host of problem areas such as racism, sexism, age discrimination, and discrimination against the handicapped. More than good intentions are necessary here. Throughout the range of applications discussed above, the psychologists must work to balance the societal demands for fairness in work settings and the practical interests of employers, sometimes having to endure criticism for even the most ingenious of solutions.

For example, if an employer finds the company must increase its number of Hispanic workers, vigorous recruiting is an excellent first step; yet it may prove expensive enough to aggravate the employer. If recruiting is not successful because would-be applicants doubt the employer's sincerity, both they and the employer will be unhappy. If recruiting is successful in generating interest, but many interested individuals are unqualified, providing them special training could be a reasonable solution. Applicants might feel it degrading, however, to be required to undergo more training than others before them, and/or the employer might balk at the extra cost involved.

The first industrial psychologists needed little more than solid training in their discipline to achieve success. Their descendants need, beyond training in a discipline that has enlarged enormously, the talents of diplomats.

Context

Between about 1880 and the beginning of the twentieth century, psychology moved away from its origins in philosophy and aligned itself with science, both in method and in intended usefulness. Work in the early laboratories, modeled after the pioneer laboratories of Wilhelm Wundt in Germany and William James in the United States, convinced the second generation of scientific psychologists that objective evidence should be the basis for knowledge and, borrowing directly from the physical sciences, taught them techniques for gathering it. Declaring that psychology should be a science and working to make it one encouraged psychologists to seek knowledge with practical value and to put what they learned to use. The new psychology was expected to benefit people, and the likelihood that it might do so through their vocations was readily accepted.

Psychologists were certainly not the first to study work settings and suggest changes, or even the first to apply the scientific method to the enterprise. For example, Frederick Winslow Taylor and Frank Gilbreth were industrial engineers who considered workers not too different from cogs in the machines also involved in industry. Their "time and motion" studies sought to discover how workers could most efficiently carry out their parts of the enterprise. Although their conclusions are often now cited as examples of inhumane manipulation of workers for companies' benefits, Taylor and Gilbreth envisioned that both workers and employers were to gain from increases in efficiency. Not surprisingly, most of what industrial engineering studied was appropriated by industrial psychology and remains part of I/O psychology— usually under the designations job design and human factors engineering in the United States, or the designation ergonomics elsewhere.

Early psychologists had an advantage over the others studying and offering advice about work. They were popularly identified as people experts, and for the many problems thought to be based on human characteristics or limitations, their expertise was acknowledged even while it was very modest. The advantage of being expected to make valuable contributions was put to good use, and within the first two decades of the twentieth century, industrial psychology became a recognized discipline with the ability to deliver most of what was expected of it.

Ironically, wars materially aided the early development of industrial and organizational psychology. World War I provided psychologists unprecedented opportunities to try intelligence testing on a very large scale and to develop and implement a very large personnel program. Robert Yerkes directed the intelligence testing of more than one million men between 1917 and 1919, and Walter Dill Scott and Walter Van Dyke Bingham interviewed and classified more than three million men before the war ended.

Testing, interviewing, and classification were also part of industrial psychologists' efforts during World War II, and many other lines of research and application were also pursued. For example, the previously mentioned human factors engineering, which emphasized machine design tailored to the people who would use the device, was greatly advanced by the necessity that people be able to control aircraft and other sophisticated weapons.

Following each war, some of the psychologists who had successfully worked together chose to continue to do so. Major consulting firms grew out of their associations and remain a source of employment for many industrial/organizational psychologists.

Bibliography

Dunnette, Marvin D. *Handbook of Industrial and Organizational Psychology.* Chicago: Rand McNally, 1976. Covers the full range of industrial and organizational psychology through the mid-1970's. Although much of the material is intended for specialists in the field, much also is accessible to the general reader.

Hilgard, Ernest Ropiequet. *Psychology in America: A Historical Survey.* San Diego: Harcourt Brace Jovanovich, 1987. Chapter 19, "Industrial and Organizational Psychology," is a definitive review of about eighty years of the field's advancement from a promising application of the new "scientific psychology" to a major subdiscipline of contemporary psychology. An energetic reader could use material in several of Hilgard's other chapters (for example, those on intelligence, on motivation, and on social psychology) to place industrial and organizational psychology in the context of its parent discipline.

Jewell, Linda N., and Marc Siegall. *Contemporary Industrial/Organizational Psychology.* 2d ed. St. Paul, Minn.: West, 1990. A text for an introductory college course offering excellent coverage of the discipline's topics. Written for students majoring in business as much as for those majoring in psychology. A book that almost anyone can understand, even enjoy.

Rosenzweig, Mark R., and Lyman W. Porter, eds. *Annual Review of Psychology.* Stanford, Calif.: Annual Reviews. Most volumes of this highly respected series contain a chapter or two on I/O psychology, indexed under "Personnel-Organizational Psychology." Each volume also contains a chapter title index for at least the previous decade, making location of particular topics reasonably easy.

Harry A. Tiemann, Jr.

Cross-References

Ability Tests: Uses and Misuses, 27; Achievement Motivation, 96; Career and Personnel Testing, 467; Group Decision Making, 1114; Human Resource Training and Development, 1197; Leadership, 1419; Work Motivation, 2654.

INFANT PERCEPTUAL SYSTEMS

Type of psychology: Developmental psychology
Fields of study: Auditory, chemical, cutaneous, and body senses; infancy and childhood; vision

Infants' sensory and perceptual systems function at birth and develop rapidly during the early months of life. The study of infant perception addresses theoretical issues raised by empiricist and nativist philosophies, provides information about how infants make sense of their environment, and has implications for medical and child-rearing practices.

Principal terms
CRITICAL PERIOD: the time during which the developing organism is sensitive to certain inputs or experiences necessary to foster normal development
EMPIRICISM: a philosophy which holds that knowledge is learned through experience and that infants begin life like blank slates, learning about their environment through experience
HABITUATION: a decrease in response to repeated presentations of a stimulus that is not simply caused by fatigued sensory receptors
NATIVISM: a philosophy which holds that knowledge is innate and that the neonate enters the world prepared for certain kinds of environmental inputs
PERCEPTION: the act of processing and interpreting inputs from sensory systems
SENSATION: the act of basic processing of inputs from sensory receptors

Overview

The intriguing question of how infants experience the world around them has triggered substantial research on the development of sensory and perceptual abilities. The infant's sensory systems are functional at birth, or even prenatally, and continue to develop during the early months of life. Newborn infants can discriminate among basic taste sensations. They distinguish sugar solutions from water, showing preferences for sweeter substances. Like adults, infants respond to sweet, sour, and bitter substances with different facial expressions. Young infants also discriminate different odors, showing facial expressions of displeasure in response to odors that adults rate as unpleasant, such as odors of fish and rotten eggs, and facial expressions of pleasure to odors that adults rate as pleasant, such as odors of banana and vanilla. Breast-fed infants demonstrate recognition of scent as early as one week postnatally. When presented with cotton pads scented from the underarm or breast of their mothers and of strangers, they turn toward their mother's odor.

The sense of touch has social and perceptual facets. Pediatrician T. B. Brazelton proposed that touch plays a critical regulatory role in development. Touching and patting can calm a fussy infant or rouse a drowsy one. Neonates respond to various types of tactile input. Stimulation by touch or air puff to the body leads to cardiac and behavioral responses. Painful stimulation, such as a heel prick to draw blood, leads to cries and movement.

An obvious demonstration of hearing in neonates (newborns) is that they are startled by sudden, loud sounds. Further characterization of their auditory abilities is based on studies of behavioral responses such as head turning or physiological responses such as brain wave changes. Generally, newborns have higher auditory thresholds than adults—that is, they require louder sounds. Loudness thresholds vary, however, with sound frequency. Human adults detect sounds in a broad frequency range of 20 to 20,000 cycles per second. Young infants appear to be especially sensitive to sound frequencies in the range of human speech. At these frequencies, their loudness thresholds approach those of adults.

The young infant's ability to localize the source of sounds is immature. Neonates can turn their heads in the direction of a sound coming from their left or right side. The newborn's motor control, however, is relatively poor, and the head-turning response is not completely reliable. By three to four months, infants demonstrate more accurate sound localization.

Infants appear especially interested in human speech sounds. In studies in which sound is used as a reinforcement for pacifier sucking, infants show a greater increase in response if reinforced by speech than by nonspeech stimuli. They show preferences for high-pitched, expressive voices. Young infants are able to make fine discriminations between human speech sounds, such as *b* and *p* in "ba" and "pa." By four to five months, infants can match vowel sounds to faces posed as if they were making that sound—for example, a rounded mouth with the sound of the vowel *a* as in "spa."

Newborns, once thought to be blind at birth, have functional vision, but their visual acuity is much poorer than normal adult acuity. A newborn can see a pattern from 6 meters away with the same clarity as can an adult with normal vision from 90 to 150 meters away. Because of their poor acuity, young infants are more likely to prefer patterns with sharply defined, high-contrast borders, such as black-to-white, rather than shades of gray. As acuity improves over the first few months of life, infants tend to prefer patterns with elements that optimally stimulate their visual system. Thus, a neonate may look preferentially at a two-by-two black-and-white checkerboard pattern, whereas a three-month-old might prefer a more complex, six-by-six checkerboard. By the end of the first year, infant acuity approximates adult acuity.

It is difficult to determine whether young infants see and discriminate color hues. Hue and brightness often vary together, so simply demonstrating that infants discriminate red from green does not prove that they see color; the discrimination could be based on brightness alone. By four months, infants perceive colors and categorize color similarly to adults. For example, infants habituated to a blue hue showed renewed response to a new green hue but not to a new blue hue, even though both new hues were equally different in wavelength from the original blue.

Although newborns can move their eyes to a visual stimulus and fixate it, the efficiency of scanning improves postnatally. Newborns tend to scan in a limited manner, fixating on high-contrast borders of patterns. By two to three months, infants scan central features of a pattern. Similarly, eye movements to track a moving stimulus are immature and jerky in newborns but become more mature by two months.

Young infants show some ability to adjust their eyes to objects at different distances, but these movements are inconsistent prior to two months. Size constancy, or the ability to perceive the size of an object as the same regardless of distance, emerges at four to six months. The ability to use binocular cues to determine depth also emerges around this time. In classic studies on a "visual cliff," Eleanor Gibson and Richard Walk demonstrated that once infants begin to crawl, they respond to depth cues. Gibson and Walk constructed a Plexiglas platform, half directly over a checkerboard pattern and the other half over a drop-off with a checkerboard pattern at the bottom. Infants between six and fourteen months in age would crawl readily over the shallow side of the surface, but would refuse to crawl over the deep side.

Applications

Knowledge of infant perception has led to further understanding of what qualities and quantities of stimulation are optimal for normal development. The term "critical period" implies that certain experiences must occur during that time period in order for development to proceed normally; omission of that experience causes permanent deficits. A similar term, "sensitive period," implies that certain experiences must occur during that time period in order for development to proceed optimally.

Kittens that were experimentally deprived of visual input to one eye during an early sensitive period later failed to develop adequate binocular vision. Human children who have abnormal binocular experience between about four months and three years because of disorders in eye alignment, such as strabismus, or "lazy eye," may fail to develop fully normal binocular vision. Studies of early visual deprivation that results from cataracts showed that after cataract removal children had more pronounced deficits in visual acuity if the deprivation occurred between birth and age three.

Experience with self-produced locomotion, that is, moving oneself around the environment, may facilitate depth perception. Kittens who were allowed to move actively in their environment showed normal depth perception responses. They extended their paws when lowered to a visual surface, and they avoided the deep side of the visual cliff. Kittens that were passively moved in the environment did not demonstrate these normal responses.

Critical periods also occur in language development; in fact, there may be a critical period for language learning. Case studies of children deprived of any language input throughout most of their infancy and childhood suggest that it is nearly impossible to develop linguistic competence at a later age. A more specific example of a sensitive period involves native speech sound discrimination. Young infants discriminate among sounds that are not found in their native language—sounds that are indistinguishable to adults. As infants become familiarized with sounds in their native language, their ability to discriminate the foreign sounds disappears. For example, native English-speaking and Japanese-speaking infants both show discrimination of the sounds *r* and *l* as in "ra" and "la." These sounds are used distinctly in English but not in Japanese. While English-speaking children and adults continue to make this auditory discrimination, Japanese-speaking children and adults can no longer discriminate between the two sounds. The developmental loss of this ability occurs near the end of the first year of life.

Laboratory research with rats reared in sensory-enriched or sensory-deprived environments suggested that enriched environments stimulate brain development and increase rates of maze learning. Early studies of institutionalized infants found that introducing visual displays such as mobiles or colorful crib bumpers into the environment promoted attentiveness and reaching behaviors.

Concerns about stimulating environments for infants have influenced parenting magazines and books as well as toy manufacturers. Toys and accessories for young infants were once available predominantly in pastel colors but, in the 1990's, became more readily available in primary colors and in black-and-white. Some of these toys include instructions to parents on how to determine whether their infants are enjoyably stimulated or overstimulated by the patterns.

Medical advances leading to the ability to sustain life in young preterm infants have triggered controversy about appropriate stimulation for infants. Preterm infants were initially kept in isolettes and treated as too fragile to tolerate extra stimulation. In the 1960's and 1970's, worries about whether these infants were suffering sensory deprivation and whether parent-infant social interaction was adversely affected by early separation led to research on intervention programs to increase stimulation. It was later recognized that the levels of stimulation in the neonatal intensive-care units were already quite high, with bright lights, loud background noise, and repeated handling for medical examinations. For extremely young or ill preterms, additional stimulation may not be advisable. Other preterms apparently benefit from intervention programs. Studies have shown increased weight gain and improved health in preterms who were exposed to additional stimulation regimens. These intervention programs include the use of specially designed water beds to stimulate the somatosensory and vestibular systems, or manual stroking and limb flexion techniques. Further reasearch is needed to determine the optimal use of stimulation for preterm infants.

Context

Historically, interest in infant perception was triggered by the contrasting views of nativist and empiricist philosophies. Empiricist John Locke argued that infants were born as tabulae rasae, or blank slates, and that their knowledge was determined by experiences after birth. Nativists asserted that infants at birth have some innate knowledge and that many perceptual abilities were present at birth.

The influence of these contrasting viewpoints remains noticeable in current developmental theories of perception. Early psychophysical and information-processing approaches descended largely from the empiricist approach, assuming that perceptions are built up from basic component features. The nativist approach influenced Eleanor and James Gibson's ecological theory of perception, which suggests that infants are active perceivers and that the information available in the environment directly leads to perception. It is probable that the empiricist and nativist extreme views are unrealistic and that any aspect of perceptual development has innate and experiential components. Continuing studies of perceptual development will undoubtedly explore how experience combines with innate predispositions to provide a human's sights, sounds, tastes, touches, and smells of the world.

William James, in 1890, speculated that the infant experienced the world as a "blooming, buzzing confusion." James suggested that the senses were integrated at birth and later differentiated into distinct sensory modalities. In Jean Piaget's theory of cognitive development, infant perceptual abilities in the early sensorimotor stages of development provided the foundation for later cognitive maturation. Piaget proposed that the senses were differentiated at birth and later integrated as the infant learned about objects in the environment.

In addition to understanding each sensory system separately, another goal of infant perception research is to describe the interaction among sensory modalities, or "cross-modal" perception. The different predictions of James and Piaget may each be partially correct. It is possible that neonates and young infants respond to the overall quantity of stimulation, integrating modalities into a global sensory experience. It is not until four to five months, however, that infants clearly demonstrate transfer of information between modalities. By this age, infants can recognize visually an object they previously touched, or reach out in the dark for a luminous object, or match a videotaped bouncing ball with a synchronous noise. Future research will continue to examine how the sensory systems interact during early development.

In addition to advancing scientific knowledge, the study of infant perception provides useful information on normative perceptual development for pediatricians, parents, and child care workers. Applications of such research help to advance medical treatment of infants and children and also to provide a foundation for developing improved methods of communication and experiences for individuals who have sensory impairments.

Bibliography

Bower, T. G. R. *The Perceptual World of the Child.* Cambridge, Mass.: Harvard University Press, 1977. A brief (83-page), basic introduction to issues in infant perception. Includes a thorough discussion of how physical growth from infancy through adulthood provides challenges for perceptual systems. Covers some classic studies of perceptual development. Written for a general audience.

Fogel, Alan. *Infancy: Infant, Family, and Society.* St. Paul, Minn.: West, 1984. A text for introductory college courses on infant development. Chapters are organized chronologically, with aspects of perceptual development covered for the newborn and for early-, middle-, and late-infancy periods. Useful for brief overviews and for linking developments in perception to developments in other aspects of the infant's life.

Gottlieb, Gilbert, and Norman Krasnegor, eds. *Measurement of Audition and Vision in the First Year of Postnatal Life: A Methodological Overview.* Norwood, N.J.: Ablex, 1985. Detailed chapters cover behavioral, physiological, and psychophysical measures of auditory and visual development. Good resource for information on methods for experiments in perceptual development and for discussion of the inferences drawn from such studies. Written for researchers and students of infant perception.

Maurer, Daphne, and Charles Maurer. *The World of the Newborn.* New York: Basic Books, 1988. An excellent introduction to the young infant, from the transitions of birth through early perceptual, cognitive, and social development. Emphasizes findings from scientific research and concludes with an integrated view of infancy. Written for the nonspecialist. Includes pictures and thorough notes with bibliographic information on all cited research.

Pick, Anne D., ed. *Perception and Its Development: A Tribute to Eleanor J. Gibson.* Hillsdale, N.J.: Lawrence Erlbaum, 1979. Reviews areas of perceptual development influenced by Gibson's theory of perceptual development, concluding with a chapter by Gibson herself. Covers depth perception, pattern perception, the perception of meaning, and selective attention. Provides detailed examples of the implications of Gibson's theoretical approach for empirical studies of perception.

Marie T. Balaban

Cross-References

Birth: Effects on Physical Development, 429; Development: Theoretical Issues, 804; Developmental Methodologies, 817; Motor Development, 1623; Physical Development: Environmental versus Genetic Determinants, 1823; Prenatal Physical Development, 1861; Sudden Infant Death Syndrome, 2495; Visual Development, 2616.

INHIBITORY AND EXCITATORY IMPULSES

Type of psychology: Biological bases of behavior
Fields of study: Nervous system; organic disorders

Two types of processes occur in neurons: those that excite the cell to react to a stimulus and those that inhibit the cell. Cells receive many impulses of both types and must integrate the incoming messages to determine what response should be produced.

Principal terms

ACTION POTENTIAL: a rapid change in electrical charges on a neuron's cell membrane, with depolarization followed by repolarization, leading to a nerve impulse moving down an axon

AXON: the single fiberlike extension of a neuron that carries information away from the cell body toward the next cell in a pathway

DENDRITE: a branching extension of a neuron through which information enters the cell; there may be one or many dendrites on a neuron

DEPOLARIZATION: a shift in ions and electrical charges across a cell membrane, causing loss of resting membrane potential and bringing the cell closer to the action potential

EXCITABILITY: the ability of neurons to be excited by a stimulus and to respond by producing an electrical impulse transmitted down the axon

ION CHANNEL: a pathway through the cell membrane, controlled by gates and used for passage of ions during electrical impulse generation

NEUROTRANSMITTER: a chemical produced in a neuron and released by axon terminals to stimulate the next cell in the neuronal pathway

POSTSYNAPTIC POTENTIAL: a chemical stimulus produced in a postsynaptic cell; may excite the cell to come nearer to electrical firing, or inhibit firing

RESTING MEMBRANE POTENTIAL: the maintenance of difference in electrical charges between the inside and outside of a neuron's cell membrane, keeping it polarized with closed ion channels

SYNAPSE: the space between two neurons or between a neuron and an effector cell, across which neurotransmitters pass to carry a chemical message between cells

Overview

An unstimulated neuron—one which is neither receiving nor transmitting an impulse—maintains a difference in ions on either side of its cell membrane. While many positively charged potassium (K^+) ions are present within the cytoplasm of a cell, proteins and other large molecules located there carry more numerous negative charges, making a negative net charge inside the membrane. Large numbers of positively charged sodium ions (Na$^+$) are located on the outside of the cell in the intercellular space, giving it a net positive charge. Thus, in a resting neuron, there is a positive charge on the outside of the cell membrane and a negative charge on the inside. This charge difference is called the resting membrane potential. It is usually expressed as -70 millivolts, meaning that the inside of the cell is seventy thousandths of a volt more electrically negative than the outside.

The resting membrane potential is maintained by active transport of ions across the cell membrane. Sodium and potassium ions move across the membrane by diffusion, with sodium leaking into the cell and potassium leaking out. These ions are said to be moving down their concentration gradients, going from an area of higher concentration of each ion to an area of lower ion concentration. Such movement occurs passively, without the addition of energy by the cell. If this movement were allowed to continue uninterrupted, the resting potential would be lost fairly quickly, as the ions would reach equilibrium where they would be at the same concentration on both sides of the membrane. This is prevented from happening by the active transport process of the sodium-potassium pump. Active transport is a means of moving materials across the cell membrane from an area of lower concentration to an area of higher concentration. It cannot occur by diffusion, but requires the input of energy from the cell, released by breakage of a molecule by adenosine triphosphate (ATP), the energy currency of the cell. The sodium-potassium pump is a protein that spans the cell membrane and acts as a channel through which both sodium and potassium are pushed against their concentration gradients by the cell's energy. Much of the ATP made by every cell is used to run this pump and maintain the resting potential, not only in neurons but in all other cells as well. The sodium-potassium pump moves two potassium ions into the cell and three sodium ions out of the cell for each ATP molecule broken.

The electrical difference between the sides of the cell membrane is particularly important in neurons, since it is through a change in this difference that a message is passed along the surface of a single neuron. In this information transmission, an electrical impulse passes down an excited, activated neuron's axon to the "output" end of the cell, the axon terminal. There the electrical impulse causes tiny vesicles or sacs filled with a chemical called a neurotransmitter to move to the cell membrane and fuse with it, emptying the contents of the vesicles into the space between cells, which is called a synapse. The cell that releases its chemical messengers at the synapse is the presynaptic neuron, and the cell which receives the message is the postsynaptic neuron. The message of the neurotransmitter is received by the second cell when the chemical binds to a protein receptor on the surface of the postsynaptic cell, usually on a dendrite or the cell body. This message may be interpreted as an excitatory stimulus or as an inhibitory stimulus. Either kind of stimulus causes a change in the properties of the receptor and of the postsynaptic cell to which it belongs, generally by changing the permeability of the cell's membrane.

When the stimulus is excitatory, the charge difference on the two sides of the membrane is at first lowered. A threshold level of electrical charge is reached, about

−55 millivolts, and an action potential is generated, followed by the firing of the neuron. A self-propagating wave of depolarization results from an excitatory stimulus that causes the neuron to reach threshold. Special proteins called sodium gates open in the cell membrane, forming a channel that allows sodium ions from outside the cell to flow rapidly down their concentration gradient into the cell's interior. As the net charge inside the cell becomes positive, the charge outside the cell becomes negative. There is a sharp rise, then a decline of the charge within the cell, called a spike, that reaches as high as +35 millivolts with the inflow of sodium ions. The action potential that results from this entry of ions acts according to the all-or-none law. A neuron will either reach the threshold and respond completely or will not reach the threshold and will not respond at all; there is no partial response. After sodium ions rush into the cell, the sodium gates close and potassium gates open, allowing potassium ions to flow out of the cell, restoring the negative charge inside the cell. The sodium-potassium pump then must reestablish the relative ion concentrations across the membrane, necessitating a period in which the cell cannot respond to an excitatory impulse, called the absolute refractory period.

When the message imparted by the neurotransmitter is inhibitory, a different response occurs in the postsynaptic neuron. Instead of depolarizing the membrane by changing the membrane potential from −70 to −55 millivolts, the inhibitory message causes hyperpolarization, raising the difference in charge between the inside and outside of the membrane. The interior of the cell becomes more negative, reaching −80 millivolts or more, thus inhibiting the generation of an action potential in that cell. The inhibitory impulses help prevent the chaos that would result if excitatory impulses were firing with nothing to regulate the chain of stimulation. They also help fine-tune sensory perceptions; they can make sensations more exact and sensitive by blocking the firing of neurons around a specific point, such as the precise place on the skin that a touch is felt.

Applications

Transmission of information in the form of electrochemical messages is the job of the entire nervous system. One of the ways in which understanding of this information movement is applied is through the study of neurotransmitters. Different parts of the nervous system show the action of many different chemicals that either excite or inhibit the passage of information by means of generation of an action potential in a postsynaptic neuron. The response of the postsynaptic neuron that leads to firing of an action potential is called an excitatory postsynaptic potential (EPSP). If such firing is instead prevented, the response is called an inhibitory postsynaptic potential (IPSP). Together these are referred to as PSPs.

An important aspect of the generation of these excitatory and inhibitory postsynaptic potentials is that they may be cumulative, with numerous different presynaptic cells sending different messages to the same postsynaptic cell. The messages may all be the same, leading to summation of the information. This would allow a neuron to fire even if each individual excitatory PSP is unable to reach threshold by itself, since the effect can be additive over time (temporal summation, with several messages received from the same cell in a short time) or over space (spatial summation, with several axons sending impulses at the same time). Inhibitory PSPs also have a cumulative effect, but the result of several of these would be to make it harder for the neuron to reach threshold and the development of an action potential. Alternatively, the messages coming into a neuron from several different presynaptic cells might be conflicting, some excitatory and others inhibitory. In this case, the postsynaptic cell would act like a computer and integrate the information from all presynaptic cells to determine whether the net result allows threshold to be reached. If threshold is achieved, the cell fires and a nerve impulse is generated. If threshold is not achieved, the cell does not fire, but it will be brought closer to the action potential by reduction of the voltage difference across the membrane. Since development of an action potential is an all-or-none response, no matter how the threshold is reached the same level of information passage will result. Behavior of an individual organism thus results from the actions of each separate neuron in determining the net balance of incoming information and determining whether an action potential is reached.

Neurotransmitters are the chemical messengers that act in the nervous system to excite or inhibit the postsynaptic neurons. At least four neurotransmitters have been studied in detail: acetylcholine, norepinephrine, dopamine, and serotonin. Other transmitter substances have also been examined, such as the amino acids glutamate, aspartate, gamma-aminobutyric acid (GABA), and glucine. From these studies it has been shown that the interpretation of the message lies within the postsynaptic neuron, since the same neurotransmitter may be either inhibitory or excitatory, depending on the tissues in which it is found.

Acetylcholine, for example, is found in both the brain and the peripheral nervous system. Since the peripheral nerves are more accessible to study, more is known about the activities of acetylcholine there than in the brain. Two types of cholinergic receptors (those for acetylcholine) are found in the peripheral nervous system, called muscarinic and nicotinic receptors. Acetylcholine has an excitatory effect on nicotinic receptors, as in causing the contraction of skeletal muscles, but an inhibitory effect on the muscarinic receptors, as in slowing the heartbeat. This neurotransmitter is also believed to cause excitation of tissues in the brain and in autonomic ganglia. In the cerebral cortex, acetylcholine is thought to be involved in cognitive processes, while in the hippocampus it appears to be linked to memory; in the amygdala, it seems to help control emotions.

Norepinephrine, dopamine, and serotonin are monoamines, neurotransmitters that act by means of a second messenger system to produce a postsynaptic response. In this system, cyclic adenosine monophosphate (cAMP) is produced within the cell when a neurotransmitter binds to its receptor, and the cAMP opens the ion channels that cause excitation or inhibition to be produced. This causes a longer-lasting effect on the postsynaptic neuron, and the neurotransmitters that utilize this system are apparently involved in long-term behaviors that include memory, emotion, and motivation. Like acetylcholine, norepinephrine is formed in both the brain and the peripheral nervous tissues, while dopamine and serotonin have been localized to brain tissues only. In the peripheral nervous system, norepinephrine interacts with two kinds of adrenergic receptors on muscle cells, the alpha and beta receptors. Alpha receptors are found on blood-vessel cells, where an excitatory effect results from binding norepinephrine. Beta receptors are seen in the lungs, heart, and intestines, tissues in which norepinephrine has different effects. Binding of the neurotransmitter to beta receptors in cardiac tissue causes excitation, while binding to lung and intestinal receptors inhibits their activities. It is still unclear how the same kind of beta receptor can have different responses in different tissues to the same chemical message.

In the brain, a diffuse system of neurons produces norepinephrine, so its effects are widespread, affecting emotion, learning, memory, and wakefulness. Dopamine is produced by cells found in the substantia nigra, the hypothalamus, and the ventral tegmental areas of the brain, where abnormal levels cause profound behavioral disorders. The related monoamine, serotonin, has distribution and behavioral effects similar to those of norepinephrine. In the upper regions of the brain, the presence of serotonin stimulates higher sensory states and sleep, while reduced levels are associated with severe depression. Since most of the effects of raised or lowered quantities of these mood-altering neurotransmitters seem to cause depression and psychoses, their study has been of great interest. Many of the drugs that have been found to elevate mood clinically act by enhancing or interfering with the action of these neurotransmitters. Through their control of excitation and inhibition of the neural impulse, neurotransmitters control an incredibly complex system of neural interconnections and neuroneffector cell interactions. If this system were under less strict control, behavioral chaos would result, as it does in certain psychiatric and psychological disorders. Applications of knowledge in this area of behavioral research may eventually lead to the ability to control such disorders chemically.

Context

Studies on the mechanisms of action of the neuron have been ongoing since the 1930's in giant axons of the squid nervous system. Discovered by J. Z. Young, these axons are so large that a single cell can be dissected out and examined in the laboratory. Much of what is known about the human nervous system's response to excitatory and inhibitory stimuli comes from pioneering work done on these marine mollusks. K. C. Cole and coworkers developed a voltage clamp system of electronic feedback to maintain a constant membrane potential at a chosen voltage level. The axons are penetrated by tiny electrodes and used to measure how electrical transmission occurs in different areas of the neuron across the cell membrane. A later development is the whole cell patch recording, used to examine a small area of the neuron's cell membrane with ion channels more or less intact. A classic series of papers published by Andrew Huxley and Alan Hodgkin in 1952 explained the regulation of electrical conductance along the neural membrane, including movement of ions across the sodium and potassium channels after excitatory stimulation. Huxley and Hodgkin received a

Nobel Prize in 1963 for their work on squid axons.

Another way that excitatory and inhibitory responses are studied is with the muscarinic and nicotinic cholinergic receptors, which are inhibited from working by the actions of the drugs muscarine (from poisonous mushrooms) and nicotine (from tobacco). The drugs mimic the action of acetylcholine on these different kinds of molecules on target tissues. Less is known about the effects of acetylcholine on brain tissues, but this area of research is getting widespread attention because of the evidence that the neurotransmitter appears to be related to the development of Alzheimer's disease. Acetylcholine deficiency in the nucleus basilis is a general finding at autopsy in patients with this disease of aging, which is accompanied by loss of memory and intellectual ability and by profound personality changes.

Behavioral disturbances, including depression and mania, are also caused by abnormally high or low concentrations of norepinephrine in the brain. Some of the drugs used to treat depression are able to do so by controlling the levels of norepinephrine and thus the stimulation of excitatory and inhibitory pathways in the brain. Dopamine is associated with Parkinson's disease, in which there is an abnormally low level in the substantia nigra of the brain, and the condition can be treated by increasing the amount of dopamine and by slowing its breakdown in this region. In addition, an abnormally high level of dopamine in other parts of the brain has been associated with causing schizophrenia, suggested by the fact that drugs which block the actions of dopamine also reduce the behavioral aberrations seen in this disease. Since brains of patients with these diseases are studied at autopsy and not during the actions that cause the behaviors, it is difficult to tell what actually occurs at the synapses and whether actions are attributable to inhibition or excitation of particular neurons.

Other transmitter substances include amino acids and neuropeptides, but less information has been gathered on these chemicals, and less is known about their activities in the nervous system and behavior. Glutamate and aspartate are amino acids that are thought to be the main excitatory chemicals in use in the brain, while GABA and glycine are inhibitory. GABA is thought to be the most widespread neurotransmitter in the brain, particularly in functions involving movement. Neuropeptides include endorphins, but the mechanisms by which they act are less well known. It is thought that certain cells are able to produce and release both a neurotransmitter such as dopamine as well as a neuropeptide, giving the nervous system more versatility and complexity in its decision-making capabilities. Perhaps both excitation and inhibition may be handled by the same cell at different times in its regulation of behavioral activities.

Bibliography

Carlson, Neil R. *Physiology of Behavior.* 3d ed. Boston: Allyn & Bacon, 1986. An excellent resource for the psychology student on the biological aspects of behavior. The second and third chapters cover communication within and between cells of the nervous system. Emphasis is on research methods in physiological psychology.

Kolb, Bryan, and Ian Q. Whishaw. *Fundamentals of Human Neuropsychology.* 2d ed. New York: W. H. Freeman, 1985. The second chapter of this undergraduate textbook covers the physiology of the nervous system, including the function of the synapse and its excitatory and inhibitory activities. References at the end of the chapter.

Levitan, Irwin B., and Leonard K. Kaczmarek. *The Neuron: Cell and Molecular Biology.* New York: Oxford University Press, 1991. Designed to incorporate neurophysiology into an undergraduate curriculum, this text is very thorough on the concepts of cellular and molecular function of the neuron. Several chapters are devoted to the generation of the action potential, ion channels, and other aspects of intercellular communication. Excellent coverage of research techniques used to study excitation and inhibition. Includes a large bibliography and many diagrams.

Ornstein, Robert Evan, and Richard F. Thompson. *The Amazing Brain.* Boston: Houghton Mifflin, 1984. An excellent book on the structure and function of the brain for the general reader. Chapter 3 covers neurons and how they work, including the activities at the synapse. Many pictures but no references.

Restak, Richard M. *The Mind.* Toronto: Bantam Books, 1988. Published to accompany the Public Broadcasting Service television series of the same title, this well-illustrated book discusses behavior as affected by neurotransmitters in chapters on aging, addiction, and depression. While not involved with inhibition and excitation processes per se, this book does address the behavioral effects of neurotransmitter action on the brain.

Schneider, Allen M., and Barry Tarshis. *An Introduction to Physiological Psychology.* 3d ed. New York: Random House, 1986. This undergraduate textbook gives a thorough coverage of the neural impulse and the synapse in chapters 7 and 8. Several diagrams aid the discussion of the impulse cycle. Neural transmission is tied to adaptive behavior.

Tortora, Gerard J., and Nicholas P. Anagnostakos. *Principles of Anatomy and Physiology.* 6th ed. New York: Harper & Row, 1990. A text for undergraduate college students, this book covers excitatory and inhibitory nerve impulses in Chapter 12 on nervous tissue.

Villee, Claude Alvin, et al. *Biology.* 2d ed. Philadelphia: Saunders College Publishing, 1989. Chapter 46 of this freshman college text covers neurons, including a lengthy discussion of transmission of a neural impulse. The effects of neurotransmitters in exciting and inhibiting depolarization of the membrane are also covered.

Jean S. Helgeson

Cross-References

The Autonomic Nervous System, 362; The Central and Peripheral Nervous Systems, 494; Endorphins, 973; Neurons, 1661; Neurotransmitters, 1673; Synaptic Transmission, 2514.

INSOMNIA

Type of psychology: Consciousness
Field of study: Sleep

Insomnia is a complaint of poor, insufficient, or nonrestorative sleep; it may be experienced for a few nights or for a lifetime. Daytime functioning is often affected. Insomnia may be caused by an underlying physiological or psychological disorder, or by substance abuse, but it can also occur independently of these factors.

Principal terms
CHRONOTHERAPY: the systematic adjustment of an individual's sleep-wake cycle to align it with the person's circadian rhythm
CIRCADIAN RHYTHM: a rhythm, such as the human sleep-wake cycle, that follows a roughly twenty-four-hour pattern
PERSISTENT PSYCHOPHYSIOLOGICAL INSOMNIA (PPI): behavioral insomnia that may be caused by sleep-incompatible behaviors (such as stimulant intake) or by chronic anxiety or stress
POLYSOMNOGRAPHY: a technique employed in a sleep laboratory to monitor the electrical activity, respiration, heart rate, and movements of the body during sleep
TRANSIENT INSOMNIA: a period of insomnia lasting no more than three weeks

Overview

Insomnia is defined as a person's perception that his or her sleep is inadequate or abnormal. It may include difficulty initiating sleep, short sleep time, frequent awakenings from sleep, and sleep that is nonrestorative. The daytime symptoms of insomnia include fatigue, excessive daytime sleepiness (EDS), mood changes, and impaired mental as well as physical functioning. Insomnia can be caused by conditions such as stress, anxiety, depression, substance abuse, medical illness, or other sleep disorders, but it may stand alone in some patients, separate from any known underlying disorders. The occurrence of insomnia increases with age; one study estimates that approximately 50 percent of persons between the ages of sixty-five and seventy-nine experience trouble sleeping.

The Association of Sleep Disorders Centers (ASDC) recognizes that there are two general types of insomnia. Classified on the basis of the duration of the period in which the person experiences insomnia, these two types are transient insomnia and primary insomnia. Transient insomnia is seen when persons have had a history of normal sleep but experience a period of insomnia which lasts less than three weeks; the patient returns to normal sleep after the insomnia period. The insomnia period is usually tied to a specific experience or situation, and it is believed that there are two common processes that are involved in transient insomnia. The first involves central nervous system arousal and any condition which may cause such arousal, whether it is psychological or environmental. There is no clear physiological disorder associated with this condition, but some research suggests that individuals who are likely to be aroused by stress may be more vulnerable to this type of insomnia than other people. Some sleep researchers indicate that emotional disturbance may play a role in up to 80 percent of transient insomnia cases.

A second process involved in transient insomnia results from persons having a sleep-wake schedule that is not aligned with their own circadian (twenty-four-hour) rhythms. Biological rhythms control many bodily functions, such as blood pressure, body temperature, hormonal activity, and the menstrual cycle, as well as the sleep-wake cycle. Insomnia can be caused by a sleep-wake cycle which is misaligned with the circadian rhythm, such as that which occurs when persons travel across many time zones or engage in shift work. Circadian rhythm disorders can last for periods of more than six months, in which case the problem would be considered chronic.

Primary insomnia is diagnosed when the patient's insomnia is not secondary to problems such as depression, anxiety, pain, or some other sleep disorder, and it lasts for a period longer than three weeks. Two types of primary insomnia are persistent psychophysiological insomnia (PPI) and insomnia complaints without objective findings. PPI is commonly known as learned, or behavioral, insomnia, as it is caused or maintained by maladaptive learning—that is, by the occurrence of sleep-incompatible behaviors, such as caffeine intake before bedtime. PPI is diagnosed when the patient demonstrates sleep difficulties which are verified in a sleep laboratory and are then traced to their behavioral causes. Figures vary, but approximately 15 percent of those patients diagnosed as having insomnia probably have PPI. One common feature of PPI is excessive worrying about sleep problems. Great efforts are made to fall asleep at night, which are unsuccessful and lead to increased sleep difficulty; however, the patient may fall asleep quite easily when not trying to fall asleep.

One theory concerning how persistent psychophysiological insomnia can develop suggests that some people have a poor sleep-wake system, which makes it more difficult for them to overcome sleep-inhibiting behavior. For example, it is possible for persons to become so anxious concerning their poor sleep that even the thought of their own bedroom causes them stress, which further increases their sleep problems and creates a cycle of increasingly difficult sleep. This cycle would eventually end for persons with normal sleep cycles, but it is much easier for these events to disrupt those who already have the poor sleep-wake cycle suggested by this theory. Although PPI may begin in response to stress or an emotional situation, it should again be noted that in PPI this type of learning or behavior plays the major role in the insomnia complaint.

Most insomnia patients will exhibit irregular sleep patterns or polysomnographic findings when tested in a sleep laboratory; however, there are those who complain of insomnia yet show no irregular sleep patterns. In the past, these people were viewed as having "pseudoinsomnia," and they were even thought of as possibly using poor sleep as an excuse for being lazy. Those who have insomnia complaints without objective findings do not show any physiological or psychological disorder and do not exhibit any sleep-incompatible behaviors, yet they commonly respond to treatment of their insomnia as would a verified insomnia patient.

One study found that insomnia was associated with anxiety, depression, psychiatric distress, and medical illness in 47 percent of the cases. The medical and psychiatric disorders, as well as the pharmacological substances, that can cause insomnia are too numerous to list here. James Walsh and Roger Sugerman note three theories which attempt to explain the occurrence of insomnia in psychiatric disorders that may prove helpful in understanding the process. The first suggests that insomnia results from a psychological disturbance that goes unresolved and leads to arousal that prevents sleep. The second states that neurochemical abnormalities may be the cause of insomnia in psychiatric disorders. The final theory asserts that affective (emotional) disorders may disturb the biological rhythms that control sleep.

Applications

The importance of a greater understanding of the mechanisms of sleep and insomnia can be appreciated by everyone. Anyone knows that when one feels truly sleepy, it is difficult to concentrate, perform simple tasks, or maintain patience with other people. If this situation were to last for a week, a month, or several years, one would at least wish for it to end and at most find it nearly intolerable.

A National Institute of Mental Health survey reported that approximately 17 percent of a nationally representative sample had experienced "serious" trouble sleeping in the year prior to the survey. Other research suggests that as many as 38 percent of adults in the United States experience trouble sleeping. It is likely that at some time in their lives, nearly everyone has experienced some difficulty sleeping.

The trouble that many people face when trying to get a good night's rest is not the only problem caused by insomnia. Insomnia may have drastic effects on behavior during the day. As stated previously, fatigue, excessive daytime sleepiness, mood changes, and impaired mental and physical functioning are all frequently caused by insomnia. Difficulties in the workplace, as well as increased health problems, are also associated with complaints of insomnia, though they are not necessarily caused by insomnia. Insomnia is not a problem that the individual faces only at night.

Diagnosis of insomnia depends on an accurate evaluation of the circumstances surrounding the complaint. The clinician must take many things into account when diagnosing each particular case, as insomnia may be the result of any number of factors in the patient's life. Questions concerning behavior should be asked to determine if the insomnia is caused by sleep-incompatible behaviors. Polysomnographic testing in a sleep laboratory may be necessary in order to determine which type of insomnia the patient has.

Once properly diagnosed, insomnia may be treated in a number of ways, all of which are dependent on the type of insomnia with which the clinician is faced. While the classical treatment for sleeping problems in the past has been "sleeping pills," and treatment of transient insomnia today may still involve small doses of a short-acting drug (such as benzodiazepines) when necessary, merely counseling or educating patients concerning situations that may increase their sleep problems is frequently found to be effective. If the transient insomnia is caused by disrupting sounds in the sleeping environment (such as snoring or traffic noise), devices that mask the noise may be used; earplugs and placing a fan in the room to mask the noise are two simple examples of this method. If the sleep disturbance is associated with misaligned circadian rhythms, the person's bedtime may be systematically adjusted toward either an earlier or later hour, depending on what time they presently go to sleep. Strict adherence to the adjusted sleep-wake schedule is then necessary in order for the individual to remain on a regular schedule. This method is referred to as chronotherapy.

Peter Hauri suggests that treatment of persistent psychophysiological insomnia will typically involve aspects of three "domains": sleep hygiene, behavioral treatment, and the use of hypnotics. Methods involving sleep hygiene focus on educating the patient concerning proper sleep habits. Hauri states that the goal is for the patient to avoid all thoughts that may stimulate or arouse the patient. This is done by focusing on or engaging in monotonous or nonstimulating behaviors at bedtime such as reading or listening to pleasant music.

Behavioral methods include relaxation therapy, limiting sleep time to a few hours per night until the patient is able to use the time in bed as "true" sleeping time, and using "stimulus control" therapy. This method requires the patient to get out of bed whenever she or he is not able to sleep. The process is aimed at reducing the association between the bedroom and the frustration with trying to go to sleep. Finally, the use of hypnotic medications is indicated in patients who have such a need for sleep that they "try too hard" and thus become aroused by their efforts. As with transient insomnia, a small dose of a short-acting drug is suggested in order to break this cycle of frustration. The treatment for patients who exhibit no objective polysomnographic findings is similar to that for patients with any other type of insomnia. Such patients also tend to respond to behavioral, educational, and pharmacological methods.

Context

The discovery of the methods used to monitor electrical activity in the human brain during the late 1920's essentially ushered in the modern era of sleep research. With this development, sleep stages were discovered, which eventually led to a greater understanding of what takes place in both normal and abnormal sleep.

A. Michael Anch, Carl Browman, Merrill Mitler, and James Walsh write in *Sleep: A Scientific Perspective* (1988) that most insomnia research prior to 1980 treated insomniacs as one group, with little attention paid to differences such as duration or causal factors in the subject's insomnia. While this limits the ability to generalize the earlier findings, these authors concede that the inclusion of different types of insomnia in studies eventually came to increase knowledge of the psychology of sleep and insomnia.

With regard to the treatment of insomnia, much has been learned that allows doctors and psychologists to treat the different types of this disorder more effectively. The myth of the "cure-all" sleeping pill has been replaced with a more sophisticated approach, which includes educational and behavioral practices. Medications are still used, but treatment options have increased so that clinicians are not as limited as they once were.

As the study of sleep disorders has developed in terms of scientific sophistication, researchers have been able to learn the importance that sleep holds in day-to-day functioning. They have also discovered how detrimental sleep loss or disruption of the sleep-wake cycle can be. Aiding in the discoveries have been scientific developments in neurobiology, behavioral medicine, physiology, and psychiatry that allow analysis of the mechanisms in normal and abnormal sleep. It is hoped that as scientists gain a further understanding of insomnia through research, they will also understand, more generally, the true purpose of sleep.

Bibliography

Anch, A. Michael, Carl P. Browman, Merrill M. Mitler, and James K. Walsh. *Sleep: A Scientific Perspective*. Englewood Cliffs, N.J.: Prentice-Hall, 1988. A comprehensive work on the field of sleep disorders that also provides a concise history of the science. Chapter 9 covers insomnia, but the entire book is noteworthy for its broad coverage of historical as well as modern research and treatment of sleep and its disorders. A very helpful work for those interested in learning about any aspect of sleep.

Dement, William C. *Some Must Watch While Some Must Sleep*. San Francisco: W. H. Freeman, 1974. A book by a scientist who many consider to be the leading authority in the field of sleep studies. Easily readable by high school or college students. Very informative; provides an excellent starting point for further study.

Kryger, Meir H., Thomas Roth, and William C. Dement, eds. *Principles and Practice of Sleep Medicine*. Philadelphia: W. B. Saunders, 1989. An extremely thorough collection of articles written by many of the leaders in sleep research and treatment. It is an advanced work to some extent, but is written in a style that allows the novice reader to understand many technical concepts with little difficulty. Section 4 (chapters 46-52) deals exclusively with insomnia and includes further information on many subclassifications of insomnia as well as on the medical and psychiatric illnesses commonly associated with insomnia.

Mendelson, W. B. *Human Sleep: Research and Clinical Care*. New York: Plenum Medical Book Company, 1987. Provides an overview of research and treatment practices for a number of sleep disorders. Recommended for the college student, but may be understood by those having a basic knowledge of sleep.

Nicholson, Anthony N., and John Marks. *Insomnia: A Guide for Medical Practitioners*. Boston: MTP Press, 1983. Though the title may sound imposing to those who are new to the study of insomnia, this book is quite easily understood by those with a limited knowledge of sleep disorders. The entire work is devoted to insomnia, and it provides information on diagnosis and treatment of various types.

Alan K. Gibson

Cross-References

INSTINCT THEORY

Type of psychology: Motivation
Fields of study: Biological influences on learning; motivation theory

Until behaviorism, which rejected instincts, became the dominant theoretical model for psychology during the early decades of the twentieth century, instinct theory was often used to explain both animal and human motivation. As behaviorism faded, aspects of instinct theory returned to psychology—modernized, but still recognizable as parts of the oldest theory of motivation.

Principal terms
BEHAVIORISM: a school of psychology that had a commanding influence on American psychology from the 1920's to the 1950's; it dictated that scientific psychology could work only with directly measurable factors
INSTINCT: an inherited, unlearned, complex sequence of behaviors, uniform in their expression and universal in a species
MOTIVATION: an inferred inner force that instigates, directs, and sustains behavior, as opposed to the "outside" environmental forces that influence actions
REFLEX: an inherited simple response of one part of the body to a specific stimulus, made without thought—for example, closing the eye when a flying insect hits the eyeball
SCIENTIFIC METHOD: an approach to gaining knowledge that involves proposing a hypothesis, rejecting or accepting it on the basis of evidence gathered, and sharing what was learned with others
TROPISM: an inherited, fairly complex behavior of an entire organism—for example, a moth's being attracted to light

Overview

When instinct theory was incorporated into the new scientific psychology of the late nineteenth century, it was already centuries old. In its earliest form, instinct theory specified that a creature's essential nature was already established at birth and that its actions would largely be directed by that nature. A modern restatement of this notion would be that creatures are already programmed, as computers are, at birth and that they must operate according to their programs. Charles Darwin's theory of evolution through natural selection, first published in 1859, led to great controversy in the late nineteenth and early twentieth centuries. It also fostered speculation that, if humans were evolved from earlier forms and were therefore more closely related to other animals than had once been believed, humans might have instincts— inherited behaviors—as other animals were observed to have. William McDougall was one of the main early instinct theorists; he suggested a list of human instincts in

1908 that included such varied behaviors as repulsion, curiosity, self-abasement, and gregariousness. Many researchers came up with their own lists of human instincts; by the 1920's, more than two thousand had been suggested.

A computer program can be printed out and studied, but an instinct in the original sense cannot so easily be made explicit. At best, it can be inferred from the behavior of an animal or person after other explanations for that behavior have been discounted. At worst, it is simply assumed from observing behavior. That a person has, for example, an instinct of argumentativeness could be assumed from the person's arguing; arguing is then "explained" by declaring that it comes from an instinct of argumentativeness. Such circular reasoning is unacceptable in scientific analyses, but it is very common in some early scientific (and many modern, popular) discussions of instinct.

As is often the case with ideas that have long been believed by both scientists and the general public, instinct theory has separated into several theories. The earliest form, mentioned above, was accepted by Aristotle, the ancient Greek philosopher/scientist. He wrote in his *Politics* that "a social instinct is implanted in all men by nature" and stated that "a man would be thought a coward if he had no more courage than a courageous woman, and a woman would be thought loquacious if she imposed no more restraint on her conversation than the good man." The first comment declares an inherent quality of people; the second, inherent qualities of men and women. Very likely, Aristotle's beliefs were based on careful observation of people around him—a good beginning, but not a sufficient basis for making factual comments about people in general.

Aristotle's views were those of a scientist of his day. Centuries later, a scientist would not hold such views, but a layperson very well might. Over the many centuries since Aristotle expressed his views on instinct theory, "popular" versions of it have been more influential than the cautious versions offered by later scientists.

Modern science reaches conclusions based, to the greatest extent possible, on evidence gathered and interpreted along lines suggested by theories. Traditional instinct theory is especially weak in suggesting such lines; usually it put early psychologists in the position of trying to support the idea that instinct had caused a behavior by demonstrating that nothing else had caused it. Rather than supporting one possibility, they were attempting to deny dozens of others. Even worse, they were forcing thought into an "either-or" pattern rather than allowing for the possibility that a behavior may be based on inherited influences interacting with learned ones.

For example, to try to evaluate the possibility that people are instinctively afraid of snakes, one could begin by finding a number of people afraid of snakes, followed by an attempt to discount all the ways in which those individuals might have learned their fear—that they had never been harmed by a snake, never been startled, never been told that snakes are dangerous, and so on. The task is all but impossible, almost guaranteeing that a researcher will conclude that there are several ways that the fear could have been learned, so there is no need for an instinct explanation. The fact that people who fear snakes can learn not to fear them can be offered as further evidence that they had learned their original fear—not a particularly compelling argument, but a good enough approach for a researcher who wants to discount instinct.

When behaviorism became the predominant theoretical stance of psychology in the 1920's, the problems with instinct as an explanation of motivation were "resolved" simply by sidestepping them. Instincts were discarded as unscientific, and other concepts—such as needs, drives, and motives—were substituted for them. Psychology's dropping the term instinct from its jargon did not, either for lower animals or for people, eliminate the behaviors it had originally labeled; dropping the term did, however, separate even further the popular views of instinct from the scientific ones.

Applications

Instinct theory's purpose in psychology's infancy was the same as it had once been in the distant past: to explain motivation of a variety of species, from the simplest creatures up through people. Unfortunately, it had also served other purposes in the past, purposes which often proved unwelcome to early behavioral scientists. To declare people superior to other animals, or men superior to women, or almost any target group better or worse than another was not a goal of psychology.

Worse than the heritage of centuries of misuse of the concept of instinct, however, was the accumulation of evidence that instincts (as originally defined, as completely unlearned behavior) were limited to simple creatures and were virtually nonexistent in people. Psychology and related sciences virtually eliminated instinct as a motivational concept for decades, yet they could not avoid bringing back similar notions. The term "instinct" was gone, but what it tried to explain was not. For example, social psychologists, working in the 1940's to find alternatives to the belief that aggression is instinctive in humans, proposed that frustration (goal blocking) is a major cause. When pressed to explain why frustration led to aggression, many indicated that this is simply part of human nature. Some years later, it was demonstrated that the presence of some sort of weapon during a frustrating experience enhanced the likelihood of aggression, apparently through a "triggering effect." Instinct as a concept was not invoked, but these ideas came very close.

Even closer was the work of another group of scientists, ethologists, in their explanations of some animal behaviors. Evaluating what might be thought a good example of instinct in its earliest definition, a duckling following its mother, they demonstrated that experience with a moving, quacking object is necessary. In other words, learning (but learning limited to a very brief period in the duckling's development) led to the behavior. Many other seemingly strong examples of instinct were demonstrated to be a consequence of some inner predisposition interacting with environmental circumstances. A new, useful rethinking of the ancient instinct concept had begun.

A 1961 article by Keller and Marian Breland suggested that instinct should still be a part of psychology, despite its period of disgrace. In training performing animals, they witnessed a phenomenon they termed "instinctive drift." (It is interesting to note that although other terms, such as "species-specific behavior," were at that time preferred to "instinct," the Brelands stated their preference for the original label.) Instinctive drift refers to the tendency of a creature's trained behavior to move in the direction of inherited predispositions.

The Brelands tried to teach pigs to place coins in a piggybank; they found that although the pigs could easily be taught to pick up coins and run toward the bank, they could not be stopped from repeatedly dropping and rooting at them. Raccoons could be taught to drop coins in a container, but could not be stopped from "dipping" the coins in and rubbing them together, a drift toward the instinctive washing of food. Several other species presented similar problems to their would-be trainers, all related to what the Brelands willingly called instinct.

Preparedness is another example of an instinct/learning relationship. Through conditioning, any creature can be taught to associate some previously neutral stimuli with a behavior. Dogs in Ivan Pavlov's laboratory at the beginning of the twentieth century readily learned to salivate at the sound of a bell, a signal that food would appear immediately. While some stimuli can easily serve as signals for a particular species, others cannot. It seems clear that they are prepared by nature for some sorts of learning but not others. Rats can readily be trained to press a lever (a bar in a Skinner box) to obtain food, and pigeons can readily be trained to peck at something to do so, but there are some behaviors that they simply cannot learn to serve that purpose.

Conditioned taste aversion is yet another example of an instinctive influence that has been well documented by modern psychology. In people and other animals, nausea following the taste of food very consistently leads to that taste's becoming aversive. The taste/nausea combination is specific; electric shock following a taste does not cause the taste to become aversive, nor does a visual stimulus followed by nausea cause the sight to become aversive. Researchers theorize that the ability to learn to detect and avoid tainted food has survival value, so it has become instinctive.

Context

In popular use, belief in instincts has confused and hurt people more than it has enlightened or helped them. Instinct theory often imposes a rigid either-or form on people's thinking about human motivation. That is, people are encouraged by the notion of instinct to wonder if some behavior—aggression, for example—is either inherent in people or learned from experience.

Once one's thoughts are cast into such a mold, one is less likely to consider the strong likelihood that a behavior has multiple bases, which may be different from one person to the next. Instead of looking for the many possible reasons for human aggression—some related to inherent qualities and some related to learned qualities—one looks for a single cause. Often, intently focusing on one possibility to the exclusion of all others blinds people to the very fact that they are doing so. Searching for "the" answer, they fail to recognize that their very method of searching has locked their thinking onto a counterproductive track.

Instinct theory has been invoked to grant people special status, above that of other animals. Generally, this argument states that people can reason and rationally control their actions, while lower animals are guided solely by instincts. At best, this argument has been used to claim that people are especially loved by their God. At worst, the idea that lower animals are supposedly guided only by instinct was used by René Descartes to claim that animals are essentially automata, incapable of actually feeling pain, and that therefore they could be vivisected without anesthesia.

Instinct theory has also been used to support the claim that some people are more worthy than other people. Those with fewer "base instincts," or even those who by their rationality have overcome them, are supposedly superior. Acceptance of such nonsense has led to very real errors of judgment and considerable human suffering. For example, over many centuries, across much of the world, it was believed that women, simply by virtue of being female, were not capable of sufficiently clear thinking to justify providing them with a formal education, allowing them to own property, or letting them hold elected office or vote. Anthropologist Margaret Mead, in her 1942 book *And Keep Your Powder Dry: An Anthropologist Looks at America*, reports reversal of the foolish claim that women inherently lack some important quality. Young women in her classes, when told the then-prevailing view that people had no instincts and therefore that they had no maternal instinct, according to Mead, became very upset, believing that they lacked something essential. Many minority racial or ethnic groups have suffered in similar fashion from claims that, by their unalterable nature, they are incapable of behaving at levels comparable to those in the majority.

Instinct theory has been used to suggest the absolute inevitability of many undesirable behaviors, sometimes as a way of excusing them. The ideas that philandering is part of a man's nature or that gossiping is part of a woman's are patently foolish uses of the concept of instinct.

Bibliography

Birney, Robert Charles, and Richard C. Teevan. *Instinct: An Enduring Problem in Psychology.* Princeton, N.J.: Van Nostrand, 1961. A collection of readings intended for college students. Contains fourteen articles, ranging from William James's 1887 discussion of instinct to Frank Beach's 1955 "The Descent of Instinct," in which Beach traces the idea of instinct from the time of the ancient Greeks up to the 1950's and concludes that "the instinct concept has survived in almost complete absence of empirical validation."

Breland, Keller, and Marian Breland. "The Misbehavior of Organisms." *American Psychologist* 16 (November, 1961): 681-684. In the process of training performing animals, the Brelands were forced to contend with inherited behaviors of their pupils. This article alerted a generation of psychologists to the possibility that instinct had been inappropriately eliminated from their thinking. The writing is clear and amusing, and the article should be fairly easy to locate; most college and university libraries will have the journal.

Cofer, Charles Norval, and M. H. Appley. *Motivation: Theory and Research.* New York: John Wiley & Sons, 1964. Long regarded as a classic on the topic of motivation, this book includes (in chapter 2, "Motivation in Historical Perspective") thirty-two pages of material that traces instinct through the centuries. Chapter 3, "The Concept of Instinct: Ethological Position," discusses ways the once discredited concept was returning to psychology in the early 1960's.

Hilgard, Ernest Ropiequet. *Psychology in America: A Historical Survey.* San Diego: Harcourt Brace Jovanovich, 1987. The material Hilgard covers is often complex, but his clear organization and writing make it accessible to most readers. Material related to instinct in several chapters (for example, those on motivation, comparative psychology, and social psychology) can help a reader gain further background on instinct's place in psychology.

Watson, John Broadus. *Behaviorism.* Rev. ed. Chicago: University of Chicago Press, 1930. The fifth chapter of Watson's popular presentation of the new psychology he was sponsoring ("Are There Any Human Instincts?") nicely illustrates how behaviorism handled instinct. This chapter contains Watson's famous declaration, "Give me a dozen healthy infants, well-formed, and my own specified world to bring them up in and I'll guarantee to take any one at random and train him to become any type of specialist I might select. . . ." Watson's writing is still charming, but his position is today mainly a curiosity.

Weiten, Wayne. *Psychology: Themes and Variations.* 2d ed. Pacific Grove, Calif.: Brooks/Cole, 1991. Introductory psychology texts all have some coverage of instinct's return to psychology and, more important, describe how several other concepts have been introduced to deal with topics with which instinct was once inappropriately linked. Weiten's text is one of the best: easy and interesting to read, yet strong in its coverage of scientific psychology.

Harry A. Tiemann, Jr.

Cross-References

Aggression: Definitions and Theoretical Explanations, 162; Behaviorism: An Overview, 401; Defense Reactions: Species-Specific, 775; Drive Theory, 843; Ethology, 992; Imprinting and Learning, 1262; Preparedness and Learning, 1866; Taste Aversion and Learning Theory, 2520.

INSTRUMENTAL CONDITIONING: ACQUISITION AND EXTINCTION

Type of psychology: Learning
Field of study: Instrumental conditioning

Unlike Pavlovian conditioning, which deals with reflexive behaviors, instrumental conditioning deals with learned behaviors that are nonreflexive. The consequences of responding and how those consequences are presented to the organism determine how these behaviors are learned and maintained. Instrumental conditioning techniques have been successfully applied to a wide variety of areas, including classroom learning and treatment of mental disorders.

Principal terms
EXTINCTION: the removal of reinforcement and the subsequent ceasing of the instrumental response
INSTRUMENTAL CONDITIONING: a type of conditioning in which the organism is the agent or instrument in causing behavior to occur; differs from Pavlovian conditioning, in which the organism plays a passive role
LAW OF EFFECT: Thorndike's basic law of instrumental conditioning, which holds that responses followed by certain events will be either more or less likely to recur
OPERANT: the basic response unit in instrumental conditioning; a response which, when emitted, operates upon its environment and is instrumental in providing some consequences
PUNISHER: a possible consequence of emitting a response which reduces the likelihood of repeating the response and can be positive or negative
REINFORCER: a possible consequence of emitting a response which increases the likelihood of repeating the response and can be positive or negative
SHAPING: the acquiring of instrumental behavior in small steps or increments by reinforcing successively closer approximations to the desired final behavior
SKINNER BOX: the most commonly used apparatus for studying instrumental conditioning; manipulation of a lever (for rats, monkeys, or humans) or an illuminated disk (for pigeons) produces consequences

Overview

Instrumental, or operant, conditioning is involved with the acquisition and maintenance of responses that, unlike the responses of Pavlovian conditioning, are nonreflexive. Instrumental responses appear to be flexible, intelligent, complex, farsighted, and controlled by their consequences. This is in marked contrast to the rigid, simple, and automatic appearance of Pavlovian responses, which are elicited by preceding (rather than consequent) stimuli. Although instrumental conditioning has been used since ancient times, its identification and discovery are credited to the psychologist Edward L. Thorndike.

At the end of the nineteenth century, Thorndike confined hungry cats in a puzzle box and placed food outside the box. A cat could get to the food by correctly manipulating a latch inside the box, which opened the door. Thorndike showed that with repeated trials, the time it took the cat to press the latch decreased. Thus, through repeated trials, the cat acquired a new behavior and became increasingly efficient at performing it. From these experiments, Thorndike formulated his law of effect in 1911. Responses which are followed by a particular consequence become connected to the situations, so that when the situation recurs, the response is more or less likely to recur. If the response is more likely to recur, the consequence is called a reinforcer. If it is less likely to recur, the consequence is called a punisher. When a cat pressed the latch, it obtained food. Pressing the latch became associated with the box and with obtaining food. The cat was more likely to press the latch and press it quickly upon being reintroduced to the box. (Food is thus a reinforcer.) If the cat had instead received an electric shock, it would likely have ceased responding. (Electric shock would be a punisher.)

As Thorndike so ably demonstrated with his puzzle box experiments and law of effect, the hallmark of instrumental conditioning is that the response must first occur before the consequence can be given and eventually exert control over the behavior. That is, a contingency or association between the behavior and what follows must be developed. If the response is simple, as with Thorndike's puzzle box, the organism can usually acquire the correct response through trial and error without assistance. If the response is more complex, however, or if rapid acquisition of a simple response is desired, then assistance will be required. If the organism is a human, verbal instruction or modeling the correct behavior may be sufficient.

If the organism is not human, or if the behavior cannot be adequately described verbally or modeled, shaping will have to be used. With this procedure, the desired behavior is acquired by successively reinforcing small steps, or increments, of behavior which increasingly approximate the final behavior. The size of the steps is small enough to ensure a smooth transition from one response to the next. For example, if the task were to cause a rat to press on a bar to receive food in a Skinner box, the researcher could shape the rat by first reinforcing responses that are oriented toward the bar, then reinforcing movements toward the bar, then reinforcing the placing of the rat's paws on the bar, and finally reinforcing the pressing of the bar.

Shaping is made possible by the processes of differential reinforcement and induction. By differentially reinforcing the desired response and not reinforcing incorrect responses, the researcher causes the desired response to become more frequent. As the correct response becomes more frequent, similar responses which have not previously occurred also become more probable. These new responses are natural variations of the correct response, and some of these responses will be even closer approximations of the desired behaviors. This process is called induction. These new responses can then be differentially reinforced until the final desired behavior is shaped.

Reinforcement is critical to the successful acquisition, and then maintenance, of instrumental behavior. If reinforcement is withdrawn, the behavior will undergo extinction; that is, it will cease to occur. All instrumental behavior will extinguish if it is not reinforced. The important question then becomes how long it takes the behavior to extinguish. The most important factor determining the course of extinction is the schedule of reinforcement that is used to maintain the behavior. Each correct response can be either reinforced or not reinforced every single time it occurs during maintenance. It is well established that behavior that is only intermittently or partially reinforced is much more resistant to extinction than behavior that is reinforced every time. A good example of this partial-reinforcement extinction effect is provided in a study done by Donald J. Lewis. Five groups of college students were permitted to play a slot machine. Depending upon the group, the slot machine was rigged to pay off on either one, two, four, six, or all eight (continuous reinforcement) of the initial plays. The machine then stopped paying off altogether (extinction). Lewis found that the one-, two-, four-, and six-payoff groups all continued to pull the handle more often and longer than did the eight-payoff group before they finally stopped responding. Furthermore, resistance to extinction was inversely related to the number of payoffs; that is, the one-payoff group took longest to extinguish and made the most pulls, and the eight-payoff group made the least.

During the acquisition of instrumental behaviors, each correct response should be reinforced so that correct behavior will not have a chance to extinguish. Once the behavior is acquired, however, not every occurrence of the correct response need be reinforced. Fewer reinforcers will be required, and the behavior will be stronger.

Applications

Since instrumental (operant) conditioning stresses the control of behavior by the consequences produced by that behavior, it provides a powerful tool for teaching new behaviors.

Animal trainers rely on it to teach their animals new tricks. For example, Gunther Gebel-Williams, the legendary animal trainer with the Ringling Bros. and Barnum & Bailey Circus, used shaping with his lions and tigers. Unlike rats or pigeons, lions and tigers must begin learning their routines when they are young, around fifteen months old ("You can't take a grown-up lion and say, 'Come on, get on the horse,' " Gebel-Williams wryly observed). In one instance, lion cubs learn tiny bits of behavior that might later be integrated into a routine. For example, the cubs are urged to run across the center ring, jump onto a small platform, and then jump onto a dummy horse that a circus hand is pulling about the ring. When each phase is performed correctly, the cub receives meat, petting, and praise. Mild aversive stimuli are sometimes used, too. A cub learns to stand on its hind legs when meat is held above its head. Additionally, short, sharp taps from a stick help the cub assume the right position. Once this is done, however, the aversive stimulus ceases (a behavior is strengthened through removal of a consequence, or negative reinforcer), and the cub receives affection and food (a behavior is strengthened through presentation of a consequence or positive reinforcer).

Mild aversive stimulation can also be useful for teaching tricks to killer whales. Since killer whales have no natural enemies, force cannot be used to get them to do a trick. Rather, food and affection are used as the primary reinforcers. The whales, not their trainers, design the activities that are eventually performed. The routines consist of movements that are natural to the whale. Each day, the trainer gets in the water and plays with the whale. When the trainer sees a behavior that could be part of the routine, the behavior is reinforced. Killer whales are highly intelligent, so they readily repeat the behavior. If the whale performs incorrect responses during acquisition, however, affection is withheld; the trainer simply walks away (negative punishment, in which a behavior is suppressed through removal of a consequence). The whale must ask the trainer to come back. If the whale performs properly, then affection is restored (positive reinforcement). Through this method, the whale quickly picks up the appropriate routine.

Instrumental conditioning procedures have also been used extensively to facilitate new behaviors in individuals with severe mental disorders. Theodore Allyon and Nathan Azrin provided schizophrenic and mentally disordered hospital patients with candy, cigarettes, or extra coffee or milk if they picked up a knife, fork, or spoon while passing by the service counter. The reward procedure had no noticeable effect; the frequency of the desired behavior remained very low. Then, as the patients passed in line, the attendant verbally instructed them to "please pick up your knife, fork, and spoon, and you have a choice of extra milk, coffee, cigarettes, or candy." The addition of these verbal instructions produced an immediate increase in the desired behavior. It is likely that picking up the silverware could have been shaped in successive approximations without the verbal instructions; however, this experiment shows how effective verbal instructions can sometimes be with humans. The verbal instructions act as a controlling stimulus to call attention to the desired behavior.

As a last example, instrumental procedures have been used in classrooms to help promote and maintain discipline. David R. Adamson has offered a number of tips for both correcting misbehaviors and promoting good behaviors. Simple solutions should be sought. If students return late from recess, the teacher should time exactly how late the last person arrives and deduct that amount of time (negative punishment) from the whole class's next recess. Tighter rules should be imposed. The teacher should list the consequences for breaking rules and follow through consistently from the first moment if those rules are broken.

Good behavior should be rewarded. This helps disruptive students identify appropriate behaviors. The teacher should write out behavior contracts listing the desired instrumental behavior (for example, raising one's hand before talking), how often the behavior must occur (for example, 100 percent of the time), the positive reinforcers the student will receive for behaving appropriately (for example, a ten-minute recess from class each day), and the length of the contract (for example, one week or less). The teacher should use unexpected reinforcers occasionally when the students behave appropriately. For example, a special film can be shown. The teacher should be certain that the students know the reinforcer is a direct result of their good behavior.

Context

Learning became a central part of American psychology with the development of Pavlovian conditioning and Watsonian behaviorism in the late nineteenth and early twentieth centuries. Interest focused on how behavior was modified in response to ever-changing conditions in an organism's environment. John B. Watson adopted Pavlovian conditioning as his model of learning. Watson discarded instincts and other inherited behaviors, leaving as the remaining unit of unlearned behavior the unconditioned reflex (UR), which was elicited by the unconditioned stimulus (US). The unit of habit or learning was the conditioned reflex (CR). Human behavior was the product of conditioning of URs. Animals and people were born with a limited number of US-UR relationships. By conditioning and association of USs with conditioned stimuli (CSs), these CSs produced the more complex, learned behaviors of the adult. Watson ignored the implications of Thorndike's instrumental conditioning as a model for a second type of learning.

In two important articles published in 1935 and 1937, however, B. F. Skinner convincingly argued that Thorndike's law of effect described most of the behavior of organisms. Skinner further demonstrated the powerful effect of the consequences rather than antecedents of behavior in modifying and strengthening behavior by forming a contingency, or connection, between the response and its consequence. Skinner referred to this behavior as produced by operant conditioning (a term he preferred to instrumental conditioning), which, he argued, should be the concern of psychologists; Pavlovian conditioning should be the concern of physiologists.

In the beginning of his 1979 book, *The Road Less Traveled*, M. Scott Peck states, "Life is difficult. This is a great truth, one of the greatest truths. . . . Life is a series of problems." The solutions for which people strive to resolve life's problems describe how well they fit or match with their world, how able they are to change or modify their behavior successfully in response to a changing environment, and how well they control their environment in order to enhance their lives.

Instrumental conditioning is a better model than Pavlovian conditioning for explaining how most changes in behavior occur. This is not to deny the importance of Pavlovian conditioning. Nevertheless, most of people's adaptations to their changing world require the acquisition of behaviors that are spontaneous, modifiable, intelligent, goal-oriented, and farsighted, rather than rigidly controlled or elicited by definite external events. It is the instrumental conditioning model that captures these characteristics.

Bibliography

Baldwin, John D., and Janice I. Baldwin. *Behavior Principles in Everyday Life.* Englewood Cliffs, N.J.: Prentice-Hall, 1981. A very readable introductory text which presents a lucid discussion of instrumental/operant conditioning, as well as numerous examples of it in everyday life.

Ferster, Charles B., and Stuart A. Culbertson. *Behavior Principles.* 3d ed. Englewood Cliffs, N.J.: Prentice-Hall, 1982. Similar in orientation to the Baldwin and Baldwin book cited above, but more advanced in its discussion of instrumental/operant conditioning and presentation of examples.

Ormrod, Jeanne E. *Human Learning: Principles, Theories, and Educational Applications.* Columbus, Ohio: Charles E. Merrill, 1990. Another very enjoyable and readable presentation of instrumental/operant conditioning, with specific applications to the classroom.

Skinner, B. F. *Cumulative Record: A Selection of Papers.* 3d ed. New York: Appleton-Century-Crofts, 1972. A varied selection of important papers on instrumental/operant conditioning by the most important and influential psychologist in this area. Presents both theoretical and applied papers.

_____. *Science and Human Behavior.* New York: Macmillan, 1953. A thoughtful and thought-provoking discussion of instrumental/operant conditioning from the perspective of its usefulness in improving life on the individual and societal levels.

Ullman, Leonard P., and Leonard Krasner. *Case Studies in Behavior Modification.* New York: Holt, Rinehart and Winston, 1965. A thorough treatment of the application of instrumental/operant conditioning to the understanding and treatment of mental disorders.

Laurence Miller

Cross-References

Behavioral Family Therapy, 394; Behaviorism: An Overview, 401; Operant Conditioning Therapies, 1714; Pavlovian Conditioning: Acquisition, Extinction, and Inhibition, 1757; Punishment, 2016; Radical Behaviorism: B. F. Skinner, 2045; Reinforcement Schedules, 2077; Reinforcers and Reinforcement, 2084; Rule-Governed Behavior, 2115.

INTEGRITY: ERIKSON

Type of psychology: Developmental psychology
Fields of study: Adulthood; aging

"Integrity," as used by Erik Erikson, refers to a sense of wholeness and complete-ness. According to Erikson, the task of the last stage of development is to achieve integrity and overcome the despair that can be associated with the review of one's life. The attainment of wisdom is the final outcome of the struggle between integrity and despair and can be achieved through life review.

Principal terms
>DESPAIR: the feeling that life has been full of too many regrets and too many lost opportunities
>ID: the part of the mind containing powerful basic drives, such as the need to express anger
>IDENTITY: a distinctive personality established over time, based on the foundation laid in childhood and the expectations associated with reaching adulthood
>INTEGRITY: the need to integrate life events into a complete picture of the self that begins around the age of seventy and ends at death
>LIFE REVIEW: the process of reviewing one's life to achieve a better understanding of its meaning
>REMINISCENCE: the process of thinking or talking about the past
>SUPEREGO: the collection of moral behaviors learned from parents, teachers, and other authority figures that affect the decisions people make
>UNCONSCIOUS MOTIVES: the forces of which individuals are usually unaware, that underlie behavior; they have been said to result from the desires of the id and/or the superego
>WISDOM: as defined by Erikson, an informed and detached concern for life in the face of death

Overview

The concept of integrity is a difficult one to define. For most people, it means honesty and good character. According to Erik Erikson, in his work *Childhood and Society* (1950), integrity means a sense of wholeness and completeness. Individuals who fail to find integrity in their lives may be left with feelings of despair and worthlessness. The conflict between integrity and despair occurs, according to Erikson, in the final stage of development. Individuals who are approaching the last part of their lives have already gone through seven stages of development and have resolved or have failed to resolve issues such as trust, identity, and intimacy. The final stage of development is called the integrity-versus-despair stage. It begins at about age seventy and lasts for the rest of an individual's life.

This last stage of life is characterized by a need to review one's life and make sense out of the events that have occurred in earlier stages of growth. Individuals looking back over their lives may need to make peace with their past, accept some events as unchangeable, acknowledge their mistakes, and seek reconciliation with significant others in their lives. In the last stage, unlike earlier stages in which the focus of an individual's life is on others, individuals turn inward. More time is spent alone, reviewing the past, looking for themes that tie a person's life together, and finding ways to make sense of all the good and bad things that have occurred.

The end result of the struggle toward integrity is wisdom. Older persons who have looked back over their lives, acknowledged their failings, and made peace with their past have a depth of understanding that others can only achieve when they too approach the end of their lives. A sense of dignity is achieved and maintained despite the physical and sometimes financial problems that often accompany the aging process. The wisdom attained during this period of development is often shared with the next generation, adding even more worth and completeness to a person's life.

Not everyone is able to look back over his or her life and put things together to create the wholeness that characterizes the wise and dignified individual. Those who have made mistakes that they have been unable to forget or for which they have been unable to make amends are likely to experience feelings of despair. Those who dwell on missed opportunities may experience a sense of worthlessness. Those who are unable to reconcile broken relationships may experience feelings of anxiety and restlessness. There may be a sense that important activities have been left undone and that there is no time left to complete them. Physical deterioration and social isolation may add to the feelings of despair and increase the desire to hurry the arrival of death. The increase in depression and suicide rates that accompanies the aging process attests the fact that not all older individuals resolve the integrity-versus-despair conflict successfully.

It might be tempting to conclude that a person who appears to have the wisdom associated with successful resolution of the final stage of development has no self-doubt or uncertainty; wisdom, however, is not gained without moments of despair. The dynamic interplay between finding meaning in one's life and grieving over unfulfilled goals is at the center of wisdom. Learning to acknowledge the moments of despair and finding ways to reconcile relationships and overcome or accept the mistakes in one's life serve as the foundation for the integrity that is developed. Often the deepest moments of despair can make individuals aware of the need to come to terms with the past in order to make the most of the time they have left.

Clearly, not every individual reaches the final stage of development. Some are cut short by untimely death; others suffer from diseases that render them incapable of remembering their past. Still others fail to acknowledge that they are going to die and remain in earlier stages of development until they are too sick to do the hard work associated with life review. Most individuals who survive into their seventies, however, acknowledge their mortality; they understand that their lives will end sooner rather than later. This realization often comes because physical impairments and chronic illnesses remind them of their approaching death. Those who do accept the reality that they are in the final stages of life, no matter how physically impaired they might be, have an opportunity to accept their lives and, in so doing, approach their pending deaths with dignity.

Applications

Increasing interest in adult development and particularly in aging has led to several investigations involving the application of the concept of integrity. One of the most common applications of Erikson's ideas concerning the final stage of life can be found in the use of autobiographical, biographical, and even fictional information to provide insight into the process of aging. In a book he edited entitled *Adulthood* (1978), Erikson devotes a chapter he himself wrote to a review of Ingmar Bergman's film *Smultronstället* (1957; *Wild Strawberries*, 1959). In the review, Erikson uses his ideas about integrity and despair to find meaning and purpose in the life of the film's central character, Dr. Isak Borg, a retired Swedish doctor.

This process of using life reviews found in biographical works to identify the development of integrity in a person's life has been applied to many famous and some not-so-famous individuals. An extensive description of the application of Erikson's ideas to the understanding of the life of Vera Brittain, a British feminist and pacifist, was written by Abigail J. Stewart, Carol Franz, and Lynne Layton and published in *Journal of Personality* 56 (March, 1988). A similar technique has been applied to study the lives of Augusta Turnley (a fictional character from the 1975 novel *Perilous Voyage*, written by Lael Wertenbaker), Florida Scott-Maxwell (an author and psychologist), and Arie Carpenter (a woman born and reared in rural North Carolina). This type of application is described in an article in *International Journal of Aging and Human Development* 27, no. 1 (1988), written by Natalie Rosel. The reviews of the lives of these individuals show the universality of Erikson's ideas and the diverse ways in which people reach and maintain a sense of dignity in their lives. The concepts of dealing with despair and the achievement of wisdom are made concrete through examples from the biographies and autobiographies that serve as the data base for the studies.

Though a clearer understanding of the attainment of integrity is achieved by applying Erikson's theory to biographical sketches, there is much to be gained by applying his ideas to the lives of those who are still living. In a study involving a group of elderly nursing home residents, published in 1990, Lois Taft and Milton F. Nehrke explored the development of integrity. The authors wanted to discover whether people whose conversations about the past (a phenomenon called reminiscence) involved a review of their lives would have a stronger sense of integrity than those who used reminiscence as a tool for education or as a way to discover solutions for problems. Those nursing home residents who reported spending more time reviewing their lives when reminiscing about the past agreed more strongly with statements indicating the presence of integrity, such as "I am proud of what I have done" and "I am satisfied with my life so far." The authors of the study concluded that people benefit from reminiscing about their past and that the listeners also benefit from the wisdom, knowledge, and insight that emerges from those actively involved in the life-review process.

The results of the nursing home study suggest two things. First, even people who are no longer able to take care of all their daily needs (for example, meal preparation, housekeeping, and monitoring medication) may benefit from the life-review process. They may be able to achieve a sense of dignity despite their impairments. The results obtained in the nursing home study also suggest that therapists who work with clients in the final stage of development might use life review as a way to help them deal with many of the issues that arise during the integrity-versus-despair stage of development.

Studies such as the one done with the nursing home residents continue to show the importance of Erikson's developmental theory. His work has led to improved therapeutic interventions for older adults. Counselors are incorporating the idea that development continues throughout the life span into their treatments. They have recognized that older individuals can and do benefit from therapeutic interventions designed to deal with their specific needs. The symptoms of depression and the emotions associated with losing a spouse are being identified and treated in the older population. Negative feelings arising from the adjustments required during retirement are also being identified, and therapists are responding with interventions unique to an older population. Counselors are in the process of helping older adults deal with their pending deaths and are helping them make the most of what remains of their lives. Social workers in nursing homes are helping residents remain oriented to time and place and are working with them to improve the quality of their lives. Clearly, Erikson's identification of the conflict between integrity and despair in the final stage of life has contributed to the enhancement of the therapeutic interventions for older adults.

Context

Erikson's thoughts on the development of wisdom emerging from the struggle between integrity and despair have roots in the philosophy of Søren Kierkegaard. Robert Coles, the author of *Erik H. Erikson: The Growth of His Work* (1970), argues that Kierkegaard's concept of the mind as a battleground in which selfish desires of individuals fight against the needs of society may have been one of the foundations of Erikson's conceptualization of the eight stages of development.

In each of the proposed developmental stages, the actions of the individual in the context of the society in which he or she is reared plays a central role in the conflict that must be resolved in that stage. In the integrity-versus-despair stage, individuals fight to maintain their dignity in a body that is failing them in the context of a society that may not value their insight and experience.

Erikson's ideas were also heavily influenced by one of his teachers, Sigmund Freud. Like Freud, Erikson believed in the existence of unconscious motives that could be responsible for behavior. The conflict between the desires of the individual (represented by the id) and the standards set by parents, teachers, and the culture (represented by the superego) is at the heart of both Freud's and Erikson's work. Erikson, in contrast to Freud, put more emphasis on the importance of the environment and was more interested in development across the life span than was his teacher.

Building on the foundation laid by Kierkegaard and Freud, Erikson spent many years studying American Indians, veterans returning from World War II, and children and adults from diverse backgrounds. His development of the ideas concerning integrity and despair were derived from these experiences but were particularly influenced by his interest in people such as Martin Luther, Albert Einstein, and Mahatma Gandhi. In studying their lives, he saw the development of integrity out of despair. He argued that in all people's lives there are moments of regret and lost opportunities that they must accept and from which they must learn; in so doing, they can attain wisdom.

Erikson's theory of development, as introduced in his book *Childhood and Society*, is explained in more detail in several subsequent works. His most detailed discussion of the final stage of life is developed in a book coauthored with Joan Erikson, his wife, and Helen Kivnick entitled *Vital Involvement in Old Age* (1986). Through the information obtained from clients (called informants), the authors provide examples from each of the conflicts that are present in each of the eight stages of development. The emphasis is on the importance of the struggles encountered in earlier stages and their influence on the development of integrity in the final stage.

Erikson's thoughts about development are important in a variety of ways. He was one of the first theorists to propose a developmental theory acknowledging that growth occurs across the life span, culminating only in death. Furthermore, his work expanded on Freud's by including the important role that the culture in which individuals are reared plays in development.

Despite these important contributions, Erikson, like most developmental and most personality theorists, has been criticized. The most frequently cited problems with the theory involve the difficulty that investigators have in testing the concepts it proposes. Investigators cannot easily define integrity or wisdom, or measure integrity or despair. These are difficult but not insurmountable problems.

The work done with life review suggests that some progress is being made in understanding the final stage of development, and it provides hope that more of Erikson's ideas will be tested in the laboratory and used in the therapist's office in the future. Despite the many problems with testing Erikson's assumptions about development, his theory continues to play a vital role in the understanding of personality across the life span.

Bibliography

Coles, Robert. *Erik H. Erikson: The Growth of His Work.* Boston: Little, Brown, 1970. A definitive work on the historical and psychological roots of Erikson's theory and on his writings. Fascinating reading for those who attempt to understand a theory by understanding the person who developed it. Some background in philosophy and some prior exposure to Freud are helpful.

Erikson, Erik H., ed. *Adulthood.* New York: W. W. Norton, 1978. The first chapter, written by Erikson, uses the life of the Swedish doctor portrayed in Ingmar Bergman's film *Wild Strawberries* to highlight the concepts of integrity and despair. Both the film and the chapter are highly recommended. The remainder of the work is also well presented but not as relevant to the concepts of integrity and despair as the first chapter.

_____. *Childhood and Society.* New York: W. W. Norton, 1950. Lays the foundation for and explains Erikson's theory of development. Erikson's psychological training, his artistic background, and his excellent command of the language are evident throughout the book. The clinical method of study is described and then applied to children and to Native Americans. The concept of the ego is developed and explored through biography and literature as well as clinical case histories. Should be read by anyone with an interest in personality or development.

_____. *Identity and the Life Cycle.* New York: International University Press, 1959. Reprint. New York: W. W. Norton, 1980. Expands on the earlier thoughts communicated in *Childhood and Society.* Thoughts about the importance of the historical backdrop in which people develop are more fully expressed than in earlier works. The growth of the individual as reflected in the healthy personality is described in some detail. The writing is dense and may be difficult for the reader who has not had much exposure to Erikson's work.

Erikson, Erik H., Joan M. Erikson, and Helen Q. Kivnick. *Vital Involvement in Old Age.* New York: W. W. Norton, 1986. Published when Erikson was well into his eighties. Describes the stages of the life cycle in reverse chronological order, emphasizing the importance of and dependence on earlier stages of development in successful aging. Clinical examples are abundant and help illustrate the many nuances of Erikson's theory. Not an easy read for those unfamiliar with Erikson's ideas, but a delightful and telling example of Erikson's own generativity and integrity.

Gross, Francis L., Jr. *Introducing Erik Erikson: An Invitation to His Thinking.* Lanham, Md.: University Press of America, 1987. Introduces the thoughts of Erikson through brief historical excerpts and anecdotes from Erikson's life. Explanations of his theory are also included. Written for the novice and enhanced by frequent examples from classic and popular literature. The writing style is engaging and frequently humorous.

Lori L. Temple

Cross-References

Aging: Cognitive Changes, 180; Aging: Physical Changes, 192; Death and Dying:

INTELLIGENCE:
DEFINITION AND THEORETICAL MODELS

Type of psychology: Intelligence and intelligence testing
Fields of study: General issues in intelligence; intelligence assessment

Intelligence is a hypothetical concept, rather than a tangible entity, that is used by psychologists and other scientists to explain differences in the quality and adaptive value of the behavior of humans and, to some extent, animals. Its meaning and the theoretical models used to explore it are as varied as the field of psychology itself.

Principal terms
COGNITIVE PSYCHOLOGY: an area of psychology that deals with all aspects of experience that pertain to the process of knowing
CORRELATION: the degree of correspondence between two variables, which is usually expressed by a coefficient that can range from $+1.00$ to -1.00; 0.00 signifies no correspondence
FACTOR: a purely descriptive and hypothetical entity that is identified by examining the pattern of results of a factor analysis
FACTOR ANALYSIS: a statistical technique wherein a set of correlated variables can be regrouped in terms of the degree of commonality they share
HERITABILITY: the quality that allows a given characteristic or trait to be passed on through genes from one generation to another

Overview

The idea that human beings differ in their capacity to adapt to their environments, to learn from experience, to exercise various skills, and in general to succeed at various endeavors has existed since ancient times. Intelligence is the quality most often singled out as responsible for successful adaptations. Up to the end of the nineteenth century, notions about what constitutes intelligence and how differences in intelligence arise were mostly speculative. In the late 1800's, several trends converged to bring about an event that would change the way in which intelligence was seen and dramatically influence the way it would be studied. That event, which occurred in 1905, was the publication of the first useful instrument for measuring intelligence, the Binet-Simon scale, which was developed in France by Alfred Binet and Théodore Simon.

Although the development of intelligence tests was a great technological accomplishment, it occurred, in a sense, somewhat prematurely, before much scientific attention had been paid to the concept of intelligence. This circumstance tied the issue of defining intelligence and a large part of the research into its nature and origins to the limitations of the tests that had been devised. In fact, the working definition of intelligence that many psychologists have used either explicitly or implicitly in their scientific and applied pursuits is the one expressed by Edwin Boring in 1923, which holds that intelligence is whatever intelligence tests measure. Most psychologists realize that this definition is redundant and inadequate in that it erroneously implies that the tests are perfectly accurate and able to capture all that is meant by the concept. Nevertheless, psychologists and others have proceeded to use the tests as if the definition were true, mainly because of a scarcity of viable alternatives. The general public has also been led astray by the existence of "intelligence" tests and the frequent misuse of their results. Many people have come to think of the intelligence quotient, or IQ, not as a simple score achieved on a particular test, which it is, but as a complete and stable measure of intellectual capacity, which it most definitely is not. Such misconceptions about what intelligence-test scores represent also have led to an understandable resistance toward and resentment of intelligence tests.

Boring's semifacetious definition of intelligence may be the best known and most criticized one, but it is only one among many that have been offered. Most experts in the field have defined the concept at least once in their careers. Two of the most frequently cited and influential definitions are the ones provided by Alfred Binet himself and by David Wechsler, author of a series of "second-generation" individual intelligence tests that overtook the Binet scales in terms of the frequency with which they are used. Binet believed that the essential activities of intelligence are to judge well, to comprehend well, and to reason well. He stated that intelligent thought is characterized by direction, knowing what to do and how to do it; by adaptation, the capacity to monitor one's strategies for attaining a desired end; and by criticism, the power to evaluate and control one's behavior. In 1975, almost sixty-five years after Binet's death, Wechsler defined intelligence, not dissimilarly, as the global capacity of the individual to act purposefully, to think rationally, and to deal effectively with the environment.

In addition to the testing experts (psychometricians), developmental, learning, and cognitive psychologists, among others, are also vitally interested in the concept of intelligence. Specialists in each of these subfields emphasize different aspects of it in their definitions and research.

Representative definitions were sampled in 1921, when the *Journal of Educational Psychology* published the views of fourteen leading investigators, and again in 1986, when Robert Sternberg and Douglas Detterman collected the opinions of twenty-four experts in a book entitled *What Is Intelligence? Contemporary Viewpoints on Its Nature and Definition.* Most of the experts sampled in 1921 offered definitions that equated intelligence with one or more specific abilities. For example, Lewis Terman equated it with abstract thinking, which is the ability to elaborate concepts and to use language and other symbols. Others proposed definitions that emphasized the ability to adapt and/or learn. Some definitions centered on knowledge and cognitive components only, whereas others included nonintellectual qualities, such as perseverance. In comparison, Sternberg's and Detterman's 1986 survey of definitions, which is even more wide ranging, is accompanied by an organizational framework consisting of fifty-five categories or combinations of categories under which the twenty-four definitions can be classified. Some theorists view intelligence from a biological perspective and emphasize differences across species and/or the role of the central nervous system. Some stress cognitive aspects of mental functioning, while others focus on the role of motivation and goals. Still others, such as Anne Anastasi, choose to look upon intelligence as a quality that is inherent in behavior rather than in the individual. Another major perspective highlights the role of the environment, in terms of demands and values, in defining what constitutes intelligent behavior. Throughout the 1986 survey, one can find definitions that straddle two or more categories.

A review of the 1921 and 1986 surveys shows that the definitions proposed have become considerably more sophisticated and suggests that, as the field of psychology has expanded, the views of experts on intelligence may have grown farther apart. The reader of the 1986 work is left with the clear impression that intelligence is such a multifaceted concept that no single quality can define it and no single task or series of tasks can capture it completely. Moreover, it is clear that in order to unravel the qualities that produce intelligent behavior one must look not only at individuals and their skills but also at the requirements of the systems in which people find themselves. In other words, intelligence cannot be defined in a vacuum.

Applications

The lack of a universally accepted definition has not deterred continuous theorizing and research on the concept of intelligence. The central issue that has dominated theoretical models of intelligence is the question of whether it is a single, global ability or a collection of specialized abilities. This debate, started in England by Charles Spearman, is based on research that uses the correlations among various measures of abilities and, in particular, the method of factor analysis, which was also pioneered by Spearman. As early as 1904, Spearman, having examined the patterns of correlation coefficients among tests of sensory discrimination and estimates of intelligence, proposed that all mental functions are the result of a single general factor, which he later designated g. Spearman equated g with the ability to grasp and apply relations. He also allowed for the fact that most tasks require unique abilities, and he named those s, or specific, factors. According to Spearman, to the extent that performance on tasks was positively correlated, the correlation was attributable to the presence of g, whereas the presence of specific factors tended to lower the correlation between measures of performance on different tasks. By 1927, Spearman had modified his theory to allow for the existence of an intermediate class of factors, known as group factors, which were neither as universal as g nor as narrow as the s factors. Group factors were seen as accounting for the fact that certain types of activities, such as tasks involving the use of numbers or the element of speed, correlate more highly with one another than they do with tasks that do not have such elements in common.

Factor-analytic research has undergone explosive growth and extensive variations and refinements in both England and the United States since the 1920's. In the United

States, work in this field was influenced greatly by Truman Kelley, whose 1928 book *Crossroads in the Mind of Man* presented a method for isolating group factors, and L. L. Thurstone, who by further elaboration of factor-analytic procedures identified a set of about twelve factors that he designated as the "primary mental abilities." Seven of these were repeatedly found in a number of investigations, using samples of people at different age levels, that were carried out by both Thurstone and others. These group factors or primary mental abilities are verbal comprehension, word fluency, speed and accuracy of arithmetic computation, spatial visualization, associative memory, perceptual speed, and general reasoning.

As the search for distinct intellectual factors progressed, their number multiplied, and so did the number of models devised to organize them. One type of scheme, used by Cyril Burt, Philip Vernon, and others, is a hierarchical arrangement of factors. In these models, Spearman's g factor is placed at the top of a pyramid and the specific factors are placed at the bottom; in between, there are one or more levels of group factors selected in terms of their breadth and arranged according to their interrelationships with the more general factors above them and the more specific factors below them. In Vernon's scheme, for example, the ability to change a tire might be classified as a specific factor at the base of the pyramid, located underneath an intermediate group factor labeled mechanical information, which in turn would be under one of the two major group factors identified by Vernon as the main subdivisions under g—namely, the practical-mechanical factor. The hierarchical scheme for organizing mental abilities is a useful device that is endorsed by many psychologists on both sides of the Atlantic. It recognizes that very few tasks are so simple as to require a single skill for successful performance, that many intellectual functions share some common elements, and that some abilities play a more pivotal role than others in the performance of culturally valued activities.

Another well-known scheme for organizing intellectual traits is the structure-of-intellect (SOI) model developed by J. P. Guilford. Although the SOI is grounded in extensive factor-analytic research conducted by Guilford throughout the 1940's and 1950's, the model goes beyond factor analysis and is perhaps the most ambitious attempt to classify systematically all the possible functions of the human intellect. The SOI classifies intellectual traits along three dimensions—namely, five types of operations, four types of contents, and six types of productions, for a total of 120 categories ($5 \times 4 \times 6$). Intellectual operations consist of what a person actually does (for example, evaluating or remembering something), the contents are the types of materials or information on which the operations are performed (for example, symbols, such as letters or numbers), and the products are the form in which the contents are processed (for example, units or relations). Not all the 120 categories in Guilford's complex model have been used, but enough factors have been identified to account for about 100 of them, and some have proved very useful in labeling and understanding the skills that tests measure. Furthermore, Guilford's model has served to call attention to some dimensions of intellectual activity, such as creativity and interpersonal skills, that had been neglected previously.

Contemporary theorists in the area of intelligence have tried to avoid the reliance on factor analysis and existing tests that have limited traditional research and have tried different approaches to the subject. For example, Howard Gardner, in his 1983 book *Frames of Mind: The Theory of Multiple Intelligences*, starts with the premises that the essence of intelligence is competence and that there are several distinct areas in which human beings can demonstrate competence. Based on a wide-ranging review of evidence from many scientific fields and sources, Gardner has designated seven areas of competence as separate and relatively independent "intelligences." His list includes some familiar categories, such as linguistic, spatial, and logical-mathematical intelligences, as well as the more unusual categories of musical, bodily-kinesthetic, and personal intelligences.

Another theory is the one proposed by Robert Sternberg in his 1985 book *Beyond IQ: A Triarchic Theory of Human Intelligence*. Sternberg defines intelligence, broadly, as mental self-management and stresses the "real-world," in addition to the academic, aspects of the concept. He believes that intelligent behavior consists of purposively adapting to, selecting, and shaping one's environment and that both culture and personality play significant roles in such behavior.

Theories of intelligence are still grappling with the issues of defining its nature and composition. Generally, newer theories do not represent radical departures from the past. They do, however, emphasize examining intelligence in relation to the variety of environments in which people actually live rather than to only academic or laboratory environments. Moreover, many investigators, especially those in cognitive psychology, are more interested in breaking down and replicating the steps involved in information processing and problem solving than they are in enumerating factors or settling on a single definition of intelligence. These trends hold the promise of moving the work in the field in the direction of devising new ways to teach people to understand, evaluate, and deal with their environments more intelligently instead of simply measuring how well they do on intelligence tests.

Context

The most heated of all the debates about intelligence is the one regarding its determinants, often described as the "nature-nurture" controversy. The "nature" side of the debate was spearheaded by Francis Galton, a nineteenth century English scientist who had become convinced that intelligence was a hereditary trait. Galton's followers tried to show, through studies comparing identical and nonidentical twins reared together and reared apart and by comparisons of people related to each other in varying degrees, that genetic endowment plays a far larger role than the environment in determining intelligence. Attempts to quantify an index of heritability for intelligence through such studies abound, and the estimates derived from them vary widely. On the "nurture" side of the debate, massive quantities of data have been gathered in an effort to show that the environment, including factors such as prenatal care, social-class membership, exposure to certain facilitative experiences, and educational opportunities of all sorts, has the more crucial role in determining a person's level of intellectual functioning.

Many critics, such as Anastasi (in a widely cited 1958 article entitled "Heredity, Environment, and the Question 'How?' ") have pointed out the futility of debating how much each factor contributes to intelligence. Anastasi and others argue that behavior is a function of the interaction between heredity and the total experiential history of individuals and that, from the moment of conception, the two are inextricably tied. Moreover, they point out that, even if intelligence were shown to be primarily determined by heredity, environmental influences could still modify its expression at any point. Most psychologists now accept this "interactionist" position and have moved on to explore how intelligence develops and how specific genetic and environmental factors affect it.

Bibliography

Fancher, Raymond E. *The Intelligence Men: Makers of the IQ Controversy.* New York: W. W. Norton, 1985. Presents the history of the various debates on intelligence in a highly readable fashion. The lives and ideas of the pioneers in the field, such as Alfred Binet and Francis Galton, are described in some detail.

Gardner, Howard. *Frames of Mind: The Theory of Multiple Intelligences.* New York: Basic Books, 1983. Gardner's description of the talents he designates as "intelligences" and explanation of the reasons for his selections provide a fascinating introduction to many of the most intriguing aspects of the field, including the extremes of prodigies and idiots savants.

Guilford, Joy Paul. *The Nature of Human Intelligence.* New York: McGraw-Hill, 1967. Guilford describes the foundation of his theory of the structure of the intellect and in the process reviews the history of research into and theorizing about intelligence. This volume is an important contribution to the field.

Sternberg, Robert J. *The Triarchic Mind: A New Theory of Human Intelligence.* New York: Viking Penguin, 1988. Sternberg reviews and criticizes the limitations of traditional views of intelligence and presents his own variations on that theme. The book is addressed to a general audience and contains a number of intellectual exercises aimed at enhancing the reader's performance on cognitive tests.

Vernon, Philip Ewart. *Intelligence: Heredity and Environment.* San Francisco: W. H. Freeman, 1979. Presents a thorough and thoughtful review of research on both sides of the "nature-nurture" debate on the development of intelligence. The issue of racial differences in intelligence is also discussed at length.

Susana P. Urbina

Cross-References

INTELLIGENCE: GIFTEDNESS AND RETARDATION

Type of psychology: Intelligence and intelligence testing
Field of study: General issues in intelligence

Giftedness and retardation can be seen as occupying two extremes of the continuum of intelligence. The two conditions may be diagnosed through intelligence testing; each of them presents its own needs and dilemmas.

Principal terms
   ADAPTIVE BEHAVIOR: certain common skills and abilities—such as eating, communicating, dressing, grooming, shopping, and working—that enable one to function in the world
   GIFTEDNESS: a marked ability to learn more rapidly, perform intricate problems, and solve problems with a higher degree of rapidity; operationally defined as an IQ score above 130 on an individually administered test
   INTELLIGENCE: as David Wechsler defines it, the aggregate or global capacity of an individual to act purposefully, think rationally, and deal effectively with his or her environment
   PRODIGY: a very gifted child whose skills and abilities are readily apparent early in life
   RELIABILITY: the ability of a test to measure a construct or skill with a high degree of consistency
   RETARDATION: a condition, measured by an IQ score of less than 70, wherein a person has mental abilities that are far below average; other skills and abilities, such as adaptive behavior, may also be marginal
   VALIDITY: the extent to which a test measures what it purports to measure

Overview

The terms "giftedness" and "retardation" are frequently used to identify opposite ends of the spectrum of intelligence. These two categories reflect two extremes of the population, and they embody different, disparate domains. Giftedness has typically been defined by using intelligence quotient (IQ) scores from an individually administered intelligence test given by a school psychologist or other professional. Although there is some variation from state to state and from program to program, the generally accepted cut-off point is an IQ score of 130 or above for placement in a gifted program or recognition as a gifted student.

Gifted individuals generally show greater problem-solving skills, manifest a greater degree of insight, and tend to learn more rapidly than the average person. They may show greater interest and curiosity in the world and may have been identified as "more intelligent" early in their lives. There are also many children, however, who drift through school (and do quite well) without being recognized as gifted until they find a subject in which they become passionately interested; their giftedness then becomes manifested.

Some gifted children, seen by their peers as outsiders, may be taunted or ostracized; this situation can leave lifelong emotional scars. Another problem is that parents may put unrealistic expectations on gifted children or try to live vicariously through them; these situations also create emotional problems for the children.

The Wechsler Intelligence Scale for Children-Revised (WISC-R), developed by David Wechsler in 1974, is generally the most commonly used IQ test for the determination of giftedness, although other tests, such as the Stanford-Binet test, are used for placement. Much concern has been voiced about the reliability and validity of intelligence tests; some tests that are administered in groups, for example, may be less reliable or valid than individually administered tests, which require a highly trained examiner. Individual tests yield clinical, educational, and other information. It should also be noted that there has been much discussion and theorizing concerning what, exactly, "intelligence" is. Some theorists hold that it reflects the speed of information processing—that is, how fast one learns and processes new information. Others believe that it is the difficulty of the problems that one can solve that more accurately reflects one's intelligence. Still others believe that the interaction of one's personality, environment, motivation, and natural skills makes up the construct of intelligence.

In some school districts, achievement test scores are used for placing children in gifted-student programs. Such children may show exceptional talents or skills in one or a variety of areas—mathematics, science, reading, spelling, and so on. Teachers often nominate students for inclusion in gifted programs. Parents, too, may believe their child to be gifted and expect the school system to provide the enrichment that they think is necessary for the child to develop fully.

On the other end of the intelligence spectrum is mental retardation. While the causes of mental retardation vary, the intellectual and cognitive deficiencies do not; there is a marked deficiency in intellectual thinking processes. There are several classifications of mental retardation, based primarily on IQ scores. In a general sense, these classifications are borderline mental retardation (IQ of 70-79), mild mental retardation (IQ of 50-55 to 70), moderate mental retardation (IQ of 35-40 to 50-55), severe mental retardation (IQ of 20-25 to 35-40), and profound mental retardation (IQ below 20 or 25). These scores should be viewed with some caution, however, as different IQ tests vary greatly in their theoretical orientation. Some are more verbal in nature, while others rely more on performance aspects as criteria of intellectual ability. There may also be secondary handicapping conditions, as well as motivational or transitory factors, that influence a person's performance on an IQ test. Medical conditions (such as cerebral palsy) or emotional problems such as low frustration tolerance, impulsivity, or an inability to pay attention are among those factors that may affect a mentally retarded person's test scores.

There may also be discrepancies among different skills. Some mentally retarded persons are able to do performance-based tasks very well—some can perform a number of routine mechanical tasks quite well but have very poor verbal and other language-based skills, arithmetic skills, and abstract thinking skills. This may also take the opposite form, in which verbal and vocabulary skills might be well developed but gross and fine motor coordination and manual dexterity are poor.

Terms that refer specifically to the retarded person's ability to learn and need for care are frequently used, and they relate generally to the type of IQ categorization given above. The terms educable mentally retarded, trainable mentally retarded, dependent, and custodial are often used as global terms to reflect a person's level of competence. There may be gross discrepancies, however, between IQ and level of functioning. For example, a mentally retarded person may have a relatively high IQ yet be unable to tie shoelaces or dress or groom himself or herself. On the other hand, a person with a lower IQ might be able to perform fairly complex procedures such as cooking, cleaning, or even changing the oil on a car or repairing machines. These anomalies are a challenge to psychologists' understanding; one theory is that they may reflect damage to a part of the brain at birth or in early childhood.

Some mentally retarded people need institutional care or even extreme one-on-one assistance. Some are able, with considerable supervision, to live in community group homes. On the other hand, a number of mentally retarded people can perform simple repetitive tasks in a wide variety of settings. Some hold jobs wherein they are supervised closely by a foreman; others are employed in what are termed sheltered workshops. In these facilities, the mentally retarded may work assembling objects or help on projects in the community. Some mentally retarded people have other medical or psychological problems that require attention and considerable assistance; many have secondary handicaps such as cerebral palsy or epilepsy.

The mentally retarded person may also manifest many deficits in adaptive behavior in several areas. As the level of retardation increases, the level of deficiency in adaptive behaviors generally increases. Many retarded people do need to be fed, dressed, and groomed; some are incontinent. Mentally retarded individuals may also become lazy or withdrawn; in particular, this occurs if they are not being challenged but are left simply to watch television or listen to the radio. Severely and profoundly retarded individuals may show behavioral manifestations of retardation such as perseveration (repetitious rocking or repeated words over and over), drooling, poor attention to dress and grooming, and attention-seeking behaviors. Skills that were once possessed can also be lost; this is especially true of educational skills.

Applications

The gifted person apparently has more sophisticated thinking skills, an ability to process more information in a more rapid manner, and a greater ability to sift salient information from meaningless information than does the average person. The gifted person also seems to have a higher degree of insight. The three germane components of insight—selective encoding, selective comparison, and selective combination—have been deemed crucial factors in giftedness. Gifted people seem to encode (or learn) important material more rapidly, compare it to previously learned information quite easily, and then combine, synthesize, and integrate information more readily than less gifted individuals.

Howard Gardner, in his book *Frames of Mind: The Theory of Multiple Intelligences* (1983), wrote on another aspect of giftedness: the various types of skills, abilities, and talents that are possessed by artists, musicians, and others. Gardner hypothesized that there are six domains of intelligence: linguistic, musical, logical-mathematical, visual-spatial, bodily-kinesthetic, and interpersonal and intrapersonal. Different cultures emphasize different aspects of intelligence—people in Japan, India, and Australia, for example, place emphasis on different skills, abilities, and talents than do people in the United States. In the United States, it is not uncommon for talented children with exceptional thespian, public speaking, creative, or writing skills to be ignored; perhaps American society is unsure how to encourage and nurture those skills. Mentoring has been seen as one avenue toward the encouragement of those gifts (Shaughnessy, 1989).

Several explanations have been given to as to why exceptionally intelligent people do not always achieve at a level equal to their potentials. Robert Sternberg (1986) postulated twenty reasons for this; among them are lack of motivation, lack of impulse control, lack of perseverance, using the wrong abilities, inability to translate thought into action, fear of failure, excessive self-pity, distractibility and lack of concentration, and inability or unwillingness to "see the forest for the trees." Sternberg and others believe that it is most important to look at what a person does with the amount of intelligence that he or she possesses rather than at the sheer amount of measured intelligence. Personality, motivation, and a host of other factors contribute to intellectual and cognitive success.

Sternberg also developed what he termed a "triarchic theory" of intelligence. He posits that IQ tests have changed very little since the beginning of the twentieth century, whereas Western culture and society have changed considerably. In his book *Beyond I.Q.: A Triarchic Theory of Human Intelligence* (1985), Sternberg discusses his three subtheories of intelligence—exponential, contextual, and componential—and further subdivides them into more specific aspects.

Some theorists (as well as many parents of gifted children) believe that special skills and training are needed to teach gifted children. There are master's degree and doctoral programs designed to train teachers to work with gifted students and high achievers. Some educators advocate grade skipping or independent study for gifted children. Some gifted children take college courses from local universities; others attend special camps or residential schools. One such school, the Hollingsworth School in Maine, only admits students with IQs of 160 or higher. Special summer programs for the mathematically or scientifically precocious are offered at The Johns Hopkins University and other major universities. There are also a number of national and international societies and groups for highly gifted and intelligent students.

The needs of the mentally retarded vary considerably, according to the severity of the retardation; these needs can be examined as they relate to the five categories of retardation noted earlier. Borderline individuals may be able to live independently, work in the community, travel within their town, cook, and clean their homes. They may be unable to do tasks such as filling out their income tax forms, however, that require some sophisticated mathematics and reasoning skills. Those people with mild mental retardation usually have more difficulty with academic tasks such as reading instructions on the job, filling out an employment application, or balancing a checkbook. They may not be able to perform complex tasks and may require a considerable amount of supervision on the job—if they are performing at a level that enables them to procure employment.

Moderately retarded individuals typically are able to work in a sheltered workshop, with much supervision and assistance. They may need assistance in grooming (bathing, shaving, hygiene, and so on). They may get lost in their own locality if they travel, may be unable to make changes, and may engage in inappropriate behavior.

The severely or profoundly retarded person has extreme difficulties functioning independently. Some may need to be fed; some may not have any language skills other than a few words, such as "mama," "dada," or "want food." Others need assistance in dressing or may wear pull-over clothes (with no buttons) and shoes that do not lace (as they cannot perform the fine motor skills necessary for lacing). These individuals may sit for long periods in front of the television and move only when prompted. Some have slurred speech and difficulties in communicating. Many are at least occasionally incontinent and require prompting and assistance with toilet behaviors.

Since the 1970's, there has been remarkable progress using behavior modification techniques to shape and reinforce behaviors that help the mentally retarded to function with minimal adult assistance.

Context

As society becomes increasingly sophisticated and complex, intelligence is of greater and greater importance in terms of human functioning. A computerized society requires advanced intellectual skills; moreover, with increasing automation, jobs that can be performed by people with impaired intellectual abilities become fewer. Those people who are borderline mentally retarded may have much greater difficulty functioning and obtaining employment. Schools and even preschool and kindergarten facilities screen children for learning problems or developmental disabilities. Many psychologists and educators believe that it is important for those who are mentally retarded or have intellectual or language delays to receive as much early intervention as possible. Others, however, suggest that such early labeling tends to bring about lower expectations and therefore less investment in the child. It is important that this debate among educators and parents be kept active.

There are a number of federal laws regarding the mentally retarded and the amount of services they are legally entitled to receive. Most special educators, for example, are aware of laws specifying that those in special education programs or with hand-icapping conditions are entitled to receive certain services and should be educated in the "least restrictive environment" possible. A multidisciplinary treatment team should be involved in creating a treatment plan that indicates specific goals and how they should be achieved. What constitutes the "least restrictive environment" is not clearly specified, however, and is often difficult to determine. Many handicapped people still do not receive all the benefits to which they are entitled by law. At the other end of the spectrum, there is very little legislation concerning gifted people and gifted education programs. Much more needs to be done in this area in order to assist the academically, artistically, and intellectually gifted.

Bibliography

Feldman, David Henry, with Lynn T. Goldsmith. *Nature's Gambit: Child Prodigies and the Development of Human Potential.* New York: Basic Books, 1986. Feldman presents a number of case studies of prodigies and their growth and development. One of the best books on the subject.

Gardner, Howard. *Frames of Mind: The Theory of Multiple Intelligences.* New York: Basic Books, 1983. Gardner outlines his conceptions of intelligence and his do-mains of talent. A classic book that outlines different types of intelligence.

Shaughnessy, Michael F. "Cognitive Structures of the Gifted: Theoretical Perspec-tives, Factor Analysis, Triarchic Theories of Intelligence, and Insight Issues." *Gifted Education International* 6, no. 3 (1990): 149-151. Presents a perspective on how intellectually gifted people think and discusses research in this area. As psycholo-gists increasingly study gifted children and adults, they must pay more and more attention to the way in which these individuals learn and process information.

_____. "Mentoring the Creative Child, Adult, and Prodigy: Current Knowl-edge, Systems, and Research." *Gifted Education International* 6, no. 1 (1989): 22-24. Reviews the process of mentoring with various special groups. As men-tored people seem to do very well in life, it is important to study this process; this article provides a "how to" overview for the beginner.

_____. "What's New in I.Q.?" *Creative Child and Adult Quarterly* 10, no. 2 (1985): 72-78. This article outlines theories of intelligence. Presents a very good summary of the theories of Gardner, Sternberg, and other theorists in the field.

Sternberg, Robert J. *Beyond I.Q.: A Triarchic Theory of Human Intelligence.* New York: Cambridge University Press, 1985. An excellent book on reconceptualizing intelligence for the 1990's and beyond. It is heavy reading in places but is impor-tant for those people genuinely interested in understanding intelligence and Stern-berg's theories.

_____. *Intelligence Applied: Understanding and Increasing Your Intellec-tual Skills.* New York: Harcourt Brace Jovanovich, 1986. Helps one understand one's intelligence and provides exercises to increase it; for those people who want to work at being more intelligent and using their skills optimally.

Wechsler, David. *Manual for the Wechsler Intelligence Scale for Children-Revised.*

New York: Psychological Corporation, 1974. Contains information about the most widely used contemporary IQ test for children. This test has been revised, however, so many people will encounter the WISC-III.

Michael F. Shaughnessy

Cross-References

Ability Tests: Design and Construction, 13; Creativity: Assessing Special Talents, 726; Creativity and Intelligence, 731; Intelligence: Definition and Theoretical Models, 1328; Intelligence Tests, 1341.

INTELLIGENCE TESTS

Type of psychology: Intelligence and intelligence testing
Fields of study: Ability tests; intelligence assessment

Individual intelligence tests are used by psychologists to evaluate a person's current cognitive ability and prior knowledge. The intelligence testing movement has a long history, including the development of numerous group and individual tests to measure one aspect of a person's overall intelligence, which frequently changes over time.

Principal terms
> AGE NORM: on an aptitude test, the median score made by children of a specific chronological age
> COGNITION: ways of knowing and intellectual processes; thinking, problem solving, remembering, and understanding
> INTELLIGENCE: among many definitions, David Wechsler's "the aggregate or global capacity of the individual to act purposefully, to think rationally and to deal effectively with the environment" is widely accepted
> INTELLIGENCE QUOTIENT (IQ): a unit showing the relative standing of an individual's ability as measured by intelligence tests
> MENTALLY GIFTED: a person significantly above average in intellectual functioning, with an IQ of 130 or higher
> MENTALLY HANDICAPPED: a person significantly below average in intellectual functioning, with an IQ of 69 or below
> PERCENTILE: a score or point in a distribution at or below which a given percentage of individuals will fall; for example, if a student has a test score at the 99th percentile, his or her score is equal to or higher than scores of 99 percent of cases
> PERFORMANCE TESTS: tests on which the examinee is required to manipulate various objects
> SENSORIMOTOR TESTS: tests designed to measure sensory, perceptual, and psychomotor skills separately or in juxtaposition
> VERBAL TESTS: tests requiring written, oral, or numerical answers

Overview

Although means for measuring mental ability date as far back as 2000 B.C., when the ancient Chinese administered oral tests to determine a candidate's fitness for carrying out the tasks of civil administration, the modern intelligence test has its origins in the nineteenth century, when Jean-Étienne-Dominique Esquirol drew a clear distinction between mentally deranged people ("lunatics") and mentally retarded people ("idiots"). Esquirol believed that it was necessary to devise a means of gauging "normal" intelligence so that deviations from an agreed-upon norm could be ascertained, and he pointed out that intellectual ability exists on a continuum extending from idiocy to genius. His work coincided with studies in Europe and the United States that were designed to develop a concept of "intelligence" and to fashion a means of testing this capacity. Work done by Sir Francis Galton in the United Kingdom on hereditary genius, by James McKeen Cattell in the United States on individual differences in behavior, and by Hermann Ebbinghaus in Germany on tests of memory, computation, and sentence completion culminated in the 1905 Binet-Simon scale, created by Alfred Binet and Théodore Simon. It was the first practical index of intelligence measurement as a function of individual differences. This test was based on the idea that simple sensory functions, which had formed the core of earlier tests, are not true indicators of intelligence and that higher mental processes had to be included.

French psychologist and educator Binet founded the first French psychological laboratory. He was a pioneer in the study of individual differences in abilities and introduced intelligence tests that were quickly accepted and widely used in Europe and the United States. His work stemmed from a commission from the minister of education in Paris, who gave him the task of devising a way to distinguish between idiocy and lunacy, as Esquirol had defined them, and normal intelligence, so that handicapped students could be given special instruction. He and Simon used many items that had been developed by earlier examiners; the key advances they made were to rank items in order of difficulty and to register results in terms of age-based cognitive development. Their scale reflected the idea that intelligence was a combination of faculties—judgment, practical sense, and initiative—and contained measures related to memory, reasoning ability, numerical facility, and object comparison.

Binet and Simon's work demonstrated the feasibility of mental measurement, assessing intelligence for the first time in general terms rather than measuring its component parts. Binet revised the test in 1908, and another revision was published in 1911, the year of his death. Advances in his basic design led to the development of tests that could be used for all children (not only those considered mentally limited) in assessing their "mental quotient," a ratio adapted by Lewis Terman of Stanford University. It was obtained by dividing mental age (as determined through scores on a test) by chronological age. Terman renamed the term the intelligence quotient (IQ), and his 1916 version of the Binet-Simon scale became known as the Stanford-Binet test, the most common intelligence test administered in the United States during the twentieth century. It was revised and updated in 1937, 1960, 1972, and 1986, when a point-scale format was introduced for the first time.

Binet's test depended on an age scale; that is, the questions which were answered correctly by a majority of ten-year-old children were assigned to the ten-year age level of intelligence. A more sophisticated version of the test was devised by Robert Yerkes, which depended on a point scale for scoring; this format was fully developed by David Wechsler. While the Binet-Terman method used different tests for different age groups, Wechsler worked toward a test to measure the same aspect of behavior at every age level. The goal of his test was to measure intelligence in a holistic (encompassing the larger whole of personality) fashion that did not depend on the verbal skills that the Stanford-Binet tests required. Wechsler thought of intelligence as a multifaceted complex of skills, the total of an effective intellectual process; he wanted his test to show the way intelligent people behaved as a consequence of an awareness of the results of their actions. He thought that those actions would be more rational, worthwhile (in terms of social values), and meaningful than those of less intelligent people.

Wechsler's first test (the Wechsler-Bellevue Intelligence Scale) was published in 1939, and it awarded points for each answer depending on the level of sophistication of the response. The test consisted of six verbal subjects (information, comprehension, arithmetic, similarities, vocabulary, and digit span) and five performance subtests (picture completion, picture arrangement, block design, object assemblies, and digit symbols). The division into verbal and performance skills permitted the calculation of three intelligent quotients: a verbal IQ based on the sum of the verbal tests, correlated with norms of age, a performance IQ based on the sum of performance tests, and a full-scale IQ derived from the sum of all the answers. The test was standarized on a sample of adults, and it could be used to test individuals who had linguistic or sensorimotor handicaps. The pattern of scores on the separate tests could also be used to diagnose learning disability or, in some situations, clinical disorder or dysfunction.

The original test was limited by the sample used for standardization, but the 1955 Wechsler Adult Intelligence Scale (WAIS) provided a basis for testing adults from sixteen to seventy-five. Further revision in the standard scale (including the WAIS-R, 1981) updated the test to coincide with changes in cultural experience. In addition, a Wechsler Intelligence Scale for Children (WISC) was designed to cover ages five to fifteen in 1949 and was revised (WISC-R) in 1974 to cover ages six to sixteen. In 1991, another revision was introduced. Subsequent modifications also led to a test suitable for preschool children, the Wechsler Preschool and Primary Scales of Intelligence (WPPSI) of 1967, which covered ages four to six-and-one-half and included mazes, animal figures, and copying geometric designs. This test was revised in 1981 (WPPSI-R) to extend its range over three years to seven years, three months. Further adjustments have also been made to account for a candidate's sociocultural background in a test called the System of Multi-Cultural Pluralistic Assessment (SOMPA, 1977).

Recent definitions of intelligence have resulted in further development of testing instruments. Raymond Cattell's proposal that intelligence could be divided into two types—fluid (or forming) and crystallized (fixed)—led to a test that used figure classification, figure analysis, and letter and number series to assess the essential nonverbal, relatively culture-free aspects of fluid intelligence; it used vocabulary definition, abstract word analogies, and general information to determine the skills that depend on exposure to cultural processes inherent in crystallized intelligence.

Other theories, such as Jean Piaget's idea that intelligence is a form of individual adaptation and accommodation to an environment, led to the development of a test which measures mental organization at successive ages.

Applications

There has been a tendency at various times during the twentieth century to regard intelligence assessment as an answer to questions of placement and classification in almost every area of human experience. The most effective and scientifically valid uses of tests, however, have been in predicting performance in scholastic endeavor, in revealing disguised or latent ability to assist in career counseling, in determining the most appropriate developmental programs for handicapped or mentally handicapped individuals, in locating specific strengths and weaknesses in an individual, in measuring specific changes associated with special programs and forms of therapy, and in comparing a child's mental ability with other children observed in a similar situation to establish a profile of cognitive skills.

One of the most widespread and effective uses of intelligence tests is the determination of possible problems in a child's course of basic education. As reported by Lewis Aiken in his *Assessment of Intellectual Functioning* (1987), a typical case involved an eight-year-old boy with a suspected learning disability. He was given the WISC-R test in 1985, and his full-scale IQ was figured to be 116, placing him in the high average classification. This provided an assessment of general intelligence and scholastic aptitude. His verbal IQ was 127, placing him in the ninety-seventh percentile, indicative of exceptional verbal comprehension. This suggested that he could reason very well, learn verbal material quickly, and process verbal information effectively. His performance IQ of 98 placed him in the average category, but the magnitude of the difference between his verbal and performance IQs is very unusual in children of his age. It pointed to a need for additional interpretive analysis, as well as further study to reveal the reasons behind the discrepancy. Close scrutiny of the test results showed that low scores on the arithmetic, digit span, and coding subtests might indicate a short attention or memory span, poor concentration, or a lack of facility in handling numbers. While no absolute conclusions could be drawn at this point, the results of the test could be used in conjunction with other procedures, observation, and background information to determine an appropriate course of action.

Another common use of an intelligence test is to help an examinee determine specific areas of ability or aptitude which might be useful in selecting a career route. As reported in Aiken, a college senior was given the Otis-Lennon School Ability Test (O-LSAT, Advanced Form R) just before her twenty-second birthday. She planned to enroll in a program in a graduate business school and work toward a master of business arts degree. The O-LSAT is designed to gauge general mental ability, and it includes classification, analogy, and omnibus (a variety of items to measure different aspects of mental functioning) elements. The omnibus includes verbal comprehension, quantitative reasoning, and the ability to follow directions. The examinee was able to complete the test in thirty-five minutes and used the remaining allotted time to check her answers. Her raw score (number of items answered correctly) was 64 (out of 80), her school ability index was 116—which approximated her IQ—and her percentile rank among candidates in the 18-plus range was 84. These scores were in the average range for college seniors, indicating an overall intellectual ability that could be classified as "high average" in terms of the general population. Of the sixteen items answered incorrectly, a superficial analysis pointed toward some difficulty with nonverbal reasoning, but no conclusions could be reached without further examination in this area. There was no significant pattern of errors otherwise, and the random distribution offered no additional guide to areas of weakness. The initial conclusion that was drawn from the test was that a career in business was appropriate, and that with hard work and the full application of her intellectual abilities, she would be able to earn an M.B.A. at a reputable university.

A particularly important application of intelligence assessment is the identification and guidance of a child with advanced intellectual abilities. In a case reported in Jerome M. Sattler's *Assessment of Children* (1988), a three-year-old boy was tested repeatedly from that age until his sixth birthday. This procedure required the implementation of the Stanford-Binet Form L-M, the WPPSI, and the Peabody Individual Achievement Test (PIAT) for grade equivalents. The Stanford-Binet scores were 127 (at age three), 152, 152, and 159+ (with a linear extrapolation to 163). During his first test he was anxious and did not give long verbal responses, but the range of his scores indicated a very superior classification. He did not cooperate with the examiner on the WPPSI vocabulary and animal subtests (the examiner believed that he was not interested), but his performance at age four placed him in the superior range. On the PIAT, he was consistently above average, earning a grade equivalent above 4.0 at the age of six, with a grade equivalent of 7.4 (his highest score) in mathematics; the average grade equivalent for age six is 1.0.

As Sattler points out, the case illustrates "a number of important principles related to testing and assessment." In the largest sense, it illustrates the way different tests measuring general intelligence may yield different results (although all pointed toward superior mental development). The same test may also yield different scores at different age levels. The child's motivation (among other factors) may also play an important part in his results. More specifically, since the boy showed more interest in reading at age three and mathematics at age six, the test could not be considered a useful predictor of later interest, although an interest in solving perceptual-logical problems remained consistent throughout. Finally, since the parents had kept a detailed record of the boy's early development in a baby book, the rich history recorded there was corroborated by the test results which reaffirmed their initial suspicions that the boy was unusually gifted. During his first year in school, he tended to play alone and had frequent minor tantrums which affected his performance in school subjects. When he became accustomed to the social process of school life, however, he was able to demonstrate the ability that his parents had observed at home and which the initial tests validated.

Context

While intelligence tests of some sort appear in human history as early as the Old Testament Book of Judges (7:3-7, 12:6), which indicates that early Jewish society used questions and observations in personnel selection, the intelligent test as it is known today can be traced to Renaissance Europe. In 1575, the Spanish physician Juan Huarte wrote *Examen de Ingenios*, a treatise concerning individual differences in mental ability with suggestions for appropriate tests. His work, and that of other investigators and theorists, was the result of the rise of a middle class with aspirations to productive employment. Previously, the aristocracy had controlled everything, and fitness for a position was determined by lineage. Once this monarchical rule began to break down, other means were necessary for determining who was fit for a particular occupation and what might be the most productive use of a person's abilities. When it became apparent that royal blood was no guarantee of competence, judgment, or mental acuity, the entire question of the origins of intelligence began to occupy members of the scientific community. For a time, the philosophy of empiricism led scientists toward the idea that the mind itself was formed by mental association among sense impressions, and sensorimotor tests were particularly prominent. As the results of these tests failed to correlate with demonstrations of mental ability (such as marks in school), however, other means were sought to measure and define intelligence. The interest in intelligence testing in the nineteenth century was an important aspect of the development of psychology as a separate scientific discipline, and the twin paths of psychometric (that is, the quantitative assessment of an individual's attributes or traits) and statistical analysis on the one hand and philosophical conjecture concerning the shape and operation of the mind on the other were joined in experimentation concerning methods of assessing intelligence.

From their first applications in France as a diagnostic instrument, intelligence tests have been used to help psychologists, educators, and other professionals plan courses of action to aid individuals suffering from some mental limitation or obstacle. This role has been expanded to cover the full range of human intellectual ability and to isolate many individual aspects of intelligence in myriad forms. The profusion of tests has both complicated and deepened an understanding of how the mind functions, and the continuing proposition of theories of intelligence through the twentieth century has resulted in an increasingly sophisticated battery of tests designed to assess and register each new theory.

In addition, technological developments, particularly the growing use of computers, will permit a wider use of flexible testing in which the decision about what item or task to present next depends on the previous answer. Computers are also useful in "number crunching," so that such basic components of a test system as norms, derived scores, and reliability and validity coefficients (the basic statistical material behind the calculation of scores) can be assembled more quickly and efficiently. Computers will also make it possible to administer tests at multiple sites simultaneously when an individual examiner's presence is not necessary. Nevertheless, the human capacity for judgment and analysis in the interpretation of results will remain crucial to test procedures.

Intelligence testing is likely to continue as a primary means of predicting educational or vocational performance, but tests designed to measure the mind in terms of its ability to process information by shifting strategies in response to a changing environment are likely to become more prevalent. The proliferation of more detailed, separate sets of norms for different groups (age, sex, ethnic origin, and so on) is likely to continue. Also, the relationship between intelligence per se and behavioral attitudes that seem to resemble aptitude rather than personality measures is part of the heredity-environment controversy that will continue. Finally, advances in studies on the neurophysiological bases of intelligence will be reflected in tests responsive to a growing understanding of the biochemical aspects of cognition. As an operating principle, though, professionals in the field will have to be guided by a continuing awareness that intelligence testing is only one aspect of understanding a person's total behavior and that the limitations involved in the measuring process must be understood to avoid incorrect or inappropriate diagnoses that might prove harmful to an individual.

Bibliography

Aiken, Lewis R. *Assessment of Intellectual Functioning.* Boston: Allyn & Bacon, 1987. An extremely good source, clearly written and comprehensive; with a historical overview, descriptions of crucial tests, many examples, theoretical discussions of concepts of intelligence and useful statistical tables. Includes a glossary of terms, a list of standard tests, a detailed bibliography, and several indexes.

Cohen, Ronald Jay, et al. *Psychological Testing: An Introduction to Tests and Measurement.* Mountain View, Calif.: Mayfield, 1988. A basic book providing the reader with background information on assessment issues, including intelligence and personality assessment. Also provides the reader with an excellent chapter on the science of technological measurement.

Modgil, Sohan, and Celia Modgil, eds. *Arthur Jensen: Consensus and Controversy.* New York: Falmer Press, 1987. A must for anyone interested in the effects of cultural differences on the science of measurement, with an emphasis on African-American experiences. The volume is a collection of essays by outstanding contributors in the field of contemporary intelligence assessment. The last chapter is a competent response to the previous essays by Jensen, an extremely controversial figure in the field.

Sattler, Jerome M. *Assessment of Children.* 3d ed. San Diego, Calif.: Author, 1988. An outstanding text, including a thorough history of intelligence tests, a survey of issues involved in measurement, specific discussions of many individual tests, considerable scientific and statistical material, many tables, photographs, extensive references, and separate name and subject indexes.

Wolman, Benjamin B., ed. *Handbook of Intelligence: Theories, Measurement, and Applications.* New York: John Wiley & Sons, 1985. A very good source, containing thirty-five contributions by experts covering the entire field of measurement and assessment. The book was written as a tribute to David Wechsler and honors his pioneering work. The first section covers theories and conceptual issues, and the second addresses measurement issues and specific tests (and their limitations). The conclusion deals with the application of various tests to specific settings.

Leon Lewis
James R. Deni

Cross-References

Ability Testing: Individual and Group, 1; Ability Tests: Design and Construction, 13; Ability Tests: Uses and Misuses, 27; Intelligence: Definition and Theoretical Models, 1328; Intelligence: Giftedness and Retardation, 1334; Race and Intelligence, 2031; Testing: Historical Perspectives, 2540.

INTEREST INVENTORIES

Type of psychology: Personality
Field of study: Personality assessment

Interest inventories are questionnaires that have been developed for the purpose of assessing an individual's patterns of interest in or preference for a variety of activities. Most commonly, the interest inventory is designed to assist a person in making decisions about future educational and career directions.

Principal terms

CRITERION GROUP: a group used for validating a measurement
instrument; in the case of interest inventories, it refers to persons in a
particular occupational group
HOLLAND'S TYPOLOGY: a career theory developed by John L. Holland
that involves six occupational themes or types
INVENTORY: a questionnaire-type device used to assess various
components of personality such as attitudes, interests, and behaviors
REFERENCE GROUP: a group of individuals representing a sample of
"people in general"
RELIABILITY: the consistency and stability of test scores (or, in this case,
inventory scores) upon repeated administrations
TRAIT-FACTOR APPROACH: a method of educational and vocational
counseling that utilizes measures of an individual's personal traits
and organizes those traits into broad constellations or factors
VALIDITY: the extent to which a test (or an inventory) actually measures
what it is intended to measure

Overview

Since the inception of the interest inventory in the late 1920's, its development in the context of educational and vocational counseling has expanded considerably. Simply put, the interest inventory is a questionnaire-type device designed to measure the intensity and breadth of an individual's interests. Most often, the specific interests measured by an inventory relate to a variety of vocational and avocational activities. The term "interest" refers to a very specific aspect of human behavior. An interest is an enduring trait, a predilection for a particular activity, avocation, or object. It is a special attitude that engages the individual and motivates him or her to move toward the object of interest.

An interest inventory is distinct from both an achievement test and an aptitude test. An achievement test measures an individual's current ability to perform a particular task. An aptitude test measures potential or capacity for performing that task in the future. An interest inventory, on the other hand, measures a person's liking for a particular task without reference to the individual's actual ability to perform the task or potential for doing so in the future. For example, a high school student may show a high interest in the field of nursing. This interest alone, however, does not mean that he or she has any current nursing skills, nor does it indicate that the student has the mental ability, physical stamina, or emotional makeup for succeeding in the nursing field.

What then is the rationale for examining patterns of interest? First, interest in a particular activity provides some motivation for engaging in that activity. Therefore, when one identifies areas of interest, one is also identifying areas in which a person might have the degree of motivation necessary for following through on that activity. Second, the scores obtained from an interest inventory are helpful in pointing out which groups of persons an individual most resembles. Finally, it has been shown that there is some relationship between a person's domain of interest and the occupational field that that person may eventually choose.

The construction of an interest inventory may be empirically based (that is, based on observation of factual information), or theory-based (based on systematic principles concerning occupational categories). Some inventories have utilized a combination of these approaches. In its development, the empirically based inventory would be administered to various criterion groups of successful persons representing particular occupations. The inventory would also be given to a reference group, a large group representing people in general. The items on the inventory that set apart a particular criterion group from the larger reference group would then become part of the scale for that occupation. A person would be considered to have a high score on a particular occupational scale if he or she has interests that closely match the criterion group's interests.

Other inventories are simply based on occupational theory. One well-known theory that has been utilized in the construction of interest surveys was first set forth in John L. Holland's 1973 publication *Making Vocational Choices: A Theory of Careers.* The theory involved the categorization of occupations into the following six types: realistic, investigative, artistic, social, enterprising, and conventional. Other occupational categories have also been devised and utilized as the bases for interest inventory construction and scoring. Interest inventories also differ on the basis of the format used in the construction of the items. Some inventories ask the individual to indicate the degree of interest he or she has in a particular activity, whereas others use a forced-choice format, asking the testee to make an either/or choice between two activities.

In their book *Career Guidance and Counseling Through the Life Span* (1984), Edwin L. Herr and Stanley H. Cramer reviewed some commonly used interest inventories. Some of the inventories, such as the well-known Strong-Campbell Interest Inventory (SCII), the Career Assessment Inventory (CAI), and the Vocational Preference Inventory (VPI), yield results based on Holland's six general occupational themes. Others, such as the Career Occupational Preference System (COPS) and the Vocational Interest Inventory (VII), are constructed around Anne Roe's eight occupational groups. Interest inventories also differ in terms of their intended use. The Interest Determination, Exploration, and Assessment System (IDEAS) was developed for grades six through twelve; the Geist Picture Interest Inventory (GPII) is intended for culture-limited and educationally deprived populations, and the Kuder Occupational Interest Survey (KOIS) is for high schoolers and adults. The scope of occupations explored is another variable. The Minnesota Vocational Interests Inventory (MVII) deals with skilled occupations, while the COPS, Form P, deals with professional occupations. Some inventories are hand-scored, while others are scored by computer. Tests such as the Strong-Campbell Interest Inventory can be computer-administered as well. Some of the inventories are designed to be used in conjunction with the *Dictionary of Occupational Titles*, published by the U.S. Employment Service, or the *Occupational Outlook Handbook*, published by the U.S. Department of Labor, Bureau of Labor Statistics. The Kuder Occupational Interest Survey and the Ohio Vocational Interest Inventory (OVII) are two such examples.

There are various ways to judge the relative value or dependability of these measurement devices. First of all, one must consider the reliability of the inventory. Interests are human traits with a somewhat enduring quality. They are not expected to change radically over a short period of time. The reliability of the inventory is a measurement of how stable scores on the inventory would be if the inventory were administered to the same person over a period of time. A second consideration in determining the value of an inventory is its validity. Though there are many ways to approach test validity, the aim is to determine if the inventory is really measuring interests as opposed to some other traits. Studies are often undertaken to see if scores on one interest inventory are consistent with scores on another interest inventory which is considered to be a valid measure. Another test of validity involves giving the interest inventory to persons in that occupation to see if their interest scores emerge in the direction expected. Information about the specific reliability and validity of a particular interest inventory are reported in the manual developed for its use.

Of particular concern in evaluating an interest inventory is the possibility of sex-role bias. The extent to which an interest inventory is constructed to perpetuate stereotypic male and female roles is a major issue. The SCII, for example, attempted to use both male and female criterion groups for each occupation on the inventory. This posed some problems, such as finding sufficient numbers of males or females in certain occupations. Care was also taken in revisions to eliminate inappropriate references to gender; for example, "policeman" was changed to "police officer."

Applications

Interest inventories are typically used in educational and vocational counseling. Most interest inventories are devised to assist a person in pinpointing possible career options. This entails assessing not only his or her interests in terms of particular careers but also interests related to college majors. Often an interest inventory will be helpful in determining where an individual's interests lie in relation to larger clusters of occupational groupings. Interest inventories are also used by researchers in obtaining information about the vocational interests of specific groups for the purpose of planning and implementing career training programs and noting overall occupational trends.

The case study presented below serves as an illustration of the practical use and interpretation of the interest inventory. It includes a student profile based on the Kuder Occupational Interest Survey (KOIS) and the recommendations a counselor might make to this student in the light of the results obtained.

"John" is a seventeen-year-old adolescent in his junior year of high school. He is enrolled in a college preparatory program and has often verbalized at least a tentative interest in following in the footsteps of his father, who works in commercial real estate appraisal. His grades in art and drafting classes indicate that he has a propensity for visual thinking and illustration. John would be the first to admit, however, that his interests are very practical in nature, and he is not drawn toward philosophical debates. John's entire class was administered the Kuder Occupational Interest Survey through the counseling and guidance department of his school. The tests were computer-scored, and results were distributed to the students during individual appointments with the school counselor.

John's KOIS report form indicated that his results appear to be dependable. His interests in ten vocational activities are ranked in order of his preference for each. As compared with other males, his top interests, which are literary, persuasive, artistic, and mechanical, are average in intensity. The two areas ranked least interesting to John are social service and musical. John's patterns of interest as compared with men in many different occupations are most consistent with the auto salesperson, the photographer, the travel agent, the buyer, the retail clothier, the radio station manager, and the real estate agent. Furthermore, John showed an interest pattern most similar to men in the following college majors: business administration, physical education, economics, and engineering.

John's counselor reminded John that the KOIS measures interests, not aptitudes or other personal variables that go into a successful career match. The counselor observed that John's KOIS profile does accentuate some of the areas of interest to which John had alluded during his high school years. She noted that on the KOIS there were several indications that John might like an occupation related to business and sales.

As a follow-up to the KOIS, the counselor pointed out that John could benefit from exploring various school programs which offer the college majors that surfaced on his report form. She encouraged John to talk to college representatives about his particular interests. She suggested that John look into some of the occupations that appeared on his KOIS report and possibly utilize such resources as the U.S. Department of Labor's *Guide for Occupational Exploration* in learning about working conditions, employment prospects, promotion opportunities, and related occupational opportunities. The counselor also encouraged John to talk with persons working in those general areas of employment that appeared on his KOIS. Exploration of other careers in the same job families as those which appeared on his report form might also prove beneficial. For John, the KOIS was probably the most beneficial in providing him with the impetus for continued career exploration.

In another application, the counselor, in perusing all the scores of the junior class members with whom she is working, may note overall patterns of interest appearing in the KOIS report forms. This information may lead her to make certain provisions for those interests in the school's career awareness program, in the type of invited speakers, and in the kinds of college and training program representatives invited to make presentations at the school. While John was given the opportunity to take an interest inventory in high school, there are other situations in which a person may do so. Professional career counselors offer such opportunities to interested parties through college and university career centers and vocational rehabilitation services, in workshops for those planning second careers, and in private practice settings.

Context

Interest inventories can be situated in the overall context of vocational counseling, a field whose origins stemmed from the focus on job productivity and efficiency that arose during the Industrial Revolution. Frank Parsons is credited with laying the foundation for the field of career development. In his book *Choosing a Vocation* (1909), Parsons articulated a conceptual framework for career decision making. He emphasized that career decision making must be based upon a clear understanding of one's personal attributes (such as aptitudes, interests, and resources) as related to the requirements of the job field. Parsons' theory provided the theoretical backdrop for the more scientifically oriented trait-factor approach to vocational counseling which would soon follow.

Getting displaced American workers back on the job was a major impetus in vocational counseling after the Great Depression. During that era the University of Minnesota became a center for the development of new assessment devices to measure individual differences, and researchers there designed instruments that became part of test batteries used in counseling centers around the country. E. G. Williamson's work in career counseling research led to the publication of the *Dictionary of Occupational Titles* by the U.S. Employment Service in 1939. D. G. Paterson and J. G. Darley were also prominent among those psychologists who developed what is referred to as the "Minnesota point of view," or trait-factor theory.

This trait-factor approach has been the basis for many of the interest inventories which have been devised. Attempts were made to match the personal traits (in this case, interests) of the individual with the requirements of particular careers and job environments. The two interest inventories discussed below have been the most widely used.

The first version of the Strong-Campbell Interest Inventory (SCII) was published in 1927 by Edward K. Strong, Jr., from Stanford University; this inventory has been in use for more than sixty years. At that time it was known as the Strong Vocational Interest Blank (SVIB), a project on which Strong worked tirelessly, revising and improving it until his death in 1963. In that same year, David P. Campbell at the University of Minnesota Center for Interest Measurement Research assumed the task of continuing to update Strong's work. Along with Jo-Ida Hansen, Campbell produced the interest inventory that was redesignated the Strong-Campbell Interest Inventory in its fourth (1985) edition.

Probably the most common alternative to the SCII is the Kuder Occupational Interest Survey (KOIS), which was first published by G. Frederic Kuder as the Kuder Preference Record. Differences can be noted between the KOIS and the SCII in terms of their technical construction and scales.

While many interest inventories have been devised since the idea was first conceived, most of these inventories have focused on interests in career activities and related college majors. The 1970's, however, brought about the notion of inventories designed to measure leisure interests. Richard N. Bolles, in his book *The Three Boxes of Life* (1981), indicated that, in addition to meaningful work, people need to engage in the pursuit of two other "boxes," that of learning/education and that of leisure/playing. This more holistic approach may be more evident in the interest inventories yet to be developed.

Bibliography

Bolles, Richard N. *The Three Boxes of Life.* Berkeley, Calif.: Ten Speed Press, 1981. This popular book on life and work planning contains one of the simplest interest inventories devised. Based on Holland's typology, it is called "The Party" and appears on page 127.

Cottle, William C. *Interest and Personality Inventories.* Boston: Houghton Mifflin, 1968. Part of the publisher's Guidance Monograph series. Geared to the reader seeking a comprehensive overview of interest inventories.

Fogarty, Pat. "Using an Interest Inventory." *Academic Therapy* 22 (November, 1986): 209-212. Focuses on the usefulness of interest assessment in discovering the aspirations of children and in designing appropriate educational experiences for them. Does not require knowledge of technical vocabulary.

Frisbie, G. R. "Measurement of Leisure Interest." *Journal of Career Development* 11 (December, 1984): 101-109. Places the measurement of leisure interests in the overall context of career assessment. Presents the college-level inquirer with the rationale for developing an interest inventory that addresses both work and leisure activities. Examines one such inventory.

Graham, John R., and Roy S. Lilly. "Measuring Interests, Values, Attitudes, and Personal Orientation." In *Psychological Testing.* Englewood Cliffs, N.J.: Prentice-Hall, 1984. Provides the college-level reader with a concise historical overview of the development of interest inventories. Sample score reports and interpretive information are given for the Strong-Campbell Interest Inventory (Form T325) and the Kuder Occupational Interest Survey (Form DD).

Herr, Edwin L., and Stanley H. Cramer. "Assessment in Career Guidance and Counseling." In *Career Guidance and Counseling Through the Life Span.* 2d ed. Boston: Little, Brown, 1984. Gives the reader an overview of seventeen of the most commonly used interest inventories. Surveys the kinds of interest scales or categories utilized in each. Allows the reader to compare inventories quickly and easily.

Kane, Steven T. "A Review of the COPS Interest Inventory." *Journal of Counseling and Development* 67 (February, 1989): 361-363. Examines and evaluates the COPS in a relatively nontechnical manner.

Karen M. Derr

Cross-References

Bias in Ability Tests, 7; Ability Tests: Reliability, Validity, and Standardization, 21; Career and Personnel Testing, 467; Career Selection, Development, and Change, 474; Testing: Historical Perspectives, 2540; Work Motivation, 2654.

THEORIES OF INTERGROUP RELATIONS

Type of psychology: Social psychology
Fields of study: Aggression; group processes; prejudice and discrimination

Theories of intergroup relations examine the processes that underlie relationships between individuals belonging to different groups; these theories provide insights into conflict, ethnocentrism, self-esteem, and leadership.

Principal terms

DISPLACED AGGRESSION: aggression that is directed at an object, such as a person or group, which is not responsible for the events that initiated the aggression

ETHNOCENTRISM: an attitude of uncritically assuming the superiority of the in-group culture

IN-GROUP: the select group with which one identifies and in favor of which one is generally biased

OUT-GROUP: a group with which one does not identify and against which one is generally biased

RELATIVE DEPRIVATION: the proposition that people's attitudes, aspirations, and grievances largely depend on the frame of reference within which they are conceived

SOCIAL MOBILITY: the movement of individuals or groups from one social position to another which is higher or lower in terms of status

SUPERORDINATE GOALS: goals that are desired by several groups but which cannot be achieved by any group without cooperation from all groups

Overview

The major psychological theories of intergroup relations include Freudian theory, equity theory, relative deprivation theory, social identity theory, realistic conflict theory, and the "five-stage model" of intergroup relations. The three theories listed first are the most "reductionist" and attempt to reduce intergroup relations to the level of intra- and interpersonal processes. In contrast, social identity theory, realistic conflict theory, and the five-stage model provide explanations at the level of intergroup processes.

Although Sigmund Freud did not develop a formal theory of intergroup relations, his writings on hostility and aggression have had a historic influence on most of the major intergroup theories. Freud presented an irrationalist account of group processes, arguing that conflict arises out of the irrational feelings and emotional needs of in-group members, rather than as a result of differences between the material interests of groups.

Freud proposed that feelings of both love and aversion are involved in emotional ties between individuals. Group members are bound together by the ties of love that link them all with the group leader. The corresponding feelings of hate do not disappear, but are displaced onto out-groups. Freud believed that it is possible for ties of love to bind a number of people together as long as there are some other people left over onto whom hatred can be displaced. The most likely targets for such displaced aggression would be out-groups that are more dissimilar.

Thus, for Freud, the key to understanding relations between groups lies in the nature of relations within groups, particularly relations between group members and the leader. Freud believed that the only groups worth considering are groups with leaders, because without leadership the group cannot be cohesive and effective in action.

Equity theory is also reductionist in its account of intergroup relations, but, in contrast to the Freudian model, equity theory presents a picture of humans as rational beings. The main focus of equity theory is relations between individuals, but it also has implications for intergroup relations. The starting premise is that individuals strive to maximize rewards for themselves, but this "selfishness" is pursued within the norms of justice prevalent in society.

Individuals are assumed to feel distressed when they do not achieve justice in their relationships. Justice is achieved when the ratio of a person's inputs and outcomes is equal to that of the other person in the relationship. When this ratio is not equal, justice can be restored by adjusting the inputs and outcomes, either psychologically or in practice, to arrive at an equal ratio.

What makes equity theory a psychological theory rather than simply a model of economic exchange is that it is *perceived* justice that is assumed to determine relations between group members. For example, the relations between a minority group and a majority group may in actual practice by very unequal, but the ratio of inputs and outcomes for the two groups may be seen to be equal by both groups; this perceived equality is what determines behavior.

Similar in its emphasis on purely psychological determinants of relations between groups is relative deprivation theory. This theory focuses on the conditions associated with feelings of discontent among disadvantaged individuals and, by implication, groups. Feelings of satisfaction are not assumed to be primarily determined by objective conditions, but rather by one's perceptions of one's own situation relative to that of others. Theorists disagree about the exact conditions required in order for relative deprivation to be experienced; however, two generally accepted preconditions for feelings of discontent are that individuals must, first, feel they deserve to attain a better situation and, second, believe it possible to do so.

A major European theory, and one that has probably inspired more research than any other since the 1970's, is social identity theory. This theory focuses on groups with unequal power and predicts the conditions in which people will feel motivated, individually or collectively, to maintain or change their group membership or the relations between their in-group and the out-groups. Social identity theory assumes that individuals are motivated to achieve and maintain a positive and distinct social identity. Specifically, this means that individuals will want to be members of groups that enjoy high status and are distinct in some important ways.

Social comparisons between the in-group and out-groups allow individuals to determine the extent to which the in-group provides them with a satisfactory social identity. In conditions in which the social identity of individuals is unsatisfactory and "cognitive" alternatives to the present intergroup situation are perceived, individual or collective forms of action will be taken toward achieving a satisfactory social identity. These actions range from redefining an in-group characteristic, as suggested by the slogan "black is beautiful," to direct intergroup confrontation. When cognitive alternatives are not perceived, disadvantaged group members may attempt to improve their social identity by individual mobility, or by simply comparing themselves with other members of the in-group and avoiding comparisons with members of higher-status groups.

The five-stage model of intergroup relations focuses on how disadvantaged and, to a lesser extent, advantaged group members cope with inequality. It assumes that all intergroup relations pass through the same developmental stages in the same sequential manner. During stage one, group stratification is based on rigid categories such as sex or gender. At stage two, there emerges the concept that individual effort and ability can determine group membership. It is assumed that upward social mobility will be attempted by members of the disadvantaged group, first on an individual basis, and this takes place at stage three. When individual mobility is blocked, however, during stage four, talented members of the disadvantaged group will engage in "consciousness raising" in order to try to mobilize the disadvantaged group as a collectivity. At stage five, if the challenge made by the disadvantaged group is successful and the two groups become fairly equal, there will be a healthy state of intergroup competition. If inequality persists, however, then the process of intergroup evolution begins again at an earlier stage in the five-stage cycle.

A rational and materialistic picture of intergroup relations is offered by realistic conflict theory, which addresses how conflicts arise between groups of fairly equal power, the course they take, and their resolution. At a first step, group cohesion and identity evolve as people cooperate in working toward shared goals. Intergroup conflict arises when groups interact and compete for scarce resources, such as territory or status. Conflict can be turned into peace, however, through the adoption of "superordinate goals." An example would be an environmentally safe world, a goal that is beneficial to all humankind but that cannot be achieved without the cooperation of all societies.

The similarity-attraction hypothesis and the contact hypothesis are not major theories, but they should be mentioned in any discussion of intergroup theories. The assumption that similarity leads to attraction and, by implication, that dissimilarity leads to dislike underlies several of the major theories. The contact hypothesis, in its simplest form, assumes that under certain conditions, liking increases as a result of increased contact between people.

Applications

Intergroup theories have been used to explain a wide range of behaviors involving minority and majority groups, particularly prejudice and conflict. The theories do not necessarily attempt to explain the same events and, indeed, each of them seems to have a particular strength with respect to what it can best explain and the problems for which it can provide solutions.

The Freudian model has been used with particular success for explaining hostility against minorities such as African Americans. Feelings of frustration among majority group members are channelled outside the group by the leadership and displaced onto dissimilar minorities. This process intensifies under conditions in which frustration is particularly high. For example, in conditions of economic recession and high unemployment, frustration increases and so do attacks on minorities.

A solution to conflict, following this line of thinking, is to create "safe" channels for frustration to be expressed. For example, in Japan, some companies have incorporated official exercise sessions for the employees to release their frustrations through sport. Employees can also release tensions by "beating up" dummies who might in their minds represent their boss or pet peeve at work.

Equity theory is most effective in explaining unequal relationships that from an objective viewpoint seem baffling. For example, consider the case of Jane, who is constantly abused by her boyfriend John. He is always late when they plan to go out, he never buys her presents or even remembers her birthday, and he criticizes her in public. Yet Jane not only puts up with this treatment but also describes her relationship with John as "wonderful." How is this to be explained? From the equity perspective, the answer lies in the subjective interpretation of inputs and outcomes. Jane may see herself as getting much more out of this relationship than an outside observer assumes that she is getting.

An equally puzzling aspect of social life is that unrest and revolution often occur when economic conditions are improving. Relative deprivation theory provides what is probably the best explanation of this by pointing to the role of social comparisons and rising expectations. During periods of economic growth, people have more and so come to expect more. They compare themselves with better-off others. Relative deprivation arises when the economy stops improving but expectations keep rising.

Social identity theory, developed by Henri Tajfel and his students, is particularly effective in explaining the arbitrary nature of the basis for in-group prejudice. In many situations in which social conflict occurs, the differences between the conflicting groups may appear to be rather trivial from the point of view of outsiders. For example, soccer is "only a game," but supporters of opposing teams have sometimes fought to the death to uphold their teams' honor, as in the case of British and Italian soccer fans in Brussels in June, 1985. Both laboratory studies and real-life cases suggest that in order to achieve a distinct and positive social identity for themselves, individuals will exaggerate differences between the in-group and out-groups and will give importance to differences that otherwise might be trivial.

Although social identity theory identifies a whole range of behavioral options available to disadvantaged group members, from individual acceptance to collective action, it does not specify the priorities people have for the different options. The five-stage model does identify priorities, postulating that people prefer first to improve their status individually. Thus, the five-stage model is particularly useful for explaining behavior in Western societies, which are more individualistic than collectivistic.

Among the major intergroup theories, realistic conflict theory, developed by Muzafer Sherif, has had the greatest impact in terms of applications. For example, in the context of education, the concept of superordinate goals has inspired the creation of "jigsaw classrooms," in which students work in small groups to perform a task, and each member of the group has information crucial to the group product. Thus, students work in an atmosphere of mutual dependence rather than competition. Research suggests that the jigsaw procedure not only improves the academic performance of children but also can help improve relations between ethnic groups in multiethnic classrooms. In the context of industry, the concept of superordinate goals has been used to help improve labor-management relations. The same concept has also been extended to the area of international relations. For example, world peace and survival is a superordinate goal that has helped move the superpowers out of the Cold War era.

The contact hypothesis and the similarity-attraction hypothesis have also had important applications. The assumption that contact between members of different groups leads to liking influenced the movement to desegregate schools in the United States. The assumption that people are attracted to others who are similar to themselves has been part of the reasoning for the "melting pot" or assimilation ideology in the United States. The assimilation of ethnic minorities into the mainstream is assumed to create a more homogeneous society, one in which people are more similar to one another and thus more attracted to one another.

Context

Within the general domain of psychology, intergroup theories constitute a subdiscipline of social psychology. The major books that have reviewed intergroup theories have all noted that intergroup relations is still a relatively neglected topic in social psychology. The main reason for this is that social psychology has tended to be reductionist and to seek to explain all social behavior by focusing on processes within and between individuals, rather than within and between groups.

The personal histories of researchers have undoubtably been important factors in the development of intergroup theories. For example, many of the major theories were initiated by researchers who were themselves outsiders in one way or another and who thus had firsthand experience of prejudice. These include Freud, a Jew who lived in Vienna most of his life and had to flee to escape the invading Nazis at the start of World War II; Sherif, a Turk who moved to the United States after experiencing political problems in his home country; and Tajfel, a Jewish refugee from Eastern Europe who found a home in England after World War II.

Research on intergroup relations has also been influenced in important ways by minority movements such as the "ethnic revival" and the women's liberation movement. As early as the 1940's, African-American psychologists highlighted the negative impact of prejudice on African-American children. More recently, the Black Power movement and the revival of ethnicity generally have led to a greater focus on psychological research on the treatment of ethnic minorities. Similarly, since the 1960's, there has been a greater concern for women's issues, and this has led to more emphasis on minority-majority relations. For example, the issue of how the majority influences the minority, a major topic in mainstream research, has been turned on its head to become "how the minority influences the majority."

Intergroup theories should also be considered in the context of superpower conflicts. From the 1940's until the late 1980's, the United States and the Soviet Union were considered to be superpowers of fairly equal military strength. Not surprisingly, much of the research and several of the major intergroup theories, such as realistic conflict theory, dealt with competing parties of equal strength. The focus on unequal parties came with the more recent theories, particularly social identity theory, developed in the 1970's, and the five-stage model, developed in the 1980's.

There are indications that intergroup relations is receiving more attention from psychologists and that it is gaining a more prominent role in mainstream research. This trend is likely to continue, in part as a result of the changing demographic characteristics of North American society, in which the "minorities" will soon become the numerical majority.

Bibliography

Billig, Michael. *Social Psychology and Intergroup Relations.* London: Academic Press, 1976. A critical review of intergroup relations, presented by a leading British social psychologist. Very insightful, but rather heavy reading for most undergraduate students. Extensive bibliography.

British Journal of Social Psychology 23, no. 4 (1984). A special issue of the journal devoted entirely to the topic of intergroup relations. Leading European and North American researchers present both theoretical discussions and empirical papers. Can be read by college students.

Doise, Willem. *Groups and Individuals: Explanations in Social Psychology.* Cambridge, England: Cambridge University Press, 1978. By a Swiss psychologist who has been in the forefront of intergroup research. Critically discusses intergroup research, particularly the work of Sherif and Tajfel. Translated from the French; reads well and is suitable for college students.

Katz, Phyliss A., and Dalmas A. Taylor, eds. *Eliminating Racism: Profiles in Controversy.* New York: Plenum Press, 1988. Leading researchers discuss the challenges society faces in the area of race relations. Some limited focus on theoretical concepts such as contact, but most of the issues raised are applied. Literature on "symbolic" racism is discussed in-depth.

Taylor, Donald M., and Fathali M. Moghaddam. *Theories of Intergroup Relations:*

International Social Psychological Perspectives. New York: Praeger, 1987. Each of the major intergroup theories is presented and discussed in a separate chapter. A schematic chart of each theory is provided as a simple guide to the reader. Includes suggestions for further reading after each chapter. Can be understood by the college or high school student.

Worchel, Stephen, and William G. Austin, eds. *Psychology of Intergroup Relations.* Chicago: Nelson-Hall, 1986. Presents the work of leading European and American researchers. Many of the chapters are well written and combine theoretical discussions with empirical evidence. Not all theoretical perspectives are presented, but the bibliography is comprehensive.

Fathali M. Moghaddam

Cross-References

The Contact Hypothesis, 675; Cooperation, Competition, and Negotiation, 689; Groups: Nature and Function, 1125; Effects of Prejudice, 1848; Reduction of Prejudice, 1855; Racism, 2037; Social Identity Theory, 2297; Social Schemata, 2329.

INTIMACY IN ADULTHOOD: ERIKSON

Type of psychology: Developmental psychology
Field of study: Adulthood

Erik Erikson theorized that, during early adulthood, the critical psychological growth that must occur is the development of the capacity for intimacy. If one is successful, one becomes a genuinely loving person; if not, one suffers isolation.

Principal terms
   COMMITMENT: the forming and keeping of concrete affiliations and partnerships that require significant sacrifices and compromises
   INTIMACY: the capacity for a mutually satisfying openness, interest, and acceptance of a loved other
   ISOLATION: the experience of finding oneself unable to be intimately involved with another
   LOVE: the specific psychological strength that develops as one resolves the crisis of intimacy
   MUTUALITY: the experience of one's partner's satisfaction as being intrinsically satisfying to oneself as well
   PSYCHOSOCIAL CRISIS: a time in which a basic theme of psychological development becomes ascendent and is resolved in the context of a particular psychosocial relationship
   PSYCHOSOCIAL DEVELOPMENT: the favorable resolution of a particular psychosocial crisis at the stage when it is the ascendant issue
   PSYCHOSOCIAL DIMENSION: a dimension of one's basic psychological relations with particular others that has a formative and lasting impact on one's development

Overview

Within his eight-stage model of human development, Erik Erikson articulated three stages of adult development. The first of these stages he named "early adulthood"—roughly the period of one's twenties and thirties. Each stage has its own crisis, during which a particular kind of psychological growth happens. In early adulthood, the critical growth is to become a person capable of intimacy. Facing the issue of intimacy in early adulthood is no mere coincidence. As with every stage, the timing of this crisis has two bases. First, it arises from the person's readiness for it, achieved by having resolved the crisis of the preceding stage. Second, the new crisis is propelled into ascendancy by changes in one's psychosocial situation as one begins a new stage of development.

In the preceding stage, adolescence, the critical issue was the search for personal identity. This "identity crisis" is resolved when the youth succeeds in integrating previous childhood identifications into an original synthesis, a sense of inner consistency and coherence, a sense of direction, and a feeling of place. This identity allows the youth to enter the next stage of early adulthood, wherein one's identity must be risked. As always, the precious gain of the preceding stage allows entry into the next stage, but it also must be risked to resolve the next crisis.

By attaining a sense of who he or she is, the new adult is ready to make commitments to others—the very task demanded by the new psychosocial situation. Entering adulthood means above all that the experimenting orientation of adolescence must give way to the increasingly serious requirements of marriage, family, and career. In contrast to adolescent dating relationships, becoming a spouse and parent with another is not a step to be taken casually. One cannot simply walk away from these commitments as one could from one's boyfriend or girlfriend in high school. Nor can a career, once embarked upon, be changed as easily as switching one's major after starting college. As Richard Knowles noted, one becomes aware "that the commitment is open-ended, that it involves a history, not just a moment." Whereas adolescent involvements are characterized by the fluidity and easy movement needed for exploring one's personal identity, the involvements into which one enters upon becoming an adult have a binding power that requires a new characteristic: an investment of oneself such that one risks being changed, in unforeseeable ways, by the involvement. In other words, commitment requires being willing to sacrifice the very identity gained previously, as one advances toward a more encompassing union with another beyond oneself.

It is possible to initiate adult tasks, such as marriage, family, and career, without yet having resolved the adolescent crisis of identity. It is fairly common for youths who have not yet resolved their own identity crises to get married and even have children. They may hope to grow and find themselves through their marriage and/or children. More typically, however, the reverse happens: Such persons become so overwhelmed with the new demands of being a spouse and parent that they can only foreclose, rather than truly resolve, their identity crises. The requirements to "act like" an adult interfere with the needed exploratory context, thereby preventing the completion of a real development of personal identity. As Erikson has said, "the condition of a true twoness is that one must first become oneself."

The new adult's readiness to make commitments and the increasing demand from the world to do so form the situation that propels into ascendancy the psychosocial crisis of this stage. Erikson has labeled it a crisis of "intimacy versus isolation" to communicate the task of the young adult: develop a capacity for intimacy or suffer isolation. By "intimacy," Erikson means something much broader than the usual connotation, of being sexually involved, though he points to good sexual relations as a prototypical example of intimacy. A good sexual experience is characterized by mutual satisfaction, with the other person's satisfaction being as pleasing and important as one's own. This sense of "mutuality" is the key to Erikson's understanding of intimacy. Intimacy is a "mature devotion" to another—not as a negation of oneself, but as the context within which one will grow, beyond the egocentric concerns of adolescent identity, into an authentic appreciation of being open to and truly available for an "other." This fundamental openness is what Richard Alapack meant by the term "infinite relationship": a relationship that is not bounded by any limits on knowing or being known by the other. Maggie Scarf has defined intimacy very plainly, as "a person's ability to talk about who he really is, and to say what he wants and needs, and to be heard by the intimate partner."

For many, this challenge is daunting. Such openness and commitment entails many risks, not only of committing oneself too narrowly and inappropriately but also of being misunderstood or rejected. Life does not wait, however; time never stands still. If adults do not develop intimacy they will, over time, feel an increasing sense of isolation. One will feel cut off from deep human connection, lonely, without anyone with whom to share one's deepest self. People will then retreat psychologically, to a "regressive reliving" of earlier conflicts and a using of other people in a self-centered way.

By identifying this as a "psychosocial crisis," Erikson emphasizes that it is resolved within a concrete relationship. For most, this relationship will be a marital one, though many other types of relationships can also be the context for resolving this crisis. For example, one may make deep commitments of oneself to the priesthood, to a cause, to one's life work, to an idea, or to a friendship. In whatever form, the individual must experience in that relationship a deep affiliation calling for significant compromises and sacrifices.

When this crisis of intimacy is successfully resolved, the result is the development of a new "psychological strength" (or "virtue," in the old sense of that term). The unique new strength of this stage is what Erikson calls "love." To be a truly loving person means, for Erikson, to have a "mutuality of mature devotion"—in other words, the capacity for being genuinely interested in and openly available to an other. Only by such an "experiential union" can the partners resolve the ordinary antagonisms inherent in everyday functioning together.

Applications

Erikson has called the lack of intimacy "the core pathology of early adulthood." In that sense, his depiction of intimacy and isolation is especially applicable in understanding many relationship problems in adulthood. To understand these applications, however, it is first important to grasp Erikson's key distinction between isolation and "distantiation." To Erikson, distantiation means the capacity to make or keep one's distance, and it fits on the side of intimacy in the resolution of this crisis. When one develops the capacity for intimacy, one also develops the sense that one can reject the pseudo-intimacy of a bad relationship. One is then not driven by the fear of loneliness to settle for "anyone" rather than "no one." Once one has developed the capacity for intimacy, being alone no longer necessarily means being lonely.

Isolation may develop in either of two ways, which may be demonstrated by examples. First, one may simply be psychologically unable to be involved with a partner.

Robin spends her evenings in the utter loneliness of encounters with her television set rather than a genuine other. Though she craves contact, her life is mostly an avoidance of it. A second way to experience isolation is what Erikson calls "isolation a deux"—isolation as two. One may be factually involved with another person and yet still be isolated. That may occur in any of three variations. For example, Mark has four dates every week, but they never result in lasting relationships. Though his "little black book" is filled with names and telephone numbers, Mark remains profoundly isolated. A second variation is the case of Alice, who has a series of relationships, none of which ever grows very deep. A closer look reveals that the course of these relationships is very stereotyped: On each date, Alice knows exactly what she will do, what she will talk about, and how involved she will become. Everything is prescripted, and Alice plays out the role. The problems arise when the script runs out and Alice must suddenly be herself. It is at that point that the relationship becomes boring, problematic, or too serious and finally breaks up.

In a third variation, this isolation a deux may even pervade a long-term marriage. This variation is the most tragic: Two people are seeking to love and be loved, yet are going through life merely side by side without really letting the other in. The incidence of infidelity in such marriages is high, but, as Scarf has noted, there are two very different reasons for this. A partner may become involved in an affair either to avoid intimacy with the spouse or out of a hunger for intimacy.

Psychology's understanding of intimacy is most concretely applicable for people wanting to have more fulfilling intimate relationships. There is a vast sense of yearning in contemporary society for intimacy; as wider social supports, such as communities and extended families, collapse, adults must rely more and more on their marriage for such support. Yet, sadly, those same pressures have made it harder for spouses truly to be there for each other.

One result has been an increase in the number of marriage therapists, who consequently have emerged as experts with much to say about the nurturing of intimacy in marriage. Psychiatrists Thomas and Patrick Malone, for example, have pointed out that intimacy means being in one's own space while also being in a shared space. It is not a loss of oneself, but a sharing that transforms one's own self. Through the process of being known by the other, one comes to know oneself in the other's presence; this nourishes one's own self. The Malones note that such a relationship requires reciprocity in that both members must be actively involved in what is happening. They also list other characteristics that, "if increased, make intimacy more likely": free choice, morality, acceptance, self-responsibility, attentiveness, risk-taking, presence, naturalness, participation, personal surrender, engagement, systemic detachment, and creativity.

Context

Erikson received his training from Sigmund Freud's Psychoanalytic Institute in Vienna when it was at its peak, during the years around 1930. This psychoanalytic background provided the foundation from which he created an original view of psychological development, one that took key elements from psychoanalysis yet also varied in important ways from Freud's. Erikson's own theory stresses three central features that have had a major impact on psychology, namely that development is lifelong, psychosocial, and epigenetic.

Erikson pioneered the view of psychological development as a process that does not come to an end when one reaches adulthood, as major theorists (such as Freud and Jean Piaget) had previously supposed (and is even expressed in the term "grown-up" for an adult). Rather, Erikson saw development as a never-ending lifetime process, a series of stages extending across a person's entire life span. Prior to Erikson's influence, "developmental psychology" was synonymous with "child psychology." Now, the subfield of the psychology of adult development is perhaps the greatest growth area in psychological research. Though Erikson's actual writing on adulthood has been rather brief, what he said captured so well its essential crises that it has formed the basis for later psychologists' more extensive analyses, such as that of Daniel Levinson.

Erikson also deviated from Freud's emphasis on the psychosexual dimension of development, in which each stage was anchored by a bodily zone of psychosexual arousal. Erikson added a psychosocial dimension, by his discovery of the special relationship issues at the heart of each developmental stage. He did not do so as a refutation of Freud's psychosexual theory. Indeed, he explicitly says that the two are complementary and that nothing in Freud's theory precludes the addition of this psychosocial dimension.

Erikson also specified an "epigenetic principle" as governing psychological development. By that he meant that the issues of each stage are not merely sequentially connected. Rather, they are constituents of a more holistic or "organismic" development, evident in two senses. First, the issue of each stage emerges from and is built upon all those that preceded it, and is in that sense implicated in every other. Second, the resolution of each crisis involves the reintegration of all earlier ones, so that each crisis is genuinely a confrontation with every other crisis. Thus, to learn to love in early adulthood, one must again confront all the earlier crises from childhood and adolescence: those of trust, autonomy, initiative, industriousness, and identity.

Bibliography

Douglas, Jack D., and Freda Cruse Atwell. *Love, Intimacy, and Sex.* Newbury Park, Calif.: Sage, 1988. In the past several years, there has been a virtual flood of books for the general reader about how to improve intimate relationships. This one is a representative example but perhaps is a bit better than most. It offers many examples rather than superficial techniques, and it is more literate and insightful.

Erikson, Erik Homburger. *Childhood and Society.* Rev. ed. New York: W. W. Norton, 1964. This revision of a book that first appeared in 1950 is the most widely used basis for understanding Erikson's work. It includes a variety of separately written essays, covering such topics as life history, infantile sexuality, childhood in

Native American cultures, play, cultural identity and its exemplification in the personal identities of two historical figures (Adolf Hitler and Maxim Gorky), and Erikson's first detailed presentation of his own psychosocial theory of life-span psychological development.

_____. *Identity and the Life Cycle.* New York: W. W. Norton, 1980. This collection of three previously written papers of Erikson is considered one of the best introductions of his work. The first part consists of clinical notes from field studies with Native Americans and a longitudinal study of children. The second part presents Erikson's stages of life-span psychosocial development in terms of its contributions to the development of a healthy personality. The third part addresses specifically the problem of the accomplishment of ego identity in adolescence.

_____. *The Life Cycle Completed: A Review.* New York: W. W. Norton, 1982. This work presents Erikson's updated outline of his theory of psychosocial development, written when he was already in his eighties. Interestingly, he this time depicts his life-span theory from the final stage—old age—and works backward from it, in order to show "how much sense a re-view of the completed life cycle can make of its whole course."

Knowles, Richard T. *Human Development and Human Possibility: Erikson in the Light of Heidegger.* Lanham, Md.: University Press of America, 1986. The philosophical bases of this book will be too difficult in parts for a general reader, but it provides an insightful reinterpretation of Erikson's work. Knowles examines each of Erikson's psycholosocial stages of development and adds an additional, existential level of understanding to each.

Levinson, Daniel J. *The Seasons of a Man's Life.* New York: Alfred A. Knopf, 1978. An excellent deepening of Erikson's sketch of adulthood. Levinson's understanding is based on in-depth interviews with adult males over a ten-year period. On that basis, he has been able to specify in great detail the essential phases of development in the twenties, thirties, and forties.

Malone, Thomas Patrick, and Patrick Thomas Malone. *The Art of Intimacy.* New York: Prentice-Hall, 1987. These two psychiatrists draw upon their work with adults having marital difficulties to present the meaning of intimacy and its connection with the growth of the self. The book also offers a careful analysis of ways of being in relationships, along with key distinctions between the "I, me, and self" modes of being with another.

Scarf, Maggie. *Intimate Partners: Patterns in Love and Marriage.* New York: Random House, 1987. A thoughtful analysis of problems in intimate relationships, especially of problems that have long-standing roots. Scarf depicts the essential types of interactions underlying typical problems and shows how they often perpetuate issues from one's parents' marriages.

Christopher M. Aanstoos

Cross-References

JEALOUSY

Type of psychology: Social psychology
Field of study: Interpersonal relations

Jealousy is the experience of perceiving that one's relationship is threatened; it is influenced by cultural expectations about relationships, personal self-esteem, and feelings of possessiveness. Jealousy is a common source of conflict, and it can have a destructive impact on relationships.

Principal terms

DISPOSITIONAL: relating to disposition or personality
DYADIC: pertaining to a couple
PATRILINEAGE: the tracing of ancestry through fatherhood
POSSESSIVENESS: the desire to maintain and control a resource, object, or person
SOCIALIZATION: the process of learning and internalizing social rules and standards

Overview

Jealousy is not a single emotion; it is most likely a complex of several emotions. Their central theme is the fear of losing to someone else what rightfully belongs to one. In personal relationships, jealousy focuses on fear of losing the partner; the partner is seen as a possession whose ownership is in jeopardy. Whether the threat is real or imaginary, it endangers the jealous person's self-esteem as well as the relationship. Theorists argue that three elements are central to the emotional experience of jealousy: an attachment between two people; valued resources that are exchanged between them; and an intrusion on this attachment by a third person seen to be supplanting the giver or receiver of resources.

Early theories of jealousy suggested that the jealous person fears losing possession; later conceptualizations, however, have specified that jealousy is a fear not of loss of possession but of loss of control. The intrusion of a third party also threatens the cohesiveness of the attachment, dividing partners into opponents. Insofar as the relationship has been integrated into each partner's identity, the intruder threatens not only what the jealous person has but also who he or she is. Most researchers conclude that the experience of jealousy is itself a damaging and destructive relationship event. Emotional bonds are reduced to property rights; jealousy involves the manipulation of feelings and behaviors, and it can erupt in anger or cause depression. The positive aspects of jealousy are few, but they are identifiable: It intensifies feelings, provides information about the partners, can trigger important discussions between them, and can enhance the jealous person's self-concept.

Jealousy is more likely when a relationship is intensely valued by someone; the more important it is, the more dangerous would be its loss. Social norms do not support the expression of some forms of jealousy; for example, most cultures do not tolerate expressing jealousy of one's own children. Inexpressible jealousies may be displaced onto the more tolerated forms, such as a couple's sexual relationship. Sexual attraction or behavior is often the focus of jealousy, even though sexual interaction may not be the most valued aspect of a relationship. For example, one gender difference that has been identified in the experience of jealousy (in heterosexual relationships) is that while men focus on sexual infidelity or intrusion, women express greater jealousy about the emotional attachment between a partner and a rival.

Dispositional factors in jealousy include feelings of personal insecurity, a poor self-image, and deficient education. Jealous people appear to be unhappy even before they identify a target for their dissatisfaction. Describing oneself as "a jealous person" is related to a negative attributional style; a self-described jealous person sees his or her jealous reaction as stable and uncontrollable, and thus as less likely to change. Developmental research suggests that jealous emotions originate in childhood when the child's exclusive attachment to the mother outlives the mother's intense bond to the child. Childhood jealousy also manifests itself in rivalry with one's other parent or with siblings, implying that jealousy assumes that love is a finite resource that cannot be shared without diminishment. A common theme in jealousy research is the jealous person's sense of dependence on the threatened relationship, as well as the conviction that he or she is somehow lacking. Before an intrusion appears or is imagined, therefore, a jealous person may already feel inadequate, insecure, and threatened.

Jealousy is also related to possessiveness—the desire to maintain and control a person or resource. Thus the central issue of relationship jealousy is not love but power and control. Relatively powerful people (in most societies, men rather than women) feel less possessive because they feel less powerless. Circumstances can trigger possessiveness: In all types of relationships studied, one partner feels more possessive when he or she fears that the other might have a meaningful interaction with a third person.

Cultural and subcultural norms determine the forms and incidences of jealousy. For both men and women, jealousy is related to the expectation of exclusiveness in a relationship. For men in particular, jealousy is related to gender-role traditionalism (adherence to traditional standards of masculinity) and dependence on partners' evaluations for self-esteem. For women, jealousy is related to dependence on the relationship. With these gender-role expectations, individuals decide whether they are "obligated" to feel jealous when the circumstances indicate a threat to self-esteem or intimacy.

Cultures vary widely in the standards and degree of jealousy attached to sexual relationships. Jealousy is rare in cultures that place few restrictions on sexual gratification and do not make marriage or progeny important to social recognition. In contrast, high-jealousy cultures are those that place great importance on control of sexual behavior and identification of patrilineage. Cultural researchers conclude that jealousy is not inborn but learned through socialization to what is valued in one's culture. For example, a cultural norm commonly associated with jealousy is monogamy. In monogamous cultures, alternative liaisons are condemned as wrong, and jealousy is seen as a reasonable, vigilant response. In such contexts a double standard is promoted, separating jealousy from envy, a covetous feeling about material property. While envy and greed are considered unacceptable, jealousy is justified as a righteous defense of intimate territory.

Applications

Despite the negative form and consequences of jealousy in most relationships, it is popularly associated with intensity of romantic commitment. Researchers have found that individuals who score high in measures of romanticism believe that jealousy is a desirable reaction in a partner. Perhaps because jealousy is mistakenly believed to strengthen intimacy (although research indicates that it has the opposite effect), some individuals may seek to induce jealousy in their partners. Researchers have found that women are more likely than men to induce jealousy with an expectation of renewed attention or greater control of the relationship. Five jealousy-inducement techniques have been identified: exaggerating a third person's appeal, flirting with others, dating others, fabricating another attachment, and talking about a previous partner. Theorists speculate that the gender difference in jealousy inducement reflects the imbalance of power in male-female relationships. Provoking jealousy may be an attempt to redress other inequities in the relationship.

Reactions to jealousy vary by age, gender, and culture. Young children may express rage in tantrums or attack the interloping sibling. Research has identified six common responses made by jealous children: aggression, identification with the rival (for example, crying or acting cute like a new baby), withdrawal, repression or feigning apathy, masochism (exaggerating pain to win attention), and creative competition (with the possible outcome of greater self-reliance).

Gender differences in jealous reactions include self-awareness, emotional expression, focus of attention, focus of blame, and restorative behavior. When jealous, men are more likely to deny such feelings, while women more readily acknowledge them. Men express jealousy in rage and anger, while women experience depression and fear (that the relationship may end). Men are more likely to blame the third party or the partner, while women blame themselves. Men engage in confrontational behavior and focus on restoring self-esteem. Women intensify possessiveness and focus on strengthening the relationship. In general, these gender differences reflect different sources of jealousy and different emotional and social implications. For most men, a relationship is regarded as a personal possession or resource to be protected with territorial aggression. For most women, a relationship is an extension of the self, a valued opportunity but not a personal right, whose loss is feared and defended with efforts to secure the bonds of attachment. The focus of post-jealousy behavior is guided by the resource that is most damaged or threatened by the episode: For men, this is the role of the relationship in supporting self-esteem; for women, it is the health and security of the relationship.

Cultural differences in reacting to jealousy range from extreme violence to dismissive inattention. A jealous Samoan woman might bite her rival in the nose, while a New Mexican Zuni wife might refuse to do her straying husband's laundry. Cultures may overtly or tacitly condone violence incited by jealous passion. Jealousy has been cited as a justifying factor in many forms of social violence: family murder and suicide, spouse abuse, divorce, depression, and criminal behavior. Despite cultural stereotypes of woman as more prone to jealousy, a review of murders committed in a jealous rage has revealed women to be the perpetrators in fewer than 15 percent of the cases.

Researchers have identified positive, constructive approaches to managing jealous experiences. Three broad coping strategies have been identified: self-reliance, self-image improvement, and selective devaluing of the loved one. In the first case, self-reliance involves controlling expressions of sadness and anger, and forging a tighter commitment with one's partner. In the second, one's self-image can be enhanced by making positive social comparisons and identifying and developing one's good qualities. Finally, jealousy can be reduced and the threat eliminated if one convinces oneself that the loved person is not so important after all. These approaches are all popular, but they are not equally effective. Researchers comment that self-reliance works best, selective devaluing is less effective, and self-bolstering does not appear to be effective at all.

Context

Research on jealousy has several origins. Anthropologists have long observed the dramatic cultural variations in the causes and expressions of jealousy. Psychologists have noted that jealousy has no consistent emotional expression or definition: For some people, jealousy is a version of anger; for others, it resembles sadness, depression, or fear. When research on close relationships began to develop in the 1960's and 1970's, jealousy was found to help explain the dynamics of power and conflict in intimacy. Early research produced the counterintuitive findings that jealousy hinders rather than enhances romantic relationships, and that its roots are not in intimacy but possessiveness. Jealousy was eventually found to be an aspect of self-esteem and defensiveness rather than a quality of intimacy or dyadic communication.

Jealousy has also gained attention as a social problem because of its implications in criminal behavior and domestic violence. Increases in the rate of domestic assault and murder have warranted a closer examination of the cultural assumptions and stereotypes that support jealous rage and depression. Educational programs to address self-esteem, especially in young children and adolescents, are focusing on jealousy as a symptom of pathology rather than a normal or healthy emotional experience.

Consistent discoveries of cultural differences in patterns of jealous experience have supported the view that jealousy, like many other "natural" relationship phenomena, is learned and acquired through socialization and experience. Thus, jealousy research is contributing to the "demystification" of close relationships—attraction and attachment are not seen as mysterious or fragile processes, but as learned behavior patterns that can be both understood and modified. Jealous individuals can be taught to derive their sense of self-esteem or security from more stable, self-controlled sources. Jealousy can be explained as the unhealthy symptom of a treatable complex of emotions, beliefs, and habits. Its contributions to relationship conflict and personal distress can be reduced, and its lessons applied to developing healthier attitudes and behaviors.

Bibliography

Brehm, Sharon S. *Intimate Relationships.* 2d ed. New York: Random House, 1991. This excellent text devotes one chapter to jealousy, reviewing research and putting jealousy in the context of other relationship experiences.

Clanton, Gordon, and Lynn G. Smith, eds. *Jealousy.* Englewood Cliffs, N.J.: Prentice-Hall, 1977. A short, readable, and interesting edited collection reviewing gender differences, cultural factors, and other issues in jealousy research.

Pines, Ayala M., and Elliot Aronson. "Antecedents, Correlates, and Consequences of Sexual Jealousy." *Journal of Personality* 51 (1983): 108-136. An easy-to-read, clarifying review of the causes, symptoms, and outcomes of jealousy in romantic relationships.

Salovey, Peter, and Judith Rodin. "The Heart of Jealousy." *Psychology Today* 19 (September, 1985): 22-29. This engaging article reviews research findings and suggests practical applications.

White, Gregory L., and Paul E. Mullen. *Jealousy: Theory, Research, and Clinical Strategies.* New York: Guilford Press, 1989. This well-written academic book includes chapters on romantic jealousy; the origins of jealousy in sociobiology, personality, and culture; gender effects in jealousy; pathological and violent jealousy; and strategies for assessing and managing jealousy.

Ann L. Weber

Cross-References

Attraction Theories, 332; Dissolution, 824; Emotion: Cultural Variations, 887; Emotion and Attribution Theory, 921; Love, 1486.

JUVENILE DELINQUENCY

Type of psychology: Developmental psychology
Fields of study: Adolescence; aggression; substance abuse

Juvenile delinquency refers to crime or status offenses by juveniles; the adult criminal typically began as a juvenile delinquent.

Principal terms

CRIME: activity defined as illegal by authorized officials, such as the legislature, and having punishment spelled out for violations

DELINQUENCY: violation of the law, or proof of violation of the law

JUVENILE: one below the legally established age of adulthood

PARENTAL NEGLECT: failure of parents to show proper concern for their child; failure to provide a child with such things as food, shelter, and psychological support

STATUS OFFENSE: violation of rules which the state holds to govern juvenile conduct, such as curfews, school attendance, or obeying parents

Overview

Juvenile delinquency may be defined in either of two ways. It refers either to crime or to status offenses by a person defined as not yet being an adult. The age of adulthood varies somewhat from state to state. For example, one is an adult in California at age eighteen, while one becomes an adult under Louisiana law at seventeen years of age. A crime is anything which the criminal laws of the state define as illegal. This is what most people think of when they hear the term "juvenile delinquency." There is a second category of juvenile delinquency, however, known as status offenses. These are actions for which the state holds the youth responsible, although they would not be illegal if the person were an adult. Examples include not attending school, staying out too late at night, and defiance of parents. A juvenile can be sent to a juvenile prison for a status offense. For example, in one instance a youth was sent to a juvenile prison for status offense, fell in with more criminally oriented youth, and participated in the burglary of the home of a woman who did volunteer work with the prisoners. It was rumored that she was well-to-do, although this was apparently not really the case. The youths did not find the money, but in the process of the crime they confronted and killed the woman. Thus, a youth sent to a juvenile facility for a status offense was charged with murder for his part in the affair.

Studies of juvenile delinquents often try to explain why the youth became a criminal. In many cases, especially with youths from the lower socioeconomic classes but also sometimes with middle-class or upper-class youths, the finding is that the family unit is dysfunctional. That is, the youth does not come from a normal healthy home but from a home in which there is considerable aggression among family members, either verbal or physical. Often the parents are not very supportive of the children but instead show either indifference or constant criticism. Youths who murder have often been physically and psychologically abused by their parents. For example, there is a case of a young murderer who shot and killed a female boarder in his home when he was fifteen years old. The youth had received beatings from his stepfathers. He said that the psychological abuse he suffered was even worse than the physical abuse. He gave an example in psychotherapy of one of his stepfathers telling him, "You are no better than the dog. You can go sleep outside in the doghouse to-night." With that, the adult forced him out of the house.

Many juvenile delinquents have suffered parental physical, sexual, or psychological abuse when growing up, and turning to crime seems to be one way of responding to these abuses. Too few people see the various kinds of abuse as a possible causal factor in choosing a life-style of crime. There is, however, increasing research supporting this notion. This leads to the idea that early intervention into the home may be a preventative, in that stopping some of this abuse may save some juveniles from becoming criminals. Yet not everyone who suffers such abuse becomes a criminal, so there must be many causes of crime. Some people grow up to be fairly normal despite the abuse, while others suffer various degrees of mental illness instead of becoming criminals or growing up to be normal.

In the instances where there is no obvious physical, sexual, or psychological abuse leading to juvenile delinquency, one often finds that the parents themselves are anti-social. Thus, in a sense, the child grows up following rules of socialization, but in these cases the child is socialized to antisocial choices. For example, parents may violate certain laws, often in a flagrant fashion, such as using cocaine in their child's presence. The child learns that this is the normal, approved way within his or her household, and adopts the parents' values. Thus, the road is set for the child to become a juvenile delinquent. When one thinks of crime, one may think of lower-class people, and indeed prisons are primarily filled with people from the lower socioeconomic classes, including many minorities. Middle- or upper-class youths may also be delinquent, but they are more likely to avoid going to prison, either through preferential treatment or by having better attorneys.

A totally different view of crime from the one presented thus far puts the blame squarely on the shoulders of the offender. According to this view, people have free will and commit crimes because they choose to do so. They are not seen as victims of family background but as bad people who do bad things. A slightly modified version of this approach would be that there is something in the offender that pre-disposes him or her toward committing crimes. It could, for example, possibly be brain chemistry which makes a person oriented toward thrill-seeking behavior. Per-haps some people have such a strong need for sensation-seeking that ordinary excite-ments do not satisfy them, and under the right circumstances, such as a group which encourages them, they will commit crimes. Yet another view which places the re-sponsibility primarily on the individual would be approaches suggesting that many criminals suffer from brain damage or other physical problems which interfere with good judgment.

All these explanations focus on the individual as being responsible and shy away from seeing the social setting, including the family, as having much to do with the juvenile becoming delinquent. An attempt to explain crime by saying that many criminals possess an extra Y chromosome, thus putting the cause on a genetic basis, has been shown to be inadequate. Most criminals do not possess an extra Y chromosome, and those who do seem to have low intelligence. They apparently do not become criminals because of their chromosomal abnormality.

Applications

Given that society thinks of some juveniles as delinquent, there are two general approaches to the problem. First, society needs some way of controlling those juveniles who disobey the law. Here one has the whole criminal justice system: police, juvenile courts, probation officers, prisons, and so on. Second, people can try to help the juvenile via treatment. Some would say that prison or probation is treatment, but what is meant here is the kind of intervention that a social worker, psychologist, or psychiatrist might make.

There are three kinds of prevention. Primary prevention occurs when something bad is prevented from happening before the person shows any signs of a problem. Drug education in the early school grades would be an example. Secondary prevention occurs when professionals work with an at-risk population. For example, helping a youth who lives in a high-crime area where drugs are sold and laws are often violated, but who himself or herself is not delinquent, would be secondary prevention. He or she is at risk of becoming a delinquent, given the environment, but has not become delinquent yet. Tertiary prevention occurs when the problem has already occurred and then something is done. Treating a disease after a person has become sick is tertiary prevention; so is doing psychotherapy with people who already are mentally ill, or performing some kind of intervention with someone who is already a delinquent.

Unfortunately, most of society's preventive attempts are tertiary prevention, whereas primary prevention would seem to be the most effective, followed by secondary prevention. Psychologists and psychiatrists are typically called upon for tertiary prevention. Social workers are as well, but some of the time they may intervene in a primary or secondary fashion, as when they do home visits to assess the problems in a home and devise some strategy for improving the situation. Psychologists and psychiatrists can do primary and secondary prevention, and sometimes they do, especially if they work with some agency, such as a school, and try to prevent problems before they occur. It may be too late to change most juvenile delinquents once they reach about sixteen years of age. Primary or secondary preventive efforts would seem the most effective approach. By the time an offender is sixteen, he or she may have a long history of crime and may be dedicated to an antisocial life-style. Some sixteen-year-olds can be helped, certainly, especially if they are fairly new to crime.

Many juvenile delinquents have no sense of how they could be other than a criminal. Treatment efforts need to provide them with alternatives and with the skills, via education or job training, to meet these alternatives.

Once the juvenile has been tried and convicted in a juvenile court (or in a regular adult court, if tried as an adult, as sometimes occurs in very serious cases), the court has three major dispositions it can make. The convicted juvenile may be placed on probation, ordered to make restitution if money was stolen or property damaged, or incarcerated. One would hope that fairness would prevail and that the sentences handed down from jurisdiction to jurisdiction would be similar for similar offenses. Such, unfortunately, is not always the case.

The criminal justice system is plagued with the problem of sentencing disparity. This affects juvenile and adult offenders alike. In other words, if an offender is convicted in one court, the sentence may be very different from that which is handed down in another court for the same offense, and for a juvenile with the same history. History here means that the court, legitimately, takes into account the previous arrest and conviction record of the juvenile in determining sentence. In one look at sentences given to juveniles by courts in six different sites (five different states and Washington, D.C.), all the offenders were repeat offenders convicted of serious crimes. The sentences handed down in the different sites should have been about the same. They were not. In one jurisdiction, most of the convicted juvenile offenders were incarcerated and none received probation. In the other sites, incarceration was very unlikely, and probation or restitution were frequently employed. Thus, what sentence one received depended upon where one was convicted. This is hardly an equitable application of the law. The one jurisdiction which typically used incarceration may be overly harsh, while the other jurisdictions may be overly lenient. Sometimes probation or restitution makes sense in order to give the offender another chance, while sometimes incarceration is necessary for the protection of society. The sentences should fit the needs of society and of the offender, but at times they seem to reflect the bias of the community for either harsh or lenient treatment of convicted juveniles.

Context

The idea that juveniles should be treated differently from adults is a fairly modern one. For example, in the Middle Ages people had quite a different conception of childhood. Their art often shows babies who look like small adults. Until quite recently, juveniles were often placed in prison with adults, where they were sometimes subject to rape or other abuse. Some states still place juveniles in adult prisons. Thinking of someone as a juvenile delinquent, instead of simply as a delinquent (criminal), often means that the juvenile receives what are supposed to be special considerations. For example, the juvenile may not be "convicted of a crime" but instead may have a "sustained petition" declaring him or her delinquent. The penalties may be much less than if an adult had committed the crime.

Since juveniles are treated differently, it once was held that the juvenile court was not really a court in the adult sense but a place where the judge's function was to help the youth. One consequence of this thinking was that the adult right to have an attorney was not granted universally to juveniles. Thus, those charged with juvenile delinquency would face the possibility of being convicted and sent to prison but might not have a lawyer during their trial. The United States Supreme Court changed that in 1967 in a case known as *In re Gault*, in which it ruled that juveniles are entitled to adultlike protections, including having an attorney. No longer would juveniles be tried and convicted without legal counsel.

It was previously noted that juveniles may receive lesser penalties for crimes than adults; sometimes, however, the penalties are worse. Two examples are status offenses, wherein the offense, such as disobeying parents, would not even be a crime if the juvenile were an adult, and instances where the juvenile may be confined in a juvenile prison until he or she becomes an adult. In the second case, an adult male who breaks into a warehouse may receive a three-year sentence, while a fourteen-year-old boy may be confined until he is eighteen or perhaps even until he is twenty-one. In this case, the person would have received a shorter sentence had he been an adult. The use of status offenses as a basis for charging or imprisoning juveniles has received much criticism from social scientists as unfair. Those who favor retaining it see it as an effective social control mechanism for what they consider criminal tendencies.

Bibliography

Bootzin, Richard R., and Joan Ross Acocella. *Abnormal Psychology: Current Perspectives*. 5th ed. New York: Random House, 1988. A very readable abnormal psychology text. Chapter 12, "The Addictive Disorders," deals with problems of drug dependence. Crime is related to drugs in various ways. In addition, chapter 22, "Legal Issues in Abnormal Psychology," is of interest. The authors cover the topics of psychological disturbance and criminal law, civil commitment, patient's rights, and power and the mental health profession.

Brown, Stephen E., F. A. Esbensen, and Gilbert Geis. *Criminology: Explaining Crime and Its Context*. Cincinnati: Anderson, 1991. An excellent text that gives a good overview of crime and its various explanations. While not specifically focused on juvenile crime, the book does give a good general explanation of crime from a variety of standpoints, including such things as robbery, the impact of gambling, different theories of crime, and the goals of the criminal justice system. Everything from abortion to marijuana is covered.

Eisenman, Russell. *From Crime to Creativity: Psychological and Social Factors in Deviance*. Dubuque, Iowa: Kendall/Hunt, 1991. Discusses causes of crime and makes the important point that most theories of crime are really theories of lower-class crime. The American view of the criminal, juvenile or adult, tends to be that of a person from the lower socioeconomic class, which does not allow an understanding of middle-class and upper-class crime. Both lower-class and white-collar crime are discussed. Juvenile delinquency is explored; the negative family backgrounds of juvenile delinquents are discussed.

Glueck, Sheldon, and Eleanor Glueck. *Unraveling Juvenile Delinquency.* Cambridge, Mass.: Harvard University Press, 1951. This book is one of the early classics. The Gluecks, a husband-and-wife team of researchers, use psychological and sociological concepts to try to understand why youth become delinquent. It makes sense, they hold, to look at both the personality of the offender and the social background, such as family and neighborhood.

Hunter, Mic, ed. *The Sexually Abused Male.* 2 vols. Lexington, Mass.: D. C. Heath, 1990. Since many juvenile delinquents have suffered sexual abuse, it may be that this abuse helps cause them to become criminals. Some sexually abused children do not become criminals, so this is obviously only a partial explanation. These two volumes deal extremely well with various aspects of abuse, including, but not limited to, how the abused child may go on to become a sex offender.

Monahan, John, ed. *Who Is the Client? The Ethics of Psychological Intervention in the Criminal Justice System.* Washington, D.C.: American Psychological Association, 1980. This book contains six chapters which deal with working in the criminal justice system. Ethical dilemmas abound, as the professional may have responsibilities both to the agency and to the client (such as a juvenile delinquent). Specific issues about juvenile delinquency, including theories of causation, are contained in chapter 5, "Ethical Issues for Psychologists in the Juvenile Justice System: Know and Tell," by Julian Rappaport, James T. Lamiell, and Edward Seidman. The authors suggest that community treatment of offenders may be, at times, preferable to incarceration.

Russell Eisenman

Cross-References

Abnormality: Legal Models, 67; Addictive Personality and Behaviors, 102; Aggression: Definitions and Theoretical Explanations, 162; Antisocial Personality, 265; Child Abuse, 507.

KINESTHESIS AND VESTIBULAR SENSITIVITY

Type of psychology: Sensation and perception
Field of study: Auditory, chemical, cutaneous, and body senses

Kinesthesis refers to the sense of limb movement and position. The vestibular apparatus of the inner ear provides the sense of orientation to gravity and movement of the head. Much is known about how these senses operate and about how they are linked with vision and other senses to help guide people as they move about.

Principal terms
GOLGI TENDON ORGANS: the sensory receptors that signal the level of tension on a tendon
JOINT RECEPTORS: the sensory receptors that signal the angle of a joint
MECHANORECEPTORS: the sensory receptors that are sensitive to mechanical stimulation, such as touch, movement of a joint, or stretching of a muscle
MUSCLE SPINDLE ORGANS: the sensory receptors that signal changes in the length of a muscle
SEMICIRCULAR CANALS: the three structures in the inner ear that together signal acceleration of the head in any direction
SENSORY RECEPTORS: the specialized cells that are part of the nervous system and signal the presence of stimuli
UTRICULUS: a small, saclike structure in the inner ear that contains the otoliths and sensory receptors that signal linear movement of the head

Overview

As people move about the world, they feel their own movement; this is called kinesthesis. People also feel an orientation to gravity, or a sense of "right side up." That feeling comes from a part of the inner ear called the vestibular apparatus, along with sensations of movements of the head. It is fairly easy to experience these sensations. By closing one's eyes and flexing an arm or leg, one can easily tell where the limb is in relation to the rest of the body. That feeling is provided by kinesthesis. While closing one's eyes and leaning one's head back, one continues to be aware of orientation to gravity. That is, it is still obvious which way is up. By swiveling one's head back and forth, one can feel the contribution of another part of the vestibular apparatus that signals acceleration of the head.

These sensations arise in several ways. There are actually three types of sensory receptors involved in kinesthesis. Sensory receptors are specialized cells that signal to the brain when certain stimuli are present. Rod and cone cells in the retina of the eye signal the presence of light, and cells in the inner ear signal the presence of vibration; these are all sensory receptors. The special sensory receptors involved in kinesthesis and vestibular sensitivity are called mechanoreceptors because they respond not to light or sound but to mechanical stimulation of the body, or movement. The receptors for limb movement are found in three places: joints, muscles, and tendons.

Joint receptors are special cells that are found in the linings of most joints, such as finger joints, elbows, and knees. These receptors are sensitive to pressure from the bones rubbing against the lining of the joint, and they signal that pressure to the brain, where it helps give rise to a sense of the angle at which a joint is bent. These receptors are useful only at relatively extreme angles, however, since there are few such joint receptors to signal position in the middle of the range of movement of a joint.

Muscles are attached to bones by tendons. Within those tendons are special receptors that signal the tension on a muscle, called the Golgi tendon organs (named for their discoverer, the nineteenth century neuroanatomist Camillo Golgi). The Golgi tendon organs help give rise to the sense of tension on the muscle (which may result from a person's own active contractions or from external pulling on the muscle).

The individual cells that make up most muscles run the full length of the muscle, ending in the tendons at each end, with the tendons attached to the bones to permit movement. Muscle spindle organs are attached to some of these cells and signal to the brain the degree of stretch of the muscle. For that reason, they are sometimes called stretch receptors. The muscle spindle organs play more than a sensory role, however; they form the basis for the "stretch reflex," which helps maintain limb position. Taken together, the joint receptors, Golgi tendon organs, and muscle spindle organs give rise to the perception of limb position and movement.

The vestibular senses signal the position and movement of the head, and the receptors for these senses are located in the inner ear, in close proximity to the cochlea, which contains the sensory receptors for hearing. One set of receptors for the vestibular senses lies inside two small chambers, called the sacculus and utriculus, which are coated inside with a jellylike substance into which small hairs from the receptor cells are extended. On the surface of the jellylike substance are many tiny otoliths—particles of inorganic calcium carbonate (limestone). When the head moves, the otoliths cause the jellylike material to move, deforming the hairs of the receptor cells, which results in a signal to the brain that the head has been moved. These receptors principally signal straight-line movement of the head.

The other part of the vestibular apparatus is the set of three semicircular canals. Each canal is set at right angles to the others, providing three tubes oriented in different directions. These serve to signal acceleration of the head in any direction. At one end of each semicircular canal is a slight swelling, which contains the endings of the sensory receptors. When the head moves, the fluid inside one or more of the canals moves through the canal, pushing against the sensory receptors. Since there are three canals at right angles to one another, the signals from all three can be used by the brain to determine the direction of movement of the head: One canal signals movement up and down, one right and left, and one forward and back. A combination can signal movement in any direction; however, these receptors only respond to acceleration of the head, or to change of direction. If the head is in steady motion in one direction, the fluid inside the canals is at rest, and no signal results.

Applications

The kinesthetic and vestibular senses are involved in a large number of reflexes that help control posture and movement. An important reflex of this kind is the stretch reflex. If a limb is suddenly extended by an outside force, that movement is quickly resisted by a muscle contraction. The muscle spindle organs are the principal contributors to this reflex, since they signal muscle length. A sudden change in muscle length results in a signal from these stretch receptors, which make direct connections to cells that cause the muscles to contract. The familiar knee-jerk reflex is of this kind. Here, a light blow just below the knee pulls on the tendon attaching the muscle of the upper leg to the bone of the lower leg, thus stretching the muscle. Muscle spindle organs quickly signal this stretch to the spinal cord. Signals are sent back to the muscle, causing it to contract, and thus pulling the lower leg up in a kicking motion.

One function that the Golgi tendon organs seem to play is to prevent damage from activating too much of a muscle at once. Some muscles are strong enough to damage themselves if the entire muscle were to be active at once, and the Golgi tendon organs protect against this by actively inhibiting muscle contraction when there is too much tension on the muscle. Similarly, the tendon organs signal most strongly when a limb is at full extension or contraction, thus helping to protect against over-extension.

Disturbances to the vestibular apparatus can result in dizziness as well as the awful feeling of motion sickness that some people experience riding in boats or airplanes. A similar problem that plagues astronauts on almost all space missions is "space sickness." In space, the otoliths become weightless; the sensory receptors in the sacculus and utriculus no longer signal the position of the head, but rather its acceleration. The result is much like motion sickness experienced on a turbulent plane ride or the seasickness that plagues many who travel by boat. Fortunately, people usually recover from space sickness within a few days, although many then experience "Earth sickness" upon return to the gravitational environment of Earth, since it takes some time for the brain to adapt again to the change back.

Most effects of vestibular stimulation, however, are not a direct result of signals from the sensory receptors, but rather result indirectly from the many reflexes in which they are involved. One of these reflexes is called post-rotational nystagmus. Young children are especially fond of this and will entertain themselves by whirling around in a circle, then stopping. This act results in both dizziness and a sensation that the world is now spinning in the opposite direction. This results from small reflex eye movements that go slowly in the direction opposite to the former rotation, then snap quickly back the other way. When ballet dancers perform their tight spins, they avoid the dizziness and post-rotational nystagmus by fixating vision carefully on an object as they spin, then snapping their heads around to refixate the object when they have turned too far.

One aspect of movement that the brain must take into account is that input from the vestibular senses may result from the head being moved, or from a voluntary movement of the head. There is also the problem of knowing whether apparent movements of objects in the world result from those objects moving, or from the head moving. This problem is resolved in part by the use of very close connections in the brain between input from the eyes and input from the vestibular senses, which can take into account the movement of the head and translate that into a perception of self-movement, or use the lack of indication of head movement to indicate that the movement is of objects "out there." These vestibulo-ocular reflexes help the visual system distinguish self-movement of the body and eyes from movements of objects, but are also rather sensitive. For example, alcohol can disrupt some of these reflexes, resulting both in dizziness and in an inability to make smooth-pursuit eye movements. Most eye movements are very quick and jerky, but a person can also follow objects that are moving by using the smooth-pursuit eye movements. A roadside test for drunkenness that is sometimes used by police is to ask a person to follow an object such as a pencil with their eyes as it is moved in front of them. At a high enough level of blood alcohol, the person is unable to make a smooth-pursuit movement, but instead makes a series of jerky movements.

Context

Muscle spindle organs, Golgi tendon organs, and joint receptors all are involved in various reflexes, but a long-running dispute in psychology and physiology has concerned which of the sensory receptors gives rise to the conscious perception of limb position. In *The Integrative Action of the Nervous System* (1906), the great neurophysiologist Sir Charles Scott Sherrington suggested that the muscle spindle organs were the principal contributor. In the 1950's, however, the case for a "muscle sense" seemed rather thin. For example, it was claimed that subjects could not detect movements imposed on the eye when vision was blocked by an opaque lens. More recent evidence, however, makes it clear that Sherrington's original view is correct.

Joint replacement surgery for arthritis, in which an entire joint (such as a finger joint or hip) is actually replaced by a plastic or metal prosthesis, results in the complete removal of the joint receptors, yet the sense of limb position is not much affected. Other patients have been studied who were undergoing surgery under local anesthetic for carpal-tunnel syndrome in the wrist. Pulling on the tendons that run through the wrist from muscles in the forearm to the fingers with a forceps resulted in a clear perception that a finger was being moved, even though no actual movement of the finger took place. Finally, detailed studies of the joint receptors have shown that they do little through most of the range of movement, signaling mainly when the joint is fully extended.

Another approach to the issue of kinesthesis and vestibular sensitivity has resulted from arguments put forth by James Gibson, who points out that a person's general sense of position is enormously affected by vision. After all, as one moves, what one sees changes. A person who is standing "still," if observed carefully from the side, will actually be seen to sway forward and back. A number of reflexes dependent on input from the muscle spindle organs serve to keep a person upright. When a person sways forward, those stretch receptors detect the fact and signal for a muscle contraction to correct the sway, resulting in a sway backward. If the eyes are closed, however, body sway increases dramatically (it is also greater in blind persons). Psychologist David Lee, pursuing Gibson's ideas, built a small room that was suspended inside a regular room so that it could be moved slightly. A person standing facing the wall will typically show an exaggerated sway if the wall is moved only an inch toward or away from him or her. If the wall is moved away, the visual impression is of the body swaying backward, and the brain quickly acts to correct this, resulting in a sway forward. Indeed, young children tested the same way will usually fall down as a result of the corrections their bodies make to what are perceived as movements of the body rather than the room. These results make it clear that kinesthesis cannot be spoken of in isolation. Instead, many senses contribute to the sense of movement and limb position in everyday life.

Bibliography

Bridgeman, Bruce. *The Biology of Behavior and Mind.* New York: John Wiley & Sons, 1988. Includes a discussion of kinesthesis within the context of the control of movement, rather than its perception, which places it within a larger context. Also includes a particularly good discussion of vestibular sensitivity which emphasizes the experience of vestibular signals, rather than only the biology.

Dickinson, John. *Proprioceptive Control of Human Movement.* Princeton, N.J.: Princeton Book Company, 1974. Proprioception is an umbrella term encompassing perception of movement based on muscle, joint, and tendon receptors, as well as vestibular input. Dickinson presents an unusually good discussion of all these senses, within the context of their role in the control and learning of human movement.

Gibson, James Jerome. *The Ecological Approach to Visual Perception.* Boston: Houghton Mifflin, 1979. Presents a detailed argument for considering vision as a contributor to kinesthesis. While Gibson's views on perception remain controversial, they continue to inspire much interesting research.

Lee, David N., and Eric Aronson. "Visual Proprioceptive Control of Standing in Human Infants." *Perception and Psychophysics* 15 (June, 1974): 529-532. Although this article appears in a usually daunting scientific journal, it is an easily readable account of research on the role of vision in kinesthesis. The "swinging room" demonstrates nicely that vision and kinesthesis are usually tightly linked in everyday life. An easily readable scientific article.

Matthews, P. B. "Where Does Sherrington's 'Muscular Sense' Originate? Muscles, Joints, Corollary Discharges?" In *Annual Review of Neuroscience* 5. Palo Alto,

Calif.: Annual Reviews, 1982. Reviews the history and recent evidence concerning the source of a sense of limb position and movement, focusing on whether the joint receptor or muscle spindle organ is the better candidate. Concludes that joint receptors contribute little, and that voluntary effort must also be taken into account (especially for perception of heaviness of lifted objects).

Schiffman, Harvey Richard. *Sensation and Perception.* 2d ed. New York: John Wiley & Sons, 1982. Reviews sensation and perception generally, including particularly clear descriptions and illustrations of the vestibular apparatus, though his discussion of kinesthesis and the issue of the contribution of the muscle spindle organs is less adequate.

James D. St. James

Cross-References

The Auditory System, 344; The Central and Peripheral Nervous Systems, 494; Motion Perception, 1600; Reflexes, 2066; Sensory Modalities and Stimuli, 2214; Touch and Pressure, 2578.

LANGUAGE: THE DEVELOPMENTAL SEQUENCE

Type of psychology: Language
Field of study: Infancy and childhood

Like any ability, a child's skill with language does not appear all at once but emerges in stages of development. The child proceeds through babbling, single-word speech, and two-word sentences, and then learns to elaborate and combine these primitive sentences. The field of language acquisition has studied the development of this sequential process in children learning a number of different native languages.

Principal terms
ARTICULATION: the physical process of producing a speech sound
FUNCTION WORD: a word which has little meaning in itself yet signals relationships between other words in a sentence, such as an article ("the" or "a") or a preposition (for example, "in," "on," "of")
GRAMMATICAL MORPHEME: a minimal unit of meaning whose principal function is to signal relationships among elements in a sentence; function words and inflections are both grammatical morphemes
INFLECTION: an addition to the stem of a word which indicates subtle modulations in meaning, such as plurality (more than one) or tense (present time or past time); in English, inflections are all suffixes (that is, they are added to the end of the word stem)
OVEREXTENSION: the application of a word to more instances in the world than ordinary adult usage allows
PASSIVE VOICE: a sentence structure in which the agent of the action does not serve as the grammatical subject of the sentence; the sentence "The ball was thrown by the boy" is a passive-voice sentence (as opposed to its active counterpart, "The boy threw the ball")
PROPOSITION: an utterance having a subject and a predicate; often used as a synonym for "sentence," although a sentence may actually contain more than one proposition
REFERENT: an object in the real world to which a word refers
SALIENT: characterized by something which stands out from the background because it is perceptually prominent

Overview

Even before they are ready to walk, most babies are busily engaged in acquiring their native languages, and they do so with startling rapidity. The typical four-year-old child is already in command of most of the major structures that characterize the language of adults. The details of exactly how children are able to extract such complex rules from the language of the community into which they have been born are largely unknown; however, there is considerable information about the stages—the developmental sequence—of language development.

Young infants do not talk, but an observer witnessing a "conversation" between mother and baby might think they do, for a mother treats a tiny baby as a conversational partner, allowing the baby's burps, coughs, or cries to stand for a "turn" in the communication exchange and responding to these vegetative sounds with comments such as "Oh, you're hungry, aren't you?" or "Well, excuse you!" As the infant matures, the mother ceases to respond to involuntary noises and treats only higher-quality vocalizations such as babbling as a conversational turn. By the time a child reaches one year, a mother accepts only words or approximations to them as attempts at language. In the first year of life, then, the child is encouraged to talk through the speech exchange known as conversation.

Although infants burp, cough, and cry, such noises are not in fact language, nor are the earliest additions to this repertoire, such as cooing and babbling. Babies coo in the early weeks of extrauterine life, but they do not actually begin to utter intentional strings of what might be called speech sounds until around the middle of the first year, at about six or seven months of age. These intentional sequences of sounds are called babbling, and they usually consist of a repeated, or reduplicated, consonant-vowel string, such as "babababa" or "dadadada." The purpose of such babbling seems to be vocal play or practice. Children will babble to themselves or take turns babbling with a playful adult, using various pitch patterns on the babble to indicate glee, anger, discomfort, and so on. Typically, babies babble only a limited number of possible speech sounds, favoring consonants formed at the front of the mouth, such as /b/, /m/, /p/, or /d/, and avoiding those produced at the back, such as /k/ or /g/. Their preferred vowel sounds are those represented by the letter *a* in the words "father" or "daddy" (different sounds, in spite of the use of the same letter).

Although some variation exists, children generally produce their first real words based on the adult language around one year of age. These early words usually contain the same speech sounds the child favored in babbling. If, for example, a child's preferred babble string was "dadadada," a list of the child's first words might include "duck," "daddy," "shoe" and "sock," not necessarily because the concepts housed in these words are inherently interesting to the child but because they begin with /d/ or with consonants produced at nearly the same place in the mouth.

Children typically pass through a phase during which they speak one word at a time. In some ways, these utterances are not true words at all since they tend to convey much more information than a single word would. For example, if a child says "Cookie!" he or she probably wants to be given one, so the word is not a mere label for an object. Moreover, many of these one-word utterances demonstrate an "overextension" of the meaning of the adult word. For example, the child may use "duck" to indicate a duck, a sea gull, a mug with a protruding handle, or Daddy holding a cookie between his teeth. That is, the child may identify the word not with the entire original referent but with one or more salient features associated with it.

The one-word period is rapidly supplanted by the two-word stage. During this stage, the child unites two words in a single utterance. "Cookie allgone" or "Airplane bye-bye" are utterances typical of English-speaking children in the second half of the second year of life, and similar two-word sequences have been found in the speech of many different children acquiring many different native languages. Some children seem to use a formulaic approach; that is, they use one or two words frequently and combine these with a large number of other words. Children who take this approach may be heard to say "Hi Daddy," "Hi doggie," "Hi kitty," "Hi car," or "See car," "See duck," and so on. Other children tend to use two-word utterances to express a number of relationships they have observed, such as actor-action ("Doggie run") or possessor-possessed ("Baby blanket").

Regardless of which strategy the child employs, he or she quickly moves beyond the two-word stage. English-speaking children typically add to the length of their sentences by combining two or more two-word utterances and by adding one or more of the grammatical morphemes of English to the words comprising their utterances. That is, whereas previously the child may have said "Daddy drive," and "Drive car," he or she can now combine these two utterances into one: "Daddy drive car." In addition, the child's speech ceases to be telegraphic; that is, it no longer resembles a telegram in its omission of function words such as "the" and "is," and inflections such as *-s*, *-ed*, and *-ing*. Thus, forms such as "eating," "cookies," and "baby's" begin to enter the child's utterances. A sentence such as "That baby eating cookies" is not in the least unusual for a child at this stage.

It is important to understand that the child acquiring language is not parroting adults but is formulating a set of rules which will allow him or her to produce an indefinite number of novel utterances. One indication that children's language is rule-governed behavior and not imitation is the overgeneralization they so frequently produce. Having learned that *-s* signals plural and that *-ed* marks past tense in English, for example, children typically add these morphemes to exceptional nouns and verbs that are differently inflected. Thus, a child is likely to say "maked" instead of "made," "drawed" instead of "drew," "foots" instead of "feet," and so on, even though he or she has never heard these forms in the speech of adults. Moreover, a child is likely to resist correction of these forms, being certain that his or her own extraction of the rules is correct and that the rules apply without exception. These errors are creative, and, while they are errors, they indicate that the child has accurately assessed the rules of the language. Similar overgeneralization has been observed in children acquiring many different native languages, and thus appears to be a universal tendency. Children are left with the developmental task of determining the exceptions to their rules.

By the time a child is three years old, he or she probably has a fair-sized vocabulary and has mastered many of the grammatical morphemes. Whereas previously the child combined words to form two-word sentences, and two-word sentences to form more complete simple sentences, the child now begins to combine sentences by the process of coordination (tying ideas together through the use of function words such as "and") and through subordination (having one proposition serve as a modification for another). The child begins to make utterances such as "I played tag and I singed a song," "I'll be right there after I eat my cookie," "That's a man that wears a hat," and "I'd better eat my nuts before the dinosaur eats them." The child uses language to explain, to lie, to pretend, and to tell a story. Passive forms also appear, usually in shortened and colloquial form: "I got put in time-out."

By the age of five, a child has many of the forms of adult speech under his or her command. The child must still learn to make sentences cohere to produce a good story, to specify appropriately the antecedents (the full nouns) for pronouns, and to apply language skills to reading and writing.

Applications

The study of language acquisition has applications in the fields of education, second-language teaching, and speech pathology. How successful a child may be in learning to read and write may depend on how closely the teaching-learning situation resembles the situation in which the primary linguistic skills of talking and comprehending were acquired in the home. Many educators contend that the school-room should provide as natural a context as possible for the acquisition of reading and writing, and so teachers create situations in which children have to write real letters to real people, not just learn the form of letter writing by copying sample letters. Teachers who take this approach help children learn to read and write by having them compose their own stories and produce their own books. In other words, the children learn in a context where their words will be read by others as well as themselves, and so the material they learn from has intrinsic value; it is written by the children for the purpose of communication, just as early language is spoken by children in order to communicate. Language, after all, is acquired not for its own sake but to express desires, needs, hopes, and, eventually, thoughts. That literacy skills should be similarly acquired is the guiding principle of the school of educational practice called "whole language." Children are given a chance to make their own progress, perhaps halting at first, just as their progress with talking was. They are encouraged to produce whatever level of literacy they can, just the way mothers encourage their babies' vocalizations, and they are encouraged to move up to higher levels of abilities. The idea is to make the learning natural and to respect the child's own degree of progress.

In addition, knowledge of language development has enhanced the teaching of second languages in the classroom. Since the acquisition of second languages has often been studied by comparing the sequence of second-language acquisition to that of first-language acquisition, the explanations of similarities and differences can then be used to improve instruction in second-language teaching. In particular, the teaching of English as a second language in the United States to children from newly immigrated families has benefited from a knowledge of developmental sequence. How can educators make the learning situation in the second language as natural and effortless as was the acquisition of the native language? Will drills work? What about teaching the child to translate or memorize?

Such methods are only minimally successful, if at all. Children acquiring their native languages do not memorize vocabulary in context-free drills, nor do they practice meaningless changes in the forms of sentences—exercises frequently employed in the second-language classroom. Children acquiring both first and second languages learn by attempting utterances and modifying them when not understood, by trying out new words to see if they really understand them, and by attempting to get things done with words—explaining, requesting, and expressing ideas. Because children acquire their first language in the process of trying to communicate, they can acquire a second language most successfully when they are similarly immersed in the language and learn to "swim" in it. Children learn their way around a second language in the same manner as they master the first. They have no other option if they want to communicate.

A third area of application is a clinical one. Speech pathologists use the insights gained from language acquisition studies to help children who are having difficulties in normal speech development. For example, research on normal language development shows that many children pass through a phase in which they substitute the consonants /t/ and /d/ in all places where the adult language has /k/ and /g/; eventually, they learn the correct tongue positions for the correct articulation of various consonants. The question is, When should such substitutions cease? When is intervention by a trained practitioner necessary? The answers lie in what language behavior is typical of a sample of children at a particular age. Speech pathologists are trained to assess the developmental progress of children's language on the basis of what is normative so that they can recommend some specific steps for clinicians, parents, teachers, and other care givers to take. In this way, faulty articulations and problems with syntax which get in the way of the child's comprehensibility and social acceptance—and subsequent success in school—can be remedied.

Context

Parents with an eye for detail have recorded their children's progress with language at least since evolution theorist Charles Darwin took notes on his son's development and published his observations in 1877. In 1907, the German psychologists Clara and Wilhelm Stern published the first edition of their masterful analysis of their own children's acquisition of German in *Die Kindersprache* (child language). Other parents around the world similarly kept track of their children's development in their native languages, but a systematic scientific investigation of the acquisition process did not actually begin until 1962, when Harvard psychologist Roger Brown, equipped with tape recorders, gifted student assistants, and Noam Chomsky's theory of generative transformational grammar, set out to chart the course of development of three English-acquiring children, who were given the pseudonyms "Adam," "Eve," and "Sarah." Through careful systematic analysis, Brown charted the children's first stages of language development, and a developmental order for the acquisition of the grammatical morphemes of English was established. Brown published the findings of his research group, along with a discussion of the methodology they used, in a book called *A First Language: The Early Stages* (1973).

In the late 1970's and 1980's, as knowledge about the early form of children's utterances increased, research began to turn toward factors responsible for the shape and content of children's speech. Investigators studied the meanings of early words and sentences and how these meanings change with time. They studied the "pragmatics" of young children's speech, that is, the particular forms children use to accomplish specific goals. For example, researchers sought to determine the developmental sequence of request forms and other speech acts and to study the development of extended discourse such as conversation and narrative.

In addition, many students of child language began to examine the sequence of acquisition of semantic (meaning) notions cross-linguistically. That is, they studied children acquiring the native languages of many different cultures in order to separate acquisition factors caused by constraints in cognitive development from factors that result from the structure of particular languages. They sought to determine whether children acquiring a particular language expressed a specific type of idea late because its meaning was difficult for a child to grasp conceptually or because the language itself had a means of expressing the notion that was especially difficult for children to learn. By comparing how children acquiring a number of different types of languages developed, investigators attempted to separate the universal from the particular—the strategies all children everywhere tend to use as opposed to the strategies which the structure of a particular language may suggest.

A third area of interest to have emerged is that of individual differences. During the 1960's and 1970's, the theoretical foundation for the study of language laid by linguist Noam Chomsky led researchers to assume that all children proceeded in the same way. As work progressed, however, it soon became evident that children may take alternate routes to the same goal. For example, as has been discussed, when children begin combining words to form primitive sentences, they may take a formulaic approach ("Hi car") or a relational approach ("Mommy do"). Even before the two-word stage, however, children may differ from one another in their approach. Some children at the one-word stage are "referential": Their early vocabularies include primarily words for objects, and they acquire new words relatively rapidly. Other children are "expressive": They use fewer nouns, preferring pronouns, modifiers, and function words. It should be kept in mind that these categories are ends of a continuum; children are rarely all one or all the other, but are more or less referential or expressive.

Since its inception in the early 1960's, the field of language acquisition study has grown enormously, and so has knowledge of the strategies children around the world use in developing what is quite possibly their most important intellectual skill, fluency in their native language.

Bibliography

Brown, Roger William. *A First Language: The Early Stages.* Cambridge, Mass.: Harvard University Press, 1973. This account of early language development in English and in several other languages is a classic, and it is accessible to the careful reader interested in the early work which laid the foundation for modern language acquisition research.

Bruner, Jerome S. *Child's Talk: Learning to Use Language.* New York: W. W. Norton, 1983. Looks at the acquisition process from the point of view of pragmatics; investigates how a child comes to use language to accomplish various goals in the world and how, from limited beginnings, the child learns to expand his or her uses of language. A well-written and succinct contrast to the syntactic approach espoused by Roger Brown.

De Villiers, Peter A., and Jill G. de Villiers. *Early Language.* Cambridge, Mass.: Harvard University Press, 1979. Written specifically for the nonspecialist. Provides a clear and accessible account of children's first sounds, words, and sentences, as well as a discussion of the nature of speech addressed to children and its possible role in facilitating language development.

Kessel, Frank S., ed. *The Development of Language and Language Researchers: Essays in Honor of Roger Brown.* Hillsdale, N.J.: Lawrence Erlbaum, 1988. An anthology of essays written by former students and colleagues of Roger Brown. Includes overviews of several of the subfields of language acquisition, as well as autobiographical accounts of several researchers' own development in thinking about language development issues. Of particular interest to the beginner are the selections by Dan I. Slobin, Melissa Bowerman, and Jill de Villiers.

Werner, Heinz, and Bernard Kaplan. *Symbol Formation.* New York: John Wiley & Sons, 1963. Uses information provided by numerous diary studies of language and language acquisition to provide a psychological account of the development of language, connecting changes in expressive language with developmental change in general. The first two parts of this five-part account will be of particular interest to the novice trying to understand the cognitive basis of language acquisition.

Marilyn N. Silva

Cross-References

LANGUAGE ACQUISITION THEORIES

Type of psychology: Language
Fields of study: Behavioral and cognitive models; infancy and childhood

Three theories of how children learn to talk have provided differing interpretations of the roles played in this acquisition by inborn predispositions and by particular features of the environment. The debate among these theories, known as the behaviorist (or empiricist) approach, the innatist (or rationalist) approach, and the interactionist approach, echoes the controversies in other fields of psychology concerning the nature of knowledge.

Principal terms

CONDITIONING: a process by which a behavior comes to be paired with an environmental event; if a behavior results in a positive outcome (reward), the organism will tend to repeat that behavior; if the behavior results in a negative outcome (punishment), the organism will tend to avoid it

EMPIRICISM: a philosophical position which maintains that knowledge is a sum of sense impressions; that is, knowledge is derived from experience

NATURE: a philosophical term for the particular genetic endowments— the inborn capacities—of an organism

NURTURE: the philosophical term for the effect of the environment on knowledge, personality, and so on

REINFORCEMENT: the reward provided in a conditioning situation; negative reinforcement is the punishment that may be provided in a conditioning situation

SCAFFOLDING: a term used to describe the structured interaction by which American babies, at least, are introduced to language

Overview

Children all around the world, regardless of ethnicity or national origin, acquire the language of the group into which they are born with seeming ease and in essentially similar ways. Explaining exactly how two- to three-year-old children, who are as yet incapable of abstract reasoning, formulate the complex and abstract principles which allow them to comprehend and produce language has been the goal of three broad explanations of linguistic development. These explanations include the behaviorist approach, in which nurture is given paramount importance, the innatist approach, in which nature is given prominence, and the interactionist approach, in which nature and nurture are given equal importance, with both considered necessary and neither sufficient.

In the behaviorist view of language acquisition, imitation and conditioning account for language development. That is, proponents of this school of thought claim that children try to imitate the language they hear around them and pair the words and sentences they hear with environmental events. They receive social rewards such as smiles and other forms of approval for being increasingly correct in both pronunciation and meaning, and their initially babyish attempts at language eventually become replaced with appropriate adult forms. As is consistent with the behaviorist approach, the mental events which may accompany such responses are not included in this account of language development, because mental events are not open to direct observation. The basics of this theory are the stimulus, which may be an environmental occurrence such as the appearance of a cat and the expression of the word "cat" by an adult, and the response, the child's attempt to imitate the word he or she hears.

The behaviorist account seems plausible, but certain observations about what children actually do in the process of acquiring a language present a number of problems for the contention that imitation plays a significant role in language learning. For example, children will produce—and retain, even in the face of correction by adults—such erroneous forms as "throwed" or "readed," which they never hear in the language of the adults around them and which cannot therefore be the result of imitation. Second, when children have been explicitly asked to imitate adult sentences, they frequently substitute forms more in line with their own systems of language for some of the appropriate adult forms. Finally, the most damaging evidence against the behaviorist position is that in ordinary everyday interaction children produce completely novel utterances, utterances which they have not previously heard in the speech of adults. The creative nature of children's errors, imitations, and spontaneous utterances argues quite cogently against the contention that imitation plays the primary role in language acquisition.

The problems for the behaviorist account do not end with imitation, for it has been widely observed that parents reward truthfulness rather than grammatical correctness in the speech of their children. That is, children usually learn to speak quite grammatically without any reinforcement for their syntactic errors. The reinforcement component of the behaviorist tradition thus seems to be largely inoperative in language acquisition.

A second account of language acquisition is the innatist position advocated by the linguist Noam Chomsky. Using as evidence the idea that every sentence uttered is novel rather than a routine memorized by rote and the fact that native speakers of a language have intuitions about whether sentences never heard before are grammatical, Chomsky held, unlike the behaviorists, that linguistic science must investigate the source of this creativity and intuition, namely the set of mental events that are called "grammar." Furthermore, pointing to the numerous false starts, hesitations, and errors that occur in the speech around them, Chomsky contended that only an innate language faculty would enable children who could not deal with abstraction in other contexts to extract from this impoverished data a grammar capable of generating a potentially infinite and completely well-formed array of sentences. Chomsky, therefore, posited that human beings are born with a faculty he called the "language acquisition device" (LAD), which, equipped with a set of possible forms that grammars of human languages can take, allows children, on the basis of very limited data, to choose those rules of sentence formation which best characterize the sentences of the language to which they are exposed.

Since Chomsky's goal was to account for the ability of the finite human organism to produce a potentially infinite set of sentences, his emphasis fell on the syntax of language—that is, those rules of language which determine appropriate word order for sentences and which govern how certain sentences are systematically related to other sentences. For Chomsky, syntax was the central concern of language science. Implicit in this account is the notion that the child's interaction with others is not crucial to the theory of language acquisition. This model assumes that all that is necessary is for the child to be exposed to a language, and LAD will take over. With interaction not an essential component, it is clear that the innatist approach focuses on the structure of language (which is unique in all the communication systems found in nature) rather than on the function of language, communication.

No child acquires language in a vacuum, however, and many researchers contend that interaction is the crucial ingredient in the acquisition recipe. The interactionists do not dispute that humans are innately predisposed to acquire language, but they do question the necessity of positing anything so definite as a language acquisition device. Instead, the interactionist solution takes one of two forms, the cognitivist school or the social interactionist school.

The cognitivist position follows the theory of the Swiss psychologist Jean Piaget in that it contends that the child constructs language just as he or she constructs knowledge in other cognitive areas—by interacting with the environment. Through such interaction, innate reflexes begin to be elaborated and transformed into higher-order cognitive structures. The particular course that cognitive development takes is uniquely and universally human. Language, however, does not have a privileged position in this development; as a cognitive achievement among other important cognitive achievements, it rests on the same foundation and therefore is not separate from cognitive development, but rather follows from it.

The social interactionist approach, on the other hand, gives language special status yet does not focus on what might be innate. Instead, the focus of the social interactionists is the social rather than the physical environment. Researchers who subscribe to this approach have found that from the earliest days in the life of her child, the mother treats her baby as a conversational partner, giving meaning to the baby's vocalizations before these utterances have any conventionalized form. That is, she initiates the baby into the communicative exchange and introduces the baby to the idea that he or she can use vocalizations to refer to aspects of the environment as well as to demand or to express emotion.

Applications

A distinction must be made between what adherents of a particular school of thought know about real-world events and what they consider to be theoretically relevant. That is, behaviorists know that mental events accompany language responses, but they do not consider these mental events relevant within the constraints of their model. Similarly, innatists recognize that the environment is involved in language acquisition, because if it were not, all people would speak the same language. Thus, for innatists, the environment simply provides the raw data for LAD to analyze and is not a crucial part of the model. Finally, interactionists recognize that the child probably receives approval, at least for correct vocabulary, and that the child must acquire the rules of syntax in order to produce well-formed utterances. They point to the interaction between child and caretaker, however, as creating the meaningful situation in which such acquisitions must occur. Thus, no school of thought about language acquisition denies that children acquire language in a particular environment, or that the syntax of human languages is unique among animal communication systems, or that children interact with their caretakers. Each does dispute the relative importance and theoretical significance of these factors.

In fact, each model has features that are useful in explaining certain facets of the acquisition process. The behaviorist approach may be better than the other two for explaining certain aspects of vocabulary development. For example, nearly all parents have heard their child parrot back some expression they have used (and possibly regret using) at the most inopportune moment—perhaps during Grandma's visit. Moreover, psychologists Anat Ninio and Jerome Bruner, advocates of the social interactionist approach, writing in the *Journal of Child Language* in 1978, point out that the mother of the mother/child pair they studied reinforced 81 percent of her child's correct attempts at labeling, and she did so by repeating a more accurate version of the label back to the child, by saying "yes," and by laughing.

Yet behaviorism cannot account for other aspects of acquisition, and Ninio and Bruner claim that providing a child with a word to imitate actually lessens the chances that the child will utter the word at all in an immediate response. Thus, although they can verify the significance of social reward in vocabulary development, they discount the significance of imitation. Their position is that social interaction provides the "scaffolding"—the framework which makes the acquisition possible in the first place. Since, in their view, development is nurtured by conversational exchange, the practical rules guiding such exchange also guide the development of vocabulary. Thus if one partner, in this case the mother, utters a name (a "label") for a picture in a book, there is no need for the other partner, the child, to do so; immediate imitation on the part of the child, therefore, tends not to occur. Moreover, the reinforcement provided by the mother also takes place within the confines of the conversation. Ninio and Bruner do not discount reinforcement, but they reinterpret it as part of interaction.

As important as interaction seems to be for language development, it does not really explain how it is that the child acquires syntax, the set of rules that account for sentence construction. That is, whereas it is likely that interaction plays a crucial part in the language acquisition process, interaction alone cannot account for the fact that children use correct word order in their utterances, come to understand alternate versions (paraphrases) of the same proposition, and have the potential to talk about a never-ending array of possibilities. Only a theory which could describe the mechanisms underlying this skill would be powerful enough to explain the structural component of the acquisition process.

None of these theories can account for all the details of language acquisition. Undoubtedly, a larger theory which can integrate the data reported by the three schools in a meaningful way will replace these fragmentary accounts. That is, the behaviorist, innatist, and interactionist accounts are not wrong, only incomplete.

Context

Thanks largely to the influence of John B. Watson in psychology and Leonard Bloomfield in linguistics, behaviorism dominated much of the thinking about language and language acquisition during the first half of the twentieth century. In the 1950's, however, a challenge was issued to behaviorist approaches by linguist Noam Chomsky, who, in a slender but revolutionary monograph entitled *Syntactic Structures* (1957), argued against the behaviorism advocated by Bloomfield and his followers.

Virtually simultaneous with the appearance of *Syntactic Structures* was the publication of *Verbal Behavior* by B. F. Skinner, then the most influential advocate of behaviorism. *Verbal Behavior* was an ambitious attempt to account for the acquisition of language in a behaviorist framework. In a scathing review published in 1959, Chomsky pointed to the "creative" aspects of language—the novelty of utterances—and attacked the basic tenets of Skinner's approach to language and language acquisition.

The debate between Chomsky and the behaviorists is one of the oldest debates in the history of ideas, echoing the philosophical disagreement in the seventeenth and eighteenth centuries between the British empiricists John Locke, George Berkeley, and David Hume, who claimed that knowledge of the world is attributable to a passive registration of sense impressions, and rationalists such as the French philosopher René Descartes, who claimed that much of human knowledge is attributable to innate "ideas" not derived from experience. Indeed the roots of innatism (or rationalism, as it is called in philosophical circles) go back to ancient Greece—to Plato, who originated the notion of innate ideas.

The debate between Chomsky and the interactionists, however, is more recent. In the early twentieth century, before Chomsky achieved prominence in linguistics, Jean Piaget looked at the empiricist (behaviorist) and rationalist positions and found them unable to explain the development of human knowledge. Because Piaget wrote in French, he was not much read in the United States, and the behaviorist tradition in psychology remained primary. Chomsky's challenge to behaviorist assumptions and his contentions about the nature of language acquisition had the effect of recruiting to the study of children's language a number of gifted researchers who set out to collect and interpret child language data in the light of Chomsky's model.

Much of the early work in this new field—called "developmental psycholinguistics"—involved recording and transcribing samples of young children's speech. Because the notion of the language acquisition device lay at the foundation of the model proposed by Chomsky, researchers initially kept few contextual notes about what a child was doing when speaking, and they frequently omitted or ignored what the child's adult caretaker said and did. It soon became apparent, however, that the context of the child's utterances was critical to interpretation. In 1970, language acquisition researcher Lois Bloom published *Language Development: Form and Function in Emerging Grammars*, in which she argued for "rich interpretation." That is, she contended that researchers had to do more than merely keep track of sentence growth; in order to describe a child's grammatical abilities, they had to examine the situation in which sentences occurred. Her evidence was a pair of identical two-word utterances spoken on two different occasions by the same child: "Mommy sock." On one of these occasions, the child's mother was putting a sock on the child; on the other, the child was talking about a sock that belonged to Mommy. Thus the first utterance meant approximately "Mommy is putting on my sock," and the second meant something like "Here is Mommy's sock." The relationship between the two words of the child's own utterance is clearly different on the two occasions, and only "rich interpretation" would allow the researcher to know how to provide the appropriate structural description for each utterance.

Such findings led to increasing attention to the details of context and conversation. Researchers found that mothers actually spoke quite clearly and grammatically to their babies and young children, so Chomsky's claim about the poor quality of the speech children hear was shown to be overstated. As researchers looked at mothers' speech to children, they also began to find that interaction was clearly structured to provide children with "scaffolding" to help them acquire language.

The debate continues, but since the early days of Chomsky's critique, behaviorism has generally been regarded by language acquisition researchers as lacking explanatory power, even though certain facets of the behaviorist paradigm may have become reinterpreted within a competing framework. The core of the criticism is that even if imitation and reinforcement could be shown to be crucial factors in the acquisition process, the question of how the child manages to imitate behavior as complex as language remains, as does the problem of explaining exactly how reinforcement works as a motivating device: How does the child come to make the connections between behavior and environmental reward?

These sorts of problems are not unique to the behaviorist model, however; one can aim similar ammunition at the rationalist/syntactic approach. How, for example, do children come to segment the continuous stream of speech into individual words in order to determine word order, if not through the repetition and even isolation of words that mothers and fathers provide in interacting with them? Nor is the interactionist school immune to criticism, for interaction alone cannot account for the acquisition of the most complex part of human language, its syntax, which provides language with its infinite potential.

Bibliography

Bohannon, John Neil, III, and Amye Warren-Leubecker. "Theoretical Approaches to Language Acquisition." In *The Development of Language*, edited by Jean Berko Gleason. Columbus, Ohio: Charles E. Merrill, 1989. This chapter in a language acquisition textbook provides a comprehensive overview of the theoretical approaches, outlining their general assumptions and evaluating each in terms of supporting and contrary evidence. It critically discusses the most plausible formulation of the rationalist approach, learnability theory.

Campbell, Robin, and Roger Wales. "The Study of Language Acquisition." In *New Horizons in Linguistics*, edited by John Lyons. Harmondsworth, Middlesex, England: Penguin Books, 1970. This essay constitutes an early critique of Chomsky and the psychologists he influenced, faulting them for not attending to the communicative function of language.

Gleitman, Lila R. "Biological Dispositions to Learn Language." In *Language Learning and Concept Acquisition*, edited by William Demopolous and Ausonio Marras. Norwood, N.J.: Ablex, 1986. In a highly readable article, Gleitman describes a number of observations which support the notion of the innateness of language-specific faculties.

McNeill, David. "The Creation of Language." In *Language*, edited by R. C. Oldfield and J. C. Marshall. Harmondsworth, Middlesex, England: Penguin Books, 1968. NcNeill provides a succinct, nontechnical discussion of language acquisition from the Chomskyan perspective. Although some particulars of linguistic theory presented here are somewhat dated, the thought which guides the rationalist approach, including a discussion of the language acquisition device, is clearly presented, along with some data supporting the rationalist thesis.

Piattelli-Palmarini, Massimo, ed. *Language and Learning: The Debate Between Jean Piaget and Noam Chomsky.* Cambridge, Mass.: Harvard University Press, 1980. Represents the proceedings of a conference held in October, 1975, which constituted the only meeting between Piaget and Chomsky. Given that they are the founders of two radically different theories involving the nature of knowledge, this book is required reading for anyone interested in the debate. It is lengthy (more than 400 pages long) and not easy, but the fact that practitioners of different disciplines and methodologies were meeting face-to-face means that the language employed in the book does not become overly technical. Of great value are the discussions at the ends of the presentations and an entire section devoted to commentary on the debate.

Marilyn N. Silva

Cross-References

Behaviorism: An Overview, 401; Bilingualism: Acquisition, Storage, and Processing, 408; Cognitive Development Theory: Piaget, 553; Grammar and Speech, 1100; Language: The Developmental Sequence, 1387; Language in Primates, 1407.

LANGUAGE AND COGNITION

Type of psychology: Cognition
Field of study: Cognitive processes

Cognition and language are complex psychological processes that are central to understanding the human mind. Language is used both to facilitate and to communicate thought. Thought may be constrained by language, but language may also be determined by the underlying structure of thought.

Principal terms
ARTIFICIAL INTELLIGENCE: the use of computers to simulate aspects of human thinking and, in some cases, behavior
BEHAVIORISM: a theoretical approach which argues that the proper subject matter of psychology is observable behavior, not internal mental processes
LINGUISTIC RELATIVITY HYPOTHESIS: the idea that the structure of particular languages people speak affects the way they perceive the world
LINGUISTICS: the study of the structure of language
PROPOSITION: the smallest unit of knowledge that can be stated; mental representations that resemble the underlying structure of language

Overview

Humans are thought to be unique among all the creatures of the world in their ability to use complex thought and to communicate with language. Are language and thinking simply different labels given to the same, uniquely human mental ability, or are language and thinking separate psychological processes? If language and thinking are in some sense distinct mental processes, how might they interact? Does language determine thought, or does thought determine language? Questions such as these puzzled the ancient Greek philosophers and continue to be addressed by philosophers, linguists, and psychologists today.

Psychologist John B. Watson, a founder of behaviorism, believed that thought and language were identical. Watson proposed that what is called thought is actually the faint motor movements of speech. While this subvocal speech is generally unobservable in adults, Watson noted that thinking-as-speaking can easily be seen in young children. Today, few would agree that thought and speech are the same, and speech is not viewed as identical to language. In contrast to Watson, Noam Chomsky, a contemporary cognitive scientist, believes that thought and language are separate processes. Chomsky argues that language is an internal grammar of the mind, universal in humans, which may be manifested in speech. Chomsky conceives of language as an encapsulated mental module, separate from thinking.

A middle position between the extremes of Watson and Chomsky is suggested by cognitive psychologists such as John Anderson. Anderson believes that thinking and language are separable but that both derive from the same internal mental structure. In Anderson's theory, the mind is described as composed of propositional networks. Propositions are abstract, quasi-linguistic forms of representing the world; these are combined in networks of association which provide the foundation for both language and thinking. People's abilities to learn and remember are dependent upon the way concepts have become associated in memory; propositions are communicated to others through language.

Within the framework of Anderson's propositional network theory, thought may be viewed as determining language. That is, the structure of language is viewed as dependent upon the underlying propositional structure of thought. In support of this viewpoint, Anderson notes that in the grammars of almost all languages, sentences are arranged such that the subject comes before the verb and the object. This corresponds with the human sense of the world in which agents (subjects) act upon objects. Propositions are assumed to have a subject-object phrase structure.

Clearly, thought and language are intimately associated with each other. While thought may, at least in part, determine language, the reverse may also be true. That is, the particular language one speaks may influence one's perceptions of the world. For example, it is argued that since Arabic languages have many words for the animal which in English is simply called "camel," Arabic speakers are able to see more variations in camels than are speakers of English. This notion, that language at least partly determines thought, has been termed the linguistic relativity hypothesis, because one's thinking is seen as relative to the specific language one speaks. The linguistic relativity hypothesis was advanced by anthropologist Edward Sapir and was developed and popularized by Benjamin Lee Whorf in 1956. Sometimes it is referred to as the Sapir-Whorf hypothesis or simply the Whorfian hypothesis.

In its strongest form, the linguistic relativity hypothesis asserts that language invariably imposes a particular view of the world. This suggests that speakers of the English language cannot see variations in camels, while Arabs, with their many words for this animal, can. Certainly, people do develop a larger vocabulary for objects or concepts which are prevalent or significant in their lives. The skier has many words for different types of snow; the gardener has many words for different types of soil. It is unlikely, however, that the specific language one uses actually controls one's ability to perceive differences in objects. Infants clearly distinguish among objects long before they are able to use language to describe them; animals have concepts, distinguish among important objects in their world, and solve problems.

A weaker version of the linguistic relativity hypothesis is more likely to be valid. This holds that language may influence thought when the type of thinking called for specifically depends upon the properties of one's language system. Thus, the skier may remember variations in snow from one day to the next better than the non-skier, because he or she encodes those variations in memory in terms of previously learned labels. To the extent that memory depends upon attaching meaning in terms of language, the skier will be at an advantage for remembering snow.

Clearly, the relationship between thought and language is complex. Language can facilitate memory, transmit knowledge, and help people solve problems. People's experiences, what they think about, and what is significant to them may influence the words in their language—and perhaps even affect how language is structured. Beyond the recognition of this complexity, psychology can draw no firm conclusions about the mechanism through which language and thought interact.

Applications

Language is an important tool both for the expression of thought and for the development of complex thinking itself. The written and spoken word allow humans to transmit knowledge to others; they transmit culture. Language aids learning. The meaningfulness of new concepts is enhanced by elaborating them in language, and this makes them memorable. Writing or speaking with others about one's thoughts can enhance and transform ideas.

It has been very difficult to test the relationship between language and thought empirically. In the heyday of behaviorism, in the 1940's, attempts were made to test Watson's proposition that thinking was nothing more than subvocal speech by measuring any vibrations made by the vocal chords while a person silently thought. In many cases, such vibrations could be measured, lending support to Watson's notion, but the fact that sometimes vibrations were not recorded left room for doubt. The issue was resolved when a researcher, Steven M. Smith, allowed himself to be temporarily paralyzed with curare. Curare paralyzes muscles, so Smith was unable to move his vocal chords at all; indeed, he was kept breathing by a respirator. Curare does not interfere with awareness, however, so Smith was able to see and hear during the experiment. He found that he could solve problems, learn, and remember during his paralysis. These results cast grave doubt on Watson's notion that thought was only subvocal speech.

Research on other aspects of language and thinking has not reached such unambiguous conclusions. In part, difficulties arise because contemporary theories conceive of both language and cognition as internal psychological processes. Such internal processes cannot be directly observed, and the relationship of observable speech and behavior to internal language and thinking is not always clear. For example, while it is fascinating to note that different languages label the world in different ways, the import of these differences is not at all obvious. Does the fact that Eskimos have many words for snow and the Hanunoo people of the Philippines many words for rice mean that their perceptions of snow and rice necessarily differ from each other—and from English speakers who have only a single word for each? Empirical tests of this question require both that speakers of different languages be tested and that a means to measure perceptions and/or thinking separate from language be found.

The research of Eleanor Rosch fulfills these criteria. She examined the possibility that the Dani of New Guinea, who have only two words for color, perceive colors differently from speakers of English, who have eleven basic color terms. Rosch found that although the Dani only use two color terms, they can readily distinguish among the eleven colors labeled in English. In subsequent research, it has been found that across cultures, regardless of the specific color terms available in a language, those eleven colors, termed "focal colors," are easily discriminated and remembered. This research often is cited as evidence that spoken language itself does not determine one's perceptions of the world. Indeed, there may be many universal concepts which, like focal colors, constrain the sorts of labels the various languages of the world place on them. For example, the naming of plants and animals seems to be constrained such that the basic level (for example, "bird," as opposed to "bluebird" or "goldfinch") is remembered easily and (if named) is named simply in all languages.

While the linguistic relativity hypothesis is called into question by findings such as those described above, other well-designed studies produce more ambiguous results. John B. Carroll and Joseph B. Casagrande conducted a study with Navajo youths. In the Navajo language, different verb forms for "handling" are used, depending on the form of the material being handled. For example, one would use a different form of "to handle" when the object handled was a stick as opposed to a rope. The researchers found that when primarily Navajo-speaking youths were asked to sort a group of objects into meaningful subgroups, they did so on the basis of the forms of the objects. Primarily English speakers of Navajo heritage tended to sort on the basis of perceptual categories, such as color. This suggests that language indeed does influence thought, as categorization is typically viewed as the result of thinking, not language per se.

When the researchers compared the Navajo-speaking children to English-speaking children from Boston of the same age, however, they found that the children from Boston also categorized on the basis of form. The researchers suggested that the children from Boston had experience with a great variety of toys, and that this may have facilitated their categorization in terms of form. Whatever the explanation, these results render the study's implication for the linguistic relativity hypothesis ambiguous.

In sum, there is evidence suggesting both that language influences thinking and that thinking constrains language. The resolution of the conflicting results of research in this area may depend on very specific analyses of the different levels of language (for example, word, phrase, or sentence) and the different manifestations of thinking (for example, concepts, propositions, or problem-solving procedures).

Context

Cognition and language are basic to an understanding of the human mind and have long puzzled philosophers, psychologists, and others. The human capacity for thinking and language far surpasses the abilities of other creatures to think and communicate. If researchers are able to unravel the mysteries of the relationship between thinking and language, they will make major strides in understanding what it means to be human.

Although cognition and thinking are basic to the study of the mind, these topics have not always been at the core of the scientific study of psychology. Perception and thought were studied in the nineteenth century by the earliest scientific psychologists, but with the rise of behaviorism in the 1940's, many psychologists turned away from the study of the mind. According to behaviorists, the appropriate topic for scientific study of psychology is behavior, because hypothetical internal mental processes are not verifiable scientifically. Indeed, they held, such internal processes may not even exist, let alone be important to the prediction of behavior. Thus language was equated with speech, and thought was equated with subvocal speech.

Linguists and anthropologists, rather than mainstream psychologists, kept the study of language—and cognition—alive. Linguist Noam Chomsky sought to understand the internal, universal structure of language rather than its particular manifestation in speech. While Chomsky was not concerned with particularly psychological aspects of language, such as the way it is comprehended or develops in children, his theorizing is significant in that it established a cognitive approach to the internal structure of language. Anthropologists such as Edward Sapir and Benjamin Lee Whorf investigated the different languages of the peoples of the world and speculated on the relationship between thought and language. They laid the foundation for the later work of Eleanor Rosch.

The study of cognition and language as a part of psychology awaited the resurgence of cognitive psychology as a discipline. This occurred largely as the result of the computer revolution of the 1950's. Computer analogies encourage one to use an information-processing approach to the mind in which internal cognitive processes are assumed to intervene between stimulus "input" and behavioral "output." Computer programs themselves are written to develop and test specific models of thought processes. In fact, many researchers in the field of artificial intelligence, trying to formulate models of the mind, view the development of a model of natural language processes as central to their concerns. Modern cognitive scientists, be they psychologists, linguists, anthropologists, or researchers in the field of artificial intelligence, now work in an interdisciplinary fashion to unravel the mysteries of language, thinking, and their interrelationship.

Bibliography

Anderson, John R. *Cognitive Psychology and Its Implications.* New York: W. H. Freeman, 1985. Much of this sophisticated cognitive psychology textbook is based on Anderson's propositional network theory. The chapter entitled "Meaning-Based Knowledge Representations" describes the specifics of this theory; "Language: An Overview" discusses the relationship between thought and language. Suggestions for further reading are provided at the end of each chapter.

Brown, Roger. "Language and Thought." In *Social Psychology: The Second Edition.* New York: Free Press, 1986. Sophisticated but readable treatment of the relationship between language and thought. A thorough discussion of the ways thought may constrain language. Contains related chapters on "The Origins of Language" and "Nonverbal Communication and Speech Registers." References provided.

Eccles, John C., and Daniel N. Robinson. "Language, Thought, and Brain." In *The Wonder of Being Human*. New York: Free Press, 1984. Relatively sophisticated discussion of the relationship among language, thinking, and neurophysiology from philosophical, psychological, and physiological standpoints. Places the development of language in an evolutionary perspective. Contains suggestions for additional reading.

Flanagan, Owen J., Jr. "Cognitive Psychology and Artificial Intelligence: Philosophical Assumptions and Implications." In *The Science of the Mind*. Cambridge, Mass.: MIT Press, 1984. A readable introduction to the central philosophical issues addressed by cognitive psychology. Discusses mental representation in terms of propositions; language per se is not addressed in detail. The ambitions and criticisms of artificial intelligence are reviewed.

Gardner, Howard. *The Mind's New Science: A History of the Cognitive Revolution*. New York: Basic Books, 1985. An excellent review of the central issues, research, and criticisms of cognitive science. Parts 1 and 2 provide a historical account of cognitive science. Chapters on artificial intelligence and linguistics are directly relevant to cognition and language. Eleanor Rosch's research on natural concepts is discussed in "A World Categorized" in part 3.

Palmer, Frank Robert. "The Non-Linguistic Context." In *Semantics: A New Outline*. London: Cambridge University Press, 1976. Discussions of behaviorism and the linguistic relativity hypothesis from the perspective of a specialist in linguistics. Relatively sophisticated treatment. A useful complement to the psychological perspectives of Anderson, Brown, and Gardner.

Schank, Roger C. "English for Computers." In *The Cognitive Computer*. Reading, Mass.: Addison-Wesley, 1984. A readable introduction to the issues, promises, and problems of artificial intelligence. Describes the difficulties involved in writing programs that enable computers to understand natural language.

Susan E. Beers

Cross-References

Artificial Intelligence, 299; Behaviorism: An Overview, 401; Cognitive Maps, 566; Concept Formation, 637; Grammar and Speech, 1100; Language: The Developmental Sequence, 1387; Language Acquisition Theories, 1394; Linguistic Relativity Theory, 1450; Psycholinguistics, 1918; Thought Structures, 2565.

LANGUAGE IN PRIMATES

Type of psychology: Language
Fields of study: Biological influences on learning; cognitive processes

The study of language in primates is designed to examine the evolutionary factors in language development as well as to move toward an understanding of the fundamentals of language itself. This study includes the various call signals of primates as well as other types of communication, including sign language and the symbolic manipulation of colored chips.

Principal terms

ABSTRACTNESS: that characteristic of language which enables it to combine sounds to refer to a multitude of unrelated objects and incidents and thereby give them conventional meaning

CALL SYSTEM: a communication system among primates in which each call is related to one, and only one, particular message

COMMUNICATION: a system of sending messages from one or more organisms that influence the manner in which other organisms act

DISPLACEMENT: that characteristic of language which allows it to refer to past, present, and future as well as to things that have never been or may never be

LANGUAGE: a communication system characterized by openness, abstractness, and displacement

OPENNESS: that characteristic of language that enables it to combine sounds in ways to convey new meanings—that is, its productivity

SPEECH: verbal language

Overview

The study of language in primates has as its objectives the understanding of language in general, the discovery of the relationship of human language to other systems of communication, and the uncovering of language's evolutionary roots. Significant work in this area has been done since 1960 in the field, in zoos, and in laboratory settings. These studies have influenced and complemented one another.

Field studies of baboons, of rhesus monkeys, and of humans' closest relatives, chimpanzees and gorillas, among other primates, have shed much light on primate communication systems. These studies demonstrate that primates exhibit a vast repertoire of gestural, contact, and sound systems of communication. Primates may, for example, kiss upon meeting. They groom one another, picking fleas off one another's fur. Lip smacking, posing, and chest thumping, among other gestures, convey clear and definite messages. Similarly, calls communicate explicit meanings. One call may express fear, another the presence of food, still another danger, and so on. Generally, these calls cannot be combined to communicate complex messages such as, "There is an abundance of food but danger is also present!"

Attempts to teach apes, those primates most closely related to humans, systems of communication that enable them to express complex thoughts have fascinated social and behavioral scientists in recent years. Allen and Beatrice Gardner conducted the first work in teaching sign language to a chimpanzee, Washoe. They placed Washoe with a researcher at ten months of age. That researcher "spoke" to her in American Sign Language (ASL), a language developed for use among the deaf.

Not only did Washoe begin to produce her own word combinations, "water bird" for duck and "sweet water" for soda pop, but she also began to teach other chimpanzees how to sign. This rather clear display of cognitive understanding of the system and its structural constituents has been instrumental in forcing scholars to rethink their definition of language itself. It has also captured the popular imagination. When, for example, Koko, a gorilla that Francine Patterson trained to use sign language, described her dead pet cat as being in a sleep from which it would not awake (while shedding a tear), millions of Americans who saw it on television were touched and amazed.

Although the teaching of chimpanzees, gorillas, and orangutans how to sign has been the most noticeable demonstration of the nonverbal language ability of apes, there have been other studies equally important in advancing understanding of language. Ann and David Premack worked with a chimpanzee they named Sarah. They used a number of colored plastic chips, each chip representing a different word. Each chip had a different shape. In addition, the Premacks taught Sarah how to ask questions and symbols for some conjunctions (such as "and"), color terms, and various other aspects of language use.

Duane Rumbaugh has taught a chimpanzee, Lana, to use a specially constructed computer to communicate. Studies have shown that apes can learn to communicate in nonverbal language through watching other apes who have been trained to do so. Kanzi, a pygmy chimpanzee, has provided one example of this ability. Sue Savage-Rumbaugh's work with him has brought this ability to light. According to Savage-Rumbaugh, when Kanzi's friend Austin left the training site, Kanzi went to the computer and typed "Austin" and "TV," meaning that he wanted to see a videotape showing his friend Austin. When Savage-Rumbaugh did put on a videocassette featuring Austin, Kanzi calmed down and went to sleep.

These studies, along with studies conducted in natural settings by Jane Goodall, Dian Fossey, and Vernon Reynolds, among others, raise intriguing questions regarding the intellectual abilities of primates, especially apes. Many people are fascinated, others anxious, regarding the implications of these studies. They propose an entirely new understanding of the relationship between human and nonhuman primates and, consequently, a reconsideration of the nature and uniqueness of human language.

Applications

The underlying issue of primate language studies is whether human language is unique among communication systems or is simply a more developed version of other animal communication systems. In other terms, the question is whether human language is qualitatively or quantitatively different from other forms of communication. Researchers seek to discover whether it is something essentially different or a logical development of prior systems of communication.

A significant portion of the argument focuses on whether these studies reveal any significant language ability on the part of apes or merely reflect their being well trained and responding to cues, in much the same manner as a horse will count to ten when its trainer appropriately prompts it. Herbert S. Terrace, for example, maintains that chimpanzees do not have any actual humanlike language ability. Their apparent ability, he argues, results simply from training.

By true language ability, Terrace and others mean the competence to learn communication systems displaying the characteristics of arbitrariness, productivity, and displacement. Arbitrariness refers to the fact that every human language employs a limited number of sounds in combination—fewer than fifty—to refer to thousands of experiences and articles. The relationship between the combination of sounds and that to which they refer is not a necessary one. Rather, it is a purely conventional relationship.

The characteristic termed productivity refers to the ability of speakers of any language to generate an almost infinite variety of utterances which other members of that group will understand with little if any difficulty. This ability to combine sounds in a manner not encountered before allows a language to be flexible and accommodate new experiences. Finally, the characteristic of displacement allows humans to categorize experiences; discuss past, present, and future; hypothesize about relationships; imagine things that may never be found in the real world; and store a vast amount of knowledge. This characteristic of language makes it possible to learn about things one has not actually experienced oneself and to share one's experiences with others. Together, these language characteristics make human culture possible.

In a very real sense, then, the attempt to preserve the uniqueness of human language is also a venture to uphold the singularity of human culture. Although Terrace's arguments are thoughtful and require serious consideration, they have been questioned. The Premacks have responded that neither Terrace's nor Richard Sanders' arguments prove that chimpanzees are incapable of learning symbolic language. Indeed, Terrace's own research on his chimpanzee Nim Chimpsky (the name is a takeoff on the name of the famous linguist Noam Chomsky) suggests that Nim Chimpsky did employ symbolic language on occasion. For example, the sign for "more" occurred in an initial position in an impressive 85 percent of word combinations.

The argument hinges, therefore, on whether apes using computers, signs, or colored plastic shapes are really displaying the ability to use symbolic language. If they are, then room must be made for degrees of symbolic language, with human language differing in degree from other symbolic languages. Moreover, the subtleness Koko has displayed in answering questions has provided a glimpse into the emotional life of apes. For example, she refused to answer whether she liked her trainer or the assistant trainer more. She told the reporter who asked the question that it was a bad question. Moreover, her expression of affection for her pet cat, Smoke, and her expressed grief at its death certainly strongly suggests more complex emotions than had been suspected. Jane Goodall's field studies with chimpanzees have tended to support those who see strong continuities in human and ape reasoning and emotions, a position Charles Darwin himself had upheld.

Even if one agrees that there is a strong continuity between ape language and human language, however, there are still great differences. Apes learn symbolic language under highly artificial conditions. The effort required to teach an ape language is enormous compared with the relative ease with which children learn language in natural settings. Moreover, the languages apes have learned are at least in part iconic—that is, there is a connection between the symbols and the things they stand for. American Sign Language uses a symbol for book, for example, that has the two palms pushed together then has them opened, much like a person would open a real book. No ape, therefore, has yet learned a totally arbitrary language. There is, as noted earlier, still an argument regarding the role of productivity versus imitation and cue response in ape language. Nevertheless, anyone who has seen an ape signal "I love you" in an unexpected encounter in a zoo must wonder at the closeness of humans' relationship to their ape kin.

Context

The place of humans within the total animal world has long interested scholars. Modern discussions stem from the significant influence of Charles Darwin and evolutionary theory. In one form or another, that theory has inspired research in the natural, social, and behavioral sciences. Much of this research is concerned with communication. Research on ape language and primate communication is part of the overall research on nonhuman communication.

Since apes are humans' closest evolutionary relatives, ("cousins," in those terms), considerable research on nonhuman communication systems has been concerned with language in apes. Other species use sounds to communicate, and there are psychologists who study dolphins, whales, birds, monkeys, and other animals that employ call systems. The study of apes, however, holds the most promise in answering the question of whether other species have the faculty to learn symbolic language. No one is claiming that other animals have developed that faculty independently in a natural state. The question is simply whether that capacity exists.

It was important for reseachers to realize that apes could not readily produce verbal language. The first reported research (in the 1930's) concerned a chimpanzee named Gua, that W. N. and L. A. Kellogg raised with their son Donald. Not surprisingly, Donald made the expected progress in language learning and Gua did not. Moreover, in the early 1950's, when Keith and Cathy Hayes did teach their chimp, Viki, to speak, the results of three words—"cup," "mama," and "papa"—hardly seemed worth three years of effort. They did demonstrate that the brains of chimpanzees are not organized for verbal language. Furthermore, their vocal tracts, unlike human vocal tracts, are not physiologically fit for speech.

Once that lesson was learned, researchers in the 1960's began to design the laboratory work that has proved so vital to clarifying understanding of language. At the same time, field studies of primates in natural settings revolutionized comprehension of these animals. Since that time, the heat of the debate concerning primate signal systems, ape language, and human language suggests that vital issues in the definition of human faculties and culture are in question.

Future research is likely to seek clarification of the meaning of language itself as well as the concepts of "word," "syntax," "grammar," "semantics," and other linguistic elements. Moreover, greater attention to the manner in which children actually learn and develop their linguistic competence will become of greater concern in this discussion. Field studies will continue to play a prominent role in providing empirical material regarding the actual processes of primate social life. Definitions of human language and culture will undergo serious modification in order to accommodate new advances. These advances will further expose the genius of Darwin's vision as people gain new insights into the evolutionary threads that resulted in human language and culture.

Bibliography

Chomsky, Noam. *Syntactic Structures.* The Hague: Mouton, 1971. Chomsky's book put forward the basic ideas of generative grammar, which revolutionized the science of linguistics. Chomsky argues for a universal language acquisition device in humans as well as for the underlying unity of all human language.

Gardner, R. Allen, and Beatrice Gardner. "Teaching Sign Language to a Chimpanzee." *Science* 165 (August 15, 1969): 664-672. The Gardners argue for the continuity of human language with that which preceded it among the higher apes. They indicate that nonhuman primates are not able to achieve verbal language for physiological reasons. They are, however, capable of signing nonverbally and can communicate symbolically with humans.

Goodall, Jane. *In the Shadow of Man.* Boston: Houghton Mifflin, 1971. Goodall examines the chimpanzees in Gombe, Tanzania. Her work is based on intensive field observation of the colony there. Describes their use of tools and employment of other symbolic devices.

Kellogg, W. N., and L. A. Kellogg. *The Ape and the Child.* New York: McGraw-Hill, 1933. The Kelloggs describe the early developmental period of a chimp raised with their young child. Their argument that apes are incapable of language stood almost unchallenged until later research on apes and nonverbal language.

Premack, David. "On the Assessment of Language Competence in the Chimpanzee." In *Behavior of Nonhuman Primates,* edited by Allan M. Schrier and Fred Stollnitz. 2 vols. New York: Academic Press, 1965. Premack outlines the basic lines of the argument on chimpanzee language ability. He is fair in providing space for both sides.

Frank A. Salamone

Cross-References

Emotion in Primates, 947; Ethology, 992; Language Acquisition Theories, 1394; Language and Cognition, 1401; Nonverbal Communication, 1681; Psycholinguistics, 1918; Reinforcers and Reinforcement, 2084.

LAW AND PSYCHOLOGY

Type of psychology: Social psychology
Fields of study: Group processes; prejudice and discrimination; social perception
and cognition

The legal decisions made by juries are intended to be uncontaminated by evidence not presented within the court case. Psychologists, however, have found that factors such as defendant attractiveness, race, and moral character do, in fact, bias these legal decisions. Experts within both the psychological and legal fields have begun to propose guidelines to minimize this effect.

Principal terms

AUTHORITARIAN SCALE: a measurement of the extent that a person accepts authority; those who score high tend to favor blind submission to authority and are characterized by rigidity and intolerance

EXTRANEOUS VARIABLES: factors such as defendant attractiveness, race, or morality which should be irrelevant to a jury in their decision-making process

FORENSICS PSYCHOLOGY: a science that deals with the relation and application of psychological concepts and theories to legal problems

MOCK JURORS: within a psychological experiment, people playing the role of jury members in order to examine psychological phenomena

NEGLIGENT HOMICIDE: the act of killing someone unintentionally or accidentally

SIMULATED COURTROOM: within a psychological experiment, a classroom or laboratory converted into an artificial courtroom in which mock jurors make legal decisions

UNBIASED DECISIONS: decisions influenced only by relevant factors and not influenced by information beyond the evidence of the court case

Overview

Imagine that a man is sitting in his living room watching television when, all of a sudden, a police officer knocks on his door, asks him to step outside, and then informs him that he is being arrested on suspicion of burglary. He claims that he is innocent, but six months later he finds himself on trial for this crime and in front of a jury. Should it make any difference to the jury whether he has a good or bad character, whether he is attractive or unattractive, or whether he is white, black, or Hispanic? The American legal system is designed to yield objective, unbiased decisions based on a set of rules and procedures intended to focus on evidence presented at the trial. Yet Clarence Darrow, one of America's most famous lawyers, bluntly saw it otherwise: "Jurymen seldom convict a person they like, or acquit one that they dislike. The main work of the trial lawyer is to make a jury like his client, or, at least, to feel sympathy for him; facts regarding the crime are relatively unimportant." Research in the field of forensic psychology confirms Darrow's 1933 statement by indicating that human beings do not always conform to such idealistic principles as complete objectivity. Though moral character, life-style, attractiveness, race, and related factors have little, if anything, to do with the evidence presented in a given case, research shows that they nevertheless affect the outcome of both real and simulated trials.

An example of a powerful but supposedly irrelevant variable is the moral character or life-style of the person on trial. An early study by David Landy and Elliot Aronson in 1969 provided support for this claim when people acting as jurors in a simulated courtroom read facts about a negligent homicide case in which a pedestrian was run over and killed on Christmas Eve. Mock jurors read either positive or negative character descriptions of the defendant. In the positive character case, the defendant was described as an insurance adjuster, a widower, and going to spend Christmas Eve with his son and daughter-in-law. In the negative character case, the defendant was described as a janitor, twice divorced, possessing a criminal record, and going to spend Christmas Eve with his girlfriend. Mock jurors were asked to judge whether the defendant was guilty or innocent and, if guilty, to decide how many years he should spend in jail. When the person on trial was described as having a positive character, mock jurors sentenced him to two years in jail; when he was described as having a negative character, they sentenced him to five years in jail. This clearly suggests that the life-style and moral character of people on trial do dramatically influence jury decisions.

The attractiveness of the person on trial has also been found to affect the verdict reached by jurors. Michael Efran in 1974 wondered whether physical attractiveness might bias students' judgments of another student who was accused of cheating. He had college students act as school jurors. Students received a photograph of the fellow student and a written description of the cheating case. All students read the same case description. Half had an attractive photograph attached, however, whereas the other half saw an unattractive photograph. Those with the attractive photograph attached judged the student to be less guilty than those with the unattractive photograph. For those found guilty of the crime, more severe sentencing was recommended for the less attractive photograph group. Evidence that attractiveness affects jury decision is found not only in simulated but also in real court cases. John Stewart in 1980 asked observers to rate the attractiveness of seventy-four male defendants tried in Pennsylvania. When he later examined the court records, he found that the more attractive defendants received the lighter sentences. Once convicted, the more attractive defendants were twice as likely to avoid prison as those who were less attractive.

Although attractiveness often helps, there are circumstances under which good looks can actually hurt a person on trial. In 1975, Harold Sigall and Nancy Ostrove found that when mock jurors judged a woman accused of stealing $2,200 they were more lenient in their sentencing decisions when she was attractive than when she was not. When she was said to have swindled the money by charming a middle-aged man into making a phony investment, however, the beautiful defendant was sentenced more severely than her less attractive counterpart. Apparently, people react quite negatively toward someone who uses his or her appearance to commit a crime.

The race of the person on trial also seems to affect the jury decision process. Stewart found that nonwhite defendants were more likely to be convicted than were whites for comparable crimes. Further, the convicted were much more likely to be sent to prison if they were nonwhite than if they were white. Other researchers, Louis Cohen, Laura Gray, and Marian Miller, in 1990 had white students act as mock jurors in a burglary case. They all read the same burglary case, but the race of the person on trial was either black, Hispanic, or white. When the defendant was black or Hispanic, a more severe sentence was awarded than when the defendant was white. Although race of defendant should theoretically be irrelevant to a court case, it does, in fact, appear to affect the verdict.

Applications

According to the psychological research previously cited, jury decisions tend not to be completely objective, and factors irrelevant to the evidence presented in the case are often considered. That is, the character, physical attractiveness, and ethnicity of the defendant, as well as other factors such as attitude similarity between the jurors and the person on trial, all seem to impact the jury's decision-making process despite the fact that justice should be blind to these extraneous variables. Is there any way to reduce such effects and biases in the courtroom?

One way might be to eliminate from juries people who are more likely to be affected by these irrelevant factors. Henry Mitchell and Donn Byrne in 1973 showed that personality differences can affect jury decisions. People who score high on the authoritarian scale favor a blind submission to authority and tend to vote guilty more often than those who score low on authoritarianism. Mitchell and Byrne also demonstrated, however, that authoritarian tendencies interacted with characteristics of the defendant both in conviction of guilt and in recommended punishment. That is, high-authoritarian jurors were more inclined to perceive guilt and/or give more severe punishments when the defendant was described as attitudinally dissimilar from themselves or having a negative character, whereas low authoritarians did not make any distinction with regard to character. In addition, when jurors were given judicial instructions to disregard any testimony about character, low-authoritarian jurors followed these instructions, whereas high authoritarians did not. In brief, high and low authoritarians seem to attend to different aspects of evidence during the trial process, with those scoring high being more biased by evidence not presented in the case. Does that mean that attorneys should hand out personality scales before they select jury members and eliminate all those who score high on the authoritarian scale?

Unfortunately, the answer is not that simple. It has been found that people who score low on the authoritarian scale in certain circumstances will also attend to factors beyond the evidence of the trial. Jurors low on authoritarianism tend to be biased against a defendant who is an authority figure such as a police officer when he or she is accused of causing harm to a public citizen. Alternatively, high authoritarians have the opposite bias and tend to make harsher judgments when the roles are reversed and a public citizen is accused of causing harm to a police officer. That is, those who score high and low on the authoritarian scale have different expectations about how authority figures and "normal" citizens should behave that are unrelated to the facts of the trial. Thus, unfairness, punitiveness, and attention to factors beyond the evidence are not limited to those who have a high-authoritarian personality. Rather, both high and low authoritarians are affected by irrelevant factors beyond the evidence presented; they simply pay attention to different extraneous factors.

Efforts are needed to combat the psychological factors that can influence jurors and to make the legal system as fair and objective as possible. Evidence indicates that the tactic of excluding jurors who are either high or low authoritarians can produce biases in one direction or another if employed blindly; this is therefore not an answer to the problem. One might wonder whether decisions by a judge might be less biased than judgment by peers, but this appears not to be the case. That is, judges follow the same laws of human behavior; despite the fact that they have years of service, know the constraints of the law, and attend judges' schools on a regular basis, they are still influenced by extraneous variables, although to a lesser degree. Because of the importance of maintaining a jury of one's peers for fair and equitable trials, one suggestion is to inform jurors of the biases previously discussed so as to make them aware of their own limitations in objective, unbiased decision making.

Despite the fact that lawyers make use of their clients' attractiveness, dressing and grooming them appropriately for a court appearance, the idea of a trial as a beauty contest is not an appealing one. Means of diminishing the impact of physical attractiveness on legal decisions need to be established. Some researchers have proposed that attractiveness has been found to be less powerful if a sufficient amount of factual information is presented to the jury, if the judge explicitly reminds the jury of the basis on which the verdict should be reached, and if the jury is presented with transcripts of the testimony rather than being directly exposed to those who testify. These same factors should diminish the subjective impact of race as well. These, as well as many other, concerns will occupy the thoughts of many in the legal and psychological field until the American legal system becomes more objective, unbiased, and fair.

Context

The study of psychology and law, specifically decision making by a jury, is a subset of social psychology. Social psychology is often defined as the scientific field that seeks to understand the nature and causes of individual behaviors, emotions, and thoughts in social situations. Despite the fact that many social psychologists construct theories based on empirical laboratory research, there are also many social psychologists who use this basic knowledge to solve practical problems outside the laboratory. An interest in applying psychological principles to the "real" world existed almost as soon as the field of psychology was established. For example, in 1899 William James pointed out that psychological findings could be utilized to improve education. Many social psychologists since that time have devoted their efforts to applying social psychological principles to societal problems.

The idea of applying psychological findings specifically to the legal system has been discussed since the beginning of the twentieth century. In a 1906 speech to judges, Sigmund Freud suggested that psychology had some very practical applications for their field. In a 1908 book, Hugo Münsterberg, an experimental psychologist, argued that psychological principles could be applied to events in the courtroom. The famous behaviorist John B. Watson also argued in the early 1900's that lawyers and psychologists had many common interests. Despite this early enthusiasm, little empirical social psychological research of direct relevance to the legal system was carried out in the first half of the century. It is only since the 1960's that there have been a number of studies attempting to answer questions of both legal and psychological interest.

In the 1960's and 1970's, forensic psychologists primarily focused on how evidence, both relevant and irrelevant to the facts of the case, is used. More recently, the field of psychology and law has expanded greatly. Research has focused on such topics as jury selection and jury functioning, social influence as it occurs in the courtroom, the deterrence value of capital punishment and the length of jail sentences, the validity of expert witnesses, and the effect of memory on eyewitness identifications. These areas of psychological application to the legal arena provide a wealth of information that not only will make people aware of potential problems within the judicial system but also will, it is hoped, help provide solutions to make the system as unbiased and objective as possible.

Bibliography

Hastie, Reid, Steven D. Penrod, and Nancy Pennington. *Inside the Jury.* Cambridge, Mass.: Harvard University Press, 1983. This book emphasizes how the experimental method within psychology creates an invaluable approach to studying the jury deliberation process. It focuses on how juries make decisions as well as on the product of those deliberations. Provides an extremely detailed and scientific approach to the jury process.

Kassin, Saul M., and Lawrence S. Wrightsman. *The American Jury on Trial: Psychological Perspectives.* New York: Hemisphere, 1988. An authoritative review of the entire process of trial by jury, from jury selection to verdict. Includes a review of the history of the jury, of jury research, and of highly publicized trials. The presentation of information about specific trials is very interesting and enjoyable to read.

Landy, David, and Elliot Aronson. "The Influence of the Character of the Criminal and His Victim on the Decisions of Simulated Jurors." *Journal of Experimental*

Social Psychology 5 (1969): 141-152. One of the earlier experimental articles examining the impact of irrelevant variables on the jury decision-making process. Both defendant character and attractiveness were manipulated and found to have an effect on the determination of guilt or innocence and the number of years of imprisonment.

Loftus, Elizabeth F. *Eyewitness Testimony.* Cambridge, Mass.: Harvard University Press, 1979. This book provides a comprehensive account of the reliability—or, more appropriately, the unreliability—of remembering people and events from the scene of a crime. Her description of psychological experiments providing evidence for the way people reconstruct memories is both interesting and provocative.

Loftus, Elizabeth F., and Katherine Ketcham. *Witness for the Defense.* New York: St. Martin's Press, 1991. In this book, Loftus continues her exploration into the fallibility of eyewitness testimony. The presentation of her experiences as a consultant in several court cases, such as those of Ted Bundy and Nazi war criminal Ivan the Terrible, makes this extremely interesting and fascinating reading.

Nemeth, C. J. "Jury Trials: Psychology and Law." In *Advances in Experimental Social Psychology*, edited by Leonard Berkowitz. New York: Academic Press, 1981. An extremely complete account of the psychological research completed on a diverse range of topics related to trial by jury. Provides extremely important historical background information on the jury in America, then discusses a number of factors that affect the jury decision process. A fairly technical account of this information.

Amy Marcus-Newhall

Cross-References

Attraction Theories, 332; Attributional Biases, 338; Group Decision Making, 1114; Memory and Eyewitness Testimony, 1544; Effects of Prejudice, 1848; Racism, 2037; Social Perception: Others, 2311.

LEADERSHIP

Type of psychology: Social psychology
Field of study: Group processes

Leadership involves a complex set of interactions between an individual and a group. The conclusion of extensive research on leadership is that good leaders come in many forms; there is no one best type of leader. Effective leadership has been shown to depend on characteristics of the group and its environment as well as those of the leader.

Principal terms
CONSIDERATION: the expression of concern for employees' values and
needs
CONTINGENCY THEORY: Fred Fiedler's theory that optimal leadership
style depends on the combination of leader-member relations, task
structure, and position power
INITIATING STRUCTURE: an orientation toward task accomplishment
LEADER-MATCHING TRAINING: a program to assist leaders in structuring
their situations to match their leadership styles
LEAST-PREFERRED COWORKER: a measure of leadership style in Fiedler's
contingency theory
TRANSFORMATIONAL LEADERSHIP: a style that succeeds in getting
followers to exceed their expectations for performance

Overview

Much of the behavior of individuals is shaped and influenced by other people. Someone who has relatively more influence over others than they do over him or her—for better or worse—can be called a leader. This influence can arise naturally through personal interactions, or it may be attributed to a structuring of relationships whereby one person is designated as having power over, or responsibility for, the others.

In general, theories of leadership make a distinction between two broad types of behavior. One type, often called "consideration," revolves around the leader's relationship with the group members. The leader who exhibits this type of behavior shows warmth, trust, respect, and concern for the group members. Communication between the leader and the group is two-way, and group members are encouraged to participate in decision making. The second type of leader behavior concerns "initiating structure." This construct refers to a direct focus on performance goals. The leader who is high in initiating structure defines roles, assigns tasks, plans work, and pushes for achievement.

Over the years, theorists differed in their views on the optimal mix of consideration and initiating structure in their conceptions of the ideal leader. Those advocating a human-relations approach saw leadership success resulting from high consideration and low initiating structure. Others, however, argued for the intuitive appeal of a leader being high on both dimensions. Research soon revealed that there was no single best combination for every leader in every position.

One approach to the study of leadership, Fred Fiedler's contingency theory, is founded on the assumption that effective leadership depends on the circumstances. Every leader is assumed to have either a work focus or a worker focus. This is measured by the "least-preferred coworker" scale. By asking people a series of questions about the person with whom they have worked least well, the procedure permits an evaluation of the degree to which one can keep work and relationships separate.

Three characteristics of a situation are deemed important in determining which style will work best. First and most important is the quality of the relations between the leader and members of the group. To assess leader-member relations, a leader is asked to use a five-point scale to indicate extent of agreement or disagreement with statements such as "My subordinates give me a good deal of help and support in getting the job done." After scoring the leader's responses to such items, the leader-member relations are characterized as "good" or "poor."

The second most important feature of a situation is the amount of task structure. A situation is classified as "high" or "low" depending on the leader's rating of the frequency with which various statements are true. The statements ask whether there is a quantitative evaluation of the task, whether roles are clearly defined, whether there are specific goals, whether it is obvious when the task is finished, and whether formal procedures have been established.

According to contingency theory, the third—and least important—characteristic of a situation is the degree of power inherent in the leader's position. Position power is assessed by asking questions such as whether the leader can affect the promotion or firing of subordinates and if the leader has the necessary knowledge for assigning tasks to subordinates. As with the other features, there are two types of position power, strong or weak.

In summary, there are eight possible types of situations, according to contingency theory: every possible combination of leader-member relations (good vs. poor), task structure (high vs. low), and position power (strong vs. weak). These eight combinations vary along a continuum from high situational control (good leader-member relations, high task structure, and strong position power) to low situational control (poor leader-member relations, low task structure, and weak position power). Fiedler notes that the match between situation and leader orientation is critical for effective leadership. He recommends an emphasis on task performance in the three situations with the highest situational control and in the one with extremely low situational control. For the remaining four situations, the theory suggests that a group will perform best if the leader has an employee-oriented style and is motivated by relationships rather than by task performance.

Using an alternative perspective, Bernard Bass conceptualizes leadership as a transaction between followers and their leader. He sees most leadership as characterized by recognizing what followers want and trying to see that they get what they want—assuming that the followers' behavior warrants it. In short, the leader and followers exchange rewards and promises of rewards for the followers' cooperation. A minority of leaders are able to motivate their followers to accomplish more than they originally expected to accomplish. This type of leader is called "transformational." A transformational leader affirms the followers' beliefs about the values of outcomes; moves followers to consider the interests of the team, organization, or nation above their own self-interests; and raises the level of needs that followers want to satisfy. Among those who may be called transformational leaders are Alfred Sloan, for his reformation of General Motors; Henry Ford, for revolutionizing United States industry; and Lee Iacocca, for revitalizing the Chrysler Corporation. Although transformational leadership has been found in a wide variety of settings, the research on its effectiveness has been almost exclusively conducted by Bass and his colleagues.

Applications

There has been much speculation about the differences between men and women in their leadership abilities. Psychologists examine the question of differences between men and women in leadership by performing controlled studies. In two field studies of leadership in the United States Military Academy at West Point, Robert Rice, Debra Instone, and Jerome Adams asked participants (freshmen) in a training program to evaluate their squad leaders (juniors and seniors). The program consisted of two parts. First there was a six-week period of basic training covering military protocol, tradition, and skill (such as weapon use and marching). The second part was a field training program covering combat-oriented tasks (such as fabricating bridges, driving tanks, directing artillery fire, and conducting reconnaissance exercises). About 10 percent of the leaders in each program were women. The participants' responses on questionnaires showed the men and women to be comparable in terms of their success as leaders and in the nature of their leadership styles. This conclusion is in agreement with the observations of real operational leadership roles at the academy.

Although sex differences in leadership effectiveness appear to be minimal, there appear to be other group characteristics that are important determinants of leadership behavior. For example, Frank Heller and Bernhard Wilpert (1981) report different influence styles for managers from different countries. They determined the extent to which senior and subordinate managers involved group members in decisions. At one extreme, managers made decisions without explanation or discussion. At the other extreme of influence, they delegated decisions, giving subordinates complete control. Their data indicate that participation is emphasized in nations such as Sweden and France, but not in Israel. The United States is somewhere in the middle.

Regardless of the extent to which there are differences among various groups of people, it is clear that there remain individual differences in leadership style. What are the implications for attempts to improve leadership effectiveness? Recall that there is no single best leadership style for all situations. One approach is to select the leader who exhibits those characteristics that are most appropriate for the situation.

Another approach, promoted by Fiedler and colleagues, is to engineer the situation to match the characteristics of the leader. That is, people cannot change the extent of task performance or employee orientation in their leadership styles, but they can change the characteristics of their situations. The program to accomplish this uses a self-taught learning process. First the person fills out a questionnaire designed to assess leadership style. Then the characteristics of that individual's situation, leader-member relations, task structure, and position power are measured. Finally the person is taught to change the situation to mesh with his or her personality. This might involve such tactics as influencing the supervisor to alter position power or redesigning work to modify task structure. A test of this process was conducted by Fiedler and Martin Chemers (1984) at Sears, Roebuck and Company. They implemented eight hours of the leader-matching training in two of five randomly selected stores. The other stores had equivalent amounts of training discussions. Subsequent rates of the managers on eight performance scales used by Sears showed those who had received the leader-matching training to be superior on every performance dimension.

There have been other applications of leadership research that recommend that the leader choose the appropriate behavior. Victor Vroom and Philip Yetton urge leaders to adopt one of four leadership types. The autocratic leader solves the problem independently, with or without information from subordinates. A consultative leader shares the problem with individual subordinates or with the group and obtains ideas and suggestions which may or may not influence the final decision. A group leader shares the problem with an individual, and together they find a mutually agreeable solution, or with a group that produces a consensus solution that the leader implements. In the fourth type, the leader gives the problem to a single subordinate, offering relevant information but not exerting any influence over the subordinate's decision.

Which of the above four types of leadership is advocated depends on the answers to a series of questions about the need for a quality solution, the amount of information available to the leader and subordinates, the structure of the problem, and attitudes of subordinates. The questions are arranged in a decision tree, so that at each step the leader answers "yes" or "no" and then proceeds to the next step. Vroom has developed a training program based on this model. It has several components. First is an explanation of the theory. Trainees practice using the theory to describe leader behavior and deciding how they would handle various hypothetical situations. Then trainees take part in simulated leadership situations and receive feedback on their actual behavior and the leader behavior that is prescribed by the theory. Finally, there are small-group discussions about the experience. The goal is for trainees to learn how and when to adopt new leadership patterns. Reactions of participants to the program tend to be highly favorable.

Context

Concerns about leadership are evident in nearly every aspect of society. Problems such as illiteracy, inferior education, and environmental destruction are routinely attributed to misguided leadership, ineffective leadership, or an absence of leadership. Within organizations, leaders are held accountable for the work of their subordinates and the ultimate success of the organization. Because of its obvious importance, psychologists have pursued the study of leadership with the goal of developing explanations about the factors that contribute to effective leadership.

One popular conception of leadership is that it is a personality trait. If so, people vary in the extent to which they have leadership abilities. It would also be logical to expect that people in positions of leadership will have different personality characteristics from those who are followers. Yet surprisingly, the results of a large number of studies comparing the traits of leaders and followers has revealed only a few systematic differences. For example, those who are in positions of leadership appear to be, on average, slightly more intelligent and self-confident than followers; however, the magnitude of such differences tends to be small, so there is considerable overlap between leaders and followers. One problem in using this evidence to conclude that individual differences in personality determine leadership is that the traits noted may be the result, rather than the cause, of being in a position of leadership. For example, a person who, for whatever reason, is in a position of leadership may become more self-confident.

This research suggests that there are many factors besides personality that determine the ascent to a position of leadership. This is not so surprising if one considers that groups vary in many ways, as do their leadership needs. Thus there is not a clear "leadership type" that is consistent across groups. For this reason, psychologists have tended to abandon the study of leadership as a personality characteristic and pursue other approaches. The advent of an emphasis on leader behavior occurred at Ohio State University in the 1950's. Ralph Stogdill, Edwin Fleischman, and others developed the constructs of leader consideration and initiating structure. These constructs have proved to be useful in several theories of leadership and have been important in attempts to improve leader effectiveness, particularly in organizational settings.

In addition to academic settings, applied settings have been important in the history of leadership research. Studies conducted by Exxon in an attempt to improve leadership effectiveness led to the independent development of the managerial grid by Robert Blake and Jane Mouton. The two important dimensions of leader behavior that emerged from this work are concern for people and concern for production.

Bibliography

Bass, Bernard M. *Bass and Stogdill's Handbook of Leadership.* 3d ed. New York: Free Press, 1990. A complete review of the research of Bass, Stogdill, and others on differences among leaders. Somewhat technical; for advanced students.

_____. *Leadership and Performance Beyond Expectations.* New York: Free Press, 1985. Readable and thorough examination of the work of Bass and others on leadership research and practice. Emphasis on charismatic and transformational leadership.

Fiedler, Fred E., and Martin M. Chemers. *Improving Leadership Effectiveness: The Leader Match Concept.* New York: John Wiley & Sons, 1984. Discusses field tests of contingency theory and various attempts to implement leader match training. Good emphases on both theory and application.

Smith, Blanchard B. "The TELOS Program and the Vroom-Yetton Model." In *Crosscurrents in Leadership*, edited by James G. Hunt and Lars L. Larson. Carbondale: Southern Illinois University Press, 1979. A description of the work of the Kepner Tregoe organization, based in Princeton, New Jersey, on implementation of the Vroom-Yetton theory.

Yukl, Gary A. *Leadership in Organizations.* Englewood Cliffs, N.J.: Prentice-Hall, 1989. Textbook approach to leadership in the workplace. Suitable for undergraduate college students.

Janet A. Sniezek

Cross-References

LEARNED HELPLESSNESS

Type of psychology: Learning
Fields of study: Cognitive learning; critical issues in stress; problem solving

The concept of learned helplessness, first observed in laboratory animals, has been applied to humans in various situations; in particular, it has been applied to depression. The idea holds that feelings of helplessness are often learned from previous experience; therefore, it should also be possible to unlearn them.

Principal terms

ATTRIBUTION: assigning a quality or characteristic to a person or situation

HELPLESSNESS: a perception of not being able to help oneself or others

LEARNING: gaining knowledge or skill and being able to exhibit it to another person

PERSONALITY: the total physical, intellectual, and emotional structure of an individual; exhibited through consistent behavior patterns

SELF-CONCEPT: a person's view of himself or herself; it can differ from how others perceive the person

Overview

The concept of learned helplessness originated with experiments performed on laboratory dogs by psychologist Martin E. P. Seligman and his colleagues. Seligman noticed that a group of dogs in a learning experiment were not attempting to escape when they were subjected to an electric shock. Intrigued, he set up further experiments using two groups of dogs. One group was first given electric shocks from which they could not escape. Then, even when they were given shocks in a situation where they could avoid them, most of the dogs did not attempt to escape. By comparison, another group, which had not first been given inescapable shocks, had no trouble jumping to avoid the shocks. Seligman also observed that, even after the experiment, the dogs that had first received the unavoidable shocks seemed to be abnormally inactive and had reduced appetites.

After considerable research on the topic, Seligman and others correlated this "learned" helplessness and depression. It seemed to Seligman that when humans, or other animals, feel unable to extricate themselves from a highly stressful situation, they perceive the idea of relief to be hopeless, and they give up. The belief that they cannot affect the outcome of events no matter what force they exert on their environment seems to create an attitude of defeat. Actual failure eventually follows, thereby reinforcing that belief. It seemed that the reality of the situation is not the crucial factor: What matters is the perception that the situation is hopeless.

As research continued, however, Seligman discovered that exposure to uncontrollable negative situations did not always lead to helplessness and depression. Moreover, the results yielded no explanation of the loss of self-esteem frequently seen in depressed persons. To refine their ability to predict helpless attitudes and behavior, Seligman and his colleagues developed a measuring mechanism called the attributional style questionnaire. It involves twelve hypothetical events, six bad and six good.

Subjects involved in testing are told to imagine themselves in the situations and to determine what they believe would be the major cause of the situation if it were to happen to them. After subjects complete the test, their performance is rated according to stability versus instability, globality versus specificity, and externality versus internality. An example of stable, global, internal perceptions would be a feeling of stupidity for one's failure; an unstable, specific, and external perception might consider luck to be the cause of the same situation. The questionnaire has been used by some industries and corporations to identify people who may not be appropriate for certain positions requiring assertiveness and a well-developed ability to handle stress. The same questionnaire has also been used to identify individuals who may be at high risk for developing psychosomatic disorders so that early intervention can be implemented.

Perhaps the primary significance of learned helplessness is its model of how a person's perception of a life event can influence the person's behavior—and can therefore affect his or her life and possibly the lives of others. Seligman believes that the way people perceive and explain the things that happen to them may be more important than what actually happens. These perceptions can have serious implications for a person's mental and physical health.

Applications

The human mind is so complex, and the cognitive process so unknown, that perception is one of the most confusing frontiers facing social scientists. Why do people perceive situations as they do—often as events far different from the ones that actually transpired? If a person is convinced that an event occurred the way he or she remembers it, then it becomes that person's reality. It will be stored that way and may be retrieved that way in the future—perhaps blocking opportunities for positive growth and change because the memory is based on an inaccurate perception.

If children are taught that they are "stupid" because they cannot understand what is expected of them, for example, then they may eventually stop attempting to understand: They have learned that their response (trying to understand) and the situation's outcome are independent of each other. If such helpless feelings are reinforced, the individuals may develop an expectation that no matter what they do, it will be futile. They will then develop a new feeling—hopelessness—which can be generalized to a new situation and can interfere with the future. Various studies have indeed shown that many people have been "taught" that, no matter what their response, the outcome will be the same—failure—so there is no reason to bother to do anything.

One example of this can be demonstrated in the area of victimized women and children. Halfway houses and safe houses are established in an attempt both to protect and retrain battered women and children. Efforts are made to teach them how to change their perceptions and give them new feelings of potency and control. The goal is to teach them that they can have an effect on their environment and have the power to administer successful positive change. For many women, assertiveness training, martial arts classes, and seminars on how to make a strong positive statement with their self-presentation (such as their choice of clothes) become matters of survival.

Children, however, are in a much more vulnerable situation, as they must depend on adults in order to survive. For most children in the world, helplessness is a reality in many situations: They do not, in fact, have much control over what happens to them, regardless of the response they exhibit. Adults, whether they are parents, educators, church leaders, or older siblings, have the responsibility of being positive role models to help children shape their perceptions of the world. If children are allowed to express their feelings, and if their comments are listened to and considered, they can see that they do have some power over their environment and can break patterns of learned helplessness.

A therapist has described "Susan," a client who as a youngster had lived with the belief that if she argued or asserted her needs with her parents they would leave her. She became the "perfect" child, never arguing or seeming to be ungrateful; in the past, if she had, her parents would often get into a fight and one would temporarily leave. Susan's perception was that if she asserted her needs, she was abandoned; if she then begged the parent who remained to tell the absent parent that she was sorry and would never do it again, that parent would return. In reality, her parents did not communicate well and were using their child as an excuse to get angry and leave. The purpose was to punish the other adult, not hurt the child.

When Susan became an adult, she became involved with a man who mistreated her, both physically and emotionally, but always begged forgiveness after the fact. She always forgave him, believing that she had done something wrong to deserve his harsh treatment in the first place. At her first session with a therapist, she was reluctant, having been referred by a women's shelter. She missed her second session because she had returned to her lover, who had found her at the shelter. Eventually, after a cycle of returns to the shelter, the therapist, and her lover, Susan was able to break free and begin the healing process, one day at a time. She told the therapist repeatedly that she believed that no matter what she did the outcome would always be the same—she would rather be with the man who abused her, but paid attention to her, than be alone. After two difficult years of concentrating on a new perception of herself and her environment, she began to experience actual power in the form of positive effectiveness on her life. She became able to see old patterns before they took control and to replace them with new perceptions.

Another example of the power that perceptions of helplessness can have concerns a man ("John") who, as a young boy, was very attached to his father and used to throw tantrums when his father had to leave for work. John's mother would drag him to the kitchen and hold his head under the cold water faucet to stop his screaming; it worked. The child grew up with an impotent rage toward his mother, however, and disappointment in his father for not protecting him. He grew up believing that, no matter how he made his desires known, his feelings would be drowned, as they had been many years before. As a teenager, John grew increasingly violent, eventually getting into trouble; he did not realize that his family was dysfunctional and did not have the necessary skills to get better.

John was never able to believe in himself, even though—on raw rage and little confidence—he triumphed over his pain and terror to achieve an advanced education and black belt in the martial arts. He even developed a career teaching others how to gain power in their lives and how to help nurture the spirit of children. Yet after all this, he still does not have much confidence in his abilities. He is also still terrified of water, although he forces himself to swim.

Feelings of helplessness can also affect a person's health. Research is being conducted on ways of healing that involve perceptions of helplessness or power; in a sense, this involves healing by positive thinking, a very controversial area of science. There has been evidence that the mind and body are inseparable, that one influences the other even to the point of breakdown or healing. There have been many anecdotal reports of people who successfully combat cancer for years after it has been diagnosed as terminal. On the other hand, many people have learned to react in helpless ways to stress, becoming afflicted with migraine headaches, ulcers, and severe back problems, and possibly even causing certain types of terminal illnesses in themselves. Tremendous amounts of money are spent treating stress-related disorders, many of which could be avoided if people could learn that they can have a positive effect on their environment and themselves. There are many effective ways that people can assert power over their lives. Learned helplessness need not be terminal.

Context

The concepts of helplessness and hopelessness versus control over life situations are as old as humankind. The specific theory of learned helplessness, however, originated with the experiments conducted by the University of Pennsylvania in the mid-1960's by Martin E. P. Seligman, Steven F. Maier, and Bruce Overmier. The idea that helplessness could be learned has opened the door to many exciting new approaches to disorders formerly considered personality or biologically oriented, such as psychosomatic disorders, victimization by gender, depression (the "common cold" of mental disorders), and impaired job effectiveness.

The idea that they actually do have an effect on their environment is of tremendous importance to people suffering from depression, because most such people mention a general feeling of hopelessness, which makes the journey out of this state seem overwhelming; the feeling implies that one is powerless over one's reactions and behavior. Research-based evidence has shown that people do have the power to influence their perceptions of their environment and, therefore, change their reactions to it.

Research has provided validity to the suspected link between how a person perceives and influences his or her environment and the person's total health and effectiveness. Leslie Kamen, Judith Rodin, and Seligman have corroborated the idea that how a person explains life situations (a person's explanatory style) seems to be related to immune system functioning. Blood samples were taken from a group of older persons who had been interviewed about life changes, stress, and health changes. Those whose interviews revealed a pessimistic or depressive explanatory style had a larger percentage of suppressor cells. Considering the idea that suppressor cells are believed to undermine the body's ability to fight tumor growth, these discoveries suggest a link between learned helplessness (as revealed by attitude and explanatory style) and susceptibility to diseases.

Studies have also been conducted to determine whether learned helplessness and explanatory style can predict illness. Results, though inconclusive, suggest that a person's attitude and perception of life events do influence physical health some twenty to thirty years later and can therefore be a valuable predictor and a tool for prevention. Particularly if an illness is just beginning, a person's psychological state may be crucial to healing.

If the research on perception and learned helplessness is accurate, a logical next step is to find out how explanatory style originates and how it can be changed. Some suspected influences are how a child's first major trauma is handled, how teachers present information to be learned (as well as teachers' attitudes toward life events), and parental influence. Perhaps the most promising aspect of the research on learned helplessness is the idea that what is learned can be unlearned; therefore, humans really do have choices as to their destiny and quality of life. Considerable importance falls upon those who have a direct influence on children, because it is they who will shape the attitudes of the future.

Bibliography

Abram, Harry S., ed. *Psychological Aspects of Stress.* Springfield, Ill.: Charles C Thomas, 1970. In this collaboration of chapters on six different stressful situations and how they affect the human being, the different contributors, all medical doctors, examine and discuss the human response to stressful events in life, both pathologically and physiologically. Covers topics from human precognitions to outer-space stressors and intimates that preconceived thought influences future perceptions. Excellent references at the end of each chapter.

Applebee, Arthur N. *The Child's Concept of Story, Ages Two to Seventeen.* Chicago: University of Chicago Press, 1978. An innovative approach and eight thought-provoking chapters give this book an edge on some of the classics in this field. The author examines the use of language and how perceptions can be influenced by it. Demonstrates an adult's and child's sense of story, as well as the responses of adolescents. The author shows how perceptions are easily manipulated by skillful use of phrasing. There are three appendices: a collection of analysis and data, elements of response, and a thorough supplementary table.

Bammer, Kurt, and Benjamin H. Newberry, eds. *Stress and Cancer.* Toronto: Hogrefe, 1981. This edited group of independently written chapters presents thirteen different perspectives from a variety of professionals working in the field of cancer and stress. Well-written; achieves its goal without imposing editorial constraints. Perception of events is emphasized as a major determinant of healing. Excellent resources.

Coopersmith, Stanley. *The Antecedents of Self Esteem.* San Francisco: W. H. Freeman, 1967. Emphasizes the importance of limits and boundaries of permissible behavior in the development of self-esteem. Discusses the mirror-image idea of humans emulating society as it develops through the parent/child relationship. There are four very helpful measuring devices in the appendix.

Seligman, Martin E. P. *Helplessness: On Depression, Development, and Death.* San Francisco: W. H. Freeman, 1975. This easily read and understood book was written by the master researcher in the field of learned helplessness. Covers such areas as anxiety and unpredictability, education's role in emotional development, experimental studies, and how perception influences everyday life. Excellent references. This book is a must for anyone interested in the topic.

Frederic Wynn

Cross-References

Causal Attribution, 487; Cognitive Maps, 566; Depression: Theoretical Explanations, 789; Escape Conditioning, 985; Instrumental Conditioning: Acquisition and Extinction, 1315; Learning: Concept, Expectancy, and Insight, 1431; Learning: Generalization and Discrimination, 1437; Observational Learning, 1694; Theories of Stress, 2432.

SURVEY
OF
SOCIAL
SCIENCE

ALPHABETICAL LIST

CATEGORY LIST